Constructing Meaning

Balancing Elementary Language Arts

Third Edition

Joyce Bainbridge
University of Alberta

Grace Malicky
University of Alberta

With a Chapter on Drama by

Patricia A. Payne
University of Alberta

THOMSON
NELSON

Australia   Canada   Mexico   Singapore   Spain   United Kingdom   United States

THOMSON

NELSON

Constructing Meaning: Balancing Elementary Language Arts, Third Edition

by Joyce Bainbridge and Grace Malicky

Editorial Director and Publisher:
Evelyn Veitch

Executive Editor:
Joanna Cotton

Acquisitions Editor:
Cara Yarzab

Marketing Manager:
Chantal Lanning

Developmental Editor:
Glen Herbert

Production Editor:
Natalia Denesiuk

Copy Editor and Proofreader:
Rodney Rawlings

Indexer:
Noeline Bridge

Senior Production Coordinator:
Hedy Sellers

Creative Director:
Angela Cluer

Interior and Cover Designs:
Gabriel Sierra

Cover Image:
Cathy Melloan Resources/Photo Edit

Compositor:
Andrew Adams

Printer:
Transcontinental

COPYRIGHT © 2004 by Nelson, a division of Thomson Canada Limited.

Printed and bound in Canada
2 3 4 07 06 05 04

For more information contact Nelson, 1120 Birchmount Road, Toronto, Ontario, M1K 5G4. Or you can visit our Internet site at http://www.nelson.com

ALL RIGHTS RESERVED. No part of this work covered by the copyright hereon may be reproduced, transcribed, or used in any form or by any means—graphic, electronic, or mechanical, including photocopying, recording, taping, Web distribution, or information storage and retrieval systems—without the written permission of the publisher.

For permission to use material from this text or product, contact us by
Tel 1-800-730-2214
Fax 1-800-730-2215
www.thomsonrights.com

Every effort has been made to trace ownership of all copyrighted material and to secure permission from copyright holders. In the event of any question arising as to the use of any material, we will be pleased to make the necessary corrections in future printings.

National Library of Canada Cataloguing in Publication

Bainbridge, Joyce, 1944–

Constructing meaning: balancing elementary language arts / Joyce Bainbridge, Grace Malicky; with a chapter on drama by Pat Payne. — 3rd ed.

Includes bibliographical references and index.
ISBN 0-17-622491-2

1. Language arts (Elementary)
2. English language—Study and teaching (Elementary) I. Malicky, Grace, 1944– II. Title.

LB1575.8.B34 2004 372.6'044
C2003-907069-7

Preface

Research has long shown that children develop their language abilities through interacting meaningfully with people in their daily lives—in storytime, at mealtimes, during chores, and while playing. When children enter school, they continue this process through using language in purposeful ways across the entire school curriculum. Learning is enhanced through interactions with teachers, parents, and others both within and outside the school context. In the school setting, teachers play a crucial role in maximizing children's language development. They serve as language models, providing a stimulus for thinking and for exploring ideas and talking about them, and in demonstrating literacy in action.

This textbook is an introduction to teaching elementary language arts from an integrated, balanced, and social constructive perspective. It is intended for both preservice and inservice elementary school teachers. As in the first two editions, we provide a comprehensive theoretical framework accessible to beginning teachers and a range of ideas related to different areas of the language arts. New in this edition, however, is more explicit reference to provincial, territorial, and regional curriculum documents as well as to national and regional initiatives. We also place more focus on Canadian issues such as those involving Aboriginal education.

Another significant change in this edition is the addition of an appendix presenting grade-appropriate book lists highlighting Canadian authors. We have also made significant changes to the chapter on technology, partly as a result of the rapidly changing nature of this field, but also because we wanted to present both media and technological literacies within a critical literacy framework. We have updated all chapters in the textbook, significantly changing sections on assessment in several chapters to reflect current policies and practices, and provided additional information on current practices such as guided reading, levelled texts, and Reading Recovery. Throughout the text, we have attempted to place whole language and phonics within a balanced perspective without becoming embroiled in the reading wars of the last half-century.

Consistent with social constructivist views, we continue to introduce each chapter with a graphic organizer that provides readers with an overview of topics and subtopics to be considered. To invite readers to construct their own meaning as they read, we present brief scenarios at the beginning of chapters, pose questions based on these scenarios, and use transitions between major sections of chapters to encourage reflection and prediction. Definitions of terms in boldface type are presented in a glossary at the end of the book. Included in many chapters are book lists, examples of teaching/learning activities, and samples of children's reading, writing, and oral language. We end each chapter with a summary, a short annotated list of selected professional resources for readers who wish to pursue an area further, and lists of both children's and professional materials referenced. We rely more heavily on Web resources in this edition than in previous ones and frequently include them in our lists of suggested professional resources for teachers.

In Chapter One, we present our theoretical framework and encourage readers to reflect on their notions of how children learn. We also introduce the dimensions of language learning included in most language arts programs: speaking, listening, reading, writing, viewing, and representing. Because we hold a social constructivist view of learning, we devote considerable attention in this chapter to the social context of learning. We end the chapter with an indication of what we mean by balance in language arts classrooms.

Chapters Two through Nine provide specific suggestions for assessment and instruction in speaking, listening, reading, and writing. In Chapter Two, we describe the structure of language and present perspectives on language acquisition. This is followed by an exploration of how language functions in different social contexts and how language functions in learning in general. At the end of the chapter, we present suggestions for enhancing listening and speaking in classrooms and for assessing children's oral language abilities.

The focus of Chapter Three is emergent literacy. In this chapter, we begin by describing perspectives on early reading and writing development, as well as components of emergent literacy. We then provide suggestions for assessing young children's literacy development and for planning appropriate programs to meet their needs. We end the chapter by describing specific instructional techniques to foster early literacy development.

Reading is the focus of Chapters Four through Six. We begin in Chapter Four by describing various theoretical perspectives on reading and techniques for assessing children's reading abilities and needs. In Chapters Five and Six, we suggest specific instructional techniques to help children develop reading strategies, beginning with comprehension and then moving to word identification and fluency.

Chapters Seven, Eight, and Nine are devoted to writing. In Chapter Seven, we examine models and forms of writing, the process of composing, and guidelines for implementing a writing workshop. In Chapter Eight, we focus on the role of writing in learning across the curriculum, describing strategies for working with journal writing, learning logs, research reports, and study skills. The final chapter on writing deals with techniques for assessing children's writing as well as conventional aspects of writing.

We believe that children's literature has a critical role to play in children's language development. Therefore, in Chapters Ten and Eleven, we provide lists of children's books (with a heavy emphasis on Canadian content), as well as information on selecting children's literature and on responding to literature through a range of activities involving response groups, journals, drama, and visual arts.

Chapters Twelve and Thirteen focus on viewing and representing. In Chapter Twelve, Patricia A. Payne introduces various forms of drama and shows how these can be used in the classroom to help children represent meaning. In Chapter Thirteen, we begin with a focus on critical literacy and then use this as a framework for discussion of goals, instruction, and issues in media and technological literacies.

The final chapter is designed to help teachers plan and implement language arts programs to meet the needs of all learners. We begin in Chapter Fourteen by acknowledging that no one organizational structure is best for all classrooms. We go on to suggest ways that materials, time, space, and students can be organized to maximize learning in different contexts. The chapter concludes with a brief section on parents as partners.

Acknowledgments

We wish to thank all the children, teachers, undergraduate students, graduate students, and colleagues who have helped us understand the nature of the teaching and learning of language arts during our years as students and teachers. Particular appreciation is expressed to the teachers who took the time to write about their classroom experiences and to the children who provided samples of their reading, writing, and oral language.

We wish to acknowledge the significant contribution of Pat Payne, who drew on her knowledge of language arts to write the chapter on drama. One of the most complete descriptions of drama available in any language arts textbook, this chapter models integration in action.

As well, we are very grateful to John Proctor, who made a significant contribution to the writing of the first chapter and the chapter on technology in the language arts. Pat Campbell's contribution to the section on miscues in the chapter on assessment, Sylvia Pantaleo's contribution to the chapters on children's literature, and Shelley Peterson's contributions to the chapters on writing are also gratefully acknowledged.

We also appreciate the assistance of Tracey Derwing in providing feedback on the linguistics aspects of the chapter on oral language, and the research assistance of Nicole Green and Susan Larison in updating the lists of children's books. In addition, we received valuable comments and suggestions from instructors at our own and other universities, as well as from the following reviewers selected by Nelson: Ian J. Cameron, University of Victoria; Mary Clare Courtland, Lakehead University; Nancy L. Evans, Okanagan University College; Virginia McCarthy, Malaspina University-College; Janet McIntosh, Nippissing University; and Sharon J. Rich, University of Western Ontario.

Finally, we wish to thank the editorial staff at Nelson for encouraging us to write a third edition of this book and for providing advice and support during its development.

Joyce Bainbridge
Grace Malicky
University of Alberta

Contents

Chapter 4:
The Nature and Assessment of Reading 111

Chapter 5:
Reading Comprehension Strategies 137

Chapter 6:
Word Identification Strategies and Fluency 165

Chapter 7:
The Process of Writing 191

Chapter 8:
Writing Across the Curriculum 220

Chapter 9:
Assessment and Conventions of Writing 240

Chapter 13:
Critical, Media, and Technological Literacies 387

Chapter 14:
Planning and Organizing Language Arts Programs 431

Chapter

Introduction to Language Learning

From the Great Debate to Reading Wars

The Context of Language Learning

- Prior Knowledge
- Ways of Using Language
- Ways of Telling Stories
- English-Language Proficiency
- Gender

Models of Knowledge and Learning

- The Transmission Model
- The Constructivist Model
- The Social Constructivist Model

Introduction to Language Learning

Balanced Language Arts Programs

- Ownership and Control
- Phonics and Meaning
- Teaching and Practice of Language
- Dimensions of Language Arts
- Level of Difficulty

Language Learning in Canadian Classrooms

- Dimensions of Language Arts
- Integrating the Language Arts

Chad Lee is enrolled in his first university course in language arts education, and *Constructing Meaning: Balancing Elementary Language Arts* has been assigned as the required text for the course. As he reads the title, he is pretty sure he knows what we mean by the word *meaning* but wonders about the term *constructing meaning*. He has a visual concept of balance (something on one side weighing the same as something on the other side) but little idea of how this applies to teaching language arts. When he moves to the graphic organizer, he is surprised to see the term *reading wars*. As a student in elementary school, Chad was not aware that there was heated debate among educators on how to teach reading. Recently, however, he has heard advertisements for phonics programs that imply these programs meet needs not currently being met in schools. He is also aware that classes in many elementary schools are more ethnically and culturally diverse than when he was in school.

As is true of many of you, most of Chad's ideas of language learning and teaching come from notions of how he personally learned to read and write in elementary school. He knows his ideas need to be developed and honed if he is to be effective in helping 25 to 30 children become competent and confident readers and writers. He begins by thinking about what he needs to learn:

- What does it mean to have students construct meaning, and how does this differ from transmitting knowledge?
- What is a balanced language arts program, and how do teachers achieve balance in their language arts programs?
- Do schools teach **phonics** and if so, how does it fit into the rest of the language arts program?
- How can language arts programs meet the needs of the diverse population of students in today's schools?

These are some of the questions Chad asks himself as he starts his first course in language arts education. Before you begin reading this chapter, take a few minutes to think about your past experiences and about what you will soon face in your own classroom. What are some of your questions?

FROM THE GREAT DEBATE TO READING WARS

In this section, we present a brief overview of a debate that has dominated reading research and instruction for the past five decades, a debate that has become so intense in recent years that writers are calling it "the reading wars."

Those of you who entered first grade in the 1960s or early 1970s likely remember reading about Dick and Jane from a popular basal reading series published by Gage. Dick and Jane were members of a middle-class white family in which the father worked outside of the home and the mother was a full-time homemaker. This series reflected a whole-word or controlled vocabulary approach in which approximately 50 words were taught as sight words prior to the introduction of phonics. Sight words were introduced and repeated in a controlled manner until the end of third grade. Those of you who received instruction from this or a similar basal reading series likely remember that a reading lesson went something like this:

- The teacher introduced new words before you read a new story,
- You read the story silently in a small group,
- After you finished reading the story silently, the teacher asked comprehension questions,
- You reread the story orally in a round-robin fashion, and
- You completed workbook pages or worksheets following the story.

This approach was successful in helping most but not all of you learn to read.

It was concern for those children who were not successful that lead to Rudolf Flesch's (1955) book entitled *Why Johnny Can't Read*. In this book, Flesch blamed the whole-word method for reading failures and presented phonics as the panacea. Although basal readers continued to dominate reading instruction through the remainder of the 1950s and into the 1960s, the U.S. Department of Education funded a series of large-scale comparative studies in the 1960s in an attempt to determine the best method for teaching beginning reading. Results were inconclusive; all methods worked for some children, but no one method worked for all children. Indeed, it appeared that the teacher was a more important factor in children's reading success than the method employed (Bond and Dykstra, 1967). Overall, however, some evidence suggested that basal reading series plus phonics worked better than basal readers alone.

On the basis of these findings, Jeane Chall, in her influential book entitled *Learning to Read: The Great Debate* (1967), presented the case for an increased focus on phonics in reading programs. The use of phonics workbooks increased and phonics-based series appeared in some Canadian classrooms in the 1970s. At the same time, however, an alternative approach to beginning reading began to appear in the 1970s and was predominant throughout the 1980s and early 1990s.

Frank Smith (1971) and Kenneth Goodman (1970) both viewed meaning, rather than phonics or sight words, as the centre of reading instruction. They argued that learning to read was primarily a process of predicting words on the basis of passage meaning and prior knowledge. Both opposed part-to-whole pedagogy involving isolated letters and sounds, and instead championed whole-to-part pedagogy employing real children's literature. Over time, these ideas were developed into what became known as the **whole-language** approach (Goodman, 1986), an approach that many of you experienced when you were in elementary schools in the 1980s and early 1990s.

Whole language was a philosophy or set of beliefs rather than an approach or technique (McKay, 1993). At the core of whole language was a focus on meaning as the essence of language learning, and on children learning language through using it. Writing was also viewed as a fully integrated component of beginning language arts programs. Children were engaged in "real" reading and writing rather than completing exercises in workbooks and worksheets. They read high-quality children's literature, often **trade books,** rather than material written to teach children to read, and teachers observed them as they engaged in language activities rather than assessing them with standardized tests (Altwerger, Edelsky, and Flores, 1987).

But not everyone was convinced that whole language was the best way to go. In 1990, Marilyn Jager Adams published *Beginning to Read* (1990) in which she concluded, from an extensive review on beginning reading, that direct and systematic phonics instruction is the most effective way to teach reading. Research had revealed that whole language was effective in developing prereading skills, in increasing children's tendency to engage in literate activities, and in producing more sophisticated responses to literature (Pressley, Allington, Warton-McDonald, Block, and Morrow, 2001). However, there was little evidence to demonstrate increased scores on reading tests and some evidence that whole language was less effective than other approaches with weaker readers. By the early-to-mid-1990s, the debate over whole language had become so intense and acrimonious that the term "reading wars" began to appear in the literature (Pressley et al., 2001). This war was waged both in professional journals and the mass media (see, for example, the May 1998 issue of *Reader's Digest* for a vehement condemnation of whole language by Claudia Cornwall).

Weary from the pendulum effect of reading practices swinging from one extreme to the other decade after decade, several writers (e.g., Reutzel, 1999a) began to argue for a more balanced approach to language arts instruction, combining skills instruction with whole-language components. Promising as this direction is, however, the 20th century ended with one more attempt to determine what works best in beginning reading instruction. A National Reading Panel was established in 1997 to assess the research on effectiveness of various approaches to teaching children to read. Among other results, the National Reading Panel (2000) reaffirmed Jager Adams' findings regarding the effectiveness of phonics instruction. This sparked a whole new round of debate both about the way the National Reading Panel conducted its review and the way results were interpreted (e.g., Allington, 2002; Cunningham, 2001; Garan, 2001). The war is not over yet!

One positive outcome of the ongoing debate is that it has kept reading and writing on the political agenda, resulting in additional government funding for early **literacy** programs in many school jurisdictions. However, it has also resulted in many educators throwing out what was good about old approaches when new ones came along (Fox, 2001). How can educators avoid become blinded by every new approach that comes along? And how can they combine the best from each approach into an effective **balanced language arts** program?

We believe that this can be achieved if educators have a coherent theoretical framework about how children learn. Only by framing best practices and balanced literacy within a coherent theory will teachers have an adequate basis for meeting the needs of individual learners in today's classrooms. Without a coherent theory of language learning, educators remain vulnerable to "the fads of literacy instruction" (Hiebert, 1991, p. 4).

That's what this book is about—helping teachers like you construct the theoretical and practical knowledge of language learning that you need in order to develop and implement an effective balanced language arts program. We begin by delving into what it means to know something and how knowledge is developed.

MODELS OF KNOWLEDGE AND LEARNING

As a learner, you probably focus most of your attention on what you are learning and pay little attention to how people learn or what it involves. As a teacher, it is vitally important that you become aware of and reflect on your views of learning as these views will affect everything you do in your classroom. In this section, we consider three ways of thinking about knowledge and learning—transmission, **constructivism**, and social constructivism.

The Transmission Model

In this model, learning is often equated with transmitting information. Knowledge is what students can recall. It is a quantitative notion, emphasizing facts and someone else's knowledge to be learned and reproduced on demand. Teachers have the knowledge, and it is their job to transmit this knowledge to their students. They often appear to assume that there is a direct conduit between their minds and those of their students and that knowledge can travel, unchanged, through this conduit.

Although the transmission model was more predominant in the past, it still dominates in some classrooms. In these classrooms

- tasks are defined and set by the teacher,
- the teacher is entirely responsible for monitoring students' progress and evaluating their learning,
- learning is thought of as linear and proceeding in incremental stages,
- skills, knowledge, and attitudes are viewed as separate, and the teacher assumes responsibility for building student competence in each area,
- teacher talk predominates, and
- students' learning is equated with their ability to correctly answer questions, complete workbooks and skillsheets adequately, and score well on objective tests.

In language arts classrooms where transmission is the underlying theory, teachers provide the type of instruction presented in Box 1.1.

Box 1.1   Sample Activities in Transmission Language Arts Classrooms

- Teachers assign the topics children write about and evaluate their writing.
- Teachers assign children stories to read from basal reading series and rely on teacher guides for activities and instructional ideas.
- Teachers set purposes for reading and determine the ways students respond to the reading.
- Teachers teach word recognition and comprehension as separate components or aspects of reading.
- Teachers ask questions about stories to test children's understanding of the author's ideas.
- Teachers present skills in a sequential order.
- Teachers rely on workbooks and skillsheets to provide practice in reading and writing skills.

The Constructivist Model

Today, few educators believe that direct transmission of information between two people's minds is possible. Think about the last time you went to a movie with your friends and discussed the movie afterwards. Although there may have been many similarities in the meaning constructed by each of you, there were also likely some subtle and sometimes not-so-subtle differences. You might think that meant your friends were not paying attention or that they didn't understand the movie. In fact, however, it reflects the constructive nature of all meaning making and the impact of individual experiences on that process.

Today, many educators emphasize the individual or personal construction of meaning and understanding (Brooks and Brooks, 1993; Lauritzen and Jaeger, 1997). The focus is on students actively making meaning and solving problems. Students make connections between new experiences and their prior knowledge, constructing and testing hypotheses as they create meaning.

The theoretical base for this thinking comes from the work of Piaget (1972), who focused on the individual meaning-making process and on the development of higher levels of thinking. He conceptualized cognitive operations as being the same across cultures and social contexts. His ideas have been translated into hands-on activities designed to develop children's concepts and thinking processes (Richardson, 1997).

Box 1.2 presents some of the types of activities that predominate in language arts classrooms where constructivism is the underlying theory. As you can see, there are substantial and profound differences between transmission and constructivist classrooms.

If constructivism is new to you, you likely have many questions at this point. For example:

- Are all interpretations or compositions equally valid and "good" if no one meaning of a text is *the* meaning?
- What role does the teacher play in helping children with reading comprehension or written composition if the construction of meaning is primarily an individual process?
- How are shared meanings developed?

Social constructivism deals with these kinds of questions.

Box 1.2   Sample Activities in Constructivist Language Arts Classrooms

- Children choose their own topics for writing.
- Children brainstorm ideas and jot these down to serve as a reference as they write.
- Children make decisions about form, format, and style and evaluate their own effectiveness as writers.
- Teachers use "high-quality" children's literature, both fiction and nonfiction, in the classroom.
- Teachers provide opportunities for children to interact with what they are reading by making predictions, forming hypotheses, and asking questions before and during reading.
- Children respond personally to what they read.
- Teachers teach reading and writing skills and strategies on the basis of children's needs as they engage in "real" reading and writing.

The Social Constructivist Model

Let's return to the example of you and your friends discussing a movie you attended together. Equally important as differences among your constructions of meaning are similarities. None of us constructs meaning in a vacuum. Instead, we make sense of our experiences within a particular social group, and this occurs within a broader societal and cultural context. The more similar the sociocultural backgrounds of you and your friends, the more similar will be the meanings you construct. In other words, the social context of learning has a significant impact on the construction of meaning.

Social constructivism has its origins in the work of Vygotsky (1978), who theorized that the ways we think are learned primarily through social interactions and that the ways we learn language develop as a result of our use of language in social contexts. According to Vygotsky, children are active in their own development, but other people in their immediate social context also play an important role. When they work collaboratively, people negotiate and develop shared meanings. Wells (2001, p. 180) puts it this way:

> Knowledge is constructed and reconstructed between participants in specific situations, using the cultural resources at their disposal, as they work toward the collaborative achievement of goals that emerge in the course of their activity.

But not everyone has an equal voice in these negotiations. The view of one person or group is often privileged over that of others. To illustrate this, we return one last time to the movie discussion with your friends. Even within your small group, some people's meanings are given greater credibility than others'. Your gender, race, socioeconomic status, and language abilities all have an impact on how your ideas are viewed by other people. Social constructivists who take a critical stance recognize these inequalities and encourage each of us to become aware of our biases and of how we may knowingly or unknowingly value the ideas of one gender, race, or class over those of another.

To help teachers become aware of these inequalities, Edelsky (1994) presents the following questions:

- Who decides what is a "good" story?
- Who decides what children write about?
- Who decides whose turn it is to talk?

- Who decides whose meaning of a text is acceptable?
- Who decides what books are in the classroom?
- Whose view of the world is represented in these books?

When teachers base their teaching on social constructivism, they actively and consciously go beyond the activities that characterize constructivist classrooms to recognize the social nature of all learning. Some go even further, helping children develop awareness of how systems of meaning and power affect people and the lives they lead. These teachers involve children in conversations about fairness and justice, and encourage children to ask why some people are positioned as others (Leland, Harste, Ociepka, Lewison, and Vasquez, 1999). A primary concern with literacy education from this perspective is the improvement of society and with enabling individuals to contribute to a democratic society and to achieve their human potential (Wells, 2001). Teachers and children in social constructivist classrooms engage in the types of activities presented in Box 1.3.

A summary of the three major theories of learning discussed in this section is presented in Table 1.1. As authors of this text, we continue to construct and reconstruct theories of language learning with each new conversation, teaching experience, or article we read. At this point, however, the social constructivist view most adequately reflects what we believe about language learning. You may or may not hold a similar view, but you now have some understanding of what educators mean when they talk about constructing meaning.

LANGUAGE LEARNING IN CANADIAN CLASSROOMS

Although education is a provincial and territorial responsibility, there is considerable similarity across Canada in how language learning is viewed. In all parts of the country, language is seen as central to thinking and learning, as reflected in the following statements taken from provincial and regional documents:

Box 1.3   Sample Activities in Social Constructivist Language Arts Classrooms

- Children brainstorm ideas and share their ideas with others.
- Children share their writing with one another, discuss revisions in the group context, and engage in peer editing.
- Teachers provide opportunities for children to share ideas when making predictions, forming hypotheses, and discussing responses to their reading.
- Children work cooperatively on activities designed to help them develop reading and writing strategies.
- Children and teachers discuss how people of different genders, races, cultures, socioeconomic groups, and age levels are portrayed in stories and books.
- Children and teachers examine and explore themes that focus on and celebrate diversity, acceptance, care, and mutual support.

Table 1.1   Three Orientations to Teaching and Learning

	Transmission	Constructivism	Social Constructivism
Underlying assumptions	Reality is objective and exists outside the individual. Knowledge is transmitted—meanings are reproducible and constant.	Reality is subjective and exists only as it relates to the individual. Knowledge is constructed—meanings vary with the individual.	Reality is a social construct. Knowledge is negotiated—meanings vary with the context or situation.
Goal of education	Development of specialized knowledge and skills (Bershied, 1985)	Development of personally relevant knowledge and skills	Development of socially relevant knowledge and skills
Role of the teacher	Develop and manage teaching sequences and schemes. Present information, instruct, transfer knowledge.	Create learning contexts that involve active learning. Scaffold or support individual learning.	Create learning contexts that encourage ownership of learning. Support individual and collaborative learning.
Role of the learner	Essentially passive—externally motivated	Active—internally motivated	Active—internally and socially motivated

- "Language is the basis of all communication and the primary instrument of thought. ... Thinking, learning, and language are interrelated. From Kindergarten to Grade 12, students use language to make sense of and to bring order to their world. They use language to examine new experiences and knowledge in relation to their prior knowledge, experiences, and beliefs" (*Western Canadian Protocol for Collaboration in Basic Education: The Common Curriculum Framework for English Language Arts: Kindergarten to Grade 12*, 1998, pp. 1–2).
- "Language Learning is central to every learning project, for language is a vital aspect of communication and represents a vehicle for learning used in all subjects. ... Since it provides access to knowledge, it is an essential tool for creating, analyzing, exercising critical judgment and describing or expressing ideas, perceptions and feelings" (*English Language Arts Program of Study*, Quebec Ministry of Education, 2001, p. 70).
- "Language is central to students' intellectual, social, and emotional growth, and must be seen as a key element of the curriculum. ... Whether they are studying literature or history, or learning science, students need fundamental language skills to understand information and express their ideas" (*The Ontario Curriculum: Grades 1–8: Language*, 1997, p. 5).
- "Language is the primary instrument of thought and the most powerful tool students have for developing ideas and insights, for giving significance to their experiences, and for making sense of both their world and their possibilities in it" (*Atlantic Canada English Language Arts Curriculum: Grades 4–6*, p. 3).

Box 1.4 presents Web site addresses for provincial and regional language arts curriculum documents available on the Internet.

Box 1.4 Provincial and Regional Curriculum Documents on the Internet

Atlantic Canada

Foundation for the Atlantic Canada English Language Arts Curriculum (1996)
  Available: apef-fepa.org/pdf/english.pdf

Atlantic Canada English Language Arts Curriculum: Grades K–3 (1999)
  Available: www.gnb.ca/0000/publications/curric/englangartsk-3.pdf

  Available: www.gov.nf.ca/edu/sp/eng_lang_arts_prim.htm

Atlantic Canada English Language Arts Curriculum: Grades 4–6 (1998)
  Available: www.gnb.ca/0000/publications/curric/englangarts4-6.pdf

  Available: www.gov.nf.ca/edu/sp/eng_langarts_ele.htm

Quebec

English Language Arts Program of Study (2001)
  Available: www.meq.gouv.ca/degj/program/pdf/educprog2001bw/educprog2001bw-051.pdf

Ontario

The Ontario Curriculum: Grades 1–8: Language (1997)
  Available: www.edu.gov.on.ca/eng/document/curricul/curr971.html

Western Canada

Western Canadian Protocol for Collaboration in Basic Education: The Common Curriculum Framework for English Language Arts: Kindergarten to Grade 12 (1998)
  Available: www.wcp.ca

English Language Arts K–7: Integrated Resource Package (1996) British Columbia
  Available: www.bced.gov.bc.ca/irp/elak7/elacons.htm

English Language Arts K–9 (2000) Alberta
  Available: www.learning.gov.ab.ca/k_12/curriculum/bysubject/english/default.asp

English Language Arts: A Curriculum Guide for the Elementary Level (2002) Saskatchewan
  Available: www.sasked.gov.sk.ca/docs/ela/index.html

English Language Arts: Manitoba Curriculum Framework of Outcomes and Standards
  Available: edu.gov.mb.ca/ks4/cur/ela/index.html

Dimensions of Language Arts

There is also considerable similarity across Canada in the dimensions of language learning included in curriculum documents. Although these dimensions are called *strands* in Ontario* and Saskatchewan, *processes* in the Atlantic provinces, *communication forms* in

*Ontario combines the first two and last two dimensions into a strand labelled Oral and Visual Communication.

British Columbia, and *language arts* in Alberta and Manitoba, the following dimensions are included in all of the documents:

- speaking
- listening
- writing
- reading
- viewing
- representing

The first four dimensions have been included in language learning programs for many years and are familiar to all of you. However, the last two have appeared more recently in curriculum documents as the marked increase in technology and media broadened the range of "texts" that students create and from which they construct meaning. In "Foundation for the Atlantic Canada English Language Arts Curriculum" (1996) the meaning of "texts" is extended to describe any language event, whether it be a poster, television program, or multimedia production.

Integrating the Language Arts

All provincial curriculum documents indicate that the language arts are interrelated and interdependent, and stress the importance of teaching the language arts in an integrated manner. There are at least three different levels of **integration** that can be considered in elementary classrooms. One involves the integration of the dimensions of language learning with one another. This capitalizes on reading–writing connections, speaking–writing connections, viewing–representing connections, and so on. For example, knowledge about how stories are organized helps children to construct meaning when both reading and writing. Knowledge about the relationship between letters and sounds helps children to both spell and identify words. Teaching the language arts in an integrated way helps children transfer strategies and knowledge developed in one language context to another.

A second level of integration involves language across the curriculum, a movement founded in the United Kingdom in the 1960s by James Britton and his colleagues at the London Institute for Education. More recently, the concepts of this movement have become known simply as language for learning. There are no aspects of the school curriculum where language does not play a major part. Music, health, mathematics, science, social studies, art, and physical education all have subject-specific language—a vocabulary and a way of speaking about that subject that must be learned.

The third level of integration goes beyond the curriculum when children bring their own knowledge and experience of the world into the classroom and take what they learn in the classroom to their home and community contexts. Integration at all these levels is illustrated in the work of one Grade 4 classroom in Nova Scotia.

As the children learn about expository writing, they put together a book on the history of one small community in their area. The books are printed in paperback by a local publisher and sold in the community (Petite Rivière, 1993). The work involves both social studies and language learning, and the teacher combines the available time from both subject areas in order to maximize the time for the project. During the process, the children collect information from community members, learn how to search for material for the book, and make decisions about what to include and what to leave out, how to lay out pages, and how to select illustrations. They discuss what they have read and heard, including the meanings of words used in the past but no longer in common usage today.

They write, read, conference, draft, edit, and generally engage in truly integrated learning activities that connect their own lives and experiences with life in the classroom.

Most of the chapters in this book are organized around the dimensions of language learning identified above. Chapter Two focuses on talking, Chapter Three on reading and writing, Chapters Four to Six on reading, Chapters Seven to Nine on writing, and Chapters Twelve and Thirteen on viewing and representing. Within these chapters, we draw links across dimensions when appropriate and, in the final chapter, tie the pieces into an integrated language arts program.

THE CONTEXT OF LANGUAGE LEARNING

You were a language user long before you set foot in school, and you continued to develop language facility as you interacted with others in your home, community, and broader society as well as in school. Our primary focus throughout this section is on diversity within society and its implications for language arts learning and instruction.

We live in an increasingly diverse society. When children arrive at school, they bring with them a wide range of cultural, societal, and home influences that, taken as a whole, means each child views the world differently and interacts with others in unique and special ways. These differences involve gender, race, class, language, and culture. A major challenge for public schools is to provide equal educational opportunities for all children. Studies suggest, however, that outcomes of schooling are far from equal. Data reveal that 1 362 000 children in Canada (or one in five) are living in poverty (Hay, 1997). This is an increase of 46 percent since 1989. Poor children are twice as likely to have difficulties with academic achievement as children from mainstream homes, and are twice as likely to drop out of school. Low-income earners, the long-term unemployed, Aboriginal peoples, seniors, prisoners, people with disabilities, and racial and cultural minorities all have higher-than-average rates of under-education and poverty. Some Canadians interpret these results to mean that people are poor because they are illiterate. However, the National Anti-Poverty Organization (1992, p. 1) maintains "It is poverty and other forms of inequality that create the barriers to good education for many Canadians." In his book *Savage Inequalities*, Kozol (1991) points out large disparities in the United States in levels of funding for public education of middle-class and poor children. Put simply, less money is spent to educate children from poor than middle-class homes.

In recent years, it has become apparent that schools do not meet the needs of children from poor and minority homes as well as they do those from middle- and upper-income homes. To meet the needs of all the children in our classrooms, we need to be aware of diversity among the children and make a conscious effort to adjust instruction to reflect this diversity.

Prior Knowledge

What is already known and what is already experienced form the basis for new knowledge that children develop. Most teachers are aware of differences in prior experiences that children from different backgrounds bring to language learning classrooms. For example, urban children will likely have far less knowledge about farm animals than children who live on farms. And among the latter, those on mixed farms will have far more knowledge about farm animals than those on grain farms.

The prior knowledge we develop from past experience does not consist of a series of isolated facts or concepts, but is instead a mental framework that influences our expectations and imposes structure on the information we receive. Through relating new experiences and old ones, we build these organized frameworks that many theorists (e.g., Rumelhart, 1980) refer to as **schemata**. Frank Smith (1975, p. 11) expresses this idea as a "theory of the world in the head."

These schemata, or theories of the world, develop through repeated experiences in a particular context. For example, children who are taken to McDonald's by their parents begin to develop a schema for going to a restaurant. They know that it is a place where they get food to eat, that they place an order at a counter, that someone at the counter takes the order, that the person at the counter puts the food on a tray, that the food is paid for, that one takes the food to a table to eat, and so on. When their parents take them to another restaurant where they sit down and someone comes to take their order, the children extend their schema for going to a restaurant to include features of that type of restaurant as well. Eventually, children who are taken to eat at a range of different restaurants will establish a schema that is sufficiently well developed to apply to most restaurants.

So far we have focused on relatively minor differences in background knowledge. Teachers provide opportunities for these children to relate new experiences to what they already know in order to help them develop increasingly elaborate and complex schemata. They engage children in discussions, **semantic mapping**, or other activities that involve building networks of ideas. However, many Canadian children come from very different cultural backgrounds than their teachers. Some of this reflects immigration patterns but it also reflects the presence of Aboriginal people (called First Nations in some regions) across the country.

Most provinces recognize that Aboriginal children bring very different world views to schools, and that these views need to be taken into account when planning programs. It is difficult to generalize one Aboriginal view, because, as Weber-Pillwax (2001) points out, there never was one Nation in North America. However, in a collaborative project, Elders and educators from the Northwest Territories, Yukon Territory, British Columbia, Alberta, Saskatchewan, and Manitoba produced what they refer to as an Aboriginal perspective (*Western Canadian Protocol for Collaboration in Basic Education: The Common Curriculum Framework for Aboriginal Language and Culture Programs*, 2000). This perspective reflects the view that survival is dependent upon respectful and spiritual relationships with oneself, other people, and the natural world. Good relationships mean good lives (Weber-Pillwax, 2001).

Froese (1997) labels programs that focus on differences in food and holidays "naive multiculturalism." These types of programs are clearly insufficient (not to mention condescending) in bridging the gap in experiential knowledge between mainstream teachers and Aboriginal children. Better are the efforts of many teachers to bring Aboriginal children's literature into the classroom and to integrate Aboriginal content into other areas of the curriculum. This not only provides Aboriginal students with content related to their experiential knowledge, but also increases the awareness of other children of Aboriginal cultures. Many Aboriginal people consider this also to be insufficient. In order to preserve Aboriginal culture, they believe that Aboriginal people need to assume control of the education of Aboriginal students and that, because culture and language are inextricably linked, Aboriginal cultural content should be taught in the Aboriginal languages (Kirkness, 1998).

Ways of Using Language

Closely related to diversity in prior knowledge are differences in language use, since it is through language that we develop our culture and make sense of experience and the world. Differences in language use were the focus of Heath's (1983) highly influential study of children from three communities in the Carolina Piedmont region of the United States who attended school together following desegregation. The teachers and parents wanted to find out why the children and teachers frequently could not understand one another. Specifically, they wondered why children who never stopped chattering at home rarely talked in class, and why children who were unable to answer simple questions in class could explain a rule for a ball game on the playground.

Heath found that the children from the three communities had experienced different ways of learning and using language at home. The experiences of some children matched the ways language was learned and used in the school better than the experiences of other children did:

- In "Maintown," a middle-class, school-oriented community, the focus of literacy-related activities was on labelling, explaining, and learning how to display knowledge. The children from this community were socialized into the interactional sequences that commonly occur in classrooms.
- Families in "Roadville," a white working-class community, also focused on labelling and explanations, preparing children for literal comprehension tasks in the classroom. However, these children were unprepared for reading activities that involved reasoning or affective responses.
- In "Trackton," a black working-class community, the children were not taught labels or asked for explanations in their homes, but instead were asked to give reasons for and personal responses to events.

When children from all three communities arrived at school, the predominant type of questions asked by teachers involved having children name attributes of objects taken out of context, for example, "What colour is the horse in this picture?" The children from Trackton had not been asked these kinds of questions by their parents, and they thought these were dumb questions because their teachers already knew the answers. When teachers incorporated questions similar to those the Trackton children were asked at home, the children participated much more frequently and eventually responded to more school-based questions as well.

There have been no comprehensive studies of the language use of children in different cultural groups in Canada. However, the work of Scollon and Scollon (1981) did suggest some differences in the use of language by Athabaskan and mainstream English-speaking Canadians that have implications for children in schools. Athabaskan languages are spoken by Aboriginal people in the northern parts of Manitoba, Saskatchewan, Alberta, and British Columbia, as well as in the Northwest Territories. Scollon and Scollon found that Athabaskan speakers avoid conversation unless the point of view of all participants is well known, whereas English speakers feel that the main way to get to know the point of view of people is through conversation with them. This leads English speakers to feel that Athabaskan speakers are very taciturn or silent and Athabaskan speakers to feel that English speakers talk too much. Scollon and Scollon also found that how much people talk is related to social relations of dominance. In schools, children are expected to show off their abilities to the teacher who is in the spectator role. This is different for Athabaskan speakers because in their culture adults are expected to display abilities for the child to learn. The adult is in the exhibitionist role while the child is in the spectator role. These differences have the potential to lead to misunderstanding.

Misunderstanding was evident in a study conducted by Ward (1990) in a Canadian kindergarten classroom in which there were nine Native and five non-Native children. She found that Native children had difficulty understanding rules of instructional dialogue. They answered questions less frequently and less appropriately than non-Native children, and differences between the two groups increased across the school year.

Ways of Telling Stories

Differences are also evident in the ways people tell stories and in what they think are good stories. This was highlighted in research by Michaels and Cazden, who listened to children and teachers during sharing time in kindergarten and Grade 1 classrooms (Cazden, 1988). Sharing time, sometimes called "show and tell," is a common activity in primary classrooms when children are invited to share a story or personal experience about their lives outside of school.

Michaels and Cazden found that teachers' reactions to children's stories revealed specific expectations about what the stories should be like. "Good" stories were those with a beginning, middle, and end, with all the ideas related to one topic. In one classroom, 96 percent of the stories told by white children met these criteria, but only 34 percent of those told by black children were topic-centred. Instead, many black children provided chains of loosely related actions or events, often with the topic left unstated. An example of these episodic stories follows:

> I went to the beach Sunday and to McDonald's and to the park and I got this for my birthday. [*Holds up purse.*] My mother bought it for me and I had two dollars for my birthday and I put it in here and I went to where my friend named Gigi. I went over to my grandmother's house with her and she was on my back and I and we was walking around by my house and she was heavy. She was in the sixth or seventh grade. ... (Cazden, 1988, p. 13)

Teachers tended to react negatively to episodic stories, whereas they praised children who produced topic-centred stories. Michaels and Cazden subsequently presented a selection of both topic-centred and episodic stories to black and white teachers and asked them to comment on how well-formed the stories were. Teachers were also asked to predict the probable academic success of the child who told each story. White teachers frequently rated episodic stories as hard to follow and predicted the children would be low-achieving, while black teachers rated both topic-centred and episodic stories positively.

Episodic stories are also common in Aboriginal groups. It is not that children from these communities cannot tell stories; it is that the stories they tell do not match their teachers' expectations. Because Aboriginal society is primarily oral, it's not only the forms of their stories that are different but also the purposes of their stories as well as their protocols for storytelling. They use stories to teach and to provide history as well as part of spiritual ceremonies. "Certain persons tell particular stories at certain times of the year and during certain events or situations" (Weber-Pillwax, 2001, p. 156). Publishers and educators frequently mislabel Aboriginal legends and narratives as fairytales and myths (Corbiere, 2000).

Many teachers are not aware of the mismatch between their sociocultural backgrounds and those of the children in their classrooms. The first step in providing appropriate classroom instruction is awareness; the second is adjusting instruction so that children are entitled to tell their stories and to tell their stories their way (Bloome, 1991). It is also important to include stories from all cultural heritages in a respectful and valued way to develop students' self-concept and identify as well as an appreciation of Canada's multicultural diversity.

English-Language Proficiency

So far, we have dealt with differences in people's stories and in the ways they use language in their homes. Many children arrive at school speaking a language other than English or using a nonstandard form of English. In some Canadian cities, such as Vancouver, more than half of the school population comes from homes in which languages other than English are spoken (Froese, 1997). There are many other homes in which a nonstandard form of English is used.

For children with a first language other than English or French, there is controversy regarding the role of first-language instruction in language arts programs. Many language experts recommend that initial literacy instruction be provided in a learner's first language (e.g., Hudelson, 1987; Allen, 1991). To take advantage of language knowledge and abilities children bring to school, immersion and bilingual classrooms have been set up across the country to enable children to read and write in languages such as Spanish, German, Arabic, Cree, and Mandarin. However, not all children whose first language is not English have access to these classrooms. The others are immersed in classrooms where English is the language of instruction, often without any special assistance to support them as they learn English.

For children who enter schools speaking a nonstandard **dialect** of English, one issue teachers face involves the extent to which children's oral language should form the basis for instruction compared with having them learn standard English. If teachers do not adjust instruction in relation to the language these children bring to school, the children frequently have difficulty learning to read and write. This occurs because of the discrepancy among their oral language, the language of books, and teachers' expectations of the children's writing.

However, if teachers introduce these children to reading using language written in their dialect, they may not learn the standard English necessary to succeed in mainstream society. According to Delpit (1988, p. 287), we do children who speak nonstandard dialects of English no service to suggest, even implicitly, that standard English is not important. Children do need to learn to spell correctly and to use correct grammatical forms in order to gain access to higher education and jobs. The challenge for language arts teachers is to balance instruction that builds on the language children bring to the classroom with their need to communicate through standard English. It appears to be more a matter of when, rather than if, the standard form is introduced to children in elementary classrooms.

Gender

Evidence has shown for many years that girls outperform boys in reading in the elementary grades, but until the last two decades, boys began to pull ahead by the secondary level (Wilkinson and Marrett, 1985). By the early 1990s, however, an international assessment of literacy revealed that girls read better than boys in 19 of 27 countries at ages 9 and in 13 of 31 countries at age 14. Canada was among those countries with the largest gender differences at age 14. A subsequent international assessment of 15-year-olds in 2000 revealed that girls achieved higher scores than boys on combined reading literacy in all 32 countries included (Shiel and Cosgrove, 2002).

Large-scale writing examinations in Canada, Great Britain, and the United States showed that girls scored consistently higher than boys on writing as well (Peterson, 2001), and recent results in the United Kingdom showed that girls outperformed boys in all areas of the curriculum (Barrs, 2000). In the United States, boys are 50 percent more likely to be retained than girls, and 55 percent of the students who drop out of schools are boys (Young and Brozo, 2001).

These results have led to considerable controversy about both why girls are doing better than boys in school and what should be done to redress the differences. Some educators focus on teacher's expectations, indicating that teachers tend to expect girls to be more successful than boys when they arrive at school. Others identify the feminization of elementary schools. They argue that since most teachers in elementary schools are female, boys have few male role models. Still others suggest that there is a "poor fit between the culturally prescribed male gender role and the student role that has become institutionalized in American elementary schools" (Brophy, 1985, p. 118). Boys are expected to be active, exploratory learners in our society, but schools traditionally have valued passive, recipient learners.

Another difference between boys and girls involves what they read. Surveys of reading preferences report that girls read more romance and horror, while boys opt for action and science fiction (Millard, 1997). In writing, researchers have also found that stereotypical gender roles and relationships are reflected in the characters, plots, and styles of children's stories (Peterson, 2001). Characters in girls' stories demonstrate more emotion and pro-social behaviours whereas those in boys' stories exhibit more aggressive behaviour and engage in high-intensity, dangerous actions. Research also shows that boys actively resist the kind of living through or **aesthetic** reading of fictional texts described by Rosenblatt (1989) and have difficulty expressing their feelings in their peer group about what they have read. In addition, some types of reading tests favour girls over boys. Boys tend to do better on multiple-choice tests whereas girls tend to do better on more open-ended measures (Barrs, 2000).

How do we go about improving the literacy levels of boys? The education minister in the United Kingdom recently urged schools to spend more time having children read nonfiction texts rather than fiction (Barrs, 2000). However, Moss (2000) found that boys' apparent preferences for nonfiction were more related to their attempts to escape judgments by their peers than a desire to read that type of material. Nonfiction texts were not as obviously graded as fiction, and by "Steering round these texts via the pictures, and ignoring the verbal text, weaker readers could nevertheless stake out territory as 'experts,' on a level with peers who read more competently" (Moss, 2000, p. 103).

Brozo (Young and Brozo, 2001) provides another suggestion for improving the literacy level of boys. He recommends the use of books with strong masculine themes so that boys lives are not demeaned, and they become engaged with reading. Engagement, for him, is the prerequisite to skilful reading. The problem with this approach is that it serves to reinforce gender stereotypes and biases (Young in Young and Brozo, 2001).

Rather than gearing curriculum and assessment to approaches which are thought to favour boys, several writers (e.g., Barrs, 2000; Moss, 2000; Young in Young and Brozo, 2002) recommend that we create classrooms that nurture all students as literacy learners. In her research, Moss (2000, p. 105) found that the most effective practice to increase boys' literacy involved building and sustaining a reading culture that encompassed the full range of interests in the class and also substantially expanded them.

The first step in dealing with diversity in language arts classrooms is becoming aware both of the knowledge and abilities children bring with them to school and of our own biases and preconceptions about the learning abilities of different children. Only with this awareness are we in a position to provide a learning environment that is equitable for all children.

BALANCED LANGUAGE ARTS PROGRAMS

In this last section of the chapter, we revisit the great debate introduced earlier, to construct an understanding of the concept of balanced literacy. We begin by presenting a position statement from the International Reading Association.

> There is no single method or single combination of methods that can successfully teach all children to read. Therefore, teachers must have a strong knowledge of multiple methods for teaching reading and a strong knowledge of the children in their care so they can create the appropriate balance of methods needed for the children they teach. (1999, p. 1)

What does balance look like? Initially, balance was defined in a simplistic way as a combination of phonics and whole language. However, as Reutzal (1999b) and many other writers have pointed out, the concept of balanced instruction goes well beyond this simplistic representation.

Fitzgerald (1999) defines balance as a set of beliefs, a perspective to instruction. She argues that, "There is no one right or wrong balanced approach, and likewise, there are many different manifestations of balanced reading approaches. ... Balance does not mean 'one size fits all'" (p. 102–105). Balanced approaches take on different faces at different grade levels and with different children. Fitzgerald believes that a balanced perspective includes a focus on multiple kinds of knowledge about reading, multiple sources of this knowledge, and multiple ways of learning. An overview of our multidimensional perspective on balance is presented in Box 1.5. We begin our discussion of these dimensions with a focus on sources of knowledge and whose knowledge counts.

Ownership and Control

According to Edwards (1980), there is a sharp distinction in most classrooms between the teacher ("the one who knows") and the students ("the many who do not"). Because of this distinction, the major role of students is to listen and that of teachers is to tell. In addition, it is often the teacher who decides what counts as knowledge and who "owns" instructional talk. The teacher determines which students speak and then what they talk about, how long they talk, and how well they talked. In the end, it is the teacher who does most of the talking, and when he or she does ask questions, they nearly all require students to provide information that the teacher already knows.

The most common **discourse** pattern in classrooms is a three-part sequence of "teacher-initiation, student-response, teacher-evaluation" (the IRE pattern, Cazden, 1988). When children come to school, those from some homes are more familiar than others with this structure. The children from Trackton in Heath's study described earlier, for example, were far less familiar with this type of interaction than those from Maintown. The IRE pattern is consistent with a transmission model of knowledge and appropriate for some purposes (e.g., having children learn number facts), but it is far less consistent with constructivist views and inappropriate for supporting children's responses to literature. Although it is easy to imagine talk in which ideas are explored, it is much harder to make this a reality of daily classroom life. It is more than a matter of who talks when, involving a significant change in conceptions of knowledge and teaching and in how ownership is shared by children and teachers.

Box 1.5   Variables in a Balanced Literacy Program

Ownership and Control

Hierarchical relationships	Collaborative relationships
Teacher ownership	Student ownership
Competition	Co-operation

Phonics and Meaning

Focus on words	Focus on meaning
Teaching from parts to wholes	Teaching from wholes to parts

Teaching and Use of Language

Deductive	Inductive
Systematic	Incidental
Isolated	Contextualized

Aspects of Language Arts

Focus on reading	Focus on all aspects of language

Level of Difficulty

Common expectations	Different expectations
Relatively easy tasks for automaticity	Challenging tasks for new strategies
Independent learning	Scaffolding

As Wells and Chang-Wells (1992) note, the important point is not whose vision—the teacher's or children's—will prevail, but rather what can be done to create a context in which meaning is co-constructed by the teacher and children together.

> In such a context, the teacher remains in charge, but his or her exercise of control is manifested not in a once-and-for-all choice between intervening with the correct answer or standing back and leaving the students to find their own solutions, but in the making of moment-by-moment decisions about how to proceed, based on knowledge of the topic, understanding of the dynamics of classroom interaction, intentions with respect to the task, and a continuous monitoring of the ongoing talk. (pp. 46–47)

Thus, the issue is not whether but *how* the teacher intervenes.

Clearly, the constructivist teacher assumes a role different from that of the traditional teacher who is "dispenser of information and authority on all things to be taught and learned in the classroom." And what might that role be, on the basis of a social constructivist model of learning? The role is obviously a multifaceted one, including at least the following dimensions:

- The teacher is a *provider* of resources, and an *organizer* of space and time so that children have the opportunities and materials they need for learning (Lindfors, 1987).
- In the role of *demonstrator* (Smith, 1983), the teacher shows how something is done and demonstrates through actions that he or she is a reader, writer, and thinker.

- Learning is a lifelong activity, and it's important for children to see the teacher's own enthusiasm and questioning as a *learner*.
- The teacher is a *responder*. When we are learning something new, it is helpful to have someone respond to our questions, question us further, support our learning, and let us know how we are doing. That is not the same as judging our performance. Response is genuine and productive, and occurs as the teacher actively follows what children are trying to do and attempts to further that learning.
- In the role of *observer*, the teacher gains insight into the children's learning processes and comes to understand what children know and can do.

In the classroom incident described in Box 1.6, Linda Graves shares an experience in which she played all the roles described above. She was a provider of resources, demonstrator when she read her own writing, observer as she examined the leads Desira had written, and responder when she encouraged Desira to make her own choice. But most of all she was a learner. Her interaction with Desira helped her to more fully understand the importance of guiding children to gain control over their own writing.

As teachers' roles become more consistent with social constructivism, children take responsibility for more of their own language learning, and the relationship between teachers and children becomes more collaborative and less hierarchical (Vygotsky, 1978). By working collaboratively in classrooms, children develop a sense of ownership of both their knowledge and language. By making choices about their language learning, children begin to feel like readers and writers—they feel that they belong to the literacy club (Smith, 1988).

This last point emphasizes the social rather than individual nature of learning. Social constructivists place a focus on the social nature of language learning and on children working together, whereas transmission models tend to value individual learning and achievement. Although there is greater emphasis on cooperative learning and peer assessment in schools today than in the past, most schools continue to focus more on individual competition than on cooperation and assessment of group outcomes.

Phonics and Meaning

The dichotomy between phonics and meaning focuses on the kind of knowledge about reading and other aspects of language that educators believe children need to learn. Many educators in the late 1980s and early 1990s placed meaning at the centre of instruction and encouraged children to focus on meaning-making when reading and writing rather than on accuracy of spelling and word identification. Instead of providing a systematic set of planned lessons in phonics and spelling, these teachers believed that skills were best taught incidentally in mini-lessons when they noted a particular need in children's reading and writing. While this might be sufficient for some children, it is now generally recognized that others require direct teaching of skills in a sequential manner to become fluent readers and writers (Pressley and Rankin, 1994; Beck, 1998). However, does this mean that meaning should be placed on a back burner and replaced by sequential phonics and spelling programs? Few academics or educators would go that far. As Cunningham and Allington (1999, p. xiii) point out, "Children do need phonics, but phonics is not all they need."

Most educators now recognize that part of what children need in literacy programs is balance between a focus on words and a focus on meaning. This idea has been championed in books on balanced literacy by Fountas and Pinnell (1996) and Cunningham and Allington (2003). As the authors of this text, we, too, recognize that this is critical and

---

Box 1.6   Teacher Roles: A Specific Example

Linda Graves shares an experience with a young student writer in her Saskatoon classroom.
I remember a time when I was working with Desira in our Writer's Workshop. Desira had written a wonderful story about Fluffy, her cat. The lesson I had introduced to the students that morning was on leads. We looked at lots of books and discussed how the authors began their stories. Students were eager to share their favourite books and why they thought each lead was used to introduce each story. We also looked at our own writing and shared our leads. I read to the students my writing about our class cat, Kizmit. The children had lots of helpful suggestions on how I could "hook" the reader. I asked the students to think of two or three different ways they could write a lead on the story they were currently working on. Off they went to their special places in the classroom and hallway to weave more ideas on leads.

Desira was sitting quietly in a corner of the classroom hard at work. She had written three leads and was trying to decide which one she would like to use. I pored over her work with her, asking her to read me the leads.

Once there was a cat who's name was Fluffy. he is potty trained. and he tears all the walls up. Sometimes he bites and scratches me and my sister but he thinks he's playing.

there was a cat his name is Fluffy. he always crys for food. When we say no to him. he jumps in the Garbage can.

Meaww Meaww Where's my Dinner cried Fluffy no food said Desira.

I loved them all, but my favourite was "Meaww Meaww." That is the one I wanted Desira to choose. With my teacher control finger poised on the start button, I almost said to her, "Desira, this is the best one. Why don't you lead your story with that?" But I stopped and told myself, "If you want these children to be the masters of their own writing, then you must allow them to make the choices they want." A rather tough thing for me to do. Regaining my composure, I then asked Desira what lead she was going to choose. She did not choose my preferred lead, but rather chose one that perhaps was more conventional and more like the leads she had read in other books. Desira was either not willing or not ready to take a risk that day and I had to support her decision, hoping a day would come when she would take a risk.

Desira learned something about leads that day, but perhaps it was I who learned the most. We must allow students to make choices for themselves if we truly want to empower them, to help them become masters of their own destinies. Desira went on from this day with the feeling that she had control over her writing, and that is exactly where the control should be. We must guide student writing, not take ownership for it. Thanks, Desira—you were my teacher that day!

---

hence include suggestions to help children develop strategies for both words and meaning in our chapters on emergent literacy, reading, and writing.

Teaching and Practice of Language

In the 1980s and early 1990s, it was not unusual to hear educators talking about children learning "naturally" by being immersed in rich literacy experiences with relatively little

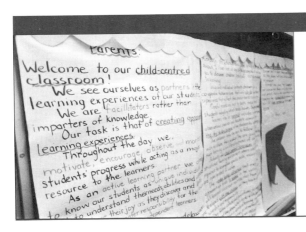

Communicating teachers' roles to parents.

formal instruction. Today, few educators or parents would question Gaffney (1998) when she says that the key to children learning to read can be summed up in one word—teaching. It's the *how* of teaching that's currently open to debate (Cambourne, 1999).

Explicit Versus Implicit Instruction

One question in this debate involves whether explicit or implicit instruction is more effective. Explicit or direct teaching is often associated with a transmission model of knowledge. Teachers present knowledge and have students use that knowledge in new situations. It includes three phases when applied to **strategy** instruction:

1. Teachers identify what a specific strategy is, explain why the students are learning the strategy and when and where they should use it, and model the strategy to make the mental processes visible to the students.

2. Teachers involve students in guided practice during which teachers provide support but require students to take more and more responsibility for the strategy.

3. Teachers provide students with opportunities for independent practice and application, monitoring their performance and reinstating support if necessary. (Armbruster and Osborn, 2002, p. 70)

In contrast, implicit or inductive teaching is more consistent with constructivist views of learning. Teachers begin with data and help students build generalizations about those data. For example, rather than teaching children the "final *e* rule," teachers present words that do (e.g., *kit, kite*; *fat, fate*; *cub, cube*) and do not (e.g., *love, give, some*) exemplify the pattern and ask children to figure out how the sounds and letters work. Proponents of inductive teaching maintain that because students are actively engaged in gathering and interpreting information, they more readily retain the knowledge they construct. This is highly motivational and leads to the development of self-directed learners. However, opponents point out that inductive teaching is less efficient, and that some children have great difficulty learning without direct instruction (Grimmett, 1994).

Constructivist teaching does not mean that children have to figure out how written language works all of the time, that they have to reinvent *everything* on their own. The question is not which is best—implicit or explicit instruction—but which will serve a child's needs at any specific point in time. When constructivist teachers decide to use explicit instruction, however, they know that no two children will develop exactly the same understanding of what's being taught.

Incidental Versus Systematic Instruction

Another major question faced by teachers is whether skills instruction should be provided incidentally in mini-lessons or sequentially in a systematic set of planned lessons. Should practice be provided on an occasional basis or on a continuous basis? The answer will depend, as it did for implicit and explicit teaching, on each child's daily needs.

Sometimes incidental instruction or occasional practice will be sufficient, but often it is not. Many times it is possible to teach strategies *as* children read and write, but again this is not always the case. Once more, balance is needed. By carefully observing children in the classroom, teachers decide when and how to provide instruction at any point in time. They also decide how much practice children need in order to generalize skills and strategies to other reading and writing contexts.

Isolated Versus Contextualized Instruction

Another question related to the "how" of teaching involves whether skills should be taught as separate components of the language arts program or in the context of real reading and writing. Furthermore, should practice be provided with isolated words and tasks, or should it involve authentic language activities? (The latter is supported by thinking that says to become good at doing anything, whether it's riding a bike, swimming, or writing, we need to spend time actually doing it.)

Many children spend relatively little time at school actually reading or writing. In the 1980s, Anderson, Hiebert, Scott, and Wilkerson (1985) reported that the average daily time children devoted to reading in the primary grades was only seven minutes. They found that most time allocated for reading consisted of the teacher talking about reading or the children completing worksheets. While there is little doubt that children need to spend time reading at home as well as in school, Stanovich (1986) has shown that this happens more frequently with good readers than poor readers. For many poor readers, their *only* reading is done at school.

Dimensions of Language Arts

Until the past two decades, most language arts time was allocated to reading instruction and restricted largely to using one basal reading series. In the 1980s, the work of educators such as Graves (1983), Calkins (1986), and Atwell (1987) led to a sharp increase in the time children spent writing in elementary schools. Indeed, many educators appeared to assume that children would learn to read by reading their own writing and by reading and responding to the writing of their peers. Now, as the current reading wars intensify, there is a danger that a swing back to a renewed concentration on reading will result in minimal attention being paid to writing and other critical areas of language learning.

A balanced program does not mean that the same proportion of language arts instruction is devoted to speaking, listening, reading, writing, viewing, and representing every day. Rather, it means that children spend at least some time in each of these modes of language every day, and that over time they receive instruction to maximize their language growth in *all* areas.

Level of Difficulty

Many children in language arts classrooms experience daily frustration because they are unable to complete tasks that are too difficult for them. Others are not sufficiently challenged to maximize their learning. Only by having language arts activities at an appropriate level of difficulty will children experience success *and* reach their potential. There are three major ways teachers can achieve this type of balance:

- by adjusting their expectations for performance during the initial stages of learning something new,
- by setting different expectations for different children on the same learning task, and
- by providing different levels of materials and tasks for different children

There is a marked contrast between how young children learn to talk at home and how they are later generally taught to read and write. Parents try to understand their children even when their oral language is far from the adult form. They reinforce their children's efforts to communicate by responding in a meaningful way. As Holdaway (1979) points out, no one expects a young child to speak in grammatically correct sentences with perfect pronunciation the first time he or she talks. In reading and writing, however, accuracy is often required from the beginning, both at home and at school. Teachers help children feel successful by having realistic expectations when they are learning something new.

Because children are not all at the same place in their language proficiency, teachers can also balance level of difficulty by expecting children to perform differently on the same learning task. For example, in a kindergarten class, the teacher might have very different expectations for what children will be able to do with a predictable book after it is read to them. That is:

- Some children will be able to identify words in the book as they reread it.
- Other children may point to the words as another child reads them, developing an understanding of the one-to-one relationship between words in oral and written language.
- Still other children may listen and chime in ("talk like a book" [Clay, 1972]), developing an understanding of how written language sounds.

In other words, different children do different things with the same book in order to achieve different objectives.

Sometimes, however, the teacher needs to adjust the level of materials and tasks for different children. For example, an important goal for all children is to become fluent, automatic readers. It is estimated that children need to read a minimum of three-and-one-half hours per week to achieve this goal (Rossman, 1987), and during this time, they need to be reading books that they can handle without assistance from others. In any classroom, books at a range of levels are required for this independent reading. The higher the grade level, the greater this range needs to be.

Although children need practice with reading and writing activities they can handle independently, they will not learn to their potential without activities that challenge them. At least some of the time, they need to be working in their **zone of proximal development** (Vygotsky, 1978). At this level, work is too difficult for them to complete independently, but they can achieve success with the support of their teacher or other students.

This support is frequently referred to as *scaffolding*, a term used by Bruner (1975, p. 12) to refer to interaction between a young child and its mother, in which the mother supports the child "in achieving an intended outcome." The child decides to do something and the mother provides the assistance (such as a helping hand, gesture, or word) that allows the child to manage to do it. In schools, teachers use scaffolds as temporary supports to help children extend their skills and knowledge to a higher level of competence (Dorn and Soffos, 2001). **Guided Reading** is a teaching process designed by Fountas and Pinnell (1996) to scaffold students' selection and application of a range of effective reading strategies (see Chapter Five for a description of this teaching process). To maximize the effectiveness of Guided Reading, Fountas and Pinnell recommend that children be matched with books that provide an appropriate level of challenge and familiarity to support their development of self-extending reading strategies. In the past, this level was called the child's instructional reading level.

The term **instructional reading level** has been used for decades in the field of reading to indicate the need to select materials that are neither too difficult nor too easy for instructional purposes. In recent years, this need has lead to a focus on what is referred to as **levelled text** (Brabham and Villaume, 2002). Levelled text refers to reading materials that represent a progression from simple to more complex and challenging texts. Text leveling originated in New Zealand with Clay's (1991) work, and it's use is increasing in both the United States (e.g., Fountas and Pinnell, 1999) and Canada (e.g., Rog and Burton, 2002).

> As we conclude this section, we return to the scenario at the beginning of the chapter in which Chad poses several questions about language arts instruction. The conclusion that both you and he have probably reached is that there are few simple answers. There is no one best way to facilitate children's language learning. In our discussion, we not only identified the need for a coherent theoretical framework, but also asked you to incorporate apparently irreconcilable approaches into a balanced language arts program in order to meet the needs of all children. Your most pressing question at this point is probably "But how do I do it?" Our main goal in the remainder of this book is to help each of you construct your own answers to this question.

SUMMARY

For the past five decades, educators and parents alike have engaged in a search for one best way to teach children to read and write. In the 1950s and 1960s children learned to read from basal reading series with a whole-word approach. By the 1980s to mid-1990s, educators had moved to whole language, with an emphasis on meaning and "real" language experiences. Periodically throughout these decades, writers decried the lack of attention to phonics instruction and portrayed phonics as the answer to reading problems. By the mid-to-late-1990s many educators were calling for balanced language arts programs employing "best practices." However, many programs are still not being driven by a coherent theoretical framework.

There are three major theoretical perspectives on knowledge and learning: transmission, constructivism, and social constructivism. Skills-based instruction reflects a transmission model in which teachers have knowledge and transmit this knowledge to their students. Whole language instruction is more consistent with constructivism, where the focus is on actively making meaning, rather than on reproducing existing knowledge. But constructing meaning does not occur in a vacuum; social constructivism acknowledges the impact of the social context and social interactions on learning.

There is considerable similarity in how language learning is viewed in curriculum documents produced across Canada. Language is central to all learning and thinking, and elementary language arts programs generally include the following dimensions: listening, speaking, reading, writing, viewing, and representing. Through these dimensions, children construct and share meaning with others. Teaching language arts in an integrated way helps children transfer strategies from one language arts dimension to another, use developing language strategies in all subject areas, and link what they learn in the classroom to their home and community contexts.

A major challenge for schools is to provide equal educational opportunities for all children. Children differ in the prior experience they bring to classrooms, in the ways they use language in their homes, in the stories they tell, in their proficiency with the English language, and in their gender. An important step in dealing with diversity in language arts classrooms is becoming aware both of the knowledge and abilities children bring with them to school and of our own biases and preconceptions about the learning abilities of different children.

Many educators argue that balance is crucial to meeting children's needs. The term "balanced literacy" is generally used to refer to programs that maintain a balance between work on words and work on meaning. Balance does not stop there, however. An important aspect of balance involves ownership and control. In social constructivist classrooms, children take more responsibility for their own learning, relationships between children and teachers become more collaborative and less hierarchical, and greater emphasis is placed on cooperation than competitiveness. Another aspect of balance involves providing instruction in all dimensions of the language arts rather than emphasizing one or two areas at the expense of the others. Still another aspect involves balance between the amount of time spent on teaching and that spent on using language strategies. Sometimes children learn inductively, whereas at other times they need deductive instruction. Sometimes incidental instruction is sufficient, whereas at other times direct, systematic instruction is critical to learning. And, to become good at any activity (including reading, talking, or writing), children need to spend time doing or practising it. Balance also relates to the difficulty level of tasks and materials. Children do not learn when tasks are too difficult, but they also do not learn unless they are sufficiently challenged. Teachers balance the level of difficulty by setting different expectations for different children, by varying the amount of teacher or peer support they provide to help children as they learn new strategies and establish mastery of these strategies, and by varying the level of difficulty of learning activities.

SELECTED PROFESSIONAL RESOURCES

Fitzgerald, J. (1999). What is this thing called "balance"? *Reading Teacher, 53* (2), 100–107. In this article, Fitzgerald summarizes some of the dominant definitions of balance and points out similarities and differences between them. She argues that there is no single, right balanced approach to teaching reading and instead, presents balance as a philosophical perspective on what children need to know about reading and how they should learn it. She then draws implications from this view of balance for classroom instruction.

National Reading Panel (2001). *Teaching Children to Read.* Available: www.nationalreadingpanel.org. This Web site includes two volumes that present information on how the National Reading Panel was set up, the topics it chose to investigate, its procedures and methods, and its findings. The five areas dealt with in the report are alphabetics (phonics and phonemic awareness), fluency, comprehension, teacher education and reading instruction, and computer technology and reading instruction. The site also includes guides for parents and teachers based on the findings of the National Reading Panel.

Cunningham, P. M. and Allington, R. L. (2003). *Classrooms That Work: They Can All Read and Write* (3rd ed.). New York: Longman. Cunningham and Allington provide a compelling argument for combining best practices into a balanced literacy program. They also provide a practical guide for language arts teachers in the elementary grades.

REFERENCES

Adams, M. J. (1990). *Beginning to read: Thinking and learning about print.* Cambridge, MA: MIT Press.

Allen, V. G. (1991). Teaching bilingual and ESL children. In J. Flood, J. M. Jensen, D. Lapp, and J. R. Squire (eds.), *Handbook of research on teaching the English language arts* (pp. 356–364). New York: Macmillan.

Allington, R. L. (2002). *Big brother and the national reading curriculum.* Portsmouth, NH: Heinemann.

Altwerger, B., Edelsky, C., and Flores, B. M. (1987). Whole language: What's new? *Reading Teacher, 41,* 144–154.

Anderson, R., Hiebert, E., Scott, J., and Wilkerson, I. (1985). *Becoming a nation of readers.* Washington, DC: National Institute of Education.

Armbruster, B. B. and Osborn, J. H. (2002). *Reading instruction and assessment: Understanding the IRA standards.* Boston: Allyn and Bacon.

Atlantic Canada English Language Arts Curriculum: Grades K–3 (1999). Governments of New Brunswick, Newfoundland and Labrador, Nova Scotia and Prince Edward Island. Available: www.gnb.ca/0000/publications/curric/englangartsk-3.pdf.

Atlantic Canada English Language Arts Curriculum: Grades 4–6 (1998). Governments of New Brunswick, Newfoundland and Labrador, Nova Scotia and Prince Edward Island. Available: www.gnb.ca/0000/publications/curric/englangarts4-6.pdf.

Atwell, N. (1987). *In the middle: Writing, reading, and learning with adolescents.* Portsmouth, NH: Heinemann.

Barrs, M. (2000). *Gendered literacy? Language Arts, 77* (4), 287–293.

Beck, I. L. (1998). Understanding beginning reading: A journey through teaching and research. In J. Osborn and F. Lehr (eds.), *Literacy for all: Issues in teaching and learning* (pp. 11–31). New York: The Guilford Press.

Bloome, D. (1991). Anthropology and research on teaching the English language arts. In J. Flood, J. M. Jensen, D. Lapp, and J. R. Squire (eds.), *Handbook of research on teaching the English language arts* (pp. 46–56). New York: Macmillan.

Bond, G. L. and Dykstra, R. (1967). The cooperative research program in first-grade reading instruction. *Reading Research Quarterly, 2,* 1–142.

Brabhan, E. G. and Villaume, S. K. (2002). Leveled text: The good news and the bad news. *Reading Teacher, 55* (5), 438–441.

Brooks, J. G. and Brooks, M. G. (1993). *In search of understanding: The case for constructivist classrooms.* Alexandria, VA: Association for Supervision and Curriculum Development.

Brophy, J. (1985). Interactions of male and female students with male and female teachers. In L. C. Wilkinson and C. B. Marrett (eds.), *Gender influences in classroom interaction.* Toronto: Academic Press.

Bruner, J. S. (1975). The ontogenesis of speech acts. *Journal of Child Language, 2,* 1–40.

Calkins, L. (1986). *The art of teaching writing.* Portsmouth, NH: Heinemann.

Cambourne, B. (1999), Explicit and systematic teaching of reading—A new slogan? *Reading Teacher, 53* (2), 126–127.

Cazden, C. B. (1988). *Classroom discourse: The language of teaching and learning.* Portsmouth, NH: Heinemann.

Chall, J. S. (1967). *Learning to read: The great debate.* New York: McGraw-Hill.

Clay, M. M. (1972). *Reading: The patterning of complex behaviour.* Auckland, NZ: Heinemann Educational Books.

Clay, M. M. (1991). *Becoming literate: The construction of inner control.* Portsmouth, NH: Heinemann.

Corbiere, A. I. (2000). Reconciling epistemological orientations: Toward a wholistic Nishaabe (Ojibwe/Odawa/Potowatomi) education. *Canadian Journal of Native Education, 24* (2), 113–119.

Cornwall, C. (May 1998). Scandal of our illiterate kids. *Reader's Digest,* 77–82.

Cunningham, J. W. (2001). Essay Book Review: The National Reading Panel Report. *Reading Research Quarterly*, 36 (3), 326–335.

Cunningham, P. M. and Allington, R. L. (1999). *Classrooms that work: They can all read and write* (2nd ed.). New York: Longman.

Cunningham, P. M. and Allington, R. L. (2003). *Classrooms that work: They can all read and write* (3rd ed.). New York: Longman.

Delpit, L. (1988). The silenced dialogue: Power and pedagogy in educating other people's children. *Harvard Educational Review*, 58, 280–298.

Dorn, L. J. and Soffos, C. (2001). *Shaping literate minds: Developing self-regulated learners.* Portland, ME: Stenhouse Publishers.

Edelsky, C. (1994). Education for democracy. *Language Arts*, 71 (4), 252–257.

Edwards, A. D. (1980). Patterns of power and authority in classroom talk. In P. Woods (ed.), *Teacher strategies: Explorations in the sociology of the school* (pp. 237–253). London: Croom Helm.

English language arts K–9 (2000). Alberta Learning. Available: www.learning.gov.ab.ca/k_12/curriculum/bysubject/english/default.asp.

English language arts K–7: Integrated resource package (1996). British Columbia Ministry of Education. Available: www.bced.gov.bc.ca/irp/elak7/elacons.htm.

English language arts: Manitoba curriculum framework of outcomes and standards. Manitoba Education and Youth. Available: www.edu.gov.mb.ca/ks4/cur/ela/index.html.

English language arts: A curriculum guide for the elementary level (2002). Saskatchewan Education. Available: www.sasked.gov.sk.ca/docs/ela/index.html.

English language arts program of study (2001). Quebec Ministry of Education. Available: www.meq.gouv.ca/degj/program/pdf/educprog2001bw/educprog2001bw-051.pdf.

Fitzgerald, J. (1999). What is this thing called "balance"? *Reading Teacher*, 53 (2), 100–107.

Flesch, R. (1955). *Why Johnny can't read—And what you can do about it.* New York: Harper & Row.

Foundation for the Atlantic Canada English language arts curriculum (1996). Governments of New Brunswick, Newfoundland and Labrador, Nova Scotia and Prince Edward Island. Available: apef-fepa.org/pdf/english.pdf.

Fountas, I. C. and Pinnell, G. S. (1996). *Guided reading: Good first teaching for all children.* Portsmouth, NH: Heinemann.

Fountas, I. C. and Pinnell, G. S. (1999). *Matching books to readers: Using leveled texts in guided reading*, K–3. Portsmouth, NH: Heinemann.

Fox, M. (2001). Have we lost our way? *Language Arts*, 79 (2), 105–113.

Froese, V. (1997). Basic issues of language instruction. In V. Froese (ed.), *Language across the curriculum* (pp. 2–16). Toronto: Harcourt Brace & Company, Canada.

Gaffney, J. S. (1998). The prevention of reading failure: Teach reading and writing. In J. Osborn and F. Lehr (eds.), *Literacy for all: Issues in teaching and learning* (pp. 100–110). New York: The Guilford Press.

Garan, E. M. (2001). What does the report of the National Reading Panel really tell us about teaching phonics? *Language Arts*, 79 (1), 61–70.

Giroux, H. A. (1987). Critical literacy and student experience: Donald Graves' approach to literacy. *Language Arts*, 64 (2), 175–181.

Goodman, K. S. (1970). Behind the eye: What happens in reading. In K. S. Goodman and O. Niles (eds.), *Reading: Process and program* (pp. 3–38). Urbana, IL: National Council of Teachers of English.

Goodman, K. S. (1986). *What's whole in whole language?* Richmond Hill, ON: Scholastic-TAB.

Graves, D. H. (1983). *Writing: Teachers and children at work.* Exeter, NH: Heinemann Educational Books.

Grimmett, P. P. (1994). Induction and inductive teaching. In A. C. Purves (ed.), *Encyclopedia of English studies and language arts* (pp. 622–624). New York: Scholastic.

Hay, D. I. (1997). Campaign 2000: Child and family poverty in Canada. In J. Pulkingham and G. Ternowetsky (eds.), *Child and family policies: Struggles, strategies and options* (pp. 116–133). Halifax: Fernwood Publishing.

Heath, S. B. (1983). *Ways with words: Language, life and work in communities and classrooms.* Cambridge, MA: Cambridge University Press.

Hiebert, E. H. (1991). *Literacy for a diverse society: Perspectives, practices, and policies.* New York: Teachers College Press.

Holdaway, D. (1979). *The foundations of literacy.* Gosford, Australia: Ashton Scholastic.

Hudelson, S. (1987). The role of native language literacy in the education of language minority children. *Language Arts, 64,* 827–841.

Kirkness, V. J. (1998). The critical state of aboriginal languages in Canada. *Canadian Journal of Native Education, 22* (1), 93–107.

International Reading Association (1999). *Using multiple methods of beginning reading instruction: A position statement of the International Reading Association.* Newark, DL: Author. Available: www.reading.org/pdf/methods.pdf.

Kozol, J. (1991). *Savage inequalities: Children in America's schools.* New York: Crown Publishers.

Lauritzen, C. and Jaeger, M. (1997). *Integrating narrative through story: The narrative curriculum.* Albany, NY: Delmar Publications.

Leland, C., Harste, J., Ociepka, A. Lewison, M., and Vasquez, V. (1999). Exploring critical literacy: You can hear a pin drop. *Language Arts, 77* (1), 70-77.

Lindfors, J. W. (1987). *Children's language and learning* (2nd ed.). Englewood Cliffs, NJ: Prentice-Hall.

McKay, R. (1993). Whole language: Defining our beliefs, examining our practices. In L. L. Stewin and S.J.H. McCann (eds.), *Contemporary educational issues: The Canadian mosaic* (pp. 482–504). Toronto: Copp Clark Pitman.

Millard, D. (1997). *Differently literate: Boys, girls, and the schooling of literacy.* London: Falmer Press.

Moss, G. (2000). Raising boys' attainment in reading: Some principles for intervention. *Reading, 34,* 101–106.

National Anti-Poverty Organization. (1992). *Literacy and poverty: A view from the inside.* Ottawa: National Anti-Poverty Organization.

National Reading Panel (2001). *Teaching children to read.* Washington, DC: National Institute of Child Health and Human Development. Available: www.nationalreadingpanel.org.

The Ontario curriculum: Grades 1–8: Language (1997). Ontario Ministry of Education. Available: www.edu.gov.on.ca/eng/document/curricul/curr971.html.

Peterson, S. (2001). Teachers' perceptions of gender equity in writing assessment. *English Quarterly, 33* (1 & 2), 22–30.

Petite Rivière Elementary School. (1993). *History of Crousetown.* Lunenburg County, NS: Petite Rivière Publishing.

Piaget, J. (1972). *Insights and illusions of philosophy.* New York: Routledge and Kegan Paul.

Pressley, M., Allington, R. L., Wharton-McDonald, R., Block, C. C., and Morrow, L. M. (2001). *Learning to read: Lessons from exemplary first-grade classrooms.* New York: The Guilford Press.

Pressley, M. and Rankin, J. (1994). More about whole language methods of reading instruction for students at risk for early reading failure. *Learning Disabilities Research and Practice, 9* (3), 157–168.

Reutzel, D. R. (1999a). On balanced reading. *Reading Teacher, 52,* 2–4.

Reutzel, D. R. (1999b). On Welna's sacred cows: Where's the beef? *Reading Teacher, 53* (2), 96–99.

Richardson, V. (1997). Constructivist teaching and teacher education: Theory and practice. In V. Richardson (ed.), *Constructivist teacher education* (pp. 3–14). London: Falmer Press.

Rog, L. J. and Burton, W. (2002). Matching texts and readers: Leveling early reading materials for assessment and instruction. *Reading Teacher, 55* (4), 348–356.

Rosenblatt, L. (1989). Writing and reading: The transactional theory. In J. M. Mason (ed.), *Reading and writing connections* (pp. 153–176). Boston: Allyn and Bacon.

Rossman, A. D. (1987). Reading automaticity: The essential element of academic success. *Principal, 67,* 28–32.

Rumelhart, D. E. (1980). Schemata: The building blocks of cognition. In R. J. Spiro, B. C. Bruce, and W. F. Brewer (eds.), *Theoretical issues in reading comprehension* (pp. 33–58). Hillsdale, NJ: Lawrence Erlbaum Associates.

Scollon, R. and Scollon, S.B.K. (1981). *Narrative, literacy and face in interethnic communication*. Norwood, NJ: Ablex Publishing Corporation.

Shannon, P. (1989). The struggle for control of literacy lessons. *Language Arts, 66* (6), 625–634.

Shiel, G. and Cosgrove, J. (2002). International assessments of reading literacy. *Reading Teacher, 55* (7), 690–692.

Smith, F. (1971). *Understanding reading*. Hillsdale, NJ: Erlbaum.

Smith, F. (1975). *Comprehension in learning*. New York: Holt, Rinehart and Winston.

Smith, F. (1983). Reading like a writer. *Language Arts, 60* (5), 558–567.

Smith, F. (1988). *Joining the literacy club: Further essays into education*. London: Heinemann.

Stanovich, K. E. (1986). Matthew effects in reading: Some consequences of individual differences in the acquisition of literacy. *Reading Research Quarterly, 21* (4), 360–406.

Vygotsky, L. S. (1978). *Mind in society: The development of higher psychological processes*. M. Cole, V. John-Steiner, S. Scribner, and E. Souberman (eds.). Cambridge, MA: Harvard University Press.

Wason-Ellam, L. (2002). Interwoven responses to critically conscious stories. *Query, 31* (1), 21–26.

Weber-Pillwax, C. (2001). Orality in Northern Cree Indigenous worlds. *Canadian Journal of Native Education, 25* (2), 149–165.

Wells, G. (2001). The case for dialogic inquiry. In C. G. Wells (ed.), *Action, talk, and text: Learning and teaching through inquiry*. New York: Teachers College Press.

Wells, C. G. and Chang-Wells, G. L. (1992). *Constructing knowledge together: Classrooms as centers of inquiry and literacy*. Portsmouth, NH: Heinemann.

Western Canadian protocol for collaboration in basic education: The common curriculum framework for Aboriginal language and culture programs (2000). Governments of Alberta, British Columbia, Manitoba, Northwest Territories, Saskatchewan, and Yukon Territory. Available: www.wcp.ca.

Western Canadian protocol for collaboration in basic education: The common curriculum framework for English language arts: Kindergarten to Grade 12 (1998). Governments of Alberta, British Columbia, Manitoba, Northwest Territories, Saskatchewan, and Yukon Territory. Available: www.wcp.ca.

Wilkinson, L. C. and Marrett, C. B. (1985). *Gender influences in classroom interactions*. Toronto: Academic Press.

Young, J. P. and Brozo, W. G. (2001). Conversations: Boys will be boys, or will they? Literacy and masculinities. *Reading Research Quarterly, 36* (3), 316–325.

Chapter 2

Language Development and Oracy

The Purposeful Nature of Language

- Learning How to Mean
- Halliday's Functions of Language

Perspectives on Language Acquisition

- Behaviourist View of Language Learning
- Innatist View of Language Learning
- Interactionist View of Language Learning

Language Development and the Social Context

- Preschool Language Development
- Language Development in Elementary School
- Language at Home and at School
- Communicative Competence

Language Development and Oracy

Language in Learning

- Language and Thinking
- Language Across the Curriculum

Language Structures

- Semantics
- Syntax
- Phonology
- Pragmatics

Oral Language in the Classroom

- Listening
- Talking
- Assessing Oracy (Listening and Talking)
- Promoting Oral Language Growth in the Classroom
- Helping Children Become Effective Listeners
- Vocabulary Development

Ms. Moorhouse has successfully taught reading and writing to her Grade 2 students for the last three years. Ms. Moorhouse, however, doesn't have a BA in English, and she is coming to feel that she needs to know more about the English language itself. Ms. Moorhouse listens to her students talking in class and on the playground, and often hears statements such as "My brother, he got the measles." She is aware that some of the children need help in refining their oral language abilities. She would like to know more about how to address children's nonstandard oral language habits so that her students will become more articulate as they share their ideas in class and with their peers and families at home. What do teachers need to know about language in order to be able to teach oral language skills to children? If children have learned the essentials of their language before they come to school, what is left to teach in school, other than reading and writing?

As they strive to help children express themselves clearly and in appropriate language, many teachers find themselves asking questions about language as well as about how children learn language in the years before they come to school. This chapter describes the basic elements of language and how children learn to construct meaning through language. It explores language development in children both before they enter school and during their years in the elementary grades. Teachers model appropriate language in their interactions with their students, and they make every effort to understand important concepts and principles about language development. They appreciate, like Ms. Moorhouse, that understanding the nature of language development also facilitates an understanding of the role of language in learning. In school, children do two major things in their language development: they continue to learn and refine their language abilities, both written and spoken, and they learn how to use language in order to learn.

THE PURPOSEFUL NATURE OF LANGUAGE

In this section, we draw heavily on the work of Michael Halliday. Halliday was one of the most influential researchers and writers on language learning in the 1960s and 1970s and his work continues to influence research and practice in the language arts today.

In answering the question, "What is language?" Halliday (1969) maintains that the answer lies in the purpose or intention behind the language event. He believes that language is, for children, defined by its usefulness, by what language can do for them. Children learn language because there is something they need to *do*, and in order to do it, they need to communicate their intentions to another person (Box 2.1). There is almost no limit to what children can do with language. From birth onwards, children develop the ability to communicate their intentions, and they develop that ability long before they develop language. Their gestures direct the behaviour of the adults around them: they hold up their arms to be lifted up, and they point when they drop a favourite toy. At other times they play, gurgling and repeating the sounds and rhythms they have learned, evoking playful responses from their caregivers.

Halliday's Functions of Language

Michael Halliday identified seven "functions" of language (Box 2.2), which are summarized here. In everyday life we encounter *instrumental language* every time we ask another person to help us. When we order a meal in a restaurant, we are using the instrumental function of language. Closely related to this is the *regulatory function*. Sometimes it is difficult to tell these two functions apart, since when we regulate someone else's behaviour, it is often in order to meet our own needs. A "No Smoking" sign, a handbook on how to make a kite, the requirements for an assignment for a university class—all are examples of this. *Interactional language* is the language we use to maintain and establish relationships (or to have an argument, which is another way of maintaining a relationship). It is the social chat we engage in over coffee, and the conversations we have with friends and colleagues. *Personal language* is used when we tell about ourselves—our feelings, thoughts, and beliefs. Our personal language reveals part of our unique identity. **Heuristic language** is used when we explore and question and when we wonder and hypothesize. We hear it when a child says, "I wonder what would happen if …" The *imaginative* function

Box 2.1   Learning How to Mean

Michael Halliday maintained that children know what language is because they know what language does. In other words, children learn about language through using it. It was Halliday (1975) who coined the phrase "learning how to mean."

Halliday explained that

- children learn language to express meanings to others and to construct meaning for themselves. Most thinking is done through language. Although we sometimes think in feelings and images, we construct our most abstract thoughts through the vehicle of language.
- children learn language in real situations where something is being accomplished; for example, the singing of a song at bedtime, the talk mothers engage in while changing a child's clothing, the conversation that goes on around the dinner table, the choice of a television program, or the completion of a job in the yard.
- children are included in conversations even when they are not yet capable of speaking in complete sentences—an example is when older siblings ask infants what toys or books they would like to play with.
- children come to understand language from their own experiences of language in use. For example, children do not learn explicitly what a noun is, but they do learn to label. They do not understand what **grammar** is, yet they learn how to string words together into sentences that make sense to them and to the people with whom they intend to communicate.
- the **discourse** that contributes most to the growth of children's language learning is the discourse that actively involves the child. Interaction, particularly with significant adults or more mature language users, is necessary for language development to occur.
- watching television and being talked *at* are no substitutes for involvement. Genuine involvement and purposeful talk *with* children are the most important conditions upon which language development rests.

of language comes into full play when we write stories or poetry, or when we daydream, make a wish list, or engage in play with a child. Jokes, riddles, and cartoons are part of this realm. *Representational language* is the language of reports, lectures, documentary programs on television, and textbooks. As teachers and students, we become very familiar with this type of language because it predominates in classroom discourse.

Of importance to teachers is Halliday's observation that probably the most useful functions of language in a classroom are heuristic and personal. However, he showed that the most common functions in classroom use are representative and regulatory. In constructivist classrooms, teachers are aware that all language use has a purpose behind it. They provide a wide range of experiences so that children have opportunities to use language in different functions across the school day.

Halliday's work suggests that children do not develop language in a haphazard or purposeless way. On the contrary, children develop language because they have needs that must be fulfilled, and they quickly see that language enables them to make sense of and, to some extent, control their world. Through language, children can have their needs met, live in the world of the imagination, inquire, tell about who they are, tell what they know, and develop relationships. As children interact with others in classrooms, playgrounds,

Box 2.2   The Seven Functions of Language

On the basis of his observations of young children's language development in the early years, Halliday (1969) proposed a model that categorized language use according to seven functions.

Function

1. Instrumental (language as a means of getting things, satisfying material needs)
2. Regulatory (controlling the behaviour, feelings, or attitudes of others)
3. Interactional (getting along with others, establishing relative status and separateness)
4. Personal (expressing individuality, awareness of self, pride)
5. Heuristic (seeking and testing knowledge)
6. Imaginative (creating new worlds, making up stories, poems)
7. Representational (communicating information, descriptions, expressing propositions)

Example

"I want."

"Do as I tell you."

"Me and you." or "Me against you."

"Here I come."

"Tell me why."

"Let's pretend."

"I've got something to tell you."

Source: Based on M.A.K. Halliday, "Relevant models of language," *Educational Review, 22* (1), pp. 26–37.

stores, and other public places, they use language with amazing proficiency. When children enter kindergarten classrooms, their language reflects an implicit knowledge of the rules of grammar and appropriate language usage. In their five years of life they have mastered the most complex learning task they will likely ever have to accomplish—the learning of language—and they can use that language to do a multiplicity of tasks. Most of this language is learned in a two-year period, between the ages of 2 and 4. At this age, children have often been called linguistic geniuses. By the time children are in school, they take language completely for granted.

LANGUAGE STRUCTURES

The next section of the chapter examines language itself. How do linguists describe language? What does language consist of? What do the terms "semantics," "syntax," and "phonology" mean? How do these systems connect to language arts in the elementary grades? These are the questions Ms. Moorhouse was asking as this chapter opened.

As adults, we do not usually remember exactly what facets of language we learned as children, but we are all aware that we did once learn language. We also teach language to our own children without having any training in how to do it, and usually without a conscious awareness that we are teaching it. We talk to children, listen to them, play with them, read and tell stories to them, and they seem to learn language without much effort or direct teaching. What is it that children learn and that adults take for granted?

Linguists describe language in terms of three systems: **semantics**, **syntax**, and **phonology**. In addition, we learn the **pragmatics** of language. The ability to manipulate the basic language elements of semantics, syntax, phonology, and pragmatics with relative ease and fluency is called **native speaker ability**. It is part of what we know when we understand the difference between "That mom is awesome" and "That, Mom, is awesome." It's what helps to create the humour in children's books such as *Amelia Bedelia* (Parish, 1963), when Amelia "checks the laundry," "dresses a chicken," and "draws the drapes." A whole array of cultural, social, and contextual factors influence native speaker ability. Although all of the systems of language are interrelated, for clarity we discuss them independently in this section of the chapter.

Semantics

Semantics refers to the meaning component of language. A basic element of the meaning system of language is its **morphology**. *Morphemes*, the building blocks of meaning, are the smallest meaning units of language. Helping to create meaning within words and sentences, they consist of root words, or *free morphemes* (such as *ball*, *girl*, *play*, and *fast*) and *bound morphemes* (such as the *ed* suffix denoting past tense, the *s* suffix denoting plural, and the *er* suffix denoting "one who does"; e.g., a singer is one who sings). Prefixes are also examples of bound morphemes (e.g., *anti*, as in antihistamine or antiseptic). Bound morphemes do not stand alone, but have meaning only when attached to a free morpheme. The morphology of our language is extremely complex, yet children learn this aspect of language at the same time they learn the other systems that make up language.

Idioms and *compound words* are also part of the system of semantics that native speakers learn. Idioms are phrases whose meaning is not related to the meanings of the individual words in the phrase. For example, "to kick the bucket" has nothing to do with either kicking or a pail: it means "to die." The meanings of idioms have to be learned in the same way as individual vocabulary items—they are unique and have to be understood in the context of their use.

In the same way, native speakers learn compound words, two separate words that together create a new, single meaning. Native English speakers understand what a houseboat and a housefly are, and know the difference between them. They know that a houseboat is "a house that is also a boat," and that a housefly is not "a house that is also a fly," but a fly that lives in houses. They know they can say that a plate broke or a briefcase handle broke, but they would not say that a sweater or a newspaper broke. These are examples of the colloquial restrictions that native speakers learn. All of this is part of our semantic knowledge.

More than simply the words and phrases we learn and use, semantics includes the highly cultural nature of language—how our language performs the job the culture requires it to do. Every culture has its own world view, which is encompassed in its language. All members of a culture tacitly agree on the meanings of words and phrases. In English we have a verb tense system that marks when an event occurs. Some languages, however, do not mark verb tenses in the same way as English. They might say, for example, to indicate that something happened in the past, "before now." The way in which a culture chooses to classify the world is arbitrary. The English language has many words for colour, for example, whereas some languages make only a binary distinction (roughly equivalent to light and dark), although the physical perception skills of all people are the same.

When teachers teach lessons on suffixes or on compound words, they are teaching the semantic system of language. Synonyms, antonyms, and homonyms are also examples of the semantics of language taught in elementary classrooms. These aspects of language are most effectively taught in the contexts of speaking, listening, reading, and writing, where they are likely to occur naturally rather than as isolated exercises or drills.

Syntax

The basic unit in syntax is the sentence. Syntax refers to the way words are strung together to create meaning. Every language has its own syntax. In English, syntax and word order are almost synonymous: a change in the word order of a sentence almost always has an effect on meaning—sometimes minimally, sometimes drastically. "The dog bit the man" is very different in meaning from "The man bit the dog." Often a similar meaning is conveyed by two sentences that have different structures, as in "The child collected the books" and "The books were collected by the child." Rarely, however, do changes in syntax have *no* effect on meaning. To illustrate the role of syntax, take the sentence "I saw the kitten in the garden" and insert the word "only" at various points throughout to see the major shifts in meaning. For example, "Only I saw the kitten in the garden" is quite different in meaning from "I saw only the kitten in the garden," "I saw the only kitten in the garden," and "I saw the kitten only in the garden." Thus, the rules for ordering words in English are extremely important, because changes in syntax affect meaning. (And sentences following no rules of syntax—for example, "The I saw kitten the only garden in"—are clearly meaningless.) In elementary school classrooms, syntax is usually taught under the heading of "grammar."

As children mature, they have a growing capacity to embed more and more meaning into each sentence they speak or write by using clauses and phrases, making the sentence more compact and yet richer in meaning (Hunt, 1965). A young child may say in conversation with a partner, "I have a cat. He's called Sam. I like him. He's grey. He's my friend." An older person might combine these basic (or kernel) sentences and say something like, "I have a grey cat called Sam, whom I like very much because he's so friendly." The result is a more fluent language style as well as a more economic way of expressing meaning— in short, a more mature form of syntax.

Sentence-combining and sentence-building activities are often helpful to students because they demonstrate how language can be manipulated, and they provide alternatives for children in constructing sentences. They are also frequently enjoyable and playful activities with no right or wrong answers—just many alternatives. There are, for example, many ways of combining these four kernel sentences:

The puppy is black.

The puppy barked at the rabbit.

The puppy belongs to Janet.

Janet lives on Third Street.

Alternatives include "The black puppy belonging to Janet, who lives on Third Street, barked at the rabbit," or "Janet, who lives on Third Street, has a black puppy that barked at a rabbit." Clearly, there are many other combinations that students can create as they manipulate word order and come to a fuller understand of the role of syntax in the construction of meaning.

Although the words "grammar" and "syntax" are frequently used interchangeably, they do have different definitions. Syntax is a term linguists use to describe how human beings organize their language structures. Grammar is a term teachers have traditionally used to define a prescriptive set of rules. Syntax and grammar are both derived from the spoken language, but when grammar is taught in school, it usually pertains to writing. Educators and researchers (see Braddock, Lloyd-Jones, and Schoer, 1963) have long believed that grammar should not be taught in elementary schools in a formal manner. However, it is certainly helpful for children to know the difference between what is acceptable or appropriate and what is considered poor grammar. Unacceptable grammar is reflected in such commonly used sentences as "I borrowed him my pencil" and "I should of went earlier." The labels describing parts of speech (such as nouns, adjectives, adverbs, and so on) are also helpful to students, because they enable teachers and students to talk about language and how we use it, especially in the context of a writing workshop. Grammar is rarely studied as a set of rules in isolation today. There is a far greater interest in children being able to use these rules in their speech and writing rather than in identifying them. The focus is more on appropriateness in various contexts than on correctness. This aspect of language teaching and learning is dealt with in later chapters, notably in Chapter Nine.

Phonology

The phonology of a language is its sound system. Every language has a set of sounds that enables its users to communicate meaning. The smallest units of sound in a language are *phonemes*. The English language has between 45 and 52 different phonemes (depending on the classification system and dialect). Phonemes are not the same in all languages, and what constitutes a phoneme in one language may not constitute one in another. English has the phonemes *l* and *r*, but these are not meaningful sounds in Japanese, for example. As a result, Japanese people who learn to speak English tend to confuse these sounds because they were not distinguishable in their first language. In the same way, English speakers have difficulty pronouncing many Swahili words beginning with *ng*, as in *ngoma*, which means "drum." Even though this sound is a separate phoneme in English (note the difference between "rim" and "ring"), English speakers do not hear it at the beginning of a word and hence have difficulty pronouncing it when it appears there. The nearest we have to this sound in English occurs in the words *ring* and *think*.

When the phonology of a language is transcribed into symbols, it is referred to as the **graphophonic** system. In English, these sounds are represented by the 26 letters of the alphabet. Understanding the sound–symbol relationship is one of the key learnings children accomplish in their literacy development. The manipulation of the graphophonic system forms the basis for children's reading and writing development in the primary years. It is important to note that the phonological system (sound system) and the orthographic system (written system) are two distinct systems of language, each with its own conventions. This is just one of the reasons why learning to read and write in English is a complex undertaking, especially where spelling is concerned.

A further element of phonology is intonation, which consists of stress, pitch, and juncture. Stress is the emphasis placed on different words, pitch is the level of the voice, and juncture is the pause that adds or emphasizes meaning. We provide intonation clues in writing through the use of punctuation.

The phonology of a language varies from one **dialect** to another. Dialect refers to variations in language based on social class, ethnic group, and geographic location. To some Canadians, the words *metal* and *pedal* rhyme, and the *t* in "congratulations" sounds like the *d* in "graduation." The words *cot* and *caught* are homonyms in Canadian English, but for some American or British speakers, the words have very different vowel sounds. These differences in speech patterns can sometimes create difficulties for people in communicating meaning, but on the whole, we manage to communicate orally in English whether we are from India, South Africa, Australia, Pakistan, Wales, or Canada.

Pragmatics

When two or more people talk together, it takes a lot of coordination to keep the conversation flowing smoothly. Although we are not normally aware of it, the various speakers are careful not to talk at the same time, or to interrupt each other or to fail to answer a question when a question is asked. It is these common understandings of the "rules" of language use that constitute pragmatics. *Pragmatics* refers to the ways in which speakers use language in context. For example, when a person says "The phone is ringing," it is often a request for someone else to answer it, not simply a statement of fact. It is the speaker's intent that is of concern.

Children do not learn language in isolation. The sounds, meanings, and grammatical principles learned are embedded in the social-interactive framework of the child's world. The rules governing how language is used in this social context make up the pragmatic component of language. As they become effective communicators, children learn to take both the speaker's and the listener's roles and perspectives into account at the same time. They learn how to initiate a conversation, contribute to the topic, request clarification, create smooth changes in topic, provide both verbal and nonverbal feedback to keep the conversation going, monitor timing and pauses in the dialogue, and conclude the interaction appropriately. They also learn how to modify the usage of words such as *here* and *there*, *this* and *that*. They learn how to say, for example, "I will put my cookie *here*. You can put your cookie *there*," or "I will have *this* one, and you can have *that* one."

Language use also varies according to the social norm, an aspect of language known as *register*. Children learn, for example, a range of registers and styles that help them to function appropriately in situations ranging from formal (making a speech at high school graduation) to informal or nonstandard (playing in the park with friends, reading a comic book). Students who come from sociocultural settings where nonstandard English is used are usually able to read textbooks and listen to television newscasts that are in standard English. They seldom have problems with comprehension. Competent speakers learn to control a range of registers that allow them to function in diverse situations in society. As they make the transition from student to teacher, some preservice teachers have to work at mastering standard English and a more formal register of language use. This is a necessary step if they are to be appropriate role models in the classroom and perceived as functioning professionals.

People who have strong pragmatics abilities are usually considered to be socially competent and confident These skills, together with linguistic competence, form what is known as *communicative competence*.

Intercultural Differences in the Pragmatics of Language

An interesting aspect of pragmatics is that of timing and pauses. Scollon and Scollon (1983), whose work we mentioned in Chapter One, write, "In interethnic communication there are often differences in the systems of the speakers, so that mistakes happen that lead to further misunderstandings" (p. 22). They use the Athabaskan family of languages as an example. When an Athabaskan speaker and an English speaker converse, it is most likely that the English speaker will speak first. Where the Athabaskan feels it is important to know the relationship between the two speakers *before* speaking, the English speaker feels that talking is the best way to *establish* a relationship (and frequently ask questions to foster the relationship). An Athabaskan speaker will usually initiate a conversation only where there is a longstanding relationship. Scollon and Scollon go on to say that the person who initiates a conversation usually also controls the topic of the conversation. The differences in the discourse systems can lead to misunderstandings: Athabaskan speakers can feel ignored, or may feel that English speakers are egocentric and focused only on their own ideas. English speakers may feel that Athabaskan speakers do not have any ideas of their own or that when new ideas are introduced they are off-topic.

Pausing between turns is yet another area where difficulties may arise in interethnic conversations. To continue Scollon and Scollon's example, speakers of Dene Soun'line (a member of the Athabaskan language family) in Fort Chipewyan, Alberta, allow a slightly longer pause between sentences than English speakers. Where English speakers generally allow one second before beginning another sentence or entering a conversation, Dene Soun'line speakers, along with speakers of other Athabaskan languages, allow one-and-a-half seconds. That half-second is long enough for English speakers to innocently jump in and dominate a conversation, not allowing Athabaskan speakers long enough to continue their flow of ideas. Such subtle differences in discourse patterns can result in strong stereotypical responses to the opposite ethnic group.

Researchers (Scollon and Scollon, 1983; Cleary and Peacock, 1989) have identified Aboriginal cultures as being High-Context and English Speaking cultures as Low-Context. Table 2.1 outlines the communication characteristics of the two cultures.

When non-Aboriginal teachers do not understand the differences in discourse patterns, misunderstandings and frustrations can occur in communications with their Aboriginal students. Non-Aboriginal teachers, in trying to elicit greater clarity and depth in their students' responses, will often elaborate on the original response, or may eventually stop asking questions of the Aboriginal students altogether (Delpit, 1995). Further misunderstandings can be caused by the difference in the standard wait and response times typical of these two cultures. Non-Aboriginal teachers leave a shorter wait time after their questions and comments before assuming that if the students have not responded within this time, they have nothing to share or they have finished sharing. However, because the Aboriginal students' average response time is longer than that of the non-Aboriginal English-speaking Canadian, the Aboriginal student is interrupted or cut off by their non-Aboriginal teacher. This then feeds into the stereotype of the "nonverbal Aboriginal child" and the pushy, aggressive non-Aboriginal teacher (Delpit, 1995).

In addition, Aboriginal students do not necessarily maintain eye contact with other speakers, as lack of eye contact is considered a sign of respect. Non-Aboriginal teachers, however, often feel uncomfortable, irritated, or hurt by what they consider disrespectful behaviour (Cleary and Peacock, 1989). What the non-Aboriginal teacher perceives as a lack of "assertiveness" in their Aboriginal students' softer and slower communication style contrasts starkly with the Aboriginal students' perceptions of the unfamiliar loudness and speed with which their non-Aboriginal teachers speak (Delpit, 1995). Aboriginal students

Table 2.1 Communication Characteristics of Aboriginal and Non-Aboriginal Canadians

English-Speaking Aboriginal Canadians (High Context)	English-Speaking Non-Aboriginal Canadians (Low Context)
• Most communicated information is either in the physical context or internalized in the person, while very little is in the coded, explicit, transmitted part of the message. • Reliance is less on spoken words and more on non-verbal information. • If a statement, thought, or idea has once been made, it is not made again. • Words are often not said, as situated factors deliver the greater part of the intended meaning. • Speakers pause on average for a longer period of time between their own and other speaker's thoughts than do non-Aboriginal English speaking Canadians. • Voices are usually softer and language is spoken slower than non-Aboriginal English-speaking Canadians. • Speakers will not necessarily make eye contact with other speakers.	• The mass of information is communicated in the explicit code and therefore is highly verbal. • Most messages are conveyed through conversation. • Explanations are belaboured rather than risking unsuccessful communication. • Speaker pauses between thoughts/sentences are, on average, shorter than those of Aboriginal speakers. • Voices are generally louder and language is spoken faster than English-speaking Aboriginal Canadians. • Speakers will generally make eye contact with other speakers.

can understandably be left puzzled and annoyed that their comments and explanations are seemingly inadequate. Non-Aboriginal teachers can feel frustrated that their Aboriginal students appear to be disengaged with the verbal landscape of the classroom. A classroom environment that promotes positive communication for Aboriginal English-speaking students (as well as for all students from minority groups) can be created when teachers are sensitive to their own discourse patterns and to the discourse patterns of the students in their classrooms.

PERSPECTIVES ON LANGUAGE ACQUISITION

The next section of this chapter addresses the various hypotheses proposed by researchers to account for children's language learning. The early acquisition of language by young children remains something of a mystery to educators and researchers alike. There is a great deal still to be learned about language acquisition. Teachers continue to be intrigued by the phenomenon, because language abilities are so very important to a child's later learning both inside and outside school.

Behaviourist View of Language Learning

Until the 1950s, researchers believed that children learn language through the feedback they receive to their utterances. Children were seen as passive in their language learning—not initiating, but reacting and responding to the language of others. This was a behaviourist view of learning, postulating that children learn language as they are reinforced for their responses to a variety of stimuli (Skinner, 1957; Staats, 1971). The reinforcement could be either positive or negative, depending on the appropriateness of a given response. For example, if a child says "Ma-ma-ma-ma," there will likely be a positive response from the caregiver, just as when a child first waves a hand in a gesture of farewell. Children receive cuddles, smiles, frowns, angry retorts or soft verbal responses from their caregivers as they explore their environment and experiment with language. However, as researchers continued to explore children's language development, it became apparent that the behaviourist view of language acquisition could not account for all the things a child learns to *do* with language, nor for the vast amount of language a child learns or the unique utterances a child makes.

The behaviourist view subsequently gave rise to a plethora of language learning research with chimpanzees, mules, and other animals. Much of the research was carried out by Terrace (1979) who, after working in this field for five years, finally recognized that what the animals were learning was not a language in the sense that humans use language. The animals were responding to their trainers through printed and verbal symbols, but it was not language. Certainly, some of what children learn in their early years is attributable to behaviouristic responses from caregivers, but the majority of language learning is far too complex to occur solely as a result of this effect.

Innatist View of Language Learning

In the 1950s, Noam Chomsky, a linguist at Harvard University, developed a completely new view of language learning that became known as the *innatist* view. He argued strongly that children have a predisposition for learning language, that some built-in device enables them to learn it quickly and easily. This device, which Chomsky labelled a Language Acquisition Device (LAD), has only to be triggered by language input of some kind and children will learn language. It is as though children have a custom-built software package that allows them to access language and use it after minimal "messing around" and "testing" of the program.

Shortly after the publication of Chomsky's major work (1957), Eric Lenneberg (1964) postulated that language must be learned in stages, such as those stages in children's physical development. Lenneberg pointed out some parallels between physical development and language development. He also maintained that there is a critical period for language development—from birth until about the age of 13, when the brain has largely matured. Lenneberg's work supported the innatist claim that genetic inheritance does not simply give human beings a mental ability for learning in general, but that it also provides a specific language learning ability. Lenneberg believed that exposure to language in the environment was a necessary and sufficient condition for language learning to occur, whereas Chomsky believed this capacity to be some kind of unconscious knowledge of language universals, built into the brain and activated when young children encounter a stream of meaningful language around them.

In a completely different approach to exploring language development, some researchers (including Donaldson, 1978) suggested that all children possess a general capacity for inference, a capacity that allows them to develop language. A child actively tests hypotheses and makes inferences in order to learn language.

All these approaches to language learning focus on the nature of the child's innate ability to learn language. It was not until the early 1980s that an approach to language learning was formulated based on a totally different set of principles or assumptions—an *interactionist* approach. In many ways this approach has at its base the old "nature versus nurture" controversy, for it involves the role of both the individual and the culture in the development of language.

Interactionist View of Language Learning

The interactionist view of language development maintains that there must be a fully functioning human being (i.e., biologically intact, capable of developing language) and a fully functioning social system (i.e., an intact social environment) in place before language development can occur (John-Steiner and Tatter, 1983). In other words, language is contextualized; it happens in real situations for real purposes. If there is no intact social system in place, or if a child is disabled in some way, then normal language learning may not take place. If there is no interaction between the child and the social system, this will create a lack in language learning. Rather than seeing culture, society, and the child's psychological makeup and cognitive abilities as separate entities, the interactionist views all of them as interdependent, much like a woven tapestry. The child is part of the culture as much as the culture is part of the child. Language learning involves both learning *about* the culture and learning about being an individual who is a *part of* the culture. These facets of human life cannot be separated and examined in isolation. They are each part of the other, interacting and contributing to the unique development of all individuals.

Researchers working from a behaviourist perspective on language learning believed that children's language acquisition was entirely a result of the reinforcement they received for their utterances. In the 1950s, Chomsky theorized that children possess some kind of language acquisition device, something like the hard drive of a computer that pre-wires children for language learning. The LAD allows them to learn language after the device has been triggered by a minimal amount of language input from caregivers. The most recent view of language learning is much more complex than either of these. The interactionist view postulates that children learn language as a result of the interaction of the human being, the social situation, and the culture. Language is contextualized and is learned through its use. This view of language development has powerful implications for teaching language arts and for using language in learning across the curriculum.

LANGUAGE DEVELOPMENT AND THE SOCIAL CONTEXT

The next section of this chapter addresses the continuing development of children's language abilities from preschool through elementary school. In particular, attention is paid to the social context of language development and to the factors that influence the development of children's language.

Preschool Language Development

Most caregivers talk to their infants as though they are equal participants in conversation. When a mother changes a baby's diaper she usually talks to the child, smiles, tickles the infant, and converses as though the infant understands the language and will respond. We hear a mother saying:

Do you want your diaper changed? Oh, you're all wet! No wonder you were making a fuss. Let's see what we can do. There, does that feel better? Let's go see what Jennifer's doing.

This type of interaction is vitally important to young children, and before long they, too, begin to make sounds, to babble and coo and explore the sounds they are capable of making. By the time children are nine or ten months old, they can make all the sounds that are used in all the languages in the world. At this stage, children with normal hearing suddenly begin to stop making some sounds, continuing only with those they hear around them. They also adopt the intonation pattern and rhythm of the language they hear. By the time children are about one year to eighteen months old, the sounds they make are more and more like words. Children who have hearing problems, however, will stop all the sounds they have been making and either not develop speech or be delayed in speech development, depending on the severity of their hearing problem.

The first stage of language development is that of the holophrase, or one-word utterance. Here a child uses one word to communicate myriad meanings. *Puppy* can mean anything from "Look at the puppy" to "I want to hold the puppy" to "That is a puppy." Children know what they mean, however, and if they don't get an appropriate response, they will let their conversational partners know. Halliday (1969) first identified his seven functions of language when he was exploring this very early stage of language development. Children learn to create words and string words together because they have things they want to *do*. They have needs, ideas, and relationships that are important and can best be expressed through language. It is the use of language that is the driving force behind its development.

Children speak their first words generally anywhere between the age of ten months and two years. Their age when this happens does not seem to influence their language development in any significant way. The first words spoken are usually labels for items in the child's environment that he or she acts on, such as *cookie, milk, kitty, ball, sock,* and *daddy*. Words unlikely in that list are *crib* (unless the child has learned to let down its side!), *diaper, powder,* and any others used to label something in the child's world that he or she has no control over and that is not relevant to his or her intentions.

The second phase of development is the two-word utterance, where children string two words together to create more specific and detailed meanings. "Daddy gone," "More milk," "Cup fall" are examples of speech at this stage of development. The stage marks a breakthrough in language, because children move from simple labelling and the use of one word to a more sophisticated use of language. This stage is followed by telegraphic speech, where children string three or more words together to create meaning. Because they don't use structure words, their language sounds like a telegram. For example, a child might say, "Mummy go store" or "Nana come now." From here, children move on to creating complete sentences, and by the age of four, their language is likely to sound very much like that of adults. Brown (1973) at Harvard University was one of the key researchers who described in detail the sequential development of children's speech. Brown studied the development of questioning and sentence-combining, while researchers such as Clark and Clark (1977) studied children's early interactions with their caregivers. Research shows that although there are general patterns and trends in language development, every child passes through these stages and phases at different rates. However, the most important influence on the child's language development is the language and playful interactions that take place between him or her and the primary caregiver.

Language Development in Elementary School

When children enter school at the age of five or six, they have mastered the complexities of the language system. They understand syntax and phonology, and they can create a multitude of meanings from what they say and hear around them. They are aware of the printed symbols they see in their environment and can recognize print symbols, such as those on cereal boxes and in grocery stores and fast food restaurants. Most children know how to handle books by this age and take delight in being read to by a caregiver. They take pleasure in playing with language, and are beginning to understand the subtleties of language that underlie the creation of humour.

Early in the 1950s, Walter Loban (1963) undertook a longitudinal study of children's language development. He tracked one group of children in the Oakland area of California throughout their years of schooling from kindergarten to Grade 12. The study proved to be a landmark in our understanding of children's language development during the elementary years. Loban showed that children who enter school with low language ability are likely to remain lower than other children in their language ability throughout their schooling. Likewise, children who enter school with high language ability retain that advantage throughout their schooling. Not only that, but those children with high language proficiency make the greatest progress and improve their language ability the most, while children who have low language ability fall further and further behind their peers. This finding was one of the motivating forces that led to the development of Head Start programs in the United States in the 1960s (an initiative in which early intervention and support services are provided for poor preschool children and their families to try to break the poverty cycle). Loban also demonstrated that the direct teaching of grammar has little or no impact on the language development of elementary school children. Since this research was published in 1963, curriculum developers have struggled to create programs of study that balance instruction in the forms of language with the purposeful use of appropriate language in classrooms. A third major finding of Loban's study was that reading and writing abilities are related, and a fourth was that boys more than girls are more likely to have problems with language or, conversely, to appear in the group with the highest language ability. Overall, Loban showed that children learn language by using it, and that children's progress on this lifelong journey is strongly affected by what happens to them before they enter school.

Throughout the school years, children continue to develop and refine their language abilities in all areas, especially language structure, language use, and **metalinguistic awareness** (the growing ability to use language to talk about language as a formal code) (Lindfors, 1987). Metalinguistic awareness is part of children's thinking in general. Donaldson (1978) posited that young children's thinking is embedded; they make sense of language in the context of their everyday lives and experiences. In other words, children relate what they learn to what they know, and make sense of new experiences only in the context of what is familiar. A six-year-old child, hearing that the family was going to Seattle, said that he didn't want to go to Seattle because "I don't even know who Attle is anyway." Donaldson showed that children also make sense of tasks they are asked to do in school in similar ways. If children are introduced to new concepts by working with concrete objects in the context of a familiar situation (e.g., learning about fractions through cutting pizza or apples), they are more likely to understand the concept than if they are taught without concrete objects and in an unfamiliar context (learning about fractions through manipulating numbers on a whiteboard). As children get older they are able to understand language and thinking without embedding it in their everyday experiences. Donaldson maintains that by the age of eleven children are usually able to consider language outside the context of their own experiences. They can reflect on language as an entity separate from themselves, and hence manipulate it and learn about it with a new awareness.

Language at Home and at School

From birth onwards, children creatively develop language in social situations. They actively figure out how language creates meaning by observing what it does. Children use forms of language they have never encountered before, which refutes a totally behaviouristic theory of language learning. From birth to age six, children learn an astounding average of 21 new words a day (Miller, 1977). They attend to language selectively, however, using whatever is relevant to them. They speak and take note of how others respond, they notice how other people express meanings, they ask questions and imitate what other people say (and how they say it), and they use some general principles for figuring out how language works.

The primary social context for children's language learning is, of course, the home. Here, children first learn language in interaction with their caregivers. Slowly, the child's world gets larger. Children visit other homes, the daycare centre, stores, the playground, the doctor's office, and so on. When they enter school, they encounter a whole new social context, where adults' use of language is often different from what children have encountered in their homes. Generally, there is far less personal interaction in school than there is at home.

Some remarkable studies have explored the language environments of both home and school. Tizard and Hughes (1984) examined the language at home and at school of four-year-old children in nursery schools in the United Kingdom. Their finding was that children do not encounter a richer language at school than at home (contrary to popular belief) primarily because of the nature of the interactions. Teachers have less time to devote to individual children, and are busy with the organizational aspects of teaching. They are not usually involved in doing things *with* children, which is when most language interactions occur with children at home (whether we are making dinner together or watching television together). Teachers speak *to* children but generally not *with* them.

Probably the most extensive study of language development completed in the social contexts in which children live is the Bristol Study conducted in England by Gordon Wells (1986). Wells followed 32 children from the ages of 2 to 9 years, tape-recording a number of 15-minute segments of their oral language interactions every day. The children were fitted with radio microphones, so the data were collected at various times and in a variety of contexts. The talk was analyzed for grammatical complexity and for the functions of language used. Wells challenged previous research findings (Tough, 1976) by showing that children from homes of low socioeconomic status did *not* exhibit impoverished language use. At home, those children used language much the same as the children of high socioeconomic status. However, what Wells also found was that the language of all 32 children was suppressed at school. He states, "For no child was the language experience of the classroom richer than that of the home—not even for those believed to be 'linguistically deprived'" (1986, p. 87). Wells discovered that teachers dominated conversation and that much of the talk children engaged in at school was inauthentic, lacking the purpose and spontaneity of real talk. These findings coincide with Tizard and Hughes's findings regarding the language of four-year-olds. Clearly, there is a problem with oral language interactions in classrooms. These studies indicate that educators need to explore possibilities for expanding children's "oracy" in school, and determine the causes of the current failure to address this important area of language arts.

In the constructivist world of home, playground, street, shopping mall, club, and so on, children continue to expand their language strategies. As they interact with more people, and with people in different social contexts, they continue their efforts to make sense of language and to expand their phonological, morphological, syntactic, semantic, and pragmatic knowledge. In this capacity, the classroom is particularly important, as children learn language most effectively with teachers who support and stretch their efforts in language development. In constructivist classrooms, teachers and children learn and interact in language contexts that enable them to communicate and express their own thoughts and feelings. In other words, children develop language abilities most effectively when they use language in school for the same purposes for which they use language out of school. They write real letters to real people for real purposes, share their stories with people who are interested in hearing and responding to them, read books and magazines for pleasure and information, and generally engage in real-world language events, including listening and speaking.

Learning in a school context provides numerous opportunities for children to use language to solve problems and interact with the world, calling into play all of their linguistic knowledge and skills. Harste, Woodward, and Burke (1984, p. 9) suggest that "control of form is not a prerequisite to the language process." Unfortunately, much of school learning has, in the past, divorced meaning from form (Ferreiro and Teberosky, 1982). James Britton (1970) used the phrase "dummy runs" to describe many of the language experiences children are required to engage in at school. He maintained that children must *practise* language in the sense that a doctor practises medicine and a lawyer practises law, and *not* in the sense that a juggler practises a new trick before performing it. When doctors practise medicine, they are totally engaged in problem solving with their patients in a professional capacity that calls upon all their knowledge and skills. When jugglers practise tricks, they repeat the same moves over and over as a rehearsal for the time when they will finally perform in front of an audience. Children do not need to rehearse language in school for a time when they will have to use it in the "real world." In a constructivist classroom, the activities children engage in across the curriculum are also activities that teach language. Children, as they use language in their learning, are encouraged to solve problems, make inferences, and express their own opinions and ideas. In such a context, children do not need rehearsals.

Communicative Competence

"Communicative competence" is the ability to combine and use all aspects of language, including nonverbal communication, and to use them as a native speaker does. It is not simply linguistic competence, where a speaker knows the language and the rules of that language; it is the ability to make sense of the world through language, and to use language in diverse ways and situations to accomplish specific purposes.

Communicative competence, then, refers to language in use. A large part of communicative competence includes the pragmatics of

Children learning in a school context.

understanding the appropriateness of interactions. Most interactions we encounter are comfortable and acceptable. When an interaction is neither of these, we are sensitive to it. Sometimes, we are face-to-face with our interlocutor and we can take note of the non-verbal aspects of the communication—for example, the expression on a person's face or the distance between ourself and our partner. But even if we are not in face-to-face communication, we might have the feeling that something is not appropriate. We might begin to question the interaction and ask, "What is really going on here?"

The following excerpt from a telephone conversation demonstrates a lack of communicative competence in Anne, one of the speakers:

Anne: You know what?

George: No, I don't know, Anne. Tell me.

Anne: You know what?

George: No, Anne, tell me what you've been doing today.

Anne: Are you there?

George: Yes, I'm here, Anne. What have you been doing today?

Anne: You know what?

This exchange took place during a call between a resident of a group home and one of her caregivers. Anne, who initiated the call, appeared to lack social competence because she seemed to have difficulty in establishing the conversation with George. She violated basic rules of conversation (pragmatics), and it might have been difficult for George to know the purpose of her call. In fact, Anne did not have the communicative competence necessary to state her purpose and relay her message to George. The conversation continued only because George understood Anne's difficulty and was able to help Anne move into a conversation where she could narrate the day's events to him and share her excitement. The one essential element of communication is that it be purposeful. When the purpose of a conversation is not apparent, the whole event can become confusing and difficult.

Communicative competence includes the pragmatics of knowing how to open a conversation, establish rapport, take turns, get to the point, ask questions, clarify, check for understanding, be relevant, not talk for too long, supply all necessary information, and be truthful, clear, and comprehensible. If any of these elements is missing, a distortion in communication can occur. Usually, the conversational partner will correct the situation by asking relevant questions, focusing the speaker, paraphrasing, or stating directly that a problem exists (e.g., "I'm not sure what you mean by that. Are you saying that ...?"). Naturally, we try to be as tactful as possible in a conversation to keep it focused and flowing.

Children develop communicative competence when they are using language to achieve their own specific purposes. The seven functions of language Halliday (1969) noted in young children drive children to learn and to participate in language events as equal and demanding partners. The more they spend time with others, with an agenda of their own and freedom to explore their world, the more children will become competent communicators. The classroom, where there is a great diversity of background experiences, family lifestyles, and cultural mixes, provides a rich opportunity for developing communicative competence. Children learn to narrate, which is a fundamental way of making sense of the world (Rosen, 1984), to explain and inform, and to express their personal ideas and opinions. They also learn to adapt their communication to the situation, to the age and status of the conversational partner, to whether this is a family member or not, to their familiarity with their partner, and to the physical location of the communication. In short, a child speaks differently on the playground than in the classroom, in the doctor's office, or at church or temple. The development of these competencies at school is the focus of the remainder of this book.

LANGUAGE IN LEARNING

To this point, this chapter has focused on how children learn language. The next part of the chapter focuses on how language helps children to learn, or how language influences cognition. Everyone has a theory of how the world works, and we develop that theory through our experiences of the world. Language plays a very large role in this process as we replay events to ourselves and others and, in doing so, make greater sense of them. We listen to or read others' opinions and ideas and clarify our own ideas, thus adding to our learning. We relate new experiences to old ones and continue to make sense of them all. The language we have at our disposal enables us, to a large extent, to perform this learning. Language allows us to shape our thoughts, to ask questions, to explore, to clarify, and to create meaning. Words allow us to put meanings together, and to create new understandings. In both children and adults, we can see the same processes taking place.

When Ms. Moorhouse was an undergraduate student in education, she read many chapters from textbooks and was later tested on the content. She learned the material well and answered the questions on the test to the satisfaction of the examiner. But how much had really made sense to her? How much of her learning would she to be able to apply in her field experiences? It is actually quite likely that during student teaching Ms. Moorhouse would consider teaching as she herself was taught, and that choice would likely be "transmissive." Parents might also pressure her to teach the way they were taught, because that's what they are most familiar with. In fact, Ms. Moorhouse didn't come to understand what she knew and what she didn't know until she engaged in conversations with her instructors and fellow students and was challenged by the learning needs of the children in her student teaching classroom. Only then were her understandings truly tested. What had those book chapters been referring to? How would this knowledge affect Ms. Moorhouse's planning for instruction? And how would her own learning relate to the learning accomplished by the students in her classroom? It was when these questions were raised and discussed that new understandings began to emerge for Ms. Moorhouse, and new ways of approaching learning and teaching became apparent.

Language and Thinking

Information is not simply processed in isolation, but is shared, built on with peers, and discussed as it relates to real people and real contexts. This aspect of learning is one of the strongest reasons for having students engage in group projects, where they can study and work together, pooling information and helping one another to clarify and test out specific learnings. Through group interaction and exploratory talk, students question, make meanings more precise, and reinterpret past experience (which is why a personal story is often told to make a point). Interaction becomes crucially important as learners stretch their limits and move into areas that are uncertain, going beyond personal experience and specific situations. It is this concept of the role of language in the learning process that has caused educators to focus on processes such as collaboration, cooperation, group work, and the value of oral language in the classroom.

Sometimes we talk ourselves into understanding, and sometimes we write our way into understanding. Writing can create new worlds for the writer (and reader), but it may be that writing, even more than speech, "not only reflects our knowing ... but ... also causes our knowing" (Dillon, 1985, p. 9). We write letters, lists, papers, reports, and notes, and we also write for ourselves (poetry, stories, notes, diaries, logs). Journal writing is one of the ways in which we write for ourselves, as we attempt to recall and understand. Writing and then rereading our thoughts, pondering them, and revisiting them kindles personal and cognitive growth that we often cannot complete with other people. It is a task we have to accomplish alone. Writing encourages us to make our ideas separate from ourselves—putting our thoughts out there so we can examine them and hold on to them for future reference and ongoing reflection. This process is part of the decontextualization of thought (what Donaldson, 1978, calls "disembedded thought"). We can move into a more detached realm and see our thoughts as things to be played with and built on. Our thoughts, we find, are not only part of our self, but part of a larger world with more abstract and less personal meaning. We move from the contextualized (embedded) to the decontextualized (disembedded), and we move from the known to the unknown. We begin with our own experiences and our own ideas, but then we pass beyond them to a wider world, accommodating and assimilating the new.

Language Across the Curriculum

The work of Michael Halliday, James Britton, James Moffett, and Douglas Barnes has provided educators with valuable structures for analyzing, understanding, and creating language learning opportunities in diverse areas of the school curriculum. Now armed with a basis for developing language learning tasks that are meaningful, purposeful, and cohesive, many teachers have been helped to answer the critical question "How can I help my students to learn?" The guiding principles outlined in this chapter can be applied to learning activities not only in language arts, but also in subject areas such as social studies, science, music, and health.

Halliday's functions of language have proved to be especially helpful to teachers because they focus the learning activity on a combination of knowledge about the topic *and* knowledge of how the form, purpose, sender, and receiver of a communication event interact. Box 2.3 presents a series of learning activities for a Grade 6 social studies unit on Ancient Greece. The activities illustrate the range of learning opportunities that can be generated in social studies.

ORAL LANGUAGE IN THE CLASSROOM

During the elementary school years, children continue to refine and extend all the language competencies that allow them to be full conversational partners in all walks of life, with many people, in many contexts. The research cited earlier in this chapter suggests that children learn these competencies most effectively when teachers talk *with* children on

Box 2.3   Activities for a Grade 6 Social Studies Unit on
Ancient Greece

1. Instrumental

Oral: The Delian League was a group of Greek city-states that banded together to protect each other from aggressive forces. Your class constitutes the members of the city-state of Athens, the largest and strongest member. Chios, also a member of the Delian League, has requested your help in battle against Persian aggressors. In a group debate, decide whether you should get involved in the war and help Chios.

Written: You are an accomplished athlete, but you have not been chosen to engage in the special training necessary to compete in the Olympic Games. You are unhappy and wish to participate in the games. Write a letter to the selection committee asking them to intercede on your behalf so that you can participate in the training.

2. Regulatory

Oral: You, as citizens of Athens, are concerned about the civil rights of slaves in Athenian society. In small groups, discuss the present slave regulations and devise a new set of civil rights that will allow slaves the same rights as Athenian citizens. You will present these civil rights to the assembly.

Written: You are a rich Athenian citizen and, like all rich citizens of Athens, you buy and sell slaves regularly. You have just purchased a slave to help in the running of your household. Make a list of daily household chores for the slave to fulfil while she or he is living with your family.

3. Interactional

Oral: You are citizens of Troy and are awaiting a message from the town crier (played by the teacher) after being summoned for an important meeting. The town crier arrives and says, "There is a giant wooden horse outside the city gate, left as a peace offering from Greece. We must decide among ourselves whether or not to accept this horse. We must also decide what to do with it, if we choose to accept it." As a class, discuss how you will make this decision. What will you as a group say?

Written: Women in Athenian society were confined to the home and denied the privileges of men. You are all Athenian women who feel you deserve the same rights as men. Discuss these issues among yourselves and write, for publication in the *Grecian Gazette*, individual editorials arguing the rights you desire.

4. Personal

Oral: You are Athenian slaves waiting to be sold. A reporter (played by the teacher in role—see the chapter on drama) interviews you to determine your emotional reactions to being sold.

Written: In Athens, many landowners frequently found themselves heavily in debt and often had to resort to selling their own children into slavery. You are a child who has to be sold into slavery. Write a diary entry that describes how you are feeling the night before you are to be sold.

Continued

Box 2.3   Activities for a Grade 6 Social Studies Unit on
Ancient Greece   *continued*

5. Heuristic

Oral: Citizens of Ancient Greece believed in a direct democracy where all free adult males were equal and contributing members of the government. Some of you are members of the Athenian Assembly, while the rest are reporters who interview the assembly about why they have chosen a direct democracy rather than electing one leader.

Written: Imagine that the Olympic Games are coming to your country this year. You are chosen to make the public aware of how the first Olympic Games in Greece were conducted. Write a report that describes these games. Provide information on such topics as athletic events, opening and closing ceremonies, and prizes awarded. Your report will be published in the local newspaper.

6. Imaginative

Oral: You are in charge of entertainment at an Athenian banquet. To entertain your guests, you have decided to compose poetic "Who am I?" riddles based on mythical Greek gods. In groups of three, compose and audiotape these riddles.

Written: One of the mythical Greek gods of Mount Olympus has been killed in a fierce battle. You have been summoned by Zeus, ruler of the Olympic gods, to create a replacement. Write a story about a new god, and describe where and how your god originated, what he or she is the god of, and what powers he or she possesses. You may also want to give a physical description of your god. You will send your story to Zeus.

7. Representational

(The following task involves modern technology in the context of Ancient Greece.)

Oral: You are a member of the Athenian Tourist Bureau. Your job is to make a television commercial to entice people to visit Ancient Greece. In small groups, compose and dramatize a television commercial.

Written: You are the editor for *Ancient Greece Abroad*, a magazine for travellers. Design a brochure for these travellers that illustrates the culture of Ancient Greece. You may want to include aspects such as food, entertainment, and art.

It is important to note that many of the above activities fulfil more than one language function. In (5), for example, the written task meets the representational function as much as it does the heuristic one. To complete a representational task, a certain amount of heuristic language must first be used. In (7), the activity draws on the heuristic, representational, and regulatory functions. All of the activities described here are examples of language arts tasks that also meet many of the objectives of the specific provincial programs in social studies. Such objectives include understanding that all people have similar physical, social, and psychological needs, and that Greek values, beliefs, and ideas have strongly affected Western civilization. In particular, these activities help to provide a fuller context for the communication skill objectives of writing a summary of the main points, collecting and organizing information into a short report, and sharing ideas through drama and role play.

topics that are of interest to children, and in a manner that enables children to participate as *legitimate conversational partners*.

The term *oracy* was coined to refer to auditory and spoken language. The study of oracy in classrooms is a relatively new development. Oral language skills form the foundation for literacy development. Children come to Canadian classrooms from a vast range of ethnic, racial, political, and social backgrounds. They bring with them a similar range of oral language abilities. Many children arrive with well-developed oral language. They ask questions, tell about themselves, engage in play, listen to and read stories, and know how to interact with teachers and other children in diverse situations. Other children may be shy or withdrawn, unwilling to participate, and unable to read. It may be that at home they have not been encouraged to ask questions, have not been exposed to books, or have different values about what is appropriate and acceptable from those of most children in white, middle-class classrooms. The studies by Loban, Wells, Heath, and Tizard and Hughes remind educators to examine their classroom practices, and to pay attention to listening and speaking and the ways in which these facets of language are facilitated by instructional programs.

Listening

Of all the modes of language used in the elementary school classroom, listening is undoubtedly the most prevalent and the most important. Children make sense of oral language through attending, anticipating, predicting, focusing, visualizing, making connections, generalizing, and evaluating. Their success in school depends largely on their listening abilities. A teacher's success in telling stories, providing instructions, organizing students and activities, and teaching concepts all depend on the abilities of the students to listen and to understand. Much of what students listen to in classrooms is not information as such, but directions about how to do something and what to do next. Children in the primary grades can easily be confused if they do not hear directions or do not understand the teacher's instructions. Being able to listen attentively and respond appropriately accounts for a large part of a child's success in a primary classroom. Even in the upper elementary grades, listening remains important in coping successfully with schooling.

Listening is probably the most used of the language modes from birth onwards. Infants listen in order to learn language, to communicate with others, and to construct meaning in their world. The need to listen continues in school and through adulthood. Many teachers today comment on what seems to be the short attention span of some children in their classrooms. These children, the teachers say, have difficulty in listening and paying attention to what is happening in class. At the same time, however, some research has demonstrated that in fact many teachers have poor communication skills: they talk too much, explain too much, and do not actively listen to their students (Cazden, 1988; Berry, 1985). Thus, by modelling appropriate listening behaviours (among other strategies), it would seem that teachers can actually help children to listen effectively throughout the curriculum.

Listening is not the same as hearing. According to Freshour and Bartholomew (1989), listening consists of six components:

1. receiving—hearing the sounds in the environment,
2. attending—paying attention selectively to those sounds that are important,
3. understanding—creating pictures and mental images or making connections to concepts already understood,
4. analyzing—raising questions and interrogating the validity of what is heard,

5. evaluating—accepting or rejecting what is heard, and

6. reacting—responding to what has been heard, either emotionally, physically, or cognitively

Listeners understand speech at about double the rate a speaker can produce it, and so the mind tends to wander away from the topic of conversation and onto something else. Research tells us the average length of time a listener can attend to one specific thing is only 20 seconds (Moray, 1969). To lengthen that attention span, most people learn how to listen actively by nodding, agreeing with the speaker, making notes on a paper, focusing on key words, formulating questions, and generally engaging in the stages noted above. When helping children to become active listeners, teachers can help children to establish specific purposes for listening. They can also provide them with lots of purposeful opportunities for listening and responding in the context of meaningful oral language experiences (Cox, 1999, p. 152). Saskatchewan Education provides examples of effective listening activities online at: www.sasked.gov.sk.ca/docs/ela/listening01.html.

The purpose of listening to a message, as with any other language act, drives the way in which the listening takes place. If children understand why they are to listen to a message, a story, a poem, or a list of instructions, they are more likely to listen effectively and focus on the appropriate element of the communication. When educators state reasons or purposes for listening and focus children's thinking on ways they can accomplish the task, children's listening skills are enhanced.

Talking

"Talk is an essential part of communicating, thinking, and learning. It allows students to express themselves, to negotiate relationships, to give definition to their thoughts, and to learn about language, themselves, and their world. Talk lays the foundation for reading and writing" (Saskatchewan Education, 2002). Research suggests that oral language skills are developed through modelling and through practice—that students learn about language and how to use it effectively through opportunities to interact with different people in different contexts to accomplish different purposes (British Columbia Ministry of Education, 1988, p. 1.1).

For most people, talking is the primary means of communication. Through oral language and nonverbal gestures, we communicate most of our needs, fears, and dreams to the people we encounter in our day-to-day lives. Through oral language we frequently work out our ideas, "bounce" ideas off colleagues and friends, and communicate the most prosaic, yet necessary, messages to those closest to us. It is therefore of utmost importance that children's oral language abilities be fostered throughout elementary school. Oral language cannot be taken for granted or ignored.

Talk is a major part of classroom life every day, every year, in every grade. Oral language is used by students and teachers for all the purposes Halliday outlined—to have their needs met, to regulate the actions of others, to express who they are, to interact with peers and colleagues, to ask questions and wonder, to represent what is known, and to enter the world of the imagination. Students often need to talk their way into understanding before they begin a writing task. Sometimes, they also need to talk *while* they are writing, and they need to check out meanings and understandings with their peers. Speech facilitates thought, especially in the higher-level thinking required of problem solving (Vygotsky, 1962; Fillion, 1983; Wilkinson, 1984). The teacher's role in facilitating oral language development in the classroom is a crucial one. Research, as already noted, has demonstrated that teachers usually talk too much and do not listen to their students enough (Berry, 1985). Teachers in constructivist classrooms ensure that students engage in small group work that will enhance oral language and thinking, and they facilitate oral language development whenever possible.

Much of the business of the classroom is conducted orally. Teachers give directions and instructions orally, present information orally, and organize classroom life orally. Students ask questions orally, and establish and maintain their social relationships orally. In the classroom, learning outcomes for oral language development include:

- varying speech to meet the needs of the situation (small group, whole class, one on one),
- speaking clearly (with good pronunciation) so that communication is enhanced, and
- speaking expressively and avoiding a monotone.

Assessing Oracy (Listening and Talking)

Listening and talking usually occur together in any social or school situation. It is difficult to assess either one in isolation from the other. When teachers observe their students' listening strategies and abilities, it is likely to be in the context of group work the students are engaged in: a reader response group, a drama activity, a writing conference, a conversation with another student, a science activity, a parent–student conference, interactions on the playground, and physical education or art classes. Those are the same contexts in which they will also collect information about students' speaking abilities. Much of the information teachers collect about their students' oral language proficiencies is anecdotal—it occurs in everyday contexts and is noted as it occurs. Teachers keep notebooks about their students' progress in all areas of the curriculum. These notes complement the students' portfolios of writing, artwork, and so on. The notes can help teachers make instructional decisions that affect their students' learning. If a child is experiencing difficulty in participating in a literature circle, for example, the teacher will want to observe the interactions more closely and decide how the student can be helped to participate more fully.

Teachers are becoming increasingly aware of their students' cultural backgrounds, and they understand that certain oral language behaviours considered appropriate and desirable in a European/Canadian context are not considered so in many other cultures. Some of these behaviours include:

- contributing without invitation to conversation or group discussions,
- sharing ideas and feelings,
- looking at the person being addressed,
- asking questions for clarification,
- inviting other people to contribute to the conversation,
- taking turns,
- assuming a leadership role,
- volunteering to begin the discussion,
- dealing with any conflict of opinion, and
- remaining courteous throughout.

Although teachers encourage these behaviours in their students in Canadian classrooms, they are also sensitive to the diversity of oral language values their students bring to the classroom.

The British Columbia Ministry of Education developed a resource package, *Enhancing and Evaluating Oral Communication in the Primary Grades* (1988), to assist teachers in developing and assessing children's oral communication skills. It is a comprehensive document that serves as a central source of information for this section of the chapter. Listed in the document are seven areas of communicative competence:

1. *Affective behaviours.* Those aspects of communication that reveal attitudes and values. For example, did the students participate in a certain activity willingly and enthusiastically? Can they articulate their responses in a diverse range of media (writing, drawing, mime, puppetry, artwork, dance)?

2. *Language awareness.* The actual knowledge students possess about their own language use and learning. For example, how did the students perform a certain math activity? Did they feel it was easy for them? What was the most important thing they learned?

3. *Listening comprehension.* The students' abilities to construct meaning from what they hear. For example, did the students meet the requirements of the task? Did they follow directions appropriately? Did they accomplish the task set out for them? How much support did the students need from the teacher or from peers?

4. *Speech communication.* The assessment of how successful the students are in accomplishing the objectives of their speech. How much support do they need in order to accomplish their speech goals? Do they attempt to expand their repertoire of speaking strategies by experimenting with new forms?

5. *Critical/evaluative behaviour.* The students' abilities to monitor their own speech and the messages they receive from others. Are they aware of whether their message has been understood? Are they able to question and clarify messages received from others?

6. *Interpersonal strategies.* Those behaviours that allow students to create relationships with others. Children learn how to do this through their play and work in school. Interpersonal strategies include conversing, solving problems, sharing stories, and participating in drama activities.

7. *Oral language codes.* Those aspects of language that allow us to communicate effectively to different people in different situations. Children learn a wide repertoire of language codes as they participate in relationships with a diverse group of people—grandparents, parents, friends, teachers, salespeople, and so on. Children learn to be aware of their audience, the content to be communicated, and the most appropriate ways to communicate their thoughts and feelings. Do the students attempt to extend their range of language codes? Do the students possess a range of language codes that work for them in different situations?

The authors suggest that these areas be assessed in three ways: through observing students as they communicate; through listening to what students say in conversations, group conferences, and other classroom activities; and through reading what students write.

Saskatchewan Education (2002) provides on its Web site a range of assessment strategies for listening and speaking. Box 2.4 displays a sample listening checklist.

A further resource for assessing language abilities is the *English Profiles Handbook,* which provides a series of assessment strategies for oral language. Published by the Department of School Education in Victoria, Australia (1991), the document outlines nine "bands" of proficiency in oral language and provides descriptions and assessment practices for each. The handbook emphasizes the importance of talking with and listening to students, and of involving them in drama; listening to songs, poems, and stories; choral reading; sharing time; cooperative writing; group activities; instruction designing; readers' theatre; improvisation; cooperative "cloze" activities (discussed in Chapter Six); storytelling; role-playing; group discussions; cross-age tutoring; and reporting.

Box 2.4   Sample Developing Phase Listening Checklist

Student's Name: _____

Class: _____

Listening Behaviours	Yes	No	Comments and Dates Assessed
Focuses on the task and listens with obvious intent	—	—	
Understands reasons for listening	—	—	
• listens to learn	—	—	
• listens to enjoy	—	—	
Follows straightforward two and three-step directions	—	—	
Listens sensitively and responsibly to others	—	—	
Distinguishes fact from opinion	—	—	

Listens to and retells a narrative using details and personal interpretation:

	Yes	No	
• remembers sequence of events accurately including main characters and setting	—	—	
• is aware of story plot	—	—	
• makes and confirms predictions	—	—	
• makes and confirms inferences	—	—	
• recognizes cause and effect relationships	—	—	
• recognizes imagery in stories and poems	—	—	
• responds to the mood and emotions expressed	—	—	
• responds by evaluating (judging) what was heard	—	—	

Listens to and recalls nonfiction presentations:

	Yes	No	
• recognizes key ideas and pertinent details	—	—	
• recognizes text structures	—	—	
• recognizes when words are used to convince or persuade	—	—	
• makes notes using note grids (what, when, how, who, where)	—	—	
• summarizes information	—	—	
• draws conclusions	—	—	
• recognizes facts and opinions	—	—	
• answers questions beyond literal level	—	—	
• judges ideas heard	—	—	

Additional Comments:

The assessment records in the handbook are organized into two categories: use of oral language and features of oral language. Spoken-language "band D" (approximately Grade 4) lists the following attributes:

Use of Oral Language

- tells personal anecdotes, illustrating in a relevant way the issue being discussed,
- recounts a story or repeats a song spontaneously,
- retells scenes from a film or drama,
- offers predictions about what will come next,
- recites poems,
- asks questions in conversation,
- has a second try at saying something to make it more precise, and
- arouses and maintains audience interest during formal presentations (e.g., report to class, announcements)

Features of Oral Language

- uses a range of vocabulary related to a particular topic,
- maintains a receptive body stance in conversation, and
- speaks in a way that conveys feelings (while keeping emotions under control)

Teachers might want to make these lists of attributes into a checklist that could be augmented with comments on the oral language behaviours of each individual child. The assessment of oral communication abilities relies heavily on the teacher *listening* to children—not only listening to *what* children have to say and responding appropriately, but also listening to *how* children create and communicate meaning. Lists like those above can be helpful in tracking children's abilities and growth in this very important area.

When using checklists and rubrics, it is helpful to teachers if they are familiar with the statements of attainment for children both younger and older than the grade level at which they teach. In any one classroom there will be a wide range of oral communication competencies. Familiarity with a broad range of abilities helps teachers to understand their own students' oral language development more clearly.

Promoting Oral Language Growth in the Classroom

Many children talk with ease on the playground, but have difficulty expressing themselves adequately in the classroom or school office. Some children feel comfortable moving from one language register to another and speak easily to different people in different contexts. Other children are limited by their experiences of language use. While students are usually comfortable in using oral communication to get their needs met or to regulate the actions of others, they may not be as comfortable or as adept in using persuasive language, giving directions, or making inquiries in school. These functions of language can be taught through the everyday classroom interactions that occur among children, and between teacher and students, helping students to become more articulate, precise, and confident in their spoken language.

Thoughtful teachers and adults working with students nurture and support their oral language. If a child is having difficulty describing something, the teacher asks questions; if a child has difficulty explaining something, the teacher prompts and encourages. Activities that promote the functions of language, such as those outlined in Box 2.3, also promote the development of oral language. In addition, most drama activities enhance oral language development—both talking and listening. The teacher's role is to provide challenges to students in their oral language capacities, and also to support students in their oral language efforts. One of the conclusions reached by Loban after his longitudinal study of language development (1963) was that children who have well-developed oral language skills tend to learn to read more easily and become better readers than children who do not have strong oral language skills. It is clearly important that teachers understand the role of oral language in the classroom, and that they encourage children to use oral language effectively for a variety of purposes.

Many adults can remember being corrected in their language as children, or remember being told that their dialect was not appropriate and they should not speak in a certain way. Comments of this kind silence children and are equivalent to telling children they can sing in the choir, but must only mouth the words. Oral language is part of our familial and cultural heritage and an important part of who we are as human beings. Correcting a child's grammar or usage is not the same thing as facilitating oral language competency. The language students bring to school is to be accepted, and then it is to be built upon so that children can refine their knowledge and skills and become more articulate and confident speakers in a range of social situations.

In promoting oral language growth in classrooms, it is helpful for the teacher to give students opportunities to hold conversations with one another and with teachers, janitors, office staff, and visitors. Some of these situations will be unstructured, as when students play together at recess or chat while they set up activities. Other situations will be more structured, such as the talk that occurs when children are discussing science activities, creating dramatic episodes in social studies, sharing ideas in writing conferences, and participating in reading workshops. Purposeful talk includes that which surrounds journal writing, and the inevitable talk that provides much of the basis for written composition itself, particularly in the primary grades. In constructivist classrooms, oral language is the basis for much classroom learning as well as for the personal growth that occurs in children. All talk is purposeful to the speaker. Whether it is about last night's hockey game or a classroom project, an intention is being realized. Children grow and learn through their talk, and there is room in the classroom for many kinds of talk on different topics.

Box 2.5 contains an excerpt from a transcript of a social studies/drama class. The excerpt demonstrates how children use talk for many purposes and how they change register depending on the context. Clearly, the students in this class were actively engaged with the drama activity and were generally using language appropriate to the situation. They engaged in problem solving, brainstorming, and sharing their solutions. The students had to think as though they were pioneers themselves, and they quickly moved into role and took over the language and thinking of a family with a problem to solve. The students became more focused, and the teacher observed that they seemed to learn more through these activities than they did through only reading and writing about the topic.

To facilitate talk, classrooms can be organized so that children are able to talk to one another easily without having to move from their desks or speak in loud voices. Grouping desks together or seating children around small tables works effectively. It is also important to consider the purpose of the grouping, and to group children differently at different times. Most of the time, heterogeneous grouping is most effective, as it facilitates children's engagement in conversations, expressing what they know and asking questions of one another. Grouping of this kind enables children to help another and develop expertise independently from the teacher.

Box 2.5   Purposeful Talk in a Drama Context

Jewel Bondar, a special education teacher, had taken her primary adaptation students on a field trip to Fort Edmonton Historical Park. In Alberta, children in an adaptation classroom are usually at least two years below the accepted standard of competency in at least four subject areas in school. The Alberta Grade 3 social studies curriculum requires that students study the history of their community. During a visit to the 1846 fort, one of the last students to leave the ice house had left the door open. The tour guide reprimanded the students for this and raised questions about the consequences of such forgetfulness for residents of the fort in 1846. On returning to the school, Jewel decided to engage the children in a group drama session about this action. She worked in role as the mother of a pioneer family.

Jewel:	Are you ready to begin drama time?
Children:	Yeh!
Jewel:	When your father gets home he will whip you soundly—all of you!
[Silence]	
Jewel:	Was it you, John? Jake?
Boy:	It was him. He got you, us all, in trouble.
Jewel:	Do you have a name?
Girl:	That guy there is Tom.
Jewel:	And you?
Girl:	Rebecca.
Jewel:	Who did it?
Children:	Did what?
Jewel:	Look over there. What do you see?
Girl:	Wolf tracks.
Jewel:	What else?
Girl:	Trees and a cookhouse and water.
Jewel:	Good eyes, daughter. What else?
Boy:	I see a door open over there.
Jewel:	Look children! A door is open!
Jewel:	I wonder what sort of person would go into someone else's …
Boy:	I told him not to, but he done it.
Jewel:	What did he do?
Boy:	A traveller came by in the night.
Jewel:	How do you know?
Jewel:	[Out of role and into real life:] Do you want to be frightened by this?
Children:	Nope, pioneers were tough, a kid done it.
[Back in role:]	
Boy:	Somebody forgot to lock it.
Boy:	I told him where the food is, like when my brother tells me where the stuff, the good stuff is hid.
Girl:	Look, mother, it is yucky. A door is open.
Jewel:	What do you think is the problem? Why would that door be open?
Boy:	He was hungry.

Continued

Box 2.5   Purposeful Talk in a Drama Context   *continued*

Jewel:	Who?
Boy:	The traveller, so he stole some food.
Jewel:	Oh no! The door to the ice house has been left open and our meat for winter is sure to spoil.
Boy:	I'll shoot a crow or somethin'.
Boy:	A crow would not even fill you up and we got no guns.
Girl:	There aren't no berries like we had for breakfast in winter.
Boy:	Nope and a lotta snow.
Girl:	Could we trap?
Boy:	Trap what?
Boy:	Buffalo.
Girl:	Ain't no trap big enough.
Girl:	I know, we could get beavers and rabbits and stuff.
Girl:	We'll starve on small things like that. Do we have to feed all of us all winter long?
Boy:	Of course, there ain't no Safeways.
Girl:	You dumby.
Jewel:	[Out of role and in real life:] Stop. Is this the way pioneer children would talk to one another?
Children:	Nope, they'd get beat, it's not appropriate, no put-downs remember?
Jewel:	Do you want to continue?
Children:	Yes, let's find out, come on you guys. I like this, yeah.

[Back in role:]

Jewel:	Any ideas on what to do about the meat supply? What might we do?
Girl:	I got an idea. We could set a trapline like we did last day.
Boy:	We'll starve on small things like that.
Boy:	How much meat we got now?
Girl:	What meat? It stole and rotten, ain't it?
Children:	Pew! It stinks, there are bugs, it's green, yuk.
Jewel:	[In real life:] Stop. Put your head down on the table and close your eyes. I want you to think about the ice house. What is it similar to today? I want you to think what rotten meat would smell like, look like, taste like. What would the pioneers do for food in the winter if the meat spoils? In your tables, groups, I want you to help solve the problem. Somebody has left the ice house door open. The meat is warming and sure to rot if a solution or answer is not found soon.

[Students brainstormed together for ten minutes and Jewel circulated among the groups. Table two needed assistance in focusing on the problem.]

Jewel:	Give me five! [Classroom control signal] [Back in role:] I don't believe someone has been so careless. Well, can any of you suggest what to do before your father comes home from his voyage? [Several hands go up.]
Jewel:	[Out of role and in real life:] I am going to ask each group to show the class how they think the ice house problem was solved. When I say freeze, I want

Continued

> ### Box 2.5　Purposeful Talk in a Drama Context　*continued*
>
> you to stop like I expect in physical education class. In drama this is called a still image because it is similar to taking a picture, the people are in a pose. Kathy, can you stand over here, please? Brush your hair. Freeze—very good listening. Kathy brushed her hair and then when I said freeze, she gave a still image. Do you all understand freeze means to stop everything, not fall over or fall down?
>
> **Children:**　Yes, we do.
>
> And so the drama continued. All the groups shared their tableaux, still image, and "thoughts in the head" (see Chapter Twelve).

Source: J. Bondar and J. B. Edwards, "Charting new territory: Pioneers in an adaptation classroom," *Ohio Journal of the English Language Arts, 36* (2), 11–19.

Helping Children Become Effective Listeners

As in any other area of the language arts, children learn best when they are provided with opportunities to listen in the context of their learning. They do not generally need exercises and drills on listening. Teachers can show children how to vary their listening according to the specific purpose for listening, and can help children develop specific listening strategies. Some students have only one strategy for listening no matter what the purpose—to listen hard and remember everything. Children can be helped to understand that once a purpose is established for listening, they can vary *how* they listen and hence be more effective listeners.

Listening for pleasure (appreciative or aesthetic listening) to a story such as *Baseball Bats for Christmas* (Kusugak, 1990) allows students to enter the world of the imagination; to create images of the setting, characters, and events; and to respond emotionally and intellectually to the narrative. Children can be encouraged to create pictures in their minds as they listen to the story. Listening later on to the teacher talk about the author, Michael Kusugak, requires a different kind of listening (comprehensive or efferent listening). Here students attempt to make sense of information about Michael Kusugak, including his childhood in Repulse Bay, where Kusugak now lives and works; how he began writing for children; why he enjoyed listening to his grandmother's stories; and how he first learned English. Understanding this information add richness to the story Kusugak wrote. Yet another kind of listening (critical listening) is required when students and teacher talk together about how Michael Kusugak went by plane, at age six, to a school far away from his home, returning only in the summers. At school, Kusugak had to learn to speak and read English and was forbidden to use his own language. As students ponder the dilemma of having young children stay at home versus providing them with a formal education, and forcing them to speak English rather than their own language, they are required to listen critically, assess what they have heard, make judgments about situations, and perhaps attempt to understand two sides of a debate.

Later in this book, in Chapter Eight, a Grade 4 oral history project is described. The students in this Grade 4 classroom taperecorded interviews with local residents, searched archives and local libraries, and eventually wrote a history of one of the local communities. The project had a specific purpose. When the students were conducting the interviews, they were aware that they would later be using this information to write a book that would be sold in the community. Their listening was focused on the information they could use in the book. The project is an example of the integration of all the language arts modes—listening, speaking, reading, writing, viewing, and representing. The students completed individual work, group work, and whole class work as they produced the history book. Clearly, listening played a large part in the success of the project.

Most of the strategies teachers find helpful in enhancing listening in the classroom fall into the realm of management rather than the language arts. Before classroom activities begin:

- Ensure all children have a clear view of the teacher and the main teaching area.
- If necessary, increase the distance between students desks.
- Consider the seating plan and seat students where they will be able to focus most attentively.
- Seat children at the front and toward one side of the classroom if they experience difficulty in listening attentively.
- Do not seat children close to high traffic areas such as the pencil sharpener, cubbies, and the door.
- Ensure that recess snacks, lunches, toys, and coats are not brought to the students' work areas.
- Ensure desktops are completely clear.
- Set regular times for activities to occur.

Further classroom strategies that enhance effective listening are listed in Box 2.6.

The English Language Framework (Ministry of Education, Victoria, 1988) makes the following suggestions for enhancing listening in the classroom. All the suggestions can be implemented by both teachers *and* students:

- Respect the opinions of others.
- Be a considerate listener.
- Negotiate rather than argue stubbornly.
- Share discoveries and queries.
- Interact in group discussions.
- Recall facts.
- Repeat instructions.
- Respond to what is heard.

Students can be encouraged to engage in active listening when they participate in writing conferences with their peers, engage in group projects, take part in drama activities, and read to each other in shared reading experiences.

Vocabulary Development

Children learn new words both from reading and from listening to the constant stream of oral language around them. We each have a receptive and an expressive vocabulary. The receptive vocabulary is generally much larger than the expressive vocabulary—we can understand many more words than we actually use in speaking and writing. Young children's vocabulary development depends heavily on the oral language they hear around them, but as they get older, this development depends increasingly on their reading (McKeown and Curtis, 1987). Teachers in constructivist classrooms are aware that vocabulary develops most effectively when students are engaged in activities that stretch them to say new things in new ways. Thus, teachers play an important role in children's

Box 2.6   Classroom Strategies to Support Effective Listening

Experienced teachers set the stage for effective listening. They

- discuss with the students what good listeners look and sound like. They brainstorm a list and place it in the classroom.
- discuss with students the reasons why effective listening is important.
- develop a language or "secret code" in the classroom, which signals students to listen, for example, hold up the right index finger and thumb outward to form the letter "L." Students respond by doing the same, signalling that the teacher needs to talk and the students are ready to listen. Alternatively, they say, "I need to see eyes listening, ears listening and feet listening," which indicates that hands need to be still, eyes need to be on the speaker, and feet need to be forward.
- clearly state positive consequences for listening. These might include words and gestures of praise, centre time, extra responsibility in the classroom or "glad-notes" and phone calls home to parents.
- clearly state negative consequences of not listening. These might include a reminder phrased as "I need you to …," "head down on desk," or "time out."

During their teaching, experienced teachers

- give instructions as simply and briefly as possible.
- ensure the language they use is appropriate for the students' developmental levels.
- emphasize critical words such as "first, then, afterwards."
- display an agenda and directly encourage students to follow along with the lesson.
- use gestural cues, for example, point to the face or point at the picture in the book if the child needs to look at it.
- model good attending behaviours and reinforce those students who are doing the same.
- if needed, verbally redirect or prompt children who are experiencing difficulty.
- are consistent in the wording of routine instructions.
- complement oral instructions with written instructions.
- ensure their voice is interesting and not monotonous when presenting information.
- have manipulatives and visuals in clear sight of children.
- consistently ask one or two students to repeat what has been said by the teacher or by other students.
- invite students turn to a neighbour and share what has been discussed in the classroom.
- follow up on negative or positive consequences.

vocabulary development when they introduce new vocabulary in their classroom talk and draw their students' attention to those words.

New words generally enter our expressive vocabularies slowly, for users usually need to feel confident about the meaning and context of new words before they use them with ease in their oral or written language. When people hear or read a new word and pay attention to it, they might use the word in their speech, but only if they feel confident enough. Once a word is comfortably fixed in a speaking vocabulary, it is more likely to be used in writing, where it becomes more permanent. Some words become fashionable for a while and quickly move into the general lexicon. Words such as "viable," "interface," "cognizant," and "explicate" are all words that have appeared in common academic usage in the past 20 years and then have faded. Similarly, children have their own language (or slang) in which certain words attain powerful meaning before becoming outdated. Vocabulary generally cannot be taught through word lists and definitions, since words have to be used meaningfully. However, teachers can certainly help their students by showing them how to use a dictionary to check the meanings of any words they are unsure of and to cross-check the meanings against the context in which the words are used.

Maintaining a vital oral language curriculum means that classrooms cannot be quiet places. Teachers distinguish between the busy chat and movement of actively engaged children and the noise created by off-topic talking and irrelevant behaviour. Teachers in constructivist classrooms understand the need to develop learning activities that engage children's interests and stimulate oral language. They capitalize on activities such as literature circles, reader-response groups, and drama activities in an effort to enhance their students' abilities to articulate their thoughts and feelings clearly and with confidence.

At the beginning of this chapter, Ms. Moorhouse asked what it is she needs to know about language, and about children's learning of language, that will enhance her classroom instruction in the language arts. Understanding these concepts makes teaching the language arts more meaningful and purposeful. It is clear from the research conducted in this field that most of children's learning in school, including their reading and writing development, rests largely on oral language ability—the ability to listen and talk in a variety of registers and social contexts. Because this area of the language arts is so vital to children's success in school, it is important that they have the opportunity to talk in situations that encourage or challenge them to extend their talk repertoire. Since what is taught and valued in school contexts is normally assessed, it is important that children's oral language development be noted by teachers and feedback be provided to students and their parents.

SUMMARY

In constructivist classrooms, teachers make every effort to understand how children learn language, and to understand language itself. Language is probably the most complex and sophisticated of all human behaviours—many researchers maintain that it is the use of language that sets human beings apart from other animals. Language consists of four major elements: semantics, syntax, phonology, and pragmatics. Semantics refers to the meaning element of language; syntax to the organization of language; phonology to the sound system of language; and pragmatics to the ways in which language is used to communicate.

Over the years, theories of language acquisition have developed and changed. It was once believed that language was learned through the purely Skinnerian model of behaviourism: children make an utterance and learn whether it is correct through the reactive behaviour of those around them. It eventually became apparent that this explanation was not sufficient to account for the great range of words and sentence structures that children learn so quickly in the first four years of their lives. Behaviourist psychology cannot totally account for that kind of learning and thinking. In the 1950s, Noam Chomsky proposed the theory that language structures are innately present in children, and that when children encounter spoken language, these structures are activated and language learning progresses. Today, an interactional approach to language development prevails, whereby language acquisition is seen to be the result of a child's interaction with caregivers and the sociocultural environment. From a balanced perspective, it is likely that some aspects of all three of these theories apply when children learn language.

The social context of language development has also received attention from researchers. Longitudinal studies by Loban, Heath, and Wells have demonstrated the effects of the social system, and especially the classroom, on children's language learning and language use. Although it was once believed that a school environment could provide a richer language environment for children than they were likely to experience at home, research has shown that this is not so. Children's language use in classrooms is generally suppressed and not as rich as children are likely to experience in their homes.

Language and learning cannot be separated. Much of what children learn, both in and out of school, takes place through the vehicle of language—both written and oral. The processing of thoughts cannot be separated from the use of language. How would we think if we didn't have language? Teachers in constructivist classrooms understand that children, to learn effectively, need the opportunity to work purposefully in groups, sharing ideas, questions, suggestions, and problem-solving strategies. As we talk through ideas, we think about them further, clarify them, refine them, and enhance our knowledge and understandings.

The oral language competencies of young children have been shown to be related to reading and writing abilities. Children entering school with strong oral language competencies are more likely to experience success in their literacy endeavours. Although the focus of elementary language arts is generally on literacy development, a great deal of classroom communication occurs orally. Children can be helped to expand their listening and speaking skills so that they can maximize their learning opportunities. It is therefore important that oral language be nurtured and supported in classrooms so that children become effective listeners and speakers wherever they are. It is also important that children's oracy be assessed on an ongoing basis through informal observations and anecdotal records. Children need to know how strengthening their oral language abilities can improve their learning overall.

SELECTED PROFESSIONAL RESOURCES

British Columbia Ministry of Education. (1988). *Enhancing and evaluating oral communication in the primary grades: Teacher's resource package*. Victoria, BC: British Columbia Ministry of Education. A comprehensive resource for teachers, these materials combine background information with specific, practical strategies. Resource packages are also available for the intermediate and secondary grades. The packages can be used by educators to help plan and monitor oral language learning across the curriculum, make decisions about the oral language development of students, plan instructional strategies, and develop evaluation formats.

Saskatchewan Education. (2002). *English language arts—A curriculum guide for the elementary level*. Regina, SK: Saskatchewan Education. Available: www.sasked.gov.sk.ca/docs/ela/index.html. The *Guide* contains suggestions for enhancing oral language in the classroom, focusing on practical activities across the curriculum. Listening and speaking activities are listed separately. The *Guide* also provides, in the assessment and evaluation section, some excellent ways to assess children's listening and speaking competencies.

Ministry of Education, Victoria. (1988). *English language framework, P–10: Language for living*. Melbourne, Australia: Victoria Ministry of Education. The book lists goals for the oral language curriculum from kindergarten to Grade 9, and describes the teacher's role, the context, and specific learning activities in some detail.

CHILDREN'S BOOKS NOTED IN CHAPTER TWO ▬▬▬

Kusugak, M. (1990). *Baseball bats for Christmas*. Toronto: Annick Press.
Parish, P. (1963). *Amelia Bedelia*. New York: Harper and Row.

REFERENCES ▬▬▬

Barnes, D. (1976). *From communication to curriculum*. Harmondsworth, UK: Penguin Books.

Berry, K. (1985). Talking to learn subject matter/learning subject matter talk. *Language Arts, 62* (1), 34–42.

Bondar, J. and Edwards, J. B. (1995). Charting new territory: Pioneers in an adaptation classroom. *Ohio Journal of the English Language Arts, 36* (2), 11–19.

Braddock, R., Lloyd-Jones, R., and Schoer, L. (1963). *Research in written composition*. Champaign, IL: National Council of Teachers of English.

British Columbia Ministry of Education. (1988). *Enhancing and evaluating oral communication in the primary grades: Teacher's resource package*. Victoria: British Columbia Ministry of Education.

Britton, J. (1970). *Language and learning*. Harmondsworth, UK: Penguin Books.

Brown, R. (1973). *A first language*. Cambridge, MA: Harvard University Press.

Cazden, C. (1988). *Classroom discourse: The language of teaching and learning*. Portsmouth, NH: Heinemann.

Chomsky, N. (1957). *Syntactic structures*. The Hague: Mouton & Co.

Clark, H. and Clark, E. V. (1977). *Psychology and language*. New York: Harcourt Brace Jovanovich.

Cleary, L., and Peacock, T. (1998). *Collected wisdom: American Indian education*. Needham Heights, MA: Allyn & Bacon.

Cox, C. (1999). *Teaching language arts: A student- and response-centered classroom*. Boston, MS: Allyn and Bacon.

Delpit, L. (1995). *Other people's children: Cultural conflict in the classroom*. New York: The New Press.

Department of School Education. (1991). *English profiles handbook*. Melbourne, Australia: Victoria Department of School Education.

Dillon, D. (1985). Editorial. *Language Arts, 62* (1), 9.

Donaldson, M. (1978). *Children's minds*. New York: W. W. Norton & Co.

Ferreiro, E. and Teberosky, A. (1982). *Literacy before schooling*. Exeter, NH: Heinemann.

Fillion, B. (1983). Let me see you learn. *Language Arts, 60* (6), 702–710.

Freshour, F. and Bartholomew, P. (1989). Let's start improving our own listening. *Florida Reading Quarterly, 25* (4), 28–30.

Halliday, M.A.K. (1969). Relevant models of language. *Educational Review, 22* (1), 26–37.

Halliday, M.A.K. (1975). *Learning how to mean*. New York: Elsevier North-Holland Inc.

Harste, J., Woodward, V., and Burke, C. (1984). *Language stories and literacy lessons*. Portsmouth, NH: Heinemann.

Hunt, K. (1965). *Grammatical structures written at three grade levels*. NCTE Research Report Number 3. Urbana, IL: National Council of Teachers of English.

John-Steiner, V. and Tatter, P. (1983). An interactionist model of language development. In B. Bain (ed.), *The sociogenesis of language and human conduct* (pp. 79–97). New York: Plenum.

Lenneberg, E. H. (1964). The capacity for language acquisition. In J. A. Fodor and J. J. Katz (eds.), *The structure of language* (pp. 580–605). Englewood Cliffs, NJ: Prentice-Hall.

Lindfors, J. W. (1987). *Children's language and learning* (2nd ed.). Englewood Cliffs, NJ: Prentice-Hall.

Loban, W. (1963). *The language of elementary school children*. NCTE Research Report Number 1. Urbana, IL: National Council of Teachers of English.

McKeown, M. G. and Curtis, M. E. (eds.). (1987). *The nature of vocabulary acquisition*. Hillsdale, NJ: Lawrence Erlbaum Associates.

Miller, G. (1977). *Spontaneous apprentices: Children and language.* New York: Seabury Press.

Ministry of Education, Victoria. (1988). *English language framework, P–10: Language for living.* Melbourne, Australia: Victoria Ministry of Education.

Moffet, J. (1968). *Teaching the universe of discourse.* Boston: Houghton Mifflin.

Moray, N. (1969). *Listening and attention.* Baltimore: Penguin Books.

Rosen, H. (1984). *The importance of story.* Sheffield, UK: National Association for the Teaching of English.

Saskatchewan Education. (2002). *English language arts—A curriculum guide for the elementary level.* Available: www.sasked.gov.sk.ca/docs/ela/speaking01.html.

Scollon, R., and Scollon, S. (1983). *Narrative, literacy, and face in interethnic communication.* Norwood, NJ: Ablex.

Skinner, B. F. (1957). *Verbal behavior.* Englewood Cliffs, NJ: Prentice-Hall.

Staats, A. W. (1971). *Child learning, intelligence, and personality: Principles of a behavioral interaction approach.* New York: Harper & Row.

Terrace, H. S. (1979). How Nim Chimpsky changed my mind. *Psychology Today, 13* (6), 65–76.

Tizard, B. and Hughes, M. (1984). *Young children learning.* Cambridge, MA: Harvard University Press.

Tough, J. (1976). *Listening to children talking: A guide to the appraisal of children's language use.* Portsmouth, NH: Heinemann.

Vygotsky, L. S. (1962). *Thought and language.* Cambridge, MA: MIT Press.

Wells, G. (1986). *The meaning makers.* Portsmouth, NH: Heinemann.

Wilkinson, L. (1984). Peer group talk in elementary school. *Language Arts, 61* (2), 164–169.

Chapter

Emergent Literacy

Perspectives on Early Literacy

- Reading Readiness
- Emergent Literacy

Emergent Literacy

Components of Emergent Literacy

- Cultural Views and Functions of Written Language
- Nature and Forms of Written Language
- Speech–Print Relationship

Assessing Emergent Literacy

- Observing Children
- Interviews
- Samples of Children's Work

Planning for Instruction

- Rich Literacy Environment
- Daily Reading and Writing
- Control over Literacy Learning
- Acceptance of Approximations
- Differences Among Learners
- Sequence of Instruction

Experiences That Facilitate Literacy Development

- Reading to Children
- Shared-Book Experiences
- Shared Writing: The Language Experience Approach
- Writing
- Functional Interactions with Print

When the children arrive at Iris Li's kindergarten class each day, they meet together on the rug in one corner of the classroom and update the calendar and weather report. Iris has written the days of the week on cards, and the children select the card that shows what day it is, talking about what letter they see and what sound they hear at the beginning of the word. They describe the weather, and Iris prints what they say on a whiteboard. The children watch and listen to her say each word as she prints it. This type of activity has been taking place in kindergartens for decades. What is different now is that we are more aware of how this helps children construct knowledge about the connection between oral and written language.

There are other differences too. Rather than worksheets and visual discrimination activities with shapes and pictures, the children are engaged in a wide range of reading and writing activities. Every day Iris shares a story with the children, sometimes from a big book with print large enough so that all the children can see it as she reads. Iris carefully guides the discussion before, during, and after reading this book, focusing on both meaning and print. There is also a writing centre in the room where children go to write stories, letters, and recipes.

Print is everywhere in Iris's classroom. In one corner is a store centre with labelled cans and packages, as well as a cash register, pencils and paper for making grocery lists, and signs showing where different products are kept. As the children write grocery lists and identify products from their labels, they learn what print is for and how it relates to what they say.

Iris uses the term **emergent literacy** to describe her students' learning experiences. This term, which began to replace **reading readiness** in the late 1970s, signalled a significant change in the way literacy programs for young children were conceptualized and implemented.

- What do the terms "reading readiness" and "emergent literacy" mean to you?
- What types of reading and writing activities do you think are appropriate for young children?
- How can teachers figure out what young children know about reading and writing and what they need to learn?

The purpose of this chapter is to help you construct answers to these and other questions you might have about the early stages of learning to read and write.

PERSPECTIVES ON EARLY LITERACY

If you were in kindergarten or Grade 1 in the 1970s, you likely completed reading readiness activities. If you entered school in the 1980s, it's more likely that you were immersed in the types of learning experiences in Iris Li's classroom. In this section, we present an overview of these two perspectives. Although most of the discussion over the past century has been focused on reading, the perspectives that have evolved also have implications for early writing.

Reading Readiness

This concept, which has driven early reading instruction since the beginning of the 20th century, is rooted in the work of influential psychologists such as Stanley G. Hall (Durkin, 1983). Hall emphasized the impact of heredity on development and indicated that everyone went through the same stages of development in the same order. The term "reading readiness" first began to appear in the 1920s when educators, concerned about the number of Grade 1 children who had difficulty learning to read, applied maturationist notions to reading. They hypothesized that children who failed to learn to read were simply not yet at the appropriate stage of development. Since maturation rather than instruction was seen as necessary to move children to the next stage of development, the solution to reading problems was to delay instruction (Durkin, 1983).

The notion that children needed to reach a certain age to be ready to learn to read received increased credibility through the results of an influential study by Morphett and Washburne in 1931. They examined the relationship between children's reading achievement and their mental age and concluded that children needed to reach a mental age of 6 1/2 before they could profit from reading instruction. Although other researchers found that learning to read was more dependent on the nature of the reading program than the child's mental age (Gates, 1937), the maturationist perspective continued to prevail until the 1950s. By this point, another view was influencing how educators approached reading instruction for young children.

Rather than sitting back and waiting for children to get ready to learn to read, proponents of a developmentalist perspective believed that prereading experiences could hasten children's readiness. The reading readiness workbook was born. These workbooks were often part of basal reading programs and focused primarily on three areas: language development, visual–motor abilities, and auditory discrimination (deHirsch, Jansky, and

Langford, 1966). Typical activities in reading readiness workbooks involved colouring pictures of words that rhymed, choosing pictures of objects that faced the same direction, arranging pictures in order, and drawing lines between pictures of objects related in some way (e.g., mothers and babies or shoes and feet). Almost none of the activities involved written language, since the children were not considered ready for reading. Although some children already knew how to read when they arrived at school, it was common for all children in Grade 1 to complete reading readiness activities before beginning formal reading instruction. By the mid-1960s, however, constructivist views were beginning to affect the field of early literacy.

Emergent Literacy

The term *emergent literacy* was first used by Marie Clay in 1966 (Crawford, 1995). She found that young children came to school with considerable knowledge about reading and writing and that they were able to use this knowledge in meaningful ways. The term *emergent* was used to indicate that learning to read and write involves growth along a continuum rather than mastery of prereading skills. The term *literacy* reflected a broader perspective than reading readiness, embracing both reading and writing. From an emergent literacy perspective, there is no sharp distinction between not being literate and being literate. Instead, literacy development is viewed as continuous, beginning with children's earliest experiences with print at home. Hence, in contrast to reading readiness, which was associated with kindergarten and the first few months of Grade 1, emergent literacy is seen as encompassing a considerable period of time. It begins very early in life for almost all children in a literate society (Teale, 1995) and continues to age eight or nine for some children (Sulzby, 1991).

Whereas in the past, parents had often been cautioned not to teach their children to read and write, proponents of emergent literacy view parents as playing a vital role in literacy development. They believe that young children sort out what print is for and how it works as they engage in a wide range of activities and experiences involving printed language. For instance:

- When they are read to by their parents, children not only experience the pleasures of a good story, but construct a schema for what stories are like and what book language sounds like.
- When they see their parents making lists to take to the supermarket and refer to these lists as they shop, children begin to understand that print carries ideas across time and space.
- In the morning as they eat breakfast, children become aware that there is a relationship between the words they say and hear and what is on the cereal box.

Today, *emergent literacy* is a term that pervades descriptions of early reading and writing development. Most educators who use it hold a constructivist view of knowledge. They believe that children develop literacy by being actively engaged in meaningful literacy activities rather than being taught skills directly. They further believe that children need to be immersed in print-rich environments where they have opportunities to experiment with reading and writing. However, they still also feel that children develop literacy through a series of stages.

In contrast, social constructivists hypothesize that there are no qualitative differences in the processes of literacy used by readers and writers at different ages and levels of experience (Crawford, 1995). Rather than there being stages of development, social constructivists believe that literacy is specific to different cultures and that literacy learners construct meaning within their social context. Some social constructivists go even further, claiming that schools provide a more appropriate environment for some children to learn to read and write than they do for others. These educators maintain that a match between what children bring to school and what happens there is critical to literacy development. Purcell-Gates (1998) writes about the "terrifying mismatch" that often occurs between beginning reading instruction and the knowledge children have about literacy when they enter school.

Table 3.1 summarizes the similarities and differences between the two perspectives described in this section. From even a cursory examination of the comparisons provided, it is obvious that these perspectives on early literacy are related to the three major theoretical perspectives on language learning presented in Chapter One. Reading readiness perspectives reflect transmission models, and emergent literacy perspectives reflect constructivist and social constructivist models.

While Table 3.1 portrays the most pervasive perspectives on literacy instruction across the 20th century, it fails to reflect the diversity of current perspectives on beginning reading. In particular, it does not reflect the work of connectionists, who believe that, from the beginning, the focus should be on print with direct, explicit instruction in phonics (Adams, 1990). Connectionists believe that children progress through several stages as they learn to read and that reading should be broken down into a series of skills organized from easy to more difficult, with each skill taught directly and in sequence. Although connectionists acknowledge that young children need to be placed in print-rich environments,

Table 3.1 Perspectives on Emergent Literacy

| Reading Readiness | | Emergent Literacy | |
Maturationists	Developmentalists	Constructivists	Social Constructivists
• Readiness is discrete, separate from reading and writing development. Emergent literacy is continuous, part of reading and writing development.		• Emergent literacy is continuous, part of reading and writing development.	
• Reading and writing development begins at school.		• Literacy development begins at home and occurs from infancy to age 8 or 9.	
• Children need time to mature before beginning formal reading and writing instruction.	• Nonprint activities develop readiness for formal reading and writing instruction.	• Literacy learning occurs in a print-rich environment where children are actively engaged in meaningful reading and writing.	
• Literacy development progresses through a series of stages.		• Literacy development progresses through a series of stages.	• Literacy is culturally specific and there are no universal developmental stages.
• Goal is to prepare children for schools and literacy instruction.		• Goal is to prepare children for schools and literacy instruction.	• Goal is to change schools and literacy instruction to meet the needs of the children.

they place priority on children learning phonics to identify words, which is seen as a means to fluent reading and comprehension.

> Our view of early literacy builds on a social constructivist perspective. Like the connectionists, we believe that immersion in a print-rich environment is a necessary but not sufficient condition for many young children to learn to read and write. Explicit instruction is needed in literacy programs for young children. In contrast to the connectionists, however, we believe that early literacy development involves far more than learning sound–letter relationships. In the next section, we provide a comprehensive model of the components of emergent literacy.

COMPONENTS OF EMERGENT LITERACY

Some writers define emergent literacy by differentiating young children's interactions with print from conventional reading and writing (e.g., Sulzby, 1985). However, as Harste, Woodward, and Burke (1984, p. 69) argue, even the term *emergent literacy* implies that proficient language users engage in a process that is "psycholinguistically different from the process young children engage in." Working with young children from age three, they found no compelling evidence that this is so. For example, when young children sit down to write, they use marks on a page to communicate a message. Although the marks may not yet be accurate spelling, the process of encoding meaning through symbols is similar to that used by the proficient writer.

Neuman and Roskos (1998) indicate that a major problem with using the terms *emergent* and *conventional* to describe literacy development is the implication that there is a distinct point at which children move from emergent to fully mature reading and writing. This raises the question of just when it is appropriate to label what the children do as "conventional" reading or writing. What percentage of words do children need to identify correctly in order to call what they are doing conventional reading? What percentage of words must be spelled correctly before we say children are engaged in conventional writing?

While some writers have adopted instead the term *early literacy* to avoid these types of questions (e.g., Christie, Enz, and Vukelich, 2003), we continue to use *emergent literacy* in this book because of its importance in changing the face of reading and writing instruction for young children. As Sénéchal, LeFevre, Smith-Chant, and Colton (2001) point out, this term indicates a clear break from readiness views of reading and acknowledges that children learn a great deal about literacy before entering school. It is important to note, however, that even though we use this term, we view reading and writing development as continuous, beginning with the child's earliest attempts to interact with print and progressing to proficient reading and writing. Hence, we refer to all young children's attempts to work with print as reading or writing, recognizing that over time these attempts will have more and more in common with the reading and writing of independent readers and writers.

The following section, organized around major dimensions provided by Purcell-Gates (1998), attempts to capture the complexity of children's emergent literacy development. An overview of these dimensions is presented in Box 3.1. It is important to note that there are large individual differences among children in literacy development and that the age at which children develop understandings within each of these dimensions varies considerably.

Box 3.1   Components of Emergent Literacy

Cultural Views and Functions of Written Language

- Expecting meaning from written language
- Engaging in purposeful reading and writing

Nature and Forms of Written Language

- Understanding that oral and written language are related
- Matching words heard with those in print (eye–voice matching)
- Internalizing the language of books

Speech–Print Relationship

- Differentiating between pictures and print
- Understanding how print works (conventions of print)
- Matching sounds and letters in words (alphabetic principle)
- Understanding terms related to books, reading, and writing

Source: Major headings extracted from V. Purcell-Gates, "Growing successful readers: Homes, communities, and schools," in J. Osborn and F. Lehr (eds.), *Literacy for all: Issues in teaching and learning* (New York: The Guilford Press, 1998), p. 54.

Cultural Views and Functions of Written Language

Children's views about the value and functions of written language are a direct reflection of their experiences within their family and the wider social context. In many families, children are read to from birth and literacy is a part of the very fabric of family life (Taylor, 1982). Although young children in these homes may not recognize letters and words as such, many do understand that what they see written in books, or written by parents as lists, memos, notes, and cards, contains meaning. From the age of about two onward, as soon as children can grasp a pencil or crayon, they become involved in representing and expressing meaning. As adults read books to them, children come to expect pleasure and that books will make sense. In turn, they try to make meaning as they interact with books independently.

Children in these types of homes see their mothers and fathers using reading and writing for a wide range of purposes. Their parents read manuals of directions to assemble new toys, furniture, and tools. They read items in the newspaper for both information and entertainment, and write letters for a wide variety of purposes. By talking to their parents about what they are doing and imitating or taking a reader/writer role alongside them, children learn why people read and write—for the fun of it, to find out something, to learn how to do something, or to communicate with someone.

However, not all children are born into or raised in literate environments. Studies by Taylor and Dorsey-Gaines (1988) and Purcell-Gates (1998) examined the literacy experiences of children in homes of low-socioeconomic-status families. They found great variation in these homes in the extent to which people read and wrote and in the way they used reading and writing. Overall, many children from these homes came to school with either fewer or different types of print experiences than children from middle-class homes. Rather than labelling these children as deficient, social constructivists recommend that schools be prepared to provide for a wide range of individual differences when planning beginning reading and writing instruction.

Nature and Forms of Written Language

A major understanding that children develop when they are read to involves the relationship or connection between oral and written language. Temple and Gillet (1989, p. 113) indicate that children need to know "that the talk that is inspired by a text is not a free-form commentary on the pictures, nor a story that changes a little with each telling, but rather a sort of frozen discourse that must come out just so every time the text is read." While this seems self-evident to adults who know how to read, few of us can remember when we reached this realization. One way children demonstrate an understanding that the story is a "frozen discourse" is by becoming intolerant if their parents do not read every word in the text exactly. They also demonstrate an understanding that spoken messages can be written down in their early writing when they produce scribbles or letters and ask that these be read back to them.

But children need to go beyond this general understanding of the relationship between oral and written language to a more specific understanding that each written word is related to one word they hear or say. By asking their parents to read the same book again and again until they have virtually memorized the text, children are able to begin matching words on the page with words in memory. This is frequently referred to as eye–voice pointing or speech-to-print matching. The child looks at each word at the same time as he or she is saying it.

It is not only experiences with books that contribute to awareness of the relationship between oral and written words. Torrey (1969) described a young boy who learned to read from exposure to advertisements on television, and others have documented the impact of **environmental print** on children's literacy development (Mason, 1984). In the supermarket, young children see products being named as they are selected, and they are frequently asked to find particular products. Television commercials, household products, and signs attract attention to print and help children become aware that every word they hear is linked directly to a word in written language. This is critical because it enables children to focus attention on the appropriate units of print as they attempt to read.

Through experiences with books, children also become aware that there are differences between the language in books and the spoken language they use in their daily lives. We rarely talk like the three little kittens who cried, "Oh Mother dear, we sadly fear / Our mittens we have lost." Doake (1988) refers to this as learning the language of books, and Clay (1972, p. 28) refers to it as "talking like a book." Knowledge about the language of books is reflected in the stories children tell and in what they say when they read. Applebee (1978) examined the stories told by young children and found that even at two years old, children who have been read to begin to differentiate storytelling from talking.

Speech–Print Relationship

Perhaps the most basic knowledge children construct about print is that there is a difference between it and pictures. This is evident in children's writing when they begin to differentiate between what they write and what they draw (Harste, Woodward, and Burke, 1984). Understanding the difference between pictures and print is also evident when children point to print rather than pictures when reading a book from memory.

However, this is only the beginning of what children learn as they figure out how print works. In alphabetic languages, a few symbols are arranged in different orders to produce all the words in the language (referred to by Clay, 1975 as the "generating principle"), and these symbols are rarely repeated next to each other more than twice. Ferreiro and Teberosky (1982) studied the developing awareness of young children about this aspect of the printed language. As one task, they presented children with cards containing strings of printed symbols and asked the children to indicate which could be read and which could not be read. They found that the children tended to reject cards with fewer than three letters as not being readable (they were "too short"), as well as rejecting those with the same letter repeated several times ("It's all the same").

Early writing usually begins with scribble—large, rounded gestures or scratchy straight lines. As the scribble evolves in form toward print, letters and familiar shapes emerge that children repeat as they perceive a likeness to models in their own world. Marie Clay (1975) has shown that this early writing plays a significant role in developing children's knowledge about how print works. Children come to understand that the same letter can be written in various ways (referred to by Clay as the "flexibility principle"). We see this when a child fills a piece of paper with different versions of the letter *A*, for example. We might see tall, thin *A*'s, wide, fat ones, ones that are upside-down, and ones with no stroke across the middle.

Children also learn about directionality as they engage in early writing. They learn

- that print begins at the top of a page and continues to the bottom,
- that we read and write from left to right on the page,
- that the front of a book opens on the right, and
- that directionality is important to the identity of letters.

These directional principles are different for other languages, such as Hebrew and Mandarin. Many teachers and parents express concern when young children write their names backwards or confuse the letters *b* and *d*. However, until children encounter written language, they have an implicit understanding that directional orientation does not affect the identity of an object. For example, a cup is still a cup, whether the handle is turned toward the left or the right. We are still the same people whether we're lying down or standing on our heads. Directionality has not been used to differentiate objects in the child's environment, but with letters and numbers, all that changes. Nines and sixes are entirely different numbers, *b*'s and *d*'s are different letters, *on* and *no* are different words.

Perhaps the most critical understanding that young children construct about print involves the connection between letters and sounds. Many researchers hypothesize that a first step in developing this understanding involves awareness that words can be segmented into phonemes, or sound units. Adams (2002, p. 76, italics in the original) maintains that children need to discover that "*every word can be conceived as a sequence of phonemes. It is this discovery—this insight—to which the term 'phonemic awareness' refers.*"

From the review of research on beginning reading conducted by the National Reading Panel, Ehri, Nunes, Willows, Schuster, Yaghoub-Zadeh, and Shanahan (2001) concluded that **phonemic awareness** (the ability to focus on and manipulate phonemes in spoken words) is significantly related to learning to read. However, they also indicated that phonemic awareness training is more effective when it is taught with than without letters. What this suggests is that it is not so much the ability to hear sounds in words that is important in learning to read but rather children's understanding of the connections between letters and sounds. Many people refer to this as understanding the **alphabetic principle**—that letters in written words stand for sounds in spoken words (Muter, Hulme, Snowling, and Taylor, 1997).

Although it is largely an artifact of reading instruction, children also learn the terms we use to talk about reading and writing. They come to understand what teachers mean when they say, "Find the word *cat*," "What sound do you hear at the beginning of the word *cat*?" and "Read the first sentence" (Mason, 1984). Many writers refer to terms about reading and writing as "metalinguistic knowledge" and note that young children frequently have quite different concepts from adults about terms such as *word, letter, sentence,* and *sound* (Reid, 1966; Downing, 1979). Other conventions they learn involve our use of punctuation and the associated terminology, as well as words we use to describe books (e.g., *front, back, author, cover*).

ASSESSING EMERGENT LITERACY

Some children arrive at kindergarten with very little understanding of what written language is for or how it works. Others come to school already reading and writing independently. Christie, Enz, and Vukelich (2003) note that it is not unusual to find as much as a five-year range in children's literacy development in a kindergarten classroom. As their teacher, you need to know what understandings your students have constructed about literacy in order to plan and provide appropriate experiences. In this section, we present suggestions for how you can informally assess the emergent reading and writing development of your students. But first, we provide a rationale for using informal assessment as compared to standardized tests with young children.

Standardized reading readiness tests were widely used in the past to determine children's readiness to learn from formal reading instruction, and they are beginning to be used in some school jurisdictions again due to increased concern about accountability. These tests traditionally assessed areas often only peripherally related to reading achievement, such as vocabulary development and visual and auditory discrimination. The major purpose of traditional reading readiness tests was to predict a child's readiness to learn from formal reading instruction. They provided little information on a child's specific instructional needs.

With the movement from reading readiness to emergent literacy in the late 1970s, informal assessment became the recommended means for teachers to discover what children know about literacy and where they are in their literacy development. Several advantages of informal assessment have been identified (Teale, Hiebert, and Chittenden, 1987):

- In contrast with formal testing, informal assessment is part of instruction. It is not separate from the teaching/learning process and, hence, does not take time away from instruction the way standardized testing does.
- Informal assessment is more broadly based than formal assessment. The focus is on all the literacy activities the child completes in the language arts classroom rather than what the child does on contrived test items.
- Informal assessment occurs continuously rather than at one or two points in the year.

As such, informal assessment provides a basis for daily lesson planning and responsive instruction.

Four major types of informal assessment have been described in the literature. The first three—observation, interviews, and samples of children's work—involve informal assessment by the teacher. The last involves student self-assessment.

A few years ago, Yetta Goodman coined the term *kid watching* to refer to the ongoing observation by teachers of children in classrooms. She suggests that kid watching is likely not as conscious as it needs to be for teachers to "gain the greatest insights from it" (1991, p. 58).

Teacher questioning has been a very common part of language arts instruction, and as Durkin (1978–79) has pointed out, this questioning has been primarily used to evaluate rather than to enhance children's understanding. In order to maximize insights from children's answers, however, it is crucial that we go beyond evaluating those answers as right or wrong and move on to determining what they tell us about children's literacy development. Interviewing generally refers to more structured interactions between teachers and children than those that occur in the classroom on a daily basis. Interview questions are usually organized around a specific topic or aspect of language learning, and the teacher may use the questions as prompts to gather information from children on an individual basis.

A third type of informal assessment involves gathering samples of children's work. This is not a new idea, but it has recently received considerable attention through the movement to "portfolio assessment." The term comes from artists' portfolios, in which they collect and display their best work. Portfolios of children's reading and writing are generally not restricted to their best work; instead, they are meant to contain samples across time that indicate children's efforts, progress, and achievements. Serafini (2001, p. 388) cites the purposes of portfolios as "to uncover the possibilities for students, to understand each child as a whole, and to attempt to provide a window into a student's conceptual framework and ways of seeing the world." From a collaborative perspective, one of the major advantages cited for portfolio assessment is the potential it has for children to become involved in self-assessment. This is achieved by having children both select some of what goes into the portfolio and collaborate with their teacher in assessing what is there. Thus, portfolios have the potential to create a more democratic language arts classroom.

Observing Children

As teachers, we gather information every time we interact with children, whether we are aware of it or not. However, even though these observations are often not recorded, they might still influence our instructional decisions. Some teachers keep anecdotal records, jotting down key observations of their students' reading and writing during or at the end of the day. For example, a teacher may note what books a child selected during free time or that a child was able to find the word *cat* in the language experience story that day. Teachers use these informal notes to track individual growth, ascertain the effectiveness of their instruction, and plan future class and small group activities.

Most beginning teachers find it useful to be more systematic in gathering and recording information. One way to do this is by using a checklist. Chittenden and Courtney (1989) recommend that observations be organized according to the contexts in which children learn language. The learning contexts described later in this chapter involve

- reading to children,
- shared-book experiences,
- shared writing (language experience approach),
- writing, and
- functional interactions with print.

Earlier in this chapter, we presented a comprehensive model of the components of emergent literacy, indicating the understandings that young children construct in the early stages of learning to read and write. The checklist in Table 3.2 is organized around attitudes and

Table 3.2 Emergent Literacy Checklist

Attitudes and Understandings	Learning Contexts	Behaviours	Comments and Examples
Positive attitude to books and print	Reading to children Shared-book experience Language experience Writing Functional interactions with print	___ Enjoys story time ___ Chooses books as free-time activity ___ Rereads language experience stories in free time ___ Chooses to write during free time ___ Shows interest in print around the classroom, school, community	
Written language is meaningful	Reading to children and shared-book experience Shared-book experience Shared-book/language experience Language experience and inter-active writing Interactive and independent writing Functional interactions with print	___ Makes comments or asks questions during story reading ___ Predicts meaningful words during completion reading or when words are covered ___ Reproduces meaning as a whole during rereading ___ Contributes ideas during story writing ___ Produces meaningful message when reading what has been written ___ Responds meaningfully to labels, calendar, charts in classroom	
Message stays the same	Reading to children, shared-book and language experience Functional interactions with print	___ Chimes in during reading ___ Knows when teacher or another child makes a mistake during rereading ___ Responds to labels/words the same way every time	
How written language sounds	Shared-book experience Language experience and writing	___ Memorizes favourite books ___ "Talks like a book" when rereading ___ "Talks like a book" when dictating/writing stories	
Story sense	Reading to children and shared-book experience Language experience/writing	___ Predicts what will happen in a story ___ Retells beginning, middle, and end of stories ___ Is able to draw or dramatize stories ___ Includes beginning, middle, and end in stories	Continued

Table 3.2   Emergent Literacy Checklist   *continued*

Attitudes and Understandings	Learning Context	Behaviours	Comments and Examples
Importance of print	Shared-book and language experience Writing Functional interactions with print	___ Points to print during reading/rereading ___ Makes letters or letter-like forms when writing ___ Points to print in classroom, school, and community	
Directional aspects of print	Shared-book and language experience Shared book Writing	___ Begins reading at top of page ___ Points from left to right when tracking print ___ Reads left page before right page ___ Writes from top to bottom of page ___ Writes left to right across page	
Speech-to-print match	Shared-book and language experience	___ Points to each word while saying it during reading/rereading	
Terms and concepts of print	Shared book and language experience Writing Shared-book/language experience, and writing	___ Uses terms *letters* and *words* while reading, e.g., "What's this word?" ___ Leaves a space between words ___ Uses terms *letters* and *words* while writing, e.g., "How do you spell the word *on*?" ___ Uses terms *author*, *page*, *sentence* while reading and writing	
Decoding/encoding strategies	Shared-book/language experience, and functional print Writing	___ Identifies same word in different contexts ___ Uses initial letter sound to help identify words ___ Verbalizes letter sounds while writing ___ Bases spelling on letter names or sounds	

understandings related to literacy. For each attitude or understanding, behaviours are listed that indicate a child has developed an attitude or understanding in specific learning contexts.

The checklist can be used either as a general guide for unrecorded observations or in a more systematic way to record information on some or all of the children in the class. Used at regular intervals, it provides an indication of a child's progress toward constructing particular understandings and is a very useful component in the portfolios of children who are not yet reading independently. The right-hand column in the checklist is a space to record specific comments and examples. For instance, if the teacher has checked "Chooses books as free-time activity," this column could include information on what types of books the child chooses (big books, animal books, familiar books), how frequently this happens (every day, once a week), and whether the child reads alone or with another child.

Information gathered on a checklist such as the one in Table 3.2 leads directly to instruction, since specific learning contexts are included as one organizer for the information collected. Consider the following examples of how information collected on this checklist might be interpreted:

- Children who are beginning to point globally at print as they read or reread books are showing that they understand the importance of print (as compared with pictures) in reading.
- When they point to words as the teacher reads, or they read a familiar book or language experience story as the teacher points, children demonstrate that they are ready for speech-to-print matching activities.
- Children who have achieved the speech-to-print match when rereading familiar books or language experience stories show that they are ready for instruction that involves identifying specific words, first in familiar books and language experience stories, and later in less familiar materials.

Interviews

Parents have a great deal of information that can serve as a basis for planning instruction. Box 3.2 presents questions that teachers can use to solicit information from parents about the reading habits of family members in the home, as well as about the home reading and writing experiences of young children. The children themselves are also able to provide information about their home reading and writing experiences when asked questions such as those provided in Box 3.3.

Although teachers gain considerable information about an individual child's concepts and knowledge by observing them during shared-book experiences, there are times when further information is needed. Several people have developed interview schedules for this purpose. The one in Table 3.3 (p. 82) incorporates questions and concepts from book-handling interviews suggested by Doake (1981), Alberta Education (1993), and Clay (1993).

Teachers use information gathered through interviews to supplement that gained as they observe a child's daily reading and writing in the classroom. This information helps the teacher ask a child to respond in ways during shared-book experiences that are consistent with the child's literacy concepts and knowledge. For example, it makes sense to ask a child to find a specific word on a page in a big book only if the child understands the significance of print and knows terms such as *word* and *letter*.

Samples of Children's Work

Emergent Writing

It is much easier to gather the artifacts of children's writing rather than their reading. Teachers often collect writing samples throughout the school year and keep them in a child's writing folder or portfolio. These samples are then analyzed to describe the development of the child's writing.

Box 3.2   Parent Interview Questions

Reading and Writing Habits of Family Members

1. Who reads and writes at home? (mother, father, siblings, others)
2. How much does X (repeat question for each person named in #1) read and write? (every day, twice per week, once per week)
3. What does X read and write? (newspapers, magazines, TV guide, children's books, cookbooks, letters, grocery lists)
4. Why does X read and write? (to learn, for pleasure, to accomplish a particular task)

Reading to the Child

5. How often is your child read to? (every day, once per week)
6. Who reads to your child? (mother, father, sibling, other)
7. What books are read? (titles or types of books)
8. What are some of your child's favourite books? (titles)
9. How many books does your child regularly have access to? (at home, the library)
10. How does your child feel about books and being read to? (positive, negative)
11. What does your child do when being read to? (mumbles along, asks questions, wanders away)
12. What does your child do independently with books? (nothing, looks at the pictures, reads aloud to him- or herself)

The Child's Writing

13. What types of writing behaviours does your child exhibit? (scribbling, using single letters for words, spelling some words phonetically)
14. How often does your child write? (every day, once per week)
15. What kinds of questions and comments does your child make when he or she is writing? (none, asks about spelling, talks about what he or she is writing)

Generally, the following stages can be used to describe young children's development of knowledge and concepts related to written language (Neuman and Roskos, 1993):

1. uses drawing for writing,
2. uses pictures and scribble for writing,
3. uses scribble for writing,
4. uses letter-like forms for writing,
5. uses letters (not based on sound) for writing,
6. uses letter names for **invented spelling,**
7. uses letter sounds for invented spelling, and
8. uses conventional spellings.

Not all children go through all these stages in this order, but a child who is still using scribble for writing is clearly not ready for a heavy focus on conventional spelling. Children also demonstrate growing awareness of directional principles in their writing, moving from scribbles placed in no particular order on the page, to some awareness of directional patterns, to the correct directional pattern (top to bottom, left to right, spaces between words).

Box 3.3   Child Interview Questions

Family Reading and Writing Habits

1. Who reads at home?
2. What kinds of things does X (mother, father, sibling, other person) read?
3. Why do you think X (repeat for each person named in #2) reads these things?
4. Who writes at home?
5. What kinds of things does X write?
6. Why do you think X writes these things?

Child's Home Reading Experiences

7. Who reads to you at home?
8. Do you enjoy reading? What do you like most about reading?
9. How often does X read to you?
10. Tell me the names of some of your favourite books.
11. Do you read to yourself at home? If so, how often? What do you read? What do you do when you read?
12. Do you write at home? If so, how often? What do you write? What do you do when you write?

Although much of the focus of research has been on the forms of emergent writing, it is important to look beyond these forms to determine children's understanding of the purposes of writing. Even when children scribble, they are indicating that they realize writing and drawing are different. As they begin to use letter or letter-like forms, they show an awareness that writers use symbols when they write. They begin to talk about what they have written (or ask someone to tell them what they have written), indicating that they are aware that written language holds meaning. As they continue to grow, they produce invented spellings and are aware that a message is encoded in the words they write.

David, a first-grader whose writing is presented in Exhibit 3.1, talked out loud to himself as he wrote, demonstrating clearly that he was aware he was encoding a message in print. He also reviewed what he had written at one point before writing more. In addition, his writing indicated that he was aware of the importance of directionality to letter identity and that he used letter sounds for spelling. At one point he printed the letter *d* at the top of the page and asked if that was right before writing a word in his story. However, he also used an arithmetic symbol to represent the word *plus* and needed help from his teacher to spell the words *trolls*, *live*, and *mushroom*.

David's writing reflects a greater understanding of the nature of written language than that of another first-grade child, Jillian. When asked to write a story, she produced a labelled drawing (shown in the top part of Exhibit 3.2, p. 84) for her friend Ashley. She said that she did the same type of thing when asked to write at school. When asked to write all the words she could, Jillian produced the list at the bottom of Exhibit 3.2. Many of the same words appear on both lists, and several are the names of important people in her life, including her parents, friend, and sister. In relation to components of emergent literacy, Jillian showed that she was developing an understanding of how we use print to relate to other people. She also knew that words are used in writing, although her picture conveyed most of the message. She demonstrated only a beginning understanding of the alphabetic principle at this stage in her literacy development.

Table 3.3   Book-Handling Interview

Questions	Literacy Concepts and Knowledge	Comments
1. How books work • Can you show me the front of the book? • Where is the title? What does it tell you? • Open the book so we can start reading at the beginning of the story	___ Identifies front of book ___ Identifies title ___ Identifies first page of story	
2. Importance of print • Show me with your finger where to start reading	___ Points to print	
3. Directional aspects of print • Show me the top/bottom of this page. • Show me which page to read first. • Show me with your finger which way I go as I read this page.	___ Identifies top/bottom of page ___ Reads left page before right ___ Points left to right across line of print	
4. Speech-to-print match • Point to the words as I read.	___ Partial matching ___ Exact matching	
5. Terms and concepts of print • Point to one letter/word. • Point to the first/last letter in a word. • Point to an upper-/lowercase letter.	___ One letter ___ One word ___ First letter ___ Last letter ___ Uppercase letter ___ Lowercase letter	
6. Letter/word identification • Point to the letter ___ (name two letters on the page). • Point to the word ___ (name two high frequency words on the page).	___ Letter names ___ Words	
7. Meaning in written language • Tell me the story	___ Retells by naming pictures ___ Retells part of story ___ Retells beginning, middle, and end	

Exhibit 3.1 David's Writing in Grade 1

Although general developmental patterns are useful to teachers in assessing children's progress in learning to write, Sulzby (1991) has pointed out that many children, even until mid- or late Grade 1, move between forms and understandings of writing. Whereas a child may write a short sentence using invented spellings and be able to read this sentence accurately on request, he or she might revert to scribbling on a more difficult task such as writing a whole book. From her research, Sulzby feels that this movement between more and less sophisticated writing is part of normal development. With this in mind, we recommend that teachers collect many samples in a variety of contexts rather than a single sample, to provide a more comprehensive picture of a child's literacy than might otherwise result.

Emergent Reading

When children read orally or silently, no permanent record remains of their reading. While some teachers tape the reading of their kindergarten or Grade 1 children, it is not easy to use these tapes to assess growth. In addition, it takes a great deal of time to listen to tapes of children reading, and it is difficult to remember what the child did on one tape when listening to the next. A practical solution to this challenge is for the teacher to make a written record of a child's reading. Clay (1993) recommends that teachers take "running records" of their children's reading.

To take a running record, the teacher has a child read a book, and as the child does so, the teacher notes in writing what the child says and does. This can be done in one of two ways. In the first, the teacher makes a copy of the text the child will be reading and marks what the child says on that copy. Alternatively, the teacher can use a blank sheet of paper

Exhibit 3.2 Jillian's Writing in Grade 1

and put a mark for each word the child reads correctly and note any deviations from the text. These two options are shown in Box 3.4. For children in the emergent stage of literacy development, it is more appropriate to use books that they have some degree of familiarity with when taking running records, although it is useful at times to see what they do with a completely unfamiliar book.

One way of analyzing children's reading is to examine their running records in relation to stages reported in the literature. The following stages are based on the work of Sulzby (1985) and Neuman and Roskos (1993):

1. pays attention to pictures, labelling objects rather than forming a story,

2. pays attention to pictures, making up a story from the pictures,

3. pays attention to pictures, telling a version of the story,

4. pays attention to pictures, and talks like a book,

5. pays attention to print, identifying some words and inventing the rest to produce a meaningful version of the story,

6. pays attention to print, focusing primarily on word identification, and

7. pays attention to both print and meaning cues, reading fluently

All children do not go through all these stages, but it is clear that most begin by focusing on pictures and most need to spend some time internalizing and telling stories before they are ready to profit from a heavy focus on print. David, whose **miscues** are shown in Box 3.4, was paying attention to both print and meaning cues and was approaching reading fluency.

Another way of analyzing running records is to code deviations from the text in relation to what type of information the child used to produce these deviations. Goodman (1969) coined the word **miscues** to refer to these deviations rather than the word "errors" because he believes that they provide us with a great deal of useful information about how children read. As they read, he says, they are constantly using picture, print, and context cues to predict words, and their miscues provide insight into which cues they are using. Miscue analysis involves looking at each miscue the child has made and relating it to the information sources being used by the child. For classroom purposes, we recommend a simplified system for analyzing miscues, although more sophisticated systems may be necessary for children who have significant difficulty learning to read.

Children use two major sources of information as they read: print information and background knowledge. To become good readers, they need to integrate both sources of information so that what they read makes sense and is consistent with the print information. In our simplified miscue analysis, we recommend that you look at each miscue a child made and ask yourself two questions:

Box 3.4   Taking a Running Record

Marking System for Running Records

- A stroke (/) indicates word read correctly.
- A substituted word is written above the text word.
- An omission is indicated with a circle around the word.
- T indicates the word was provided by the teacher.
- SC indicates that a miscue was self-corrected.

Text: _Whistle, Mary, Whistle_ by Bill Martin, Jr.

Option 1: Making a Copy of the Text the Child Is Reading

        T

"Whistle, Mary, Whistle, and you shall have a trout."

        fell

"I can't whistle, Mother, because my tooth is out."

"Whistle, Mary, Whistle, and you shall have a rabbit."

      I   my tooth

"I can't whistle, Mother, because I've lost the habit."

        dandy

"Whistle, Mary, Whistle, and you shall have a daisy."

        T

"I can't whistle, Mother, because it looks so crazy."

Option 2: Using a Blank Sheet of Paper	**Coding**
"Whistle, Mary, Whistle	/ / /
and you shall have a rabbit."	/ / / / / / (used picture cue for rabbit)
"I can't whistle, Mother,	/ / / /
because I've lost the habit."	/ I / my tooth
	I've the habit
"Whistle, Mary, Whistle,	/ / /
and you shall have a daisy."	/ / / / / dandy
	daisy
"I can't whistle, Mother,	/ / / /
because it looks so crazy."	/ / / / T

1. Does the word the child said look like the word in the text (thus indicating use of print cues)?
2. Does the word the child said make sense (thus indicating use of background knowledge)?

If the word the child says contains any of the letters in the text word, write the letter _P_ above the word to indicate use of print cues. If the miscue makes sense up to that point, write the letter _M_ above it to indicate use of meaning cues. Box 3.5 shows how David's miscues were coded using this simplified system of analysis.

Miscues are then interpreted as follows:

- Miscues with only a *P* above them indicate that the child uses print cues, but does not rely on his or her knowledge to make a meaningful prediction.
- Miscues with only an *M* above them indicate that the child uses his or her knowledge to predict a word that makes sense, but does not use print cues.
- Miscues with both a *P* and an *M* above them indicate that the child may be using both print cues and background knowledge.
- Miscues with neither a *P* nor an *M* above them indicate that the child is unable to make effective use of either print cues or background knowledge.

A simple count of the number of miscues of each type in Box 3.5 shows that two were coded as meaningful, one as using print cues, and two as using both print and meaning cues. In addition, David waited for help from the teacher on two words, suggesting that he was focusing on print cues, even though he was unable to identify the words from these cues. Overall, this analysis of David's miscues shows that he is attending to both meaning and print cues but does not always use the cues together. He also does not correct any of his miscues, which suggests that either he is unaware that what he is reading doesn't make sense or look right or he has not yet developed enough facility with using print and meaning cues to self-correct.

In the actual classroom situation, we would want to analyze a larger sample of David's miscues to confirm this interpretation. However, from both the running record in Box 3.4 and the writing sample in Exhibit 3.1, it is clear that David has considerable knowledge about how books work. He also knows that written language is meaningful and is developing strategies for encoding and decoding words on the basis of print and sound cues. He has constructed many of the understandings involved in emergent literacy and is rapidly reaching independence in reading and writing.

Box 3.5 Coding of David's Miscues on a Predictable Book

- P: miscue contains at least one letter in the text word
- M: miscue makes sense in relation to prior text

T

"Whistle, Mary, Whistle, and you shall have a trout."

M

fell

"I can't whistle, Mother, because my tooth is out."

"Whistle, Mary, Whistle, and you shall have a rabbit."

PM   M   PM

I   my tooth

"I can't whistle, Mother, because I've lost the habit."

P

dandy

"Whistle, Mary, Whistle, and you shall have a daisy."

T

"I can't whistle, Mother, because it looks so crazy."

As with writing, Jillian's stage of reading development is different from David's. When asked if telling and reading a story are the same, she answered, "Yes," and she also indicated that people can't read with their eyes closed because they can't see the pictures. When asked to read a familiar, predictable book (*A Dark, Dark Tale*), she was highly successful, relying primarily on memory of sentence patterns and picture cues. When introduced to an unfamiliar, predictable book, she was able to use her excellent auditory memory and language abilities along with picture cues to read the book with a high degree of accuracy after only two readings. When asked what kinds of books she read at school, Jillian proceeded to "read" one without the text in front of her. She used storybook language and maintained a high degree of accuracy with the absent text, making a correction at one point to insert a line she had forgotten to include. Although Jillian knew a lot about books and book language, she was just beginning to develop an understanding of the forms of written language and of how written and oral language are related.

> Finding out where children are in their literacy development is a necessary component of effective instruction, but it is clearly not enough. The biggest challenge is planning programs to meet the needs identified. The next two sections are designed to help you construct ideas to meet this challenge.

PLANNING FOR INSTRUCTION

We begin by presenting some general guidelines for planning literacy instruction, and follow with a section on specific instructional strategies that facilitate young children's literacy development.

Parents are no longer told not to teach their children to read and write at home as they were in the middle of the 20th century. Instead, it is now almost universally accepted that the home plays a crucial role in literacy development, and parents are being urged to read to their children from an early age. Research on early neurological development indicates that there are critical periods, many before the age of six, when young children require stimulation to establish neural pathways in the brain in order to optimize learning throughout life (McCain and Mustard, 1999).

Children's literacy learning at home is frequently referred to as natural, and some educators argue that the developmental model used in the home should be extended to educational contexts in both the community and school. These educators have done much to foster meaningful literacy programs for young children, and some of the principles outlined below are based on their work (e.g., Holdaway, 1979; Cambourne, 1995).

Other educators question whether the obvious lessons derived from home literacy can or should lead to prescriptions for the classroom (Sulzby, Teale, and Kamberelis, 1989). They contend that a heavy focus on natural literacy learning may lead to literacy programs devoted entirely to providing children with opportunities to read and write but little more. Most educators today agree that direct, explicit instruction is needed for most children learning to read and write. It is the focus of this instruction that is in question.

Some of the differences of opinion relate where and how early childhood programs are offered. In most provinces and territories, formal literacy education begins at school in kindergarten at age five, although some provinces such as Ontario and Quebec offer a discretionary additional year of kindergarten beginning at age four. Most other early childhood services and programs are offered by community agencies rather than school districts. However, a commitment of funding to early childhood development by the federal government as part of its National Children's Agenda (socialunion.gc.ca/nca_e.html) beginning in 2001/2002 has recently lead to greater involvement of provincial and territorial ministries of education in the development of early childhood programs for young children.

The following general instructional guidelines reflect a range of perspectives as well as the recognition that children come to early childhood programs from a wide variety of literacy environments. We focus much of our discussion on school-based programs beginning at the kindergarten level, although the guidelines are appropriate for teachers working in community-based programs with younger children as well.

Rich Literacy Environment

Children who learn to read early are generally immersed in a literate home environment. They own books and are read to regularly by their parents. They are surrounded by print in their homes and communities, ranging from books to television commercials, signs, toys, newspapers, letters, and bills. They see their parents and other people in their home and communities reading and writing on a daily basis. Kindergarten and first-grade classrooms that are print-rich enable children to be involved daily in meaningful, purposeful literacy activities. When written language is used in authentic ways by their teacher and others, children are encouraged to view reading and writing as functional and worthwhile.

The following two examples help to distinguish between authentic literacy experiences and those that are more contrived. In one classroom, a teacher decides to increase the children's familiarity with signs in their community and to do so develops worksheets depicting frequently occurring signs such as stop signs, walk lights, restaurant signs, and signs on washroom doors. The teacher asks the children to say what they think the signs mean and what they should do when they see each sign. The teacher then puts the words on flash cards for the children to practise reading. Contrast this with another classroom where the children are planning to bake cookies and need to go to a local store to buy the ingredients. They first consult a recipe to determine what ingredients are needed, and then make a list to take to the store. On the way to the store, they talk about traffic signs. Once at the store, they locate the products needed. The major difference between these two classrooms is that, in the first, the goal is the reading of signs for their own sake. In the second, which involves more authentic learning, the goal is to get to a store to purchase products in order to make cookies.

Daily Reading and Writing

Children do not learn to read and write by cutting out or colouring pictures, although this may develop their fine motor coordination. Similarly, children do not learn to read and write by working together to build a house out of blocks, although they may learn to work cooperatively and develop visual–motor perceptual skills.

In addition to being immersed in print-rich environments, we believe that children need to interact with books every day. For those who have been read to regularly by their parents before entering school, this will be a direct extension of home experiences, and they will know what to expect from and what to do with books. For other children, books and being read to will be less familiar. These children benefit from daily opportunities to play with and handle books, as well as from being involved in book-sharing activities. We also believe that children need to be involved in writing activities on a regular basis. Again this will be an extension of home experiences for some, but it will be relatively new for others. Through these activities, children have opportunities to see others write, to have their ideas written by someone else, and to experiment freely with their own writing.

Control over Literacy Learning

Children who learn to read and write at home frequently have considerable control over their own literacy learning (Doake, 1981; Juliebö, 1985). They decide when and how long they write, and although they may not get their parents to read to them as often or as long as they would like, children often choose the book that will be read. These children frequently select the same book day after day and, by doing so, develop favourites that they practically memorize. As they reread the books independently, they have an opportunity to engage in eye–voice matching. They engage in as much practice as they want in order to develop control over whatever aspect of written language they are ready to handle. If parents attempt to involve children in some aspect they are not ready for, children often ignore the parents' questions or stop the activity. Essentially the children choose when, how, and what they want to do or learn, and the parents help to facilitate their learning.

Parents are frequently surprised by how long their children are able to spend on a reading or writing activity. They are also often dismayed at how often their children want to have the same book read over and over again. Teachers frequently do not reread books to children, nor do they provide extensive opportunities for young children to reread the books that have been read to the class. But children need to achieve mastery over written language, and only by having numerous opportunities to practise will they develop this mastery and control.

Although children do not have as much control over what is read in the classroom as they do at home, teachers can certainly encourage their students to suggest books they would like to hear, particularly when rereading. In addition to group activities (such as compiling group language experience charts based on the experiences of several children rather than one), children benefit from opportunities to dictate stories or letters to guests or parents. Ownership is important for children as they learn how to read and write; it is even more critical to their becoming avid readers and writers.

Acceptance of Approximations

Babies are given enthusiastic reinforcement by their parents the first time they say something that even remotely resembles "mama" or "daddy." Parents are not concerned that their child does not articulate every sound correctly. Similarly, when children are rereading their favourite books or pretending to write a letter to their grandmother, parents rarely insist on accurate reading or spelling, partly because they do not view these activities as real reading and writing. Doake (1988, p. 34) presents the following example of a mother reading *Brown Bear, Brown Bear, What Do You See?* with her preschool daughter. Words the mother reads aloud are presented in bold; what Adrienne says is in italics.

Text	Adrienne and Her Mother
I see a blue horse.	**I see a** (mother pauses) … **blue** (pauses) … *horse*
Looking at me.	**Looking** (pauses) *Look … at me.*

	Tail! (Adrienne points to the tail on the horse.)
	Yes. (Mother responds and continues reading.)
Blue horse	**Blue horse**
Blue horse	*Blue horse*
What do you see?	**What do you see?**
	See?
I see a gray mouse	**I see a** (pauses)
	Gay mouse
Looking at me	**Looking** (pauses) … **at me.**

Doake notes that the whole book was read in this manner, and not once did Adrienne's mother correct any miscues. Instead, she invited her daughter to participate in the reading activity, modelling correct responses when her daughter was unable to respond and accepting approximations of correct responses. In contrast, once a child is receiving language arts instruction at school, both parents and teachers often have a difficult time accepting approximate answers.

This reflects the traditional notion that children need to engage in word-perfect reading and letter-perfect spelling right from the beginning, a notion that has come under considerable criticism in the 1980s and 1990s. Learning, when viewed from a constructivist perspective, involves exploring and actively constructing knowledge. The responses of children who learn to read and write before school entry gain closer and closer resemblance to conventional reading and writing. These children do not move from not being able to read and write one day to 100 percent perfect reading and writing the next (Doake, 1988). Children who are discouraged from reading or writing unless they can do it perfectly may become reluctant readers and writers. We are not suggesting that exact spelling and word identification are unimportant. Rather, we are arguing that this is not an appropriate goal until after a child develops an understanding of the components of emergent literacy.

Differences Among Learners

There is ample evidence that children arrive at school with differences in their knowledge about reading and writing. Heath's early study of children from different socioeconomic environments (1983), referred to in Chapter One, still provides some of the best evidence we have in this regard. While children from all three communities in her study were immersed in literate environments, only the children from Maintown and to a lesser extent Roadville were involved in the kind of environment provided in schools.

The children of Roadville were read to by their parents and involved in other literacy activities, such as writing thank-you notes to relatives. They heard their parents talk about how important reading was, but rarely saw them reading and writing. The children were expected to answer specific questions about what they had read and, when retelling a story, to stay with rather than embellish the story line. Roadville children were tended to, encouraged, talked to, and generally prepared for dealing with everyday tasks such as making cookies, mowing the lawn, and fixing a bicycle. They were "given few occasions for extended narratives, imaginative flights of establishing new contexts, or manipulating features of an event or item" (Heath, 1983, p. 352). Thus, while they were ready for some aspects of school literacy and were successful in the initial stages of literacy instruction, they were not prepared for higher-level school literacy demands.

The children from Trackton had not been read to by their parents, and no stories had been told for them by parents or older children. Instead, the children observed numerous group debates over what letters, notices, or bills meant and listened to adults tell stories to one another. Stories were rarely reflections of what actually happened or retellings of a story read. Rather, good storytellers based their stories on actual events and real people but creatively fictionalized the details surrounding the real event. The primary message was of accomplishments, victories over adversities, or cleverness in the face of an enemy, and these stories had to be good in order to hold the audience's attention. This type of storytelling did not prepare children for the decontextualized story experiences of early schooling. Their "abilities to contextualize, to remember what may seem to the teacher to be an unrelated event as similar to another, to link seemingly disparate factors in their explanations, and to create highly imaginative stories" (Heath, 1983, p. 353) were suppressed in the primary classroom, and Trackton children fell quickly into a pattern of school failure. Parents from all three communities in Heath's study had a strong desire for their children to get ahead and depended on the school to play a critical role in their children's future. However, only the Maintown people were able to provide their children with home experiences that matched the expectations of the school.

What should schools do to ensure that all children learn to read and write? Purcell-Gates (1998) believes that we need to begin with the assumption that all children are learners:

> The notion that some children, because they hold different concepts about written language, are not ready to learn is nonsense. All children are not only ready to learn, they have been learning from birth. What this not-ready-to-learn dictum is really about is the fact that not all children are ready to learn from, or can make sense of, the curriculum presented to them in schools. Thus the issue becomes one of curriculum, not children. (P. 66)

From this perspective, Purcell-Gates recommends that teachers figure out where each child is in his or her literacy development and provide appropriate instruction. This does not apply only to children from different socioeconomic environments, but also to children who have been labelled as having learning disabilities or mild mental handicaps. When teachers set appropriate goals and provide instruction to meet these goals, Purcell-Gates believes that the children will achieve success and not become discouraged.

There is considerable similarity in the literacy needs of children at the emergent stage of development regardless of whether they speak English as a first or a second language, whether they have grown up in mainstream or other cultural environments, or whether they have been labelled as special-needs learners. All benefit from being immersed in a meaningful, purposeful literacy environment and from having numerous opportunities for meaningful interaction with written language.

Teachers who have children from different cultural backgrounds in their classrooms recognize the importance of understanding and respecting the culture of all children. When teachers incorporate books and other experiences related to children's culture, the children are more likely to feel included in the classroom community. Similarly, when teachers are aware of differences in storytelling and interaction patterns in different cultural groups, they tend to accept all children's stories, and discontinuity between home and school is reduced.

Hough and Nurss (1992) believe that early childhood classrooms are generally well suited to the needs of ESL learners. Most early childhood classrooms provide numerous opportunities for concrete activities and small group interactions, and these types of literacy experiences are appropriate for both ESL learners and children whose first language is English. However, teachers of children with limited English proficiency often make two major adaptations. First, they ensure that input is comprehensible by making some changes in their language and using gestures and visual aids for the ESL learner. Second, as with all children from different cultures, the teacher takes conscious steps to ensure that ESL children feel they are part of the classroom group and that their culture is respected.

We are not suggesting that early childhood teachers can meet the needs of all children in their classrooms without assistance. Children with more severe learning problems, such

---

Exhibit 3.3   Amber Learns to Read and Write

When Amber arrived at Kathy Purkiss' Grade 1 classroom at the end of September, she appeared to have limited literacy background (Malicky, Purkiss, and Nugent, 1988–89). When asked to read predictable books (*Brown Bear, Brown Bear, What Do You See?* and *A Dark, Dark Tale*), she demonstrated a very positive attitude toward books generally and was able to "talk like a book." Her reading was meaningful although she was not yet able to match spoken to printed words or to rely on print cues to identify words. In sharp contrast with her reading, she viewed writing as a process of spelling words correctly and was very reluctant to write.

Amber was given one-to-one instruction for five months twice weekly using primarily shared reading, the language experience approach, and writing. Making steady progress in reading throughout the sessions, she was able to match spoken to printed words by mid-November and had begun to make use of print cues as she read. She also began to take familiar books and her language experience stories to her classroom to read to other children. This helped her to feel like a reader and gave her a sense of belonging to the "literacy club" (Smith, 1988) in her classroom.

Developing Amber's writing was more problematic. She was reluctant to write on her own and, when urged to try, produced short sentences of letters such as *I b swh* for "I like skipping." These written products were far less rich than the language experience stories she dictated, indicating that she thought she had to write and spell like adults do.

By late January, both of Amber's teachers were quite concerned with her progress in writing. Finally, the intervention teacher used a strategy recommended by Sulzby, Teale, and Kamberelis (1989). She assured Amber that her writing didn't have to be like grown-up writing, that no one else would read it. Tompkins (1997) has also indicated that "kid writing" is important for young children because it gives them permission

to experiment with written language. Amber then began to write, generating the piece reproduced below.

When asked to reread what she had written, she read the alphabet first (the safe part) and then, pointing to the print line by line, read, "The elves made a castle for Santa to build his toys for the kids in the L. family. Santa likes to give out toys from the Christmas tree for all the kids." She smiled happily to herself when she finished reading. With reinforcement, Amber wrote another meaning-based story in the next session. She finally felt free to engage in the type of writing most young children do in the early stages of literacy development, and this appeared to be a necessary step in her writing development. By the end of January, she was beginning to include invented spellings in her writing.

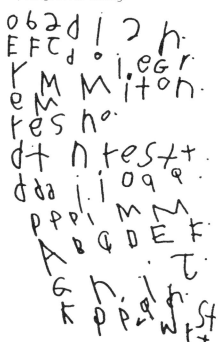

Source: Reprinted with permission of the Alberta Teachers' Association.

as language delays, attention deficit disorders, and sensory impairments, need to be referred to appropriate specialists for assistance in planning appropriate programs.

Sequence of Instruction

Although we do not believe that all children go through the same invariant stages in learning to read and write, some understandings do seem to come before others for most children. In relation to the components of emergent literacy delineated earlier in this chapter, children generally construct knowledge about the functions of written language (why people read and write) before they develop an understanding that oral and written language are related. Eye–voice matching is still a later development or construction. Similarly, for most children, being able to eye–voice match precedes understanding the alphabetic principle and being able to map letters onto sounds when spelling or to map sounds onto letters when reading (Morris, 1993).

The order of components presented in Box 3.1 provides a rough sequential order appropriate for many children. This is consistent with stages in the reading development of young children identified by Sulzby (1985) and Neuman and Roskos (1993), in which children move from a focus on pictures and meaning to a focus on print and finally to a focus on both at the same time. It is also consistent with the writing development of young children.

Harste, Woodward, and Burke (1984) have found that from the earliest stages of writing, children engage in intentional behaviour. They understand that people use "specific marks to sign specific meanings" (p. 108). Uses of written language generally precede forms in the writing development of young children. A heavy focus on form in the initial stages of learning to write often results in children becoming reluctant to write anything at all, as shown in the example presented in Exhibit 3.3. The school involved in this example is in an inner-city neighbourhood, and the first-grade child moved to the school when she went to live with her aunt and uncle at the end of September during Grade 1.

Although the development of reading and writing are not parallel, there are some similarities. Children initially approach both from a sense-making perspective, and they move from approximations of reading and writing to more conventional forms. Hence, while there is no fixed, hierarchical order to the components in Box 3.1, most children construct their understandings in approximately the order presented. Because learners are different, however, it is important that teachers continuously assess children's literacy development and base instruction on that assessment.

Purcell-Gates (1998) offers the following general suggestions. First, she notes that the literacy experiences provided at school must be appropriate for the emergent literacy component involved. For example, if we want children to learn to eye–voice match as they read, we need to use connected texts rather than isolated words. If we want them to learn the alphabetic principle, we need to have children listen to sounds in words as they write them and to look at words when they are reading. Second, Purcell-Gates recommends that, embedded in these activities, teachers give direct and explicit explanations to children. For example, when children are writing, she recommends that we point out and use labels for letters, words, and sentences. We also need to show children how to hear separate sounds in words and what letters go with these sounds. Third, Purcell-Gates recommends that some crucial constructs such as the alphabetic principle be taught systematically and explicitly. Overall, what she and many others are recommending is a balanced literacy program for young children, including a focus on all aspects of emergent literacy and involving both incidental and systematic instruction.

EXPERIENCES THAT FACILITATE LITERACY DEVELOPMENT

In this section, we present a range of literacy experiences designed to help children construct knowledge about the components of emergent literacy outlined earlier in this chapter. These are organized according to teaching/learning contexts rather than emergent literacy components, because each type of context has the potential to develop several of the components. Table 3.4 presents an overview of teaching/learning contexts presented in this section, indicating emergent literacy components that can be developed in each context.

For each of the teaching/learning contexts described in this section, we present suggestions for instruction to help children develop specific understandings about literacy and strategies for dealing with print. We recommend that, in the initial stages of literacy development, most instruction on specific skills and strategies be presented within the context of reading and writing activities. Once children have developed basic understandings about the functions, nature, and forms of written language, systematic instruction about how print works is appropriate. Suggestions for this type of instruction are provided in Chapters Six and Nine.

Reading to Children

Children's books provide the basis for a significant portion of the emergent literacy program. In her review of research on beginning reading, Marilyn Jager Adams (1990, p. 46) concluded that "The single most important activity for building the knowledge and skills eventually required for reading appears to be reading aloud to children." Not all children have equal access to this experience. Data indicated that only 45 percent of children below the age of three and 56 percent of children between the ages of three and five are read to daily in the United States (National Education Goals Panel, 1997).

At school, young children benefit from a wide range of experiences with books, including hearing their teacher read books to them, reading with their teacher, reading in groups, and reading independently. They also need exposure to a wide range of books, including picture storybooks, **predictable books**, big books, nursery rhymes and poetry, information books, and ABC and counting books. It is important to share books representative of different cultures. A list of books appropriate for reading to young children is presented in the Appendix.

While teachers have been reading to children for decades, many were not aware of all that this activity achieves, and it was often discontinued once children were able to read independently. In the past, teachers often told children to sit and listen quietly so as not to interrupt the reading. Thus, classroom reading was frequently very different from the interactive bedtime reading children experienced at home. Today, educators who hold a constructivist perspective recommend that teachers encourage children to talk about ideas in books before, during, and after the teacher reads (Mason, Peterman, and Kerr, 1989). The nature of the interaction varies depending on whether the teacher is reading a **narrative** or an informational book.

Before Reading

The major understanding children develop at this stage of the reading is that written language is meaningful. They also develop understanding of different purposes for reading as

Table 3.4 A Balanced Emergent Literacy Program

Teaching/Learning Context	Emergent Literacy Component
Reading to Children Teachers select quality children's literature and read to the whole class or small groups. They invite children to talk about ideas before, during and after the reading.	• Positive attitudes toward books and reading • Meaningful nature of written language • Language of books • Knowledge of text structure
Shared-Book Experiences Teachers and children read "big books" together. The initial reading is followed up by group and individual readings of the same book.	• Positive attitudes toward books and reading • Meaningful nature of written language • Relationship between oral and written language • Language of books • Eye–voice matching • Difference between pictures and print • Terms related to books and written language • Conventions of print • Alphabetic principle
Shared Writing (Language Experience Approach) Teachers and children write together; the children generate the ideas and the teacher does the scribing. The material generated is read by the whole class, small groups, and individuals and is also used for follow-up activities.	• Meaningful nature of written language • Relationship between oral and written language • Eye–voice matching • Terms related to reading and writing • Conventions of print • Alphabetic principle
Interactive and Independent Writing Teachers and children write together with a "shared" pen. Children also engage in daily independent writing.	• Positive attitudes toward writing • Meaningful nature of written language • Relationship between oral and written language • Terms related to writing • Conventions of print • Alphabetic principle
Functional Interactions with Print Teachers and children use print to get things done, e.g., organize the classroom, go on field trips, prepare food.	• Purposes of reading and writing • Meaningful nature of written language • Relationship between oral and written language • Eye–voice matching • Alphabetic principle

they talk about what to expect in different types of books. It is often the development of an anticipatory set that enables readers to track the meanings that are being created during reading. This set provides readers with a valuable source of information for identifying new words and self-correcting miscues.

- For all books, teachers draw children's attention to the picture on the cover and have them predict what they think the book is about. They encourage children to talk about their own experiences related to the topic or story. The children are also asked to predict whether the book will tell a story or tell about something.
- For informational books, teachers may need to demonstrate key concepts in the book if it becomes clear that several children have limited knowledge to bring to the topic.

During Reading

- While reading any book, teachers encourage the children to react to and comment on the story or ideas as they listen. Teachers also ask questions occasionally to monitor children's understanding of the story or ideas.
- For informational books, teachers may need to give demonstrations or examples of difficult ideas. These are based on the children's responses and teachers help by encouraging children to ask questions when they don't understand something.
- When reading storybooks, teachers rephrase the text when it is clear the children do not understand something. They also ask the children periodically to evaluate their earlier predictions and to formulate new ones. It is important for children to evaluate their own predictions rather than having the teacher do it for them.

After Reading

- For all books, children are asked to talk about what they have heard, relating the story or ideas to their own experiences.
- For stories, teachers often have children briefly retell the beginning, middle, and end in order to develop knowledge of story structure.

Shared-Book Experiences

To emulate the reading experience young children have in literate homes, Holdaway (1979) recommends that teachers use enlarged or "big" books so that all children can see the print and that teachers read *with* rather than *to* children. Predictable books are particularly useful for this purpose, because the repetitive and rhythmic structure of the text supports early reading attempts. A list of predictable and big books is presented in Box 3.6. More comprehensive lists of predictable books are available at the following Web sites: www.uiowa.edu/~crl/bibliographies/patterned_print.htm, compiled by S. Glenn at the University of Iowa Curriculum Laboratory, and www.earlyliterature.ecsd.net/predictable_books.htm, compiled as part of the Telus Learning Connection Project in Alberta.

Children construct different understandings about written language from shared-book experiences depending on the literacy backgrounds they bring with them. Children who have been read to a lot at home will likely construct understandings about the forms of written language and the nature of the print–speech relationship. However, for children with more limited book experience, the goal of instruction might be developing positive attitudes toward books or helping children understand the functions and nature of written language.

Box 3.6 Predictable Books

* Ahlberg, J. and Ahlberg, A. (1978). *Each peach pear plum*. New York: Scholastic Book Services.

  Aylesworth, J. (1992). *Old black fly*. New York: Henry Holt and Company.

* Baker, K. (1990). *Who is the beast?* New York: Harcourt Brace & Company.

  Baum, A. and Baum, J. (1962). *One bright Monday morning*. New York: Random House.

  Becker, J. (1973). *Seven little rabbits*. New York: Scholastic Book Services.

  Brown, K. (2001). *The scarecrow's hat*. London: Andersen Press.

* Brown, R. (1981). *A dark, dark tale*. New York: Scholastic Book Services.

  Carle, E. (1977). *The grouchy ladybug*. New York: Thomas Y. Crowell.

  Carle, E. (1983). *The very hungry caterpillar*. New York: Scholastic Book Services.

  Carle, E. (1984). *The very busy spider*. New York: Philomel.

* Cowley, J. (1980). *Mrs. Wishy-Washy*. Auckland, NZ: Shortland Publications.

* Cowley, J. (1983). *The jigaree*. Auckland, NZ: Shortland Publications.

* Cowley, J. (1983). *Who will be my mother?* Auckland, NZ: Shortland Publications.

  Cranstoun, M. (1967). *1, 2, buckle my shoe*. New York: Holt, Rinehart & Winston.

  Florian, D. (2000). *A pig is big*. New York: Greenwillow Books.

  Hoberman, M. A. (2001). *"It's simple," said Simon*. New York: Alfred A. Knopf.

* Hutchins, P. (1986). *The doorbell rang*. New York: Scholastic Book Services.

  Keats, E. J. (1971). *Over in the Meadow*. New York: Scholastic Book Services.

  Mahy, M. (1998). *A summery Saturday morning*. New York: Viking.

  Martin, Jr., B. (1970). *The haunted house*. New York: Holt, Rinehart & Winston.

  Martin, Jr., B. (1970). *King of the mountain*. New York: Holt, Rinehart & Winston.

* Martin, Jr., B. (1970). *Monday, Monday, I like Monday*. New York: Holt, Rinehart & Winston.

  Martin, Jr., B. (1970). *When it rains, it rains*. New York: Holt, Rinehart & Winston.

* Martin, Jr., B. (1972). *Brown bear, brown bear, what do you see?* New York: Holt, Rinehart & Winston.

  Mayer, M. (1975). *Just for you*. New York: Golden Press.

* Melser, J. (1980). *Lazy Mary*. Auckland, NZ: Shortland Publications.

* Melser, J. (1980). *Sing a song*. Auckland, NZ: Shortland Publications.

* Morris, W.B. (1970). *The longest journey in the world*. New York: Holt, Rinehart & Winston.

  Root, P. (2001). *Rattletrap car*. Cambridge, MA: Candlewick Press.

  Root, P. (1998). *What baby wants*. Cambridge, MA: Candlewick Press.

  Scheer, J. and Bileck, M. (1964). *Rain makes applesauce*. New York: Holiday House.

  Sutton, E. (1973). *My cat likes to hide in boxes*. New York: Parents Magazine Press.

  Tolstoy, A. (1968). *The great big enormous turnip*. New York: Franklin Watts.

* Williams, S. (1994). *I went walking*. New York: Harcourt Brace & Company.

  Wing, H. R. (1963). *What is big?* New York: Holt, Rinehart & Winston.

* Wood, A. (1984). *The napping house*. New York: Harcourt Brace & Company.

* Wood, A. (1992). *Silly Sally*. New York: Harcourt Brace Jovanovich.

* Available in "big book" form.

Although teachers sometimes group children according to literacy background, most of the time they provide shared-book experiences for the whole class. Because of differences in children's knowledge about literacy, however, teachers expect—and reinforce—different kinds of responses from different children. For example, while one child is developing an understanding of the alphabetic principle, another might be just beginning to internalize the language of books. A repetitive book is useful for both of these children, and they will both be able to predict words when teachers stop reading at predictable points during shared reading. However, only the first child will be able to respond to the teacher's invitation to point to the words in a line of print while it is being read.

Hough and Nurss (1992) believe that predictable books are well suited to the needs of children with limited English proficiency. These children can join in reading the repetitive parts of the story before individual words have become meaningful to them. Rereading both predictable and other picture storybooks is recommended for all children, including those learning English as their second language. This rereading provides ESL children with further exposure to written English and also helps them internalize the structure of stories written by authors who write from a Western cultural perspective. Having children dramatize familiar stories creates further opportunities for developing language and internalizing story structures. Picture storybooks with lots of action and repeated sequences, such as *The Three Billy Goats Gruff*, are particularly appropriate for this type of activity.

Holdaway (1979) outlines three basic steps in a shared-book experience:

1. discovery (initial reading of the book),
2. exploration (rereadings in the group), and
3. independent experience (individual and small group rereadings and follow-up activities).

Discovery

Holdaway argues that the most critical goal of the teacher when reading a new book is to provide an enjoyable experience for all children. This goal should not be sacrificed to any other purpose. The teacher encourages maximum participation of the children through talking with them about the book and asking and answering questions, as many parents do during bedtime reading. One way to encourage participation at this stage of the shared-book experience is to have children whisper a prediction to their partner once the teacher has set the stage. It is important for the teacher to organize the children so they can all see each page.

The guidelines presented above for storybook interactions before, during, and after reading are also appropriate for predictable big books. In addition, teachers may ask some children to predict words in the title before they begin reading, drawing attention to both picture and letter cues to do so.

During reading of predictable books, teachers often point to words as they read, demonstrating for the children the one-to-one correspondence between oral and written words and emphasizing the left-to-right and top-to-bottom directional nature of print. They also encourage children to read along, sometimes stopping their reading at highly predictable places so that the children can fill in the text. The children are encouraged to use both context as well as letter cues to make and confirm their predictions. Teachers talk about aspects of the text using the terms children need to learn. For example, "The first word in this sentence is ...," and "There is a question mark at the end of this sentence, so we need to sound as if we are asking a question when we read it."

Exploration

Various group activities provide further opportunities for children to interact with the book. These include

- rereadings,
- innovations on literary structures, and
- interpretations of the story through dramatization or art.

Children learn about the nature and forms of written language, and they begin to construct an understanding of the speech–print relationship through involvement in these activities.

Rereadings of predictable big books are often done at the request of children. With this type of book, children are encouraged to join in the reading as much as possible to learn the language of books. Teachers encourage group choral reading of the book, reading along with the children when they need support. By pointing to words as they read, teachers help children to hear the words as separate units and to match them with printed words on the page. By rereading the book several times, children are able to internalize the oral language they need in order to establish eye–voice matching when later reading the book independently or in a small group.

The teacher also uses the rereading time to focus on print and use of letter sounds to identify words. The teacher asks children questions such as "Where do I begin reading?" "Find words that begin with the letter *m*," and "What is this word?"

Reading nursery rhymes and other rhyming books and poetry to children helps focus their attention on the sounds in words (phonemic awareness). For many children, reading this type of material begins in the home, but teachers cannot assume children have knowledge of common nursery rhymes. Predictable books such as *1, 2, Buckle My Shoe* contain rhyming words, and children are encouraged to talk about which words rhyme. By seeing rhymes in big book format or on charts, children not only hear which words rhyme, but also learn that when words sound the same they often also look the same. When reading predictable rhyming books such as *Whistle, Mary, Whistle* to children, teachers often leave out the rhyming word so the children can predict them. For example, "Whistle, Mary, whistle, and you shall have some bread. I can't whistle, Mother, because I'm standing on my ____."

The book *The Hungry Thing* has been suggested by Yopp and Yopp (2000) as particularly appropriate for helping children focus on rhyme. In the story, a creature asks the townspeople for food, for example, "Schmancakes." After adults offer ideas, a little boy declares, "Schmancakes sound like fancakes sound like pancakes to me!" As teachers read the book to children, Yopp and Yopp suggest that they pause to encourage the children to make predictions, for example, "Feetloaf sounds like beetloaf sounds like (pause) to me?" A follow-up activity can involve the children in word play with other food words. Yopp and Yopp also suggest that teachers have children create rhyming lyrics to songs such as *Down by the Bay*. After learning verses such as "Did you ever see a whale with a polka-dot tail?" children create their own verses such as, "Did you ever see a shark strolling in the park?"

To further develop phonemic awareness, teachers can also ask children to talk about the words that begin with a particular sound. In *1,2, Buckle My Shoe*, for example, "What words begin with the sound at the beginning of the word *fun*?" When children respond, *four*, *five*, and *fat*, they are directed to the book and helped to discover that these words also begin with the same letter. Teachers are cautioned here not to isolate sounds, because many are distorted when pronounced in isolation. While it is fairly easy to isolate sounds for letters such as *s*, *f*, and *m* without distorting them, it is far more difficult to produce isolated sounds for letters such as *b*, *d*, *g*, *p*, *t*, *k*, *j*, and *ch* without distortion. The sound for *b* often ends up with a schwa (the sound at the end of the word *the*) on the end and sounds a lot like *buh*.

Research shows that in the initial stages, it is easier for children to hear rhyming words and sounds at the beginning of words than sounds in the middle or at the end (Goswami and Bryant, 1990). To encourage children to begin using knowledge of letter sounds to identify words, the teacher might also cover all except the first letter of a word in a sentence and ask the children to predict the word using cues from sentence context and the first letter. We present more systematic ways to develop phonemic awareness and phonics knowledge in Chapter Six.

Bill Martin, Jr., who has written several predictable books, recommends that teachers have children innovate on literary structures to help them develop greater awareness of the language of books. For example, near Halloween, the children can generate a Halloween book based on the structure of *Brown Bear, Brown Bear, What Do You See?* It might go something like this:

> White ghost, white ghost, what do you see?
>
> I see a black cat looking at me.
>
> Black cat, black cat, what do you see?
>
> I see a green witch looking at me.

As the children dictate, the teacher writes this story on large chart paper for them to illustrate. The story can later be used both for group and independent rereadings.

A further and often deeper interpretation of stories is achieved through giving children the chance to dramatize or illustrate what they have read. Specific ideas for incorporating drama into literacy activities are presented in Chapter Twelve.

Independent Experience

Big books that have been reread are placed in a reading centre for children to read independently or in small groups. Children reread the books as often as they wish, relying on meaning and print cues to reconstruct the text. They are encouraged to point to words as they read in order to more fully establish eye–voice matching.

To increase the exposure of young children to shared-book experiences and give them control over the number of times they hear favourite stories, a listening centre with taped books is invaluable. Tapes can be obtained commercially or produced by having volunteers or older children read and record stories.

Children's books are also now available in an interactive format for use on computers. *WiggleWorks* and *Living Books* are both highly interactive, providing children with an opportunity to listen or read along. These and other interactive books are described in more detail in Chapter Thirteen.

Perhaps most important to putting young children within easy and continuous reach of children's books is giving them regular access to a library. A classroom library is an important source of these books in kindergarten and Grade 1, but children also need to visit the school library often. This gives them an opportunity to use print to locate books and develop the habit of regular library use.

Shared Writing: The Language Experience Approach

The language experience approach builds on children's own experiences and language as a source of material to be used for reading instruction. Ashton-Warner (1986, p. 28), working with Maori children in New Zealand, viewed it as a way to build "a bridge from the known to the unknown." Children essentially tell a story or recount an experience, and the teacher acts as a scribe, writing what the children say. Although the language experience approach has been used in classrooms for several decades, understanding the nature of emergent literacy has led to an increased appreciation of its role in literacy development. As with shared-book experiences, the language experience approach is aimed at helping children construct understandings of many components of emergent literacy (see Table 3.4).

Teachers develop language experience stories with the whole class, with small groups, and with individuals. As with shared-book experiences, children at varying levels of literacy development can work effectively together on a language experience story, although the language learning will differ for each child.

The following description of the language experience approach has been adapted from ideas presented by Hall (1981). Teachers who use this approach place greater emphasis on the process of developing and using language experience stories, believing this to be more important than the final product itself.

1. *Experience.* Language experience stories begin with an experience. Trips, pets, classroom events, wordless picture books, pictures, and television provide springboards for discussion. When the children in one first-grade class visited another classroom in their school where chicks were hatching, their teacher, Susan Bennett, saw that this created an excellent opportunity to develop a language experience story.

2. *Discussion.* This is an essential step in the language experience approach, as discussion provides children with an opportunity to develop both the vocabulary and the sentence structures that will eventually be recorded. The teacher uses questions and prompts such as "I'm interested. Tell me more" to expand and clarify as well as to elevate the children's language beyond a listing of ideas. Susan Bennett had the first-grade children show how they would peck their way out of shells and asked them to imagine and talk about the first thing they might see.

3. *Recording.* As a group, children select the ideas to be recorded and provide an oral composition. This helps the children understand some of the basic differences between oral and written language. Then, as children dictate ideas, the teacher records them in large print on chart paper. As the teacher writes each word, the children watch to help them establish the link between oral and written words. The teacher makes comments and asks for help during this writing about where she or he begins writing, in what direction the print goes, about the use of capital letters and punctuation marks, and about special visual features of certain words (e.g., length, initial letter, and so on).

   If the children have some awareness of letter names and sounds, the teacher has the children suggest which letters to include in some of the words being written to further develop phonemic awareness. For example, when the children in Susan Bennett's first-grade class dictated a sentence about the chicks pecking out of their shells, she asked, "What letters do we need to write the word *peck*?" One child said "p" and another "k." Susan printed these letters and added the *e* and *c* herself, slowly articulating the sounds so the children would hear them as she wrote. She also commented on the *ck* at the end of the word. She knew the children did not have enough knowledge of letter sounds to supply these letters without help.

   A major dilemma teachers face when printing language experience stories is whether to write exactly what children say or to make changes. It is generally recommended that teachers use standard English spellings regardless of dialect (e.g., *going to*, not *gonna*) and use standard punctuation. However, controversy surrounds the question of whether or not to scribe ungrammatical sentences such as

"I don't got no pencil." The answer depends on whether you are working with a group or an individual child and on the major purpose of the language experience activity. With individual children at early stages of emergent literacy development, most educators recommend scribing children's vocabulary and grammar to help them develop an understanding of the one-to-one correspondence between oral and written words. For example, if the child dictates "Me and another chick saw a cow" and the teacher changes it to "Another chick and I saw a cow," the child will likely reread the first part of the sentence as "Me and another chick," associating the wrong spoken words with what is written.

Preserving what children have dictated is also important when working with children learning English as a second language. The context, vocabulary, and language structures will be familiar to the children, and hence will support their initial reading experiences.

However, as a general guideline when working with groups of children whose first language is English, many teachers change nonstandard English into the standard form. This practice is particularly prevalent when most of the children in the group use the standard form. This practice is also appropriate with children who are already able to match spoken and written words. One purpose of making changes to the standard form is to help children understand that there are differences between oral and written language. Children need to learn what book language sounds like to help them predict words as they read.

4. *Reading.* Immediately upon completing the story, the teacher reads it to the children, pointing to words as she or he does so. As a follow-up activity, the teacher may ask children if they want to make any changes, in order to engage them in revising what they have written. The teacher demonstrates revision by using carets and arrows, crossing out words, and writing in the margins. Once the children are happy with what they have dictated, the teacher and children read it together to ensure that their first reading will be successful. During subsequent rereadings, the children read more independently, with the teacher providing support as needed. Finally, when the children feel ready, individuals read the story alone.

5. *Follow-up activities.* A variety of follow-up activities are appropriate for both groups and individuals. Some examples follow:

   - During re-reading, the teacher asks children questions about where to begin reading, in what direction to read, how to know to stop at the end of a sentence, and so on, to develop concepts about print conventions.

   - Individual children are encouraged to read the story independently, pointing to the words as they read. Some teachers type the language experience story and make copies for the children to keep and read individually.

   - Children are asked to find words containing a common letter (e.g., all the words that begin with the letter *m*). They talk about how all of these words begin with the same sound and the fact that some of the words begin with an uppercase *M* and others with a lowercase *m*.

   - Sentences are cut apart, and children arrange the sentences in order, referring to the language experience chart if necessary. When the children are able to handle this task easily, individual sentences can be cut into words for them to put in order, again matching the words against an intact sentence strip if necessary.

   - Selected words in the language experience story are covered, and the children are asked to predict words that make sense and sound right in the space. They then check their predictions by looking at the print.

- Poetry, songs, and other material are presented to children in large print on charts. By pointing to words on a chart as the children sing, further opportunities for eye–voice matching are provided. In addition, discussing words on the chart further develops knowledge of the forms of written language and of speech–print relationships.

Writing

In this section we include both interactive writing, where children and teachers write together, and independent writing. These two types of experiences generally occur simultaneously in emergent literacy programs.

Interactive Writing

Interactive writing is an extension of shared writing, with teachers and children sharing all aspects of the writing process, including scribing (Fountas and Pinnel, 1996). It generally involves a small group and can serve as a transition to independent writing or as a teaching/learning context for children beyond the emergent stage of literacy development in which more complex skills (such as paragraphing) are demonstrated. Fountas and Pinnell (1996) recommend the following five steps in interactive writing for emergent writers:

1. The teacher and a small group of children compose a piece together, sometimes innovating on the structure of a book they have read (see the earlier section "Shared-Book Experiences" in this chapter). In the early stages of emergent literacy, Fountas and Pinnell recommend repeating the message several times and rereading it from the beginning each time a new word is completed.

2. The teacher and children share the pen. Sometimes the teacher writes the word and at other times invites children to come to the easel or whiteboard to fill in letters or known words.

3. To foster development of phonemic awareness and understanding of the alphabetic principle, the teacher selects some words and demonstrates how to articulate them slowly and connect sounds heard with letters. For example, "I stretch out the word *cat* like this, *cccaaattt*. Now I listen to the sound at the beginning of the word, *cccat*, and write the letter that goes with that sound." The teacher then invites the children to carry out a similar process, stretching words out and writing letters for the sounds they are able to hear.

4. Children quickly write known (sight) words. Others are analyzed, and different kinds of words are placed on a "word wall" to be used as a resource for further learning. Word walls will be described in more detail in Chapter Six.

5. As the piece is written, the teacher draws the children's attention to print conventions such as spacing, punctuation, and directionality.

Independent Writing

We recommend that young children have daily opportunities to write. Writing can be integrated with all the experiences described above. However, establishing a writing centre in the kindergarten or Grade 1 classroom will provide further opportunities and incentive to write. A writing centre contains a variety of writing implements and materials: paper, pencils, crayons, chalk, small chalkboards, erasers, markers, scissors, and glue. The inclusion of a computer with a word processing program for young children (see Chapter Thirteen) is useful in helping them feel their stories are like those of "real" authors.

Children in a kindergarten writing centre.

Sulzby et al. (1989) believe that all kindergarten children reared in a literate culture can and will write if the following conditions are met:

- First and most important, they suggest that in order to encourage young children to write, teachers accept the forms of writing children use.
- Second, they recommend keeping requests simple—for example, "Write a story" or "Write a letter to your mother"—and then asking children to read what they have written.
- Third, they recommend reassuring children that their writing "doesn't have to be like grown-up writing. Just do it your own way" (p. 70).

At the initial stages of children's independent writing, we recommend that teachers respond to the content or meaning of what children are writing, rather than placing a heavy focus on letter formation, spacing, and spelling. Proctor (1986) found that first-grade children in meaning-focused classrooms scored higher on both mechanical and content measures than did children in traditional skills classrooms. Children in meaning-focused classrooms wrote more and made fewer spelling errors, and their writing was characterized by a need to communicate ideas. They had a stronger sense of audience, and the ideas in their writing were more complex. Proctor concluded that when teachers focused on meaning, children not only developed their ability to express ideas with clarity and vigour, but also mastered many of the mechanical aspects of writing.

This does not mean that teachers should not provide any spelling instruction at the emergent stage of literacy development. If children are trying to write phonetically, we recommend using this as an opportunity to further develop phonemic awareness and understanding of the alphabetic principle.

One way we can help children hear sounds in words they are trying to spell is to slowly articulate each word as explained under "Interactive Writing" above and have the children repeat it slowly, listening for the sounds at the beginning, middle, and end of the word. By articulating words slowly rather than saying sounds separately, teachers are able to avoid distortion. It is also recommended that children be encouraged to represent each sound with one letter in the initial stages of writing. For example, the word *hammer* has four distinct sounds, and a young child who spells the word as *hamr* demonstrates the ability to hear all four of these sounds. As proficient readers, we need to listen closely to sounds in words to understand why young children spell words such as *hoped* as *hopt* and *dragon* as *jragn*. Like the spelling of *hamr* for *hammer*, these invented spellings indicate that children understand the alphabetic principle and that they are able to hear separate sounds in the words and map letters onto the sounds they hear. This is more important at the emergent stage of writing development than conventional spelling. In Chapter Nine, we describe stages children go through as they move toward conventional spelling, and we offer suggestions for spelling instruction.

Functional Interactions with Print

Environmental print both inside and outside the classroom provides children with functional literacy experiences. Environmental print includes such things as signs, labels, calendars, charts, and lists that can be used to organize the classroom. Putting labels and signs up in the classroom is not, by itself, sufficient to help many children construct understandings of the components of emergent literacy. Children need to interact with print in meaningful ways to maximize their learning. Examples of authentic experiences with environmental print are:

- Teachers and child make labels to identify children's cubbyholes and show where things belong.

- Calendars are used to keep track of the day of the week and of children's birthdays. Teachers also use attendance charts to help children learn to read one another's names.

- Teachers present charts or lists on the blackboard to indicate the daily schedule, classroom jobs, and who will be at which centre. Schickendanz (1989) described how one teacher used these types of lists to foster children's literacy learning. The teacher put a list of activities the children could choose from on a chart and discussed them with the children, crossing each off after it had been discussed. If the activity was a familiar one, such as blocks, she asked, "Who knows what is next on my list?" When the children replied, "Blocks," she slowly said, "Yes, b-l-o-c-k-s" and ran her finger under the word as she did so (p. 98). Once all of the possibilities had been discussed, the children make their choices. (If several children choose the same activity, the teacher makes a "turns" list.)

    The children who chose the activity of making popcorn then consulted a recipe chart. At the top was written "Things We Need," and with the teacher's assistance, the children read and located the items on the list. The teacher then read the "What to Do" part of the recipe, pointing to the words as she did so, and the children carried out the instructions. When the popcorn was finished, one child commented that they hadn't put salt on it, and the teacher referred her to the recipe, which didn't call for salt. The children decided that they wanted to use *salt* the next time, so one child put the word *salt* on the recipe chart.

- "Morning message" is a technique in which the teacher writes a brief message describing a significant event for the children that day. For example, "Today we are going to have a special visitor." Once the message is written and read, the children reread it (matching words heard to those in print as they do so) and discuss the day's upcoming events.

    After children have begun to read independently, these morning messages may be written in minimal-cues format to increase the focus on the speech–print relationship. In minimal-cues messages, the teacher leaves selected letters out of words, and the children predict what the message is on the basis of the remaining cues. For example, "We are go_ _ _ on a treasure hunt _ _day." The children predict the words and, if they are able, tell which letters go in each blank.

- Play centres can support literacy-related activities. For example, a play post office involves a variety of props such as a mailbox, stationery, envelopes, pens, pencils, stamps, address labels, and signs about mailing. Other rich contexts for literacy learning include a cooking centre, store, doctor's office, and travel agent's office.

- Field trips provide opportunities for children to use written language for functional purposes. They might consult printed material when making plans for the trip, use environmental print to find their way around during the field trip itself, and write thank-you letters after they return.

SUMMARY

Until the last two decades, the concept of reading readiness influenced the type of reading instruction provided to young children when they arrived at school. Development was thought to proceed through stages, and during the first half of the 20th century, many educators believed that a mental age of 6 1/2 was necessary to learn to read. By the 1950s, these views had changed, and children were given reading readiness activities to help them get ready for formal reading instruction.

In the late 1970s, the concept of emergent literacy began to replace reading readiness in program planning. From this perspective, literacy development is seen as continuous, beginning with children's earliest experiences with print at home. Components of emergent literacy include cultural views and functions of written language, the nature and forms of written language, and the speech–print relationship.

Children's emergent literacy is generally assessed using informal rather than standardized assessment tools. Four major types of informal assessment are used for this purpose: observation, interviews, samples of children's work, and children's self-assessment. Teachers constantly observe young children as they interact with print, and when they need a more organized record of their emergent literacy development, anecdotal notes and checklists are helpful. Interviews of both parents and children provide information about children's literacy experiences at home and about their understanding of why and how people read.

More specific information is obtained by giving children a storybook and asking them to demonstrate their understanding of how books and print work, as well as their knowledge of terms such as *letter* and *word*. Samples of children's reading and writing also provide important clues to their literacy development. Early writing attempts are examined in relation to both form (e.g., drawing, scribbling, letters) and function. Samples of children's early reading may be collected by taking running records as they read. These records are analyzed to describe children's use of picture, print, and meaning cues as they interact with print.

General guidelines for planning emergent literacy experiences have been based on the nature of literacy experiences children receive in literate homes. We recommend that young children be immersed in a rich literacy environment and involved in meaningful, purposeful literacy activities. We also recommend that children be involved in daily reading and writing, and that they be given the opportunity to have shared control of their literacy learning. Rather than requiring word-perfect reading and letter-perfect writing, it is important for teachers to reinforce children for producing approximate responses until they establish an understanding of most of the components of emergent literacy. It is also important for teachers to recognize that children come to schools from a wide range of different literacy environments and to take individual differences into account when planning instruction. All children are able to learn, and our task as teachers is to determine where they are in their literacy development and provide instruction appropriate to their needs. While all children do not go through the same invariant stages in learning to read and write, some understandings generally come before others for most children.

We recommend a balanced emergent literacy program for young children, involving a range of reading and writing experiences. Such a program includes reading to children, shared-book experiences, shared writing experiences, interactive and independent writing, and functional interactions with print. Children are encouraged to talk about ideas before, during, and after the reading of books by teachers and during shared-book experiences. Predictable big books are particularly useful for this latter activity. There are three steps in a shared-book experience: discovery or initial reading of the book, exploration or rereading, and independent experience.

The language experience approach provides the opportunity for shared writing experiences. The four stages in developing a language experience story are selecting an experience, discussing the experience to develop vocabulary and language, recording ideas as the children dictate them, and reading the story. Follow-up activities foster specific aspects of emergent literacy development. Interactive writing experiences provide opportunities for children and teachers to share both the generating and the scribing of ideas, while independent writing gives children the opportunity to explore writing on their own and with other children.

Functional interactions with print are particularly useful for helping children understand functions of written language. Labels, calendars, charts, lists, morning messages, play centres involving print, and field trips provide opportunities for children to use written language in purposeful contexts.

SELECTED PROFESSIONAL RESOURCES

Morrow, L. M. (2001). *Literacy development in the early years: Helping children read and write* (4th ed.). Boston: Allyn and Bacon. This edition of Lesley Morrow's book on literacy development from birth to Grade 3 provides a balanced approach to early literacy instruction, with a blend of constructivist ideas and explicit direct instruction approaches.

Christie, J., Enz. B., and Vukelich, C. (2003) *Teaching language and literacy: Preschool through the elementary grades*. Boston: Allyn and Bacon. Three main themes run throughout this book: a constructivist perspective on learning, respect for diversity, and instruction-based assessment. Part Two focuses specifically on emergent language and literacy learning.

Saskatchewan Education. (2000). *Early literacy: A resource for teachers*. Available: www.sasked.gov.sk.ca/docs/ela/e_literacy. This resource was developed primarily for teachers at the kindergarten and Grade 1 levels but it is also recommended for teachers of children in Grades 2 and 3 who are in the emergent phase of literacy development. The resource provides assessment tools and instructional strategies in the following four areas: supporting development of oral language, enjoying literature and learning from books, learning about sounds and letters, and supporting independence in reading and writing.

University of Connecticut. *Early literacy*. Available: www.literacy.uconn.edu/earlit.htm. This is part of a comprehensive Web site on literacy developed by the University of Connecticut. The section on early literacy contains links to several early literacy Web sites for educators, online documents about early literacy, instructional tips and activities, and links to literacy Web sites for children.

CHILDREN'S BOOKS NOTED IN CHAPTER THREE

Ahlberg, J. and Ahlberg, A. (1978). *Each peach pear plum*. New York: Scholastic Book Services.

Aylesworth, J. (1992). *Old black fly*. New York: Henry Holt and Company.

Baker, K. (1990). *Who is the beast?* New York: Harcourt Brace & Company.

Baum, A. and Baum, J. (1962). *One bright Monday morning*. New York: Random House.

Becker, J. (1973). *Seven little rabbits*. New York: Scholastic Book Services.

Brown, K. (2001). *The scarecrow's hat*. London: Andersen Press.

Brown, R. (1981). *A dark, dark tale*. New York: Scholastic Book Services.

Carle, E. (1977). *The grouchy ladybug*. New York: Thomas Y. Crowell.

Carle, E. (1983). *The very hungry caterpillar*. New York: Scholastic Book Services.

Carle, E. (1984). *The very busy spider*. New York: Philomel.

Cowley, J. (1980). *Mrs. Wishy-Washy*. Auckland, NZ: Shortland Publications.

Cowley, J. (1983). *The jigaree*. Auckland, NZ: Shortland Publications.

Cowley, J. (1983). *Who will be my mother?* Auckland, NZ: Shortland Publications.

Cranstoun, M. (1967). *1, 2, buckle my shoe*. New York: Holt, Rinehart & Winston.

Down by the bay. (1982). Port Coquitlam, BC: Class Size Books.

Florian, D. (2000). *A pig is big*. New York: Greenwillow Books.

Hoberman, M. A. (2001). *"It's simple," said Simon*. New York: Alfred A. Knopf.

Hutchins, P. (1986). *The doorbell rang*. New York: Scholastic Book Services.

Keats, E. J. (1971). *Over in the meadow*. New York: Scholastic Book Services.

Mahy, M. (1998). *A summery Saturday morning*. New York: Viking.

Martin, Jr., B. (1970). *King of the mountain*. New York: Holt, Rinehart & Winston.

Martin, Jr., B. (1970). *Monday, Monday, I like Monday*. New York: Holt, Rinehart & Winston.

Martin, Jr., B. (1970). *The haunted house*. New York: Holt, Rinehart & Winston.

Martin, Jr., B. (1970). *When it rains, it rains*. New York: Holt, Rinehart & Winston.

Martin, Jr., B. (1970). *Whistle, Mary, whistle*. New York: Holt, Rinehart & Winston.

Martin, Jr., B. (1972). *Brown bear, brown bear, what do you see?* New York: Holt, Rinehart & Winston.

Mayer, M. (1975). *Just for you*. New York: Golden Press.

Melser, J. (1980). *Sing a song*. Auckland, NZ: Shortland Publications.

Morris, W. B. (1970). *The longest journey in the world*. New York: Holt, Rinehart & Winston.

Root, P. (2001). *Rattletrap car*. Cambridge, MA: Candlewick Press.

Root, P. (1998). *What baby wants*. Cambridge, MA: Candlewick Press.

Scheer, J. and Bileck, M. (1964). *Rain makes applesauce*. New York: Holiday House.

Slepian, J. and Slepian, A. (1967). *The hungry thing*. New York: Scholastic Book Services.

Sutton, E. (1973). *My cat likes to hide in boxes*. New York: Parents Magazine Press.

The three billy goats Gruff. (1963). New York: Holt, Rinehart and Winston.

Tolstoy, A. (1968). *The great big enormous turnip*. New York: Franklin Watts.

Williams, S. (1994). *I went walking*. New York: Harcourt Brace & Company.

Wing, H. R. (1963). *What is big?* New York: Holt, Rinehart & Winston.

Wood, A. (1984). *The napping house*. New York: Harcourt Brace & Company.

Wood, A. (1992). *Silly Sally*. New York: Harcourt Brace Jovanovich.

REFERENCES

Adams, M. J. (1990). *Beginning to read: Thinking and learning about print*. Cambridge, MA: MIT Press.

Adams, M. J. (2002). Alphabetic anxiety and explicit, systematic phonics instruction: A cognitive science perspective. In S. B. Neuman and D. K. Dickinson (eds.), *Handbook of early literacy research* (pp. 66–80). New York: The Guilford Press.

Alberta Education. (1993). *Diagnostic teaching in a language learning framework 5*. Edmonton, AB: Student Evaluation Branch.

Applebee, A. (1978). *The child's concept of story*. Chicago: University of Chicago Press.

Ashton-Warner, S. (1986). *Teacher*. New York: Touchstone Books.

Cambourne, B. (1995). Toward an educationally relevant theory of literacy learning: Twenty years of inquiry. *Reading Teacher, 49* (3), 182–190.

Chittenden, E. and Courtney, R. (1989). Assessment of young children's reading: Documentation as an alternative to testing. In D. S. Strickland and L. M. Morrow (eds.), *Emerging literacy: Young children learn to read and write* (pp. 107–120). Newark, DE: International Reading Association.

Christie, J., Enz. B., and Vukelich, C. (2003) *Teaching language and literacy: Preschool through the elementary grades*. Boston: Allyn and Bacon.

Clay, M. M. (1972). *Reading: The patterning of complex behaviour*. Auckland, NZ: Heinemann.

Clay, M. M. (1975). *What did I write?* Portsmouth, NH: Heinemann.

Clay, M. M. (1993). *An observation survey of early literacy achievement*. Portsmouth, NH: Heinemann.

Crawford, P. A. (1995). Early literacy: Emerging perspectives. *Journal of Research in Childhood Education, 10* (1), 71–86.

deHirsch, K., Jansky, J. J., and Langford, W. S. (1966). *Predicting reading failure*. New York: Harper and Row.

Doake, D. B. (1981). *Book experience and emergent reading behaviour in preschool children*. PhD dissertation, University of Alberta, Edmonton, AB.

Doake, D. B. (1988). *Reading begins at birth*. Richmond Hill, ON: Scholastic-TAB Publications.

Downing, J. (1979). *Reading and reasoning*. New York: Springer-Verlag.

Durkin, D. D. (1978–79). What classroom observations reveal about reading comprehension instruction. *Reading Research Quarterly, 14* (4), 481–533.

Durkin, D. D. (1983). *Teaching them to read* (4th ed.). Boston: Allyn and Bacon.

Ehri, L. C., Nunes, S. R., Willows, D. M., Schuster, B. V., Yaghoub-Zadeh, Z., and Shanahan, T. (2001). Phonemic awareness instruction helps children learn to read: Evidence from the National Reading Panel's meta-analysis. *Reading Research Quarterly, 36* (3), 250-283.

Ferreiro, E. and Teberosky, A. (1982). *Literacy before schooling*. Exeter, NH: Heinemann.

Fountas, I. C. and Pinnell, G. S. (1996). *Guided reading: Good first teaching for all children*. Portsmouth, NH: Heinemann.

Gates, A. I. (1937). The necessary mental age for beginning reading. *Elementary School Journal, 37*, 497–508.

Glenn, S. (2001). *Patterned/predictable books*. Curriculum Laboratory, University of Iowa. Available: www.uiowa.edu/~crl/bibliographies/patterned_print.htm.

Goodman, K. (1969). Analysis of oral reading miscues: Applied psycholinguistics. *Reading Research Quarterly, 5* (1), 9–30.

Goodman, Y. M. (1991). Informal methods of evaluation. In J. Flood, J. M. Jensen, D. Lapp, and J. R. Squire (eds.), *Handbook of research on teaching the English language arts* (pp. 502–509). New York: Macmillan.

Goswami, U. and Bryant, P. (1990). *Phonological skills and learning to read*. East Sussex, UK: Lawrence Erlbaum Associates.

Hall, M. (1981). *Teaching reading as a language experience*. Columbus, OH: Charles E. Merrill.

Harste, J., Woodward, V., and Burke, C. (1984). *Language stories and literacy lessons*. Portsmouth, NH: Heinemann Educational Books.

Heath, S. B. (1983). *Ways with words: Language, life and work in communities and classrooms*. Cambridge, MA: Cambridge University Press.

Holdaway, D. (1979). *The foundations of literacy*. Gosford, Australia: Ashton Scholastic.

Hough, R. A. and Nurss, J. R. (1992). Language and literacy for the limited English proficient child. In L. O. Ollila and M. I. Mayfield (eds.), *Emerging literacy: Preschool, kindergarten, and primary grades* (pp. 137–165). Toronto: Allyn and Bacon.

Juliebö, M. F. (1985). *The literacy world of five young children*. PhD dissertation, University of Alberta, Edmonton, AB.

Malicky, G., Purkiss, K., and Nugent, B. (1988–89). Early intervention: A collaborative holistic approach. *Alberta English, 27* (1), 21–29.

Mason, J. M. (1984). Early reading from a developmental perspective. In P. D. Pearson (ed.), *Handbook of reading research* (pp. 505–544). New York: Longman.

Mason, J. M., Peterman, C. L., and Kerr, B. M. (1989). Reading to kindergarten children. In D. Strickland and L. M. Morrow (eds.), *Emerging literacy: Young children learn to read and write* (pp. 52–62). Newark, DE: International Reading Association.

McCain, M. and Mustard, J. F. (1999). *Early years: Final report*. Toronto, ON: Canadian Institute for Advanced Research.

Morphett, M. V. and Washburne, C. (1931). When should children begin to read? *Elementary School Journal, 31*, 496–508.

Morris, D. (1993). The relationship between children's concept of word in text and phoneme awareness in learning to read: A longitudinal study. *Research in the Teaching of English, 27* (2), 133–154.

Morrow, L. M. (2001). *Literacy development in the early years: Helping children read and write* (4th ed.). Boston: Allyn and Bacon.

Muter, V., Hulme, C., Snowling, M., and Taylor, S. (1997). Segmentation, not rhyming, predicts early progress in learning to read. *Journal of Experimental Child Psychology, 65*, 370–396.

National Education Goals Panel. (1997). *Special early childhood report*. Washington, DC: Author. Available: www.negp.gov/Reports/spcl.pdf.

Neuman, S. B. and Roskos, K. A. (1993). *Language and literacy learning in the early years: An integrated approach*. New York: Harcourt Brace Jovanovich College.

Proctor, J. R. (1986). *The effect of teacher's theoretical orientations on the writing produced by grade one students*. MA thesis, University of Alberta, Edmonton, AB.

Purcell-Gates, V. (1998). Growing successful readers: Homes, communities, and schools. In J. Osborn and F. Lehr (eds.), *Literacy for all: Issues in teaching and learning* (pp. 51–72). New York: The Guilford Press.

Reid, J. (1966). Learning to think about reading. *Educational Research*, 9, 56–62.

Saskatchewan Education. (2000). *Early literacy: A resource for teachers*. Available: www.sasked.gov.sk.ca/docs/ela/e_literacy.

Schickendanz, J. (1989). The place of specific skills in preschool and kindergarten. In D. S. Strickland and L. M. Morrow (eds.), *Emerging literacy: Young children learn to read and write* (pp. 96–106). Newark, DE: International Reading Association.

Sénéchal, M., LeFevre, J., Smith-Chant, B. L., and Colton, K. V. (2001). On refining theoretical models of emergent literacy: the role of empirical evidence. *Journal of School Psychology*, 39 (5), 439–460.

Serafini, F. (2001). Three paradigms of assessment: Measurement, procedure and inquiry. *Reading Teacher*, 54, 384–393.

Smith F. (1988). *Joining the literacy club: Further essays into education*. London: Heinemann.

Sulzby, E. (1985). Children's emergent reading of favorite storybooks: A developmental study. *Reading Research Quarterly*, 20, 458–481.

Sulzby, E. (1991). The development of the young child and the emergence of literacy. In J. Flood, J. M. Jensen, D. Lapp, and J. R. Squire (eds.), *Handbook of research on teaching the English language arts* (pp. 273–285). New York: Macmillan.

Sulzby, E., Teale, W. H., and Kamberelis, G. (1989). Emergent writing in the classroom: Home and school connections. In D. Strickland and L. M. Morrow (eds.), *Emerging literacy: Young children learn to read and write* (pp. 52–62). Newark, DE: International Reading Association.

Taylor, D. (1982). *Family literacy: Children learning to read and write*. Exeter, NH: Heinemann.

Taylor, D. and Dorsey-Gaines, C. (1988). *Growing up literate: Learning from inner city families*. Portsmouth, NH: Heinemann.

Teale, W. H. (1995). Young children and reading: Trends across the twentieth century. *Journal of Education*, 177 (3), 95–127.

Teale, W. H., Hiebert, E. H., and Chittenden, E. A. (1987). Assessing young children's literacy development. *Reading Teacher*, 40 (8), 772–777.

Telus Learning Connection Project. *Predictable books*. Available: www.earlyliterature.ecsd.net/predictable_books.htm.

Temple, C. and Gillet, J. W. (1989). *Language arts: Learning processes and teaching practices* (2nd ed.). Glenview, IL: Scott, Foresman & Company.

Tompkins, G. E. (1997). *Literacy for the 21st century: A balanced approach*. Columbus, OH: Prentice-Hall.

Torrey, J. (1969). Learning to read without a teacher: A case study. *Elementary English*, 46, 550–556.

University of Connecticut. *Early literacy*. Available: www.literacy.uconn.edu/earlit.htm.

Yopp, H. Y. and Yopp, R. H. (2000) Supporting phonemic awareness development in the classroom. *Reading Teacher*, 54 (2), 130–143.

Chapter 4

The Nature and Assessment of Reading

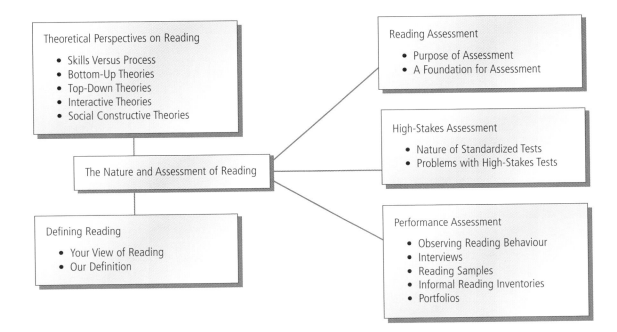

Theoretical Perspectives on Reading

- Skills Versus Process
- Bottom-Up Theories
- Top-Down Theories
- Interactive Theories
- Social Constructive Theories

The Nature and Assessment of Reading

Defining Reading

- Your View of Reading
- Our Definition

Reading Assessment

- Purpose of Assessment
- A Foundation for Assessment

High-Stakes Assessment

- Nature of Standardized Tests
- Problems with High-Stakes Tests

Performance Assessment

- Observing Reading Behaviour
- Interviews
- Reading Samples
- Informal Reading Inventories
- Portfolios

Nearly every time you turn on the radio or television, you hear an advertisement for some kind of reading program. Some advertisers promise to increase your reading rate so you will be able to read one page per second. Others promise to dramatically increase children's level of reading achievement. Many claim to achieve immediate results, particularly for children who are experiencing difficulty with learning to read in school. Your fifth-grade sister is having difficulty with reading, and your parents are wondering if they should purchase one of these commercial phonics programs. They ask for your opinion.

Thousands of parents every year are faced with this decision. The advertisers appeal to their hopes that their children will be successful in school and eventually get good jobs. The advertisers also appeal to the desire all of us have for quick-fix solutions. We would rather take a pill to lose weight than control our eating or exercise regularly. And we want easy, quick solutions to other complex problems, reading among them. From your understanding of what you read in the first three chapters of this text, you are likely dubious about the promises of the advertisers. However, before you will feel comfortable giving an opinion to your parents, you need to construct answers to some of your own questions about reading—questions that you never needed to consider as a reader but that are crucial now that you are, or are planning to become, a reading teacher.

- How *do* people read?
- How do teachers' views of reading affect the way they teach reading?
- You likely remember taking reading tests when you were in school. Are tests like the ones you remember still being used? What other ways do teachers use to find out what reading instruction their students need?

We begin this chapter with a discussion of the nature of reading, including theoretical perspectives and definitions of reading. The rest of the chapter is devoted to strategies for assessing children's reading achievement and needs.

THEORETICAL PERSPECTIVES ON READING

Psychologists have dominated views on reading and on reading instruction in the schools since the beginning of the 20th century (Huey, 1908). Behavioural psychologists focused on reading as skill development, and cognitive psychologists focused on the nature of the reading process. Only recently have theorists begun to recognize social aspects of the process. We provide a brief overview of theoretical perspectives on reading in this section, beginning with skills orientations and ending with social constructive perspectives.

Skills Versus Process

Basal reading series of the 1960s to 1970s, briefly described in Chapter One, were generally designed to teach a series of skills, often ordered hierarchically. For example, a certain number of sight words were introduced before letter sounds, and consonants were usually dealt with before work on vowel sounds. Comprehension was also broken down into component skills, with literal comprehension tasks assumed to be easier than those involving inferential and critical comprehension. Influenced strongly by behavioural theories, educators thought that reading could be taught by breaking it down into component skills to be learned one at a time, often through drill and practice.

In the 1970s, there was a major shift in the professional literature to a focus on reading processes rather than skills. Instead of asking what skills to teach, educators began to focus on how children read. This shift was reflected to some extent in basal readers used in Canada in the 1980s and early 1990s. For example, the Nelson Networks series included a book called *Reading and How* (Hughes and McInnes, 1983), focused on reading processes, at each of Grades 4 through 6.

The emphasis of the process perspective is on how the child constructs meaning from print. The focus is on learning rather than teaching, the learner rather than the teacher, and the process rather than the products of learning (Malicky, 1991). Theorists who focus on the reading process hypothesize that there are three major variables in the reading process: the text, the reader's knowledge, and the process as readers interact with the text. The extent to which readers rely on the text as compared with their knowledge formed the basis for much of the discussion of reading processes in the 1970s.

Bottom-Up Theories

Text, more specifically letters and words, has been the focus of theorists who view reading as bottom-up processing. According to this interpretation, readers begin with letters and, from them, identify words. As they identify words, they put them together to get the meaning of phrases, sentences, and passages. In other words, readers process information through a series of low-level to high-level stages. Gough (1972, p. 354), a strong proponent of the bottom-up view, stated that readers are not guessers. Although they appear "to go from print to meaning as if by magic," this is an illusion. Readers actually plod through sentences letter by letter. From a bottom-up perspective (Lipson and Wixson, 1991),

- reading is viewed as primarily a perceptual process,
- meaning resides in the text, and
- processing proceeds from parts to the whole.

Bottom-up theorists note that for readers to become proficient, processing of letter information must reach a level of **automaticity** so they can focus on meaning. Automaticity is the ability to carry out a process without conscious awareness, much like we steer a car on the highway without actively thinking about which way to turn the wheel.

Top-Down Theories

While letters and words have been the focus of bottom-up theorists, those who view reading as top-down processing emphasize the key role that readers' knowledge plays in the reading process. A proponent of this view, Goodman (1970), called reading a "psycholinguistic guessing game." He maintained that readers use their knowledge about language and the world to generate hypotheses about meaning, which are then tested against the print. From this perspective, readers are seen as problem solvers, and a complete analysis of print is not considered necessary, or even desirable, for the construction of meaning. Before encountering text, readers have expectations about what they will read. As they read, they process text in relation to these expectations, and use this information to formulate predictions about what will come in the text. If the prediction sounds right and makes sense, readers continue reading, checking out the meaning as they read subsequent text. If the prediction does not sound right or make sense, readers reformulate their predictions and reread the text to check out these new predictions. Top-down processing can explain why many writers have so much difficulty proofreading their own writing. We have such clear expectations of what we will read that we do not see deviations from what we predict on the page.

From a top-down perspective, what readers know is more important than what they see. In top-down models of reading (Lipson and Wixson, 1991),

- reading is viewed as a language-thinking process,
- meaning resides in the reader, and
- processing proceeds from whole to part.

Top-down views of reading provided the basis for reading instruction in whole language classrooms during the 1980s and 1990s.

Interactive Theories

In the late 1970s, writers such as Rumelhart (1977) and Adams, Anderson, and Durkin (1978) began to question whether either top-down or bottom-up models of the reading process were adequate. Bottom-up models were criticized for focusing on the minute analysis of words and for failing to account for either comprehension or the impact of meaning on word identification. The major criticism of top-down models was their vagueness in generating practical implications for teaching and their inability to account for research findings on the significant impact of word-level factors (such as phonemic awareness) on reading achievement. As a result of these criticisms, many educators began to consider how the two positions could be combined to produce a more adequate model of reading.

In Rumelhart's (1977) interactive model of reading, reading is viewed as neither top-down nor bottom-up, but rather as a process of synthesizing information from letters, words, sentences, and larger units of meaning. From an interactive perspective (Lipson and Wixson, 1991),

- reading is seen as a cognitive process,
- meaning results from interaction between the reader and text, and
- processing proceeds from whole to part and part to whole.

A major advantage of interactive models is that they help to account for different ways of processing information under different circumstances. For example, as good readers, we sometimes encounter material that is difficult to read, such as highly technical scientific material. When that happens, we adjust our reading to process the print information more carefully than we would when reading a novel or magazine article on a familiar topic.

Social Constructive Theories

Psychologists have been concerned with reading since at least the turn of the century resulting in a heavy focus on the individual child and on reading as an individual achievement. The social, cultural, and political aspects of reading have largely been ignored. Hence, when a child has difficulty reading, many people believe that there is something wrong with the child rather than examining the child's home, school, or society. However, as indicated in Chapter One, we need to look beyond the child to explain differences in reading achievement.

Ironically, much of the impetus for a movement toward social perspectives on reading came from the work of Vygotsky (1978), a psychologist who theorized that the way we learn language is a result of our use of language in social contexts. Some theorists who have been influenced by Vygotsky's work recognize the impact of the classroom context on children's construction of meaning, although they continue to focus heavily on what is happening inside the child's head. Ruddell and Unrau (1994), for example, view reading as a sociocognitive process. Their model of reading as a meaning-construction process includes the reader, text, classroom context, and teacher as major components. Meaning is negotiated through interaction and interchange among teachers, texts, and readers within specific learning environments.

Another major impetus to social views of reading came from literary theory, specifically from Rosenblatt's (1978) **transactional theory**. Rosenblatt sees the reader and text as having a circular rather than interactive relationship, with each affecting the other. Readers actively create meaning, relying on the text itself, their knowledge of language and the world, their background experiences, and their world view. The reader's response is conditioned by the context, depending on his or her purpose for reading a particular text. Further discussion of Rosenblatt's theory is presented later in this chapter.

According to Straw (1990), a major difference between interactive theories of reading and social constructive theories is that interactive theories are grounded in the basic assumption that reading is communication. Interactivists view reading as part of a larger language act that includes "the author as originator of meaning, the text as symbolic or representative of meaning, and the reader as receiver of meaning" (p. 171). In contrast, social constructive models perceive reading as a "more generative act than the receipt or processing of information or communication" (p. 171). In addition to the text and the reader's knowledge, meaning is constructed on the basis of the social background of the reader and the social context of the reading act, both within and outside of the school context.

By recognizing culture as "the fabric within which meaning construction occurs" (Hiebert and Raphael, 1996, p. 559), social constructivists are able to explain why more poor than rich children have reading difficulties and why girls tend to perform better than boys on measures of reading in the elementary grades. Who is regarded as a successful reader and whose meanings are regarded as "correct" are often more a matter of a child's race, class, and gender rather than of generic reading skills or strategies.

From a social constructive perspective,

- reading is seen as a socio-cultural process, and
- meaning is constructed as readers interact with texts, teachers, and peers within the classroom and broader social context.

From this perspective, reading not only is an individual achievement but also involves responding to texts in groups (Bogdan and Straw, 1993).

As you read this section, you were likely struck by the similarity between the theories of reading described here and the models of knowledge and language learning presented in Chapter One. In Figure 4.1, we summarize the theories of reading included in this section and show how we link this set of theories with the models presented in Chapter One.

DEFINING READING

Nearly everyone who is able to read has a view on what reading is and how it should be taught. As we noted at the beginning of Chapter One, most people's notions reflect their experiences of learning to read. You are likely no exception. We begin this section by asking you to articulate your views on reading, and then we present the definition we use as the basis for the remainder of our discussion of reading in this book.

Your View of Reading

Because the construction of meaning always involves background knowledge and experiences, it is useful to bring this to the foreground as you continue to construct a more

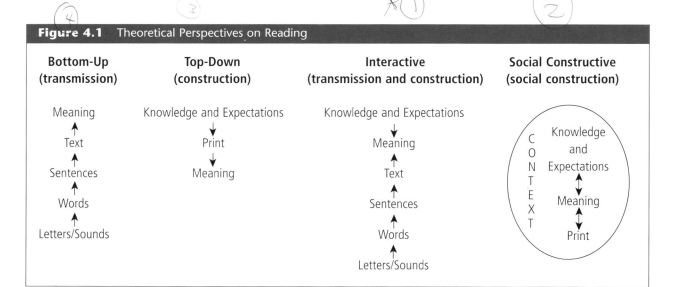

Figure 4.1 Theoretical Perspectives on Reading

Bottom-Up (transmission)	Top-Down (construction)	Interactive (transmission and construction)	Social Constructive (social construction)

coherent theory of reading. To assist with this process, we have listed several statements about reading (some adapted from DeFord, 1985) in Box 4.1. Please read each of the

---

Box 4.1 Your Theoretical Perspective

Rate each of the following statements about reading 1 (strongly agree), 2 (agree), 3 (no opinion), 4 (disagree) or 5 (strongly disagree).

_4_   1. Children should master letter sounds before reading sentences and stories.

_2_ ~ 2. When they come to a word they don't know, children should be encouraged to guess what would make sense and go on.

_4_   3. Children should use both world knowledge and letter sounds to figure out unfamiliar words.

_2_   4. Children should talk about why different people construct different meanings for the same story.

_4_   5. Flashcard drill with sight words is necessary for children to learn to read.

_4_   6. It is not necessary to introduce new words before children read them in stories.

_1_   7. Children should predict what stories will be about before they begin reading, and revise these predictions using information in the text.

_2_   8. It is useful for children to discuss texts in groups to negotiate meanings.

_5_   9. It is a good practice to correct a child as soon as an oral reading mistake is made.

_2_ 10. Teachers should use good-quality literature rather than select material on the basis of word or vocabulary difficulty.

_1_ 11. Children need to develop strategies for both comprehension and the identification of words.

_1_ 12. Children should relate what they read in stories to what they see and do in their lives outside the school.

Source: Some of these items are based on D. E. DeFord, "Validating the construct of theoretical orientation in reading instruction," *Reading Research Quarterly, 20* (3) (1985), 366–367.

statements and rate them from 1 to 5, with 1 indicating that you strongly agree and 5 that you strongly disagree.

After you have rated each statement, think about which theory each statement supports. Proponents of a bottom-up theory would strongly agree with statements 1, 5, and 9, whereas proponents of a top-down theory would strongly agree with statements 2, 6, and 10. Statements 3, 7, and 11 reflect an interactive theory of reading, and statements 4, 8, and 12 a social constructive view.

There are too few statements to clearly identify your theoretical orientation to reading. However, those of you who agreed or strongly agreed with all three statements in any of the four groupings delineated above have a leaning toward the theory associated with those statements. If you have a leaning toward one theory, think about how your school and home experiences might have led you to this view. Most likely, many of you are still in the process of developing a coherent view of reading, and as you work in classrooms you will refine this view on the basis of both your experience and your reading of the professional literature.

Our Definition

In this textbook, we define reading as the active construction of meaning from cues in the text and from readers' background knowledge within a social context. We elaborate three major components of this definition below and draw implications for teaching and learning.

Construction of Meaning

We believe that reading is a meaning-making rather than a meaning-getting process, but we are also aware that this meaning-making process varies depending upon the nature of the material being read. When you were in elementary school, your teacher likely asked you to read both stories and informational material in a similar way. With both, you were likely asked to read and then answer a series of questions about what you had read. While this may be appropriate for informational material, it is less appropriate for stories or poetry.

As Rosenblatt (1978) pointed out, we read materials differently depending on our purpose for reading. With informational material, the primary purpose is "taking away" information from what we read, whether it be following the directions for putting together a new desk or reading a science text. Rosenblatt refers to this as an **efferent** stance to reading. This does not mean that each of us will construct identical meanings for informational texts (there is no direct conduit from the author's mind to ours), but that our purpose in reading this material is to construct a meaning as similar to the author's as we can.

In contrast to efferent reading, Rosenblatt maintains that an **aesthetic** stance is more appropriate for narrative material. We enter into and live through stories rather than taking information away from them. Rosenblatt also helped us realize that we can change our stance during the reading of any one text, and that the two stances are not mutually exclusive. You can likely all think of informational texts that drew you into the world being portrayed as well as helping you construct ideas to take away. You can likely also think of novels that changed the way you view yourself or other people.

The distinction between efferent and aesthetic reading has implications for instruction. For example, if we constantly ask children literal questions about stories such as "What colour was the girl's dress?" we may give them the incorrect impression that reading is a meaning-getting process and that the meaning is in the text. Similarly, unless we accept and discuss alternative interpretations of the same story, children will quickly learn that we do not really value their responses to literature and we think there is one "right" meaning—ours. A major portion of Chapter Eleven focuses on ways teachers can foster the development of children's responses to literature.

Text Information and Knowledge

Our social constructive definition of reading supports the need for a balanced reading program. Children need to develop strategies for using both print cues and knowledge to identify words as they read. One way to do this is by presenting instruction on word identification strategies in a meaningful context. And in addition to asking "What sound does that word begin with?" when children encounter unfamiliar words, teachers also ask questions such as "What would make sense? What would sound right?" Otherwise, children may come to believe that the major purpose of reading is accurately identifying words and that meaning is secondary.

Teachers also need to take care that they present a balanced reading comprehension program that includes strategies for using both text cues and knowledge to construct meaning. A balanced program is one in which teachers encourage children to use a range of different cues as they engage in reading activities. In addition to literal comprehension questions, which are important to focus children's attention on text information, teachers ensure that children have opportunities to respond to inferential and critical questions so that they learn to use text-based and knowledge-based information together as they construct meaning. Chapters Five and Six focus on instructional strategies for helping children learn to use both text-based and knowledge-based information when they are reading.

Social Context

Finally, our definition of reading leads us to view reading in relation to the child's home, community, school, and classroom contexts. The social nature of reading underlines the importance of social experiences and interactions in classrooms. Since knowledge is socially constructed, emphasis is placed on children and teachers talking and working together in groups rather than on individuals reading in isolation.

From a broader, sociopolitical perspective, proponents of a social constructive reading theory acknowledge that classrooms are not neutral. They are inevitably more appropriate learning contexts for some children than others. The greater the discrepancy between the social background of the teacher and the children, the harder it will be to reduce discontinuities between home and school. Through instructional activities focused on **critical literacy**, teachers help children critically examine inequities based on age, gender, and race

Upper elementary child reading a nonfiction book.

to prepare them to engage in social action for change. Ways to help children develop critical literacy are described in Chapter 13.

What is important at this point is not that you have constructed a virtually identical definition of reading to the one we have shared, but rather that you have thought deeply about what you believe. This will provide you with a framework for examining the assessment and instructional strategies included in the remaining chapters devoted to reading.

READING ASSESSMENT

In this section, we begin with a focus on purposes for reading assessment and then move to an overview of the foundation for reading assessment provided in Canadian curriculum documents.

Purpose of Assessment

The major purpose of reading assessment is to obtain the information children and teachers need to optimize reading and learning. Children find out how they are doing and what they should do next. Teachers find out if what they are doing is working and what to do next. The ultimate goal in assessing any child's language learning is the improvement of instruction and of the child's reading. This sounds simple enough—figure out where the child is and go from there—but it becomes complicated by all kinds of other agendas from administrators, policymakers, parents, and taxpayers. Assessment is also conducted to provide information to these stakeholders.

Parents have a right to know how their children are learning and functioning in schools, and administrators, policymakers, and taxpayers have a right to know how effective reading programs are (Afflerbach, 1998). However, the central questions in assessment are:

- What kind of information do teachers need to serve as a basis for program planning and for enhancing children's learning?
- What are the best tools to gather this information?

Curriculum documents developed by the provinces and territories provide a starting point for dealing with these questions.

A Foundation for Assessment

With an increased focus on accountability in education in the 1990s, provinces and regions in the country redeveloped their curriculum documents to explicitly include "clear learning outcomes and high learning standards" (*English Language Arts, K–9*, 2000, Alberta Learning). Curriculum documents across the country (see Chapter One for a list of Web sites containing these documents) now present outcomes, standards, expectations, and/or objectives for elementary children, nearly always organized by grade levels.

Most documents present general outcomes, or categories of outcomes, that are broken down into subcategories and then further specified by grade level. For example, British Columbia specifies three broad categories of Curriculum Organizers: Comprehend and Respond, Communicate Ideas and Information, and Self and Society. The category Comprehend and Respond refers to students' abilities to comprehend and respond to literary and informational communications, including both print and nonprint media. The suborganizers for this category are: Strategies and Skills; Comprehension; Engagement and Personal Response; and Critical Analysis. For each suborganizer, prescribed (specific) learning outcomes, suggested instructional activities, suggested assessment strategies, and recommended learning resources are presented (*English Language Arts K–7: Integrated Resource Package*, 1996).

Most provinces and territories have developed achievement tests based on the outcomes stated in curriculum documents, and often administration of these achievement tests is mandatory. The most frequent scheduling of provincial and territorial achievement testing in reading for elementary students is at the end of Grades 3 and 6, although scheduling is different in some provinces (e.g., in British Columbia elementary students are assessed at the end of Grades 4 and 7).

The reading achievement tests are similar across the country; students read a number of passages and answer multiple-choice questions to determine whether they have met the expectations/outcomes specified in curriculum documents. Some provinces, such as New Brunswick, also require students to answer a small number of open response questions. Tests generally include both narrative and informational passages and sometimes also poetry. Example passages and questions from achievement tests administered in Alberta are available on the Internet at www.learning.gov.ab/k_12/testing/achievement/tests/previous_ach.asp.

Most provinces and territories identify a standard or expected level of student performance. They use this standard as a basis for determining how successful programs are in helping children reach expectations set out in curriculum documents and to make plans for improvement. In Ontario, for example, four levels of achievement are related to expectations in four areas of knowledge and skills: reasoning, communication, organization of ideas, and application of language conventions. Level 3 is the provincial standard, representing the expected level of achievement at each grade level. Level 1 represents achievement below the standard, Level 2 achievement approaching the standard, and Level 4 achievement surpassing the standard. A provincial report card is correlated with these achievement levels (*The Ontario Curriculum: Grades 1–8: Language*, 1997).

Results on provincial and territorial achievement tests are widely distributed, generally broken down by school district and sometimes by school. Many school districts also administer reading tests at the end of each grade, providing even more data on reading achievement levels of children in specific schools. This has the potential to significantly affect the viability of some school programs when financing is provided on a per-pupil basis. The next section examines high-stakes assessment and the potential it has to help and hinder the reading achievement of children in our schools.

HIGH-STAKES ASSESSMENT

Most of you will recall year-end reading tests when you were in school. Sometimes the results were simply placed in your file and not much else happened. Other times, the results were used by your teacher to determine a mark on your report card. In a small number of instances, the results were used as a basis for grade repetition or placement in a special class. The stakes were much higher in the last than in the first instance. In this section, we describe what is happening in high-stakes reading assessment.

On Friday, November 22, 2002, the BBC news on the Internet presented an article under the headline, "Call to close failing schools." In this article, a former government advisor called on the government to make it "clear that any school not reaching its exam performance targets in 2004 and 2006 will be expected to close." He maintains that resources from failing schools, as defined by exam results, should be switched to the expansion of good schools. If this happens, the stakes will be very high indeed.

According to the International Reading Association (1999, p. 1) "high-stakes testing means that one test is used to make important decisions about students, teachers, and schools." These decisions involve such things as promotion or retention in grades, entrance into an educational institution, teacher salary, or a school district's autonomy. The most common kinds of tests used for high-stakes decisions are standardized norm-referenced or criterion-referenced tests.

Nature of Standardized Tests

Standardized tests have been used in North American schools for many decades as one way to gather information about children's reading. In spite of changes in theories of reading, there has been little change in either the basic content or format of standardized tests since the 1930s. Most tests consist of word analysis, vocabulary, and comprehension subtests, and most comprehension subtests consist of numerous short paragraphs followed by multiple-choice questions (Hiebert and Raphael, 1996).

Standardized (sometimes called "norm-referenced") tests are developed by selecting items at a range of difficulty levels and administering them to children at various grade and age levels. Tables of norms are then developed, providing teachers with percentiles, grade equivalents, and/or standard scores corresponding to the number of items a child completes correctly. When a standardized test is administered, it determines how well the children in the class perform on the test in relation to the children in the standardization sample.

The primary reason school systems and provincial governments administer standardized tests is accountability—to show that the programs provided in the school system are producing the desired results. Administrators compare the scores of one class, school, or system with those of the standardization sample and of other classes, schools, and systems. Sometimes scores are compared across provinces, states, and even nations.

Problems with High-Stakes Testing

Standardized tests have come under considerable criticism in recent years (e.g., Pearson, 1998; Kohn, 2002). One common criticism involves the extent to which items on standardized tests are consistent with the language arts programs being implemented. In particular, criticism is directed at the nature of the passages used to assess comprehension. They tend to be short and contrived rather than high-quality children's literature. The use of multiple-choice items leads opponents to contend that standardized tests fail to measure what really counts in reading—critical thinking, construction of meaning, collaborative learning. It is questionable whether the items on most standardized reading tests are appropriate for assessing the effectiveness of the type of language learning program being recommended in this textbook or those being implemented in many Canadian classrooms. Indeed, there is a mismatch between the focus on constructivism in many provincial curriculum documents and the implementation of standardized testing programs, which are more consistent with transmission than constructivist models of knowledge and learning.

Rather than standardized tests measuring what is taught, the opposite is often the case—what is taught is determined by what is tested. Because the stakes are high, many teachers teach children what is measured on the tests. This narrows the curriculum and allows the tests to drive the curriculum, rather than the other way around (Murphy, 1998; International Reading Association, 1999). This is particularly the case in high-poverty schools that tend to have the lowest test scores. The use of high-stakes tests accelerates an emphasis on lower-level skills and drill-and-practice activities rather than higher-level thinking (Kohn, 2002).

Another, related problem involves the amount of time testing takes away from instruction. It is not only the time spent in actual testing, but also the time for preparation and recovery (Johnston, 1998; Voke, 2002). The International Reading Association (1999, p. 4) argues that the "consequences of lost instructional time, particularly for low-performing students, are too great for information that can be gathered more efficiently."

There are other problems with standardized tests. Field (1990, p. 108) notes that test items are deliberately selected "to produce failure among some and success among others." How does this happen? When items are being selected for inclusion on a particular test, those items that all students get right or all students get wrong are eliminated because they do not help to differentiate among children. In other words, unless a set percentage of children fail an item, it is not included. And by linking scores on these tests to grade equivalents, it is predetermined that some children will be at grade level, some will be above, and some will be below. In other words, when norm-referenced tests are used, half of the children will succeed and half will fail. This leads to a basic contradiction between the goals of schooling and the use of standardized tests. On the one hand, most people believe that an appropriate goal of schooling is to ensure that all children are able to read at a level appropriate to their grade. On the other hand, the use of standardized tests means that this will never be achieved. Instead, some children are identified very early as reading below expectations, the emphasis being on what they cannot do rather than what they can do.

This is by far the greatest concern with standardized tests of educators at all levels—the potentially negative impact that test results can have on individual children by marginalizing them and telling them that they are not good enough. And the children who are most often marginalized by these types of tests because of built-in bias in test items are the poor and those from minority groups (Kohn, 2002; Shannon, 1998). Indeed, it appears that these students are being forced out of schools by high-stakes testing in some states in order to increase overall results (Kohn, 2002; Voke, 2002).

Despite concerns raised about high-stakes testing, federal governments in both the United States and Great Britain are moving ahead with an accountability agenda based heavily on this type of assessment (Allington, 2002). None of the opponents of this agenda are against accountability per se. Governments, schools districts, schools, and teachers need to be accountable for the learning of children. However, opponents do question shifting instructional decision-making from local teachers and concentrating it in a central authority far away from the school and children (International Reading Association, 1999). Even more significantly, they question whether standardized tests provide the type of information teachers need to plan high-quality instruction for their students. Scores on standardized tests tell little about how children read or about their specific instructional needs.

Although there has been some movement toward high-stakes testing in Canada, all provinces and territories recognize the need for a wide range of assessment methods to inform reading instruction. In curriculum documents, they recommend what has become known as classroom-based or **performance assessment**. This type of assessment is the focus of the remainder of this chapter.

PERFORMANCE ASSESSMENT

The essence of performance assessment is its emphasis on engaging children in the process about which the examiner wishes to draw inferences (Pearson, 1998). This type of assessment is viewed as providing teachers with the information needed for the daily planning of instruction. In performance assessment, the teacher observes children as they engage in daily reading activities in the classroom, asks children to talk about their reading, and collects samples of their reading for analysis.

Several principles of classroom-based assessment are presented in provincial and territorial documents. The statements presented in Table 4.1 were selected from documents produced by governments in the Northwest Territories, Manitoba, and Newfoundland and Labrador as representative of statements found in documents across the country. In the remainder of this section, we describe various forms of performance assessment.

Observing Reading Behaviour

As noted in Chapter Three, teachers are continuously and implicitly assessing their students' reading every time they interact with them. Many educators identify classroom observation as a core tool in reading assessment (e.g., Simmons, 2000). The checklist provided in Table 4.2 is designed to help teachers observe and interpret children's reading behaviours during daily classroom reading instruction.

The headings in the left-hand column reflect those aspects of reading that are used to organize the teaching/learning techniques discussed in Chapters Five and Six. Hence, if a child does not display reading behaviours associated with a particular aspect of reading,

---

Table 4.1 Principles of Classroom-Based Reading Assessment

- Assessment is an ongoing activity for which the classroom teacher has primary responsibility.

- Assessment is a positive component of the learning experience, enhancing the student's self-esteem.

- Assessment assists in the ongoing planning of appropriate individual objectives and learning activities.

- Assessment is developmentally and culturally appropriate.

- Assessment is a collaborative and reflective process, encouraging meaningful student involvement and reflection and involving parents as partners.

- Assessment is multidimensional, incorporating a variety of tasks.

- Assessment reflects where the students are in terms of learning a process or strategy and helps to determine what kind of support or instruction will follow.

- Assessment emphasizes what students can do rather than what they cannot do.

- Assessment is integrated with instruction as a component in the curriculum rather than an interruption of it.

Source: Adapted from: *Atlantic Canada English language arts curriculum: Grades 4–6* (Governments of New Brunswick, Newfoundland and Labrador, Nova Scotia and Prince Edward Island, 1998), available: www.gov.nf.ca/edu/sp/eng_langarts_ele.htm; *English language arts classroom assessment* (Manitoba Education and Youth, undated), available: www.edu.gov.mb.ca/ks4/curr/ela/docs/ela-assess.html; *The student evaluation handbook* (Ministry of Education, Culture and Employment, Government of the Northwest Territories, 1993), available: www.ece.gov.nt.ca/02%20k_12/index.html.

Table 4.2 Reading Checklist

Aspects of Reading	Reading Strategy	Comments
Positive attitude to reading	____ Is able to name favourite books and authors ____ Enjoys reading silently in class time ____ Engages in extensive independent reading	
Integrates knowledge and text to construct meaning	____ Is able to set a purpose for reading ____ Is able to predict what a story or text will be about from the title ____ Is able to predict what will happen next in a story ____ Uses both knowledge and text information to answer inference questions ____ Retellings include inferences as well as text information	
Uses knowledge of story structure to construct meaning	____ Is able to answer questions about the setting, characters, events and ending of stories ____ Includes information from setting, events and ending in retellings of stories ____ Retells stories in sequence	
Uses knowledge of expository text structure to construct meaning	____ Is able to answer questions involving main idea, sequence, cause/effect and comparison/contrast relationships ____ Retellings reflect organizational patterns of informational texts (enumeration, cause/effect, sequence, comparison/contrast)	
Uses context cues to identify words	____ Oral reading miscues make sense and sound right in relation to prior text ____ Gives real-word rather than nonsense-word responses when reading ____ Corrects miscues that do not make sense	
Uses print cues to identify words	____ Oral reading miscues look and sound like the words in the text ____ Most sounds are represented in inventive spellings ____ Identifies words by processing letter groups, syllables or words within other words ____ Corrects miscues that do not "look right"	
Integrates context and print cues to identify words	____ Most miscues both make sense and look right ____ Corrects most miscues that change the author's meaning	
Reads with automaticity	____ Identifies high-frequency words immediately ____ Reads fluently and at an appropriate rate ____ Completes silent reading assignments in a reasonable time	

you can go directly to the appropriate section in Chapter Five or Six to select the teaching/learning techniques to use with that child. For example, a child who is not yet able to include information from the setting, events, and endings of stories in retellings would benefit from work on narrative **text structure**. A child who is not yet representing most letters in inventive spellings and whose miscues bear little resemblance to words he or she is reading would benefit from work on phonemic awareness and letter sounds.

Interviews

During classroom interactions, teachers encourage children to talk about what they read, why they read, and how they read. The interview schedule outlined in Table 4.3 is designed to help teachers collect more specific information about a child's reading interests, habits, and knowledge about reading. A range of interview schedules were consulted in devising this one, including those of Atwell (1987); Goodman, Watson, and Burke (1987); and Lipson and Wixson (1991).

You will not likely ask any child all of these questions in one sitting. Instead, you will think about what you need to know about a particular child and select those questions that might help gather this information. For example, if a child rarely chooses books to read independently, you might ask the questions about interests and attitudes. If a child appears to have few strategies for making meaning as he or she reads, you might ask the last four questions in the reading strategies section.

Reading Samples

As with emergent readers, teachers save samples of children's reading throughout the school year to assess growth. These samples take on several forms; we describe some of these forms in this section.

- Reading logs provide information on what children read and are commonly kept in their reading portfolios. In their logs, children keep a list of books they have read during the year, and make note of the amount, genre, and level of material read. Wiseman (1992) suggests that the date each book was selected and completed also be recorded in the log, along with the child's comments about the book. These entries help teachers determine children's growth in voluntary reading behaviour.
- Response to literature is another way to sample children's reading. It is crucial to examine children's written responses in terms of their ability to reflect on the text and to relate it to their own lives. Examples of children's responses to literature, as well as interpretations of these responses, are provided in Chapter Eleven. The responses illustrate how children interact with texts rather than their specific use of reading strategies. It is also important to keep in mind when examining responses that they are often as much a reflection of writing ability as reading comprehension.
- Assignments provide further information on reading comprehension strategies and achievement. Samples of written answers to questions can be included in the child's portfolio periodically throughout the school year. Again, however, it should be kept in mind that these might provide an underestimate of reading comprehension, depending on the child's level of writing proficiency.
- Running records can be used to collect samples of children's oral reading to determine what level of material is appropriate for instruction and to examine their growth in using meaning and print cues to identify words. As with young children, running records can be kept of children reading stories from basal texts, books, or

Table 4.3 Reading Interview

Area	Questions
Interests	• What kinds of things do you like to do in your spare time? • What is your favourite subject at school? Why? • What kinds of books do you like to read? • Name two books you have read recently that you liked.
Attitudes	• If you could read a story or watch it on television, which would you choose? Why? • How much time do you spend reading each day at home? at school? • How many books do you own? Do you go to the library to get books? • How do you feel about reading?

Knowledge about reading:
 	
   Functions of reading
 	
   Reading strategies
	• What is reading?
	• Why do people read?
	• Think of someone who is a good reader. How do you know he/she is a good reader?
	• How would you help someone who was having trouble reading?
	• What do you think about as you read?
	• What do you do when you are reading and come to a word you don't know?
	• What do you do when you are reading and something doesn't make sense?
	• What do you do to help you remember what you read (e.g., in social studies)?
	• Do you ever read something over again? Why?
	• Do you read some things faster than others? Why?

Self-appraisal	• How would you describe yourself as a reader? • Is learning to read easy or hard? Why? • What's the easiest thing about reading for you? What's the hardest thing? • What kind of help to you think you need with your reading?

passages specifically designed for this purpose. However, recently many educators have turned to **levelled texts** to obtain running records.

When taking running records with levelled texts, the teacher selects a book that he or she thinks will be easy for the child to read and asks the child to read orally. While the child reads, the teacher notes any errors that the child makes, and when the reading is completed, the teacher calculates the percentage of words read correctly (including errors corrected by the child). By having the child read progressively more difficult books, the teacher is able to determine what level is "just right" for instructional purposes (when the child reads 90 to 95 percent of the words correctly), what level of material the child is able to read independently, and what level is too difficult even in an instructional setting.

Oral reading errors are then analyzed to determine how the child is using cues to identify words. The coding system described below for informal reading inventories can be used for running records as well. While it is more authentic to gather running records on materials actually being used in the classroom, teachers may wish to use informal reading inventories when levelled texts are not available and with older children.

Informal Reading Inventories

Informal reading inventories usually consist of two components: a series of word lists, and a number of passages with comprehension questions at increasing levels of reading difficulty. The word lists included on the inventories are used to estimate the reading level at which to begin administering reading passages. That level is the one at which children can identify all or most of the words. This ensures that children do not spend time reading passages that are much too easy or much too difficult for them.

The teacher then has the child read passages orally and silently and answer the questions about them. The child continues to read passages of increasing difficulty until he or she is no longer able to identify 90 percent of the words or answer 70 percent of the questions correctly. As the child reads orally, the teacher keeps a running record of oral reading miscues and writes down the child's answers to comprehension questions. The marking system used for taking a running record with emergent readers is also an appropriate means of recording miscues for more independent readers. An adaptation of this system for use with independent readers is included at the top of Box 4.2.

Many teachers choose to use informal reading inventories because the passages and questions are all in one place and the teacher does not have to search out a series of books at a range of reading levels and design tasks to assess comprehension of passages in these books. Informal inventories are designed to be administered individually, so they are used primarily with children when the teacher is puzzled and needs more information to plan appropriate instruction. A wide range of informal reading inventories is available, including the *Informal Reading Inventory* (Burns and Roe, 2002), *Classroom Assessment of Reading Processes* (Swearingen and Allen, 2000), and the *Qualitative Reading Inventory—3* (Leslie and Caldwell, 2001). The last two inventories include both narrative and expository passages.

Interpreting Informal Reading Inventories

The teacher gets two major types of information from an informal reading inventory: achievement and diagnostic information. The child's level of reading achievement is the highest level at which the child meets the criteria set in the test for instructional reading level.

Although tests vary, the instructional reading level is generally the level at which the child is able to identify 90 percent or more of the words accurately *and* answer 70 percent or more of the comprehension questions correctly. The child is able to read material independently if word identification and comprehension are close to 100 percent. Material is too difficult for a child if he or she reads with less than 90 percent accuracy *or* less than 60 percent comprehension. It is important to remember that informal inventories provide only a rough indication of the level of material children can handle. Children may be able to understand more difficult material if they know a great deal about the content or are very interested in it. On the other hand, if the topic in a narrative or informational passage is unfamiliar, children may have difficulty with it even if it is at their instructional reading level as determined on an informal reading inventory.

Many informal reading inventories include an activity for children to do before they read each passage, to assess their background knowledge. On the *Qualitative Reading Inventory*, for example, children are asked to associate meanings with key concepts in passages to be read. On other inventories, they are asked to read the title and predict what passages will be about. Still others ask children to rate their knowledge about the content of the passage after they have finished reading it. From a social constructive perspective, a reader's knowledge is a critical component in the reading process.

Box 4.2   Oral Reading Miscues of a Grade 4 Boy

Marking System for Miscues

- A substituted word or mispronunciation is written above the text word.
- An omission is indicated with a circle around the word.
- A T is written above words provided by the teacher.
- An insertion is indicated with a caret.
- SC indicates that a miscue was corrected.

Coding System for Miscues

- M (meaning-based): miscue makes sense in relation to prior text and the rest of the sentence as the child reads it.
- P (print-based): miscue contains half or more of the same letters as the text word.
- I (integrative, both print and meaning): miscue contains half or more of the same letters as the text word *and* makes sense in relation to prior and the rest of the sentence.

Excerpt from a Grade 4 Passage

    I   I

Johnny   for

John first gathered bags of apple seeds. He got many of his seeds from farmers who squeezed apples to make a drink called cider. Then, in the spring, he left

                  P

            front tire SC

for the western frontier.

              I

           trees

He planted seeds as he went along. Also, he gave them to people who knew how valuable apple trees were.

John walked many miles in all kinds of weather. He had to cross dangerous rivers and find his way

                    I

                   cool

through strange forests. Often he was hungry, cold and wet. Sometimes he had to hide from unfriendly Indians. His clothes became ragged and torn. He used

       M

       his

a sack for a shirt, and he cut out holes for the arms. He wore no shoes. But he never gave up. He guarded his precious seeds and carefully planted them where they

                  P

            strange SC

had the best chance of growing into strong trees.

Source: Reading passage excerpted from B. B. Armbruster, C. L. Mitsakas, and V. R. Rogers, *America's history* (Peterborough, NH: Schoolhouse Press, 1986). © 1986 by Schoolhouse Press. Reprinted by permission of the publisher.

How the reader uses this knowledge along with print and text information is even more important. Unfortunately, because we cannot get inside children's heads to see reading as it occurs, we have to rely on indirect evidence to interpret what they are doing. Two major sources of diagnostic data from informal reading inventories that provide this evidence are oral reading miscues and answers to questions.

Miscues

Oral reading miscues are analyzed according to the same two major **cuing systems** as for emergent readers—meaning and print. The major difference is that the criteria for coding miscues with older children are more stringent. The criteria, as well as examples of miscues of a Grade 4 child, Paul, are presented in Box 4.2. The passage in this example is a goal-based narrative at the Grade 4 level from the *Qualitative Reading Inventory* (Leslie and Caldwell, 1990).

It appears from the number of miscues on this passage that fourth-grade material is at Paul's instructional level. When asked to read material at the fifth-grade level, he made well over the acceptable number of miscues. When reading material at his instructional level, however, he showed that he was able to effectively use both print and context cues to predict words that made sense, sounded right, and checked out with the print. He was able to integrate print- and knowledge-based cues to construct meaning as he read. Like many good readers, he corrected miscues when they did not make sense. He did not correct his substitution of *for* for *of* because this miscue was consistent with the meaning that he constructed. He was able to answer seven of the eight questions asked about this passage, confirming that he was able to effectively construct meaning when reading this passage.

The miscues for Kyla, a Grade 3 girl, are presented in Box 4.3. Kyla met the criteria for instructional reading level for both miscues and comprehension questions on the Grade 2 passage shown, but experienced frustration on more difficult passages. The most obvious thing about Kyla's miscues is the number she corrected. This shows that she was aware of when at least some of her miscues did not make sense or look right. Her self-corrections also indicate that she has developed some effective strategies for word identification. However, these strategies are not yet well enough developed to enable her to handle material at a third-grade level.

Effective readers use cues both in context and within words as they read. Miscues help teachers determine where to place the instructional focus at any point in time. For example:

- If children focus almost exclusively on print cues in material at their instructional level, they need less attention to cues within words for a while and a heavier focus on using context cues.
- If their miscues make sense but are not consistent with print cues, they need instruction on strategies for processing cues within words.

As soon as children begin to show more effective use of the cuing system that is the focus of instruction, however, it is crucial to provide a balanced program so that children learn to use multiple sources of information to identify unfamiliar words.

An analysis of Paul's miscues shows that he is able to use print and meaning cues, and that he can integrate them to construct a message consistent with that intended by the author. Kyla was also able to do this most of the time when reading a Grade 2 passage, but she needs to develop further strategies for dealing with both print- and knowledge-based information so that she can handle material consistent with her grade placement.

Box 4.3   Oral Reading Miscues of a Grade 3 Girl

Excerpt from a Grade 2 Passage

It was a Saturday morning. John looked at the toys in his room. They were all old and he wanted something new. John went to his mother. "All my toys are old," he said. "I want something new to play with."

His mother looked at (him) "John, we don't have

SC

All

the money to buy you anything new. You'll have to find a way to make something new." John went back to his room and looked around at the toys. There were many toys that were fun. But he had played with them so much that they weren't fun anymore.

 SC

They

Then he had an idea. His friend Chris wanted a truck

M

one   SC

just like his red truck. And John wanted a car like the (one) Chris got for his birthday. Maybe they could trade. John ran down the street to Chris's house. "Hey, Chris would you like to trade your car for my truck?" "Sure," said Chris. "I'll trade. Later we can trade something else.

 P   P   SC

They   well   away

That way we'll always have something new to play with."

Source: Reading passage excerpted from L. Leslie and J. Caldwell, *Qualitative reading inventory* (New York: HarperCollins Publishers, 1990), p. 117. Reprinted by permission of Addison-Wesley Educational Publishers Inc.

Questions

Teachers use question data to determine what types of questions a child is able to answer. If children are successful in answering factual questions, they appear to be able to use text information to construct meaning. If they are successful in answering inferential questions, they appear to be able to integrate their world knowledge with text information to construct meaning as they read.

Children who are able to answer factual but not inferential questions may think reading is a meaning-getting rather than meaning-making enterprise, or they may not know how to use their knowledge along with text to construct meaning. They benefit from the teaching/learning strategies described in Chapter Five in the section on integrating knowledge-based and text-based information.

Children who are able to answer inferential questions better than factual ones may be relying too much on their background knowledge to construct meaning. Often, if they're asked to retell what they have read, they demonstrate limited processing of text information. They frequently benefit from teaching/learning strategies designed to help them use the structure of narrative and expository texts to construct meaning.

Portfolios

Portfolios have been defined as "collections of artifacts of students' learning experiences assembled over time" (Valencia, Hiebert, and Afflerbach, 1994, p. 14). The reading portfolio provides information on children's reading, including strategies that they use in a range of everyday reading activities. The process of developing and discussing the portfolio is also intended to help children develop **metacognition** as they reflect on their reading (Wiener and Cohen, 1997).

There are two major types of portfolios: the working portfolio and the showcase portfolio (Christie, Enz, and Vukelich, 2003). The items in the working portfolio represent a child's typical, everyday performance. From the working portfolio, children and their teachers select pieces to include in the showcase portfolio that contains the child's best work.

Content of Portfolios

The content of reading portfolios reflects the reading theories of teachers, the reading programs in classrooms, the type of portfolio, and children's interests, goals, and strategies. Hence, there is considerable diversity in the nature of portfolios across children and classrooms. In addition to information obtained from observations, interviews, and reading samples as outlined above, portfolios often include

- anecdotal notes,
- learning logs,
- reading and content area projects,
- family information, and
- (sometimes) the results on standardized reading tests.

Anecdotal records are teacher notes describing a child's behaviour. While anecdotal notes are less systematic than use of checklists to guide observations, it is often helpful to focus on questions such as "What can this child do?" or on specific children having difficulties to make the task more manageable (Christie, Enz, and Vukelich, 2003).

Learning logs are used by children to keep a record of their learning in the classroom. Students' logs generally focus on what they learned, what they didn't understand, and what they liked or didn't like. Teachers use this information to modify plans for subsequent lessons.

Projects usually involve the preparation of a report based on research conducted in and/or out of school. Students are involved in reading a wide range of types of print media and often present reports using media as well. Projects reveal how effectively children use their reading strategies on an authentic reading activity, independently or in collaboration with their peers, and how well they integrate all aspects of the language arts.

Purpose of Portfolios

Portfolio assessment has become so popular in recent years that it seems in danger of becoming another bandwagon in reading education. As Murphy (1998) has pointed out, portfolio assessment often focuses on the form rather than the process of assessment. Similarly, Serafini (2000/2001) notes that in some contexts portfolio assessment focuses on the procedures of assessment (what types of folders to use or how to pass them on to the next grade level) rather than on the purpose of assessment. This procedural focus is most likely to occur when external stakeholders rather than teachers and students make the decisions concerning how and why to use portfolio assessment. He gives the example of Arizona where portfolio assessment was initiated by school district administrators in response to a state-mandated directive. In this context, the teachers collected children's writing samples, used a generic rubric to score each sample, and submitted scores for students to district offices.

Serafini's example illustrates what can happen when educators attempt to replace standardized testing with portfolio assessment for accountability. Pearson (1998) and Hiebert and Raphael (1996) question whether portfolio assessment is appropriate for high-stakes decisions regarding accountability or placement of children in special programs, because teacher ratings lack consistency and comparability across classrooms and jurisdictions.

Portfolio assessment is much more appropriate as a process of inquiry and interpretation used to promote reflection concerning children's understandings, attitudes, and reading abilities (Serafini, 2000/2001).

> In this paradigm, portfolios are seen as a vehicle for promoting student and teacher reflection, self-evaluation, and goal setting. These portfolios are an ongoing collection of work used to understand a student's interests, abilities, needs, and values. (p. 387)

The critical difference between this paradigm and the assessment as procedure paradigm is in why teachers implement portfolio assessment. The content of portfolios might not be different but what is done with the information is very different.

A major difference is the extent of involvement of children in the assessment process. This involves much more than a change in how assessment is done. It suggests a fundamental change in the way power relationships are constituted between teachers and children. Children participate in decisions not only about what goes into portfolios, but also about what counts as "good" reading.

Many teachers ask children to select at least some of the reading samples included in their portfolios. They sit down with children periodically to look at and talk about the reading growth shown in their portfolio samples. Children share their portfolios with their parents when they visit the school. When teaching a new reading strategy in the classroom, teachers invite children to comment on whether the strategy works for them and why or why not. These and other comments are included in learning logs in portfolios.

A FINAL COMMENT

It does not appear that one type of reading assessment can meet the needs of all stakeholders in education—students, teachers, parents, policymakers, administrators, and the public. Standardized tests are more appropriate than performance assessment to answer the questions of policymakers, administrators, and taxpayers about the effectiveness of reading programs. This does not mean that standardized tests cannot be improved, particularly in light of their mismatch with current theories and practices in reading. Nearly all standardized tests reflect a transmission model of knowledge and learning whereas most Canadian classrooms reflect constructive or social constructive models.

Performance or classroom-based assessment with a process focus is consistent with constructivist views of knowledge and learning. However, for performance assessment to achieve its potential, we need to resist pressure to reduce the contents of portfolios to those pieces that answer the question of whether a child has met the standards for his or her grade level. Only when the information in portfolios is dedicated to describing children's reading will teachers have the information they need to plan appropriate instruction. And only when children are significant partners in the assessment process does portfolio assessment reflect the democratic principles consistent with a social constructivist view of learning. Reading assessment is not valuable for its own sake, but only if the information gathered is used to plan effective reading instruction and experiences for children in classrooms. Our goal as reading teachers is to match instruction and experiences with children's reading levels, interests, and strategy development in order to maximize their reading growth.

SUMMARY

Psychological theories dominated the field of reading throughout most of the 20th century. Behaviourist theories lead to skills models, in which reading is broken down into component skills to be learned one at a time. Cognitive theories place the focus on the reading process. In bottom-up theories of reading, the focus is on print, and processing proceeds from parts to wholes. These theories reflect a transmission model of knowledge and learning. In top-down theories, the focus is on readers' knowledge, and processing proceeds from wholes to parts. These theories reflect a constructive model of learning. Interactive models of reading combine ideas from bottom-up and top-down theories and reflect both transmission and constructive models of learning. Meaning is viewed as resulting from interaction between the reader and text, and processing of parts and wholes occurs simultaneously.

Recognizing the importance of social interactions and social contexts in learning underlies social constructive theories of reading. These theorists see meaning as being constructed by readers during the act of reading, rather than being transmitted from authors to readers. We define reading in this textbook as the active construction of meaning from cues in the text and from the reader's background knowledge within a social context.

A major goal of language learning assessment is to improve instruction in order to maximize children's reading growth. The objectives and standards in provincial and territorial curriculum documents provide a foundation for assessment instruments. Two major types of assessment tools are standardized tests and performance assessment. Standardized tests measure a child's reading achievement in relation to other children's, and the primary purpose of this type of assessment is accountability. It is referred to as high-stakes testing when important decisions about children, teachers, and schools are made on the basis of the results from one standardized test. Teachers need different information to serve as a basis for daily planning, and performance assessment is widely employed for this purpose. The focus of this type of assessment is on what children do as they read.

Checklists and interviews are used to assess how children use print-based and knowledge-based cues to construct meaning as they read. Reading logs are records of what children have read, response journals provide an indication of how children interpret and react to literature, and running records indicate what level of text is "just right" for instruction. Samples of children's oral and silent reading can be collected using informal reading inventories and results provide an indication of their instructional reading level.

Examining answers to comprehension questions and oral reading miscues reveals information on children's use of print-based and knowledge-based cues as they read.

Portfolios are collections of artifacts documenting children's reading growth and development over a period of time. Some of these artifacts include checklists, interview data, anecdotal notes, reading and learning logs, written responses to literature, running records, completed projects, and sometimes results on standardized tests. Portfolio assessment can either be completed within a procedural framework where the focus is on the collecting and scoring of information or within a process framework where the focus is on reflection concerning children's understandings, attitudes, and reading abilities.

More than one type of assessment is used to meet the needs of all the stakeholders involved in education. Standardized testing, which reflects a transmission model of knowledge and learning, tends to be used primarily for accountability. Performance assessment is more consistent with constructivist views of learning and provides the type of information teachers need to plan instruction to maximize children's reading growth.

SELECTED PROFESSIONAL RESOURCES

International Reading Association. (1999). *High-stakes assessments in reading: A position statement of the International Reading Association.* Newark, DL: Author. Available: www.reading.org/pdf/high_stakes.pdf. The International Reading Association developed this position statement because of the increased use of high-stakes testing in the United States over the past decade and concern that testing has become a means of controlling instruction rather than gathering information to foster children's reading growth. The statement discusses what high-stakes testing means and what some of the problems with it are. It also provides recommendations for teachers.

Rhodes, L. K. (1993). *Literacy assessment: A handbook of instruments.* Portsmouth, NH: Heinemann. Rhodes pulls together informal assessment tools from a wide range of sources and includes interview schedules, checklists, miscue analysis, self-assessments, and observation schedules in this handbook. These assessment tools focus on emergent literacy, reading, and writing.

Serafini, F. (2000/2001). Three paradigms of assessment: Measurement, procedure, and inquiry. *Reading Teacher, 54* (4), 384–393. In this article, Serafini examines the differences between standardized and classroom-based assessment against the backdrop of transmission and constructive models of knowledge. He shows how portfolio assessment can reflect either a transmission or constructive view depending on why it is being done.

REFERENCES

Adams, M. J., Anderson, R. C., and Durkin, D. (1978). Beginning reading: Theory and practice. *Language Arts, 55,* 19–25.

Afflerbach, P. (1998). Reading assessment and learning to read. In J. Osborn and F. Lehr (eds.), *Literacy for all: Issues in teaching and learning* (pp. 239–263). New York: The Guilford Press.

Allington, R. (2002). *Big Brother and the National Reading Curriculum: How ideology trumped evidence.* Portsmouth, NH: Heinemann.

Atlantic Canada English language arts curriculum: Grades 4–6 (1998). Governments of New Brunswick, Newfoundland and Labrador, Nova Scotia and Prince Edward Island. Available: www.gov.nf.ca/edu/sp/eng_langarts_ele.htm.

Atwell, N. (1987). *In the middle: Writing, reading, and learning with adolescents.* Portsmouth, NH: Heinemann.

Bogdan, D. and Straw, S. (1993). Introduction. In S. B. Straw and D. Bogdan (eds.), *Constructive reading: Teaching beyond communication* (pp. 1–14). Portsmouth, NH: Heinemann.

Burns, P. C. and Roe, B. D. (2002). *Informal reading inventory* (6th ed.). Chicago: Rand McNally.

Call to close failing schools. BBC News on the Internet. Available: news.bbc.co.uk/1/hi/education/2500453.stm.

Christie, J., Enz. B., and Vukelich, C. (2003) *Teaching language and literacy: Preschool through the elementary grades.* Boston: Allyn and Bacon.

DeFord, D. E. (1985). Validating the construct of theoretical orientation in reading instruction. *Reading Research Quarterly, 20* (3), 351–367.

English language arts K–9 (2000). Alberta Learning. Available: www.learning.gov.ab.ca/k_12/curriculum/bysubject/english/default.asp.

English language arts K–7: Integrated resource package. (1996). British Columbia Ministry of Education. Available: www.bced.gov.bc.ca/irp/elak7/elacons.htm.

English language arts classroom assessment. Manitoba Education and Youth. Available: www.edu.gov.mb.ca/ks4/curr/ela/docs/ela-assess.html).

Field, J. C. (1990). *Educators' perspectives on assessment: Tensions, contradictions and dilemmas.* PhD dissertation, University of Victoria, Victoria, BC.

Goodman, K. S. (1970). Behind the eye: What happens in reading. In K. S. Goodman and O. Niles (eds.), *Reading: Process and program* (pp. 3–38). Urbana, IL: National Council of Teachers of English.

Goodman, K. S., Watson, D. J., and Burke, C. L. (1987). *Reading miscue inventory: Alternative procedures.* New York: Macmillan.

Gough, P. B. (1972). One second of reading. In J. Kavanagh and J. G. Mattingly (eds.), *Language by ear and eye* (pp. 331–358). Cambridge, MA: MIT Press.

Hiebert, E. H. and Raphael, T. E. (1996). Psychological perspectives on literacy and extension to educational practice. In D. C. Berliner and R. C. Calfee (eds.), *Handbook of educational psychology* (pp. 550–602). New York: Macmillan.

Huey, E. B. (1908). *The psychology and pedagogy of reading.* New York: Macmillan.

Hughes, M. and McInnes, J. (1983). *Reading and how.* Scarborough, ON: Nelson Canada.

International Reading Association. (1999). *High-stakes assessments in reading: A position statement of the International Reading Association.* Newark, DL: Author. Available: www.reading.org/pdf/high_stakes.pdf.

Johnston, P. (1998). The consequences of the use of standardized tests. In S. Murphy (ed.), *Fragile evidence: A critique of reading assessment* (pp. 89–101). Mahwah, NJ: Lawrence Erlbaum Associates.

Kohn, A. (2002). Poor teaching for poor kids. *Language Arts, 79* (3), 251–255.

Leslie, L. and Caldwell, J. (1990). *Qualitative reading inventory.* New York: HarperCollins.

Leslie, L. and Caldwell, J. (2001). *Qualitative reading inventory—3.* New York: HarperCollins.

Lipson, M. Y. and Wixson, K. K. (1991). *Assessment and instruction of reading disability: An interactive approach.* New York: HarperCollins.

Malicky, G. V. (1991). Myths and assumptions of literacy education. *Alberta Journal of Educational Research, 37* (4), 333–347.

Murphy, S. (1998). *Fragile evidence: A critique of reading assessment.* Mahwah, NJ: Lawrence Erlbaum Associates.

The Ontario curriculum: Grades 1–8: Language. (1997). Ontario Ministry of Education. Available: www.edu.gov.on.ca/eng/document/curricul/curr971.html.

Pearson, P. D. (1998). Standards and assessments: Tools for crafting effective instruction? In J. Osborn and F. Lehr (eds.), *Literacy for all: Issues in teaching and learning* (pp. 264–288). New York: The Guilford Press.

Rhodes, L. K. (1993). *Literacy assessment: A handbook of instruments.* Portsmouth, NH: Heinemann.

Rosenblatt, L. (1978). *The reader, the text, the poem: The transactional theory of the literary work.* Carbondale, IL: Southern Illinois University Press.

Ruddell, R. B. and Unrau, N. J. (1994). Reading as a meaning construction process: The reader, the text and the teacher. In R. B. Ruddell, M. R. Ruddell, and H. Singer (eds.), *Theoretical models and processes of reading* (pp. 996–1056). Newark, DE: International Reading Association.

Rumelhart, D. E. (1977). *Introduction to human information processing theory*. New York: John Wiley & Sons.

Serafini, F. (2000/2001). Three paradigms of assessment: Measurement, procedure, and inquiry. *Reading Teacher, 54* (4), 384–393.

Shannon, P. (1998). A selective social history of the uses of reading tests. In S. Murphy (ed.), *Fragile evidence: A critique of reading assessment* (pp. 75–87). Mahwah, NJ: Lawrence Erlbaum Associates.

Simmons, J. (2002). *You never asked me to read: Useful assessment of reading and writing problems*. Boston: Allyn and Bacon.

Straw, S. B. (1990). The actualization of reading and writing: Public policy and conceptualizations of literacy. In S. P. Norris and L. M. Phillips (eds.), *Literacy policy in Canada* (pp. 165–181). Calgary: Detselig Enterprises.

The student evaluation handbook. (1993). Ministry of Education, Culture and Employment, Government of the Northwest Territories. Available: ece.gov.nt.ca/02%20k_12/index.html.

Swearingen, R. and Allen, D. (2000). *Classroom assessment of reading* (2nd Edition). Boston: Houghton Mifflin Company.

Valencia, S. W., Hiebert, E. H., and Afflerbach, P. P. (eds.). (1994). *Authentic reading assessment: Practices and possibilities*. Newark, DE: International Reading Association.

Voke, H. (2002). What do we know about sanctions and rewards? *Infobrief, 31*, pp. 1–10. Available: www.ascd.org/readingroom/infobrief/issue31.html.

Vygotsky, L. S. (1978). *Mind in society: The development of higher psychological processes*. M. Cole, V. John-Steiner, S. Scribner, and E. Souberman (eds.). Cambridge, MA: Harvard University Press.

Wiener, R. B. and Cohen, J. H. (1997). *Literacy portfolios: Using assessment to guide instruction*. Columbus, OH: Prentice-Hall.

Chapter 5

Reading Comprehension Strategies

Overview of Comprehension Instruction

- Skills
- Response to Literature
- Strategy-Based Instruction

Integrating Knowledge-Based and Text-Based Information

- Directed Reading–Thinking Activity
- KWL
- Questioning the Author
- Question–Answer Relationship
- Reciprocal Teaching
- Think-Alouds
- Semantic Webs

Reading Comprehension Strategies

Using Text Structure

- Narrative Texts
- Informational Texts

Studying

- Using Comprehension Strategies
- SQ3R

A group of children in Grade 5 have just finished reading an informational text on the Cariboo Gold Rush, and their teacher is leading a discussion to determine what meaning they have constructed. When she asks where gold was discovered in 1958, most of the children reply that it was near the junction of the Fraser and Assiniboine rivers, but Daniel says, "I think it was in Alaska. I heard about that in a TV program." Daniel is relying too heavily on his own knowledge at this point and not enough on the text. At another point in the discussion, the teacher asks the children to think about how the prospectors felt who did not strike it rich. Immediately, Heather answers, "It didn't say." In contrast with Daniel, Heather is not making enough use of her background knowledge.

From a social constructive perspective, both text cues and background knowledge are crucial to constructing meaning while reading, and one important goal of reading instruction is to help children learn how to use these sources of information in an integrated manner. Some of your questions as you prepare to teach reading comprehension might include:

- How can I help children like Daniel make more effective use of cues in the text when constructing meaning?
- How can I help children like Heather make more effective use of their background knowledge when reading?
- How can I help children use both text cues and background knowledge to constructing meaning as they read?

It is important to note that constructing meaning is only one aspect of reading. Equally important is responding to text and analyzing or interrogating texts from a critical perspective. Ways to develop children's response to literature are presented in Chapter Eleven and suggestions for developing critical literacy are provided in Chapter Thirteen.

The focus of this chapter is on instructional techniques to develop reading comprehension strategies. These techniques are organized according to information sources used by readers. Some techniques foster an integrated use of both knowledge-based and text-based information, whereas others focus on the use of text structure. Most of the techniques included in this chapter can be used to help children construct meaning from texts in social studies and science classes as well as in language arts classes.

We begin, however, by asking you to think back to the reading instruction you received when you were in elementary school. As you read the overview of reading comprehension instruction described below, which type of instruction is most familiar to you?

OVERVIEW OF COMPREHENSION INSTRUCTION

Reading comprehension instruction across the past half-century has generally been focused on one of the following three aspects: skills, response to literature, or strategies. The first focus, skills-based instruction, reflects a transmission model of learning. Strategy-based and response-based instruction are more consistent with constructivist models.

Skills

Basal readers from the 1950s through 1970s had a skills focus and used the Directed Reading Activity (DRA) as the basic format to provide reading instruction to ability groups. The DRA generally contained the following five components (Tierney and Readence, 2000):

- *Readiness.* The teacher developed background knowledge, introduced new vocabulary and established a purpose for reading.
- *Directed silent reading.* Children read the selection silently to seek answers to the teacher's purpose-setting questions.
- *Comprehension check and discussion.* The teacher asked questions to check and extend comprehension.
- *Oral rereading.* Children reread the selection orally, often in round-robin fashion.

- *Follow-up activities*. These activities focused on either skill development or enrichment such as creative work or extended reading.

While the teacher worked with one group on the first four steps of this activity (there were often three ability groups), the other children completed worksheets, skillsheets, or other follow-up activities.

Although questions were considered a major way to teach comprehension in basal reading series, researchers found that the questions teachers asked during DRA generally tested whether children had constructed the teacher's meaning rather than taught them how to comprehend texts (Durkin, 1978–79).

Researchers also examined the level of questions teachers asked. The questions included in most basal reader guidebooks were designed to assess three levels of thinking (Bloom, 1956):

- *Literal*. Reading the lines to comprehend what the author says.
- *Inferential*. Reading "between the lines" to infer relationships among ideas and draw conclusions intended but not explicitly stated by the author.
- *Critical*. Using knowledge to make objective or subjective evaluations of the ideas in the text.

Research showed that teachers asked far more literal questions than ones involving inference, evaluation, or other higher-level thinking skills. A steady diet of factual questions may communicate to children that the meaning is on the page. It is little wonder that when asked an inferential question, some children such as Heather in the example at the beginning of this chapter respond, "It didn't say."

Besides questioning, basal reading series traditionally included exercises to develop comprehension skills such as finding the main idea, recalling details, and drawing conclusions. These exercises were generally presented in workbooks or on worksheets, often with little or no teaching beforehand of the skills needed to complete them. There is little support in the research for these types of skill-based exercises (Pearson and Fielding, 1991).

Response to Literature

With the movement to whole language in the 1980s and 1990s, the DRA was no longer consistent with the major goals of language arts instruction. Instead, many teachers framed instruction within a Reading Workshop format which involved the following four elements (Atwell, 1998):

- time for "real" reading
- forums for response to literature
- conferences with teachers
- mini-lessons on reading strategies

The Reading Workshop approach is described in detail in Chapter Eleven.

Strategy-Based Instruction

Although reading strategies were developed through mini-lessons in the Reading Workshop, strategies were not the primary focus of that approach. By the 1990s, cognitive and metacognitive strategies became a major focus in reading comprehension instruction. According to Forrest-Pressley and Waller (1984, p. 6), "Cognition refers to the actual processes and strategies that are used by the reader" whereas metacognition "refers to what a person knows about his or her cognitions and second, to the ability to control these cognitions."

Metacognition

In relation to the first aspect of metacognition, what a person knows about his or her cognitions, readers have the following types of knowledge:

- They have knowledge about *factors that affect reading* (Jacobs and Paris, 1987; Flavell, 1979). For example, a reader may know that he or she is good at figuring out hard words but has difficulty finding main ideas. A reader may also know that he or she is a better reader than most other children in the class, that there is a limit to how fast most people can read, and that it is generally easier to recall the gist of a story than to remember it word for word.
- They have knowledge about *reading strategies*. For example, they know how to figure out difficult words or how to study for a multiple-choice test.
- They know *when and why to apply particular strategies*. For example, they know they don't need to use a phonic strategy to identify a word they have already established as a sight word.

The regulative or control dimension of metacognition involves readers in planning and monitoring their reading. Proficient readers are able to plan what they will do as they read—for example, using the headings and subheadings to predict what a passage or chapter will be about before they begin reading. They evaluate their reading to determine whether what they read makes sense, and make corrections if it does not. For example, if you reached the end of this paragraph and decided that the meaning you constructed did not make sense, you might decide to reread the paragraph. Alternatively, you might decide to read to the end of the section to see if that helped you to make sense out of what you had been reading.

Researchers have generally found that young children are less likely to display metacognitive abilities than older children (Paris, Wasik, and Turner, 1991). However, children's understanding and control of strategies increase with reading proficiency and age. The National Reading Panel (2000), in its analysis of the scientific literature on reading, concluded that instruction on comprehension monitoring improves most readers' comprehension.

Cognitive Strategies

In his review of the literature on the impact of strategy instruction on reading comprehension, Pressley (1998) concluded that strategies that have proven their worth include activating prior knowledge, constructing mental images, analyzing stories into their story grammar components, generating questions, and summarizing. These strategies can be applied before (e.g., making predictions based on prior knowledge), during (e.g., mental imaging), and after (summarizing) reading.

Two years later, the National Reading Panel (2000) concluded that there is a scientific basis for the following types of strategy instruction:

- use of graphic and semantic organizers (including story maps),
- question answering (children answer teachers questions and receive immediate feedback),
- question generation (children ask themselves questions about the text),
- story structure (children use story structure to aid recall to answer questions), and
- summarization (children integrate ideas and generalize from text information)

Research also shows that some of these types of instruction are more effective when used as part of a multiple-strategy approach than alone, e.g., as in reciprocal teaching.

The National Reading Panel noted that teaching reading comprehension strategies is complex at all grade levels, and that to be effective, teachers need:

- a firm grasp of the content presented in the text,
- substantial knowledge of the strategies themselves,
- knowledge of which strategies are most effective for different students, and
- knowledge of how to provide explicit explanation and modeling of the thinking processes involved in successful reading comprehension

Guided Reading

Drawing on the work of New Zealand educators such as Marie Clay (1993), Fountas and Pinnell (1996) developed Guided Reading to help primary children become strategic, independent, and self-extending readers. They view guided reading as a critical component of a balanced literacy program that also consists of reading aloud, shared reading and writing, interactive writing, guided writing, and independent reading and writing. In 2001, Fountas and Pinnell extended Guided Reading to the upper elementary level, with Guided Reading again viewed as one aspect of a literacy program.

At both the primary and upper elementary levels, guided reading is an instructional setting with a small group of students using materials at a moderate degree of difficulty. To facilitate the selection of appropriate materials, Fountas and Pinnell provide lists of levelled texts for children across the elementary grades (Fountas and Pinnell, 1999; Pinnell and Fountas, 2002).

Once an appropriate text has been selected, *guided reading* involves the following steps:

- *Introducing the text to students.* The introduction is intended to create interest, raise questions, prompt expectations, and highlight or foreshadow information, concepts and strategies.
- *Reading the text.* At the primary level, children read quietly or silently while at the upper elementary level they read silently. While the children read, the teacher confers with individual children. A child is asked to read aloud, and the teacher observes and notes how the child is processing text, occasionally providing guidance in use of reading strategies. At the upper elementary level, the teacher might ask children to make notes on their reading in lieu of individual conferences.
- *Discussing and revisiting the text.* Following the reading of the text, the children discuss what they have read and the problem-solving strategies they used. They might reread a portion of the text to provide evidence for their thinking.
- *Teaching for processing strategies.* The teacher selects a strategy that the students need further help with, and explains and demonstrates the strategy.
- *Extending understanding* (optional): The children might extend their understanding through writing or drama.

While the term *guided reading* is used by Fountas and Pinnell to refer to a specific procedure, other educators use it in a broader sense (Villaume and Brabham, 2001). Cunningham and Allington (2003) say that guided reading occurs when a teacher guides students—whole group, small group, or individual—through an activity designed to help them apply reading strategies. Like Fountas and Pinnell, Cunningham and Allington view guided reading as one component of a balanced reading program that consists of four "blocks" (guided reading, self-selected reading, working with words, and writing). However, unlike Fountas and Pinnell, Cunningham and Allington do not organize children into ability groups for guided reading. They choose materials either at the average level of the class or at an easier level than the average. The purpose of guided reading is to expose students to a wide range of literature, teach them comprehension strategies, and teach them how to read progressively more difficult materials.

Using a "4-Blocks" perspective, Sigmon (www.teachers.net/4blocks/article14.html) outlines the following three phases in the guided reading block:

- *Pre-reading.* The teacher builds knowledge of the topic, introduces a few vocabulary words, presents a mini-comprehension lesson, and sets a purpose for reading the text.
- *Reading.* The format of the reading depends on what level of support the teacher determines that the children need to read the text. Support ranges from a teacher read-aloud providing the greatest level of teacher assistance, to choral reading, echo reading, or shared reading which also provide a high level of support, to partner or independent reading where there is less teacher assistance.
- *Post-reading.* The teacher brings closure to the block with an activity to see how the students applied the comprehension strategy taught in the mini-comprehension lesson.

We agree with Villaume and Brabham (2001) that effective guided reading instruction depends less on doing it the "right" way and more on reflecting on its purposes. We recommend that teachers critically examine all instructional techniques in relation to both the needs of the children in their classrooms and the curriculum guidelines for their jurisdictions. No program will be effective unless both the teachers and students understand what a strategy involves as well as why, how, and when to use the strategy. Strategy instruction will not reach its potential of developing active, strategic readers unless it is taught in thoughtful rather than perfunctory ways (Villaume and Brabham, 2002).

Many instructional techniques foster strategy development. We are very selective in this chapter, choosing strategies supported by research that are appropriate for helping children use both knowledge-based and text-based information in narrative and informational texts.

INTEGRATING KNOWLEDGE-BASED AND TEXT-BASED INFORMATION

The focus of the techniques described in this section is on helping readers use what they know and what is on the page together as they read. An overview of the techniques and specific objectives for each technique are presented in Table 5.1. We recommend that the strategies described in this chapter be applied across the curriculum as well as during language arts classes.

Directed Reading–Thinking Activity

The directed reading–thinking activity (or DRTA) is an instructional technique for use with narrative material. Students first predict what they will read, and then they check their predictions through subsequent reading. Formulated by Stauffer (1975), the tech-

Table 5.1 Instructional Techniques for Integrating Knowledge-Based and Text-Based Information

Technique	Material	Helps Children:
Directed reading–thinking activity	Narrative texts with strong plot lines	• Set purposes for reading narrative texts. • Make and evaluate predictions during reading.
KWL	Informational texts	• Set purposes for reading informational texts. • Ask and answer questions during reading.
Questioning the author	Narrative and informational texts	• Construct meaning during reading. • Monitor meaning during reading. • Understand character and plot. • Fill in gaps in text. • Summarize text information.
Question–answer relationship	Narrative and informational texts	• Determine which information sources are required to answer specific questions. • Answer text-based and knowledge-based questions.
Reciprocal teaching	Informational texts	• Summarize text information. • Ask questions. • Clarify parts of texts that are confusing. • Make predictions.
Think aloud	Narrative and informational texts	• Make predictions. • Form visual images as they read. • Link prior knowledge with text information. • Monitor ongoing comprehension. • Correct comprehension confusions.
Semantic webs	Narrative and informational texts	• Activate knowledge before reading. • Construct relationships among ideas. • Relate text information to prior knowledge.

nique helps students actively seek information from the material they read. The teacher acts as a catalyst to thought by asking such questions as:

- What do you think?
- Why do you think so?
- How can you support it?

As readers predict what they will read, they rely on their knowledge, and as they check their predictions, they use cues in the text.

The DRTA is most appropriate for narrative material with a clearly defined plot that can easily be read in one sitting. Short mystery stories are ideal for this activity. The basic steps in the technique are outlined here and summarized in Figure 5.1.

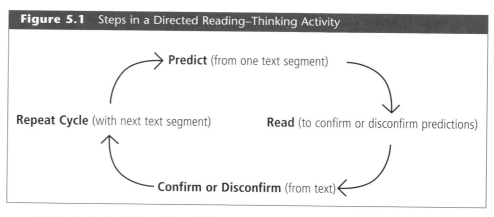

Figure 5.1 Steps in a Directed Reading–Thinking Activity

Predict (from one text segment)

Read (to confirm or disconfirm predictions)

Confirm or Disconfirm (from text)

Repeat Cycle (with next text segment)

1. On the basis of the title and illustration or first paragraph of a story, the teacher asks students to predict what will happen by asking questions such as:

   • What do you think this story will be about?
   • What do you think will happen in this story?
   • Why do you think so?

   This last question is particularly important, because it gives children an opportunity to refer to both their knowledge and the cues in the title, picture, or first paragraph.

   During the prediction process, the teacher's role is not to evaluate predictions, but rather to activate thought by asking students to defend their hypotheses. In Grade 1 classrooms, some teachers have the children whisper their predictions to a partner to ensure that all are engaging in the predicting process. The children then share their predictions in the group context, and the teacher writes them on the board for later reference. Once children are able to read and write independently, they can fill in prediction charts and share them with partners.

2. Students are then asked to read silently to a certain point in the material to confirm or disprove their hypotheses. It is particularly effective to have children stop at suspenseful points in the story.

3. After the students have read to the designated point, they discuss which of their hypotheses were confirmed. The teacher asks for evidence from the text to support the plausibility and accuracy of the hypotheses.

   • What do you think now?
   • Find the part in the text to confirm or disconfirm your prediction.

   Students might read aloud a sentence or paragraph to provide this evidence. Again, this helps to focus attention on both text-based and knowledge-based information.

4. After students have completed the three-step process (predict, read, prove) with one segment of the material, they go on to the next segment. The process continues until they have read the entire text. Throughout, the teacher serves as a mentor to refine and deepen the reading–thinking process, but takes care not to evaluate the students' predictions. It is also useful to emphasize the importance of evaluating and finding proof in the text rather than deciding who is right or wrong. The DRTA is not a contest; it is a technique to make sure individuals start thinking before they begin to read.

   Gillet and Temple (1994) suggest no more than five stops in one story in one sitting so as not to interrupt the students' reading too frequently. The DRTA is particularly helpful for those children who take a passive approach to reading and who appear to believe that the message is in the book. However, the technique will help these children become active, purposeful readers only if they know why they are doing it and how they can use a similar strategy when they read independently.

KWL

The KWL technique helps children construct meaning when reading **expository writing**. Modelling the active thinking involved in reading for information (Ogle, 1986), the technique involves children using the following three basic steps:

1. accessing what they *know*
2. deciding what they *want* to learn
3. recalling what they did *learn* as a result of reading

The children use a group or individual chart like the one in Box 5.1 to guide them through these steps.

1. *K: What I know.* The children brainstorm information they know about the topic or a key concept in the material (e.g., wolves). The teacher records what the students brainstorm on the board or an overhead. The goal of this brainstorming is to activate whatever knowledge the readers have that will help them construct meaning as they read. Ogle (1986) suggests deepening students' thinking by asking questions such as:

   - Where did you learn that?
   - How can you prove that?

   To avoid implying a transmission model of knowledge, some teachers have children differentiate between ideas they are sure about (everyone agrees) and those they are not so sure about (some agree).

   Some teachers also ask children to complete a second, optional part of this step—thinking about what general categories of information they are likely to encounter when they read. The children consider the information they have brainstormed and group it into more general categories (e.g., what wolves eat, where they live).

2. *W: What I want to learn.* As the children think about what they know on a topic and what categories of information might be included in what they read, questions emerge. After the group discussion, each child records his or her own questions in the W column to focus attention during reading. The children then read the material.

3. *L: What I learned.* After the children finish reading, they write down in the L column what they learned from reading. The role of the teacher is to have them locate cues in the text that they used to construct this information.

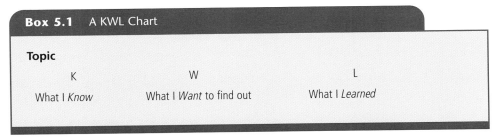

Box 5.1   A KWL Chart

Topic

K	W	L
What I *Know*	What I *Want* to find out	What I *Learned*

Source: Adapted from D. M. Ogle, "KWL: A teaching model that develops active reading of expository text," *Reading Teacher, 39* (6) (1986), 565.

If not all of the children's questions are answered in the material, the children generate a list of "Questions I would like answered," and the teacher suggests further reading on the topic. This ensures that the children's desire to learn takes precedence over what the author has chosen to include.

Sampson (2002) has extended the KWL technique by adding a confirmation component to deal with instances of children providing incorrect information in the *What I Know* column, for example, "a whale is a really big fish," and the proliferation of questionable information on the Internet. Sampson suggests changing the heading of the K column to *What We Think We Know*. This provides support for brainstorming without giving the illusion that the items listed are all accurate. After the students brainstorm what they think they know and what they want to know, they search for sources to either confirm information in the *What We Think We Know* column or answer questions in the *What We Want to Know* column. Columns labelled *Source* are inserted beside both the *What We Think We Know* and the *What We Learned* column, and sources (books, Internet addresses, magazines, electronic media) related to each item or question are listed as students locate them. A check mark is placed beside a brainstormed item in the *What We Think We Know* column when students are able to confirm it with a minimum of two sources. Sampson's extension is appropriate to help upper elementary students learn to do research, check resources, and evaluate accuracy of information.

Questioning the Author

Beck and McKeown developed the QtA technique to help upper elementary and middle-school children construct meaning during reading of both expository and narrative texts. The technique brings the author to the foreground, and students learn to question the author with a "reviser's eye" (Beck, McKeown, Hamilton, and Kucan, 1997).

Planning

Teachers begin planning a QtA by a careful reading of the text the students are going to read. As they read, the teachers identify major ideas students are to construct and potential problems they might encounter. They then segment the text so they can have students stop reading where the major ideas are or where the students might have problems. Finally, they develop queries, which are different from questions in that they are not used to assess comprehension after reading but rather to help students construct meaning *during* reading. There are three different types of queries: initiating, follow-up, and narrative.

1. *Initiating queries*. Draw attention to major ideas and the fact that ideas are written by the author.

   - What is the author trying to say here?
   - What is the author's message?

2. *Follow-up queries*. Help students construct the meaning behind the actual words of the author, connect ideas previously learned with the text, and figure out why the author included certain information.

   - What does the author mean here?
   - Does the author explain this clearly?
   - Does this make sense with what the author told us before?
   - Why do you think the author tells us this now?

3. *Narrative queries*. Deal with characters and plot.

   - From what the author has told us, what do you think this character is up to?
   - How does the author let you know that something has changed?

Implementation

1. *Introduction of QtA*. Beck and McKeown recommend that the classroom be arranged in a U shape to facilitate discussion, and, the first time QtA is used, that teachers tell students they will be discussing a text in a way they have not done previously. The teacher talks about author fallibility, indicating that sometimes ideas are not as clear as they might be. The students' job is to figure out what the author is trying to say. The teacher then demonstrates through a think-aloud the kind of thinking involved in constructing meaning from a text and that characterizes a QtA discussion. Following the demonstration, students are given the opportunity to ask questions about what the teacher was doing and what the author was trying to say.

2. *QtA process*.

   - As students read a text, the teacher asks them to stop at the end of each segment and poses queries to initiate discussion.
   - The students contribute ideas that can be refined, challenged, or developed by the students and the teacher. The students and teacher work collaboratively to grapple with ideas and construct understanding.
   - The teacher serves as an initiator, facilitator, guide, and responder. In addition to queries, teachers use the first three "moves" listed below to make ideas students have offered in the discussion more productive and the next three to bring themselves into the interaction with students more directly:

      - *Marking*—paraphrasing or explicitly acknowledging an ideas importance,
      - *Turning back*—turning students' attention back to the text or turning responsibility back to the students for figuring out ideas,
      - *Revoicing*—rephrasing ideas students are struggling with,
      - *Modelling*—showing the students strategic processes they can use to grapple with text,
      - *Annotating*—providing information to fill in gaps or add information, and
      - *Recapping*—pulling information together or summarizing the major ideas students have constructed to that point in the discussion. Students assume greater responsibility for recapping over time.

Question–Answer Relationship

Raphael (1986) presented this technique, the question–answer relationship (or QAR), for enhancing children's ability to answer questions. The technique is based on Pearson and Johnson's (1978) taxonomy of questions:

- textually explicit (answer in the text)
- textually implicit (answer involves use of both knowledge and text)
- scriptally implicit (answer is in child's knowledge)

A QAR focuses on two major categories of information used for answering questions:

- *in the book* (text-based information)
- *in my head* (knowledge-based information)

Each of these two categories is subdivided into two question types as shown in Table 5.2.

Raphael recommends introducing students to the two major categories—*in the book* and *in my head*—before having them deal with the four question types. In the initial stages of instruction, the students' answers to questions are less important than their being able to indicate which source of information is required. Raphael suggests the following steps in teaching QARs:

1. The teacher begins by explaining to the children that they are going to talk about questions and the best way to answer them. Some questions ask for information that the children can easily find in the book. Other times, they won't find it there and will need to use what they know to answer the questions. Each question can be answered by figuring out where to get the information needed for the answer.
2. The teacher asks specific questions, and discussion focuses on where the children get information to answer each question.
3. The teacher gives the children short passages and questions for which both answers and QARs are provided for further discussion.
4. The teacher gives the children short passages with questions and answers, and the children indicate which QAR each belongs to.
5. The teacher gives the children passages and questions, and they identify both the QARs and the answers to the questions.
6. The children then move to the two questions for in the book and in my head categories and eventually to longer passages.
7. The teacher provides regular review and extends the use of QARs to content area texts.

The terms "in the book" and "in my head" can be confusing for primary children. Some teachers have found that substituting the terms "on the page" and "off the page" helps primary children gain a better understanding of the QARs involved in this instructional strategy.

Reciprocal Teaching

Reciprocal teaching (Palincsar, 1986) is a dialogue between a teacher and children to jointly construct meaning as they read. It is designed to promote four comprehension strategies:

1. summarizing a passage in a sentence
2. asking one or two good questions about the passage
3. clarifying parts that are confusing
4. predicting what the next part will be about

The teacher models these strategies using expository passages, and then the students assume the role of teacher using segments of the text.

1. *Modelling the strategy.* The teacher meets with a small group of students, each of whom has a copy of the same content area material, and models the four comprehension strategies while reading a paragraph from the material.

   a. The teacher summarizes the paragraph, and the students decide whether the summary is accurate.

Table 5.2 Question–Answer Relationships

In the Book	In My Head
Right There The words in the question and in the answer are "right there" in one sentence. Find the words used to make up the question and look at the other words in that sentence to find the answer. **Think and Search (Putting It Together)** The answer is in the story but you need to find it in more than one sentence or paragraph. The answer comes from more than one part of the text.	**Author and You** The answer is not in the story alone. You need to think about what you know and what the author tells you and fit it together. **On My Own** The answer is not in the story. You need to use what you already know.

Source: Adapted from T. Raphael, "Teaching question-answer relationships," *Reading Teacher, 39* (6) (1986), 519.

b. The teacher asks questions about the paragraph, and the students tell whether the questions involve important information in the passage and then answer the questions.

c. The teacher identifies parts of the paragraph that could be confusing and, with the students' help, clarifies these parts.

d. Finally, the teacher predicts what the next passage will be about, and the students judge whether the prediction is logical.

2. *Students assume role of teacher.* After the teacher has modelled the procedure with several segments of text, he or she asks a student to be the teacher. As the student teacher summarizes, asks questions, identifies confusing parts, and predicts what will come next, the adult teacher provides feedback and coaches him or her through the strategies. The other students are asked to judge the adequacy of the summary, importance of the questions, and logic of the predictions, as well as to help clarify points and support the student teacher. The following steps indicate how reciprocal teaching is used when students assume the role of the teacher:

a. The teacher presents the children with the title of the material they will be reading and asks them to use background knowledge they have about the topic to predict what they will learn in the material. A student teacher is then appointed for the first part of the material, and the group reads it.

b. The student teacher asks a question that the other students answer, and then summarizes what has been read. The students judge the accuracy of the summary and the importance of the questions.

c. A discussion follows about clarifications that the student teacher and other students made while reading, or about points that they think still need to be made.

d. Finally, the student teacher and other students make predictions about the next segment of the material, and a new student teacher is appointed.

Throughout this dialogue, the adult teacher provides the students with feedback and instruction on how to use the four strategies more effectively. For example, the teacher might help the students to produce shorter summaries or to ask questions about main ideas as well as details.

At the end of a half-hour reciprocal teaching session, the teacher sometimes gives the children a passage they have not read before and asks them to summarize it or answer a few substantial questions about it. Reciprocal teaching is more appropriate for students at the upper elementary level than for primary children.

Think-Alouds

"Think-alouds" are used to help readers clarify their views of reading and their use of strategies. Davey (1983) recommends the following four steps:

1. *Teacher modelling.* The teacher verbalizes his or her own thoughts while reading orally to provide a "model." The teacher selects a short passage that contains points of difficulty, contradictions, ambiguity, or unknown words. As the teacher reads the passage aloud, students follow silently, listening to how the teacher thinks through the reading. The following are examples of points that can be made during reading to help children develop metacognitive awareness and control (Davey, 1983):

   - Make predictions. (The teacher shows the children how to make pre-dictions during reading.)

     "From the title, I predict that this story will be about a boy who wanted to fly."
     "In this next part, I think we'll find out why the boys got into a fight."

   - Describe the picture you're forming in your head from the information. (The teacher demonstrates how to develop images during reading.)

     "I have a picture of this scene in my mind. The boy is walking through a dark alley and there are no other people around."

   - Share an analogy. (The teacher links prior knowledge with new infor-mation in text. Davey calls this the "like-a" step.)

     "This is like a time we went to West Edmonton Mall and Sean got lost."

   - Verbalize a confusing point. (The teacher shows children how to mon-itor their ongoing comprehension.)

     "This just doesn't make sense."
     "This is not what I thought would happen."

   - Demonstrate fix-up strategies. (The teacher shows children how to cor-rect their comprehension confusions.)

     "I'd better reread."
     "Maybe I'll read ahead to see if it gets clearer."
     "I'd better change my picture of the story."
     "This is a new word to me—I'd better check context to figure it out."

2. *Practise with student partners.* After several modelling experiences, children work together with partners to practise think-alouds. The partners take turns reading and thinking aloud with short passages.

3. *Independent practice.* Children practise independently with the use of checklists such as the one in Box 5.2.

4. *Use in other subject areas.* Teachers both model and provide opportunities for children to practise using think-alouds with content area materials. This helps chil-dren learn when and why to use certain strategies.

Box 5.2 Checklist for Think-Alouds

	Not Very Much	A Little Bit	Much of the Time	All of the Time
Predicting				
Picturing				
"Like-a"				
Identifying problems				
Using fix-ups				

Source: Adapted from B. Davey, "Think aloud—Modeling the cognitive processes of reading comprehension," *Journal of Reading, 27* (1) (1983), 46

Semantic Webs

A **semantic web** is a visual representation of relationships among ideas. These graphic arrangements (sometimes also referred to as semantic maps) show the major ideas and relationships in texts (Sinatra, Stahl-Gemake, and Berg, 1984) or among word meanings. A web consists of nodes containing key words, with connecting lines between nodes.

Joyce Bodell, an elementary teacher in Coquitlam, B.C., uses prior- and post-knowledge webs to achieve a number of significant purposes. Before beginning a new unit or theme, she has her students individually web everything that they already know about the topic. She writes the topic or idea on the board, reads it aloud, and then asks the children to take a minute or two to think of everything that they know about it and to record their ideas on a piece of paper.

This activity is completed individually for two reasons:

- First, Joyce wants to know what level of understanding each child is bringing to the unit of study. This informs her teaching and enables her to plan for content and lessons that will meet the children's needs most effectively.
- Second, it enables children to recognize for themselves how much they already know and to raise questions about particular ideas, facts, or aspects that they are not sure about.

After the webs are finished, Joyce collects and reads them, and then stores them away until the students have finished their unit.

At this point, Joyce usually does a whole-class brainstorming activity and records it on chart paper. This provides a written record of the children's combined knowledge, which Joyce leaves posted in the classroom. The children often refer back to it during whole-class lessons and discussions when they learn something that validates (or invalidates) what they thought they knew, or when they find an answer to a question that someone raised.

At the end of the unit, Joyce gives individual webs back to the children and asks them to use a coloured pencil to add their new knowledge to their webs and to cross out ideas that didn't really belong. The result is a two-colour web that provides the children with a powerful visual representation of all the learning they accomplished. Often, children ask for a second, larger piece of paper so that they can fit in all of their new ideas. They glue the original web in the centre and branch out onto the larger sheet. If a whole-class web was done, Joyce revisits this with the entire group, and together they build on their combined prior knowledge, adding all of the new information and understandings that they acquired. In the semantic web shown in Exhibit 5.1, the ideas within thick lines indicate the children's prior knowledge about Canada. The rest of the ideas indicate what they learned.

Exhibit 5.1 A Semantic Web of Canada

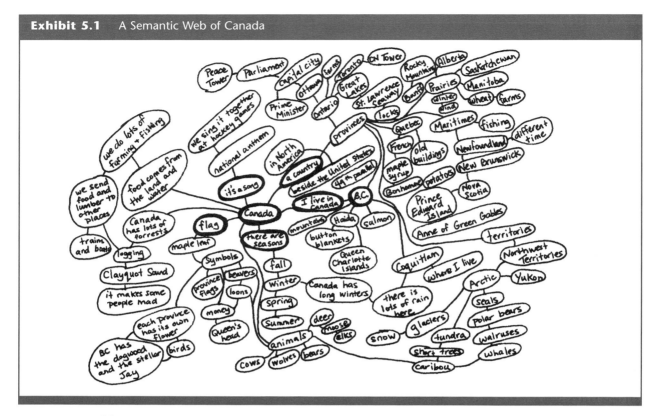

Source: Joyce Bodell. Reprinted with permission.

This second round of webbing offers the teacher a valuable assessment/evaluation tool. It demonstrates the breadth and depth of understanding that each student acquired. It can also be used to note what has not been learned, either by individuals or by most of the class. For example, if an important concept seems to be missing from most of the post-knowledge webs, it might indicate to the teacher that some additional instruction time needs to be spent on that area before the unit is drawn to a close.

All of the instructional techniques included in this section have the potential to help children develop awareness and control over their reading. This potential will only be achieved, however, if the teacher models strategy use and the children have opportunities to talk about and use the strategies being demonstrated. We also recommend having children evaluate which strategies work best for them in different contexts and for different purposes.

USING TEXT STRUCTURE

This section deals first with helping children develop their knowledge of the structure of stories and then moves to informational texts.

As noted in Chapter Three, young children who have had stories read or told to them on a regular basis learn what stories are like, and the stories they tell reflect the structure of the stories they have heard. It's easier for children to construct meaning when reading stories if they are familiar with the structure of stories, because they will be able to relate ideas as they read and anticipate what comes next. Similarly, it's easier for children to construct meaning when reading informational texts if they know how authors organize and relate ideas in these texts. Since few parents will have read as much informational as narrative material to their children, fewer children come to school with an awareness of the structure of informational texts.

Narrative Texts

Story grammars are attempts to delineate the basic elements of a well-formed story (e.g., Mandler and Johnson, 1977). Nearly all stories written in the Western tradition contain a setting, which introduces the main characters and tells where and when the story takes place, and a series of episodes. Although episodes are represented differently in different story grammars, common elements include a problem, attempts to resolve the problem, outcomes, and a resolution. Sometimes these elements are not presented in this order when authors use flashbacks in their writing.

There is considerable controversy about using story grammars with children. Stories written by authors from other cultures do not always conform to what these story grammars depict as well-formed stories. As children read more multicultural literature, story grammars will be less useful as a guide for their reading. Another problem is teaching story grammar for its own sake rather than to help children construct meaning. A related problem involves the often-heavy focus on children learning specific terms related to story elements, such as characters, episodes, and so on. Rather than imposing this terminology on children, it is more useful for them to generate their own terms, such as *who* and *what happened*.

The best way to build knowledge of story structure is to provide children with experiences with stories on a regular basis. However, some explicit attention to story structure will benefit children with limited story experience and those who do not appear to reflect this knowledge in their storytelling or writing.

1. *Story maps.* The teacher prepares a chart, such as the one in Table 5.3, reflecting the structure of a typical story. Cochrane, Cochrane, Scalena, and Buchanan (1984) suggest that the best type of story to use for story mapping is a problem-centred one. The teacher reads the story to the children, and as a group, they analyze the story, filling in a large copy of the story map. This can be followed up with a range of activities, such as rearranging the parts of a well-formed story in order and filling in a missing story element.

2. *Questions based on story grammar.* Vacca, Vacca, and Gove (1991) suggest that teachers use story grammars to generate questions about stories. These questions can then be used to guide discussions both during and following reading. For example:

Setting

- Where did the story take place?
- When did the story take place?
- Who is the main character?

Problem/Internal Conflict

- What is the problem of the main character?
- What did _____ need?
- Why is _____ in trouble?
- What conflict does the main character have?
- What does _____ decide to do?
- How did _____ feel about the problem?

Table 5.3 Story Map	
Setting	
When	
Where	
Who	
Events	
Problem/internal conflict	
Attempt(s) and outcome(s)	
Resolution/reaction	

Attempts/Outcome

- What did ____ do about ____?
- What happened to ____?
- What will ____ do now?

Resolution

- Was the problem solved? If not, why did the author do this?
- If so, how did ____ solve the problem?
- How did ____ feel at the end?
- What would you do to solve ____'s problem?

It is crucial that children understand why they are being asked these questions and how the information required to answer the questions relates to the overall structure of the story. Unless children are clear on the purpose for this activity, it will test their comprehension but not teach them how to construct meaning.

Informational Texts

People read informational material to gain information. Authors generally use one of four types of organization to reflect different ways ideas are related, although they occasionally use narrative to inform as well. For example, although the purpose of this book is to inform, we occasionally share a short story about a child or classroom event to illustrate a point. Most of this book, however, uses informational text structures.

The four most common types of organizational patterns for informational material are enumeration, sequence, cause–effect and comparison–contrast. In the enumeration pattern, information about one topic is listed, but the order in which the information is presented is not important. We used the enumeration pattern to write the paragraph you are currently reading. The topic is organization patterns for informational material, and the

Three upper elementary children reading an informational book.

four types are listed and defined, with examples provided for clarification. The sequence pattern, which presents information in time order, is commonly found in historical texts, recipe directions, and scientific experiments. We used this pattern to list steps in instructional techniques in the preceding section of this chapter. Cause–effect and comparison–contrast patterns appear in a wide range of content areas. We used the comparison–contrast pattern in Chapter Three when we contrasted concepts of reading readiness and emergent literacy. An overview of these four organizational patterns for informational texts, including characteristics, signal words, examples, and graphic organizers, is presented in Table 5.4. Other graphic organizers are provided in Schools of California Online Resources at www.sdcoe.k12.ca.us/score/actbank/sorganiz.htm.

Enumeration Pattern

This is the pattern typically used in "main idea activities" in classrooms. Pearson and Johnson (1978, p. 89) state, "We know of no aspect of comprehension so universally accepted yet so often confused as the notion of 'Finding the Main Idea.'" The term *main idea* is variously used to refer to the most important idea, the topic, the title, or the theme. In fact, "main idea–detail" is a "logical relation between more general and more specific propositions" (p. 90). "Main idea" is the generalization arrived at by determining what the specific details have in common.

Much nonfiction material is organized in this pattern, so being able to understand how ideas are related in these types of texts is crucial for content area reading. Authors provide "signals" (connective words) to readers to help them construct relationships among ideas. Signals to the enumeration pattern include words such as *several*, *other*, *also*, and *for example*.

Classification of Words. Pearson and Johnson (1978) note that children need to engage in the same kind of thinking to understand main idea–detail relationships as they use on classification tasks with words. For example, in the list of words

jump ropes

kites

toys

dolls

the word *toys* is the generalization, or the class, that all the others belong to. The following activities are useful for introducing this concept to children:

Table 5.4 Organizational Patterns for Informational Texts

Pattern	Signal Words	Example Passage	Graphic Organizer
Enumeration Lists features, characteristics, and examples	some, several, other, many, also, too, for example	There are several good rules for bicycle safety. For example, always use hand signals. Another good rule is to ride on the right side of the street. Still others are not to go too fast and not to ride barefoot. (McGuire and Bumpus, 1973, A4, Level P)	*Good Rules for Bicycle Safety* → Always use hand signals / Don't ride barefoot / Ride on right side of street / Don't go too fast
Sequence Lists events or items in order	first, next, last, finally, then, how to, directions	Here are the directions for making a ham sandwich. First, take two pieces of bread. Then, put some ham on one piece. Finally, spread some mustard on it and cover. (McGuire and Bumpus, 1973, B2, Level P)	*Directions for Making a Ham Sandwich* ▼ Take two pieces of bread ▼ Put ham on one piece ▼ Spread mustard on it ▼ Cover
Comparison–Contrast Tells how people, places, things, and ideas are the same and/or different	different, like, however, same, both, but	Brian's new kite is different from Bill's new kite. Brian's kite is blue. It is shaped like a fish. Bill's kite is red. It is shaped like a diamond. (McGuire and Bumpus, 1973, A2, Level P)	*Attribute* | *Brian's Kite* | *Bill's Kite* — Colour | Blue | Red — Shape | Fish | Diamond
Cause–Effect Links one or more causes with one or more effects	because, why, so, reasons, therefore, as a result	"Why did you choose a goldfish for a pet?" asked Bruce. "Because they are easy to care for," said Cheryl. "They eat only a few times a week. You don't have to brush them, either. And they are fun to watch." (McGuire and Bumpus, 1973, B3, Level P)	*Cause (Why?)* Easy to care for / Eat only a few times a week / Don't have to brush them / Fun to watch → *Effect (What happened?)* Choose a goldfish for a pet

- The teacher presents to children word lists containing the classification label (such as the one above) and discusses the nature of the relationship among words in the lists (e.g., "How are these words the same? A jump rope, a kite, and a doll are all toys, so *toys* is the word that tells about all the others.").
- After children are able to describe relationships among words in lists containing the class label, the teacher presents lists of words without this label, for example

screeching siren

crash of thunder

booming gun

Discussing how the word or phrase generated by the children shows what the items in the list have in common (in this instance, something like *loud noises*) is essential so that students consciously think about the general–specific relationship. Traditional basal readers and workbooks contain numerous classification exercises that can be used both to help children learn how to classify and conceptualize generally as well as to provide material for the introductory step in work on main idea–detail relationships.

Passages. When children understand the nature of the relationship between a generalization and specific ideas, they are ready to look for this pattern in passages. Some children need to work systematically through the steps outlined below. Others are able to move quickly into longer paragraphs that do not contain an explicitly stated main idea.

1. Well-organized passages are presented in which the author explicitly provides a generalization (main idea) in the first sentence. For example,

   The chair was a great place to play games of make believe. Sometimes Miguel would pretend he was stunt flying. At other times he would make up games he called Hoopa Loopa and Twisto-Chairisto. Still other times he just sat very still and dreamed about things he might do someday. (McGuire and Bumpus, 1973, A4, Level I)

   Students read the paragraph and think about what all of the sentences have in common. They then determine whether one of the sentences reflects this shared meaning. The teacher also helps them see that authors use certain words to signal the way ideas are related. Signal words such as *sometimes* and *at other times* suggest that each sentence is a specific example of something. The objective of the discussion is to help children construct relationships among ideas rather than to label one sentence as the main idea. An example of the kind of discussion that teachers might use to help children understand how ideas are related in this type of paragraph is presented in Box 5.3.

2. Well-organized paragraphs where the author leaves the main idea unstated are then presented. For example:

   Some seeds travel with the wind. Elm and Maple seeds do this. Other seeds are hitchhikers. Burrs stick to dogs, for example. Birds carry berry seeds, too. Still other seeds pop right out of their pods. (McGuire and Bumpus, 1973, B3, Level P)

   Again, the teacher guides children in a discussion of what these sentences have in common, underlining key words to focus on areas of similarity. They then construct a general statement that captures the common meaning of the sentences.

Box 5.3 Illustrative Lesson on Enumeration (Main Idea–Detail) Pattern

1. The teacher provides students with copies of a short, well-constructed paragraph, such as:

   The moving ice did great things for Canada. It scraped a thick layer of topsoil off the Canadian Shield. This left the minerals near the surface where people could reach them. It carried good soil south to southern Canada where the climate is suitable for farming. Most interesting of all, it made Canada beautiful.

2. The teacher says, "Let's read this paragraph to find out the writer's main idea. We are going to underline the key words as we read. Let's look at the second sentence. What are the key words in this sentence?" Answers will probably be *scraped, topsoil,* and *Canadian Shield*. Students underline these words in the sentence. The teacher then asks the students to read on, underlining key words. When the children finish reading and underlining words, they share their underlined words with the group, and the teacher lists words for each sentence on the board. Discussion will lead to a list something like the following:

   - ice did things Canada
   - scraped topsoil Canadian Shield
   - left minerals near surface
   - carried good soil southern Canada
   - made Canada beautiful

3. The teacher then guides a discussion focused on the nature of the relationships among the ideas in the five sentences. This discussion leads the students to conclude that sentences (b), (c), (d), and (e) are specific things ice did, while sentence (a) contains a general statement. Each of sentences (b), (c), (d), and (e) indicate one of the great things ice did for Canada. Sentence (a) is the general overall statement arrived at by determining what the specific ideas have in common. This is the main idea of the paragraph.

4. As a follow-up activity, students discuss the main idea of paragraphs selected from content area textbooks.

Source: Adapted from an illustrative lesson for upper elementary students presented in an unpublished paper by Phillis Sutherland, a former teacher and remedial specialist in Edmonton Public Schools.

The paragraphs included in the examples to this point have been very well organized, with the authors using specific signal words to help readers construct relationships among ideas. Although this type of material is useful for helping children understand how ideas are related in the enumeration pattern, most material is not this tightly organized, nor do authors always provide so many cues to help readers construct relationships. Once children are familiar with the pattern and the relationships within this pattern, the teacher guides their reading of paragraphs in which ideas are not so clearly related and authors provide fewer cues (i.e., signal words or the explicit statement of main ideas) to help children construct relationships among ideas.

Outlining and Graphic Organizers. Pearson and Johnson (1978) suggest two techniques other than discussion to help clarify the relationship between main ideas and details: outlining and diagramming. Generally, the teacher models these techniques to visually show the relationships before asking students to generate their own outlines or diagrams. An example of a graphic organizer for the enumeration pattern is shown in Table 5.4.

Both outlining and diagramming can also be used for organizing ideas for written composition. Once a topic is identified, the children generate a number of ideas related to it through brainstorming. The children then organize these ideas using diagrams or outlines before they begin to write. Having children use diagrams for both reading and writing helps them understand how these language processes are related, and this in turn helps them transfer what they are able to do in one mode of language to the other.

Sequence Pattern

Exercises on sequence patterns run a close second to those on main ideas for causing students difficulty. The most common type of exercise involves giving students sentences that are out of order. Students are asked to place a number beside each sentence to indicate what order they should be in. There are several reasons why this task is difficult, particularly for young children. One is that we generally use numerals (1, 2, 3) to indicate quantity rather than sequence. When numerals are used to indicate sequence, they are generally transformed to ordinals—*first*, *second*, and so on. As well, there is often no logical reason for one event to occur before another in the exercises given to children. In other words, the sequence is essentially arbitrary. Pearson and Johnson (1978, p. 116) point out that primary children find reversible relationships (where there is no logical reason for one thing to occur before the other and the order is essentially arbitrary) more difficult to understand than irreversible relationships (where one thing logically follows another). For example:

> *John watched television before he ate dinner.* (reversible)

> *John closed the door. Then he bolted it.* (irreversible)

In addition, young children tend to pay attention to the order in which events are presented rather than to signal words (e.g., *then*, *before*, *after*) when sorting out the sequence of events. Hence, young children often interpret the sentence *Before Mary ate dinner, she read a book*, as first Mary ate dinner and then she read a book. Finally, many young children find that reordering sentences in their heads is too abstract.

We provide the following suggestions for planning instructional activities with texts written in the sequence pattern:

- Begin by having students understand the sequential relationships in familiar experiences before moving to unfamiliar material. Language experience stories are ideal for this.
- Present students with texts that illustrate irreversible events before reversible ones.
- Have students read material where the order of presentation matches the time order. Students need considerable instruction with temporal connectives before they can use them to aid comprehension.
- Have students recall the order in which events occurred rather than having them order sentences, unless the sentences can be physically moved to place them in order of occurrence.
- Have students use a time line or other type of graphic organizer (such as the one in Table 5.4) to show temporal relationships among ideas. Again, these types of graphic organizers can be used to generate ideas for written composition when the topic involves a sequence of events.

Cause–Effect Pattern

Understanding the cause-and-effect pattern is crucial to constructing meaning from both narrative and informational material. Plots often revolve around cause–effect relationships in stories, and causality is important for understanding historical, social, and scientific issues.

Children need to learn several points about cause–effect relationships:

- One is the reciprocal relationship between cause and effect.
- Another is the chaining of causes and effects—that is, a cause produces an effect, which in turn causes another effect, and so on.
- A third is the meaning of causal connectives such as *because, since, therefore, why,* and *as a result.* Young children often use words such as because as if they were causes themselves rather than words to link causes and effects.

To help children construct causal relations as they read,

- Begin with texts that illustrate single-cause–single-effect relationships, then move to those that illustrate single-cause–multiple-effect and multiple-cause–single-effect relationships, and finally to those with chains of cause–effect relationships.
- Discuss the nature of cause–effect relationships with children. Throughout discussion, it is important to talk about the function of causal connectives, and to help children use these words in their own writing.
- Charting cause–effect relations helps many readers conceptualize the relationships among ideas. (Table 5.4 shows such a chart.) These charts may also help children organize ideas involving causality for written composition.

Comparison–Contrast Pattern

Comparison–contrast patterns are used by authors when they are describing characters and settings. They are also used in content area materials. We recommend using

- discussion focused on common attributes of people, places, things, and ideas being compared, and on the features that differentiate those being contrasted,
- discussion to direct children's attention to specific words that indicate comparisons or contrasts, such as h*owever, on the other hand, both,* and *alike,* and
- charts to help children understand comparison–contrast relationships.

Teachers can give students a chart like the one in Table 5.4 before reading to guide their construction of comparison–contrast relationships as they read. Students can also use them after reading to guide recall or as a study guide, or to organize ideas when writing paragraphs comparing or contrasting places, people, things, or ideas.

We have included only a few possible instructional techniques for developing comprehension strategies in this section. Other techniques are described in the "Selected Professional Resources" listed at the end of this chapter. It is important to note, however, that these will not be effective unless children know why, how, and when to use strategies and are able to use the strategies before, during, and after reading.

STUDYING

When asked how they study, many children say they just read the material again and again. Do you have a strategy for studying? If so, is it similar to any of the strategies described in this chapter?

Studying is a special kind of reading. As with all reading, the major goal is to construct meaning on the basis of text-based and knowledge-based information. However, individuals also need to organize information in order to enhance retrieval of the meanings they have constructed.

Using Comprehension Strategies for Studying

Some of the instructional techniques described above can help children organize and retrieve information. For example, KWL helps children think about what they learned after they finish reading. The techniques included in the section on informational text structure help children to organize ideas in content area texts, and we know that it is easier to remember related ideas than isolated details. In addition, Standal and Betza (1990) suggest helping children develop the following strategies for both reading and studying:

- Scanning involves sampling the text. Readers rapidly search through the text to locate specific information or answer a specific question. They learn to focus on headings, pictures, summaries, illustrations, and key words rather than reading every word.
- Skimming is a quick survey of the text to get an indication of what it is about.
- Outlining helps children understand and retain relationships among ideas. Mapping can be used to teach outlining.
- Underlining and highlighting make it easier to refer to important points when reviewing information. (Because elementary children are rarely able to mark in their books, Cunningham and Allington, 2003 suggest that children use stickies to mark important points.)
- Note-taking can be introduced in the upper elementary grades.

These study skills are most effective when taught to children within the context of materials in the content areas.

SQ3R

This classic technique, developed by Robinson (1961), continues to provide students with an organized, systematic approach to studying. Before beginning to read, students *survey* what they will read and ask *questions*. This ensures that when they do *read*, they are actively engaged in searching for answers. After they finish reading, they put what they have read into their own words (*recite*) or make notes about the questions generated from their survey of the material. Finally, they use these notes to *review* the major ideas and details in the passage. Throughout this process, they are continuously using information from both the text and their knowledge. Students can be given a guide such as the one that follows to help them apply the steps in SQ3R:

1. *Survey*. Read the title and headings in the chapter to see the few main points. This should take no more than a minute and will show the three to six core items around which the rest of the ideas cluster. If the chapter has a final summary paragraph, this will also list the ideas developed. This orientation will help you organize the ideas as you read them later.
2. *Question*. Turn the first heading into a question. This will arouse your curiosity and so increase comprehension. It will bring to mind information you already know, thus helping you understand that section more quickly. And the question will make important points stand out from details.

3. *Read.* Read to answer the question. This is not a passive plowing-along-each-line exercise, but an active search for the answer.

4. *Recite.* When you have read the first section, look away from the book and try briefly reciting the answer to the question in your own words. If applicable, give an example. If you can do this, you know what is in the book. If you cannot, glance over the section again. Another way to recite is by jotting down key words and phrases in outline form in a notebook.

Repeat steps 2, 3, and 4 for each section.

5. *Review.* When you have read through the chapter, look over your notes to get a bird's-eye view of the points and their relationships. Check your memory about the content by covering up your notes and trying to recall the main points. Then expose each major point and try to recall the subpoints listed under it.

The balance of opinion among researchers is that SQ3R is effective, but this conclusion is by no means unanimous (Manzo and Manzo, 1997). Instruction on how to use SQ3R is most effective when given with materials students are actually studying for an examination. The teacher models the steps with part of one chapter from the text, thinking out loud. Students and teacher work through the next part together, with the teacher guiding students through the steps. Students then use SQ3R in small groups or individually.

One of the major obstacles to study strategy instruction is changing habits. Think about your own study habits and how easy it would be to incorporate the SQ3R steps into your study process. To be effective, study strategies need to become automatic so students are able to focus on the content of what they are studying rather than on the process of studying itself.

SUMMARY

Three major aspects of reading comprehension have been the focus of instruction over the past 50 years: skills, response to literature, and strategies. Basal reading series of the 1950s through 1970s used the Directed Reading Activity as a lesson framework, and two major types of comprehension activities were included—questioning and comprehension skill exercises. Teacher questions generally test rather than teach comprehension, and more are literal than inferential or critical. There is little evidence to support teaching a series of reading comprehension skills.

In the 1980s, the focus shifted to response to literature, and the Reading Workshop was used as a lesson framework for this work. By the 1990s, there was increasing emphasis on cognitive and metacognitive strategies, and guided reading, of both a specific and a broader nature, has been developed to provide a framework for development of these strategies.

Several techniques can be used to help children integrate knowledge and text cues to construct meaning as they read. Some of these include the directed reading–thinking activity, KWL, questioning the author, question–answer relationships, reciprocal teaching, think-alouds, and semantic webs. To help children use story structure to construct meaning, we suggest the use of story maps and questions focused on story components. There are four major types of organizational patterns in informational texts: enumeration, sequence, cause–effect, and comparison–contrast. Discussion, charting, and diagramming can help children to construct relationships among ideas in these patterns. Many of these techniques are also useful as study strategies, although some children and teachers find specific study strategies useful as well.

SELECTED PROFESSIONAL RESOURCES ▬▬▬▬▬

Fountas, I. C. and Pinnell, G. S. (2001). *Guiding readers and writers, Grades 3–6: Teaching comprehension, genre, and content literacy.* Portsmouth, NH: Heinemann. In this book, Fountas and Pinnell extend their work on guided reading at the primary level to students in Grades 3 to 6. They provide a comprehensive literacy framework designed to help students develop a broad and integrated range of reading, writing, and language abilities. The Reading Workshop block consists of independent reading, guided reading, and literature study.

4-Blocks™. Available: www.blocks4reading.com. This Web site provides information on the multi-method, multi-level literacy framework developed by Pat Cunningham and Dottie Hall at Wake Forest University. The four blocks include guided reading, self-selected reading, working with words, and writing. The site provides the following information on guided reading: goals, strategies, activities, and formats.

Tierney, R. J. and Readence, J. E. (2000). *Reading strategies and practices: A compendium* (5th ed.). Boston: Allyn and Bacon. The authors present a wide range of instructional techniques to facilitate reading development. The major focus is on comprehension, although attention is also given to study skills, word identification, assessment, and other aspects of reading instruction.

REFERENCES ▬▬▬▬▬

Atwell, N. (1998). *In the middle: New understandings about writing, reading, and learning.* Portsmouth, NH: Heinemann.

Beck, I., McKeown, M., Hamilton, R., and Kucan, L. (1997). *Questioning the author: An approach for enhancing student engagement with text.* Newark, DE: International Reading Association.

Bloom, B. (1956). *Taxonomy of educational objectives: Cognitive domain.* New York: McKay.

Clay, M. M. (1993). *Reading recovery: A guidebook for teachers in training.* Portsmouth, NH: Heinemann.

Cochrane, O., Cochrane, D., Scalena, S., and Buchanan, E. (1984). *Reading, writing and caring.* Winnipeg: Whole Language Consultants.

Cunningham, P. M. and Allington, R. L. (2003). *Classrooms that work: They can all read and write* (3rd ed.). New York: Longman.

Davey, B. (1983). Think aloud—modeling the cognitive processes of reading comprehension. *Journal of Reading, 27* (1), 44–47.

Durkin, D. D. (1978–79). What classroom observations reveal about reading comprehension instruction. *Reading Research Quarterly, 14* (4), 481–533.

Flavell, J. H. (1979). Metacognition and cognitive monitoring: A new area of cognitive-developmental inquiry. *American Psychologist, 34,* 906–911.

Forrest-Pressley, D. L. and Walker, T. G. (1984). *Cognition, metacognition and reading.* New York: Springer-Verlag.

Fountas, I. C. and Pinnell, G. S. (1996). *Guided reading: Good first teaching for all children.* Portsmouth, NH: Heinemann.

Fountas, I. C. and Pinnell, G. S. (1999). *Matching books to readers: Using leveled texts in guided reading, K–3.* Portsmouth, NH: Heinemann.

Fountas, I. C. and Pinnell, G. S. (2001). *Guiding readers and writers, Grades 3–6: Teaching comprehension, genre, and content literacy.* Portsmouth, NH: Heinemann.

Gillet, J. W. and Temple, C. (1994). *Understanding reading problems: Assessment and instruction.* New York: HarperCollins.

Jacobs, J. E. and Paris, S. G. (1987). Children's metacognition about reading: Issues in definition, measurement, and instruction. *Educational Psychologist, 22* (3 and 4), 255–278.

McGuire, M. L. and Bumpus, M. J. (1973). *Croft skillpacks*. Old Greenwich, CT: Croft Educational Services.

Mandler, J. and Johnson, N. (1977). Remembrance of things parsed: Story structure and recall. *Cognitive Psychology*, 9, 111–151.

Manzo, A. V. and Manzo, U. (1997). *Content area literacy: Interactive teaching for active learning*. Columbus, OH: Prentice-Hall.

National Reading Panel. (2000). *Teaching children to read: An evidence-based assessment of the scientific research literature on reading and its implications for reading instruction*. Washington, DC: National Institute of Child Health and Human Development. Available: www.nationalreadingpanel.org.

Ogle, D. M. (1986). K-W-L: A teaching model that develops active reading of expository text. *Reading Teacher*, 39 (6), 564–570.

Palincsar, A. S. (1986). Metacognitive strategy instruction. *Exceptional Children*, 53 (2), 118–124.

Paris, S. G., Wasik, B. A., and Turner, J. C. (1991). The development of strategic readers. In R. Barr, M. L. Kamil, P. B. Mosenthal, and P. D. Pearson (eds.), *Handbook of reading research*, Vol. 2 (pp. 609–640). White Plains, NY: Longman.

Pearson, P. D. and Fielding, L. (1991). Comprehension instruction. In R. Barr, M. L. Kamil, P. B. Mosenthal, and P. D. Pearson (eds.), *Handbook of reading research*, Vol. 2 (pp. 815–860). New York: Longman.

Pearson, P. D. and Johnson, D. D. (1978). *Teaching reading comprehension*. New York: Holt, Rinehart & Winston.

Pinnell, G. S. and Fountas, I. C. (2002). *Leveled books for readers, Grades 3–6*. Portsmouth, NH: Heinemann.

Pressley, M. (1998). Comprehension strategies instruction. In J. Osborn and F. Lehr (eds.), *Literacy for all: Issues in teaching and learning* (pp. 113–133). New York: The Guilford Press.

Raphael, T. E. (1986). Teaching question–answer relationships. *Reading Teacher*, 39 (6), 516–522.

Robinson, F. (1961). *Effective study*. New York: Harper & Row.

Sampson, M. B. (2002). Confirming a K-W-L: Considering the source. *Reading Teacher*, 55 (6), 528–532.

Sigmon, C. S. *Guided reading the 4-Blocks way*. Available: teachers.net/4blocks/article14.html.

Sinatra, R. C., Stahl-Gemake, J., and Berg, D. N. (1984). Improving the reading comprehension of disabled readers through semantic mapping. *Reading Teacher*, 38 (1), 22–29.

Standal, T. C. and Betza, R. E. (1990). *Content area reading: Teachers, texts, students*. New York: Prentice-Hall.

Stauffer, R. G. (1975). *Directing the reading–thinking process*. New York: Harper & Row.

Tierney, R. J. and Dishner, E. K. (2000). *Reading strategies and practices: A compendium* (5th ed.). Boston: Allyn and Bacon.

Vacca, J. L., Vacca, R. T., and Gove, M. K. (1991). *Reading and learning to read* (2nd ed.). New York: HarperCollins.

Villaume, S. K. and Brabham, E. G. (2001). Guided reading: Who is in the driver's seat? *Reading Teacher*, 55 (3), 260–263.

Villaume, S. K. and Brabham, E. G. (2002). Comprehension instruction: Beyond strategies. *Reading Teacher*, 55 (7), 672–675.

Chapter 6

Word Identification Strategies and Fluency

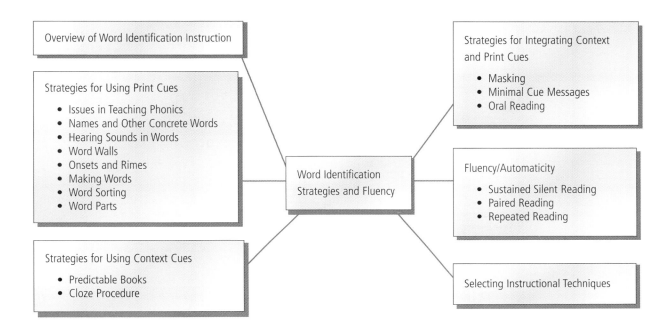

Overview of Word Identification Instruction

Strategies for Using Print Cues

- Issues in Teaching Phonics
- Names and Other Concrete Words
- Hearing Sounds in Words
- Word Walls
- Onsets and Rimes
- Making Words
- Word Sorting
- Word Parts

Strategies for Using Context Cues

- Predictable Books
- Cloze Procedure

Word Identification Strategies and Fluency

Strategies for Integrating Context and Print Cues

- Masking
- Minimal Cue Messages
- Oral Reading

Fluency/Automaticity

- Sustained Silent Reading
- Paired Reading
- Repeated Reading

Selecting Instructional Techniques

You have volunteered to go into your neighbourhood school to work with individual children in Grade 2 who have reading difficulties. The teacher has selected three children for you to help. He suggests that you spend the first day listening to them read orally to get a better idea of how they read. He selects a basal reader, designed for children at the beginning of the second grade, for them to read. Sarah begins to read quite smoothly, but before she gets to the end of the first line of print she stops and looks to you for help. "I don't know that word," she says. This happens several times before she completes the first page. Jason's reading is very different. He reads in a laboured manner, slowly sounding out words letter by letter, sometimes producing nonsense words rather than words that make sense in the sentence he is reading. He makes few corrections, plowing through the page and wondering aloud by the end what the story is about. Like Jason, Tyler reads very slowly, sounding out some unfamiliar words. However, he does not produce any nonsense words and is able to talk about what he has read at the end of the page. He tells you that reading is hard and that he doesn't read very much.

Although these three children are all experiencing difficulty reading material designed for the second grade, they have little else in common. Sarah knows some words by sight but appears to have developed few strategies for identifying unfamiliar words. Jason has developed some strategies for relating sounds to letters but has difficulty making sense as he reads. Tyler has developed some effective strategies for identifying words, but these strategies are not yet automatic and he finds reading laborious. What would you do with each of these children?

- How would you help Sarah learn to use print and sound cues to identify words?
- How would you help Jason produce meaningful words and correct miscues that don't make sense?
- How would you help Tyler achieve **automaticity** in his word identification so reading would be more enjoyable?

In this chapter, we focus primarily on instructional techniques to help children develop strategies for using both **context cues** and cues within words as they read. We also provide suggestions for developing automaticity and, in the final section, relate instructional techniques to common types of reading patterns. The chapter begins with a brief overview of word identification instruction.

OVERVIEW OF WORD IDENTIFICATION INSTRUCTION

In the basal reading series of the 1950s through 1970s, word identification was taught from a skills perspective, with skills organized hierarchically into four major categories: sight vocabulary, phonics, structural analysis, and contextual analysis.

- *Sight vocabulary* refers to words that occur frequently and that readers are able to identify automatically. As skilled readers, we recognize 99 percent of the words we read by sight.
- *Phonics* is the identification of words through the relationships between speech sounds and letters, and it has been at the centre of the great debate about early reading instruction (e.g., Chall, 1967; Adams, 1990). Phonics has been broken down into more subskills than any other area of reading instruction.
- *Structural analysis* involves identifying words by larger and more meaningful units such as prefixes and suffixes. Some people include syllabication as an aspect of structural analysis, while others consider it to be a component of phonics.
- *Contextual analysis* involves using the context of sentences or of passages to predict unfamiliar words. Most educators include both grammatical cues (Does it sound right?) and meaning cues (Does it make sense?) under the rubric of contextual analysis.

Many language arts textbooks written in the 1980s and early 1990s included little information on instructional techniques for developing word identification strategies. For a time, word identification became downright unpopular. Although most language arts educators recognized that print cues were an important source of information for readers, they did not feel that direct, systematic instruction was needed to help children make use of these cues. By the mid-1990s, however, concern that many children were not becoming proficient readers led many educators to reaffirm the importance of direct teaching of strategies for word identification. The danger now is not that word identification will be neglected, but rather that educators will go too far and word identification will become an end in itself, rather than a means of constructing meaning.

The strategies described in the following sections are organized in relation to cues that readers use for word identification—those within words, and those within sentence and passage contexts. In another section, we present instructional techniques to help children integrate both types of cues. An overview of these techniques is presented in Table 6.1.

Table 6.1 Instructional Techniques for Word Identification

Instructional Technique	Cue(s)	Helps Children Develop Strategies To:
Names and other concrete words	Print	• hear sounds at the beginning of words • hear rhyming words • relate sounds with letters • differentiate upper- and lowercase letters
Hearing sounds in words	Print	• hear sounds in all word positions • relate letters with sounds
Word walls	Print	• identify common words as sight words • hear rhyming words • relate sounds with letters • use knowledge of letter sounds to identify words
Onsets and rimes	Print	• relate sounds with letters • identify new words through analogy to familiar words
Making words	Print	• relate sounds with letters • use knowledge of letter sounds to identify words
Word sorting	Print	• form generalizations about the sound and visual features of words
Word parts	Print	• use roots, affixes and syllabication to identify words
Predictable books	Context	• use meaning and language cues to predict words
Cloze procedure	Context	• use meaning and language cues to predict words • use meaning and language cues to monitor predictions
Masking	Print and Context	• use context cues to identify words • use letter sounds to identify words • use word parts to identify words

Continued

Table 6.1 Instructional Techniques for Word Identification *continued*		
Instructional Technique	**Cue(s)**	**Helps Children Develop Strategies To:**
Minimal cue messages	Print and Context	• use context cues to identify words • use knowledge of letter sounds and word parts to spell and identify words
Oral reading	Print and Context	• use context and print cues to identify words • use context and print cues to correct miscues

STRATEGIES FOR USING PRINT CUES

This section describes instructional techniques to help children use letters and word parts to identify words as they read. We begin with a discussion of issues teachers face about teaching phonics.

Issues in Teaching Phonics

As Adams (2002) points out, one of the most divisive topics in education involves whether and how to teach phonics to young children. Some people view it as a panacea—the key to teaching all children to read. Others see it as a problem—an area of instruction leading to confusion and "word calling" (e.g., Smith, 1999). We believe neither view is defensible on its own. Although it is helpful for children to be aware of the relationships between letters and sounds, knowledge of letter sounds is certainly not enough to make children good readers. It is more important that they be aware that reading is a meaning-making process and that mapping sounds onto letters is one strategy to use as they engage in this process. We do not want children to think that reading *is* sounding out words.

Our position is supported by the review of research completed by the National Reading Panel (2000). Their conclusions support the teaching of phonics but also indicate that phonics should not be taught as an end in itself. The NRP summary report states that teachers "need to understand that while phonics skills are necessary in order to learn to read, they are not sufficient in their own right" (p. 11). Phonics instruction is only one component of a total reading program.

Terminology

One of the issues teachers face when teaching phonics involves terminology. Many of you who were in elementary schools during the 1980s and early 1990s might not be familiar with the terminology of phonics instruction. There is also a question of just how much of this terminology is useful to children.

Box 6.1 presents definitions of some of the more common terms you will encounter in phonics programs. The most common terms that children learn are consonants, vowels, and long and short vowels. These terms serve primarily to facilitate communication between and among children and teachers when talking about letters and sounds in words. Because of this limited utility, it is more helpful to have children learn the possible sounds that are associated with a letter (e.g., for the letter *a* the possibilities are the sounds in *can*, *cane*, *car*, *and call*) rather than learn that these sounds are called short, long, *r* controlled, and *l* controlled.

Box 6.1   Phonics Terminology

- *Consonants.* All the letters of the alphabet except the vowels. There is one sound for most consonants, with the exception of *c* and *g* which have both hard (e.g., *car*, *go*) and soft (e.g., *city*, *gem*) sounds.
- *Consonant blends.* A combination of two or three consonants in which the sound of each of the consonants is retained and blended (e.g., *blue*, *free*, *smoke*, *street*).
- *Consonant digraphs.* A combination of two or more consonants that produce a new sound (e.g., *shoe*, *this*, *chick*, *phone*).
- *Vowels.* The letters *a, e, i, o, u* and sometimes *y* (when it is not the initial letter of a word, e.g., *my*) and *w* (when it follows a vowel, e.g., *how*).
- *Long vowel sounds.* The letter name of a vowel (e.g., *made*, *bead*, *kite*, *mope*, *flute*).
- *Short vowel sounds.* Another sound associated with single vowels (e.g., *had*, *bed*, *hit*, *mop*, *cup*).
- *Vowel digraphs.* Combinations of two vowels that have one sound (e.g., *coat*, *meat*, *wait*).
- *Vowel diphthongs.* A combination of two vowels in which the sound of each of the vowels is retained and blended (e.g., *join*, *boy*, *how*, *out*).
- *Controlled vowels.* Vowels that are followed by the letters *r* and *l* which alter the sound of the vowel (e.g., vowels influenced by *r* as in *far*, *her*, *fir*, *for*, *purr*; and *a* influenced by *l* as in *fall*).
- *Onset.* The initial consonant or consonants in a syllable (e.g., *b* in *bat*, *br* as in *brake*).
- *Rime.* (Also known as *phonogram* or *word family*.) The vowel and remaining consonants in a syllable following the onset (e.g., *at* in *bat*, *ake* as in *brake*).
- *Syllable.* A group of letters that forms a unit and has only one vowel sound.
- *Closed syllable.* A unit in which one vowel appears between consonants (e.g., *cat*, *shop*, *back*). The vowel sound is usually short.
- *Open syllable.* A unit with a vowel at the end of it (e.g., *go*, *she*, *try*, *to* in *total*). The vowel sound is usually long.

Phonic Rules

Some people argue that labels and categories are necessary so children can use phonic generalizations or rules. Some of you may recall phonic rules from your schooling, such as "When two vowels go walking, the first one does the talking." As Clymer (1963) showed in the 1960s, many phonics rules do not work often enough to make them worthwhile learning. For example, he found that the "two vowels go walking" rule only worked 45 percent of the time for words in four primary basal reading series. There are many exceptions to this rule, including all the vowel diphthongs, (e.g., *join*, *about*). Consider as well the final *e* rule. Clymer found that this rule worked only 63 percent of the time. Many common words, such as *give*, *love*, *some*, *come*, and *live*, do not follow the rule. The most reliable rules are those involving consonants, e.g., that *c* and *g* are soft following the vowels *e* and *i*.

Another major problem with phonic rules is that children are often able to recite them but are unable to use them to identify unfamiliar words. For example, a child may be able to describe in detail how the *e* at the end of the word jumps over the letter in front of it and kicks the vowel to make it say its own name, but that same child then identifies the word *mate* as *mat*. We do not recommend rule memorization as an effective way to help children learn to map sounds onto letters.

This does not mean that it's useless to help children learn the common sounds associated with vowels. In a recent reconsideration of the utility of phonic generalizations, Johnston (2001) found that some vowel pairs are more consistent with the "two vowels go walking" generalization than others. For example, the most reliable pair is *ay* at 96.4 percent. She recommends teaching vowel pairs in groupings: five vowel pairs (*ai, ay, oa, ee,* and *ey*) that are highly regular where the first vowel does the talking; and four vowel pairs (*aw, oy, oi,* and *au*) that are also highly regular but do not have long vowel sounds. Other vowel pairs have two or more sounds (e.g., *boot, book; snow, how; seat, head*) and cannot be taught so easily. Johnston indicates that students need a flexible strategy with these pairs, that is, trying more than one sound and checking the results with their oral language and context. Johnston also recommends teaching the final-*e* generalization with this same focus on flexibility.

Synthetic or Analytic Phonics

Another controversy about phonics concerns whether instruction should be synthetic, in which children are taught letter sounds and then how to blend them to pronounce a word, or analytic, in which children examine known words to discover patterns and regularities to use when identifying unknown words (Johnston, 2001). Synthetic phonics is what most people mean when they talk about children "sounding out" words.

An advantage of synthetic phonics is that children can use letter sounds to identify new words even when these words are visually dissimilar to words they know. However, it is important to keep in mind (as indicated in Chapter Three), that it's very difficult to isolate sounds for many letters without distorting them. Another problem involves using this approach with words of more than one syllable. It is not uncommon to hear young children attempting to identify words such as *hammer* by saying, "huh, a, muh, muh, eh, er," and then having no idea what the word is. These children need to learn how to organize words into syllables in order to use their knowledge of letter sounds.

Having children identify words by mapping sounds to larger chunks of letters is often referred to as *analytic phonics*. The chunks, generally labelled *phonograms* or *rimes*, consist of a vowel sound plus a consonant sound (e.g., *-ack, -ake, -eat*). These phonograms are used to create word families such as *back, pack, quack,* and *sack*. As Vacca, Vacca, and Gove (1991) point out, there are several advantages to this approach. Children find it easier to identify words using phonograms than rules, phonograms are fairly consistent, and a relatively small number of phonograms are found in many of the words in primary reading material. Still, children do come across words in which they do not recognize a phonogram and therefore need to map sounds onto smaller units of words some of the time.

The National Reading Panel (2000) did not find that one approach to teaching phonics was better than another. As in any other aspect of reading instruction, one size does not fit all. The National Reading Panel cautioned teachers to be flexible in the phonics instruction they provide in order to adapt it to individual needs.

Separate or Integrated Instruction

Another controversy about phonics involves the extent to which it should be taught as a separate entity. Several years ago, it was not uncommon for phonics instruction to be scheduled in a separate time slot and taught in virtual isolation from the rest of the language arts program. Children who received this type of phonics instruction were often able to associate sounds with isolated consonants and vowels and to recite phonics rules, but they made almost no use of this knowledge when they read. Others were able to use the knowledge to identify words in lists, but when they attempted to read texts, they were unable to make effective use of their phonics knowledge.

Today, most children with reading difficulties do not lack knowledge of individual letter sounds. What they lack are strategies for using this knowledge to spell and figure out unfamiliar words. We recommend instruction that focuses on helping children use their knowledge of letter sounds to identify and spell words in the context of real reading and writing. As the National Reading Panel (2000, p. 10) indicated, "Programs that focus too much on the teaching of letter–sound relations and not enough on putting them to use are unlikely to be very effective." The report recommends integration of phonics instruction into "complete and balanced programs of reading instruction" (p. 11).

Incidental or Systematic Instruction

A related controversy involves whether phonics should be taught through direct instruc- tion in systematic lessons, or incidentally when children experience difficulty as they are reading or writing. During the 1980s and early 1990s, phonics was frequently taught in mini-lessons as teachers identified specific needs while children were reading or writing. The National Reading Panel (2000) found scientific support for systematic teaching of phonics. Adams (2002) indicates that the power of systematic phonics instruction lies in organizing lessons so they logically reveal the nature of the alphabetic system and so instruction moves from less to more complex understandings.

We believe that some children need systematic phonics instruction but that others do not. As Johnston (2001) points out, children develop phonics knowledge two ways: through instruction and from experiences with print. Some children are better at implicit learning than others, and some aspects of phonics knowledge are easier to learn than others. She concludes, "A little phonics instruction may go a long way with some children, while others may need long-term systematic instruction to become independent readers. Teachers will need to carefully observe their students as they read and as they write to determine who needs what" (p. 141).

> Some children require specific instruction on the nature of the relationship between sounds and letters before they can develop strategies for using cues within words to identify them. For these children, we recommend the following two instructional techniques that focus on phonemic awareness. Both techniques involve looking at written letters as well as listening for sounds, because researchers have found that phonemic awareness instruction is more effective when letters are included (Ball and Blachman, 1991; Byrne and Fielding-Barnsley, 1993; Hurford et al., 1994). Once children have figured out that letters and sounds map onto one another, most ben- efit from systematic instruction on letter sounds, how letter sounds work, and how to use this information as they read and write. Following a description of the phonemic awareness activities, we present several instructional techniques to help children develop strategies for using cues within words to aid in their identification.

Names and Other Concrete Words

Cunningham and Allington (2003) suggest several activities to help build phonemic awareness as a foundation for work on word identification. The following one, involving children's names, is designed for children in kindergarten or early Grade 1.

The teacher writes the children's first names on sentence strips and cuts the names apart, with long names on long strips and short ones on short strips. Every day the teacher draws a name, and the child selected becomes "king" or "queen" for the day. His or her name becomes the focus of several language and literacy activities.

- The children interview the child, finding out what he or she likes to eat, play, and do after school, as well as how many brothers, sisters, dogs, and cats he or she has. The teacher writes this information on a chart and compiles a class book.

- The teacher focuses the children's attention on the child's name (e.g., *David*), pointing out that this word is David's name. The teacher indicates that it takes many letters to write the word *David*, and the children count the letters. The teacher then says the letter names, *D-a-v-i-d*, and has the children say them with him or her. The teacher notes that the word begins and ends with the same letter and helps the children label one uppercase and the other lowercase.

- The teacher writes the child's name on another strip as the children watch and chant the spelling of letters with the teacher. The teacher cuts the letters apart, mixes them up, and has children come up and arrange the letters in the right order to spell the child's name, using the original sentence strip as a model.

- The children write the child's name on a large sheet of drawing paper and draw a picture of the child on the other side. The featured child takes these drawings home.

- As each name is added, the children compare them, talking about which names are longer or shorter and whether the names contain any of the same letters. When two names begin with the same letter, the teacher helps the children hear that they also begin with the same sound (e.g., *Luke* and *Linda*).

- When a single-syllable name such as *Sam* is selected, the teacher has the children listen for rhyming words. For example, the teacher says pairs of words (Sam—ham, Sam—big), and the children indicate whether the two words rhyme.

- When two names that begin with the same letter but different sounds are selected (e.g., *Caroline* and *Cynthia*), the teacher uses the opportunity to help children understand that some letters have more than one sound. The teacher writes the two names on the board and has the children say the two words several times, drawing out the first sound. The teacher then says several words beginning with the letter *c* but having different sounds (e.g., *cat, celery, candy, cookies, city, cereal, cut*). For each word, the children point to either *Caroline* or *Cynthia* to show which sound they hear, and the teacher writes the word under the name on the board.

Cunningham and Allington recommend using a similar technique with other concrete words, such as the names of colours or animals. The major focus is on hearing sounds at the beginning of words and associating these sounds with letters. The following technique is designed to help children hear sounds in all word positions.

Hearing Sounds in Words

Marie Clay (1993) suggests a one-on-one modification of what is called the "Elkonin technique" to help young children hear sounds in words. The teacher begins by having children listen to figure out how many sounds there are in words, and eventually moves to having children link the sounds they hear with letters. This technique, originated by Daniil Elkonin (1973), is designed to help children make the connection between letters and sounds and to figure out how to map letters onto sounds when spelling, and sounds onto letters when identifying unfamiliar words. The steps in this instructional technique are presented in Box 6.2.

Box 6.2   Elkonin Technique

1. The teacher prepares cards on which squares are drawn for each sound unit in words of two, three, and four sounds. For example:

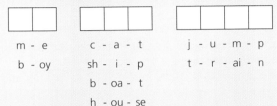

	m - e	c - a - t	j - u - m - p
	b - oy	sh - i - p	t - r - ai - n
		b - oa - t	
		h - ou - se	

2. The teacher provides a selection of counters for the children.

3. The teacher articulates a word slowly. The child watches the teacher's lips and copies the teacher.

4. The child articulates the word slowly. (A mirror can be used if it helps children become more aware of what their lips are doing.)

5. The teacher articulates the word slowly, putting one counter in each box, sound by sound.

6. The child puts the counters in the boxes as the teacher says the word slowly, or the teacher puts the counters in boxes as the child says the word.

7. The child puts counters into boxes as he or she says the word.

8. Once the child is able to hear sounds in words, this activity is applied to spelling words as he or she writes.

   a. The child is encouraged to articulate slowly the word he or she wants to spell.

   b. The teacher draws a box for each sound segment and asks, "What can you hear? How would you write it? Where will you put it?"

   c. Initially the child writes the letters he or she is able to associate with sounds heard and the teacher writes the others. For example:

   | B | i | ll |

   | b | oa | t |

   | t | r | u | ck |

9. After the child is able to hear and record most consonants and some vowels correctly, the teacher gives him or her a box for each letter. Clay suggests using broken lines initially when two letters do not represent distinct sounds. For example:

   | h | a | m | m | e | r |

Source: Adapted from M. M. Clay, *Reading Recovery: A Guidebook for Teachers in Training* (Portsmouth, NH: Heinemann, 1993), pp. 32–35.

Word Walls

Pinnell and Fountas (1998, p. 43) define a *word wall* as a systematically organized collection of words displayed in large letters on a wall. They use the term *interactive word walls* to emphasize that it is a tool rather than a display. Cunningham and Allington (2003) write about "doing a word wall" to connote the same thing. They recommend that teachers

- be very selective about the words on the wall, including only the most common words in children's reading and writing (e.g., *was, saw, of, for, from, they, that, what, with, will*),
- add words gradually—no more than five each week,
- make the word wall accessible to everyone, writing words in large clear letters,
- have children practise words by chanting or writing them, because many children can't just look at words and remember them,
- provide a variety of review activities so that children are able to identify and write words automatically, and
- make sure children spell word-wall words correctly in their writing.

Words are arranged alphabetically on the word wall, giving children an immediately accessible dictionary for the most troublesome words when they are reading or writing. The teacher and children complete several activities with words on the wall. For example:

- Children find words on the wall that rhyme with a word given by the teacher (e.g., "Find a word that begins with a *t* and rhymes with *walk*").
- The teacher writes a letter on the board and then says a sentence, leaving out a word that begins with that letter (e.g., "Write the word that begins with a *t* and fits into the sentence *Paulo wants to* _____ *on the telephone*").
- The teacher thinks of a word on the wall and gives five clues, some related to visual features ("It has three letters"), some to sounds ("It begins with the sound *s*"), and others to meaning ("It fits into the sentence 'I want to _____ the picture'"). The children write the word they think the teacher has selected after each clue.

Brabham and Villaume (2001) indicate that used effectively, word walls can be the core of systematic phonics and spelling programs as well as documenting what has been taught. In addition to the ABC word wall described above, they suggest other kinds of word walls containing:

- theme words that change as units of study are completed
- words that are examples of the different sounds each letter can represent
- commonly misspelled words
- high frequency words that lack predictable patterns
- words organized by the common spelling patterns of vowels

Brabham and Villaume indicate that some of the most powerful instruction occurs during conversations about word solving that comes up as children are reading and writing. For example, when a child asks how to spell the word *feet*, they suggest pointing to *need* on the word wall and asking how it can help. In this way, teachers scaffold the development of strategies used by skilled readers.

Onsets and Rimes

As noted above, there are several advantages to helping children develop strategies for using word families (variously called *phonograms* or *rimes*) to identify words, particularly at the primary level. Instruction begins with **onsets**, which are the consonants that precede vowels in syllables.

The sounds associated with onsets are fairly consistent, and Rasinski and Padak (2001) indicate that traditional phonics instruction for onsets works well. Rather than isolating letters and sounds, teachers teach beginning consonant sounds by associating them with words (often portrayed in pictures) that begin with these letters. Teachers may have children listen to words that begin with the sound (e.g., *bicycle, ball*), ask children to brainstorm other words that begin with the sound, read words beginning with the letter, and read texts in which many of the words begin with the targeted letter.

After the children have mastered several consonant sounds, the teacher begins concurrently teaching rimes and helping the children to use knowledge of onsets and rimes to identify words. Teachers choose rimes that are the most productive. Thirty-seven phonograms (rimes) that can be used to make 500 one-syllable and thousands of longer words are provided on the Internet at www.literacyconnections.com/phonograms.html. The following steps for instruction on rimes have been adapted from Rasinski and Padak (2001, pp. 50–56):

- Print a rime on the board (e.g., *at*) and say the sound it represents several times, asking the children to do the same.
- Brainstorm a list of words that contain the *at* rime and print them on chart paper.
- Read the words with the students, and have them read the words in groups and individually.
- Have children respond to riddles for which the answer is two or more words containing the rime (e.g., What do you get when you feed a pet too much food?).
- Introduce two or three poems, read the poems to the children pointing to the words as you read, and have the children join in when they feel comfortable. Children then read the poem chorally, read it in small groups, and finally read it individually throughout the day. Once the poem has been read many times, children are asked to find individual words and word parts in the poem. The poems can be selected from collections and anthologies (see Chapter Ten for poetry resources) or written by the teacher.
- Students are given a sheet of words containing the rime as well as the poems used for the rime. They take these home to practise reading and are also asked to write a poem of their own using words containing the rime.

The next day the students share their poems, read each others' poems, read the poems from the previous day, and identify individual words in the poems. Rasinski and Padak suggest introducing two rimes each week, with a review at the end of the week. They also suggest having children read and write books containing the rimes, use words containing the rimes for word sorts, complete cloze passages with words containing the targeted rimes, and use words containing the rimes in their daily writing. The teacher can also place some of the words on the word wall for further activities.

Making Words

In this activity, developed by Cunningham and Cunningham (1992), teachers give children letters on cards, which they use to make words. During a period of about 15 minutes, children make 12 to 15 words, beginning with two-letter words and working up to longer words until they make a target word.

The teacher prepares a set of small letter cards for each child and one set of large cards to be used in a pocket chart or on the ledge of the board. Each card has the lowercase letter on one side and the uppercase letter on the other. The teacher begins planning a lesson with a target word (e.g., *winter*) that ties in with some aspect of the curriculum and contains letter–sound patterns the children need to learn. The teacher then generates a list of shorter words that can be made with the letters in *winter* (e.g., *in*, *tin*, *ten*, *net*, *wet*, *win*, *twin*, *went*, *rent*, *tire*, *wire*, *twine*). The teacher writes these words on index cards and orders the cards from shortest to longest and according to patterns. Once these materials are prepared, the teacher follows the steps outlined in Box 6.3 (Cunningham and Allington, 2003).

Box 6.3   Steps in a Making-Words Activity

1. The teacher places the large letter cards in a pocket chart or on the board ledge.

2. Each child has corresponding small letter cards. The teacher holds up the large letter cards, names each, and asks children to hold up their matching cards.

3. The teacher writes the number 2 or 3 on the board and says a word with this number of letters in a sentence. He or she asks the children to make the word using the small letter cards (e.g., "Take two letters and make the word *in*"). The children all say the word *in*.

4. A child who has made the word correctly using the small letter cards forms the word using the large cards in the pocket chart or on the ledge, and the other children check their word.

5. This continues for other words, with the teacher giving cues such as the following: "Add a letter to make the three-letter word *tin*. Many cans are made of tin." "Now change one letter and the word *tin* becomes *ten*." "Move the letters around in the word *ten* and make the word *net*." Before telling them the last word, the teacher asks if anyone has figured out what word can be made with all the letters. If they don't know, the teacher tells them the word, and they make it.

6. Once all the words have been made, the teacher places the word cards one at a time in the pocket chart or on the board ledge, and the children say and spell them. The teacher then picks a word and asks the children to find other words with the same pattern.

7. To maximize learning, the children use the patterns they have found to identify new words written by the teacher and to spell new words dictated by the teacher.

Source: Based on P. M. Cunningham and R. L. Allington, *Classrooms that work: They can all read and write* (3rd ed.) (New York: Longman, 2003), pp. 151–158.

Word Sorting

As children become more knowledgeable about letters and words, word sorting can be used as part of the making-words technique or separately for older children. This technique is designed to focus children's attention on particular cues in words. Children compare, contrast, and sort words according to specific print or sound features. Word sorts help children form generalizations about properties of words and also help them link new words to ones they already know how to identify and spell. Teachers and/or children begin by developing a word bank of known words for word sorting.

There are two types of word-sorting activities. In a closed sort, the teacher specifies the feature the children are to use to find words (e.g., all words with the same vowel sound, all words with two syllables, all words with a soft *g*). In an open sort, the teacher does not specify how words are to be grouped—the teacher asks the children to group words so that they are all the same in some way. In both types of sorts, it is important that children talk about words as they sort them, because this helps them better understand generalizations. It is also important that the teacher model the process several times so that the children understand what to do and why they are doing it.

Pinnell and Fountas (1998) recommend the following basic approaches to sorting words:

- *Sorting words by how they sound*. Children begin with initial sounds and move to ending and middle sounds.
- *Sorting words by how they look*. Children sort words that have double letters, double vowels, double consonants, and other common patterns.
- *Sorting words by connections between meaning units*. Children sort words in relation to root words, inflected endings, prefixes, suffixes, compound words, synonyms, antonyms, and so on.

Word Parts

Structural analysis is the term traditionally used to refer to the identification of words using larger, more meaningful units than letters. It generally includes compounds, roots, affixes (e.g., *ly*), and syllabication. This area has not received the widespread attention of phonics, and much of the material available has the following types of limitations:

- First, material on compounds, roots, and affixes focuses almost exclusively on the association of their meaning to the words that contain such units, rather than on how knowledge of these units can be used to identify words.
- Second, the tasks children are frequently asked to complete, such as putting lines between syllables in polysyllabic words, don't involve reading or writing.
- Third, as with phonics, children are often required to learn terminology rather than to use word parts to identify words.
- Fourth, rules are frequently taught by memorization, particularly for syllabication. As with phonics, children may remember the rules but still be unable to identify the words to which those rules apply.

One way teachers help children learn to use structural units to identify words is by demonstrating how the children can organize difficult polysyllabic words into units. The teacher writes such a word in parts on the board (e.g., *but ter fly*), pronounces each part, blends the parts, and checks to ensure that the word makes sense in its context. The teacher then encourages children to employ a similar strategy when they encounter other unknown words as they are reading. For many children, this is sufficient to help them develop an understanding of how structural analysis works and intuitive strategies for organizing unfamiliar words into parts. Precise syllabication is generally not necessary, since context is available to check possible pronunciations. For those children who require more explicit instruction, activities such as the following are recommended:

Compound Words

A common starting point to help children who have difficulty analyzing units larger than letters is compound words. Analyzing these words into two known real words is a concrete task. It also takes advantage of words that children already know how to identify. After a brief discussion of compound words, the teacher gives students a passage containing several compound words, with the compounds underlined. He or she asks the students to read the passage silently and be prepared to talk about what they have read. When difficulties occur, compound words are written in units on the board and discussed.

Syllabication

The goal of this instruction is to have children identify syllables by hearing and seeing places in words where structural breaks occur. This is a means toward identifying longer unknown words independently. Exact division in accordance with the dictionary is unnecessary until students reach the point where they begin to hyphenate words at the end of lines in their writing. Good advice to the reader is, "Break the word down to the point where you can see how to say it, say it and move on" (Gallant, 1970, p. 93). Box 6.4 presents steps for teaching syllabication.

Box 6.4 Steps for Teaching Syllabication

1. The teacher begins by helping children develop a concept of what syllables are in the words they hear. The teacher pronounces a polysyllabic word, accentuating the syllable breaks (*in for ma tion*). The teacher and children repeat the word together in syllables. Children who have difficulty hearing syllables in words often benefit from

   - clapping every time they hear or pronounce a syllable, or
   - putting their hand under their chin and feeling it move down for each syllable

   The children then repeat the words in syllables without the teacher's aid. It is not important for the children to show how many syllables are in a word; rather, they need to be able to pronounce words in syllables.

2. To relate the concept of oral syllable to written language, the teacher presents familiar polysyllabic words to the children with syllable boundaries shown (e.g., *re port*, *fun ny*). Since the children already know how to identify these words, the focus is on syllables and how spoken syllables relate to the visual units. The children then learn the following visual clues that can be used to analyze words into syllables:

   - Prefixes and suffixes form separate syllables,
   - Double consonants or two consonants together are divided, except in the case of blends and digraphs,

Continued

Box 6.4   Steps for Teaching Syllabication *continued*

- A single consonant between two vowels often goes with the second vowel, and
- The consonant before -*le* usually goes with it.

  The teacher selects one or two words to provide a visual reminder of each clue as they are introduced. He or she prints these on a chart (with syllable divisions shown) and places them where children can refer to them when a difficult word occurs in context. Eventually the children have models for all four visual clues.

3. The teacher has the children silently read texts containing polysyllabic words, reminding them to organize words into syllables if they have difficulty identifying them. They might lightly underline words that cause them difficulty, and these can be discussed after they finish reading. The teachers or students write selected words on the board in syllables for identification and discussion.

4. Finally, children use this strategy to identify polysyllabic words when reading independently. It is important that flexibility be stressed. If the word identified does not make sense, the children are encouraged to try it another way until they get a meaningful word.

Affixes and Inflectional Endings

We do not recommend systematically working through all affixes or inflectional endings, but rather recommend focusing on specific inflectional endings (e.g., *ed*, *es*) or affixes (e.g., *pre-*, *-ness*, *-tion*) when they cause difficulty in reading and writing. What works best is beginning with familiar words and then moving on to unfamiliar ones. Another approach to affixes and inflectional endings is provided by Cunningham and Allington (2003) in their Nifty-Thrifty-Fifty list. This is a list of 50 words that contain examples for all the common prefixes and suffixes as well as common spelling changes. They recommend introducing the words gradually, with students chanting and practising them until their spelling and decoding become automatic. The Nifty-Thrifty-Fifty list can be found online at www.teachers.net/4blocks/goodies.html.

This section focused on helping children develop strategies for using cues within words to identify them. It's important that children know why they are learning these strategies. With the media's current heavy focus on phonics, you might feel considerable pressure to teach phonics for its own sake. Phonics is important, but it is best used in conjunction with other strategies for helping children identify unfamiliar words when they are constructing meaning. The next section focuses on helping children develop strategies for using cues beyond individual words.

STRATEGIES FOR USING CONTEXT CUES

In the 1980s and early 1990s, many educators championed the use of context cues as a way for children to use their language and world knowledge to identify words as they read. Other educators denigrated this approach as encouraging children to guess. We take the position that children need to use a range of strategies and cues as they read.

Context cues are one of several sources of information children have available to identify unfamiliar words. They need to use context cues *along with*, not instead of, print-based information.

Three children identifying words in context.

Predictable Books

One way teachers help young children develop strategies for predicting words as they read is by using highly predictable reading material. When reading *predictable books* to children, the teacher pauses at points in the text to provide opportunities for children to predict words that "make sense" and "sound right." When the teacher and children are reading together from big books, the teacher stops at highly predictable points to encourage the children to read on their own. When a child attempts to read a predictable book, the teacher encourages him or her to make predictions by asking, "What word would make sense? What word would sound right?"

Several series of predictable books are available, including the following:

- *Instant Readers* (Holt, Rinehart & Winston)
- *The Story Box* (Ginn)
- *Sunshine Books* (Ginn)
- *Literacy 2000* (Ginn)
- *Carousel Readers* (Dominie Press)
- *PM Starters and Books* (Scholastic)
- *Collections* (Prentice Hall Ginn Canada).

In addition, many predictable trade books are available, some of them children's classics. A selection of these was presented in Chapter Three in Box 3.6.

Cloze Procedure

In the *cloze procedure*, words are deleted from a written passage and readers fill in the blanks using their knowledge of language and the world, along with clues available from the context. Although some educators recommend beginning with cloze activities in which the reader chooses from among several possibilities the word that best fills the blank, this detracts from the meaning-making nature of reading. We do not engage in a process of elimination, but rather one of meaning construction as we read.

Material at a wide range of reading levels, including both narrative and informational texts, can be used to make cloze passages. For early readers or those experiencing difficulty, the teacher initially deletes only a few words, selecting those that are highly predictable from the context. As readers begin to make more effective use of meaning and language cues to predict words, the teacher deletes more words, including those that are less predictable. An easy way to make cloze activities is to cut up pieces of self-adhesive notes to cover selected words in texts. An example of a cloze passage created from a story in *Ranger Rick* (October 1994) is shown in Box 6.5.

Box 6.5   Sample Cloze Passage

The first paragraph (not shown here) is left intact so children will already have begun to make meaning by the time they get to the first blank. In that paragraph, Scarlett Fox and Ranger Rick Raccoon are in a picnic area near the ocean when they see a white shapeless form in the fog.

"Look, it's coming back!" Rick whispered in horror as the Thing came right toward them. Suddenly it _____ over their picnic basket and fell in a heap. Now Rick and Scarlett could see that the white thing was a _____ and out from under it crawled their friend Boomer Badger. He laughed gleefully between gulps of _____ as he tried to catch his breath.

Source: Reading passage excerpted from N. Steiner Mealy, "Adventures of Ranger Rick," *Ranger Rick*, October 1994, p. 40.

When introducing cloze activities, the teacher might begin with a whole class activity focused on material presented on an overhead projector. The teacher models the process by reading through the entire passage with the students before they try to fill in the blanks. Once all students have read through the passage, a student volunteer reads the first sentence and supplies the missing word. Other students who responded differently read the sentence and provide their responses. Class discussion centres on such questions as:

- Why did you choose this word?
- What do you know about the topic in this passage that helped you predict this word?
- What in the passage helped you to make this prediction?
- Is there a difference in the meaning when we choose your word rather than X's?
- Why did different students predict different words?

Later, the teacher gives students cloze passages to complete individually. The teacher asks children to explain in small group discussions why they used particular words, again focusing on knowledge and text cues. The small group discussions might then lead to large group discussion of some of the more interesting or controversial items.

It is not important in cloze activities for children to predict the author's exact word. As long as the predictions make sense and sound right in relation to the rest of the passage, they are accepted. By insisting on exact replacements, the teacher sends the children the message that text cues are more important than knowledge when making meaning, and the task is reduced to a "guess what word the author used" activity.

As with instructional techniques for using cues within words, it is important that children understand why they are reading predictable books and doing cloze activities. Otherwise they may not realize that they should use similar strategies to predict words when they come to unfamiliar words as they read both language arts and other materials across the curriculum.

STRATEGIES FOR INTEGRATING CONTEXT AND PRINT CUES

We believe that in a balanced literacy program most word identification techniques should help children use *both* context and print cues, rather than one or the other. This section begins with a description of how one teacher provides this type of instruction. The remainder of the section presents instructional techniques designed to help children integrate strategies for using context and print cues as they read.

In Maureen Kelly's Grade 2 classroom, the first thing children do in the morning is read the morning message to find out what they will be doing that day. Maureen omits letters from some of the words, which encourages the children to predict what words will make sense and sound right and to associate letters with sounds in those words. When she notes that several children in the class are having difficulty with marking long vowel sounds in their writing, her minimal cues message includes several words containing the final *e* (e.g., "Today we will mak_ puppets and writ_ a story about something we lik_"). As the children predict the words, they discuss what letter needs to go on the end of each word and notice that in all the words, the sound of the vowel in the middle is the same as the name of the letter.

After the morning message has been completed and the children are working on group projects, Maureen calls together the six children whose writing reflects difficulty with final *e* and provides direct instruction. She tells them what she has noticed in their writing, beginning by noting what final-*e* words they spelled correctly and then focusing on those spelled incorrectly. She gives the children word cards containing words with long vowel sounds, and they sort the words according to whether they contain the final *e* or not. Before they leave the group, the children revisit their writing and correct words containing the final *e*. When the children begin another writing activity later that morning, Maureen reminds them to think about the final *e* spelling pattern. The message the next morning again includes final-*e* words for review, but introduces two vowels together as well.

The instruction in Maureen Kelly's classroom is explicit, systematic, and at the same time integrated. In the remainder of this section, we describe instructional techniques that teachers can integrate into their language arts program to help children use both print and context cues as they read.

Masking

Holdaway (1979) describes how to use "masking" to help young children use context cues, structural units, and letter sounds to identify words. Working with either a transparency or a big book, the teacher uses a strip of paper to mask text lines and slides it aside to gradually expose parts of words, complete words, and phrases. Children read to the point where the next word is covered and predict what will come next. Then the teacher uncovers the word so the children can use print cues to check their predictions. Discussion focuses on how predictions are made and where cues come from.

Minimal Cue Messages

The morning message in Maureen Kelly's classroom described above was presented in a "minimal cue" format. Such messages, a modification of the cloze procedure, are set up to encourage integration of print and meaning cues and to aid spelling and word identification. Teachers can develop minimal cue messages to focus on specific types of print cues (e.g., endings, vowel digraphs) when the teacher identifies this need.

The teacher writes a message to the children with some of the letters missing. Dashes are generally used to show how many letters are required. For example:

Tod_ _ is a _ery sp_cial d_ _. W_ are go_ _ _ to th_ m_seu_.

These messages work best when they are relevant to the children and the language is natural and predictable. It is important that teachers discuss with the children what cues they used in unlocking the minimal cue message. Discussion focuses on both meaning and print cues, such as "I knew the word had to be *museum* because you told us yesterday that we were going to the museum today. I also saw that the word began with the letter *m*."

Initially the teacher fills in the children's predictions, but gradually the children take over the writing. Children who have been exposed to this technique often begin to write minimal cue messages to other students or the teacher.

Oral Reading

When children are reading orally, the way the teacher responds to their reading communicates a great deal about what cues and strategies the teacher thinks are important. If a teacher constantly says, "Sound it out" when the child has difficulty, the child may come to believe that reading equals sounding out. We recommend the following guidelines:

- If a child pauses during reading, wait to give the child time to use both context and print cues to identify the word. Encourage her or him to predict a word that makes sense, sounds right, and checks out.
- If a child makes a substitution while reading that is consistent with the author's meaning, ignore the miscue. Research shows that even good readers do not read with 100 percent accuracy; instead, they make some meaningful slips because of the constructive nature of reading. Ignoring such miscues communicates to children that making meaning is the essence of reading.
- If a child corrects a mistake, reinforce this by commenting on the appropriateness of the correction, rather than focusing on the error.
- If a child makes miscues that do not make sense, leave time for self-correction. If the child does not self-correct, ask whether what he or she read sounded right and made sense. Focus discussion on the meaning the child constructed from the reading.

For each instructional technique included in this chapter, we recommend having children talk about the strategies being used. Through discussion, they develop both metacognitive awareness of strategies and control of their reading. However, the ultimate goal is automatic application of word identification strategies most of the time so children are able to focus their attention on meaning. The next section deals with helping children achieve automaticity.

FLUENCY/AUTOMATICITY

Adams (2002) indicates that the amount of effort we need to invest in a task lies along a continuum with automatic processing at one end and controlled processing at the other end. We are able to complete tasks that are overlearned automatically. In contrast, we depend upon controlled processing for tasks that are not overlearned, and our mind can only focus on one controlled process at a time. During reading, the tasks of constructing and monitoring meaning place a continual demand on active attention. Hence, if we need to attend to word identification as we read, our comprehension will be negatively affected.

Although there has been considerable criticism of sight word approaches (often referred to as "look and guess"), it is now clear that a crucial factor in skilled reading is the ability to recognize words effortlessly and automatically. In order to achieve automaticity, children need to read, read, and read some more. Rossman (1987) estimates that children need to read for a minimum of three-and-a-half hours every week to achieve automaticity when reading material at their independent reading level.

The National Reading Panel (2000) states there is ample evidence that one of the major differences between good and poor readers is in the quantity of time they spend reading. Research has revealed that children in high-level reading groups tend to spend more time reading than children in lower-level reading groups (Bloome and Green, 1984). The difference between good and poor readers in the amount of time they spend reading increases during their years in school. Good readers read more both at home and at school, while poor readers read very little in either context. Stanovich (1986) refers to this as a "Matthew effect"—the rich get richer and the poor get poorer. Since good readers are more likely than poor ones to read outside the classroom, it is imperative that time be set aside in school for all children to read.

In an examination of research on the efficacy of repeated oral reading and independent silent reading, the National Reading Panel (2000, p. 12) concluded that "guided repeated oral reading that included guidance from teachers, peers, or parents had a significant and positive impact on word recognition, fluency, and comprehension across a range of grade levels." We include two oral reading techniques in this section, both of which involve considerable guidance and feedback. The results on independent silent reading were not as clear-cut because, according to the National Reading Panel, there were not enough high-quality studies available. Without contradictory evidence, we recommend that techniques such as sustained silent reading be included as one component in a balanced reading program.

Sustained Silent Reading

This activity, developed by Hunt (1971), is becoming more prevalent in schools today, and many adaptations have appeared (e.g., DEAR—drop everything and read). In addition to the opportunity it provides for increased exposure to reading, it helps create an atmosphere in which reading and books are extremely important. In the classroom, the child gains a positive image of reading by seeing the teacher and other children enjoying books.

The steps we recommend for implementing sustained silent reading (SSR) are presented in Box 6.6. Initially, the block of time should be short enough to ensure success, but gradually it can be increased to 15 to 20 minutes per day. Sometimes teachers use a timer to indicate that SSR is over. Teachers also terminate the period depending on their observations. It is important that SSR end on a positive note while children are still interested in what they are reading. Interruptions are not permitted. A sign on the door indicating that SSR is in progress will minimize interruptions. Because of the power of modelling, it is essential that teachers also read during this time rather than catching up on other work.

Box 6.6   Steps to Implement Sustained Silent Reading (SSR)

1. The teacher discusses SSR with the children so they know what they will be doing, why they are doing it, what behaviours are expected of them, and how long they will be reading. For example, all students will read a book they have chosen, everyone will be quiet, and no one will move around the room.

2. Children are given advance notice so that they will have books chosen beforehand.

3. The teacher provides children with some background for choosing what to read by acquainting them with all kinds of books and by talking about books with them. The teacher "sells" books to children by reading parts of an interesting or exciting book to them to entice them to finish the book on their own.

4. Both teacher and children settle into comfortable spots in the classroom and read silently.

Paired Reading

Paired reading, a technique developed in England by Topping (1987), involves a child reading with another reader from a book the child has selected. The other reader may be the child's parent, a volunteer, a teacher, or another child. The activity is done for 10 to 15 minutes on at least five days per week for eight to twelve weeks.

The steps in paired reading are presented in Box 6.7. Tutors praise children for appropriate signalling, self-correcting, and fluent reading. They also encourage children to talk about the meaning they have constructed both during and after reading.

Repeated Reading

This technique is designed to develop sight vocabulary and self-concept as well as increased automaticity or fluency. The technique (Samuels, 1979) involves having the student read a short, meaningful passage several times until a satisfactory level of fluency is attained. Either the teacher or the student selects the material to be read, but it should be material the student is able to read independently and that he or she is interested in. If longer stories are chosen, short selections of 50 to 200 words are marked off for rereading.

The student reads the selection to the teacher, who records reading speed and number of word recognition errors on a graph. The teacher and student set a goal for both reading speed (e.g., 90 words per minute) and accuracy (no more than five errors in a 100-word

> ### Box 6.7   Steps in Paired Reading
>
> 1. The child chooses a book to read.
>
> 2. Beginning with a prearranged signal, the child and another reader read aloud together.
>
> 3. It is important for the child to read each word correctly. If he or she doesn't, the other reader reads the word correctly, the child repeats it, and they continue reading together.
>
> 4. Using another prearranged signal (e.g., a nudge or tap), the child indicates that he or she is ready to read alone. The other reader praises the child.
>
> 5. The child reads alone until an error is made or a word is encountered that he or she cannot read in five seconds.
>
> 6. The reader immediately rejoins the child by saying the difficult word and having the child repeat it, and then they continue reading together until the child gives the signal again and the procedure is repeated or the session ends.

Source: Based on A. Brailsford, *Paired reading: Positive reading practice* (Edmonton: Northern Alberta Reading Specialists Council, 1991), pp. 3–4.

passage). The student practises reading the selection until he or she reads at or above the goal set. Then the teacher and student select another passage, and the procedure is repeated. The graph provides a visual display of the student's increasing fluency. Samuels found that both the initial speed of reading passages and the number of rereadings required to reach the goal decreased over time.

Koskinen and Blum (1986) modified repeated reading so that two children work together rather than with the teacher, making the technique more practical for the classroom context. In paired, repeated reading, children read together for 10 to 15 minutes. Each child reads a short passage at his or her independent reading level three times and then evaluates his or her own reading as well as that of a partner. Paired repeated reading involves the following steps:

1. Children choose partners or are assigned partners by their teacher.
2. Children select their own passages of approximately 50 words to read. Some children need guidance to select material at their independent level.
3. The children read their passages silently and then decide who will be the first reader.
4. The first reader reads his or her passage to a partner three times, asking for help with words if needed. After each oral reading, the reader fills in a "How well did I read?" self-evaluation sheet. This sheet consists of a Likert scale ranging from Fantastic to Terrible (Fantastic, Good, Fair, Not So Good, Terrible). For young children, teachers use pictures to represent the points on the scale. The partner listens to the child read, and after the second and third reading, tells the reader how his or her reading improved. The listener never makes negative comments.
5. The children switch roles.

Teachers introduce and model the technique for children, helping them understand (1) the procedures involved, (2) how to listen and make positive comments (e.g., "I noticed you self-corrected," "read in phrases," "read more smoothly," "knew more words"), and (3) how to select material for reading. After teachers provide supervised practice, children are able to use the technique independently.

> Although these techniques ensure that children spend at least some time reading, the ultimate goal of language arts programs is to create the context in which children *become* readers. The instructional techniques included in this chapter help children learn *how* to read. Purposeful reading experiences with a wide range of children's literature and other written material entice them into the world of readers.

SELECTING INSTRUCTIONAL TECHNIQUES

The major focus of Chapters Five and Six has been on techniques to foster the development of effective reading strategies. These techniques are appropriate for readers at all levels of reading proficiency. Research shows that instructional techniques for poor readers tend to focus more on specific skill worksheets or management rather than on text comprehension (Johnston and Allington, 1991). There is little evidence that these types of programs are effective with poor readers. Indeed, they may do more harm than good (Pearson, 1993).

What we need is differentiated instruction, and the key is matching instructional techniques to the needs of specific children. Table 6.2 summarizes common patterns of reading processing and identifies techniques that are appropriate to use with children who display each pattern.

> As a teacher, you will be bombarded on a regular basis with people who claim to have found the answer to reading problems. It may be a diet, it may be exercises, it may be a specific commercial program, it may be listening or visual devices. But whenever someone presents one answer for all children with reading difficulties, alarm bells should sound. Reading is a complex process. Reading difficulties arise from a complex interaction of factors within the child, the school, and the broader community. There are no simple answers. Each may be part of the solution for some children, but none will be the total solution for all children.

SUMMARY ▬▬▬▬▬▬▬▬▬▬▬▬▬▬▬▬▬▬▬▬▬

Word identification has traditionally been taught from a skills perspective, with a focus on sight vocabulary, phonics, structural analysis, and contextual analysis. Recently, there has been an increased call for more attention to phonics in reading programs, but children need to learn strategies for using both print-based and knowledge-based information to be able to identify words as they read. Teachers are faced with several issues when planning phonics instruction, including how much terminology to use, how to deal with phonic rules, whether to use an analytic or synthetic phonics approach, whether to provide separate or integrated phonics instruction, and, finally, whether to teach phonics incidentally or systematically.

Table 6.2 Matching Reading Patterns and Instructional Techniques

Type of Pattern	Recommended Techniques
• Child is a word caller and needs to make more effective use of background knowledge along with text to construct meaning.	• Select techniques from "Integrating Knowledge-Based and Text-Based Information" (Chapter Five).
• Child relies too heavily on phonics knowledge to decode words and produces nonsense words when he or she reads orally.	• Begin with techniques from "Context Cues" and move quickly to those for "Integrating Context and Print Cues" (Chapter Six).
• Child has few strategies for using cues within words and constructs a different meaning from text information or little meaning at all.	• Begin with techniques from "Print Cues," and as soon as the child develops some of these strategies, move to those for "Integrating Context and Print Cues" (Chapter Six).
• Child can decode short words but has difficulty with longer ones.	• Select "Word Sorting" or "Word Parts" techniques (Chapter Six).
• Child uses strategies for processing cues within words but constructs a different meaning from text information.	• Select techniques from "Integrating Knowledge-Based and Text-Based Information," emphasizing text-based information initially (Chapter Five), and from "Integrating Context and Print Cues" (Chapter Six).
• Child reads slowly and laboriously, giving so much attention to word identification that little is left for comprehension.	• Select techniques from "Fluency/Automaticity" (Chapter Six).
• Child constructs meaning when reading stories but has difficulty with informational texts.	• Select techniques from "Using Text Structure: Informational Texts" (Chapter Five).
• Child appears to think the meaning is in the text and can deal only with factual questions.	• Select techniques from "Integrating Knowledge-Based and Text-Based Information" (Chapter Five).

Instructional techniques to help children develop phonemic awareness are most effective when they involve printed letters as well as sounds. One effective technique with young children involves having them hear and see similarities and differences among their names and other concrete words. Another effective technique involves using boxes to help children hear sounds in all parts of words and to link these sounds with letters. Techniques to help children develop strategies for using cues within words and for identifying words using phonics knowledge include word walls, onsets and rimes, making words, word sorting, and word parts.

Context cues provide a way for children to use their language and world knowledge to predict words as they read. Predictable books support the use of context cues, particularly by young children. In the cloze procedure, words are omitted from passages and children use their language and world knowledge to predict words and monitor their predictions.

The most effective instructional techniques for word identification involve developing strategies for using both print and context cues. Teachers integrate techniques such as masking and minimal cue messages into daily reading activities and are thoughtful as they respond to children's oral reading, reinforcing use of print, language, and meaning cues.

The ultimate goal of word identification instruction is to help children develop automaticity in using both print and context cues so that they are able to focus most of their attention on constructing meaning. Sustained silent reading, paired reading, and repeated reading are activities that enable children to reach this goal.

None of the instructional techniques described in Chapters Five and Six will meet the needs of all children. A major goal of teachers is to assess each child's reading needs and match the program as closely as possible with these needs. This is particularly critical for children who have difficulty learning to read.

SELECTED PROFESSIONAL RESOURCES

4 Blocks Literacy Centre Web site. Available: www.teachers.net/4blocks. This site provides a forum for teachers who use the 4-Blocks Literacy Program developed by Patricia Cunningham and Dorothy Hall. It contains a monthly column that deals with specific questions or general topics, listservs, chat boards, lessons, and resources. The site deals with all four blocks: guided reading, self-selected reading, working with words, and writing.

Pinnell, G. S. and Fountas, I. C. (1998). *Word matters: Teaching phonics and spelling in the reading/writing curriculum*. Portsmouth, NH: Heinemann. Pinnell and Fountas present a concept they call "word solving." Their goal is to help children learn to take words apart, to help them in their search for meaning when reading, and to construct words from letters and letter clusters when writing. They share instructional techniques for teachers to use in three contexts—reading, writing, and word study. They also include several useful word lists for sight word and phonics instruction.

Rasinski, T. V. and Padak, N. D. (2001) *From phonics to fluency*. New York: Longman. Rasinski and Padak focus on instructional strategies for word study and reading fluency. They provide ideas for teachers on phonemic awareness, word making, word walls, word sorts, word banks, onsets and rimes, context-based strategies, and reading fluency.

CHILDREN'S MATERIAL NOTED IN CHAPTER SIX

Mealy, N. S. (October 1994). Adventures of Ranger Rick. *Ranger Rick*, 40–43.

REFERENCES

Adams, M. J. (1990). *Beginning to read: Thinking and learning about print*. Cambridge, MA: MIT Press.

Adams, M. J. (2002). Alphabetic anxiety and explicit, systematic phonics instruction: A cognitive science perspective. In S. B. Neuman and D. K. Dickinson (eds.), *Handbook of early literacy research* (pp. 66–80). New York: The Guilford Press.

Ball, E. W. and Blachman, B. A. (1991). Does phoneme segmentation training in kindergarten make a difference in early word recognition and developmental spelling? *Reading Research Quarterly*, 26, 49–66.

Bloome, D. and Green, J. (1984). Directions in the sociolinguistic study of reading. In R. Barr, M. L. Kamil, and P. B. Mosenthal (eds.), *Handbook of reading research* (pp. 395–421). New York: Longman.

Brabham, E. G. and Villaume, S. K. (2001). Building walls of words. *Reading Teacher*, 54 (7), 700–702.

Brailsford, A. (1991). *Paired reading: Positive reading practice*. Edmonton: Northern Alberta Reading Specialists Council.

Byrne, B. and Fielding-Barnsley, R. (1993). Evaluation of a program to teach phonemic awareness to young children: A 1-year follow-up. *Journal of Educational Psychology*, 85, 104–111.

Chall, J. S. (1967). *Learning to read: The great debate*. New York: McGraw-Hill.

Clay, M. M. (1993). *Reading recovery: A guidebook for teachers in training*. Portsmouth, NH: Heinemann.

Clymer, T. (1963). The utility of phonic generalizations in the primary grades. *Reading Teacher, 16*, 252–258.

Cunningham, P. M. and Allington, R. L. (2003). *Classrooms that work: They can all read and write* (3rd ed.). New York: Longman.

Cunningham, P. M. and Cunningham, J. W. (1992). Making words: Enhancing the invented spelling-decoding connection. *Reading Teacher, 46* (2), 106–113.

Elkonin, D. B. (1973). USSR. In J. Downing (ed.), *Comparative reading: Cross-national studies of behavior and processes in reading and writing*. New York: Macmillan.

4 Blocks goodies. 4 Blocks Literacy Center. Available: www.teachers.net/4blocks/goodies.html.

Gallant, R. (1970). *Handbook in corrective reading*. Columbus, OH: Charles E. Merrill.

Holdaway, D. (1979). *The foundations of literacy*. Gosford, Australia: Ashton Scholastic.

Hunt, L. C. (1971). Six steps to the individualized reading program (IRP). *Elementary English, 48*, 27–32.

Hurford, D. P., Johnston, M., Nepote, P., Hampton, S., Moore, S., Neal, J., Nueller, A., McGeorge, K., Huff, L., Award, A., Tatro, C., Juliano, C., and Huffman, D. (1994). Early identification and remediation of phonological-processing deficits in first-grade children at risk for reading disabilities. *Journal of Learning Disabilities, 27*, 647–659.

Johnston, F. P. (2001) The utility of phonic generalizations: Let's take another look at Clymer's conclusions. *Reading Teacher, 55* (2), 132–142.

Johnston, P. and Allington, R. (1991). Remediation. In R. Barr, M. L. Kamil, P. B. Mosenthal, and P. D. Pearson (eds.), *Handbook of reading research*, Vol. 2 (pp. 984–1012). White Plains, NY: Longman.

Koskinen, P. S. and Blum, I. H. (1986). Paired repeated reading: A classroom strategy for developing fluent reading. *Reading Teacher, 40* (1), 70–75.

National Reading Panel. (2000). *Teaching children to read: An evidence-based assessment of the scientific research literature on reading and its implications for reading instruction*. Washington, DC: National Institute of Child Health and Human Development. Available: www.nationalreadingpanel.org.

Pearson, P. D. (1993). Teaching and learning reading: A research perspective. *Language Arts, 70* (6), 502–511.

Pinnell, G. S. and Fountas, I. C. (1998). *Word matters: Teaching phonics and spelling in the reading/writing classroom*. Portsmouth, NH: Heinemann.

Rasinski, T. V. and Padak, N. D. (2001) *From phonics to fluency*. New York: Longman.

Rossman, A. D. (1987). Reading automaticity: The essential element of academic success. *Principal, 67*, 28–32.

Samuels, S. J. (1979). The method of repeated readings. *Reading Teacher, 32*, 403–408.

Smith, F. (1999). Why systematic phonics and phonemic awareness instruction constitute an educational hazard. *Language Arts, 77* (2), 150–155.

Stanovich, K. E. (1986). Matthew effects in reading: Some consequences of individual differences in the acquisition of literacy. *Reading Research Quarterly, 21* (4), 360–406.

Topping, K. (1987). Paired reading: A powerful technique for parent use. *Reading Teacher, 40*, 608–614.

Vacca, J. L., Vacca, R. T., and Gove, M. K. (1991). *Reading and learning to read* (2nd ed.). New York: HarperCollins.

Word families. LiteracyConnections.com. Available: www.literacyconnections.com/phonograms.html.

Chapter 7

The Process of Writing

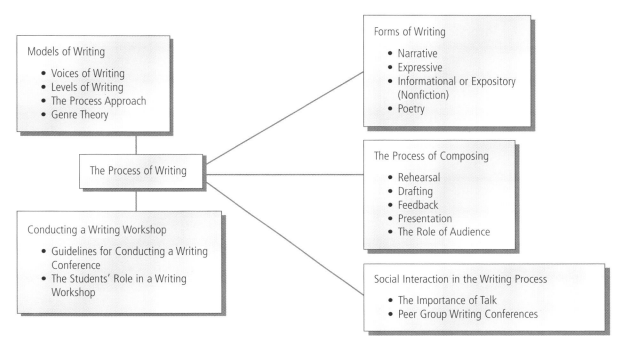

Models of Writing

- Voices of Writing
- Levels of Writing
- The Process Approach
- Genre Theory

The Process of Writing

Conducting a Writing Workshop

- Guidelines for Conducting a Writing Conference
- The Students' Role in a Writing Workshop

Forms of Writing

- Narrative
- Expressive
- Informational or Expository (Nonfiction)
- Poetry

The Process of Composing

- Rehearsal
- Drafting
- Feedback
- Presentation
- The Role of Audience

Social Interaction in the Writing Process

- The Importance of Talk
- Peer Group Writing Conferences

Dragon's Gaze

As the dragon grew upon the land, his body changed
First his hand. The scales appeared
His face was true, like a dragon's face
Then everyone knew
A shimmering glass, pink and grey in his mouth
a pearl lay
The dragon's eyes were looking at me
I looked away, towards my knee
The river full!
The thunder crackled in the sky. The splashing water on the grass
Rain!
Then I knew the dragon would be back again

"Dragon's Gaze" is a poem that was proudly shown to Monique during her first visit to her Grade 4 student teaching classroom. The writer explained to Monique that she had written it after their teacher had read Julie Lawson's book *The Dragon's Pearl* (1992) to the class. Monique was surprised to find that a student of this age could write such a vivid poem and immediately began to look forward to working with this group of student writers. Monique knew that writing instruction in elementary schools had changed dramatically over the last decade, but she wasn't exactly sure of how the changes had affected classroom instruction. Monique's cooperating teacher was encouraging and reminded Monique that a good place to start would be to reflect on her own experiences as a writer and to think about what student writers need in order to develop their abilities to create and express their ideas. The teacher suggested that Monique consider the following questions as useful entry points:

- What do children need to know and be able to do in order to develop as writers?
- What role does the teacher play in helping young writers to grow?
- How can the teacher structure writing instruction to promote growth in both fluency of ideas and control of writing skills?
- How can the teacher balance the need for creative expression with the need for clear communication?
- What forms of writing are appropriate for elementary students?

This chapter is designed to help Monique answer the above questions. It provides an introduction to models of writing, defines the writing process, and describes how the process may be realized in classroom practice.

MODELS OF WRITING

In the 1980s, teachers and researchers began to observe young writers in the act of composing (Graves, 1983; Calkins, 1986). They began to ask questions about the process that children used when writing: How do writers craft a piece of writing? How do they work on their ideas? How do they learn to shape the writing so that it is interesting and piques the interest of the audience? How do writers ensure that the piece says what they want it to say and that they have communicated the information and feelings they want to communicate? Teachers such as Graves and Calkins concluded that writing is a complex set of processes and skills that requires a command of the print code (*graphophonics*), grammar (*syntax*), and meaning-making devices (*semantics*), as well as of the physical act of creating print (handwriting or word processing). It is a generative rather than a receptive process. Like all writers, the creator of "Dragon's Gaze" generated meaning using all the cuing systems of the language and culture. Pat D'Arcy (1989), in her work as a language arts consultant, identified four elements of students' writing: processes (the thinking involved), products (the pieces of formatted writing), codes (spelling, punctuation, grammar, letters, words), and media (handwriting, word processing, notes, jottings, and so on). In a balanced instructional program, teachers help students to grow in each of these elements.

Writing is an act that is carried out with a specific purpose for a distinct audience. We use different voices, styles, genres and formats depending on the purpose and audience the writing is to serve. When student writers develop a sense of purpose and audience, they recognize that different genres help them to achieve their communication goals: letters, memos, poems, reports, editorials, invitations, journal entries, logs, diaries, essays, plays, film scripts, textbooks, novels, short stories, lists, recipes, instruction manuals, and so on. As writers, we can never separate a piece of writing from its form, function, or audience. Each one affects the others and shapes the piece of writing. We learn much of this from the reading we do every day in bus advertisements, television listings, mailbox coupons, letters to friends, application forms for jobs, cooking directions on packages of food, articles in magazines, and the novels we read. Every time we read, we learn more about writing and about what writers need to know and do to be effective.

Voices of Writing

James Britton (1970) proposed a model of writing based on the voice of the writer. **Voice** refers to the combined effects of the writer's purpose, style, tone, and other intangibles, such as commitment, energy, conviction, and personality. Britton identified three voices of writing: expressive, poetic, and transactional. The expressive voice is used when we write in a journal, write a personal letter to a friend, or write in a notebook about ideas that have lingered in our minds. It expresses who we are and what we think and feel. In expressive writing, which usually tends to be informal, we articulate ideas that are close to us, that may not yet be fully shaped. Below is an excerpt from a piece of expressive writing by a boy in Grade 4, written as he thought about the book *On My Honor* by Marion Dane Bauer (1986):

> I hate it when my friends try to convince me to do things they want to do. I think Tony is being quite mean to Joel. I think that Tony just wants Joel to do what he wants to do. I can swim but not too good. But even if I was a professional swimmer I'd never swim in a river. I think it's a bad idea because the water is pushing you. It would just suck you up. A few minutes later you'd be dead.

Poetic writing is more literary and is used in stories as well as poems. Usually created for an audience other than the self, poetic writing often contains an aesthetic element not usually present in either expressive or transactional writing. "The Dragon's Gaze" is an example of poetic writing, and so is the following poem completed by a child in Grade 3:

Cowboys

Brave and dirty,
Hazing,
Roping,
Digging their spurs into the horses.
Riding,
Racing,
Branding the cattle
Cowpunchers.

Transactional writing is used when the writer wants to convey information to others in a report, list, essay, recipe, movie review or textbook. It is usually more formal than personal, focusing principally on the effective communication of content. However, transactional writing balances information with a personal perspective, as demonstrated in

"About Seasons," presented in Exhibit 7.1. "About Seasons" was completed by a child in Grade 1 who visited the Cayman Islands with her family at Christmas time. When Tanya returned to Canada she suddenly understood the importance of seasons and realized that seasons exist all over the world, but that they vary in nature. Tanya was excited by her discovery and wanted to capture her ideas on paper so that she could present them to her classmates.

Britton noticed that young writers frequently move from one voice to another as they write. When writing a report on a pet, for example, they may add a personal anecdote about their own pet, and hence combine the expressive and transactional voices. Similarly, they may shift from the poetic to the expressive voice when writing a story, adding themselves as a character and writing in the first person. Britton terms this the *transitional voice*. In "About Seasons" (Exhibit 7.1), although it did not alter the voice of her writing, Tanya could not resist adding her address and phone number to the bottom of the page, thus ensuring her own personal stamp was placed on her piece. Usually, as writers mature, they are able to select an appropriate voice for their writing and remain consistently within that voice.

Levels of Writing

James Moffett (1979) proposed a model of writing development that suggests a hierarchy according to the skills the writer needs and the purpose the writing is to serve. The first level is that of drawing or handwriting. This is the level at which children begin writing, as they struggle to make sense of the written language system and to replicate it. The second level is copying, where children are capable of copying from a model provided by someone else. At this point, the focus is on learning the correct form of letters and sentences rather than generating ideas. The third level is transcribing or paraphrasing, where writers take someone else's ideas and write them in their own language and own words. The next level is crafting, where children generate meaning through writing in a conventional form. Here they focus on the structure of a piece and on communicating their meaning to the reader in the most effective way. The final level is what Moffett calls "the revision of inner speech." He claims this is the only true form of writing, for it involves expressing and shaping one's own thoughts. He also claims that it is rarely found in classrooms. An example of this final level is shown below. The piece was written just after the writer, in Grade 4, had read *On My Honor* (Bauer, 1986).

> Chapter eight confused me at the beginning.
> It didn't exactly say that Joel had gone home.
> When he was at home, I think I understood

Exhibit 7.1   About Seasons

About Seasons

It is almost spring. The weather changes to be warmer because the season is changing to be spring, after spring is summer which is very hot.

In some countries are even very hot during winter because they are closer to the equator, especially Africa. Some of Africa is on the equator. That's why giraffes live there.

After summer comes fall again. In fall the leaves start to fall off the trees and get ready for winter. Winter has a lot of snowstorms and people wear a lot of clothes because the weather is very cold and people think that if they wear a little more clothing they will keep warmer.

Each season is different every year.

why and how he lied. Telling the truth in tough situations is very difficult. I would never lie at all, even in a problem like that. My friend's mom just moved here a little while ago and the apartment they lived in was allowed no children. Quite absurd! She only got to live there because she said she was a doctor. Stuff like that makes me very untrusting of the world. Taking a person by how much money they have etc. When I read that chapter I felt Joel's insecurity. He seems to be not acting normal with the problems he's having. A kid dealing with something like that is real scary!

In this piece, the writer is thinking through her feelings about lying. As she writes about the character in the book, she reflects on her own experiences with telling the truth and how, at times, people are moved to lie in order to survive. The writer struggles with the ambivalence she feels, knowing that lying is wrong, but understanding a little of why at times even good people might be dishonest.

Moffett (1979) maintains that children are more likely to be successful, thoughtful, articulate, and skilful writers when they engage in all five levels of writing in the classroom. He also maintains that all levels of writing should be taught. Moffett expresses concern that if instruction is confined to copying from the board, children will be less likely to develop the skills necessary for writing their own compositions. Likewise, if children are restricted to crafting polished pieces of writing with the aim of making them public in a writing workshop, they will be denied the opportunity of learning how to use writing as a way of exploring thought. Moffett's chief concern, in 1979, was that too much of the writing children were required to do in school was for the purpose of evaluating what they had learned. This is still a concern of many educators today.

The Process Approach

In the 1970s, Donald Graves (1983) conducted research that led to a major shift in the teaching of writing in elementary schools, secondary schools, and colleges. His work, along with that of Lucy Calkins (1986 and 1991), Nancie Atwell (1998), and others, focuses on the process of writing and promotes a workshop approach to the teaching of writing. This means that children work with one another and their teachers, composing, drafting, revising, editing, and publishing their works. Graves' work enabled teachers to reconceptualize writing as a series of processes that a writer goes through when writing. When teachers take a workshop approach, they engage in writing themselves and so develop a fuller understanding of what a writer goes through to create a composition, making it clear and conventionally appropriate for an audience. The process requires time, thought, and the reworking of multiple drafts. The focus is on the process of composing and the thinking that must take place to develop a successful piece of writing. Graves' work has fundamentally changed the way educators think about the writing process and the teaching of writing in schools.

Genre Theory

The 1990s saw the implementation of a genre-based approach to teaching writing. The approach was developed in the field of educational linguistics and was based on the work of Halliday and Hasan (1985). The word "genre" is often used today to describe books, music and film. Genre theory in the teaching of writing involves identifying the language features and structures of a range of different types of written texts and teaching them explicitly. It is important to remember that genres are not static forms but that they evolve

Exhibit 7.2 Kennedy's Organization of Information from Field Notes

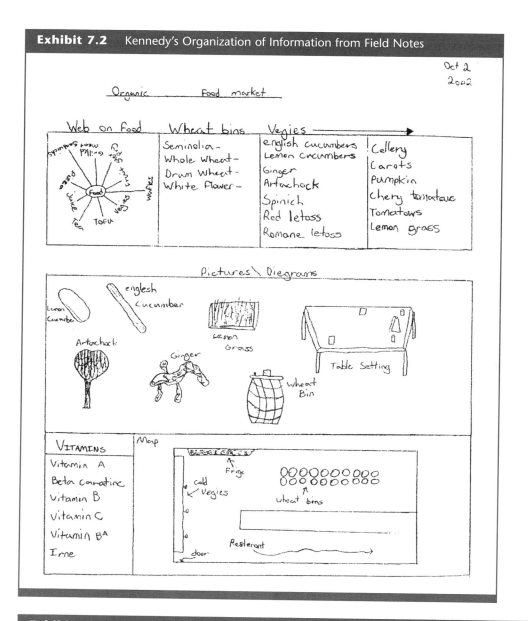

Exhibit 7.3 Marina's Restaurant Review

Harold's Veggie House

This restaurant makes the best food in the whole world. Maybe the whole galaxy. By now you are probably wondering what does this restaurant make that is so good? Five words 'sweet and sour veggie pork'. I am a vegetarian. You, I am guessing, are wondering if she is a vegetarian how can she eat pork? Simple, fake meat like tofu. My mom would agree the sweet and sour veggie pork, but she prefers the lamb curry. We both like to share the veggie hot pot. The service at this restaurant is fabulous as soon as you come to your seat. They leave you to take your coats off and get comfy.

Then they come and take your drink order. Your drink comes quickly you have to read the menu and decide what your ordering. Your food comes quickly. They check on you enough times that you know your being token care of, but not so many times that you feel as if you don't have any privacy. I would recommend this restaurant to people who like to try new things. Stop by your local veggie house today.

and change over time in response to social and cultural changes. Different types of writing, however, have recognizable organizational patterns or structures and genre theorists maintain that these forms should be directly taught in classrooms. In Australia, Martin, Rothery and Christie (1987), among others, demonstrated that only a few genres of writing were taught in elementary school classrooms and that the structures of these genres were generally not taught at all. In other words, children were experiencing a limited range of genres and teachers were not explaining how these genres were structured or what their characteristics are. It is an observation made repeatedly in Canada, the United States, and Britain, where children's writing in school consists mainly of personal expressive writing or stories.

Readers of newspapers and magazines are quick to identify different genres: recipes, movie or restaurant reviews, letters, editorials, reports, interviews, and so on. Researchers have identified seven major genres that children can master: recount (chronological retellings of events—"I went to hockey practice"), report (classificatory descriptions of processes and things—"Grizzly bears live in the Rocky Mountains"), procedure (how something is done—"First you put in the peanut butter"), explanations (how something works or occurs—"As the temperature drops below zero the water in the jar begins to freeze"), discussion (argument from a range of perspectives and with a conclusion—"Should the cat bylaw be abandoned?"), persuasion (promoting one point of view—"I think the cat bylaw should be maintained"), and narrative—"One day, the fox crept out of her den" (Bunting, 1998). The *First Steps Writing: Resource Book* (Education Department of Western Australia, 1994) is an excellent source of information and ideas for teachers who wish to work with different genres of writing in their classrooms.

The main issues in genre theory are the extent to which direct teaching of text structures should take place and the pedagogical implications of the direct teaching of linguistic forms. As with many aspects of the language arts, we feel that text structures are best taught in the context of a specific purpose and activity. Children can learn to write almost any genre if they have an authentic purpose for doing so. Teacher Julie Gellner uses the Project Approach (Chard, 1998) in her Grade 4/5 classroom. When her students worked on a restaurant project recently, they conducted extensive research and organized a "restaurant evening" at their school. The total project lasted for about three months. Ms. Gellner strove to maintain an atmosphere where the children's interests were piqued and their thinking and writing were challenged. She created a community of learners that supported one another in asking and answering questions, and where the children and teacher respected one another's ideas.

In preparation for the event, the students visited a number of restaurants and markets, and they invited guest speakers to visit their classroom. They made field notes about how the restaurants were run, wrote reviews of the restaurants they visited, explored the jobs people hold in restaurants, and how restaurants plan and organize for their patrons. Exhibit 7.2 shows how Kennedy organized his field notes after he visited a local organic market and café. Exhibit 7.3 displays Marina's review of a restaurant she visited with her mother.

Each student in Ms. Gellner's class applied for a job in the restaurant. They created letters of application and personal résumés which they sent to the manager (Ms. Gellner). Allisa's resume and letter of application are presented in Exhibit 7.4. The students decided on what dishes would be on the menu, created and wrote menus for the evening (shown in Exhibit 7.5), designed invitations for parents and friends, made placemats, and organized the various jobs, timetables, cooking schedules, and the cleanup. Will's explanation of what a waitress is expected to do is presented in Exhibit 7.6.

Exhibit 7.4 Allisa's Letter of Application and Résumé

Allisa Garden
306 Dalrymple Road
Winnipeg, MB
M9X 5P2
325-4709

Ms. Gellner, Manager
Trail End Café
Dalrymple Community School
Winnipeg, MB

Dear Ms. Gellner:

My name is Allisa Garden and I am a very talented chef. I always do my best and try really hard. So right now I am trying to get a job at the Trail End Café. I would love to be a dessert chef, a salad chef or a bar tender.

I think I would be the best person for the dessert chef job because I went to a mini-chef camp this summer for two weeks. There I made lots of good treats. My family and friends really enjoyed the pleasant treats that I made.

I hope you will consider me for the dessert chef position. I have lots of enthusiasm and you will not regret hiring me. I hope to meet you soon and I think it would be a great pleasure to work for you.

Sincerely yours,

Allisa Garden

Allisa Garden

RÉSUMÉ
Allisa Garden
306 Dalrymple Road
Winnipeg, Manitoba
M9X 5P2
325-4709

Education
September 2003
Dalrymple Community School
Winnipeg, Manitoba
Grade 5

Experience and Extra Curricular Activities
I cook with grandmother often
I help my mother make supper
I took a cooking camp at Maple College for two weeks this summer
I like swimming, rock climbing, dancing and skiing

Special Skills
I have good people skills
I am very creative
I love to cook
I like to experiment with recipes
I wash my hands frequently

Name of References
Norma Garden
Mom
Phone: 325-4709 or 562-3798

Mike Garden
Dad
Phone: 325-4709 or 562-5103

Alison Sung
Best friend
Phone: 896-3568

Exhibit 7.5 Menu for the Trail End Café

Trail End Café

Appealing appetizers

Veggies and dip	$2.50
Chips and salsa	$3.00
Hummus and pita bread	$3.00

Scrumptious salads

Caesar salad	$3.00
Tossed salad with vinaigrette dressing	$3.00

Exotic entrée

Veggie bagel melt	$4.00

Delicious desserts

Variety of squares, cookies, tarts and cakes	$2.00

Desirable drinks

Italian soda	$2.25
Shirley Temple	$2.25
Fruit punch	$2.25
Cherry cola	$2.25

Complimentary

Coffee and tea

FORMS OF WRITING

Narrative

Narrative writing links a series of events together either through a sequence in time or through cause and effect. The purpose of most narrative writing is to entertain. Much of the narrative writing completed by students in elementary classrooms is fictional, but narrative can also be used for nonfiction texts. Narrative seems to be an almost natural way for human beings to make sense of the world. Barbara Hardy (1975) says that narrative is a "primary act of mind." We seem to think in narrative retelling events to ourselves to see how the pieces fit together, or telling ourselves how something works as we try to figure out a problem.

A distinction must be noted here between a recount and a narrative story. A **recount** is simply a retelling of events with no particular attention to setting, plot, problem or conflict resolution, climax, and so on. When writers develop a *story*, however, they craft the narrative in a certain way. In Western cultures a story is usually structured around an introduction, a middle section with a problem or conflict (sometimes a series of conflicts), and then an ending, which achieves some resolution of the problem. Applebee's 1978 study of the development of children's concept of story suggests that children have to learn to do two things simultaneously to successfully write or tell a story: chain events together, and focus on a theme, problem, or character. Applebee's research demonstrated that children begin to form stories from the age of two onward, but they learn to apply these two essential elements over time, mastering the story form (or "story grammar," as it is sometimes called) over a period of years.

As children mature, their stories become more complex and cohesive. Children become aware of an audience for their writing, and strive for clarity and an engaging text. An excerpt from a story written jointly by Sharon and Erica in Grade 5 is shown in Exhibit 7.7. Unfinished at the end of the school year, the story was put "on hold" by the girls because they were not sure what to do with it next and they had another piece of writing they wanted to start. This story will be referred to again later in the chapter in the section about the importance of talk. At that point, the girls' struggle with crafting and ending the piece becomes more apparent.

Expressive

Expressive writing, found in casual letters, diaries, and journals, is the kind of personal writing we do informally as thoughts form in our mind. We rarely revise or craft expressive writing. (Britton's use of the word "expressive" to describe one of the three voices of writing differs from this use, though there is some overlap in meaning.) Expressive writing is done for an audience who knows the writer, and sometimes the audience is the self. Expressive writing is a means through which we present our ideas, thoughts, feelings, and interpretations of events. It may include responses to books we have read and movies we have seen. The two written responses to *On My Honor* (Bauer, 1986) quoted earlier in this chapter are examples of expressive writing. Expressive writing is essentially exploratory. In expressive writing, just as in expressive speech, we speculate, hypothesize, predict, and generally articulate our thoughts.

Exhibit 7.6   *"What Can I Get You?"*
A waitress is someone who serves people and asks for their orders. They use a notepad and a pen. Now the waitress brings their order to the kitchen. When they are done ordering the people have to wait for a little bit before they get their food. Finally, the waitress comes back with the food on the tray. She gives people their food. After the people are done eating the waitress takes the dirty dishes, and then goes and gets the bill. After that the waitress gets the change if necessary. So that's what the waitress does.

Exhibit 7.7 An Excerpt from "The Wellington Story"

Written co-operatively by Sharon and Erica (Grade 5)

When the story begins, Mr. Wellington, a well-known artist, and his wife are hosting a dinner party.

After [the guests] arrived they all sat down for dinner. "Cheers to Mrs. Wellington for having this party," said Miss Murphy in a loud voice. Then they all lifted their glasses and clinked them together. "I'll go get my husband for dinner," said Mrs. Wellington and left. A few minutes later, Mrs. Wellington came back into the dining room. "My husband will be coming shortly," she said as Yvette started carving the turkey. After about ten minutes had passed Mrs. Wellington asked Yvette to go see where her husband was.

Yvette left the dining room and went to the paint house. There was a moment of silence and then Miss Murphy spoke. "The strangest thing happened to me yesterday," she said. "I ... Ahhhhhh." Miss Murphy was interrupted by a loud scream. Mrs. Wellington dropped her fork.

"It's coming from the paint house," said Mr. McGregor. They all rushed out to the paint house and saw Yvette shaking, with a knife in her hand. Mrs. Wellington gasped and walked into the paint house. She saw her husband lying dead on the floor. "Yvette," she screamed.

"How could you?" Mrs. Landenburg walked into the room, looked at the body and fainted. "Somebody call the police," said Mrs. Hunt. Mrs. Wellington started to cry. Mr. McGregor called the police. About 5 minutes later they arrived. "We were in the neighborhood," they said. "Now what happened?" Mrs. Wellington explained the whole thing. "Then we walked in and saw her," she said pointing to Yvette, "standing there with a knife in her hand. She did it officer, I know she did."

"Why don't you go into the house and rest while we look around and take the body away," said the police officer. Mrs. Wellington went into the lounge with the other guests. "It's all right Margaret. It had to happen sooner or later being a famous painter and all," said Miss Murphy. "He was such a kind husband to me," said Mrs. Wellington and then started to cry. Meanwhile in the paint house officer McCarther was searching around the floor when he spotted a loose floorboard.

He pulled back the floorboard and saw a white dress with a red wine stain on it. "Hmm," he said. Then he put on a pair of rubber gloves, picked up the dress and placed it in a plastic bag. Then he took a second look, and saw the top of a broken wine bottle. He picked up the wine bottle and put it into a plastic bag. Then he walked over to where Mr. Wellington was lying and picked up the knife that Yvette dropped and went into the lounge. "I'll have to take finger prints," said officer McCarther and pulled out a stamp pad in front of Mrs. Wellington. "Are you accusing me of killing my own husband? Why would I kill him?" asked Mrs. Wellington. "You might kill him for his money and besides everyone in the room is a suspect," said officer McCarther. "Why didn't I wait until he dies?" asked Mrs. Wellington.

The girls ended the story with the following note to themselves:

tired of story change some parts
Stop story for now
want to start cat by-law not doing a play
yet at least!

Source: C. Lewis, "Partnership writing: Ten-year-olds talking and writing together," MEd thesis, University of Alberta, Edmonton, AB, 1989.

Informational or Expository (Nonfiction)

Intended to explain, persuade or instruct, expository writing requires the writer to be well organized, clear, and coherent. This writing is not meant to convey feelings or to be primarily entertaining, but is intended to pass on information to an audience. Reports, textbooks, memos, flyers, editorials, movie reviews, and the "restaurant" writing shown earlier in this chapter are examples of expository writing. Lewis and Wray (1995) identified six nonfiction genres used regularly within our society: recount, report, procedural, explanation, persuasion, and discussion. They maintain that children in the elementary grades should be taught the basic elements of these genres and should have many opportunities for using them in the classroom. An example of a Grade 4 child's report writing is shown in Exhibit 7.8.

Persuasive writing is used more often in our society than we realize. Advertising, editorials, political campaign literature, religious tracts, and much of the unsolicited junk mail that arrives in mailboxes consists of persuasive writing. Someone wants to persuade others to do something, buy something, or believe something. Children use persuasive writing when they create a poster presentation about a book or a book celebration. They write persuasively when they want something very much and have to convince an adult to allow them to have it. At school, for example, this can be channelled into writing to

---

Exhibit 7.8   Grade 4 Report Writing: Music in Crousetown

The Anglican Church in Crousetown, has the oldest pipe organ in Nova Scotia. It still is used in 1993. Every Sunday music was a big entertainment in those days and it still is today.

Most of the music of long ago was made up for fun. Some children might take some spoons and clack them against their knees, or a little boy might put some beans in a can and shake the can.

At night some people might gather together in someone's house and listen to each other play fiddles and accordians.

In those days there were no heavy rock bands or electric guitars. In the old days some homes had piano or organ they would play for sing along songs. Instead of electric guitars some people would play wooden guitars.

They had just about the same fun the old fashioned way as we do with rock bands.

Source: Petite Rivière Elementary School, *History of Crousetown* (Lunenburg County, NS: Petite Rivière Publishing, 1993), p. 4.

---

government agencies to request a change of some kind. The writing might be part of a social studies or science project, and may involve a letter-writing campaign. An excerpt from a piece of persuasive writing by a Grade 6 child follows:

> I think instead of having a curfew we should have police patrolling the streets at night as a pair. I think we shouldn't have a curfew at night because there are a lot of people out that are not vandalizing the streets.
>
> I would like to talk about why there should be two policemen in each community and how they should work the streets. In my area we have different sorts of gangs. One kid that I know was riding his bike down the street and one of the gangs called Devil's Knights, one kid threw a knife and almost hit the kid. I think the police should talk to different people and ask questions about the gangs and where they meet. I hope we can get the perfect president to run a place like this.

The writing of a recount or anecdote can form the foundation for a highly descriptive verbal picture of a scene or event. Such writing invites the reader to participate in the experience though rich sensory detail. Careful crafting can make a descriptive recount particularly dramatic. Below is an excerpt from a recount written by a student in Grade 5.

> We'd been flying for almost an hour when a grotesque aroma floated from the back of the plane and filled the air. From experience, I knew that the meal was salmon and spinach paté. My stomach turned inside out at the thought of it. The old woman who I was sitting beside didn't help my stomach because she stank of Super Polly Grip, Efferdent and cheap perfume. The clickety-clack of her knitting needles was driving me insane as I tried to write a letter to my best friend, Brooke. I knew that she was going to be knitting for a long time because she had a pattern for a large sweater taped to the back of her tray and she was still on the first cuff!

Exhibit 7.9   Grade 2 Poetry

Bad Luck

I want a Ford but I get a Toyota.
I want a brother but I get a sister.
I want my name to be Ben but my name is Sam.
I want a pool but I get a garden.
I want to live in a house but I live in a hotel.
I want a dog but I get a cat.
I want to win. I win. Yaa!

Poetry

Poetry is a genre of writing and not a specific form such as narrative or persuasive writing. We are adding a short section on children's writing of poetry, however, because student teachers such as Monique, with whom we opened this chapter, frequently ask their instructors how they can go about teaching children how to write poetry.

Poetry is a genre that attempts to capture feelings, events, places, and people in an aesthetically pleasing way. A few poetic words or phrases convey a whole set of meanings in a particularly striking manner. Poetry is not defined by a rhyme scheme or rhythm, but is uniquely artistic, although sometimes disconcerting. "The Dragon's Gaze," "Cowboys," and "Bad Luck" (presented in Exhibit 7.9) are examples in this chapter of poetry written by children in the elementary grades. The children who wrote these poems found the genre to be most effective for the meanings they wanted to convey. Children at all the elementary grade levels seem to find poetry a singularly effective genre for their writing.

Children in the elementary grades write much excellent poetry when they are encouraged to make each word do its "most effective job." We stress here that it is not helpful to provide children with a pattern for their poetry writing (such as haiku, cinquain, limerick, or diamante). When children are faced with fitting their words into an already established pattern, they frequently encounter difficulties because the constraints of the form are too limiting. Writing a good limerick or haiku, for example, is extremely difficult and takes a great deal of hard work, even for an experienced writer. Children can end up with a poorly written poem that has been created simply to fit the assigned form. Teaching children various forms of poetry and inviting them to attempt a poem of their own in that format is appropriate only insofar as they are being introduced to the form and are aware of its structure and its name.

Found Poetry

Sometimes children can be effectively introduced to writing poetry when perceptive teachers help them to recognize the poems "hidden" in their writing. It is not unusual to find a poem submerged under a welter of "hitchhiker" words—words that are simply going along for the ride. The poem emerges as these are judiciously edited out. Such poetry is often referred to as "Found Poetry." For example, Lucy, a Grade 2 student, wrote a recount about a favourite memory. In her first draft she wrote:

> When I go to see my Grandma she always has the kettle boiling on the stove.
> When the steam comes hissing out she plops a teabag in the pot and makes a
> pot of tea. Then we sit down and have a family tea.

With her teacher's help she edited out the hitchhikers. Lucy ended up with the following poem, "A Visit with My Grandma":

> Kettle boiling on the stove
> Steam whistling out
> Here comes the teapot
> Plop in goes the teabag
> Tea with Grandma.

Teachers can also prepare their students for writing poetry by encouraging them, as Lucy's teacher did, to use strong and colourful verbs and specific nouns in all of their writing, rather than decorating their writing with adjectives and adverbs. In addition, students can be encouraged to experiment with syntactical patterns to create particular effects. Notice how the effect of Lucy's poem can be changed if the last line becomes the first, or if the poem is simply entitled "A Visit." Sometimes, teachers may challenge their student writers to capture an event, scene, or idea by "saying the most with the fewest words possible." Thus, writing poetry helps students to focus their writing and to realize just how flexible and powerful written language can be.

Found poems are also created by culling words from other sources such as newspapers, magazines, advertisements, songs, and stories. They can be authored by individual children or by groups of students working together. As a reader response activity, students may collect their favourite words and phrases from a book and reorganize them to express their responses to the book. After reading *Looking for X* by Debra Ellis (1999), one group of students created the following poem, entitled "Khyber":

> Nobody looked happy
> Even though it was the end of the work week
> And they were heading home.
> "Happy," said David.
> Autism, group home, clothes and toys in boxes.
> I cried until I fell asleep.
> A van pulled up beside me
> And Elvis stepped out.
> "Winsome—You know,
> You win some, you lose some."
> Blue suitcase, great backpack.
> Keep it simple and keep it dignified.
> Now, everyone who meets me
> Will go away thinking they've met
> Someone very interesting indeed.

A number of recently published "verse novels" have fostered children's interest in writing poetry. Sharon Creech's novel *Love That Dog* (2001) is a series of found poems written by the protagonist, Jack, on the urging of his teacher. Although Jack doesn't consider himself a poet, he writes about the poems and the poets his teacher introduces to the class. His found poems reveal his thoughts and feelings about himself as a writer and about the things that are most important to him. Steven Herrick's two Australian titles *The*

Spangled Drongo (1999) and *Tom Jones Saves the World* (2002) recount the humorous and heartwarming adventures of two boys as they come to terms with the opposite sex and with parents. The books make superb "read-alouds" and they demonstrate to children how "saying the most with the fewest words possible" can create lasting images and tell intriguing stories.

THE PROCESS OF COMPOSING

Most of what is known about composing comes from the observations of real writers and authors and the insights they provide. These writers often say there is no such thing as a finished piece of writing. As they write they think, and as they think and receive feedback, they revise, develop new ideas, begin new pieces, share old ones, and continue their development. As one aspect of thinking, writing both reflects and facilitates the exploration of ideas. The composition process is more spiral than linear, for writers do not stay in the same place for long when they write. They constantly anticipate what is needed and, in the process, develop new writing strategies, techniques, and ideas.

Rehearsal

The first stage of composing is often called collecting, rehearsing, or prewriting.

At this point, writers collect ideas, memories, and experiences that help them to decide on a topic. They decide on what should be included in the composition, and what memories and recollections they can use to develop it. Writers use mixtures of people they have known, places they have visited, and their own experiences, whether real or vicarious. Writers of published works tell us that all their stories are about themselves in some way. The American children's author Katherine Paterson recalls the loneliness and alienation she felt during her Grade 1 year in the United States, having spent the first six years of her life in China (Paterson, 1989). The theme of marginalization pervades many of her novels, including *The Great Gilly Hopkins* (1978), *Bridge to Terabithia* (1977), and *The Flip Flop Girl* (1994). We retain our memories and emotions, and these become the raw material of our writing. Children are just as capable as adults of choosing a topic and working with their experiences. They need help and encouragement, but the more they have ownership of their writing (i.e., assume responsibility for key decisions about topic choice, format, audience, and production time lines) and write about topics that interest them, the more they are likely to work at their writing and improve it. We learn to write by writing.

Drafting

Once a topic has been determined, the writer begins to draft a text, putting onto paper the intentions developed in the rehearsing stage. The text may go through many drafts, and be modified and reworked, with the original intentions in mind. During the drafting stage, the writer becomes clearer about what can actually be done and what needs to be changed. The writer may play with the drafts, changing words here and there, adding to it, deleting parts that are not effective, and rewriting parts that simply don't work. It is during this stage that the writer asks, "Am I meaning what I say and saying what I mean?" Writers strive for clarity and try to maintain the interest and attention of the audience. Sometimes thoughts do not fall into place until the writer starts writing; the actual process of writing enables the ideas to flow. In a sense, writing seems to slow down thinking. As writers write, they have time and opportunity to capture their thoughts, reflect on them, and connect them to previous thoughts a generative process. Published writers go through dozens of drafts of a text before it is ready for an audience. Elementary school children might complete three drafts in total, especially if they are just beginning to work with the writing process.

As a draft takes shape, the writer revises it many times, moving parts around, editing it, and ensuring that it is ready for an audience. This work is often done with a word processor, which facilitates revision like no other writing tool. Many children now learn keyboarding skills in Grade 3 or 4. The "Track Changes" function on word processing programs makes it simple for young writers to see their changes and keep track of their work. Children love working with "Track Changes," and it makes it easy for teachers to see what their students have written and what they have edited. Editing and revision skills can be taught in mini-lessons or in the conferences that are an essential component of any writing workshop. When children are writing on paper, they can prepare for revision by writing on one side of the paper only and on every other line. These practices enable them to cross out, write over top, use carets to insert text, and make other changes without having to copy a whole piece over.

The writing shown in Exhibits 7.10 and 7.11 demonstrates the changes that Wendy, a Grade 2 student, made to her report on whales as she worked through the writing process. The two pieces presented are excerpts from the first draft and the final draft of the report.

Exhibit 7.10 Excerpt from the First Draft of Wendy's Report on Whales	**Exhibit 7.11** Excerpt from the Final Draft of Wendy's Report on Whales
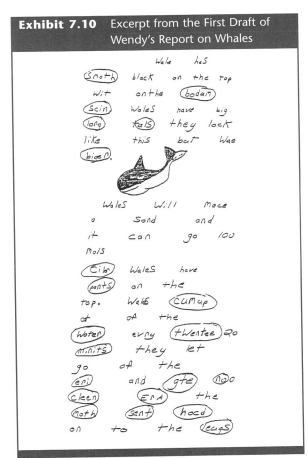	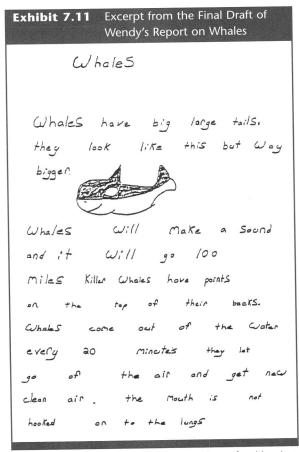

Source: F. Maaskant, "Children's perceptions of writing in a Grade One/Two classroom" (Appendix), MEd thesis, University of Alberta, Edmonton, AB, 1989.

Source: F. Maaskant, "Children's perceptions of writing in a Grade One/Two classroom" (Appendix), MEd thesis, University of Alberta, Edmonton, AB, 1989.

The children in Wendy's classroom were used to working through the writing process with both their poetic and transactional writing.

Feedback

Most student writers need feedback while they are in the process of creating a composition. Peer conferences and group or one-on-one conferences with the teacher are necessary so that children can obtain feedback on their writing when they need it, and not when it is too late to make changes. It is during these conferences that children have the best opportunity to learn about writing. Guidelines for conducting writing conferences are presented later in this chapter.

Presentation

The very last phase of the writing process is presentation, publication, or celebration. When a piece of writing is finished to an author's satisfaction, the piece can be shared with a wider audience. It might be read aloud to a whole class or group, made into a book and placed in the classroom or school library, sent to students at a nearby college, shared with residents of a seniors' home, or sent home to family. This is a time for celebrating the accomplishments of the writer. It is no longer a work-in-progress, and it is no longer appropriate for the audience to make critical comments or suggestions for change. The work will stand alone, ready for public scrutiny and the future enjoyment of reading audiences.

The Role of Audience

Establishing an authentic audience for children's writing makes a difference in how children go about the process of composition and revision, as the following story illustrates. Fran Chalmers and her teaching colleague in Edmonton assigned a writing activity on the topic of dogs to their respective Grade 1 classes. The activity "bombed" in both classrooms. The two teachers shared their dismay and tried to figure out a reason for it. Had the students not had enough time to share their thoughts with a partner before beginning their writing? Did the children lack experience with dogs? Was there enough motivation in this activity? Was it relevant to the children's lives? Did the topic not interest them? As a result of their discussion, the teachers decided to return to their classes with the news that the children were going to share their stories with their buddies in the other Grade 1 classroom. The announcement had a profound effect. The children tackled the writing with renewed interest and enthusiasm. Only 30 minutes later, 27 pairs of children were excitedly reading their stories to each other. Awareness that a real audience was going to hear the stories made all the difference. This anecdote also demonstrates how being responsive to the students in their classes, and having a willingness to question their own teaching, helped Fran and her colleague to become more effective. To the benefit of their students, the teachers changed their plans at short notice when they realized the children were not fully engaged with the activity.

CONDUCTING A WRITING WORKSHOP

The teacher/researcher who had the most influence on the teaching of writing and on writing workshops in the 1990s was Nancie Atwell. In 1987, Atwell published her first book, *In the Middle*, and in 1998 she developed a second edition of the book, modifying her ideas after many more years of classroom teaching. In the second edition, Atwell lays out the expectations she has for writers' workshops and the guidelines she uses for her students' writing sessions. Although Atwell's suggestions are made largely with students in Grades 5 to 9 in mind, many of the ideas are modifiable for teachers and children in Grades 2 to 4. Box 7.1 lists some of Atwell's suggestions for conducting writing workshops in the classroom.

Box 7.1 Conducting a Writing Workshop

1. A writing workshop has a predictable format so that students know when it is to occur, what is expected of them, and what they can expect from the teacher and the situation. Teachers work out for themselves what feels comfortable and what seems to work in their classrooms. Time is provided for children to write, as well as respond to each other, and time is also provided for teachers to respond to individual students' work. Some teachers create a schedule so that they meet with a particular group of writers on a rotating basis. Group members give feedback to one another, and when the group finishes work together, the teacher is able to work with individual students who need help that day. Some teachers also try to build into their schedules time for their own writing so that children can see them modelling the writing process.

2. A writers' workshop is something like an artist's studio and has all the necessary resources. Young children need different colours and sizes of paper, scissors, tape, felt pens, pencils, pens, and staplers so they can create their own booklets for writing and drawing. Older children need dictionaries, a thesaurus, reference books, rulers, whiteout, and staples. If there are computers in the classroom, the students need easy and regular access to them, printing facilities, a safe place to store disks, and some degree of privacy (it is interesting how passersby do not feel awkward about reading what is on a computer screen, whereas they may hesitate to look over the shoulder of someone writing with a pen).

3. A writers' workshop can be noisy because children need to talk about their writing. However, teachers try to plan quiet times when all the students are writing. These times can be agreed upon by the class as the students begin to understand and articulate what they need as writers. Many children say that they cannot do any real writing or reading at school because it is too noisy. Teachers try to respect this need as well as the need for interaction. Teachers schedule quiet time that is used for writing only, and at that time any conversation must be in a whisper. They also schedule open time, when students can write or meet together in a response group on the floor in one corner of the room. In addition, some teachers schedule planned group conferences where they interact with the children in a more traditional way.

4. A writing folder is essential for each person in the classroom, including the teacher. The folder does not have to be specially purchased; children can design and make their own. The important thing is that the folder be expandable in some way so that it can hold a stack of writing. Ideally, the folder needs two or three sections for pieces that are just being started, for works in progress, and for completed writing. Rather than have children keep these folders in their desks, it is usually easier and neater if all the folders are kept in a filing cabinet or large cardboard box that is accessible to the children at all times. A box can be decorated and kept in a prominent place. Continued

Box 7.1   Conducting a Writing Workshop   *continued*

5. All pieces of writing are dated with a draft number printed at the top. Students save all writings, even those that "don't work." This allows them to see how their work is changing. Sometimes a writer will go back to an earlier draft of a piece because it is better than a later one. When Sharon and Erica created "The Wellington Story" (Exhibit 7.7), they were unsure what to do next. They had lots of thoughts, but needed time to distance themselves from the piece so they could return to it later with fresh ideas. The piece stayed in their writing folders with various dates on it at intervals as they worked on it over a long period of time. Eventually they agreed to abandon the story, but they each kept a copy of it.

6. Students can generate a list of possible writing topics and keep them at the front of the folder, either on the cover or stapled to the inside cover. They can add to the list on a regular basis as they discover new topics and experiences that will make good stories. Teachers often encourage children to take a few minutes every few weeks to update their list of possibilities, and discuss topics students have chosen to put on their own lists.

7. Writers are encouraged not to erase their work but instead to put a line through changes and insert new material above. Writing on every other line and on only one side of the paper facilitates this process and encourages children to make changes and insertions without having to rewrite the whole piece. When children compose on a word processor it is more difficult to separate drafts, as changes are made to a text on a continuing basis. However, it is helpful if children can print drafts at various stages of development, label them, and keep them in their folder. Alternatively, drafts can be saved on the computer, numbered in the same way.

8. Writing conferences might focus on the content of a piece or on the topic or organization, clarifying the ideas and focusing the writing toward a more cohesive whole. A writing conference generally deals with only one of these elements at a time, since young writers cannot revise everything at once. The information given in a writing conference should be in small enough chunks that the writer can think about it and act on it.

9. Lessons are taught as a result of specific points that arise in a writers' workshop, usually in the context of the children's writing. These lessons can be a vehicle for teaching many writing skills, such as capitalization, the use of commas and periods, particular spelling that is difficult for a large number of children, and clarification of ideas. The craft of writing can be taught in these lessons using a piece of student writing or a piece written by the teacher and displayed on the overhead projector. Grade 5 teacher Catherine Lewis often uses a piece of her own writing to demonstrate an idea to her students, and she will ask them to make suggestions about how the piece can be improved. The aim is always to improve the piece of writing, making it more interesting, effective, and enjoyable.

10. In writing conferences, teachers almost always invite the writer to read the work aloud. The teacher is then free to listen and to encourage the writer to lead the conference as much as possible. The writer can remain in charge of the piece. The role of the teacher

and the other students is to make suggestions and share responses as interested listeners and co-writers. The conventions of writing can be attended to later in the process when the ideas and organization are firmly in place.

11. In order to be authentic and to model the writing process, teachers write themselves either with the children or at some other time if they are too busy during the writers' workshop. In addition, teachers share their writing with their students. Children need to see that even adults struggle with creating good writing. Writing is hard work, and all authors labour over their compositions. Having published authors visit the classroom to speak about their work is a particularly effective strategy. Children find these visits inspiring as well as interesting, and they benefit from knowing that books come from real people, with editors who request many drafts and revisions before the book is ready to be published. Authors struggle with their work just as much as teachers and children struggle with their writing in elementary classrooms.

Source: Some of this material is based loosely on N. Atwell, In the middle: Writing, reading, and learning with adolescents (Portsmouth, NH: Heinemann, 1987), pp. 83–84, 94.

Guidelines for Conducting a Writing Conference

Lucy Calkins (1991) and Nancie Atwell (1998) point out that young writers want to be listened to and want honest responses to their work. Sharing a piece of writing with an informed audience can be a most effective means of obtaining feedback. In the process, writers learn new ways of making meaning, building on their already existing writing skills. Teachers can teach or model feedback strategies that are productive and sensitive to the fact that every piece of writing is very special to its author. It is essentially a part of the writer, and as such, it must be respected by the audience. Students can learn how to receive the work of others gently, how to give constructive feedback and positive comments, and how to make suggestions for future drafts and new pieces of writing. Teachers who model and promote a constructive and respectful process help to ensure that, when children share their pieces of writing with a group, they will feel safe and will be able to accept the feedback.

A well-structured conference is one in which students can predict or anticipate what will happen next. In a writing conference, the writer usually reads the piece to the teacher or to the group. This enables the listener (or listeners) to focus on the ideas, wording, and flow of the piece of writing. At the elementary school level, a three-part response system works well. First, children or teacher provide a positive comment about the piece what works well or sounds good. Next, they ask questions about anything that is not clear in the piece. Finally, they make suggestions about what can be done to make the piece better. A conference might be very brief just a few minutes of conversation with the teacher or it can be a more formal and lengthy affair with a small group of students. In a conference, the teacher's goal is to provide feedback designed to improve the students' writing. The conference is effective when the teacher's responses provide strategic information that the writer can act on. Conferences can be conducted at a table in a quiet part of the room, or if the conference is one-on-one with teacher and student, it can be at the student's desk.

Atwell suggests that conferences be held about many different aspects of writing, including the ideas, information, audience, language, and format. She reminds us that the teacher and students act in conferences as mediators for learning, helping the writer to

Teacher with primary child engaged in a writing conference.

scaffold growth. Some educators maintain that it is best to focus on the content of a piece of writing during a writing conference, leaving writing conventions until much later in the process. Others feel that appropriate use of language conventions (correct spelling, punctuation, and capitalization) help in clarifying ideas and in making the piece flow more evenly. Certainly when a word processor is being used, the conventions of written language can be addressed throughout the writing process. Eventually, however, correct conventions have to be in place so that the meaning and feeling of the piece are communicated effectively to the audience. Frequent misspellings or other errors can detract from the effectiveness of a piece of writing, particularly when children have reached the age where these conventions are expected (around Grade 2 or 3) and invented spelling no longer adds to the personal voice of the writer. The conventions of language can be checked in an editing conference later in the writing process if necessary.

Just as writers need ownership of their piece of writing, they also need to feel ownership of the writing conference. Ownership can be facilitated by encouraging the writer to make decisions about the nature and the focus of the conference. Some teachers provide a box labelled "I Need an Editor" in which children can place their drafts when they are ready for the teacher to provide feedback or an editing conference. Before the conference, the teacher takes into account the student's writing stage and edits the draft for spelling and language conventions. In the process, a productive focus for the editing conference is identified. For example, the teacher may choose to review a particular spelling generalization or grammatical element with the student. During the conference, the teacher maintains this focus and encourages the student to note what was discussed for reference in future writing.

One of the key elements of a writing conference between student and teacher is response time. Most teachers find "wait time" difficult and frequently jump in with a suggestion before the student has had a chance to think and respond thoughtfully. One of the greatest challenges facing teachers in a writing conference is allowing the student time to think, not rushing in with a readymade solution for the student writer. The writing belongs to the writer, and the teacher's role is to help the student become a better writer. This will not always mean that a perfect product is produced every time. Box 7.2 contains suggestions (from Atwell, 1998) for conducting writing conferences.

Writing conferences are not restricted to poetic writing, nor is poetic writing the only kind of writing that benefits from having an audience. Transactional writing also benefits from peer and teacher responses as it is created. In fact, any piece of writing we wish to do well may require input from others along the way. Letters to a business, letters to government agencies, reports, and play scripts can all benefit from feedback from others. Writers may work on their ideas and original drafts alone, but at some point they require feedback to clarify and present those ideas to a reading public.

Box 7.2   Guidelines for Writing Conferences

1. Keep an eye on the time, and do not spend too long with one student.

2. Meet with as many writers as possible each day.

3. Circulate from one area of the room to another. Go to students' desks whenever possible.

4. Make a conference personal. It is a conversation. Kneel or sit next to the student.

5. Whisper and ask students to whisper when they confer with you. Do not distract other writers.

6. Build on what writers know and have done rather than telling them what they have not done.

7. Avoid generalized praise and moral evaluation, such as saying "good." Attending to the writer in a serious manner is more effective than giving a few words of praise.

8. Focus on one aspect of the writing in the conference, and don't try to "fix" everything or clarify all the "fuzzy" thinking.

9. Focus on meaning, and ask the questions you genuinely want to know about.

10. Invite students to note their intended actions at the end of the conference. You can add this to the conference record sheet.

11. At the end of the conference, ask the student to summarize the points discussed.

12. Be prepared to take notes of your questions and observations.

13. Don't take over the piece of writing, making it your own. Ask for permission (e.g., "May I show you a way to do this?").

Source: Some of this material is based loosely on N. Atwell, *In the middle: Writing, reading, and learning with adolescents* (Portsmouth, NH: Heinemann, 1987), pp. 94–95.

The Students' Role in a Writing Workshop

In addition to providing guidelines for teachers in conducting writing workshops, Atwell (1998) and others (e.g., Calkins, 1986, 1991) have provided suggestions for "rules" that will help students in working through drafts of their writing, eventually leading to pieces they feel proud of sharing with an audience. The rules set out in Box 7.3 are based on those Atwell provides for her students (1998, p. 115). These rules are appropriate for students engaged in poetic and transactional or informational writing, where a finished draft is important. Students who are engaged in journal writing or other forms of expressive writing may not need this structure. They do, however, need quiet time to write, assistance with the conventions of written language, and an opportunity to discuss their writing and their ideas with others.

Box 7.3   Rules for Students in a Writing Workshop

1. Save everything. You never know when you might want to refer to a piece of writing again.

2. Date and label everything so you can keep track of what you have done. This is especially important when working on a word processor.

3. When a piece of writing is finished, clip all the drafts, notes, and brainstormings together with a copy of the final draft on the top.

4. Record every piece of finished writing in a log at the beginning of the writing folder.

5. Write on one side of the paper only, and always double-space (write on every other line only).

6. Format your writing as you go (in paragraphs, lines, stanzas).

7. Try to attend to conventions as you write. Check spelling as soon as possible. Attend to punctuation as you write. Ask for help when you need it.

8. When working on a word processor, print every couple of days or every few pages of text. Read the piece through with pen in hand so that you can attend to the flow of the whole piece and not just chunks of the text as they appear on the screen.

9. Begin each writing session by reading over what you have already written. This allows you to establish where you are in the piece and creates momentum for the day's writing.

10. Writing is thinking. Don't interrupt other students while they are writing. Don't attempt to tell other people what to write.

11. If you need to talk to the teacher, speak in a whisper.

12. When you need to receive feedback from a student or teacher, move to the conference area and write down the comments as they are made. This way you will have a record of suggestions to take back to your writing.

13. Edit your work in a different colour from the text.

14. Always write as well, and as much, as you can.

Source: Adapted from N. Atwell, *In the middle: New understandings about writing, reading, and learning*, 2nd ed. (Portsmouth, NH: Heinemann, 1998), pp. 115–116.

SOCIAL INTERACTION IN THE WRITING PROCESS

Although educators have long realized that learning to talk is a social process, it is only recently that we have acknowledged the importance of social interaction when writing. If, as Moffett (1979) maintains, true writing occurs only when we revise inner speech, then children need to become aware of what the revision of inner speech entails. Teachers can encourage children to make their inner speech explicit and to wrestle with the ideas they are attempting to articulate. Moffett says that teachers "have no choice but to work in the gap between thought and speech" (1979, p. 278). He also suggests that "writing cannot be realistically perceived and taught so long as we try to work from the outside in" (p. 279). In other words, true writing comes from within the writer, who must learn to articulate thought and put it into print. When children work collaboratively in the writing process, they have opportunities to explore the gap between thought and speech. When teachers listen to them, they can find out how children negotiate meaning and the structural elements of writing. The social context of writing in the classroom and the relationships among the students influence writing enormously. Through their talk, as Michael Halliday (1969) has said, they learn "how to mean."

The Importance of Talk

As children talk together or with a teacher, continual scaffolding is evident. Through constant interaction, the students become teachers and learners interchangeably. The following excerpt is a planning session where Erica and Sharon, in a Grade 5 classroom, considered each other's opinions and incorporated them into a written discussion of the city cat bylaws (Lewis, 1989).

Sharon: Want to do a debate?

Erica: Yes, then we can each have our own opinion.

Sharon: What's yours about?

Erica: My what?

Sharon: Your issue you want to debate. I want to do the cat bylaw. OK?

Erica: OK. I'll just put "Cat Bylaw" at the top of the page.

Sharon: OK. If I was in charge of the world I'd change the cat bylaw.

Erica: Do you want to do this one [pause] together? I don't have a cat, you do, so it makes a difference, doesn't it?

Sharon: Cats should be able to walk around.

Erica: And I'm going to write against that! Cats go to the bathroom everywhere and …

Sharon: Good, we disagree then we agree on that. [Laughter.]

Erica: And it smells! Write on the top of the page "Cat Bylaw" again.

Sharon: Why?

Erica: Because we're going to do it together. ... We'll put my opinions and your opinions so we know whose is what.

Sharon: I want to ask you a question. If you don't have a cat, would you still not like the rule as much? I still think it's dumb.

Erica: Ya, but you wouldn't like it as much, like it wouldn't be. ... Even if you had a cat would you still hate it more?

Sharon: No, exactly the same.

Erica: What! I'm writing against you, right?

Sharon: Well, cats ... I agree that cats do that, go to the bathroom, I mean.

Erica: I agree in a way. [Writes this down slowly.]

Sharon: Don't write this next part down till I figure it out.

Erica: But dogs, dogs do that too [still writes slowly, thinking, pausing]. Dogs do poop on our lawn.

Sharon: Dogs usually have their owners with them.

Erica: Not always. Some people let their dogs out 'cause we've had a lot of ...

Sharon: Ya, but dogs don't come back.

Erica: Yes, they do.

Sharon: No, but cats always do in the same place.

Erica: Well, it depends on how far they go. ...

In their continuing negotiation of meaning, the two girls found that they became very aware of writing for an audience. They began to negotiate meaning and work out details, where each sentence, and at times each word, was important. Disagreements were common, and they questioned the logic of each other's ideas. The following excerpt, from a discussion Sharon and Erica held while co-writing "The Wellington Story," concerns the phrases looked closer and looked again.

Erica: "He looked closer into the hole ..."

Sharon: "He looked again" sounds better.

Erica: Well, Sharon, if you looked closer, would you stick your head right into the hole?

Sharon: It doesn't mean that.

Erica: Well it does to me!

Sharon: Closer isn't sticking your face into the hole, but "looked again" just sounds better.

Erica: Sharon, you don't listen!

Sharon: So, we don't use "closer" or "again." We say "he looked into the hole and saw the top of the wine bottle."

Erica: No, "he looked closer." A bit closer, know what I mean?

Sharon: Why would he look closer to see the wine bottle?

Erica: 'Cause the dress might have covered it up, you know. Then "he looked again" doesn't mean "he looked closer."

Sharon: Yes it does!

Erica: Sharon, I don't know. It's the way the sentence, the way …

Sharon: The way you put it sounds dumb.

Erica: Well, where did he actually look?

Sharon: Under the floorboards.

Erica: Well, I don't think he needs to get closer to see under the floorboards that's what I really mean.

Sharon: When you say "looked closer," it doesn't necessarily mean you looked closely right in the hole, it means you sort of took a second look.

Erica: Ya, that's it, he took a second look!

Sharon: Oh, wow, we got it!

Erica: Phew!

Peer Group Writing Conferences

The following group conference was initiated and conducted by four students who relied on strategies their classroom teacher had taught them. The transcript, taken from Lewis (1989), shows how the students used these conferences to further their own writing development. Erica began by reading the unfinished "Wellington" story quoted in Exhibit 7.7 earlier in this chapter.

Erica: "'It's coming from the paint house,' said Mr. McGregor. They all rushed out to the paint house and saw Yvette shaking, with a knife in her hand."

Sharon: That's as far as we've got.

Craig: I have a question. Who's Yvette?

Erica: The maid.

Craig: What's her husband's name?

Erica: The maid? She doesn't have one.

Dana: No, Craig. Mr. and Mrs. Wellington.

Craig: Oh, right.

Dana: All of a sudden you brought in that Mr. McGregor. Who's he supposed to be?

Sharon: One of the guests. When it says well, we didn't want to just list them all.

Dana: You could say, "Mr. McGregor, one of the guests ..."

Erica: Good idea.

Dana: Where do you guys go from here?

Sharon: Well, we're not sure. We have to have the loose floorboards so the police can find the ...

Erica: We also think we want it to be a play and we talked about highlighting the speaking parts, except Sharon wants to write it all out so ...

Dana: Hey, you guys, we forgot to say our favourite parts. The part about the paint house really catches my eye. Is this guy a painter, a famous one?

Erica: Ya, and that's why Yvette kills him because he painted a picture of her and she is afraid that Mrs. Wellington will find out.

Dana: Wouldn't it just be easier to destroy the painting than to kill the guy?

Sharon: Well, another idea we had is that it's not Yvette. It's the wife and she kills him for his money. We aren't exactly sure about that part yet.

Craig: I like the part where they find her holding the bloody knife.

Erica: We didn't say it was bloody.

Craig: Well, it would be, you know.

Because of the importance of talk and the amount of learning that takes place in group conferences, it is important to encourage and facilitate this kind of dialogue as part of the writers' workshop. Through interaction, students become more aware of their covert writing processes and of the conventions necessary for effective communication with an audience. Sharon said,

> I like to talk about all my ideas and I like to figure it all out with someone else. It got kind of hard, you know, because I get really excited and I yelled at Erica, she's so picky, though, you know. [Smiles.]

The following statements illustrate the students' thoughts on writing conferences:

Dana: Some days it's easy all goes well, and some days it's bad it's really hard.

Erica: Well … it's both actually easy and hard. Maybe at different times it's harder …

Craig: It helps me, I love talking to someone.

Sharon: She helps me about quotations and … other things, too.

The extensive use of expressive language enables students to clarify and extend their thoughts as they write. Children benefit from talking through their understanding at every stage of the process. Some days, there is more talk than writing, but it is through this talk that children make explicit their understandings of what writing is and what writing can do. They also articulate their understandings of literary structures and what makes a piece of writing work. In "The Wellington Story" (see Exhibit 7.7), Sharon and Erica demonstrated a command of the mystery story genre and of the conventions of story writing. Carefully crafted with an audience in mind, their story undoubtedly reflects some of their recreational reading.

SUMMARY

Writing is both an art and a skill, an activity that can give enormous pleasure to the writer as well as to the reader. Most people need to write on a daily basis, either in their jobs (a phone message, a technical report) or in their personal lives (a letter to their child's school, a grocery list, a diary, a poem). Writing instruction in the past tended to emphasize the development of competency in the surface features of language. With the advent of the process approach to the teaching of writing, teachers now help their students to develop both composition and presentation skills. Writing instruction, as a process, stresses the purpose for writing, the audience for the writing, and the relationship of these to form and function.

As they compose, students are encouraged to write for a variety of audiences and for particular purposes. James Britton (1970) pointed out that written composition can be distinguished according to purpose and intended audience. Expressive writing is written either for the self or for an audience close to the writer, and records or captures personal thoughts, feelings, and intentions. Transactional writing takes place when the writer wants to convey information to others in a formal report, list, essay, or textbook. Poetic writing is usually created for an audience other than the self. It contains aesthetic or literary elements and is the voice used in stories as well as poems. Teachers teach skills that range from drawing the letters and words (handwriting), to transcribing, paraphrasing, crafting, and revising inner speech (Moffett, 1979). In a balanced program of writing instruction, all of these voices, levels and genres of writing are taught. Students can then learn to write effectively for a range of audiences and purposes.

When composing and crafting a piece of writing, young writers need a structure in the classroom that will allow them to have large chunks of quiet writing time, conferences that provide feedback from an interested and informed audience, and the opportunity to share finished pieces with "the public." Writing conferences help writers to draft and revise their thoughts until they are sure they are saying exactly what they want to say. It is in the writing conference that most teaching occurs, and it is the entire process of drafting, revising, editing, and sharing that helps children to become better writers.

Teachers now recognize the important role that children's talk plays in their development as writers. When children are on-task and are engaged fully in a shared writing experience, they learn a great deal from one another through exchanging and negotiating ideas. The quest for clarity and appropriateness of language, the response of the readers, and the power of words to evoke images and feelings are the elements young writers learn about as they write together in the classroom.

SELECTED PROFESSIONAL RESOURCES

Atwell, N. (1998). *In the middle: New understandings about writing, reading, and learning* (2nd ed.). Portsmouth, NH: Boynton/Cook. Atwell's book is a superb resource to help in organizing writing workshops in the classroom. The book establishes rules of conduct and processes of interaction. Although Atwell describes organizational structures and procedures for reading and writing workshops for middle grade students, her book is also appropriate for elementary grade teachers who wish to organize writers' workshops in their classrooms. In detail, Atwell describes how to prepare for a writing workshop, how to get started, how to respond to writers and their writing, and how to conduct mini-lessons in writing.

Industry Canada. (2003). Canada's SchoolNet. Available: www.schoolnet.ca/home/e/resources. Retrieved: January 14, 2003. This site contains links to over 7000 educational resources for students, parents and teachers. Click on "Curriculum Areas" and then "Language Arts." This will take you to "writing" and a host of related links.

Tompkins, G. (2000). *Teaching writing: Balancing process and product* (3rd ed.). Toronto: Prentice-Hall of Canada, Inc. One of the most comprehensive books on teaching writing in the elementary school grades, this text provides an overview of the writing process, illustrated throughout with examples of children's writing. Specific chapters are devoted to journals, narrative, poetry, letters, informational or expository text, persuasive, and biographical writing. There is a chapter on writers' tools (spelling, handwriting, grammar, editing) and one on assessing student writing. The book is well laid out and easy to read. It makes an excellent resource for any teacher's professional library.

Writers in Electronic Residence (WIER). (2003). Available: www.wier.ca:8080/~wier/WIERHome.html. Retrieved January 14, 2003. This site connects elementary classrooms from across Canada with writers, teachers and one another in an exchange of original writing and commentary. Well-known Canadian authors join classrooms electronically to read and consider the students' work. They offer reactions and ideas, and guide discussions among the students.

CHILDREN'S BOOKS NOTED IN CHAPTER SEVEN ▬▬▬

Bauer, M. D. (1986). *On my honor.* New York: Bantam Doubleday Dell.

Creech, S. (2001). *Love that dog.* New York: Harper Collins.

Ellis, D. (1999). *Looking for X.* Toronto: Groundwood Books.

Herrick, S. (1999). *The spangled drongo.* St. Lucia, QLD: University of Queensland Press.

Herrick, S. (2002). *Tom Jones saves the world.* St. Lucia, QLD: University of Queensland Press.

Lawson, J. (1992). *The dragon's pearl.* Toronto: Stoddart.

Paterson, K. (1977). *Bridge to Terabithia.* New York: HarperCollins.

Paterson, K. (1978). *The great Gilly Hopkins.* New York: Thomas Y. Crowell.

Paterson, K. (1994). *Flip flop Girl.* New York: Lodestar Books (Dutton).

REFERENCES ▬▬▬

Applebee, A. (1978). *The child's concept of story.* Chicago: University of Chicago Press.

Atwell, N. (1987). *In the middle: Writing, reading, and learning with adolescents.* Portsmouth, NH: Heinemann.

Atwell, N. (1998). *In the middle: New understandings about writing, reading, and learning* (2nd ed.). Portsmouth, NH: Boynton/Cook.

Britton, J. (1970). *Language and learning.* Harmondsworth, UK: Penguin Books.

Bunting, R. (1998). From process to genre: Recent developments in the teaching of writing. In J. Graham and A. Kelly (eds.), *Writing under control: Teaching writing in the primary school* (pp. 7–16). London: David Fulton Publishers.

Calkins, L. (1986). *The art of teaching writing.* Portsmouth, NH: Heinemann.

Calkins, L. (1991). *Living between the lines.* Toronto: Irwin.

Chard, S. (1998). *The project approach: Managing successful projects.* New York: Scholastic.

D'Arcy, P. (1989). *Making sense, shaping meaning: Writing in the context of a capacity-based approach to learning.* Portsmouth, NH: Heinemann.

Education Department of Western Australia. (1994). *First Steps Writing: Resource book.* Portsmouth, NH: Heinemann.

Graves, D. H. (1983). *Writing: Teachers and children at work.* Exeter, NH: Heinemann.

Halliday, M.A.K. (1969). Relevant models of language. *Educational Review, 22* (1), 26–37.

Halliday, M.A.K., and Hasan, R. (1985). *Language, context, and text : Aspects of language in a social-semiotic perspective.* Deakin, Victoria: Deakin University Press.

Hardy, B. (1975). *Tellers and listeners: The narrative imagination.* Dover, NH: Longwood.

Lewis, C. (1989). Partnership writing: Ten-year-olds talking and writing together. MEd thesis, University of Alberta, Edmonton, AB.

Lewis, M. and Wray, D. (1995). *Developing children's non-fiction writing.* Leamington Spa, UK: Scholastic.

Maaskant, F. (1989). Children's perceptions of writing in a Grade One/Two classroom. MEd thesis, University of Alberta, Edmonton, AB.

Martin, J. R., Rothery, J., and Christie. (1987). Social processes in education: A reply to Sawyer and Watson (and others). In I. Reid (ed.), *The place of genre in learning: Current debates* (pp. 58–82). Deakin, Victoria: Deakin University Press.

Moffett, J. (1979). Integrity in the teaching of writing. *Phi Delta Kappa, 61* (4), 276–279.

Paterson, K. (1989). *The spying heart: More thoughts on reading and writing books.* New York: Lodestar Books.

Petite Rivière Elementary School. (1993). *History of Crousetown.* Lunenburg County, NS: Petite Rivière Publishing.

Chapter

Writing Across the Curriculum

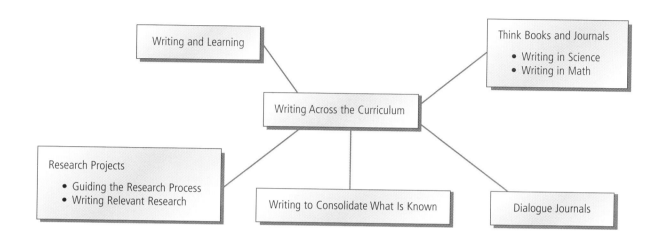

Writing and Learning

Think Books and Journals
- Writing in Science
- Writing in Math

Writing Across the Curriculum

Research Projects
- Guiding the Research Process
- Writing Relevant Research

Writing to Consolidate What Is Known

Dialogue Journals

When Jean-Pierre was placed in a combined Grade 2/3 classroom for a full term of student teaching, the teacher, Mr. Pettigrew, told him the students wrote in almost every subject area. Jean-Pierre was unsure of how this could be done. He recalled that, when he was in elementary school, any writing that he did in a subject area consisted mainly of copying notes from the board and answering his teacher's questions. Jean-Pierre was curious about what this writing across the curriculum might look like. He was intrigued by the notion of writing for learning, but he had many questions. Did Mr. Pettigrew encourage his students to write poems in science, or stories in math? How can children effectively write about their learning when many of them are only just learning how to write? Doesn't the process take a lot of class time that could be better spent on learning content material? What do the children gain from putting their learning into their own words? Considering the amount of time it takes for students to write, is it possible for a teacher to also adequately cover the prescribed curriculum? This chapter attempts to answer Jean-Pierre's questions, and explores what teachers and researchers know about learning and the importance of students talking and writing as they learn.

WRITING AND LEARNING

In many classrooms, students and teachers write as a means of engaging in ongoing dialogue about learning; dialogue with themselves, with their peers, and with their teachers or students. In these classrooms, teachers and students write to explore topics, ideas, and subject area content, as well as to demonstrate their understandings. Writing not only demonstrates what they have learned but it also provides a powerful tool that can help them to make sense of their learning as they engage in it. As Donald Murray points out, "when we write we discover what we know" (1984, p. 7).

In the 1980s, Fulwiler (1987) outlined five basic assumptions about language and learning that were approved by the National Council of Teachers of English. Three of these assumptions are particularly important to teachers with regard to writing across the curriculum:

1. When people articulate connections between new information and what they already know, they learn and understand that new information more effectively (Bruner, 1966).

2. When people write about new information and ideas—in addition to reading, talking, and listening—they learn and understand them better (Britton et al., 1975).

3. When people care about what they write and see connections to their own lives, they both learn and write with greater efficacy (Moffett, 1968).

These findings have led teachers to become acutely aware of how they can help their students to make their thinking visible, to develop confidence in their ability to think, and to value their own thoughts. Thus, writing for learning is not restricted to particular forms or genres. Journals, notes, letters, diaries, scripts, commercials, brochures, invitations, reports, and posters all provide opportunities for students to demonstrate the meanings that they have constructed. In addition, dialogue journals, think books, and learning logs allow children to share their thinking with their teacher or peers in a supportive environment that encourages students to expand and explore their ideas further.

After conducting research into young children's non-narrative writing, Thomas Newkirk (1987) concluded that the early elementary years need not be a time when "narrative must do for all." He showed that in active writing programs, the early years are a time when children make considerable advances toward mature expository writing. As illustrated in the writing done for the "Restaurant Project" (exhibited in Chapter Seven), children demonstrate the capacity they have for writing in a variety of genres to meet a range of purposes. Their writing demonstrates, in particular, their abilities to organize their thinking and record it on paper.

Newkirk hypothesized that "the abilities shown by the students are probably closely tied to the knowledge they possess on their topics and to the collaborative community in which they work" (1987, p. 141). Teachers such as Ms. Gellner, mentioned in Chapter Seven, who focus on building collaborative learning communities and developing their students' abilities to write in a variety of genres, attempt to ensure that their students

- are interested in the topic,
- have questions they want to answer, and
- are motivated to share their learning with others.

Newkirk (1987) suggested that writers should be encouraged in the early years of schooling to label, write lists, and generally sort and make sense of what they know (as Tanya did in her writing about seasons, Exhibit 7.1 in Chapter Seven). He maintained that young children learn most effectively when they write in their own voice in ways that are meaningful to them. Newkirk's data also suggest that young children develop organizational skills *as they write*. Newkirk believes that children learn and organize their ideas through writing about the world they know. Once they are comfortable with doing that, they can begin to represent their understandings of the world more abstractly. What they need is opportunity. Tanya's winter vacation in the Caribbean prompted her to think about seasons across the world. The piece suggests that although Tanya usually experiences winter as being very cold, she now understands that in some parts of the world even winter is warm. Thus the teacher encourages students to record and examine their immediate experiential world before they move on to more formal and abstract writing. Overall, it is clear that children can write in many genres, and for many purposes, from the very beginning of schooling.

THINK BOOKS AND JOURNALS

Pat D'Arcy (1989) writes that think books and journals provide the space for learners to reflect, rehearse, reshape, and redraft what they know. She quotes the Children's Learning in Science Group in the United Kingdom when she says, "If a pupil's own picture of how the world works is ignored, her ability to make sense of someone else's picture, the teacher's or the textbook writer's, is seriously impeded" (p. 3). The writing learners do as they learn—writing about emerging ideas, insights, thoughts, and reflections—is part of their own picture of how the world works. Because that picture is constantly changing, the writing is not moving toward a finished product, but is part of the process of helping learners clarify their thinking and develop new understandings. Journal writing acts as a platform on which other ideas can be built. Students can go back to the writing and reexamine the ideas captured there, reflect upon them, refine them, and build on them as they integrate new knowledge with the old. In the past, educators have frequently thought of writing as something that is done when the ideas are fully formed, but writing for learning is an intrinsic part of the total learning process. It makes learning personally meaningful and creates what we might call "action knowledge" rather than "book knowledge" (Barnes, 1976).

While academic prose tends to be logical, formal, conventional, organized, assertive, and objective, the writing in a journal is conversational in tone and reads much like talk. Journal writers begin with what they know and build their understandings as they write. The journal entry in Exhibit 8.1, written by Sarah in Grade 3, provides an example of what is meant by writing to understand. Sarah clearly explains the concept of multiplication as repeated addition, demonstrating her learning by drawing six

Exhibit 8.1 Sarah's Math Journal Entry

I did 6×7=42. I knew the answer because I know how to count by 6's. So you go 6, 12, 18, 24, 30, 36, 42. You could count by 7's or 6's. Count how many digits you wrote in the 6's or 7's. If you did 6's you needed to write by 6's like I did. Count how many digits there are. Like if you did 6×7=42, you would take the second number and plus it as many times as the first number. How many shelfs all together???

bookshelves each with seven shelves. Here, Sarah is actively making meaning from new learning. Douglas Barnes (1976, p. 76) says that writing is a means by which writers can take an active part in their own learning: "As pupils write they can—under certain circumstances—reshape their view of the world, and extend their ability to think rationally about it." James Britton (1982) refers to this same process as "shaping at the point of utterance." The advantage of students writing about their ideas as they are processing them is that they are forced to focus on them to a far greater degree than when they simply talk about them. Talked-over ideas are often lost; we may be distracted and lose the thread of our thoughts. But writing provides a record of where we have journeyed in our thinking, and points to where we might travel next.

Writing in Science

MacAlister, Kydd, and Jones (1988, p. 3) explored the value of writing in science. They write:

> The chances are that most teachers think of science notes in terms of lab write-ups, diagrams and graphs, and specialized vocabulary. ... They all have a place in science, but there are other kinds of writing that can be useful in an activity oriented classroom. ... The idea of science notebooks that blended expressive writing with occasional forays into poetic writing appealed to us. We had already agreed that "worksheet science" was detrimental to developing complete thoughts. It tended to fragment concepts as well as demanding little original writing from students. We also agreed that the formal lab write-ups required of students in higher grades were too abstract for young learners.

Teachers encourage students to write and share anticipatory questions and predictions (**heuristic** or exploratory writing) before they engage in any science activity. Students are then encouraged to write observations in their notebooks as the activity proceeds. In *Writing and Primary Science*, MacAlister, Kydd, and Jones (1988) suggest that the pieces of writing children complete in science, and the drawings and charts that accompany

Exhibit 8.2 Thomas's Writing in Science

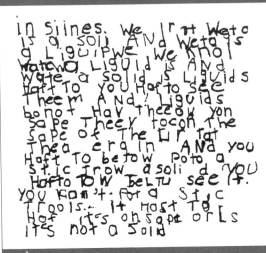

In science we learned what is a solid and what is a liquid. We know what a liquid is and what a solid is. Liquids have to, you have to see them and liquids do not have their own shape. They take on the shape of the jar that they are in and you have to be able to put a stick through. A solid you have to be able to see it. You can't put a stick through it. It has to have its own shape or it's not a solid.

Source: A. Ozdoba, "Writing to learn: Science journals in year one," MEd thesis, University of Alberta, Edmonton, 1992, p. 100.

Exhibit 8.3 Grade 1 Science Notebook

We made ice-cream using a baby food jar, and ice and salt and chocolate milk and the way we did it. And coffee container. And the way we used it. (1) One person puts milk in the jar (2) and then put the lid on (3) put some ice then salt (5) baby food jar in the ice (6) put more ice in (7) put more salt (8) put the lid on and shake. And when we opened it, it was ice cream.

We maDe ice-cream
Useing A Baby food Jar
And ice And Salt
And choclate milk
And the way we Did it
And coffe con tanne
And the way we useD it
oone Person puts milkonte
Jar And then put the liD on
put some ice then salt
Bady in the ice put mae
ice in put more salt
put the lid on And Shake
And when we open it
it wAs ice cream

Source: A. Ozdoba, "Writing to learn: Science journals in year one," MEd thesis, University of Alberta, Edmonton, 1992, p. 95.

them, can provide a rich source of evaluative and diagnostic information for teachers. "Reading an explanation written in a child's words tells the teacher more about their level of concept development than any multiple choice test" (p. 27). The specialized vocabulary of science (really, of any discipline) becomes much more important and relevant to children when they understand the concept embedded in the language. The talk that takes place when learners write in a think book, learning log, or notebook, as well as the actual writing, provides a forum for sharing and clarifying ideas that leads to understanding the concept and internalizing the specialized vocabulary. Exhibits 8.2 and 8.3 present science notebook entries from children in Grade 1 (Ozdoba, 1992).

Writing in Math

In 1989, the National Council of Teachers of Mathematics in the United States published *Curriculum and Evaluation Standards for School Mathematics*, establishing a set of principles and standards for curriculum and evaluation reform that emphasized process as well as content. A later publication, *Principles and Standards for School Mathematics* (NCTM, 2000), refined the curricular focus of the previous document, and focused on five content standards (number, algebra, geometry, data analysis, and probability), and five process standards (problem solving, reasoning and proof, connections, communication, and representation). In this document, "learning to communicate mathematically" was listed as a primary learning outcome for all students. These publications have strongly influenced Canadian provincial programs of study in mathematics.

The "communication" standard of *Principles and Standards* (NCTM, 2000, p. 402) states:

> Instructional programs from pre-kindergarten through grade 12 should enable all students to—
>
> - Organize and consolidate their mathematical thinking through communication
> - Communicate their mathematical thinking coherently and clearly to peers, teachers and others
> - Analyze and evaluate the mathematical thinking and strategies of others
> - Use the language of mathematics to express mathematical ideas precisely.

In addition, communication is inherent in all of the other standards, for whether students are problem solving, reasoning, making connections among ideas, or representing their knowledge, they are using language as a tool for thinking as well as communicating. Communication and the exploration of ideas both orally and in writing have thus taken on a more prominent role in mathematics education; a significant move away from the transmission model of mathematics teaching prevalent for many years. Students are now urged to explore, problem solve, and link learning to their own lives. They are increasingly challenged to validate their own mathematical ideas and abilities and to learn to communicate their mathematical thinking clearly. They have opportunities to express and explore their mathematical thinking through the use of manipulatives, small group discussion, and writing. The NCTM *Principles and Standards for School Mathematics* (2000) emphasizes the importance of writing: "Writing in mathematics can help students consolidate their thinking because it requires them to reflect on their work and clarify their thoughts about the ideas developed in the lesson" (p. 61).

Many high-quality resource materials are available to help teachers understand and implement writing in mathematics. *Math Is Language Too: Talking and Writing in the Mathematics Classroom* (Whitin and Whitin, 2000) is a joint publication of the National Council of Teachers of Mathematics and the National Council of Teachers of English. The book explores the ways in which grade four students use story, metaphor, and language to develop mathematical thinking skills and strategies. It contains many examples of children's writing and talking, as well as examples of children's literature that demonstrate mathematical ideas and concepts. Marilyn Burns' many publications are also highly recommended. In addition to *About Teaching Mathematics: A K–8 Resource* (2nd ed.) (2000) and *Math and Literature (K–3): Book One* (1992), is *Writing in Math Class* (1995). The latter book describes five different types of writing for math classes (journals, creative writing, explanations, math problems, and general writing assignments). It offers many tips and suggestions for classroom practice. Burns writes, "Although the final representation of a mathematical pursuit looks very different from the final product of a writing effort, the mental journey is, at its base, the same—making sense of an idea and presenting it effectively" (1995, p. 3).

Research by Edwards (1992) on the use of learning journals or think books in mathematics in Grades 2, 4, and 6 showed that journals can provide a safe and challenging environment where students can display what they know (as Sarah did in Exhibit 8.1), and they can come to terms with what they do *not* know. When students begin writing, many discover they are not as clear about their learning as they had expected. Sometimes students will express confusion and ask for help, and at that point peers or the teacher can provide support. Edwards found that learning journals took the focus away from marks and correct answers, and focused instead on what individual children understood and could clearly articulate. The writing also allowed the students to open up to other people's ideas, experiences, and understandings. Journaling provided opportunities for the teachers to recognize the children as individuals in the classroom with unique learning needs and areas of expertise. The journal writing also encouraged children to write in their own style of language, while at the same time pushing the boundaries of that language and challenging them with the language of mathematics—a language with which they became more comfortable through writing in their journals.

When the children in Edwards' study wrote in their journals, they reflected, reshaped, and redrafted as they engaged in learning—what D'Arcy calls the "three Rs of learning"—a cycle of learning that people repeat throughout their lives (D'Arcy, 1989). Shared meaning remained at the heart of these learning journals (which were also dialogue journals). The journals not only proved to be beneficial learning experiences for the children, but were powerful vehicles that encouraged teachers to examine their teaching and knowledge base in mathematics education. As teachers read the student journals, they learned much about how they could improve their own practice. They reflected on

- the complex mathematical questions children ask,
- their own knowledge and understandings of mathematics and how these could be improved,
- the need for extremely clear and explicit teaching of mathematics,
- the effectiveness of journals as informal assessment tools,
- the clues the students' writing provides as to what they understand and what they do not understand, and
- how all of this information could be used to adjust and adapt specific teaching content, methodology, and student groupings in the classroom.

Working with personal learning journals in subject areas across the curriculum requires a considerable commitment of time and energy. Teachers who embark on such a project are willing to devote a specific period of time each day, or during specified days each week, to journal writing, and they set aside that time, guarding it carefully. To be effective, writing in learning journals must be done on a regular basis. Students need to know that time will be available for their writing and that this time will not be "cancelled" to make room for something else. In other words, writing in learning journals is a priority in these classrooms and the teachers carefully guide their students through the process, ensuring their success. Teachers have found that math journals can be used effectively from Grade 1 onward. Gradually, communication skills improve, especially in the area of **expressive writing**, which in turn leads to greater facility with **expository writing**. Children need to feel their way through the concrete world of the known before they can begin to represent their understandings abstractly. Learning journals provide one vehicle through which children can do this.

DIALOGUE JOURNALS

Dialogue journals are sometimes referred to as *response journals*, but we use that term only for those journals where the students are writing in response to their learning—such as about a piece of literature or a science activity—not in response to one another. Where children are writing to a partner (whether a parent, teacher, or peer), we call those journals *dialogue journals*. (A journal can be both a dialogue journal and a response journal, but the two terms are not synonymous.)

When teachers and students engage in writing dialogue journals, a partnership is created with the person being addressed, a partnership based on compassion, acceptance, and a sincere interest in the other. Bohm (1990, p. 2) maintains that in a **dialogue**, unlike in a debate, nobody is trying to win. "In a dialogue, there is no attempt to gain points, or to make your particular view prevail. Rather, when a mistake is discovered on the part of anybody, everybody gains. ... In a dialogue everybody wins." Vygotsky (1962), Polanyi (1969), Britton (1970), and Halliday (1975) have all argued for the use of language in a heuristic or exploratory way, by students as well as teachers, so that they may make greater personal sense of their learning. Dialogue, either spoken or written, is one way for students to pursue inquiry and create personal meaning in their learning, two critical features of a constructivist approach.

Students may write dialogue journals with the teacher, parents, or a peer. The aim of a dialogue journal is to enable the learner to clarify and explore meanings in collaboration with a partner. The adage "Two heads are better than one" pertains in this situation. When students work in a small group to discuss an issue or try to solve a problem, it may take longer, but they usually learn from the experience. Adults know what happens when they discuss a book or movie with a group of friends. Their original responses are often modified, and they may find their understandings changing as they challenge themselves to expand the meanings created. The result of such dialogue is often a broader or deeper interpretation of their experiences. Teachers sometimes provide prompts for journal entries (see Atwell, 1990), while others provide a specific structure for the entry. One suggested format for a notebook or journal entry is presented in Table 8.1. This format is designed for students working in pairs. It provides prompts to help the students focus their thoughts.

Table 8.1 Model for a Science Notebook Entry

1. My observation:	
2. My conclusion: 3. What it meant to me:	4. My partner's conclusion: 5. What my partner added:
6. When we talked it over, our conclusion was:	

Two children reading a dialogue journal.

Edwards (1992) discovered that children can write in dialogue journals and respond to each other regardless of their level of writing ability or mathematical understandings. In Grade 6, the children often made a number of entries back and forth on one topic with their partner before the dialogue ended. On other occasions, there was only one entry and one response. The children enjoyed the opportunity to write to, and get responses from, many different people, and the process was structured so that they changed partners every few weeks. Some students needed additional oral dialogue with their partners in order to become totally clear about a concept. They might have many questions to ask before they would be satisfied that they had completely understood. Whether it was the peer explanation that made more sense than their teacher's, or whether it was simply the dialogue, we do not know. Their teachers reported positive class dynamics—the students were caring, compassionate, and genuinely engaged in a process of learning together—a genuine collaborative learning community.

In Grade 2, the students would often leave spaces in their math journals so their teacher could provide feedback or answer a question. Frequently, the children drew a line on which the teacher was expected to respond. For example, Julia wrote, "I get up at 7:30. What time do you come to school? ___." A further journal entry from this class is shown

Exhibit 8.4 Grade 2 Math Journal Page

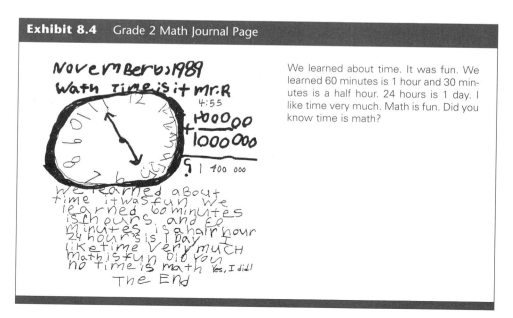

We learned about time. It was fun. We learned 60 minutes is 1 hour and 30 minutes is a half hour. 24 hours is 1 day. I like time very much. Math is fun. Did you know time is math?

in Exhibit 8.4. The children in this classroom made connections with their prior learning and were consolidating it into a more holistic understanding of the world. For example, children noticed that words used in one context could be used in a completely different context. Billy related his new knowledge of temperature and thermometers with prior knowledge in science, and observed a rule of capitalization:

> Today we learned about temperature and Celsius and Mr. Celsius. A thermometer is something that tells the temperature. Do you know what the grey stuff is in a thermometer? It is called mercury. There is a planet named Mercury. The grey stuff in a thermometer is spelled with a smaller m and the planet is spelled with a big M. Mr. Celsius is now dead. He was called Mr. Celsius! He invented the thermometer! He named the thermometer after him.

The process of writing in a dialogue journal might not always run smoothly. Experience has shown that teachers play a very important role in the success of dialogue journals even if they are not directly engaged in the dialogue itself. In one Grade 6 class, problems arose with motivation and with the meaningfulness of the journals. In that instance, the teacher gave very little guidance to the students other than telling them to write. Often, a child's entry did not receive an appropriate response from the partner. For example, Marianne wrote,

> The only part I don't get is when Mrs. Armstrong told us that when you have a question like this:
>
> $$40.8$$
> $$\times\ 80.4$$
>
> that the numbers in the ones place make up two decimal places. Then the decimal is two spots from the end.

This was met with a response from Marianne's partner about something entirely different. In the next entry, Marianne repeated her question:

> Math is pretty easy, but I still don't understand why, when you have a question like this
>
> $$40.8 \times 19.9 = 811.92$$
>
> why the decimal would be two places after the decimal in the answer.

This time her partner did respond, and said:

> I don't really understand why there has to be a two decimal place in the answer either. I wish I could do my social report on the computer. ...

Marianne was remarkably persistent, and in her third entry she again came back to the same question. Once again, she did not receive an appropriate response. However, as a result of reading Marianne's math entries, Mrs. Armstrong completed three carefully planned lessons on the topic, including guided practice for the children, helping to clarify a very important math concept that many of the children in the class had not fully understood.

When teachers use learning logs or journals in their classrooms, they

- read the student journals regularly to see how they might adapt their instruction and further facilitate their students' learning,
- encourage students to look at any questions their partners pose and consider them thoughtfully,

- provide "talk time" for pairs of students to figure out their answers to questions as well as their problem-solving strategies (some students need as long as ten minutes to read their partner's responses and discuss them),
- teach children what constitutes an appropriate response, and
- model responses on the overhead projector to help children become comfortable with a dialogue journal (not to tell children what to say, but to demonstrate a variety of ways in which they might respond to each other).

So that students can accept their partners' responses and not be hurt by a critical response, everyone in the class can be encouraged to begin their responses with a positive remark followed by a comment or recommendation. This is a response pattern many children are familiar with in writing conferences. It makes sense for children to follow this pattern in their dialogue journals as well. The following example demonstrates this twofold response pattern:

Jeremy, I like the way you explained it. It really makes sense. I also liked the way you showed an easy and a hard problem. You should talk about the remainder and tell people about estimating.

Dialogue journals are an extension of cooperative learning. Each child becomes a teacher as well as a learner. Students learn together and from one another. Most children feel good about writing and responding in dialogue journals. With carefully established procedures and regular reading by the teacher, dialogue journals are an effective and enjoyable means of learning across the curriculum.

WRITING TO CONSOLIDATE WHAT IS KNOWN

Many forms of writing serve to consolidate what a person knows, including journal writing and writing in notebooks. As we drafted the manuscript for this book, we rethought our understandings, worked through difficult ideas, consolidated what we knew about teaching and learning in language, and raised more questions. The writing of this book is part of our own continuing search for understanding. We went through all the stages that D'Arcy (1989) outlines:

1. recollecting
2. reflecting
3. reshaping
4. redrafting

Writing that consolidates what a person knows meets the representational function of language that Halliday (1975) identified, and it uses what Britton (1970) has termed the expository or transactional voice. Writing that consolidates knowledge is a reflection of what the writer knows *at the time of writing*, and it acts as a kind of summary of the learning journey.

Exhibit 8.1 demonstrates Sarah's consolidated knowledge of multiplication, and Exhibit 8.5 demonstrates how Alida, in Grade 3, consolidated her knowledge of homesteading on the Prairies.

Understanding can be consolidated at key junctures in the learning process, not only as a final activity. Students record what they have learned, with specific reference to content and processes (such as measuring or estimating in mathematics). After teaching a Grade 6 unit on scale and its uses, Ms. Redfern asked her students to write a consolidating entry about scale in their math journals. Here is a selection of the class's entries:

What I know about scale!

Scale is used for maps, to tell you how far it is from one place to another. Scale tells you the distance and how many kilometers or miles it takes to get from one place to another.

The first thing you need to know how to work on scales you need to have the mm. and the cm. in order because then you can go from cm. to km. and then you can get all your answers right. When you have a test it's not hard when you go one space up like 2m.=20cm. by adding the zero in the order.

1. Measure the length and width of tables in nearest metres because we want to find the actual measurement.

2. We have to decide what the scale will be because we have to shrink it.

3. We look at the graphing paper because we have to find out how many centimetre squares there are.

Scale is anything that you can measure in linear instead of drawing the real size of whatever it is! You have to do this because if you don't it could take the rest of your life to draw it the real size!

I know scale a little better now because I know some questions I didn't know before like who does scaling? People who build houses and cartographers. Now I know that you can measure scale with anything. What do you measure money and time with?

These five entries reveal the range of meanings children created from the unit on scale, and the ways in which they were able to apply that knowledge to the world. The writing shows how some children grasped the concept of scale very well, while others were limited to trying to manipulate numbers to make scale work for them. The writing provided excellent feedback for Ms. Redfern (who did much reteaching as a result) and also enabled the children to discover for themselves what they knew and how well they knew it. The children who were struggling to articulate their learning began to realize that they did not fully understand the concept, and some were more open to revisiting the topic as a result.

Exhibit 8.5	Homesteading

GETTING A HOMESTEAD

Many people came to ALBERTA to get a homestead. A homestead is peace of land you can farm on. To make the homestead yours you had to live on it six month of three years. You got the peace of land free but you had to pay $10.00 for the registration fee. After you pay while you live on the peace of land you had to get thirty acres planted into crops. You also had to build a house worth at least $300.00 dollars. By the way the people looking for homesteads look for water near by. They also look for people near by too. THAT'S HOW THEY GOT HOMESTEADS 100 YEARS AGO.

RESEARCH PROJECTS

In adult life, research reports are frequently written in engineering, law, medicine, social services, business, and academia, to name just a few. Reports in these contexts are always predicated on a question or line of inquiry. Researchers essentially gather data to help them answer questions. When children are required to complete research reports in school contexts, the purpose is often unclear. Children are asked, for example, to write reports on a Canadian province, an animal, or a community. But the first step in any research endeavour is to formulate questions that guide the study and provide the intrinsic motivation to complete the project. When students are required to conduct research and write a report in school, it is essential that they formulate the questions, have a genuine interest in the topic, and be motivated to discover answers to their questions. Teachers play a key role in establishing interest and motivation, in guiding students to formulate their questions, and in helping students learn relevant research strategies.

To conduct research and write research reports in school, students need to develop the ability to write exposition. As Newkirk demonstrated (1987), children's early writing is usually in the expressive voice, but as they pursue questions that are of interest and relevance to them, they learn to organize their ideas and begin to write in a variety of forms and voices. This was evident in Tanya's piece "About Seasons," in Exhibit 7.1, and also in the writing completed during Ms. Gellner's "restaurant project." However, children still benefit from instruction in expository writing, as well as in the research process. The challenge for teachers is to help students make the transition from expressive to expository writing in an interesting and enjoyable way.

For many children, the only audience for expository prose is the teacher (and that means the teacher as evaluator). But children learn by doing—they learn as they write, and through their writing they can acquire the transactional or expository voice. Exhibit 8.6 demonstrates Kelly's transactional voice in an excerpt from her report on the solar system completed in Grade 5. Kelly's teacher ensured that her students knew the audience for their writing (in this case, their peers in the classroom), and she encouraged her students to write specifically for that audience on a topic of their own choice. Kelly's writing is well

---

Exhibit 8.6 Fact or Fiction? The Solar System

True Stars are born in clouds of gas and dust called nebulas. Millions of years later the dust particles and gas are pulled together so they can heat up. When the gas is hot enough, a nuclear reation, like a bomb, sets off and it is born. Changes occur as the star gets older. Some keep growing and then shrink. Other stars project gas into space. When the stars are quit old they start to shrink and they are called white drawf stars. When they start to cool off they become black drawf stars and then the star is dead.

organized and includes information that she found to be personally intriguing as well as challenging. Kelly was fascinated by the notion that stars are born and die. Her illustration for this section of the report shows her playfulness with the idea, and, at the beginning of each page, Kelly posed the question to her classmates, "Is this fact or fiction?" Kelly's research not only started with a question, but posed a question throughout the text.

Children have a much greater chance of successfully completing a research project if the teacher provides direct and specific instruction for them. Effective teachers teach their students how to

- use library resources,
- use the table of contents and index of a book,
- locate information in books, encyclopedias, and magazines,
- interpret information from pictures, charts, graphs, videotapes, and audiotapes,
- use the Internet effectively,
- paraphrase what they read, make notes, and put what they read into their own words,
- translate information into visual form on charts, graphs, and diagrams,
- conduct interviews,
- search archives, and
- organize their findings into a report.

These strategies are best taught in the context of the research process, presenting the various strategies at times when the students need them. Teachers may begin by helping students to develop a report collaboratively. Young children learn to conduct library research and write exposition more effectively when teacher and students find information together, working as a class, than if they work independently. The more children are shown *how* to do research and the more they are actively *involved* in doing it, the more effectively they will learn.

Guiding the Research Process

Teachers in Grades 1 to 4 sometimes provide students with an outline, matrix, or web to help them organize information once they have located it. These devices help students make decisions about which information is relevant and which is not. Some devices have room for children to make their own notes in the spaces provided. These outlines, matrices, or webs are not like the typical outlines many of us were required to write in high school. Rather, they are graphic organizers that help children make sense of their research. Not all children will need such a device; however, graphic organizers do provide a sense of direction for those children who need some structure and guidance in putting together a report. An example of one graphic organizer—a data collection chart—is shown in Figure 8.1. Another form of graphic organizer is that used at the beginning of each chapter in this textbook to help the reader see the "big picture" as well as how the sections of the chapter relate to one another. Kennedy's graphic organizer (shown in Exhibit 7.2) was self-designed as he sought to make sense of the field notes he made at the market.

When one Grade 3 class was learning about animals, they focused on the concept of adaptation. The guiding question was "How do animals survive?" A class case study was created around the polar bear. Once the children began locating resources for the study, they zeroed in on the research question and found relevant information that helped them answer it. Thus, their reading was conducted from a specific perspective. Information was

Figure 8.1 Data Collection Chart, Community Services, Grade 2

noted through words, phrases, charts, diagrams, and so forth as the students collected their data. The following headings emerged as the students compiled their findings:

- physical appearance
- habitat
- food
- enemies
- migratory patterns
- conclusions (how the research answered the question)

These headings were not meant to dictate how the research report was to be written. Instead, they provided structures that guided the children's developing sense of organization.

As part of the research process, children need individual conferences with the teacher if they are to have their individual learning needs met and be assured that they are on track with their research. An anecdote here demonstrates the importance of individual writing conferences during the process of report writing.

Jared, in Grade 4, was completing a research report on fish. The report was to be made into a book to be placed in the classroom library. Jared had chosen to focus on the Mating Ritual Fish. The teacher, Mr. Johnson, felt quite sure there was no such fish, but Jared was adamant about his findings. Because of his concern, Mr. Johnson sat with Jared as Jared went over the books he had used as resources in his study. There, on one page, was a photograph of a school of fish and beneath it the caption "Mating rituals." Jared and Mr. Johnson together carefully reread this section of the book, but it took some intense discussion before Jared could recognize that this was not a breed of fish, but a process that fish engage in to reproduce themselves. Jared wrote his report on tropical fish, and was pleased with the outcome.

Because of Mr. Johnson's careful monitoring of the children's research, Jared's misinterpretation was discovered well before the report was already in progress. It would not have been helpful to Jared's self-esteem, his understanding of fish, or his confidence about library research to produce a report based on a misreading of the resource material. In this instance, Jared made a very reasonable meaning construction. In his interactions with Mr. Johnson that meaning was adjusted through discussion, providing an example of how meaning is socially constructed and negotiated.

Traditional report formats often give way today to more interactive, visual, or imaginative presentations of research. Chapter Thirteen discusses the role of technology in language arts and provides information on working with HyperStudio and other software packages in creating multimedia presentations as alternatives to the paper research report.

Children also develop new ideas for research reports from reading nonfiction books. Many current nonfiction materials available for children, such as Peter Sis's book *Starry Messenger* (1996), employ formats and strategies that are compelling and exciting. Expository prose can be full of the enthusiasm and excitement we feel when we discover something new and want to share it with a wider audience, as demonstrated in the excerpt from Kelly's report shown in Exhibit 8.6.

Writing Relevant Research

As already noted in earlier chapters, a fascinating research project completed for many years by Grade 4 children at Petite Rivière Elementary School in Lunenburg County, Nova Scotia was a series of books about the local area. Every year the children, who were bussed to the school from a wide area, selected a community within the county and pursued the questions "What makes this community unique?" and "What makes this community such a special place to live?" The project involved more than library research. The students went into the community to interview residents and businesspeople, complete correspondence, and search archives in order to answer their guiding questions. Once the research was completed, they wrote and presented the material in a final bound form that was accessible and interesting to the general public. The books were printed (complete with ISBN number) and bound by a local company and sold by the school. Stories, drawings, biographies, history, lists, poems, recipes, directions for games, minutes from meetings, maps, and posters were all included. One excerpt from *History of Crousetown* (1993) is shown in Exhibit 7.8, and a further excerpt is presented in Exhibit 8.7.

Exhibit 8.7 Stores in Crousetown

The first store in Crousetown was owned by Beechum Crouse. It used to be attached to the house that Robert Crouse is living in today. Beechum Crouse's Store sold pipes, tobacco and many different things.

Robert Crouse's father (Merle Crouse) opened a store in 1936.

Later Arthur Bolivar ran Merle Crouse's store. Merle sold the business, but he wouldn't sell the building. Arthur Bolivar then retired from the store in the early 1970s.

Johnny Himmelman had a store and a post office in Crousetown at the same time as Merle Crouse's store. John Himmelman's store is still standing across from the Community Cemetery.

Source: Petite Rivière Elementary School, *History of Crousetown* (Lunenburg County, NS: Petite Rivière Publishing, 1993), p. 24.

Before researchers begin the process of writing a research report, they try to understand their subject as much as possible so that they can communicate their findings clearly and interestingly. Mrs. Haché, the Grade 4 teacher at Petite Rivière Elementary School, writes:

Each student chose several topics that would become part of the history book. They researched their topics in the following ways: I took a group of students to the Public Archives in Halifax to research the old newspapers of that community. People from the community brought in artifacts and information to our classroom museum (a collection of old items from the community). I took the students, four at a time, after school to interview older citizens in the community (the students were prepared for the interview with questions from the whole class and a release form for each person interviewed). These interviews were videotaped and used for reference in the classroom by the students as they wrote their reports. The students checked these reports for grammar, spelling, and punctuation. The students then discussed their finished report with the teacher and proceeded to put their information and artwork together in the format for the history book.

The final stage of the project was an evening presentation in the community hall for everyone in the community. The children sent special invitations to the people they interviewed and they presented their finished books to them that evening. They prepared an evening of entertainment based on the project (readings, drama, and an old-fashioned singsong) and then served food prepared by their parents. The importance of this celebration for the community, and its impact on all the people gathered together for this special evening, cannot be overemphasized.

Mrs. Haché integrated many aspects of the language arts into this project each year. The children interviewed, discussed, listened, made notes, read, and wrote as part of the project. They worked collaboratively in some areas and individually in others. Mrs. Haché provided guidance and structure, while at the same time giving the children the opportunity to make the book truly their own. All the students had parts of their work included in the book, and the purpose of the project was clear to the children from the very beginning (as it was to the community and to the celebratory audience in the community hall). It was through their involvement in this personally and socially relevant project that the students were able to develop their ability to write effective exposition. In addition, the students learned to write for a more general audience than the immediate one they were familiar with in their classroom and homes.

The Grade 4 oral history project at Petite Rivière became a tradition. Each year's class looked forward to it, and as the children moved into Grade 5, they took care of marketing and promoting the book and handling the accounting required for publication and sales. Mrs. Haché and the children selected a different local community to study each year, so the books and the project remained unique and interesting for both the children and their teacher, as well as for community members.

Children frequently find visual depictions of their learning, such as designing and drawing posters, satisfying vehicles for representing what they have learned about a topic. Children at the beginning of the 21st century are particularly visual in their learning. They watch television and movies, play video games, and use the Internet more than any children in the past. When children combine their artwork and writing, they provide striking demonstrations of what they know. Frequently, these integrated presentation formats are more appealing to children than more traditional forms. Similarly, charts, graphs, maps, and diagrams often provide children with opportunities to share their understandings more fully. The importance of report writing lies in the fact that it remains a major format for organizing and presenting information to others. In addition, research reports provide opportunities for children to organize their thinking and learning about the world.

SUMMARY

Writing across the curriculum is much more than copying notes from the board or writing reports to demonstrate what has been learned. It is an opportunity for learners to write as they are learning, and to process that learning, making greater sense of what they know. It is a time for questioning, hypothesizing, predicting, and sometimes consolidating knowledge. Writing across the curriculum can be done from Grade 1 onward, as shown by the samples of young children's writing presented in this chapter. Writing for learning is best taught when it is modelled by teachers or developed in collaborative efforts with students and teacher working together. In addition, research and study skills are taught with the aim of helping children to become independent learners who feel confident in locating and using library resources and in accessing primary sources through such means as interviews and archival searches. Many of the skills needed to conduct research involve organizing information. This important ability can be taught collaboratively in the early grades as children become familiar with the use of webs, grids, and charts to facilitate their learning.

Being able to write thoughts on paper is one way in which people remind themselves of what they know and think. It is also a way to communicate those thoughts to others. As students develop their abilities to read and write for multiple purposes and for varied audiences, they take greater control of their own learning. The ability to recount, recapture, and reflect on their experiences and emerging understandings is a critical life skill. Most importantly, the skills students develop as they write in learning logs, think books, response journals, and dialogue journals, and the research inquiry and reporting they complete, provide them with a repertoire of powerful learning strategies. Through employing these strategies, students articulate connections between new learning and what they already know, making personal sense of their learning and becoming better writers.

This chapter opened with Jean-Pierre as he was about to begin a student teaching placement in a Grade 2/3 classroom. He raised many questions about writing for learning and had some concerns about the value of his students spending time writing and talking in subject areas across the curriculum. It didn't take long for him to discover that the students wrote in learning logs, math journals, and science notebooks, as well as in their writing folders. The idea that writing actually helped them to learn made complete sense to the students in Mr. Pettigrew's classroom. The students wrote to explore what they were learning, to ask questions when they were unsure, and to figure out meanings with a partner. The students each had a personal record of what they had learned, and they had an opportunity to receive feedback on their learning from their peers and from Mr. Pettigrew. In turn, Mr. Pettigrew had evidence of what his students were learning—and he knew which students needed help in specific areas of the curriculum. As a result of his experiences in the Grade 2/3 classroom, Jean-Pierre found that his own writing in his student teaching journal gained importance and relevance to his practice, especially when he shared some of his entries with Mr. Pettigrew and with the students in the class.

SELECTED PROFESSIONAL RESOURCES

Atwell, N. (ed.). (1990). *Coming to know: Writing to learn in the intermediate grades.* Portsmouth, NH: Heinemann. A practical approach to writing across the curriculum, this book, edited by Nancie Atwell, consists of chapters written by classroom teachers (Grades 3 through 6) who asked their students to write as scientists, historians, mathematicians, and literary critics—to use writing-as-process to discover meaning. The book describes specific classroom activities and is an excellent reference for beginning teachers. Suggestions for unit planning and for ways of incorporating writing across the curriculum are provided. In particular, the volume addresses writing reports, conducting interviews, recording observations, taking notes, and using learning logs. The book contains many examples of children's work, teachers' responses, and lists of classroom resources.

Because We Care Education Society of Alberta. (2003). *2Learn*. Available: www.2learn.ca/currlinks/croverviewmenu.html. Retrieved: January 14, 2003. 2Learn.ca provides high-quality curricular resources, tools, and support for curricular applications and integration of Information and Communication Technology Outcomes (Alberta Learning) into specific subject curricula for Grades 1–12, including writing.

D'Arcy, P. (1989). *Making sense, shaping meaning: Writing in the context of a capacity-based approach to learning*. Portsmouth, NH: Heinemann. This British book explores and describes the many different types of writing children in an elementary school can do. The book is rich in samples of children's writing and comments on the writing process. D'Arcy focuses on writing across the curriculum, and she particularly examines the writing–thinking connection and the role writing plays in stimulating thought as well as capturing it on paper.

University of Western Ontario. Education Library. (2003). *Lesson plans and other cool educational sites for teachers*. Available: www.lib.uwo.ca/education/lesson_plans_and_other_cool_sites.htm. Retrieved: January 14, 2003. This Canadian site connects teachers to a wide range of Web-based resources for use across the curriculum. It includes lesson plans, library resources, drama ideas, science, social studies, art and more—and most of it involves writing.

CHILDREN'S BOOKS NOTED IN CHAPTER EIGHT

Sis, P. (1996). *Starry messenger*. New York: Farrar Strauss Giroux.

REFERENCES

Atwell, N. (ed.). (1990). *Coming to know: Writing to learn in the intermediate grades*. Portsmouth, NH: Heinemann.

Barnes, D. (1976). *From communication to curriculum*. Harmondsworth, UK: Penguin Books.

Bohm, D. (1990). *On dialogue*. Ojai, CA: David Bohm Seminars.

Britton, J. (1982). *Prospect and retrospect: Selected essays of James Britton*. G. Pradl (ed.). Montclair, NJ: Boynton Cook.

Britton, J. (1970). *Language and learning*. Harmondsworth, UK: Penguin Books.

Britton, J., Burgess, G., Martin N., McLeod, A., and Rosen, H. (1975). *The development of writing abilities, 11–18*. London: MacMillan Education.

Bruner, J. S. (1966). *Towards a theory of instruction*. Cambridge, MA: The Belknap Press of Harvard University.

Burns, M. (1995). *Writing in math class*. Sausalito, CA: Math Solutions Publications.

Burns, M. (2000). *About teaching mathematics: A K–8 resource*, 2nd ed. Sausalito, CA: Math Solutions Publications.

Burns, M. (1992). *Math and literature (K–3): Book one*. Sausalito, CA: Marilyn Burns Education Associates.

D'Arcy, P. (1989). *Making sense, shaping meaning: Writing in the context of a capacity-based approach to learning*. Portsmouth, NH: Heinemann.

Edwards, J. (1992). Dialogue journals in math: Grades two, four and six. *Reflections on Canadian Literacy, 10* (1), 2–12.

Fulwiler, T. (ed.). (1987). *The journal book*. Toronto: Boynton/Cook.

Halliday, M.A.K. (1975). *Explorations in the functions of language*. London: Edward Arnold.

MacAlister, S., Kydd, G., and Jones, G. (1988). *Writing and primary science*. Calgary: Calgary Board of Education.

Moffett, J. (1968). *Teaching the universe of discourse*. Boston: Houghton Mifflin.

Murray, D. (1984). *Write to learn*. New York: Holt, Rinehart and Winston.

National Council of Teachers of Mathematics. (1989). *Curriculum and evaluation standards for school mathematics*. Reston, VA: Author.

National Council of Teachers of Mathematics. (2000). *Principles and standards for school mathematics*. Reston, VA: Author.

Newkirk, T. (1987). The non-narrative writing of young children. *Research in the Teaching of English*, *21*, 121–145.

Ozdoba, A. (1992). Writing to learn: Science journals in year one. MEd thesis, University of Alberta, Edmonton, AB.

Petite Rivière Elementary School. (1993). *History of Crousetown*. Lunenburg County, NS: Petite Rivière Publishing.

Polanyi, M. (1969). Knowing and being. In M. Greene (ed.), *Knowing and being: The essays of Michael Polanyi* (pp. 123–137). Chicago: University of Chicago Press.

Vygotsky, L. S. (1962). *Thought and language*. Cambridge, MA: MIT Press.

Whitin, P., and Whitin, D. (2000). *Math is language too: Talking and writing in the mathematics classroom*. Reston, VA: NCTM.

Chapter

9

Assessment and Conventions of Writing

Assessing Writing Abilities

- Purposes for Assessment
- Informal Assessment (observations, anecdotal records, conferences, self-assessment, portfolios, checklists, profiles)
- Product Assessment (analysis of writing samples, holistic scoring, analytic scales)

Teaching Spelling

- The Development of Spelling Abilities
- Invented Spelling
- Teaching Spelling in the Context of the Writing Process
- The Direct Teaching of Spelling
- A Word List Approach

Assessment and Conventions of Writing

Teaching Grammar, Capitalization, and Punctuation

- Grammar
- Punctuation and Capitalization

Teaching Handwriting

- The Perceptual Motor Approach
- Helping the Left-Handed Writer
- Printing and Cursive Writing

Self Evaluation NAME

DATE

1. Think of one or two pieces of writing that you've done this year.
   a. What have you discovered about your writing? (at least three things)
   b. What has helped you the most with your writing? (at least three things)
2. Think of 1 or 2 books that have meant the most to you this year.
   a. What have you discovered about reading? (at least three things)
   b. What has helped you the most with your reading? (at least three things)

Asha is completing her fifth week of student teaching in Grade 5. Her first student teaching placement was in a Grade 1 classroom, and so Asha is particularly conscious of the progress students make during their elementary school years. She cannot help but comment to her cooperating teacher, Ms. Hwang, how much children learn and grow in those years. The sheer amount of information they have processed is astonishing to her, but so is the development of their abilities in writing and reading. Asha asks Ms. Hwang how she records the progress the students make. How does Ms. Hwang plan for report cards and student/parent conferences? How does she know what to teach to individual students? How do the students become competent spellers? How do they learn appropriate grammar? Does Ms. Hwang teach handwriting? How did she learn to write neatly on the chalkboard? How does Ms. Hwang gather and sort information about her students into useful "chunks" that will provide feedback for her instruction in the classroom, help the children to understand their learning, and provide information to parents and a measure of instructional success for the school board?

NEL

Asha's observations and questions are important. Having taught students in Grade 1 as well as in Grade 5, she is aware that individual students require different methods of instruction depending on their varying needs. Sometimes children learn best in small groups, sharing their writing, receiving feedback, and receiving instruction through their teacher's comments and advice. At other times, students learn more effectively in individual writing conferences, and on occasion they need direct lessons in specific areas. Assessing student writing abilities is a crucial part of the planning and instruction cycle. Ongoing, formative assessment in the classroom provides teachers with the information they need to make instructional decisions that will enhance their students' learning. Summative assessment at the end of the school term or year provides the school district with a measure of the success of their programs and provides individual children with a regular statement of their progress in school. To become well-rounded writers over their years in school, children need assistance in learning the transcription skills of spelling, punctuation, and grammar, as well as involvement in writing and reading workshops. This chapter addresses the areas of assessment of writing and the direct instruction of transcription skills, often referred to as the conventions, or tools, of writing.

ASSESSING WRITING ABILITIES

Purposes for Assessment

There are ways in which the teaching of writing and the assessment of writing are so closely interconnected that teachers cannot do one without doing the other. Teachers conduct ongoing assessment in order to provide their students with appropriate feedback on their writing. This does not mean *grading* student work but *assessing* student work using appropriate criteria. Cooper and Odell (1999) remind us that one set of criteria is no longer sufficient for assessing writing, although some general concerns such as "organization" or "quality of ideas" may be valid across genres. However, as students are now encouraged to write in a range of genres, teachers need criteria appropriate to the genres, and they also need to *show* children how they can improve their writing.

In their classroom practice, teachers use a variety of strategies for assessing children's writing depending on the purpose for the assessment. Writing assessment is always focused, in some way, on improving the writing abilities of the children in our classrooms. Most often, assessment is conducted informally to guide a teacher's planning and instruction. The more information teachers possess about their students, the more effectively they can understand their students' learning and meet their students' individual needs. A second purpose for assessment is to provide feedback to students so they know what they do well and what they can focus on in order to become better writers. A third purpose is to provide information to parents and caregivers about student progress, and a fourth purpose is to provide information to school districts and provincial governments about the writing abilities of the children in their schools. Successful teachers strive to maintain a balanced approach to assessment, developing a broad picture of their students' learning. They do this through using a wide range of assessment techniques including observation, anecdotal records, checklists and profiles, portfolios or writing folders, student self-evaluation, writing conferences, analyses of samples of student writing, and provincial or local district achievement tests.

In order to describe and assess children's writing effectively, teachers attend not only to the surface features of the writing (transcription skills such as handwriting, spelling, and punctuation) but also to the content or message of what is written, which is, of course, the purpose for the writing. Rather than "marking," "correcting," or "grading" student writing, teachers usually respond to the writing or provide feedback to the student. They offer comments, either orally or in writing, on the form of the writing (the extent to which the writing meets the purpose or genre) or to the content of the piece, and only later do they attend to transcription errors. They look not only at samples of writing but also observe the students at work, listening to the running commentaries children engage in as they write, listening to student conversations and conferences with peers, watching the way they form letters or attempt to spell unknown words. In their instruction and evaluation of student writing, teachers show respect for the idiosyncratic nature of the writing process and value both the written products and the writing processes of individual students.

Box 9.1   Writing Assessment Strategies

Purpose	Informal/Formative	Product-Based/Summative
To inform instruction	• Writing conferences (group and one-on-one) • Observations of performance (including checking for spelling and other transcription skills) • Anecdotal notes • Journals/learning logs • Student self-assessment • Checklists • Review of writing folders	• Teacher-developed whole-class tests (e.g., spelling, word usage) • Whole-class writing tasks with teacher/school developed rubric • Analytical reviews of writing samples • Portfolio assessment • Student writing profiles
To inform students	• Writing conferences (group and one-on-one) • Responses to journals/learning logs • Responses to writing folder/portfolio • Checklists • Review of writing folders	• Whole-class writing tasks • Tests • Parent/child/teacher conferences • Portfolio review
To inform parents	• Portfolios of written work • Learning logs/journals • Student self-assessment • Checklists	• Whole-class writing tasks • Tests • Parent/child/teacher conferences • Student writing profiles
To inform school administration, school district, provincial Department of Education	• Writing samples with analysis	• Norm-referenced achievement tests (e.g., provincial achievement tests) • Teacher-developed tests and writing scales

Teachers and researchers now know that it is not possible to objectively assess any single piece of writing. Every reading of a text is affected by the values and cultural expectations of the reader (most often the teacher). We also know there is no *one* way to evaluate children's writing, no way to generate one mark or grade that represents the child's level of development in writing as a whole. The primary focus of assessment is on helping children to enhance their learning and on helping teachers to plan for instruction. As a result, a range of assessment strategies is necessary depending on the purpose for the assessment. Box 9.1 summarizes some of the methods teachers find useful in assessing student progress in writing in relation to the purpose for the assessment.

Informal Assessment of Writing

Teachers need to keep track of student progress in their classrooms every day. No other area of the curriculum is as complex to assess and monitor as that of writing, but teachers have found a number of informal strategies valuable when they use them regularly. These are observations, anecdotal records, conferences, student self-assessments, writing folders and portfolios, checklists and profiles.

Observations

Focused observations (and keeping relevant notes) of children as they write, participate in writing groups and conferences, revise and proofread their writing, and share their finished pieces with an audience can provide much useful information for teachers. Children's attitudes to writing, their writing strategies, how they interact with other children, and how they seek out other children for assistance or in sharing their writing can be revealed through observation. While making observations, teachers can ask the students questions to clarify what they have observed (e.g., "Would you like to share that with a partner?" "Do you have a title for this piece?"). Tompkins (2000) suggests that, while making observations, the teacher sit next to, or across from the student, and simply say "I'm going to watch you as you write so I can help you become a better writer" (p. 138).

Anecdotal Records

Notes taken by teachers informally in the classroom can be much more useful than a simple grade or mark recorded in a grade book. Anecdotal notes provide detailed information about a child's writing and knowledge of written language. These notes describe specific events and observations *without evaluation or interpretation*. They can be collected in a binder, notebook, or set of cards, and they can be entered into a database on the computer. A collection of notes taken over a period of months can provide a powerful tool for ongoing literacy assessment. Teachers usually approach their note-taking systematically, concentrating on a small number of children each day (three or four). Time is set aside for reviewing the notes periodically, rereading them, analyzing them, identifying each child's strengths and weaknesses and making inferences about children's writing development.

Teacher reviewing and discussing a child's writing.

Checklists

Many published and teacher-made checklists have been developed to aid teachers in their informal assessment of student progress in writing. Canadian teacher Stephen Leppard (1991) developed a reading–writing continuum designed to record the developing writing abilities of children as they pass from kindergarten to Grade 3. A copy of the continuum for each child is passed along from the teacher of one grade to the next throughout the primary years. The list of descriptors are read by the teacher, and those pertaining to the child being assessed are highlighted. Each assessment period (three to four months) is noted in a different-coloured highlighting pen. Thus, over a period of time, the child's progress is revealed as the different colours flow through the continuum. An excerpt from the continuum is presented in Box 9.2. The continuum is easy to use and convenient for teachers, since the observations have only to be recorded by highlighting specific characteristics.

Box 9.2   Writing Continuum

Individual Writing Stages

1. Take-Off Stage

- Can write name.
- Excited about writing.
- Wants to write (stories, lists, letters, or ideas).
- Need not rely on patterning.
- Invented (temporary) spelling becomes closer to standard.
- Writing is more meaning-centred.
- Can pick out words that are spelled incorrectly.
- Understands that each letter is a representation of a sound (phonetic understanding).
- Use of characters is moving closer to standard form.
- Sound correspondence more complete.
- Sound features of words are represented according to the child's hearing and articulation (leads to omission of preconsonant nasal, e.g., *NUBRS—numbers*).
- Realizes that print can conserve a thought statement permanently.

2. Independent Writing

- Writes stories with some sense of story structure.
- Awareness of grammar and language conventions.
- Spelling is near standard *or* spelling deteriorates because more complex words are being used.
- Understands that vowels are included in every word.
- Understands that vowels are included in every syllable.
- Vowels may be used inappropriately (e.g., *MEAK—make*).
- Developing a sense of punctuation.
- Developing an ability and desire to self-edit some corrections (spelling, simple sentence structure).
- Written work can be carried over, or continued, the next day.
- May begin to understand the inconsistencies within the English language.

Source: S. Leppard, "A Reading–Writing Continuum," in *Program continuity: The positive link*. © Access: The Education Station, 1991. Reprinted with permission.

Conferences

One-on-one or small-group conferences (two or three students) might focus on a particular topic or principle, or they can be general in scope. These conferences provide opportunities for joint assessment of student work as teachers and children discuss student progress. Unlike the instruction or process-oriented conferences listed in Chapter Seven (such as prewriting conferences, drafting conferences, and editing conferences), assessment conferences are usually held on completion of a composition. Teachers invite children to reflect on their piece of writing, their writing competencies and growth as writers. Teachers also ask students to set goals for future work. In a portfolio conference, teachers meet with students individually, review the writing samples and discuss the writing with the students. It is also a time for setting goals and reflecting on the students' growth as a writer. Teachers may also use this occasion to decide on a grade for the project in collaboration with the student.

Student Self-Assessment

In self-assessments "children pause to consider what they have learned and what has been important from their own perspectives" (Pappas, Kiefer, and Levstik, 1995, p. 317). Self-assessment is a critical aspect of evaluation and can be seen as an extension of children's engagement with learning logs or journals. When students write in learning logs they raise questions, reflect on what they have learned, and organize and reorganize their ideas. They become clearer about what they do not understand as well as about what they know. Opportunities for children to assess their progress are provided when they select writing for a portfolio or when they are at the end of a unit or writing project. Pappas, Kiefer, and Levstik (1995) point out that what students may think is significant in their learning may not seem important to a teacher or parent. Asking children to assess their own work (and providing a rationale for the assessment) is important, therefore, because it gives children the opportunity to be responsible, confident, independent, and autonomous learners. Children are required to be self-evaluative throughout the writing process when they decide on ideas for a piece of writing, make decisions about what to revise and redraft, and decide when a piece is finished or when it needs more work. These decisions and evaluations are made explicit in a student' self-assessment. Teachers often provide prompts or guidelines (questions) for student self-assessments, as shown in the photograph at the beginning of this chapter. Children who are too young to write a self-assessment may provide an oral self-assessment to the teacher and the teacher can make notes.

Portfolios

Portfolios and writing folders are used for quite different purposes. Where a writing folder is a "working file," containing work-in-progress, some finished work, and topics that might be the basis for future pieces, a portfolio is a collection of one student's completed work, carefully selected to demonstrate what that student can do. As described in chapter seven, a writing folder may contain stories, reports, poems, recipes, movie reviews, résumés, letters, and other informal material the student is working on (including notes for a forthcoming piece). Children are encouraged to keep all their drafts and finished compositions dated and clipped together, and students' self-assessments of finished work may be attached to the written pieces. If students take a piece of writing home permanently, teachers usually photocopy it for the writing folder. From time to time, children are invited to select their best pieces of writing for review, and these are placed in a portfolio. It is important that a range of genres be included in the portfolio, as the aim is to showcase the student's abilities.

The portfolio itself might be a flat-bottomed paper bag that the child has decorated, or it might be a concertina folder that expands to accommodate objects other than sheets of paper. Published books and reports might go into the portfolio, as well as comments from peers who have read or heard pieces written by the student. Students usually create a list of contents to go at the front of the portfolio and older students might add a letter stating why each piece of writing has been selected. Teachers can use the portfolios to document and illustrate a child's writing progress, and they can be used to great effect during parent-teacher conferences. When reviewing portfolios, teachers emphasize what students know and can do, rather than what students are learning to do or cannot do. Many teachers find it helpful to review portfolios with a colleague. The practice helps to inform teachers' assessment criteria and helps them develop a greater range of strategies for supporting individual children's learning.

Portfolio assessment is a form of process or performance evaluation. The aim is not to take one piece of writing in isolation, but to look at a collection of children's writings in many genres and voices. A portfolio might include stories, poems, letters, journal entries, lists, semantic maps, responses to literature, book reviews, artwork associated with the language arts, puppets, and writing from across the curriculum. In this way, children can see their writing as more than separate, isolated pieces. Portfolios also give children the opportunity to self-evaluate their work in choosing what they wish to put into the portfolio.

Farr and Tone (1994) provide many suggestions for developing and assessing portfolios. Among them is that teachers look at the volume of work in the portfolio, the interest and attitudes of the writers, and, of course, the development and growth of the writing. Farr and Tone also suggest how teachers can use portfolios to aid them in their instruction. Through discussion, writing, and reflection, portfolio assessment helps children become better thinkers and communicators. More importantly, they learn to take responsibility for their own learning. Portfolio assessment is not something teachers do *to* children but rather *with* them. Portfolio assessment is a reflection of holistic, constructive language learning and teaching in action. A sample of one teacher's comments on children's portfolios is presented in Box 9.3.

A general assessment of the portfolio can also be made using the organizational outline adopted by the Department of School Education in Victoria, Australia in their *English Profiles Handbook* (1991). An example of how this might be done is demonstrated below (p. 73):

What the writer does: Shaun edits work to a point where others can read it. He corrects common spelling errors, punctuation, and grammatical errors, especially when he reads his pieces aloud to peers. He develops ideas into paragraphs and uses a dictionary or thesaurus to extend and check his writing vocabulary.

What the writing shows: Sentences have ideas that flow. Paragraphs have a cohesive structure. Shaun shows the ability to argue and persuade. The messages in his expository and persuasive writing can be identified by others, but sometimes information is omitted. Brief passages are written with clear meaning, accurate spelling, and appropriate punctuation. Shaun can shift appropriately from first to third person in his writing. He consistently uses the correct tense in his writing. He uses compound sentences with conjunctions. His vocabulary is appropriate for a familiar audience such as peers, younger children, or adults, but he occasionally chooses an inappropriate

Box 9.3   Assessing the Contents of a Portfolio

What the Teacher Notices in the Portfolio	What That Suggests
There is little fluency and connection in pieces of writing in Keith's portfolio.	There is very little evidence that Keith thinks much about a topic before he begins writing.
This fifth-grade boy reads one comic book after another and does not record them all on his logs. Most are the funny type; many are about Garfield.	I will look for some humorous stories about cats for him to read—perhaps with a character as ornery as Garfield.
Anders has a note attached to two mysteries he has written, saying they are his favourites. He also has indicated on his log that an adventure story he wrote is his best because "it is exciting." There is not a large amount of writing in the portfolio, though.	I need to develop more opportunities for Anders to write. The adventure is a good story; perhaps if he shared it with some fellow students and saw how they enjoyed it, he would be encouraged.
Tad doesn't write a lot, but he draws well and his class-mates consider him the best artist in the class. His journal, which is spotty, is mainly about sports heroes. He also writes reviews about scary movies he has seen.	I will ask Tad if he wants to be the sports editor on the next issue of the class newspaper. He could also illustrate one of his friend Adam's stories and perhaps write a sequel to it. I will see if he might like to read *Joe Montana and Jerry Rice* by Richard J. Brenner and the mystery *Is Anybody There?* by Eve Bunting. Another book I can recommend to him is *Scary Stories to Chill Your Bones* by Alvin Schwartz. He could review the ones he reads for the paper and/or for the bulletin board.
Heriyadi's story "A Pizzaman's Adventure" is a string of events that happen to a delivery person. It uses the same character names as in his story "The City Street." Both of these stories have stringy plots but are very rich in details that build and build until they offer the reader a complete picture of the character.	There is keen evidence that Heriyadi is thinking about what he writes and its impact on his reader. It's as if he keeps wanting to ensure that the picture is really complete enough for his viewers to see it as he does.
There are no obvious sources for Benny's writing about bats and Thanksgiving. There are numerous accurate details about bats. He details the familiar feast in describing Thanksgiving.	Benny appears to have used background knowledge in writing.
Harold's "Snow Day" is about sledding, eating snow, and building a snowman. It ends with a question asking readers what they remember about snowy days.	He seems to be very audience-conscious in this piece. He anticipates that the things he likes about snow will also be what the audience likes, but he has to ask to check it out.

Source: R. Farr and B. Tone, *Portfolio and performance assessment: Helping students evaluate their progress as readers and writers* (Fort Worth, TX: Harcourt Brace & Co., 1994). © 1994 by Harcourt Brace & Co. Reprinted by permission of the publisher.

word. Shaun has a consistent handwriting style, and when using the word processor, he uses a variety of fonts and print styles appropriate for the task.

Use of writing: Shaun creates characters from his imagination and makes appropriate use of narrative and other forms of writing. He writes properly sequenced narratives with convincing settings.

Tompkins (2000) developed a writing process checklist that covers all the phases of writing, as shown in Box 9.4. The checklist can be modified by individual teachers to reflect aspects of the writing process they believe are important or that better meet the needs of the children in their classrooms.

Box 9.4   Checklist of Writing Processes

Student's Name _____

Date _____

Title _____

Prewriting

1. Considers purpose, audience, and form for writing.
2. Student gathers and organizes ideas before writing.

Drafting

3. Student writes one or more rough drafts.
4. Student labels paper as a "draft" and double-spaces text.
5. Student places greater emphasis on content rather than on transcription.

Revising

6. Student meets in a writing group to share writing.
7. Student makes changes to reflect suggestions made by classmates and teacher.

Editing

8. Student proofreads writing to identify transcription errors.
9. Student meets with teacher to identify and correct errors.

Publishing

10. Student makes a final copy.
11. Student shares writing with an appropriate audience.

Source: Based on G. Tompkins, *Teaching writing: Balancing process and product*, 3rd ed. (Columbus, OH: Merrill, 2000), p. 146. Reprinted with permission. From "Assessing the processes students use as writers," by G. E. Tompkins, *Journal of Reading*, 36 (1992), 245.

Profiles

Once data has been collected through writing conferences, observations, checklists, samples collected in writing folders, written conversations, note-taking, published writing, and discussion with parents, teachers can create writing profiles of their students. One reliable and much used resource for describing what children can actually do and how they can do it is the First Steps Developmental Continuum (1994), developed by the Education

Department of Western Australia. First Steps "recognizes that language learning is holistic and develops in relation to the context in which it is used" (p. 2). The First Steps document stresses that language does not develop in a linear sequence but that indicators do tend to cluster together. The continuum is therefore based on phases of development. The indicators listed are not, however, meant to provide evaluative criteria through which every child is expected to progress in sequential order. The document links phases of development to teaching strategies in order to help teachers make decisions about developmentally appropriate practices. First Steps pays particular attention to children who speak English as a second language. An overview of phases 1 and 2 of the continuum are presented in Boxes 9.5 and 9.6. The book contains detailed lists of indicators and teaching strategies.

Box 9.5   First Steps Developmental Continuum: Overview of Phase 1

Phase 1: Role-Play Writing

Children are beginning to come to terms with a new aspect of language, that of written symbols. They experiment with marks on paper with the intention of communicating a message or emulating adult writing.

Key Indicators

The Writer

- Assigns a message to own symbols.
- Understands that writing and drawing are
  different, e.g., points to words while "reading."
- Is aware that print carries a message.
- Uses known letters or approximations of letters
  to represent written language.
- Shows beginning awareness of directionality;
  that is, points to where print begins.

Major Teaching Emphases
- Demonstrate the connection between oral and written language.
- Demonstrate that written messages remain constant.
- Demonstrate that writing communicates a message.
- Focus on the way print works (print concepts and conventions).
- Demonstrate that writing is purposeful and has an intended audience.
- Use correct terminology for letters, sounds, words.
- Encourage children to experiment with writing.

At All Phases
- Model good English language use.
- Model writing every day.
- Encourage students to reflect on their understandings, gradually building a complete picture of written language structures.
- Ensure that students have opportunities to write for a variety of audiences and purposes.
- Encourage students to share their writing experiences.

Source: Reprinted from *First Steps in writing: Developmental curriculum* (1994).

Box 9.6 First Steps Developmental Continuum: Overview of Phase 2

Phase 2: Experimental Writing

Children are aware that speech can be written down and that written messages remain constant. They understand the left-to-right organization of print and experiment with writing letters and words.

Key Indicators

The Writer

- Reads back own writing.
- Attempts familiar forms of writing, e.g., list, letters, recounts, stories, messages.
- Writes using simplified oral language structures, e.g., "I brt loles."
- Uses writing to convey meaning.
- Realizes that print contains a constant message.
- Uses left-to-right and top-to-bottom orientation of print.
- Demonstrates one-to-one correspondence between written and spoken word.
- Relies heavily on the most obvious sounds of a word.

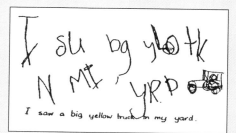

I saw a big yellow truck in my yard.

Major Teaching Emphases

- Model brief, imaginative, and factual texts and explain the purpose and intended audience.
- Help children build lists of high-frequency words from their reading and writing.
- Demonstrate the one-to-one correspondence of written and spoken words.
- Discuss how writing can be used to communicate over time and distance.
- Encourage children to talk about their experiences.
- Help children understand how written texts are composed in sentences.
- Help children develop a stable concept of a word.
- Help children relate written symbols to the sounds they represent.
- Talk about letters, words, and sentences.

Product-Based Assessment

From time to time, teachers must complete more formal assessments of children's progress in writing. These assessments may be part of the ongoing formative or diagnostic assessments that contribute to effective classroom instruction or they may be summative assessments used for report cards or end of year school district testing. This type of assessment is usually conducted through a review of written products rather than assessing the processes students engage in when writing. Assessment of a portfolio and/or writing folder, and the creation of student writing profiles, however, can also be useful summative assessment tools. However, it is frequently the finished product or the test score that parents, school administration, school districts, provincial departments of education, and employers use to judge writing abilities.

The assessment requirements of school districts and provincial governments are frequently at odds with the needs of students and teachers. Where students want to know how they can improve their writing, and teachers want to inform their planning in order to meet their students' learning requirements, school districts and provincial governments (and sometimes parents) want to know how their students' abilities compare with the abilities of students in other jurisdictions. They also want a measure of how much their students know and can do—and the more objective, the better. As a result, teachers need a broad repertoire of assessment procedures, including formal ones that demonstrate accountability to the general public as well as informal procedures designed to provide feedback to individual students and input to instructional planning.

Student performance on product-based tasks cannot be "machine scored," but must instead be judged according to well-defined criteria. The vehicle containing these criteria is commonly known as a scoring rubric—a fixed scale and a list of characteristics describing performance for each of the points on the scale (see Marzana, Pickering, and McTighe, 1993). A rubric differs from a scoring key in that a scoring key does not contain descriptive characteristics, just a list of how points are to be assigned. Various provincial ministries of education and school districts in Canada have developed their own rubrics for the assessment of student writing. Samples of these are presented later in this chapter in Boxes 9.8, 9.9, and 9.10. Teachers are trained to mark these writing tests as objectively as possible, minimizing reader bias and ensuring that scoring is consistent. Reliability checks are conducted regularly throughout the marking sessions.

Markers of student writing on large-scale tests are usually viewed as authorities who shrug aside their social values and histories when engaged in the evaluation process. However, an examination of scores assigned to the narrative writing of elementary and middle-grade students on large-scale examinations in Canada, Great Britain, and the United States reveals consistent gender patterns in the distribution of scores (Applebee, Langer, and Mullis, 1986; Stobart, Elwood, and Quinlan, 1992; Alberta Education, 1992; 1995; U.S. Department of Education, 1995). Repeatedly, greater percentages of scores at the high and medium levels for the grade are assigned to girls' narrative writing, and greater percentages of scores at the lower levels are assigned to boys' narrative writing. Does this mean that boys do not write as well as girls, or do educators describe their expectations of "good writing" in terms of the kinds of writing completed by girls? This is a question assessors keep in mind as they teach and assess writing.

Analysis of Writing Samples

When reading samples of students' writing, teachers are mindful that writing is not a single skill. Writing is a complex and sophisticated process that involves the effective utilization of syntax, organizational strategies, vocabulary, transcription tools and ideas. Each of these varies according to the purpose and audience for the writing. The purpose and intended audience for a piece of writing shape the composition. Expressive writing is writer-oriented: its purpose is to reveal feelings, attitudes, and perceptions. Expository writing is subject-oriented: it is meant to explain or present information on a subject. Persuasive writing is audience-oriented: the writer takes a position on a topic and tries to convince others about it. The stimulus, or prompt, for a writing task also frames the piece of writing and influences the piece considerably. Therefore, when teachers read and score student writing samples, they take all of these factors into consideration, varying their reading of the piece according to the purpose for the writing and the stimulus provided.

Many teachers, and language arts consultants develop rubrics and scoring guides for assessing and marking writing in their own classrooms. Frequently, these guides are developed in collaboration with the students themselves. The collaborative process facilitates three things:

1. As the students and teacher together develop the guide, they explore what constitutes a good piece of writing.

2. The students become aware of the criteria on which they will be evaluated.

3. Students remain in control of all aspects of their writing from onset to completion.

The collaborative nature of the process demonstrates the teacher's respect for students and recognizes their contributions in the classroom. Language arts consultant John Proctor developed many scoring guides for assessing writing in his work with children in schools, one of which is displayed in Box 9.7.

Box 9.7   Scoring Guide for Assessing Persuasive Writing—Grade 6

If you are going to mark my argument, here's what to look for:	Marks Possible	My Mark	Peer Mark	Teacher's Mark and Comments
A. What I said and how I said it				
I made a strong first impression	3			
I presented my point of view	6			
I presented my points in order	4			
My argument was clear and made sense	3			
B. How I presented my ideas for my reader				
I checked my spelling	2			Spelling words to work on:
I made sure my ideas were in sentences with correct capitals and punctuation	2			
My handwriting, neatness, and presentation were the best I can make them	2			
C. Working for bonus marks				
I "took out the garbage" by taking out words (such as "I feel" and "In my opinion")	2			
I made a real effort to persuade you that my argument was a good one	1			
Total marks	**25**			
Comments:				

Source: Reprinted with permission of John Proctor, University of Alberta.

Holistic Scoring

In **holistic scoring** students are evaluated on what they do *well* rather than on what they fail to do. This method encourages teachers to focus on the specifics they have in mind for rating essays and other pieces of writing before reading them. These specifics may include

- the students' attention to purpose and audience, and the ability to organize ideas according to the needs of communicating with that audience, whether through poetic, persuasive, expressive, or informative modes;
- the students' attention to the visual and verbal cues of the assignment (e.g., "Give at least one reason …");

Box 9.8 Holistic Rubric for Writing Assessment

Upper-half papers are characterized by well-supported, original ideas, clear evidence of an organizational plan, and general mastery of the conventions of standard English, although even the strongest papers may contain some developmentally appropriate errors in spelling or sentence structure.

The **"6"** paper contains sophisticated treatment of ideas, well supported by relevant details. Organization is clear and logical, with a strong lead and effective conclusion. Vivid and precise word choice, varied sentences and a clear, well-developed writer's voice combine to create a well-crafted piece of writing. Any errors in conventions are usually the result of risk-taking.

The **"5"** paper contains original treatment of ideas with relevant and appropriate details. It is well organized and usually has a strong lead and adequate conclusion. Clear and descriptive word choice and a developing writer's voice are evident. There may be some variation in sentence length and complexity. Minor errors in conventions do not interfere with the meaning of the piece.

The **"4"** paper may be somewhat mundane, but it demonstrates adequate treatment of ideas that are somewhat supported by details. Some writer's voice may be apparent. There is evidence of a good organizational plan with functional lead and conclusion. Word choice is generally appropriate, though it may be lacking in precision and originality, and sentences may lack variety. Some errors in conventions are common.

Lower-half papers lack originality or effective support for ideas. Vocabulary may be immature and control of conventions of standard English is inadequate.

The **"3"** paper is likely to contain unoriginal ideas with inadequate support, or irrelevant details that do not support the main idea. A writer's voice may or may not be evident. Word choice may be correct, but lacking maturity, and sentences tend to be simple in structure. Frequent errors in conventions are common, but the piece should be readable.

The **"2"** paper contains trivial treatment of ideas without supporting details. It is characterized by an inadequate organizational plan, immature vocabulary, short, simple sentences, and frequent errors in conventions that may, at times, interfere with understanding of the piece.

The **"1"** piece is generally characterized by such inadequate mastery of conventions of standard English that the piece may be barely comprehensible. Ideas are incomplete or confusing, there is no evidence of organization and vocabulary choice is limited.

An asterisk code (*) is used for papers that are blank, illegible, or written on a topic other than the one assigned.

Source: Based on the Regina Board of Education Scoring Guide. Originally adapted from the Northwest Regional Educational Laboratories Six Traits Writing Program by Sandra Pace, Lori Rog, Trudy Loftsgard, and Myra Froc.

- the students' developmental capabilities, allowing for the general language characteristics of children of a similar age (e.g., the invented spelling of children in the primary grades); and
- constraints of the evaluation situation—that is, the context or setting where the writing takes place (in many evaluative situations, for example, children do not have time to revise, edit, or ask for peer or teacher assistance).

A number of different methods for conducting holistic assessments have been established and many rubrics have been developed over the years. The rubric displayed in Box 9.8 was developed by the Regina Board of Education. This rubric is used for scoring writing at the Grades 4, 8, and 10 levels. An alternative method of holistic assessment, and probably the simplest, is *general impression marking*. The rater scores the paper by deciding where it fits in the range of papers produced for that assignment on that occasion. Although there is no analysis of specific features and no summary of scores, this method has high reliability because experienced raters use an implicit list of features in much the same way as do classroom teachers . If teachers were to spread out in front of them a set of writing from all the children in their class, written on the same day and on the same topic, it would be fairly clear which were the "best" pieces of writing and which were the least well developed. The middle-ranked pieces would be more difficult to arrange in some kind of order, but eventually a teacher would be able to make the decision on the basis of an implicit or internalized set of criteria. The use of this method for scoring or assessing writing can be facilitated in a school setting by a second teacher working collaboratively on the assessment. On such occasions, the teachers' implicit criteria are made explicit as problematic pieces of writing are discussed and a grade is decided upon.

Analytic Scales

Analytic scales break the writing performance down into component parts, such as organization, wording, and ideas. It takes longer to accomplish than holistic scoring, but provides more specific information and is usually regarded as being more objective. The list of features assessed may range from four to twelve, with each feature described in some detail and with high, mid-, and low points identified and described along a scoring line for each feature.

Analytic assessment of writing is used by many school districts including Edmonton Public Schools. Their Highest Level of Achievement Tests (HLATs) are administered in

---

Box 9.9 Criteria for "Excellent" Writing at Grade 3

Grade 3: Excellent

Performance Criteria: EXCELLENT

The writer fulfils the task and purposefully controls details and language to **shape the writing**.

The paper shows **overall unity** and artistry of communication.

The writing is focused, sustains the reader's interest, and **engages audience**.

The content is memorable and the topic is **skilfully** developed.

Vocabulary and usage are often clever, and **well chosen** for the form and purpose.

Continued

Box 9.9 Criteria for "Excellent" Writing at Grade 3 *continued*

The organization and style of the paper create a sense of voice **unique** to the writer.

Spelling, grammar, capitalization, and punctuation applications are **controlled** to enhance the impact of the writing; errors are hardly noticeable.

Achievement Criteria: GRADE THREE

- Audience appeal
  - _ Choose words and language patterns to create desired effects_
  - _ Hold the reader's interest in presentation of ideas
- Content and planning
  - _ support the piece of writing with some specific details
  - _ elaborate on ideas in plan and/or writing
- Vocabulary and usage
  - _ choose words appropriate to the context of their writing
  - _ use a variety of applicable words to add interest and detail
- Organization and clarity
  - _ use sentence variety to link ideas
  - _ order information in a connected sequence
  - _ provide an introduction
  - _ provide closure
- Style and voice
  - _ express thoughts and ideas using an authentic personal voice
  - _ convey personal feelings about selected topic
- Sentence structure and grammar
  - _ vary sentence beginnings by using different words
  - _ show general control of subject and verb agreement
  - _ construct complete sentences correctly
- Mechanics: spelling, capitalization, punctuation
  - _ use conventional spelling for most common words
  - _ use capitalization for sentence beginnings, proper names, I, acronyms, and titles
  - _ use end punctuation correctly (.?!)
- Editing and revising
  - _ make changes in word choices and spelling

Key:
  - _ Sample shows evidence of this criteria.
  - o No evidence of this criteria in sample.

Observations—Applying Criteria to the Sample, **Tickle Monster**

This sample was judged *excellent* because the writer purposefully controls language and engages the audience throughout. All criteria at the *Grade 3* level were met. The writer varies sentence beginnings including starting with a phrase. The choice of words reveals the writer's feelings about the game.

This writer may benefit from exposure to a variety of writing styles in literature.

Source: Reproduced from Edmonton Public Schools, Resource Development Services, *Teacher resource for Highest Level of Achievement: HLAT writing, 2002 edition* (Edmonton, AB: Edmonton Public Schools, 2002), p. 30. Reproduced with permission.

the spring of each school year and are intended to provide grade level achievement and growth data at the student, school, and district levels. Each student's writing is assessed as "excellent," "proficient," "adequate," or "limited" at each grade level. Box 9.9 presents the performance and achievement criteria for writing judged to be of "excellent" quality at the Grade 3 level. The task in 2002 was to explain to a peer how to play a game. The specific game and the context were to be selected by the individual writers. The criteria have proven useful to teachers in developing a vocabulary for discussing and conducting formal writing assessment, and in developing an explicit sense of what constitutes good writing.

Alberta Learning also uses analytic assessment in the Grades 3, 6, and 9 provincial tests of written language. The students are required to produce two writing samples: one a narrative piece prompted by a story starter, and the other a functional piece prompted by a specific purpose for a specific audience. The test provides for some choice of topic and includes time for planning and discussion with peers. The functional piece may be a business letter or a news article, for example, and is assessed according to "content" (development and organization, fulfilling the purpose, tone of the piece, and awareness of audience) and "content management" (accuracy and effectiveness of words and expressions, control of sentence structure, usage, mechanics, and format). The reporting category of content for the Grade 6 functional writing task (2002) is shown in Box 9.10. In this example, the functional writing task is a news article. Each category is scored from INS (Insufficient) through 1 to 5. Narrative writing is assessed according to five criteria: content (context, plausibility, details, awareness of audience), organization (introduction, sequencing, cohesion, and closure), sentence structure (type, length), vocabulary (specific, image-creating, accurate, and effective), and language conventions (capitalization, spelling, punctuation, format, usage, clarity, flow).

Below are the Grade 6 descriptors for a narrative text that "approaches the standard of excellence":

Content

- The context is clearly established and sustained.
- The events and/or actions are consistently appropriate for the established context.
- Supporting details are specific and consistently effective.
- The writing captivates and holds the reader's interest and is creative and/or original.

Organization (or Development)

- The introduction is purposeful; interesting; clearly establishes events, characters, and/or setting; and provides direction for the writing.
- Events and/or details are arranged in paragraphs in a purposeful and effective order, and coherence is maintained.
- Connections and/or relationships among events, actions, details, and/or characters are consistently maintained.
- The ending ties events and/or actions together.

Sentence Structure

- Sentence structure is effectively and consistently controlled.
- Sentence type and length are consistently effective and varied.
- Sentence beginnings are varied.

Vocabulary

- Words and expressions are used accurately and effectively.

Table 9.10   Alberta Learning Grade 6 Descriptors for Content (Functional Writing—News Article)

Focus

When marking CONTENT appropriate for Grade 6 functional writing, the marker should consider:

5 Meets the standard of excellence	• Effectiveness of ideas and organization of the news article • How the purpose of the assignment is fulfilled with complete and appropriate information • Appropriateness of tone for the assignment and awareness of audience
4 Approaches the standard of excellence	• The ideas are well developed and organization of the news article is clear and effective. • Complete information is presented, and this information is enhanced by precise and appropriate details that effectively fulfill the purpose of the assignment. • A tone appropriate for the assignment is clearly and effectively maintained.
3 Clearly meets the acceptable standard	• The ideas are generally well developed and organization of the news article is generally effective. • Complete information is presented, and this information is substantiated by appropriate details that fulfill the purpose of the assignment. • A tone appropriate for the assignment is clearly maintained.
2 Does not clearly meet the acceptable standard	• The ideas are adequately developed and organization of the news article is adequate. • Some sufficient information is given, and this information is supported by enough details to fulfill the purpose of the assignment. • A tone appropriate for the assignment is generally maintained.
1 Clearly below the acceptable standard	• The ideas are poorly developed and organization of the news article is ineffective. • Essential information may be missing. Supporting details are scant, insignificant, and/or irrelevant. The purpose of the assignment is only partially fulfilled. • A tone appropriate for the assignment is evident but not maintained.
INS Insufficient	• The ideas are not developed and organization of the news article is inadequate. • Essential information and supporting details are inappropriate or lacking. The purpose of the assignment is not fulfilled. • Little awareness of tone appropriate for the assignment is evident. • The marker can discern no evidence of an attempt to fulfil the assignment, or the writing is so deficient in length that it is not possible to assess content.

Note: Content and content management are equally weighted.

Please advise students that their work must be related to the assignment. Those assignments that are completely "off topic" will be awarded a mark of Insufficient.

Source: Alberta Learning, *English language arts Grade Six provincial testing bulletin*, 2002. Available: ednet. edc.gov.ab.ca/k_12/testing/achievement/bulletins/Gr6_ELA/gr6_ela_scoring.asp. Retrieved January 14, 2003. Reproduced with permission of the Minister of Learning, Province of Alberta, Canada, 2003.

• Specific words and expressions are used to create vivid images and/or to enrich details.

Conventions
• The quality of the writing is enhanced because it is essentially error-free.
• Errors, if present, do not reduce the clarity or interrupt the flow of the communication.

Box 9.11 Zulu

They came over to me talking in soft mumbling sounds that I couldn't understand. I backed into the corner of the stall and watched as they brought out a small harness. The creature reached out a hand and stroked my neck.

"He's a big one Alana, are ya still sure you want 'im?" One asked, obviously refering to me.

"Yes, the bigger they are the higher they jump."

The first speaker stepped forward and held out the soft leather thing, which they called a halter, for me to smell. It had no scent but I drew my head back and turned away. I looked for my mother, she was watching, but did nothing. The one they called Alana took the halter and slipped it over my head. I shook my head, not liking this thing tight on my face. I ran around the stall and rubbed my face on the rough wood of the wall.

"He's a spirited one alright." Henry said (The first one)

"Yeah, I don't intend to break that." Alana commented

"What are you going to call him?"

"Well his sire is Zulu Royaal and then his mother is Gotoit, so his name is Go to it Zulu. A pretty good name I think."

Henry came over, took hold of the halter and rubbed my ears. His hands were strong and gentle, I now knew why my mother was kind to these creatures.

A week passed. I got used to the halter and lead rope. I saw Henry and Alana each day. I asked my mother about them. She told me that Alana was her master and mine too. She said that I was to do what Henry and Alana wished me do and never to kick or bite. They have big plans for you, she would say, you will become great one day, till then you must do as they say.

When they came into the stall I could tell that there was something different about them. Not as happy. Alana came over to me right away and rubbed my nose and ears. I sniffed at her pockets as I had seen my mother do. She patted my side and slipped the halter over my head. I had grown much stronger over the last few days and loved to play tug'a'war with the shank. I looked at my mother, who I still would not move far from, Henry had put a halter on her too. I knew something was different today.

Analysis

Content. The piece of writing demonstrates a strong voice. Written as a first-person narrative, its details and description create an immediate engagement with the central character, a horse. The vivid description is enhanced by the use of dialogue. Rather than telling the reader that Zulu is a large horse, the writer demonstrates it in Henry's comment: "*He's a big one Alana, are ya still sure you want 'im?*" The reader is also forewarned of coming events through Alana's response: "*Yes, the bigger they are the higher they jump.*" The entire excerpt from the story is focused on the events in the stall, the early breaking of the young horse and his introduction to the harness. There are no extraneous details, no irrelevant content. The reader's interest is captivated and sustained.

Organization. The introduction is interesting and clearly establishes a setting and a point of view. The events of the story are arranged in paragraphs in a coherent sequence and are clearly connected, creating a cohesive piece of writing. The unfolding of events reveals the horse's character and situation, and the ending ties events together, as well as foreshadowing the events of the next chapter.

Continued

Box 9.11   Zulu   *continued*

Sentence structure. The sentence structure is effectively controlled, with a variety of sentence lengths and types from coordination ("*I backed into the corner of the stall and watched as they brought out a small harness*") to subordination ("*The first speaker stepped forward and held out the soft leather thing, which they called a halter, for me to smell*"). There are no sentence fragments or run-on sentences. The sentence beginnings are varied ("*When they came into the stall, …*").

Vocabulary. Words and expressions such as *halter*, *shank*, and *lead rope* are used accurately. The vocabulary is varied and colourful. Words such as *mumbling*, *creative*, *scent*, and *spirited* create vivid images and add to the rich detail presented in the piece.

Conventions. The conventions of written language are of a high standard and the piece is enhanced because it is virtually error-free. Quotation marks are used appropriately, as are question marks and periods. Paragraphs are well formed, and the indentation of paragraphs and direct speech is formatted correctly. Occasionally dialect is used, and appropriate punctuation is used to mark this (as in '*im*). There are numerous commas where periods or semicolons would have been more appropriate, but this does not reduce the clarity or break up the flow of the text ("*I looked for my mother, she was watching, but did nothing*"). This usage is likely connected to the reading the student has done. The writer's favourite book was *Black Beauty* by Anna Sewell, originally published in 1877. *Black Beauty* uses a more old-fashioned style, with the frequent use of commas to break up the text, rather than periods or semicolons.

As a demonstration, Box 9.11 presents an excerpt from a composition written by a Grade 6 student, together with an evaluation of the piece based on the above criteria.

The assessment strategies we have discussed in this chapter provide teachers with information about all major aspects of children's writing. The strategies are designed to meet the many purposes for which teachers are required to make assessments. In classrooms such as Ms. Hwang's, instructional decisions are based primarily on the students' needs. Information about those needs is gained through appropriate assessment strategies. Whether assessments are informal or formal, completed through observation, anecdotal records, checklists and profiles, portfolios or writing folders, student self-evaluation, writing conferences, analyses of samples of student writing, or provincial or local district achievement tests, the aim is always to effectively teach to the needs of students.

TEACHING SPELLING

The Development of Spelling Abilities

No aspect of the school curriculum is more researched than the teaching of spelling. Some of the very first educational research was conducted in spelling almost a hundred years ago. Researchers wanted to know whether children could spell specific words correctly or not, and which method of instruction was the most effective. During the 1970s, researchers began to explore how children develop the ability to spell correctly and the factors that affect their development. Is correct spelling tied to reading ability? Do word lists and frequent spelling tests help children become better spellers? Do children learn correct spelling as they read and write?

Invented Spelling

Children's very early writing attempts demonstrate what is known as *invented spelling*. Much research was conducted in the area of invented spelling during the 1970s (e.g., Beers and Henderson, 1977; Gentry, 1978, 1981), particularly on how children move from invented to more conventional spelling. Invented spelling is part of the developmental progression children make as they journey toward mastering orthodox spelling, and it occurs as a result of them listening acutely to the spoken language they hear around them. Young children are particularly sensitive to the sounds of words, and as they attempt to encode words into print, they try to put the sounds they hear into symbol form (Read, 1975).

During the process of acquiring orthodox spelling abilities, children generally move through five major stages of invented spelling. The process can last from age 3 or 4 through to age 11 or 12 (the Grade 6 or 7 level). Before the age of 3, most children draw and make letter shapes, but their attempts are not usually referred to as spelling, though it is recognized that these young learners are indeed "writing."

The five stages of invented spelling are

1. *Prereading or precommunicative spelling.* This stage of invented spelling consists of the random orderings of whatever letters children can draw. There is no awareness of sound–symbol relationship, and so strings of letters such as Beth's writing (in Exhibit 9.1) of *REaEoEfa aogrt NOCe baEONOEOLE* might appear on the page. Children may have their own "meaning" to go along with the letters, and may tell a coherent story to accompany them. An adult might transcribe this story onto the same page as the child's print. In Beth's case, her mother transcribed the message "I like Santa's mustache. I got my Christmas tree up last night." At this stage, Beth has no knowledge that specific configurations of letters and words are needed to create meaningful print. However, she does have a firm grasp of the message concept—that what is written on a page signifies a particular meaning.

2. *Prephonetic or semiphonetic spelling.* In this stage, children have a primitive concept of the alphabet and of letter names, and so letter names are used as clues in spelling. Children in this stage might write *NHR* for "nature," or represent a whole word with one letter, usually an initial consonant. Rarely are vowels used; a child's spelling in this stage consists almost entirely of consonants. Ian's writing, shown in Exhibit 9.2, is moving into the **phonetic** stage, but much of his spelling still reflects semiphonetic elements, as in his spelling of *GRL* for "girl" and *JWP* for "jump."

3. *Phonetic spelling.* This is the stage most commonly seen in students from kindergarten through Grade 3. Children have an understanding of sound–symbol correspondence, but they represent the features of words according to how they themselves hear and articulate the words. This often leads to the omission of preconsonant nasals, such as the *M* in *NUBERS* or the *N* in *SWIMIG*. Exhibits 9.3, 9.4, and 9.5 illustrate children's spelling during this stage.

4. *Transitional spelling.* In Grades 2 through 4, children generally include a vowel in every syllable and use familiar spelling patterns, though they are frequently used incorrectly. The word "make" may be spelled as *maek*, or "was" as *whas*. Rules are overgeneralized, and the aspects of spelling a child is currently learning become obvious through error patterns in the writing. In Exhibit 9.6, the writer spells "witch" as *wich*, and in Exhibit 9.7, "came" is spelled *caem*. Children also use the meanings of words to help them spell. One child wrote a note to his mother who was attending university at the time: "I hope you have a good time at youknowvursdy." There is no doubt that he understood that university is a place where people come "to know." Exhibits 9.6, 9.7, and 9.8 show the transitional spelling of writers in Grade 2. These students are exploring the nature of spelling

conventions such as the use of *ch*, the *ed* suffix, *ck*, and silent vowels (*caem* for "came") and are developing a core vocabulary of standard spellings (*I, my, the, on*).

5. *Standard spelling.* Generally, at about Grade 5 or later, children demonstrate a more sophisticated understanding of spelling. They understand the constraints of syntax and morphology on their spelling (i.e., the conventions of spelling), and they use dictionaries to assist in correct spelling. Children at this age have learned that correct spelling is a courtesy to the reader, as well as necessary for expressing meaning clearly to an audience.

Exhibit 9.1 Beth's Prereading Spelling

Exhibit 9.3 Omar's Phonetic Spelling

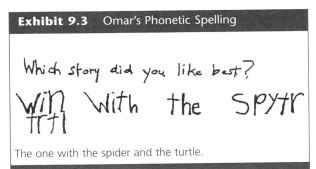

The one with the spider and the turtle.

Exhibit 9.4 Hannah's Phonetic Spelling

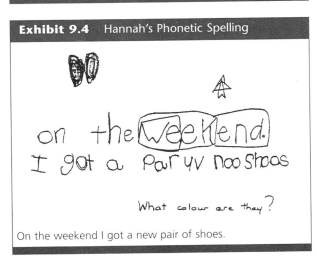

On the weekend I got a new pair of shoes.

Exhibit 9.2 Ian's Prephonetic Spelling

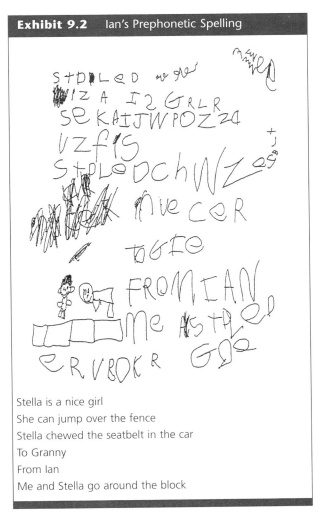

Stella is a nice girl
She can jump over the fence
Stella chewed the seatbelt in the car
To Granny
From Ian
Me and Stella go around the block

Exhibit 9.5 Gillian's Prephonetic Spelling

I can write letters to my mom.

Exhibit 9.6 April's Transitional Spelling

My favourite part was when the witch kissed Thistle.

Exhibit 9.7 Zak's Transitional Spelling

When pig blew up and the family came out of pig's stomach.

Exhibit 9.8 Michael's Transitional Selling

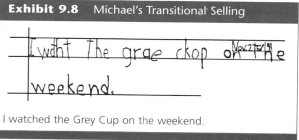

I watched the Grey Cup on the weekend.

Although these stages appear to be a natural progression for most children, the question remains as to how and when conventional spelling should be encouraged or required in classrooms. The answer is that spelling always counts, and conventional spelling can always be encouraged—but young children must first of all be helped to compose their own texts before they are *required* to adhere to the conventions of written language. In addition, it is important that teachers and caregivers focus on the words children use in their writing most frequently—words such as *I*, *was*, *and*, and *but*.

Much standard spelling can be taught during editing conferences, but some children need a more structured approach to learning conventional spelling. When adults write in journals or write letters to friends, even their spelling may not be 100 percent correct. What is important in these cases is that they make an effort to spell correctly so they can communicate with themselves (through the journal) or friends (through letters). When focusing on spelling in children's writing, it is helpful for teachers and parents to keep in mind the audience and the purpose for the writing. There are many occasions when the message to be conveyed is more important than correct spelling, especially if the piece is to be read by a limited audience.

Teachers and parents can, however, help students to become better spellers by being mindful of the things that *good* spellers do, emphasizing these behaviours in their children. Most of the time good spellers do the following:

- Recall spelling patterns and generalizations they have learned through their reading and writing
- Know about words and how to use them
- Have a repertoire of spelling strategies to choose from and do not rely only on one or two strategies
- Know which is the best strategy to apply in which situation
- Do not rely on sounding out words (too unreliable)
- Do not rely on spelling "rules" (again, too unreliable)
- Use visual memory in conjunction with other strategies

In summary, good spellers *think* about their spelling and do not rely on rote memorization.

Teaching Spelling in the Context of the Writing Process

Many children develop competency in standard spelling entirely through reading, writing, and sharing their writing with an interested audience. However, standard spelling does require effort to master; it is a discipline to be learned. An awareness of the need for correct spelling can be taught from Grade 2 onward. It is easy for any writer to become lazy about spelling, but it is essential for a committed writer to adhere to conventional forms. Habits formed in childhood often persist into adulthood, though usually adults have only one or two major error patterns in their spelling. For some, the error pattern will be confusion over double consonants (words such as *embarrass*); for others it will be problems with reversing letters, or omitting letters in a word (e.g., *contain* spelled as *contian* or *cotain*). Once adult writers become aware of the nature of their spelling difficulties, they can make efforts to learn the specific words they have difficulty with, usually words such as *embarrassment* or *containment*.

Teachers can help their students learn conventional spelling by conducting regular brief lessons using the overhead projector, focusing attention on common misspellings, and encouraging children to watch for these specific words in their spelling that particular week. More idiosyncratic misspelling can be addressed in writing conferences, but usually not until a piece is ready for a final draft unless the word is an unusual one for the child to write (e.g., *cornucopia* and *satellite*). This also applies to errors in capitalization, punctuation, and grammar. In elementary school, teachers rarely focus lengthy language arts lessons on these aspects of writing, nor do they provide worksheet exercises for the students to complete. The skills are more likely to be addressed in the context of their students' current writing, and through brief lessons interspersed with other activities.

Lessons of ten minutes' duration are usually more effective than drills and worksheet pages of exercises. It is the context of the usage and the relevance to the child that make an impact on their learning. Skills learned out of context are rarely transferred to writing completed in workshops or to writing done across curricular areas. If a number of children in the class have problems in one specific area, a group can be formed so that the teacher can give direct instruction to those who need it. There is no point in teaching to a whole class if only a few children really need to learn that skill. Through reading children's writing, and through listening to the talk children engage in while they write, teachers can gain much useful knowledge about who needs to be taught certain skills and who has already mastered them.

The presence of spell-check tools on computer word processing programs provides both advantages and disadvantages for students. Before working with the tools, students need guidance in using them effectively and appropriately. Students can be encouraged to use the tool as a first step in eliminating typographical errors and in identifying misspelled words. Following this, students must check for homonyms and homophones. Which word did they actually intend to use? The computer does not make distinctions of this nature and will not catch such misspellings. Here, the spell-check tool provides an interesting focus for instruction, teaching students an awareness of homonyms and homophones as spelling items *and* teaching young writers not to rely on computer spell-checkers completely. Many spell-check tools have an "autocorrect" feature that individual children (or the class as a collaborative whole) might want to program with their own frequent misspellings. Again, this process provides a vehicle for instruction as students identify their common misspellings and focus their attention on them.

Following are some specific strategies for aiding students in their spelling development:

- Ask students to write on every other line of a paper so that they can make changes without rewriting or erasing.
- Encourage writers to leave blank spaces for words they do not know how to spell. It is important that thoughts continue to flow; omitted words can be inserted later. Students can be encouraged to write the first few letters of the omitted word so they will have a greater chance of remembering which word they had intended to use.
- Note spelling errors by putting an asterisk in the margin of students' writing. Ask the students to find the errors themselves. Children can frequently recognize incorrect spelling, and in doing so they are reminded of the words they have difficulty in spelling.
- Encourage children to have paper at their desks so that words they are unsure of can be written down for them.
- Refrain from providing only an oral spelling of a word; always accompany it with a written model. Spelling is essentially a visual memory activity that is only conducted in writing. It is therefore important that students *see* the word they need help in spelling.
- Teach students how to use a dictionary, thesaurus, and other word books effectively, and encourage their use. A spelling dictionary is usually more effective for elementary school students than a conventional dictionary. A student who needs to spell *rein* will usually look under *ra* in a conventional dictionary, thus meeting with little success.
- Alphabet games help students to understand how dictionaries and encyclopedias are organized. Activities such as lining up in alphabetical order according to last name or first name also help children understand how to use telephone books and other reference aids.

The Direct Teaching of Spelling

Research studies have demonstrated that new and different words enter the language on an ongoing basis. Dictionaries are updated regularly, but many of the new words they contain will appear in children's writing first. Ves Thomas' landmark Canadian study (1979) showed that *more* words were used in children's writing in the late 1970s than were used 40 years before that time. Since 1979, language has changed enormously, largely through advances in science and technology that have brought new words and phrases into everyday use; words such as *mouse*, *windows*, *Internet*, *microchip*, and *browser*. At the same time these words have entered the lexicon, there has been a shift in the way writing is taught in elementary schools. Children are encouraged to write about what they do and what they think, bringing more of the child's personal world into the classroom. Characters from video games and movies now appear in children's stories, increasing the number of words children must learn to spell correctly. Children are using more words, are writing more, and are attempting to spell a greater range of words than in the past.

Spelling competence is relatively easy to test; a word list can be dictated to a student, and the examiner can check to see whether the words are spelled correctly. However, words spelled correctly on a word list do not necessarily transfer to a piece of writing created in a different context. Unless the words have been internalized and become part of the stored knowledge a writer possesses, the spelling remains in doubt. Spelling a word correctly on a test list is no guarantee that the same word will be spelled correctly in a shopping list, a journal entry, a letter, or an essay.

Adding to the problem is the fact that spelling textbooks generally do not present the teaching of spelling in ways that are consistent with research findings about learning to spell. Activities in spelling textbooks generally do not encourage risk-taking, which is a critical component of learning, and they encourage students to rely on rote memorization. Many of the activities in textbooks are repetitious and rarely help poor spellers become strong spellers. The books often contain "busy" pages with mixtures of cartoon graphics, bold colours, and many different fonts. There are frequently so many different activities on one page that it is difficult to tell what is being taught. Activities range from crossword puzzles to "Alphaspell," "Noun Hunt," "Syllable Count," "Letter Ladders," and "Word Chains." Research has shown many times that the only real way to become an effective speller is to do lots of writing for audiences other than oneself, read widely, and check spelling in a dictionary or word book whenever there is doubt. Even the most recent spelling textbooks do not focus on *teaching* spelling, but focus instead on children's word games. Teachers must ask, "What am I teaching by doing these activities, and what else could I do with this time that would be more beneficial to my students in learning how to be good spellers?"

A number of good resources are available to assist teachers in helping their students become strong and independent spellers. These include *Spelling Strategies You Can Teach* by Mary Tarasoff (1990), *Spelling: Sharing the Secrets* by Ruth Scott (1993), and *The Spelling Teacher's Handbook* by Jo Phenix (2001).

Children are more likely to become effective spellers if their motives for using correct spelling stem from communicative needs rather than a desire to please the teacher. If children have something important to say, and they have an audience they wish to address, correct spelling will help them convey their message clearly to the reader. Correct spelling is a courtesy to the reader, and is also important in transmitting a clear message. Correct spelling adds to the writer's credibility. This is especially important for teachers, who are generally perceived as role models. Teachers are expected to spell every word correctly (if a word is spelled incorrectly on a wall chart or on the chalkboard, one can almost guarantee that a visiting teacher or parent will notice it!), and certainly teachers should not send to parents or the public any of their writing that has not been carefully checked for correct spelling.

A Word List Approach

When employing a word list approach in the direct teaching of spelling, teachers ensure that they use

- a reliable word list created from either the words children in the classroom have difficulty spelling or from a reliable resource book such as Thomas (1979),
- a self-corrected pretest of ten to twelve words,
- a study procedure to ensure that children learn effective strategies for memorizing words,
- "check tests" with a buddy throughout the week,
- a mastery test of the entire list of words originally provided on day one, and
- a record of spelling achievement (on a chart at the back of the spelling scribbler).

Word Lists

When a teacher has observed children's writing and has identified those students needing direct spelling instruction (which would rarely be more than half the class), a word list approach is usually effective. The word list compiled by Ves Thomas, found in his book *Teaching Spelling: Canadian Word Lists and Instructional Techniques* (1979), remains one of the most reliable and thorough resources for teachers today. The word lists in the book are based on the frequency of usage of words in children's writing in Canada, so that the most frequently used words are on the word list for the youngest children (Grade 2), and so on up through the grades. It is suggested that word lists and study procedures *not* be used with children before Grade 2.

If teachers choose to create their own word lists, they may base them on the spelling errors they notice in the students' writing in their classroom. The use of either a preexisting list or a teacher-compiled list should provide an effective vehicle for students to study the correct spelling of words. It is not suggested that children learn spelling from lists of words compiled from current units of study across the curriculum. Words on such lists are usually used for only a short period of time, when the unit is being studied, and the words are not usually the most frequently used words in the students' writing in general. The most important factors in creating a word list are that the words be relevant to children's lives and be used regularly in their writing.

Many studies have been conducted on the most frequently used words in both adult and children's writing. It has been found that the most common 100 words used by elementary school children in their writing make up about 60 percent of all the words children write. The most common 500 words make up 70 percent of all words written, and the most common 2000 words make up 83 percent of all words written (Simpson, 1980). The average elementary school program teaches between 3500 and 4500 words over a five-year period. It is therefore essential that the words taught on those lists form part of a child's *core* spelling vocabulary. The remainder of the words children use in their writing have to be learned by memory from the simple experience of writing them and checking for correct spelling in dictionaries and other word books. Thomas' research finding (1979) that Canadian children are using an increasing number of words in their writing has implications for the teaching of spelling, since it is not possible to teach all these words by memory in the five years of an elementary school spelling program. Box 9.12 displays one well-known list of the 100 words most frequently written by children in elementary school (Carroll, Davies, and Richman, 1971).

Self-Corrected Pretest

A word list is most effectively used when it is preceded by a self-corrected pretest. All the children in a spelling group are given a test *before* the words are presented to them in list form for study. This procedure allows children to identify which words they actually have

Box 9.12	The 100 Most Frequently Used Words in Children's Writing

a	find	like	over	up
about	first	little	people	use
after	for	long	said	very
all	from	made	see	was
an	has	make	she	water
and	have	many	so	way
are	he	may	some	we
as	her	more	than	were
at	him	most	that	what
be	his	my	the	when
been	how	no	their	where
but	I	not	them	which
by	if	now	then	who
called	in	of	there	why
can	into	on	they	will
could	is	one	this	with
did	it	only	through	words
do	its	or	time	would
down	just	other	to	you
each	know	out	two	your

Source: J. Carroll, P. Davies, and B. Richman, *American Heritage word frequency book* (Boston: Houghton Mifflin, 1971). Adapted and reprinted by permission of the publisher.

difficulty spelling correctly. As children self-correct the pretest, they become aware of the spelling errors they have made, and this feature alone allows most children to correctly spell the word the next time they use it. The self-corrected pretest is probably the single most effective strategy for improving spelling ability. It provides each child with an individualized list of words that need to be studied, because the words spelled correctly can be put aside until the end of the week. At that time, a mastery test will be given that includes all the words on the original list.

It is very important that children correct their own pretest, for much learning occurs while they check their spelling. Sometimes only two or three words might be incorrectly spelled, and at other times there may be as many as five or six. If a child is presented with more than five or six words to study in one week, it is usually too many to be learned effectively. Children who experience difficulty in spelling need to work with small amounts of material and short lists of manageable words. In the early grades, a pretest of ten words is usually sufficient. In upper elementary school, the list may include from ten to twelve words.

Study Procedure

Words spelled incorrectly on the pretest are written out correctly and are used as a model for the study procedure (see Box 9.13). On the day following completion of the study procedure, students can work in pairs, giving each other buddy tests of their own personal

> **Box 9.13** Spelling Study Procedure
>
> 1. Look at the word, pronounce it, and say the letters (auditory and visual stimulation).
> 2. Listen to the sounds and notice how they are represented (sound–symbol relationship).
> 3. Close your eyes and try to see the word as you pronounce it (recall–visualization).
> 4. Keep your eyes closed and say the letters in order.
> 5. Open your eyes and check.
> 6. Write the word without looking at the model. Check writing (kinesthetic recall).
> 7. Write the word a second time and check it.
> 8. Write the word a third time. If it's correct, consider it learned.

spelling words. All students can benefit from learning a study procedure for spelling. There are many variations of study procedures, and if children do not have success with one version, they can try a modified version. For most children, the study procedure is a "key to the door" where successful spelling is concerned. Spelling is a visual memory task, and a good study procedure provides weak spellers with a concrete structure for their learning. A suggested study procedure is outlined in Box 9.13.

A sound study procedure eliminates the irrelevant and time-consuming activities sometimes found in spelling textbooks. It focuses the energies of the students on the direct learning of specific words that the individual finds difficult. There are likely to be occasions in the classroom when other methods of teaching spelling are necessary. For example, children with special needs may require alternative strategies that more specifically meet their learning requirements.

Mastery Test

A final mastery test given at the end of the week consists of the complete pretest list originally provided to the students at the beginning of the week. Spelling scores can be recorded on a chart at the back of a spelling scribbler so that children can track their own progress.

Spelling Practices to Avoid

Over the years, educators have become aware that some teaching strategies have not proven helpful in assisting children with improving their spelling:

- Pointing out the "hard spots" in words may be helpful only to a small number of children, and the hard spots are likely to be different from one child to another.
- Teaching spelling rules is not effective, since very few spelling rules can be applied regularly. Sayings such as "*i* before *e* except after *c*" may be very useful to most writers, but if they are taught as rules, then words that do not follow the rules must also be pointed out (such as *weigh* and *neighbour*). It is more effective to teach how to add suffixes (e.g., *baby* becomes *babies*) than it is to teach specific spelling rules. Most rules have almost as many exceptions as adherents (Clymer, 1963).
- Avoid having students copy spelling lists as a punishment, which establishes a negative attitude toward spelling that is not helpful to children's feelings about writing in general. Educators strive to promote enthusiasm for writing and try not to detract from the joys of writing by making writing, or any other school activity, abhorrent to children.

TEACHING GRAMMAR, PUNCTUATION, AND CAPITALIZATION

Grammar

As discussed in Chapter Two, educators often use the terms "grammar" and "syntax" interchangeably. *Syntax* is the term linguists use to describe the organization of language structures. **Grammar** is a term teachers usually use to define a prescriptive set of rules to be followed. Syntax is derived from the spoken language, but when it is taught in schools, it usually pertains to writing and is labelled "grammar." Educators and researchers have long believed that grammar should not be taught in elementary schools in a formal manner. However, children need to know the difference between what is acceptable or appropriate and what is considered poor grammar. They also need a vocabulary to be able to talk about language if they are to engage in writing conferences and develop an awareness of the writing techniques good writers use. Three basic perspectives on grammar are presented in Box 9.14 on page 270.

The teaching of grammar, usually based on the traditional, prescriptive model, was once perceived as a core feature of the elementary school curriculum. Today it is relegated to a somewhat minor role. Only a few decades ago, memorizing grammar rules, as well as memorizing poetry and quotations from plays, was believed to be good for the mind. The mind was conceptualized as a muscle, and memorization as good exercise for that muscle. Today, however, grammar is not taught as an end in itself, but as one of the tools to be used in the process of writing. Knowledge and control of grammar enables writers to strengthen their writing and clarify meaning, facilitating effective and precise communication. Correct and appropriate grammar also enables people to speak in a manner approaching "standard English," the form of English that conforms to established educated usage and is generally considered correct.

Studies in language development have shown that many concerns voiced by teachers about "grammar" are mostly concerns about usage, and usage depends on the dialect learned when children are young. A person's dialect can change when he or she moves from one area to another, or works among people speaking a closer approximation of standard English. However, the basic rules of grammar learned in childhood usually persist throughout life, and the majority of those rules are correct. By the age of six, when most children enter school, they have already mastered most of the grammar of the language, as described in Chapter Two.

Controversy has arisen in the past about whether dialect is part of a child's cultural heritage, and therefore to be protected and respected, or whether educators have the responsibility to teach children standard English so that all children will have a greater opportunity for success in higher education, business, and the professions. It is generally agreed, however, that grammar should be taught in school so that children learn to become effective writers and have the opportunity to move between dialect and standard English in speech.

It has been acknowledged for many years that teaching grammar in isolation from a child's actual writing is ineffective. Creating teaching units and providing worksheets on grammar have little effect on children's writing and speaking. More effective learning occurs when grammar is taught as part of the editing process of composition, and in brief lessons when necessary. Children can sometimes detect grammatical errors in their compositions, especially if the flow of the language or the meaning is disturbed by the error. However, much of the time, children cannot detect their own grammatical errors because the writing makes sense to them.

Box 9.14 Three Perspectives on Grammar

Linguists describe the structure of language in three ways, and all three ways influence the way grammar is taught.

1. The best known is *traditional* or *prescriptive grammar*, which provides rules for socially correct usage. This perspective dates back to the Middle Ages and has its roots in the study of Latin. The major contribution of traditional grammar is in the terminology it provides for students and teachers to talk about language. Because this form of grammar is based on Latin, it is not entirely appropriate for use with the English language, as it cannot adequately explain how language works. However, the three elements of grammar continue to be taught and prove useful to writers as they work their craft—types of sentences (declarative, interrogative, imperative, exclamatory); parts of sentences (simple, compound, complex, compound–complex); and parts of speech (nouns, pronouns, verbs, adverbs, adjectives, prepositions, conjunctions, and interjections).

2. *Structural grammar* attempts to describe how language is used. Structural grammar is not prescriptive, but descriptive, and it highlights the differences between written and spoken language patterns. The study of structural linguistics has provided detailed information about language in use, but it focuses on form and does not attempt to relate meaning to usage. Seven basic sentence patterns are identified, and it is the variations and combinations of these seven patterns that make up all the sentences people speak or write.

3. *Transformational grammar* is the most recent approach to the study of grammar. Transformational linguists attempt to describe both the way language works *and* the cognitive processes used to produce language. They refer to two levels or structures of language (the surface structure and the deep structure) to describe how meaning in the brain is transformed into the actual sentences people speak. Much research and development work was conducted during the 1960s and 1970s to make this approach viable for use in classrooms.

A thorough exploration of grammar and its teaching can be found in G. Tompkins and K. Hoskisson, *Language Arts: Content and Teaching Strategies* (3rd ed.) (Englewood Cliffs, NJ: Prentice-Hall, 1995).

As members of language communities, we accept certain phrases and incorrect usage as the norm, and it is difficult to teach children to change that usage. This is where a direct lesson is useful, because the whole group can focus on that particular item of usage and there is more likelihood that children will retain an awareness of it. One caution: students should at no time be embarrassed by their language usage. Language is an idiosyncratic part of every human being, and children (as well as adults) feel belittled if their language is criticized or faulted. Effective teachers handle this issue sensitively, aware that one dialect is not better than another, but different. Children can be taught that when playing with friends it may be acceptable to say "I should've went," but when they are in school their writing and oral language is expected to more closely adhere to standard English, and

"I should've gone" is correct and appropriate. Likewise, students need to know that writing "should of" instead of "should have" is neither acceptable nor correct.

A lesson on the differences in usage between *taught* and *learned*, *lent* and *borrowed*, or *seed* and *saw* might, for example, be necessary in some classrooms. A lesson on misplaced participles can be fun for children in the elementary years, as they can see the humour in sentences such as "I saw the lady walking down the hill with purple hair," and they enjoy figuring out why the sentence is ambiguous as well as how to fix it. It is through meaning that grammar can be taught most effectively, not through parsing sentences or learning definitions of parts of speech. Shelley Peterson has provided high-quality teacher resource material in her two books, *Becoming Better Writers* (1995) and *Teaching Conventions Unconventionally* (1997).

Knowledge of labels and definitions of parts of speech allows writers and speakers to talk about the language they are using. It is in this context that these items can be taught in school. In writing conferences and during the editing process, labels such as noun, adverb, and clause can be used. Through direct lessons they can be taught to the entire class. A brief ten-minute presentation, using examples on an overhead projector and involving the children in discussion, can be effective in reminding children about grammar and usage and in introducing certain concepts to children for the first time. Lengthy lessons with exercises on worksheets are generally not necessary. It *is* necessary, though, for children to learn these labels and their meanings so they can talk about their writing and hence improve it.

Punctuation and Capitalization

Punctuation and capitalization are the "mechanics" of written language. Writing conferences and short lessons are the most effective and appropriate vehicles for teaching the skills of punctuation and capitalization. As with grammar and word usage, worksheets of drill and skill exercises are not effective. During instruction, it is useful to refer children to the literature they are currently reading. Novels provide a quick reference for checking how direct speech, paragraphing, and the capitalization of names and places are addressed. Children often remember rules of capitalization and punctuation for a short time after they have been taught, but then forget to use them when they are composing and focusing on ideas.

Lessons are enhanced when teachers make them directly relevant to situations that affect the students—for example, through using samples of children's writing or questions children have raised themselves. It is a good idea to refer to these questions and honour their intent. Children who ask questions are the ones who want to learn. A lesson on using quotation marks might begin, for instance, with a problem raised by a student. Anne is writing a story and wants to use dialogue for two of the characters. She stops in her writing at "Who's going to run for help and who's going to stay here she asked." Anne does not know where to place the quotation marks. An overhead transparency of a comic strip can be used to demonstrate how quotation marks are used. Whenever the actual words spoken by a character are shown in a comic strip, they are inside a balloon. In a story, quotation marks are used instead of a balloon. Only the actual words spoken belong inside the quotation marks. The teacher can demonstrate this with a section of a story that includes dialogue printed on an overhead transparency (an overhead can easily be made of a page from a novel the children are familiar with). Working through Anne's original piece of student writing, the class can work with the teacher, putting in the quotation marks where they belong. As in many other learning situations, a collaborative approach is usually helpful for students, since they can engage with the problem as a group rather than in isolation. Instead of a follow-up exercise to see if the children have understood, it is more effective to observe the children's writing and remind them, when necessary, about the lesson. Lessons can be repeated, using different examples, whenever appropriate.

TEACHING HANDWRITING

It might appear, in the early years of the 21st century, that handwriting is a lost art. Certainly, the fine penmanship recognized in our grandparents is not evident in the handwriting of most students in today's classrooms. In fact, the focus of instruction has shifted from penmanship to composition. Yet legible handwriting is essential in today's world of computers just as much as it was 50 years ago. Although much writing is completed on a word processor, a great deal of what we write on a daily basis is still done by hand. Notes, jottings, journal entries, memos, and letters to friends are usually handwritten. Therefore, the need to teach handwriting in elementary school is still there, so that children can produce legible script with a minimum of *time*, *effort*, and *concentration* (the three criteria that are key to teaching handwriting). Students need to be able to read their own handwriting, and we all need to be able to read the handwriting of others.

Some points for teachers to remember:

- Students are greatly helped if they are taught to write in a way that is fluent, easy, routine, and comfortable.
- A teacher who pays little attention to handwriting is suggesting to students that handwriting is not important.
- The true test of handwriting is in situations where it is used on a day-to-day basis, doing such regular jobs as making lists, writing notes, leaving messages, and writing letters.
- In handwriting instruction, good teaching and modelling are essential, not just in the early grades, but throughout elementary school.
- A teacher's handwriting on the chalkboard, on wall charts, and on student work is a model for students of how letters are formed and what good writing looks like.

The Perceptual Motor Approach

Handwriting is more than simply a motor skill, fine muscle coordination, and practice. Children have to remember letter forms, somehow internalizing them. This is where the term "perceptual motor skill" originates. Each child has to build a perception or mental image of each letter form. It is a thinking process as well as a fine motor process. The research in this area goes back to the 1960s, to the work of Bea Furner (1969).

Furner believed that a child must first have a clear concept of how each letter appears, saying out loud how each letter is formed, while at the same time drawing it. The same process is used in teaching both **cursive writing** and **manuscript printing**. Steps in the instructional process are described in Box 9.15.

A guided practice of the manuscript letter *d* might go as follows: Pencil on the midline, go counterclockwise, round to the baseline, back up through the midline, up to the headline, retrace down to the baseline. Stop.

> **Box 9.15** Steps in Teaching the Perceptual Motor Approach to Handwriting
>
> - The teacher models handwriting instruction on the board (or an overhead projector). Clear lines are drawn on the board so that children can see the spacing of letters and the lines on which they are positioned.
> - The teacher uses a consistent writing vocabulary such as *baseline*, *midline*, *headline*, and *tail-line*.
> - As the teacher draws a letter on the board, he or she describes where the letter begins, the direction in which the hand moves, and the place where the letter ends.
> - The children describe aloud the strokes the teacher is using as the teacher draws the letter again.
> - The children draw the letter, saying aloud the description as they write, while being guided by the teacher.
> - After the letter is completed, the children compare the letter they have drawn with a model already on paper at their desks.

This would be repeated a number of times until the children begin to master the letter. A model on each child's desk provides immediate feedback as the child compares the written letter with the model. An example of one model is presented in Exhibit 9.9. The teacher attends to the number of strokes, the starting and stopping points, the direction of the strokes, and the size of the letters. The process should not be repeated more than five times during each practice session, or handwriting will lose quality—one good reason for not having children write lines or copy tedious work as a punishment.

In the intermediate grades, children may not need handwriting lessons every week, but they do need them from time to time, when the teacher can see that some children are having difficulty with a certain letter or letter combination. A lesson on the overhead projector can result in improvements in children's awareness of their handwriting and in penmanship legibility. These lessons are sometimes referred to as "maintenance lessons."

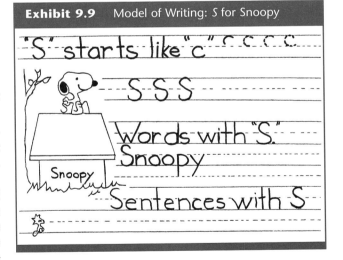

Exhibit 9.9 Model of Writing: *S* for Snoopy

"S" starts like "c" c c c c c
S S S
Words with "S."
Snoopy
Sentences with S
Snoopy

Evaluation of handwriting considers

- the form and size of the letters,
- the spacing of letters and words,
- alignment according to headline and baseline, and
- uniformity of slant.

Many handwriting scales are available for evaluating handwriting, but most do not allow for individuality in writing style. The criteria listed above are usually sufficient for providing feedback to a student and for talking about ways in which handwriting can be improved.

Helping the Left-Handed Writer

Approximately 10 percent of children in North America are left-handed. Although educators no longer insist that children write with their right hand (as was once the case), learning to write can still pose challenges for children who are left-handed. These children have unique instructional needs because of the nature of writing in the English language. English is written from left to right, thus creating a movement of the arm away from the body for right-handed children. Left-handed children physically move their arm toward their body as they write. In addition, as left-handed writers move their arm, they cover up what they have just written. Not only do they have no clear visual image of what they have written, but in covering up their writing they are also more likely to smudge their work and have further difficulty in rereading their script. Since the writing is covered by their hand, left-handed children cannot read their writing as they go, but have to stop and move their arm to reread their script.

Teachers can help left-handed children to write clearly and legibly without discomfort, developing a hand that requires a minimum of time, effort, and concentration. This is particularly important because, in order to produce clean copy and be able to read their work as they write, left-handed children frequently develop a "hooked" motion, curling their wrist over the top of the page and distorting the motions necessary to form letters. Left-handed writers may therefore require more one-on-one instruction from the teacher than right-handed writers, but sensitive teachers understand that this is necessary if the students are to be given the opportunity to develop handwriting that is legible, well-formed, evenly spaced, and with a uniform slant.

Here are some suggestions to help left-handed children at school and at home:

- Make sure the child is holding the pencil correctly—about three to four centimetres from the point and with the correct grasp by the fingers (i.e., farther away from the point than right-handed writers).
- Position the paper so that it is tilted downward at the right-hand side. This allows for an even slant and lets the child see what he or she has already written. Some teachers have found it helpful to place a piece of masking tape on the student's desk to indicate an appropriate tilt.
- Try to prevent the development of a "hooked" wrist—the habit of hooking the wrist around the writing—so as not to cover up what has been written.
- Seat the child so that light comes over the *right* shoulder and therefore the shadow of the hand does not fall on the writing.
- Provide children who need it with a lower desk surface to write on, or a cushion so that they can be higher in their seat and have a clearer view of their work.
- Do not insist on a slant to the right in letter formation. Many left-handed children write more effectively with a vertical formation.

Printing and Cursive Handwriting

Two styles of handwriting are taught in elementary school: *printing* (also called *manuscript writing*) and *cursive writing*. Children generally begin with printing, and toward the end of second grade or the beginning of third grade move into a cursive hand. The specific styles of each vary according to region and country. In North America there are a number of popular cursive styles, including D'Nealian (described below). Box 9.16 presents a comparison between traditional manuscript and cursive forms and D'Nealian script.

While many provincial and state curricula have a model of handwriting to be followed, increasingly provincial departments of education are not providing a model script. Curriculum guides and programs of study should be consulted before any handwriting style is taught, as it is important that students have a consistent style across the grades.

Toward the end of Grade 2 many children are eager to begin cursive handwriting and will begin to make the transition on their own. Other children will not be comfortable with cursive script until well into Grade 3. Many children today are expressing a preference for continuing to print, some reverting to manuscript printing in the later grades. There is no particular reason why they should move into cursive handwriting other than that it is an accepted adult convention. One of the advantages of D'Nealian script is that it was developed specifically to make the transition from printing to handwriting easier for children. A simplified form that flows from manuscript to cursive with little change in letter forms, this script is extremely legible and easy to use. Most other styles of writing are more difficult for children, and specific lessons on individual letters have to be taught. Children working with D'Nealian or similar scripts usually move into using cursive writing toward the middle of Grade 2.

The perceptual motor approach can be used for teaching cursive writing in much the same way as outlined earlier with printing. However, a new vocabulary has to be used to

---

Box 9.16   D'Nealian Script

With D'Nealian, the formation, size, slant, and rhythm learned in first grade are continued and built upon in Grades 2 and 3. As a result, second and third graders don't have to "start all over" when they begin learning cursive forms.

Source: D'Nealian® alphabet. © 1993, 1999 by Scott, Foresman. Reprinted by permission of Addison-Wesley Educational Publishers Inc.

describe the strokes necessary. Children beginning cursive writing become familiar with terms such as *undercurve*, *overcurve*, *downcurve*, and *horizontal curve*. These are the strokes necessary for linking letters to create a fluid handwriting style. The most difficult aspect of learning cursive handwriting for most children is forming capital letters. This is the area in which children generally need most guidance and practice. It is not unusual for adults to use a simplified version of cursive capital letters (and often they print them).

Handwriting habits formed in the early years of schooling frequently persist into adulthood. It is therefore essential that handwriting be taught effectively in the elementary school, with emphasis placed on legibility and comfort in writing. The example teachers set in their own handwriting has a great impact on children. Teachers' writing on the chalkboard should therefore be clear and legible, for just as with spelling, teachers are the primary models.

> The questions Asha posed to Ms. Hwang during her Grade 5 field experience provided a focus for her as she completed her final supervised teaching before embarking on her career. Critical aspects of Asha's learning included teaching the conventions of written language, helping students develop positive habits in their writing, and knowing how to assess student writing so that it could inform her instructional practices as well as inform students of their own learning. Asha began to focus on the details of teaching: developing her handwriting on the chalkboard, monitoring her own spelling, listening to students talk about their writing, following individual compositions through the writing process, talking with students about their story ideas, and observing their journals and literature response books. Asha also began to develop her own writing folder, sharing one of her pieces with the students, understanding the power of collaboration in a learning community.

SUMMARY

Assessments of student writing abilities are undertaken for four purposes: to inform teachers' instructional practices, to inform students of their progress and the areas on which they need to focus future learning, to inform parents of their children's progress, and to inform school administration and school districts about the competencies of the children in their schools. Although formal measures provide accountability for teachers, assessment is most valuable for the ways in which it helps teachers to meet the needs of individual learners. As teachers assess their students' writing abilities, they gain direct information as to what they need to teach and reteach and how they might conduct that instruction. Appropriate assessment of student writing provides invaluable feedback to teachers on what students need to learn and what teachers need to teach.

Composing a written text is a complex process. The criteria for determining *good* writing varies according to gender, personality, social group, and culture. In their instruction and assessment of student writing, teachers show respect for the idiosyncratic nature of the writing process and value both the written products and the writing processes of individual students. In constructivist classrooms, teachers focus on a wide range of writing abilities and recognize that there is no one way to evaluate children's writing, nor one mark or grade that adequately represents a student's writing development or abilities.

Writing assessments can be informal or formal, formative or summative. Informal assessment usually consists of process strategies that attempt to record the writing behaviours and attitudes of the students as well as the written product itself. Data is collected through observations, anecdotal notes, conferences, conversations with parents, portfolios of written work, checklists and writing profiles, as well as through careful reading of writing samples. Teachers make informal assessments on the basis of their reviews of collections of student writing samples in different genres—poetry, stories, learning log entries, reports, letters, persuasive pieces, explanations, response journal entries, and more.

More formal assessments of student abilities are undertaken through holistic analysis of writing samples or through the more analytic criteria-based scales. Holistic scoring is a guided procedure for sorting and ranking pieces according to general criteria or by matching them with other pieces of writing from the same class of students. Criteria-based scoring assesses writing according to component parts such as voice, vocabulary, sentence structure, conventions of written language, development and organization.

Many students learn to use the conventional transcription tools (including spelling, punctuation, capitalization, and usage) as they engage in the writing process or as teachers provide feedback during editing or writing conferences. Alternatively, these skills can be taught through direct instruction based on the children's own writing and their questions and challenges. Many students will require multiple lessons using direct instruction: demonstration, guided practice, individual application, and assessment. Teachers use a range of strategies to reteach a concept or skill until they are reasonably certain the students have successfully learned it. Children in kindergarten through Grade 2 continue to use invented spelling as they explore the written symbol system and the graphophonic system. Sound–symbol relationships are complex in the English language, and most children take a number of years to move entirely into standard spelling. Direct instruction in spelling is advised for children who experience particular difficulties in the area, but only in Grade 2 or later. Word lists with a study procedure and mastery test remain the most effective means of direct instruction.

Handwriting is taught regularly and often in the primary grades, but students in the intermediate grades also require maintenance lessons occasionally. A perceptual motor approach can be used throughout the grades, with children verbalizing letter descriptions or saying them silently as they draw the letters. A handwriting model at each student's desk is invaluable. Teachers' own handwriting, particularly their writing on the chalkboard, has a major influence on how students value handwriting and strive to achieve a legible hand. The aim of handwriting lessons is for each student to achieve legible handwriting with a minimum of time, effort, and concentration.

Young children bring to school a vast store of knowledge about language and how it is used. Teachers plan programs that allow children to use this knowledge to communicate with a wide range of audiences for a variety of purposes. An integral component of that writing program is teaching the conventions of written language. Without a working knowledge of these conventions, compositions cannot be as effective as their writers would wish. Much of the empowerment of writing comes from its precision, clarity, and imagery, whether in a novel, journal, poem, or report.

SELECTED PROFESSIONAL RESOURCES

Alberta Assessment Consortium. Available: www.aac.ab.ca. The Consortium is a nonprofit
    organization consisting of 45 school boards and the Alberta Trustees Association. The main

purposes of the organization are to develop a broad range of assessment materials, support teachers through staff development, facilitate networking and establish liaisons with other agencies. The site presents a framework for student assessment; principles of assessment, evaluation and communication; professional resources; and a newsletter, *Communiqué*.

Hodges, J., Whitten, M., Brown, J., and Flick, J. (1994). *Harbrace college handbook for Canadian writers* (3rd ed.). Toronto: Harcourt Brace and Company. This handbook is a standard reference guide for students and individual writers. It is also used as a textbook for college classrooms. The book summarizes the principles of effective writing and provides a quick and handy reference. Reflecting the Canadian context, the book contains examples from Canadian writers and the Canadian milieu. It follows MLA (Modern Language Association) style, citing rules and examples for grammar, punctuation, and usage, as well as providing the formats for documents such as business letters. It contains a glossary of terms and sections on "the whole composition" and "writing the research paper" and on the paragraph and the sentence. Information on sentence sense, parts of speech, verb forms, clauses, capitalization, spelling, and hyphenation can be found in this reference book.

Myers, M. and Spalding, E. (1997). *Assessing student performance Grades K–5. (Standards Exemplar Series)*. Urbana, IL: National Council of Teachers of English. This book grew out of the work of thousands of teachers in the United States who worked together to select and design on-demand tasks and portfolios to assess student writing competencies. On-demand tasks are those to be completed in the classroom within a specified time limit. The portfolios include a combination of assigned and freely chosen projects, both timed and untimed. The book consists mainly of selections of children's writing, along with rubrics and commentaries, that demonstrate children's wide-ranging abilities in writing across the grades from K to 5. The framework for assessment is based on three ways of knowing the language arts: knowing that, knowing how, and knowing about.

Peterson, S. (1995). *Becoming better writers*. Stettler, AB: F. P. Hendriks; and Peterson, S. (1997). *Teaching conventions unconventionally*. Stettler, AB: F. P. Hendriks. The first of the two companion volumes by Shelley Peterson is a recommended resource for the Western Canada Protocol for English Language Arts. The book contains practical information to assist teachers in passing on successful fiction-writing techniques using sample lessons, overheads, ideas for wall charts, and annotated bibliographies. The second book focuses on revision and editing strategies. It includes mini-lessons with samples of student writing, suggestions to help in planning writing conferences, and instructional strategies for teaching grammar, punctuation, and spelling. Assessment tools are included in both books, as are ideas for using literature to teach writing.

Phenix, J. and Scott-Dunne, D. (1991). *Spelling instruction that makes sense*. Markham, ON: Pembroke. This Canadian resource provides useful alternative strategies for teaching spelling in the context of a balanced literacy program. The authors trace a brief history and explain the "logic" of spelling. They include sections in the book on the developmental nature of learning to spell and suggest many learning activities for use in elementary classrooms. An especially helpful chapter suggests ways in which spelling development can be assessed and recorded, as well as ways in which parents can be kept informed about spelling itself and their children's progress.

Thomas, V. (1979). *Teaching spelling: Canadian word lists and instructional techniques*. Toronto: Gage. Thomas's book remains one of the best sources of word lists and strategies for teaching spelling. Thomas summarizes previous research findings and presents them in an accessible format. He develops a historical background for the direct teaching of spelling and presents a rationale for teaching only a core spelling vocabulary. Thomas discusses the grade placement of words on word lists and lists the 3000 most commonly used words in children's writing, breaking them into grade levels. The book also lists the 200 most frequently misspelled words in children's writing (from *about* to *writing*). The teaching strategies, activities, and record-keeping devices included in this book are of direct use to classroom teachers.

Northwest Regional Educational Laboratory. *6+1 Trait analytical model of writing assessment.* Available: www.nwrel.org/assessment/department.asp?d=1. The 6+1 Trait™ scoring procedure is based on the analytical categories of ideas, organization, voice, word choice, sentence fluency, conventions, and presentation. The term "6+1" is used because not all teachers choose to use these same six "traits." They may add one or two others, or use fewer traits. The Northwest Regional Educational Laboratory presents ways of using these traits to describe good writing at different levels of achievement. The Laboratory has also created links to instructional strategies.

REFERENCES

Alberta Education. (1992). *Achievement testing program provincial report.* Edmonton: Alberta Education.

Alberta Education. (1995). *Achievement testing program provincial report.* Edmonton: Alberta Education.

Alberta Learning. (2002). English Language Arts Grade Six Provincial Testing Bulletin. Available: ednet.edc.gov.ab.ca/k_12/testing/achievement/bulletins/default.asp. Retrieved January 14, 2003.

Applebee, A. N., Langer, J. A., and Mullis, I. V. (1986). *The writing report card: Writing achievement in American schools* (Report No. 15-W-02). Princeton, NJ: Educational Testing Service.

Beers, J. W. and Henderson, E. H. (1977). A study of developing orthographic concepts among first graders. *Research in the Teaching of English, 11,* 133–148.

Carroll, J., Davies, P., and Richman, B. (1971). *Word frequency book.* Boston: Houghton Mifflin.

Clymer, T. (1963). The utility of phonic generalizations in the primary grades. *The Reading Teacher, 4,* 252–258.

Cooper, C. and Odell, L. (eds.). (1999). *Evaluating writing: The role of teachers' knowledge about text, learning and culture.* Urbana, IL: National Council of Teachers of English.

Department of School Education. (1991). *English profiles handbook.* Melbourne, Australia: Department of School Education.

Education Department of Western Australia. (1994). *First Steps writing resource book.* Portsmouth, NH: Heinemann.

Farr, R. and Tone, B. (1994). *Portfolio and performance assessment.* Fort Worth, TX: Harcourt Brace College.

Furner, B. (1969). Recommended instructional procedures in a method emphasizing the perceptual motor nature of learning in handwriting. *Elementary English, 46* (8), 1021–1030.

Gentry, J. R. (1978). Early spelling strategies. *Elementary School Journal, 79,* 88–92.

Gentry, J. R. (1981). Learning to spell developmentally. *The Reading Teacher, 34,* 378–381.

Leppard, S. (1991). A reading–writing continuum. *Program continuity: The positive link.* Calgary: Alberta Educational Communications Corporation.

Marzana, R., Pickering, D., and McTighe, J. (1993). *Assessing student outcomes: Performance assessment using the dimensions of learning model.* Alexandria, VA: Association for Supervision and Curriculum Development.

Pappas, C., Kiefer, B., and Levstik, L. (1995). *An integrated language perspective in the elementary school: Theory into action.* White Plains, NY: Longman.

Peterson, S. (1995). *Becoming better writers.* Stettler, AB: F. P. Hendriks.

Peterson, S. (1997). *Teaching conventions unconventionally.* Stettler, AB: F. P. Hendriks.

Phenix, J. (2001). *The spelling teacher's handbook.* Markham, ON: Pembroke.

Read, C. (1975). *Children's categorizations of speech sounds in English.* Urbana, IL: National Council of Teachers of English.

Scott, R. (1993). *Spelling: Sharing the secrets*. Toronto: Gage.

Simpson, C. (1980). *The Scott, Foresman word study for spelling*. Glenview, IL: Scott, Foresman & Company.

Stobart, G., Elwood, J., and Quinlan, M. (1992). Gender bias in examinations: How equal are the opportunities? *British Educational Research Journal, 18* (3), 261–276.

Tarasoff, M. (1990). *Spelling strategies you can teach*. Victoria, BC: Pixelart Graphics; Active Learning Institute.

Thomas, V. (1979). *Teaching spelling: Canadian word lists and instructional techniques*. Toronto: Gage.

Tompkins, G. (2000). *Teaching writing: Balancing process and product* (3rd ed.). Columbus, OH: Merrill.

Tompkins, G. and Hoskisson, K. (1995). *Language arts: Content and teaching strategies* (3rd ed.). Englewood Cliffs, NJ: Prentice-Hall.

U.S. Department of Education. (1995). *Windows into the classroom: NAEP's 1992 writing portfolio study*. Washington, DC: Office of Educational Research and Improvement.

Chapter

Children's Literature for the Classroom

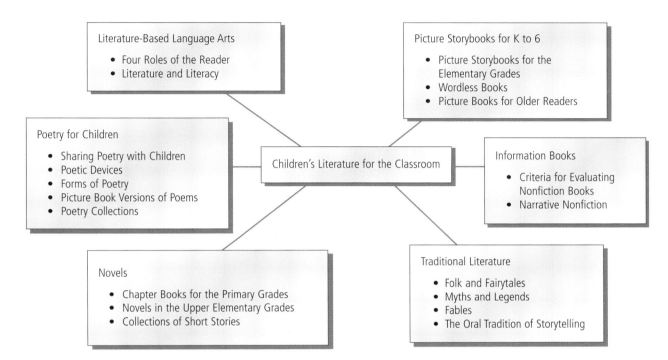

Literature-Based Language Arts
- Four Roles of the Reader
- Literature and Literacy

Picture Storybooks for K to 6
- Picture Storybooks for the Elementary Grades
- Wordless Books
- Picture Books for Older Readers

Poetry for Children
- Sharing Poetry with Children
- Poetic Devices
- Forms of Poetry
- Picture Book Versions of Poems
- Poetry Collections

Children's Literature for the Classroom

Information Books
- Criteria for Evaluating Nonfiction Books
- Narrative Nonfiction

Novels
- Chapter Books for the Primary Grades
- Novels in the Upper Elementary Grades
- Collections of Short Stories

Traditional Literature
- Folk and Fairytales
- Myths and Legends
- Fables
- The Oral Tradition of Storytelling

Jennifer is about to begin a full term of student teaching and would like to incorporate novels and literature circles into her teaching of reading, balancing the reading series generally used in the classroom. Jennifer has compiled a list of books appropriate for novel studies, but she wants to add to that list and help the teacher to develop a larger classroom collection of books for her students' selection during DEAR (Drop Everything and Read) time. Which new novels would make interesting novel studies? Should she choose novels or a combination of novels and picture books? Which poetry anthologies are available for her to use, and which nonfiction literature can she include in her reading program? How can she go about selecting high-quality nonfiction books to support the topics she will be teaching in science and social studies?

The questions Jennifer asks about suitable reading materials for her student teaching classroom demonstrate her commitment to providing the best possible learning opportunities for her students. One of the most exciting developments in language arts instruction over the last 20 years has been the shift in focus from the use of a "reading series" approach to that of incorporating **children's literature** and **trade books** into reading instruction. **Reading series** certainly have a place in elementary classrooms and can provide a range of reading experiences for children. However, the explosion of exciting trade books written and illustrated for children has made it increasingly possible to create reading and language arts programs that are literature-based. Researchers, scholars, and many classroom teachers have discovered that children's literature is an essential component of teaching children both how to read and how to appreciate reading as a pleasurable aesthetic experience.

If you take a few moments to look back on your own reading history, you may remember learning how to read. Some of the experiences might have been in school, others at home. Some might have involved teachers, while other memories may be of grandparents, older siblings, and parents sharing stories and books with you. Many people can remember the moment when they *knew* they could read by themselves. Others feel they could always read and have very few specific memories. What are some of the earliest stories you recall? Where did you read? Did you visit a library? Did your family subscribe to book clubs or to magazines? These are important questions to keep in mind when designing a literacy program, because we know that literacy learning is complex and multifaceted.

Not long ago, "children's literature" connoted an elite canon of "quality" books that largely included the classics, both old and contemporary, from *Anne of Green Gables* (Montgomery, 1908) to *Angel Square* (Doyle, 1984). In this textbook, children's literature refers to those books, both fiction and nonfiction, that are acknowledged by critics to be of high quality and well written, and that provide children with pleasurable and challenging reading experiences. The term *trade books* has a broader definition, including all books that are published for preschoolers, young readers, and young adults, but *not* as part of a basal reading series or as textbooks for use in schools. Trade books encompass many genres of literature, including comics, series books such as R. L. Stine's Goosebumps (e.g., *Welcome to the Dead House*, 1992), and magazines. The term *reading series* refers to a set of materials specifically designed for teaching reading and language arts. These used to be referred to as "basal readers" because they frequently formed the basis for an instructional program in reading. Many of the current reading series are anthologies of materials taken directly from published works of literature by well-known authors. These series generally consist of teacher guides, student anthologies, workbooks, and supplemental materials such as assessment materials, big books, correlated trade books, audiovisual aids, and computer software.

Genre, a word borrowed from French, means "literary species" or "literary form." The epic, tragedy, comedy, essay, biography, novel, and poetry are traditional genres. New forms have been added to this list over the years, and now the term is used as a convenient (and somewhat arbitrary) way of classifying literary works. Today, genre refers to a body of literature that has certain common elements. The genres usually referred to in children's literature are picture books, wordless books, concept books, biographies, classics, legends, myths, folk tales, fairytales, fables, historical fiction, contemporary realistic fiction, fantasies, science fiction, poetry, and nonfiction—and each of these may in turn be subdivided into a number of different categories or subgenres.

Competent and avid adult readers often recollect with fondness their visits to the bookmobile in the city, the arrival of the *Star Weekly* in the mailbox, comics, their first library card, favourite books, and endless series books, from the Bobbsey Twins to the Babysitter's Club. Learning from this, and from all that has been written about teaching reading and the language arts, educators have embraced the concept of literature-based reading instruction, and many have created language arts programs based on trade books of many genres. There's no doubt of the respect that teachers have today for the power of children's literature and for the authors and illustrators who create literary works for children. This is demonstrated by such events as the locally organized Children's Literature Round Table groups that meet across Canada and the excellent children's literature conferences such as Kaleidoscope, held every four years in Calgary (sponsored by the Learning Resources Council of the Alberta Teachers' Association). These conferences also underscore the recognition that children's literature is receiving in language arts education programs across all the grades, from kindergarten to high school.

Reading good books connects us with the rest of the human race and lets us know that our feelings and experiences are not unique, but part of what makes us human. Children who learn to appreciate literature are at an advantage in society and in life, not the least because good books give them a context within which to better understand the place they hold in the scheme of things.

LITERATURE-BASED LANGUAGE ARTS

In this section of the chapter, we explain the importance of children's literature in language arts programs, and the role literature plays in teaching children how to read and to become lifelong readers. This section of the chapter demonstrates why Jennifer has decided to incorporate more literature into her language arts program.

With a careful choice of books and appropriate instruction, children can learn to read from interesting and well-written, well-illustrated trade books as well as from reading series. Literature-based language arts instruction does, however, call upon increased knowledge and skill on the part of teachers. Not only must teachers know children's books (including their titles, authors, themes, plots, characters, and structures), but it is also helpful if they understand how books work and what the various literary techniques used in the books are teaching young readers. Literature-based instruction is important because it incorporates *all* of the language arts and may involve such activities as novel studies, shared reading, drama work, art activities, puppetry, journals and other kinds of writing, and book talks by children. It thus requires a good deal of organization and knowledge of strategies (e.g., literature circles and response groups). It also demands that teachers read the books their students are reading and be prepared to participate with children as they generate shared meanings from the works they read.

Four Roles of the Reader

What is the advantage of working with literature in the classroom? If children learn to read from trade books, will they lack any of the basic skills required in the early stages of independent reading? Reading is more than matching written symbols with sounds, more than acquiring a reading vocabulary, more than understanding word meanings. Reading ability is more than being able to answer someone else's questions about a text. Freebody and Luke (1990) describe four roles of a reader: code breaker, text participant, text user, and text analyst. They maintain that successful reading means being able to accomplish all four of these roles simultaneously.

- Being a *code breaker* involves understanding the sound–symbol relationship and the alphabetic principle.
- Being a *text participant* means developing the resources to engage the meaning systems of discourse (i.e., "the processes of comprehension call upon the reader to draw inferences connecting textual elements and background knowledge required to fill out the unexplicated aspects of text," p. 9).
- Being a *text user* means knowing how to use a variety of texts in real social contexts throughout daily life (i.e., knowing what to do with a text in a given social context).
- Being a *text analyst* means reading critically, or having "conscious awareness of the language and idea systems that are brought into play when a text is used" (p. 13) (i.e., being able to recognize the ideological perspective of a text and to stand outside that perspective and question it).

We already know that, before they enter school, many children learn to read from the reading materials they have in their homes, usually magazines and books. Scholars, researchers, and teachers have learned that children's literature has a greater likelihood of encouraging children to take on the four roles of the reader proposed by Freebody and Luke. The more contrived or artificial stories sometimes found in reading series are generally designed to encourage code breaking rather than any of the other three roles. Works of children's literature are more likely to challenge readers not only to be code breakers, but also to make inferences, to analyze the text, and to predict events and outcomes.

In *Come Away from the Water, Shirley* (Burningham, 1977), for example, the reader is encouraged not only to decode the text and read the words, but also to read the pictures that, at first glance, appear to have nothing at all to do with the words on the page. In order to construct a meaningful story, the reader has to engage with the book as a text participant, text user, and text analyst. There is more than one story being told in these pages. Participating only as a code breaker would create a limited story with little appeal to children. *Rosie's Walk* (Hutchins, 1969) provides a further example of this phenomenon.

There are times today when a reading series can be very useful to teachers. If a large and varied collection of children's reading material is not available, or when a student has a particular learning need, then a reading series may provide the resources necessary for instruction. In general, however, most children will learn more about reading from children's literature than from a reading series. Children clearly need to learn code-breaking skills early in their lives, but they also deserve to learn how to be text users, text analysts, and text participants if they are to become independent readers capable of constructing meaning from the texts they read. Thus, from children's literature, children are provided with the opportunity to learn both how to read *and* how to appreciate the ways in which texts work. The combination of the two creates rich possibilities for reading for pleasure and reading for information throughout life.

Literature and Literacy

Research in language learning and literacy development has consistently shown that one of the most important factors in a child's early literacy development is the amount a child is read to (and with) in the preschool years. Wells' (1986) longitudinal study of language development, conducted in Britain during the 1970s, showed that the single most important factor in reading development is the amount a child is read to during the preschool years. The study also demonstrated that

- children who are read to from infancy onwards have an enormous advantage when they begin formal schooling (this finding has significant implications for teaching those children who come from situations where reading is not common and is not regarded as a pleasurable or satisfying endeavour),

- early reading experiences affect writing as well as reading abilities, and are also influential in developing children's listening and comprehension skills, and
- the more children read and are read to, and the more children talk about what they are reading and writing, the more successful they are likely to be in school and in their literacy endeavours.

Many preschool children love books. They are fascinated by the pictures on the page and by the shared experience of reading on a caregiver's lap. This pleasurable anticipation of books provides parents and educators with the opportunity to provide quality works of literature for the young. *Each Peach Pear Plum* by the Ahlbergs (1978) is a contemporary extension of traditional literature that has become a classic. *Each Peach Pear Plum* contains illustrations rich in the detail of the nursery rhymes, folklore, legends, and fairytales of western Europe. It is a book that can be read on a range of levels. The very young child, who is still unable to follow the plots of traditional stories, can enjoy the repetition of "each peach pear plum" and the rhyming patterns, as well as the predictability of the language. Older children enjoy the humour derived from their prior knowledge of the fairytales and nursery rhymes alluded to in the book.

Children learn from books such as this that reading is an active experience. In addition to what children learn about values, culture, and life, they learn about handling and "reading" books—much of what Holdaway (1979) refers to as "literacy set." Children learn directionality: the front and back of a book, which way is the right way up, and which way the story moves through the book—in the case of *Each Peach Pear Plum*, with text on the left, pictures on the right, and a "cuing" picture above the text. Children learn that books can be actively responded to, and that books are a way into a pleasurable experience.

Children's early experiences with books such as *Each Peach Pear Plum*, and the experiences they have with reading in school, affect how they perceive themselves as readers and how they perceive reading: whether it is a relevant activity or not, whether it is a pleasurable activity or not, and whether books are worth the time and effort needed to have a truly *satisfying* reading experience. Teachers who use literature as a basis for their reading instruction demonstrate to children that books *are* worth the time and effort required of a reader, and thus children are more likely to become readers as adults. Teachers who clearly enjoy reading—and who demonstrate this joy in their daily life in classrooms—invite children into the world of books with enthusiasm and excitement.

PICTURE STORYBOOKS FOR K TO 6

This section suggests the titles of a selection of picture books for children across the elementary grades, including some books that deal with complex and difficult issues.

Every genre of literature is represented in **picture books**. The label "picture book" refers to a general category of books having the same basic format and way of communicating a message. Some books may more appropriately be called "illustrated books." True picture books involve a partnership between text and pictures, with the pictures and text *together* telling the story or presenting information. The most common genres of picture books are wordless books, concept books (such as counting and alphabet books), predictable books, easy-to-read books, and picture storybooks. There is often overlap among the genres within picture books. This section of the chapter focuses on picture storybooks rather than on the other picture book genres such as alphabet or counting books.

Picture Storybooks for the Elementary Grades

Picture storybooks are a powerful vehicle for teaching children both *how to read* and *how to become readers*. It is understood that reading should be taught in the context of real texts, but it is not until we look in detail at books such as *Come Away from the Water, Shirley* (Burningham, 1977), *Tuesday* (Wiesner, 1991), and *Zoom Upstream* (Wynne-Jones, 1992), that we fully understand the reading lessons children are receiving from picture books. Meek (1988) refers to these as "private lessons," the lessons good readers learn about reading *without* formal instruction. *Come Away from the Water, Shirley* tells one version of the story through the pictures (and through Shirley's eyes) and another version of the story through the text (and through the parents' eyes). In *Zoom Upstream*, Wynne-Jones' simple adventure story about a cat is remarkably extended by Eric Beddows' detailed and imaginative illustrations of the "catacombs" of ancient Egypt.

An example of a picture book that can be read on many levels is *Rosie's Walk* (Hutchins, 1969). It contains 1 sentence, 32 words, and 27 pages of pictures. *Rosie's Walk* is a story that, if told in words alone, would take many paragraphs and lose much of its allure. *Rosie's Walk* contains at least two stories: the story of Rosie the hen and her barnyard walk, and the story of the fox who silently follows her but is not even mentioned in the text (though he is prominent in the illustrations). The reading lesson, which transfers directly to adult books such as *The Englishman's Boy* by Guy Vanderhaeghe (1996), is an important one—there is more than one story in any book, and there is more in any book than is written on the page.

Young readers understand the way picture books work because they attend to multiple cues, not only to text. They focus on visual cues much more significantly than adults do. These young readers are engaging in completely different reading experiences today than previous generations of children did, because they have access to picture storybooks that are more challenging and interactional than before. Books such as *Rosie's Walk* and *Tuesday* are often called "writerly" texts because readers must use their imaginations to fill in the textual gaps and thus "complete" the writing of the story. Barthes (1970) used the term "scriptable" to describe texts such as these and the term *lisible* to describe what are now commonly called "readerly" texts—those in which the writer has provided most of the information for the reader, and the writer's meanings tend to be clear and direct.

Early readers need experiences with both writerly and readerly texts, and teachers can provide the instructional support children need to be able to move from one to the other. As a result of their early reading experiences with writerly texts such as *Rosie's Walk* and *Come Away from the Water, Shirley*, more children are likely to enjoy novels such as Vanderhaeghe's *The Englishman's Boy* when they grow up. They are also more likely to continue reading for pleasure as well as for information as adults.

Box 10.1 lists some picture books that are appropriate for children in the elementary grades, and Box 10.2 lists specifically Canadian picture books.

Wordless Books

Children in preschool and kindergarten enjoy sitting alone or in small groups reading wordless books. In actively encouraging emerging readers to engage with books, it is appropriate for teachers to share such books with the class, especially "big-book" versions

Box 10.1   A Selection of Picture Storybooks

Ahlberg, J. and Ahlberg, A. (1986). *The jolly postman*. London, UK: Heinemann.

Ahlberg, A. and Briggs, R. (2001). *The adventures of Bert*. London: Penguin.

Andreasen, D. (2002). *A quiet place*. New York: Simon & Schuster.

Base, G. (2001). *The waterhole*. New York: Penguin Putnam.

Brett, J. (1989). *The mitten*. New York: Scholastic.

Briggs, R. (1975). *Father Christmas goes on holiday*. Harmondsworth, UK: Puffin Books.

Browne, A. (1983). *Gorilla*. New York: Alfred A. Knopf.

Carle, E. (1974). *The very hungry caterpillar*. Harmondsworth, UK: Puffin Books.

Curtis, J. L. (2000). *Where do balloons go? An uplifting mystery*. New York, NY: Harper Collins.

Fox, M. (1990). *Possum magic*. New York: Harcourt Brace & Company.

Kent, J. (1971). *The fat cat*. Harmondsworth, UK: Puffin Books.

Peet, B. (1993). *Chester the worldly pig*. New York: Houghton Mifflin Company.

Polacco, P. (1997). *I can hear the sun*. New York: The Putnam & Grosset Book Group.

Rathmann, P. (1995). *Officer Buckle and Gloria*. New York: Putnam.

Ross, T. (1993). *The three pigs*. London: Arrow Books.

Steer, D. (1999). *Just one more story*. New York: Dutton Children's Books.

Steptoe, J. (1987). *Mufaro's beautiful daughters*. New York: Lothrop.

Van Allsburg, C. (1985). *The polar express*. Boston: Houghton Mifflin.

Van Allsburg, C. (2002). *Zathura*. New York: Houghton Mifflin Company.

Waddell, M. (1991). *Farmer Duck*. London: Walker Books.

Wagner, J. (1978). *John Brown, rose and the midnight cat*. New York: Bradbury.

Wild, M. (1990). *The very best of friends*. New York: Harcourt Brace & Company.

Yolen, J. (1987). *Owl moon*. New York: Philomel Books.

Box 10.2   Canadian Picture Books

Andrews, J. (1985). *Very last first time*. Vancouver: Douglas & McIntyre.

Bouchard, D. (2002). *Qu'appelle*. Vancouver, BC: Raincoast Books.

Eyvindson, P. (1996). *Red parka Mary*. Winnipeg: Pemmican.

Gay, M. L. (1999). *Stella, star of the sea*. Toronto, ON: Groundwood Books.

Gilman, P. (1992). *Something from nothing*. Richmond Hill, ON: North Winds Press.

Gregory, N. (2001). *Wild Girl and Gran*. Red Deer, AB: Red Deer Press.

Harty, N. (1997). *Hold on, McGinty*. Toronto: Doubleday Canada.

Jam, T. (1997). *The fishing summer*. Toronto: Groundwood Books.

Khalsa, D. K. (1986). *Tales of a gambling grandma*. Montreal: Tundra Books.

Continued

Box 10.2 Canadian Picture Books *Continued*

Lawson, J. (1997). *Emma and the silk train*. Toronto, ON: Kids Can Press Ltd.

Lawson, J. (1999). *Bear on the train*. Toronto, ON: Kids Can Press.

Lee, D. (2001). *The cat and the wizard*. Toronto, ON: Key Porter Books.

Major, K. (2000). *Eh? To zed*. Red Deer, AB: Red Deer Press.

McFarlane, S. (1991). *Waiting for the whales*. Victoria: Orca Book Publishers.

McGugan, J. (1994). *Josepha: A prairie boy's story*. Red Deer, AB: Red Deer College Press.

Morck, I. (1996). *Tiger's new cowboy boots*. Red Deer, AB: Red Deer College Press.

Morin, P. (1998). *Animal dreaming*. New York, NY: Silver Whistle Harcourt Brace & Company.

Munsch, R. (1980). *The paper bag princess*. Toronto: Annick Press.

Oberman, S. (2000). *The wisdom bird*. Honesdale, PA: Boyds Mills Press, Inc.

Oppel, K. (2000). *Peg and the whale*. Toronto: HarperCollins.

Ruurs, M. (1999). *Emma's eggs*. Markham, ON: Fitzhenry & Whiteside.

Sharp, T. (2001). *The Saturday appaloosa*. Red Deer, AB: Red Deer Press.

Simmie, L. (1995). *Mr. Got to Go*. Red Deer, AB: Red Deer College Press.

Vaage, C. (1995). *Bibi and the bull*. Edmonton: Dragon Hill Press.

Wilson, B. (2001). *A Fiddle For Angus*. Toronto: Tundra Books.

Wynne-Jones, T. and Nutt, K. (1985). *Zoom away*. Toronto: Groundwood Books.

that enable all the children to see the pictures. It is also important that teachers take a close look at the pictures before the book is shared with children (part of the preparation required in these circumstances), for children will ask many questions and make observations about the illustrations. Children focus heavily on the illustrations in books and can be particularly insightful about the details included. In their early reading experiences, children rely heavily on pictures in order to create meaning from the page. As teachers acknowledge the observations children make and the questions they ask, they enhance the children's response to the book and help expand their understanding through discussion and interaction. Box 10.3 lists wordless books that are appropriate for children from preschool to Grade 3.

Picture Books for Older Readers

Picture books are not only for pre- and beginning readers, just as wordless books, such as *Sunshine* (1981) and *Moonlight* (1982) by Jan Ormerod, are not only for children who cannot yet read. Similar to *Each Peach Pear Plum* in its intertextual references (to *Red Riding Hood* and many other folk tales and fairytales) is *The Tunnel* by Anthony Browne (1989). Intended for children in the upper elementary grades, this book requires many readings to unravel its multilayered (**polysemic**) text and illustrations. There is a great deal of reading to be done in the gaps in the turn of a page, or between text and picture. It is in these gaps that readers are invited to take an *inferential walk* (Eco, 1978) or, in other words, to read between the lines. Thus, readers learn the key role that inferencing plays in reading and in constructing meaning. Some readers may encounter difficulty in following

Box 10.3 Wordless Books

Aliki. (1995). *Tabby: A story told in pictures*. New York: HarperCollins.

Baker, J. (1991). *Window*. New York: Greenwillow Books.

Banyai, I. (1995). *Zoom*. New York: Viking.

Briggs, R. (1978). *The snowman*. New York: Random House/Scholastic.

Collington, P. (1997). *A small miracle*. New York: Knopf.

Dupasquier, P. (1988). *The great escape*. Boston: Houghton Mifflin.

Falwell, C. (1991). *Clowning around*. New York: Orchard Books.

Goodall, J. S. (1986). *The story of a castle*. New York: M. K. McElderry Books.

Goodall, J. (1988). *Little Red Riding Hood*. New York: M. K. McElderry Books.

Hoban, T. (1988). *Look! Look! Look!* New York: Greenwillow Books.

Karlin, B. (1991). *Meow*. New York: Simon & Schuster.

Keats, E. J. (1974). *Kitten for a day*. New York: Four Winds Press.

McCully, E. (1988). *New baby*. New York: Harper & Row.

Mayer, M. (1974). *Frog goes to dinner*. New York: Dial Press.

Popov, N. (1996). *Why?* New York: North-South Books Inc.

Romann, E. (1994). *Time flies*. New York: Random House.

Sis, P. (2000). *Dinosaur*. New York: Greenwillow Books.

Tafuri, N. (1990). *Follow me!* New York: Greenwillow Books.

Tanner, J. (1987). *Niki's walk*. Melbourne, Australia: MacMillan.

Weisner, D. (1992). *Tuesday*. Boston, MA: Clarion/Houghton Mifflin.

the story depicted in *The Tunnel* and feel that Browne has omitted too much, has left too many inferential gaps, and in general has created too writerly a text. These readers want the story to be laid out for them more explicitly, so that they receive a direct message from the author and don't have to create the meaning themselves. (Many adults also struggle with the story in the book and with the nature of the illustrations, because Browne manages to create allusions to several of the more disturbing aspects of relationships and growing up, leaving readers to relate their own experiences to the story and perhaps respond at deeply personal levels.) In such books, then, teachers play an important role, through dialogue and discussion groups, in helping children take inferential walks, draw inferences, make educated guesses, and understand overall that there is no correct answer when "gap filling" in texts.

Many picture books are aimed at an audience of older children, children who can already read well and who have a rich experience in working with text. Sixth-grade children respond powerfully to books such as *Black and White* (Macaulay, 1990) and *June 29, 1999* (Wiesner, 1992). *Black and White* is an adventure in **metafiction**, a constant and deliberate reminder that a book is something an author and reader create together—something that is not real and is open to many interpretations and structures. The book consists of four narrative strands, each making use of different narrative and pictorial techniques. Each double-page spread is divided into four sections so that the four narratives unfold at the same time. On the title page of the book there is a warning from the author: "This book appears to contain a number of stories that do not necessarily occur at the same time. Then again, it may contain only one story. In any event, careful inspection of both words and pictures is recommended."

In *June 29, 1999*, a very different story, student Holly Evans develops an ambitious and innovative project for her science assignment. While her classmates are sprouting seeds in paper cups, Holly launches seedlings into the sky on tiny air balloons. Although her teacher and fellow students are skeptical, only five weeks later giant vegetables begin to fall from the sky, landing in various parts of the United States. The book displays Wiesner's unconventional artwork and the same dry humour he uses in *Free Fall* (1988) and *Tuesday* (1991).

These picture books, and others created for older readers, are not necessarily easy-reading books. Many of them deal with mature themes and contain illustrations that provide powerful messages supporting and adding to the text. Two books set in Europe during World War II are *Rose Blanche* (Innocenti, 1985) and *Let the Celebrations Begin!* (Wild, 1991). In Canada, the latter book is published by Kids Can Press as *A Time for Toys*. Where *Rose Blanche* is a story about the darkness of war, *Let the Celebrations Begin!* is a story of hope. It is a tribute to the human spirit and to the survival of so many innocent people who lived for years in horrific conditions in concentration camps. In addi-

---

Box 10.4 Picture Books for Older Readers

Barbalet, M. and Tanner, J. (1992). *The wolf.* Toronto: Doubleday.

Base, G. (1997). *The eleventh hour, A curious mystery.* New York: Puffin.

Blake, W. (1993). *The tyger.* (Neil Waldman, illustrator). New York: Harcourt Brace Jovanovich.

Bouchard, D. and Vickers, R. H. (1990). *The elders are watching.* Tofino, BC: Eagle Dancer Enterprises.

Briggs, R. (1982). *When the wind blows.* New York: Schocken.

Browne, A. (1998). *Voices in the park.* New York: DK Publishing Inc.

Carrier, R. (1985). *The hockey sweater.* Montreal: Tundra Books.

Hunt, E. (1989). *The tale of three trees.* Colorado Springs, CO: Lion Publishing.

Lemieux, M. (1999). *Stormy night.* Toronto: Kids Can Press.

Macaulay, D. (1995). *Shortcut.* Boston, MA: Houghton Mifflin.

Major, K. (1997). *The house of wooden Santas.* Red Deer, AB: Red Deer Press.

Oberman, S. (1993). *The always prayer shawl.* Honesdale, PA: Boyd Mills Press.

Scieszka, J. (1995). *Math curse.* New York: Viking.

Scieszka, J. and Smith, L. (1998). *Squids will be squids.* New York: Scholastic Inc.

Spiegelman, A. (2000). *Little lit: Strange stories for strange kids.* New York: Harper Collins Publishers.

Valgardson, W. D. (1996). *Sarah and the people of Sand River.* Toronto: Groundwood Books.

Van Allsburg, C. (1984). *The mysteries of Harris Burdick.* Boston: Houghton Mifflin.

Yee, P. (1996). *Ghost train.* Toronto: Groundwood Books.

Zhang, S. N. (1993). *A little tiger in the Chinese night.* Montreal: Tundra Books.

tion to these books about Europe during World War II, there are a number of powerful picture books about the dropping of the atomic bomb on Hiroshima on August 6, 1945. These include *Hiroshima No Pika* (Maruki, 1980), *My Hiroshima* (Morimoto, 1987), *Sadako* (Coerr, 1993), and *Shin's Tricycle* (Kodama, 1995).

Although the books noted above are of a serious nature, many others for older readers are entertaining, playful, and clever, stimulating the imagination and stretching our notions of reading. Picture storybooks aimed at older readers include *Night in the Country* (Rylant, 1986), *Piggybook* (Browne, 1986), *The Widow's Broom* (Van Allsburg, 1992), and *The Mummer's Song* (Davidge and Wallace, 1993). Each of these books creates a sense of wonder and provides challenging perspectives on the reading event and on the nature of the picture book. Additional titles of picture books suitable for older readers are presented in Box 10.4.

Picture books, then, have the potential to teach important concepts about reading that can come only from working with real texts, and they are important in forming the attitudes of young children toward books in general. There is a wealth of high-quality picture books available for children in the elementary grades today, books containing artistry, excellent writing, and vivid imagery.

Take the time to locate one of the books mentioned in this section of the chapter, and see if the comments made here match the meanings you create from the book. Did the comments in this chapter help you see the book or the experience of reading in a new light? What does this experience demonstrate to you about your role in teaching reading and in mediating texts with children?

NOVELS

In the following section, we suggest a number of novels for children in Grades 2 to 6, including many Canadian titles.

Chapter Books for the Primary Grades

As children become more familiar with picture books and with story structures, and as their reading abilities become more sophisticated, they move from using pictures as a primary means of creating meaning to an increased reliance on text. Many beginning novels are available for young readers (which children in Grades 2 and 3 frequently refer to as **chapter books**), and they fall into all of the major genres. It seems that the movement from reading picture books to reading books with chapters denotes a transition in an individual's growth as a reader. This is not to suggest that children are no longer interested in reading picture books or that picture books cannot continue to capture their interest and imagination.

The reading levels of many beginning chapter books range from Grades 2 to 4 (i.e., a level calculated by the application of a readability formula). Readability does not depend on the complexity of language alone, however, but has much to do with the structure of the book and the background experience the reader is required to bring to it. Often, beginning chapter books contain illustrations, and these assist readers in the transition from picture books to novels. The content and writing style of numerous beginning chapter books are equally appropriate for older elementary students whose reading level is below grade level, and for those who simply wish to read a "good" (albeit easier) book.

There are many well-known "entry-level" novels, among them Mordecai Richler's three titles about the character Jacob Two-Two: *Jacob Two-Two Meets the Hooded Fang* (1975), *Jacob Two-Two and the Dinosaur* (1987), and *Jacob Two-Two's First Spy Case* (1995). These books are a combination of fantasy and **realistic fiction**, and are suitable for reading aloud to the class as well as for independent reading. There are also many recommended beginning novels of realistic fiction, including novels written by Canadian authors Ken Roberts, Budge Wilson, Jean Little, and Sylvia McNicoll.

In *Hiccup Champion of the World* (Roberts, 1988), Maynard Chan gets the hiccups and none of the cures generated by his family, friends, and peers are successful. However, just before Maynard is about to appear on a television show, his hiccups cease—temporarily. Budge Wilson's story, *Harold and Harold* (1995), is about a young boy named Harold whose friendship with a beautiful blue heron also named Harold assists him in being accepted by his new coastal community. Jean Little's *Lost and Found* (1985) narrates the story of Lucy, who moves to a new town and is concerned about making friends. Lucy finds a dog she names Trouble, and the dog helps ease Lucy's loneliness. In the novel *The Big Race* (1996), McNicoll tells the story of a Grade 3 boy's constant competition with a female classmate who excels at everything she does. Various events, including a broken nose, eventually bring the characters together in friendship.

A selection of beginning novels is presented in Box 10.5.

As children begin to move from picture books to chapter books, their book selection will be determined largely by the encouragement of their teacher, their peers, and their own interests. Teachers help children to grow by making book suggestions based on each child's interests and reading ability. Children benefit because a novel requires a greater investment of time and effort than a picture storybook. At the same time, children need to know that a book they select has the potential to engage their interests as well as being at an appropriate reading level. In general, reading materials of high personal interest are more fully comprehended than materials of low interest. A reader's strong interest in a topic can transcend his or her reading abilities (Hunt, 1970). Research also shows the importance of teachers reading the books their students are reading, so they can discuss the books with their students (Pantaleo, 1994). Through these discussions, teachers may challenge students to extend their interpretations and to add new dimensions to the meanings they create.

Novels in the Upper Elementary Grades

Many children begin their foray into novels with **contemporary realistic fiction**, perhaps because it is one of the avenues through which they can, on the one hand, come to know the world in which they live and, on the other, explore issues of which they have little personal experience. This genre continues to be the most widely read of them all in the upper elementary grades. In the Canadian novel *Jasmin* (Truss, 1982), Jasmin's parents seem to be unaware of the burdens their 12-year-old daughter is shouldering in helping to raise a family of six children. Jasmin is not succeeding in school and so decides to run away from the possibility of repeating Grade 6 and from the responsibilities of being the oldest of a large family. Spending time alone in the wilderness and meeting some new friends helps Jasmin in her search for independence, and brings assistance for her family.

Finders Keepers (Spalding, 1995) tells the story of two boys in Fort McLeod, Alberta, who become unlikely friends. Danny, a child of Ukrainian decent, and Joshua, a Peigan boy, find ways to help each other after Danny discovers an 8000-year-old arrowhead. Together they uncover the origin of the arrowhead and in doing so become great friends,

Box 10.5   Beginning Novels

Bjornson, H. (1997). *Raymond's raindance*. Burnaby, BC: Skoal House.

Choyce, L. (1998). *Famous at last*. East Lawrencetown, NS: Pottersfield Press.

Cleary, B. (1984). *Ramona forever*. New York: Bantam Doubleday Dell.

Croteau, M. (1996). *Fred and the stinky cheese*. Translated by S. Cummins. Halifax: Formac.

Dadey, D. *Adventures of the Bailey School kids*. Boston, MA: Little Apple.

Dahl, R. (1970). *Fantastic Mr. Fox*. New York: Knopf.

Dahl, R. (1980). *The twits*. New York: Bantam Skylark Books.

Elste, J. (1996). *True blue*. New York: Grosset & Dunlap.

Eyvindson, P. (1997). *Chubby champ*. Winnipeg, MB: Pemmican.

Fleischman, S. (1986). *The whipping boy*. New York: Greenwillow.

Gardiner, J. R. (1980). *Stone fox*. New York: Crowell.

Gauthier, G. (1995). *Mooch forever*. Translated by S. Cummins. Halifax: Formac.

Gravel, F. (1992). *Mr. Zamboni's dream machine*. Translated by S. Cummins. Toronto: James Lorimer & Company.

Hutchins, H. (1997). *Shoot for the moon, Robyn*. Halifax: Formac.

Korman, G. (1997). *Liar, liar, pants on fire*. Richmond Hill, ON: Scholastic Canada.

Lowry, L. (2001). *Zooman Sam*. New York: Dell Yearling.

MacLachlan, P. (1985). *Sarah, plain and tall*. New York: Harper & Row.

MacLachlan, P. (1994). *Skylark*. New York: Harper Trophy.

Manuel, L. (1997). *The cherry-pit princess*. Regina: Coteau Books.

Park, B. (1982). *Skinnybones*. New York: Alfred A. Knopf.

Paterson, K. (1992). *The king's equal*. New York: HarperCollins (originally published in picture book format).

Pilkey, D. (1997). *The adventures of Captain Underpants*. Boston, MA: Little Apple.

Richardson, G. (1997). *A friend for Mr. Granville*. Edmonton: Hodgepog Books.

Roberts, K. (1994). *Past tense*. Vancouver: Douglas & McIntyre.

Roy, R. (1982). *Where's Buddy?* New York: Clarion Books.

Sachar, L. (1991). *The boy who lost his face*. New York: Alfred A. Knopf.

Salata, E. (1984). *Mice at centre ice*. Scarborough, ON: Nelson Canada.

Smucker, B. (1987). *Jacob's little giant*. Toronto: Puffin Books.

Steele, M. (1993). *Featherbys*. Victoria, BC: Hyland House.

Wishinsky, F. (1998). *Crazy for chocolate*. Richmond Hill, ON: Scholastic Canada.

learning how to deal with their respective difficulties and differences (including a learning disability).

In *The Onlyhouse* (Toten, 1995), set in the 1960s, Lucija, a recent Croatian immigrant, moves to a new neighbourhood and tries to make friends. She finally discovers the joys of true friendship, but also experiences the neediness of her new friend, Jackie, and the problems of Jackie's mixed-up family. Other recommended titles of contemporary realistic fiction that focus on relationships include:

- *The Daring Game* (Pearson, 1986)
- *Afternoon of the Elves* (Lisle, 1989)
- *Maniac Magee* (Spinelli, 1990)
- *Walk Two Moons* (Creech, 1994)
- *The Watsons Go to Birmingham—1963* (Curtis, 1995)

Novels such as these encourage students to explore personal and social issues that may help them attain an increased understanding of themselves and others.

A genre much enjoyed by children in the upper elementary grades is that of mystery. These stories challenge children to become actively engaged in problem solving. Young readers enjoy putting the pieces of the puzzle together, hypothesizing, and making inferences as they act as detectives in solving the mystery. Well-formed mystery stories can be difficult to find, however, so that when children discover series books such as the Hardy Boys, Nancy Drew, or Encyclopedia Brown, they frequently read all the books in the series in their desire to remain engaged with the genre. As they become familiar with a particular series' pattern, they also become increasingly better at predicting solutions and fitting clues together. The result is that children tend to grow out of these rather predictable plots and patterns, becoming ready for something more demanding and more sophisticated. In the 1990s, children turned to the genre of horror stories in addition to mysteries. The Goosebumps series by R. L. Stine was extremely popular for a number of years, and many parents and educators expressed concern over children reading these books (see, for example, Perry and Butler, 1997; Dickson, 1998). Not unexpectedly, readers soon outgrew the books, wanting a greater challenge and a new thrill in reading.

There are, however, numerous well-written mystery stories to recommend. Betsy Byars has authored a series of mystery books about a character named Herculeah Jones. *Dead Letter* (1996) and *Death's Door* (1997) are two titles in the series. Eve Bunting wrote *Is Anybody There?* (1988) about a 13-year-old boy who is certain that someone other than a family member is regularly coming into his house. The boy has evidence to support his belief, but he needs proof to confirm his suspicions. In *Silent to the Bone* (Konigsburg, 2002) Branwell is unable to utter a word after the horrible crime that put his little sister, Nikki, into a coma. While Branwell is retained in a juvenile behavioural centre, accused of perpetrating the crime, his best friend attempts to discover what really happened to Nikki and clear Branwell's name. Other recommended titles are:

- *The Dragon Children* (Buchan, 1975)
- *Who Stole the Wizard of Oz?* (Avi, 1981)
- *Secrets in the Attic* (York, 1984)
- *Lucy Forever & Miss Rosetree, Shrinks* (Shreve, 1987)
- *Megan's Island* (Roberts, 1988)
- *The Mystery at Wolf River* (Shura, 1989)
- *The Westing Game* (Raskin, 1990)
- *Bunnicula: A Rabbit Tale of Mystery* (Howe, 1996)
- *The Chinese Puzzle* (Brouillet, 1996)
- *Sammy Keyes and the Hotel Thief* (Van Draanen, 1998)

Historical fiction is a genre that presents new challenges for many young readers, for it typically presents fictional characters in a historically accurate context. The genre often requires that the reader have some prior knowledge of the time period in which the story is set. Rosemary Sutcliff is a British author who has written many books of historical fiction for children. Her books are superbly crafted, thoroughly researched, and extremely well written. *Warrior Scarlet* (1958), for example, is set in the Bronze Age in Great Britain, a period for

Teacher and primary boy with book display.

which there is no written record and which is not connected to the real lives of most Canadian children. Readers savour her descriptive passages, and once into the story, a reader is hooked, for the book addresses issues that are as relevant today as they probably were hundreds of years ago. Historical fiction is a particularly suitable genre for teachers to share with their classes as a read-aloud. It also helps in creating a context and a deeper understanding of many social studies topics, and can inspire themes for work across the curriculum.

Books of historical fiction about Canada and by Canadian authors have become more plentiful over the last few years. Examples include *Underground to Canada* by Barbara Smucker (1977), dealing with slavery; *A Very Small Rebellion* by Jan Truss (1977), about the Riel rebellion; *The Sky Is Falling* by Kit Pearson (1989), about World War II; and *Rebellion: A Novel of Upper Canada* by Marianne Brandis (1996).

A list of historical fiction is provided in Box 10.6.

Time-slip fantasy is a genre that has become popular in recent years, though it has its roots in *Tom's Midnight Garden* (1958) by Philippa Pearce. The story usually begins in the present, and then, through some artifact from the past, the protagonist is transported into a different time, typically a specific period in history. *The Castle in the Attic* by Elizabeth Winthrop (1985) fits into this category of novel, and so does Janet Lunn's book *The Root Cellar* (1981), which is about the American Civil War. A well-known Australian time-slip fantasy is *Playing Beatie Bow* (1980) by Ruth Parks. Three Canadian time-slip fantasy books were published in 1987: *The Doll* by Cora Taylor, *Who Is Francis Rain?* by Margaret Buffie, and *A Handful of Time* by Kit Pearson. In *Who Is Frances Rain?* a pair of spectacles takes Lizzie back into the isolated pioneer times of rural Manitoba in the early part of the 20th century. Through her experiences in a different time, Lizzie is able to deal with her life in the present in a more effective and positive manner.

Fantasy literature engages the reader's imagination and gives free rein to endless possibilities. The reader is taken to worlds where animals and toys can speak, and where people can travel across time and into completely fictional worlds. The genre is popular in all the elementary grades. Young children, for example, enjoy *Charlotte's Web* (White, 1952) and *James and the Giant Peach* (Dahl, 1961). Older children enjoy *The Dark Is Rising* (Cooper, 1969) and *Harry Potter and the Sorcerer's Stone* (Rowling, 1998). Although fantasy literature has a devoted following in Grades 5 and 6, it can be a challenging genre for children *and* teachers alike because of the complexity and sophistication of the ideas embedded within it. Many books of **high fantasy** (usually quest stories), such as *The Hobbit* (Tolkien, 1937) and *The Golden Compass* (Pullman, 1996), are read by both children and adults. Much modern fantasy has its roots in ancient myths and legends,

Box 10.6 Historical Fiction

Canadian:

Attema, M. (1996). *A time to choose*. Victoria, BC: Orca (young adult).

Bellingham, B. (1985). *Storm child*. Toronto: James Lorimer & Company.

Berton, P. and Van Der Linde, H. (1996). *The Klondike stampede*. Toronto: McClelland & Stewart.

Clark, J. (2002). *The word for home*. New York: Penguin.

Ellis, S. (2001). *Prairie as wide as the sea: The immigrant diary of Ivy Weatherall* (Dear Canada Series). Markham, ON: Scholastic.

Greenwood, B. and Collins, H. (1998). *The daily life of a pioneer family*. Boston, MA: Houghton Mifflin.

Haworth-Attard, B. (2001). *Flying geese*. Toronto: Harper Collins Publishers.

Lawson, J. (2001). *Across the James Bay Bridge: Emily* (Our Canadian Girl Series). Toronto: Penguin Books Canada Ltd.

Little, J. (2001) *Orphan at my door: The home child diary of Victoria Cope* (Dear Canada Series). Markham, ON: Scholastic Canada Ltd.

Lottridge, B. (1992). *Ticket to curlew*. Toronto: Douglas & McIntyre.

Lunn, J. (1986). *Shadow in Hawthorn Bay*. Toronto: Lester and Orpen Denys.

Schwartz, V. (2002). *If I just had two wings*. Toronto: Stoddart Kids.

Stinson, K. (2001). *Dark spring: Marie-Claire* (Our Canadian Girl Series). Toronto: Penguin Books Canada Ltd.

Walters, E. (1998). *War of the eagles*. Victoria, BC: Orca Book Publishers.

Walters, E. (1997). *Trapped in ice*. Toronto: Penguin Books.

Yee, P. (1989). *Tales from Gold Mountain*. Toronto: Groundwood Books.

Non-Canadian:

Filipovic, Z. (1994). *Zlata's diary: A child's life in Sarajevo*. New York: Putnam.

Fox, P. (1973). *The slave dancer*. New York: Bradbury.

Greene, B. (1973). *The summer of my German soldier*. New York: Bantam.

Lowry, L. (1989). *Number the stars*. New York: Houghton Mifflin.

McSwigan, M. (1942). *Snow treasure*. New York: E. P. Dutton.

O'Dell, S. (1970). *Sing down the moon*. New York: Bantam Doubleday Dell.

O'Dell, S. and Hall, E. (1992). *Thunder rolling in the mountains*. New York: Bantam Doubleday Dell.

Reiss, J. (1972). *The upstairs room*. New York: Scholastic.

Speare, E. G. (1958). *The witch of Blackbird Pond*. New York: Dell Publishing.

Speare, E. G. (1983). *The sign of the beaver*. New York: Bantam Doubleday Dell.

Uchida, Y. (1978). *Journey home*. New York: Aladdin Paperbacks.

especially in the *Tales from the Mabinogian*, which is a collection of Welsh myths dating back many hundreds of years. Both Susan Cooper and Alan Garner (*The Owl Service,*

Box 10.7   Canadian Fiction for Upper Elementary Readers

Bailey, L. (2001). *Adventures with the Vikings*. Toronto: Kids Can Press.

Bradford, K. (1996). *Shadows on a sword*. Toronto: HarperCollins.

Clark, J. (1995). *The dream carvers*. Toronto: Viking.

Doyle, B. (1979). *You can pick me up at Peggy's Cove*. Toronto: Douglas & McIntyre.

Ellis, S. (1991). *Pick-up sticks*. Toronto: Groundwood Books.

Fairbridge, L. (1995). *Stormbound*. Toronto: Doubleday.

Godfrey, M. (1994). *Just call me Boom Boom*. Richmond Hill, ON: Scholastic Canada.

Heneghan, J. (2002). *Flood*. Toronto: Groundwood Books/Douglas & McIntyre.

Horrocks, A. (1996). *Breath of a ghost*. Toronto: Stoddart Kids.

Horvath, P. (2001). *Everything on a waffle*. Toronto: Groundwood Books.

Hutchins, H. (1997). *The prince of Tarn*. Toronto: Annick Press.

Matas, C. (1995). *The primrose path*. Winnipeg: Blizzard Publishing.

Pearson, K. (1996). *Awake and dreaming*. Markham, ON: Viking.

Sherman, G. T. (1997). *Grave danger*. Richmond Hill, ON: Scholastic.

Trembath, D. (2002). *The bachelors*. Victoria, BC: Orca Book Publishers.

1967) refer to the *Mabinogian* in their writing, and it is useful if readers have at least a nodding acquaintance with this material when reading these authors' books. A modern children's version by Gwynn Thomas and Kevin Crossley-Holland (1985) is a wonderful addition to any classroom library.

Additional examples of fantasy literature for children are:

- *The Wind in the Willows* (Graham, 1908)
- *The Lion, the Witch and the Wardrobe* (Lewis, 1950)
- *The Borrowers* (Norton, 1952)
- *A Wrinkle in Time* (L'Engle, 1962)
- *Tuck Everlasting* (Babbit, 1975)
- *The Keeper of the Isis Light* (Hughes, 1980)
- *Redwall* (Jacques, 1987)
- *The Giver* (Lowry, 1993)

Box 10.7 lists a selection of Canadian novels suitable for students in Grades 4 to 6.

Collections of Short Stories

The short story, as a literary form, has existed only since the middle of the 19th century. Although it has its roots in ancient tales and narratives, it was Edgar Allan Poe and Nathaniel Hawthorne, among others, who developed the short story as an art form. They were followed by writers such as Katherine Mansfield and Somerset Maugham in Britain and by Ernest Hemingway in the United States. A short story is a brief fictional narrative (though it can be anything from 500 to 15 000 words) that consists of more than just a mere record of an incident. It has a formal structure with unity of time, place, and action. Generally, a short story reveals the true nature of a character.

Today, there are a growing number of high-quality collections of short stories for children in Grades 3 to 6. These are delightful and frequently thought-provoking stories that are well-crafted pieces of writing. Readers familiar with Tim Wynne-Jones' picture books will be especially appreciative of his three books of short stories: *Some of the Kinder Planets* (1993), which won the Governor General's Award and the Boston Globe–Horn Book Award for Children's Literature, *The Book of Changes* (1994), and *Lord of the Fries* (1999). Kit Pearson has edited an anthology of short stories and excerpts from works of Canadian children's literature titled *This Land* (1998). *The Back of Beyond* (Ellis, 1998) and *Garbage Creek* (Valgardson, 1997) are also excellent collections of short stories suitable for the upper elementary grades.

TRADITIONAL LITERATURE

Traditional literature remains a staple of the elementary language arts curriculum from kindergarten to Grade 6. Today there are many beautifully illustrated retellings of traditional stories, originating from around the world. This section presents a sampling of these books.

The genre of traditional literature, which is sometimes referred to as "folk literature," includes fairytales, folk tales, Mother Goose rhymes, legends, myths, proverbs, epics, fables, and more. These are mostly short stories that reflect the values and dreams of a society, and through which societies and their cultures come alive. Traditional literature is, in general, a body of work that was originally passed from generation to generation orally. Scholars and educators agree that traditional literature is a most important genre for children, and it is frequently the first genre with which children become truly familiar. "Once upon a time" is a phrase that young children all over the Western world associate with the telling of a story. It signals the beginning of a narrative designed to take the child into the world of imagination. The classic fairytale has a structure that has become ingrained in the Western psyche. Jean Little's book, *Once upon a Golden Apple* (1991), plays with children's internalization of the structure of fairytales, and the humour in the book is based on children understanding these "rules" and knowing those rules are being manipulated.

Folk and Fairytales

Many traditional versions of folk and fairytales are available today. Some author/illustrators have become well-known for their renditions of these stories, people such as Laszlo Gal, Leo and Diane Dillon, Jan Brett, Trina Schart Hyman, Jane Yolen, Paul Galdone, Robert San Souci, and John Steptoe. Galdone's version of *Little Red Riding Hood* (1974) is particularly appropriate for young children, while Hyman's rendition of *Little Red Riding Hood* (1983) is more appropriate for older readers. *The Twelve Dancing Princesses* has been retold by Janet Lunn (1979, illustrated by Laszlo Gal), Ruth Sanderson (1990), and Marianna Mayer (1989, illustrated by Kinuko Craft). Jan Ormerod has retold *The Frog Prince* (1990 illustrated by David Lloyd), and Glen Rounds has produced a version of *The Three Billy Goats Gruff* (1993).

There are also parodies of well-known tales in books such as *The Three Little Wolves and the Big Bad Pig* (Trivizas, 1993) and *The True Story of the Three Little Pigs* (Scieszka, 1989). Both of these books are based on the traditional story *The Three Little Pigs* and depend on intertextual connections for their humour and impact.

In a number of clever retellings of fairytales, the texts deviate little from the original version, but the illustrations create a powerfully different meaning to the story. *Hansel and Gretel*, retold by Anthony Browne (1981), is one such book where the traditional story is retold in a modern setting. Ian Wallace's (1994) rendition of *Hansel and Gretel* also places the story in a contemporary setting, this time in Atlantic Canada.

Modern fairytales such as *The Tough Princess* by Martin Waddell (1986, illustrated by Patrick Benson) and *The King's Equal* by Katherine Paterson (1992, illustrated by Vladimir Vagin) play with readers' expectations and knowledge of the fairytale genre. These books raise questions about traditional gender roles and the messages implicit in most fairytales (e.g., that a woman must be rescued by a man and is then dependent on him for living happily ever after). *The Tough Princess* does this in a humorous way that questions traditional expectations from the first page. Paterson's book, *The King's Equal*, raises the same questions as *The Tough Princess*, but in a different manner, and the book accomplishes much more than a reversal of traditional gender roles. Paterson has created a story in which all the participants learn from their actions, and the presence of the mysterious wolf adds a mystical element. As teachers and students read and interact with these modern versions of fairytales, readers may discover deeper meanings in the traditional tales. They may also be moved to question them, given the context of current societal beliefs and values.

Myths and Legends

Many novels for children and adults are based on the patterns, characters, and plots of the best-known myths and legends, and certain recurring themes in literature can be traced back to myths. As a result, it is helpful for young readers to be introduced to myths and legends as part of the repertoire of elementary school reading. Greek, Roman, Celtic, and Norse myths are the better known of these stories, though many books now available are devoted to Aboriginal American, Chinese, and South American myths. Joseph Campbell (1988) argues that myths are powerful literature that should be read by everyone to help us understand ourselves as human beings and as social and spiritual creatures.

One such recent retelling of a Chinese myth, *The Dragon's Pearl* by Julie Lawson (1992), is beautifully illustrated by Paul Morin. The book won the Amelia Frances Howard-Gibbon Award for illustrations in 1993. Also illustrated by Paul Morin is Tololwa Mollel's Tanzanian myth *The Orphan Boy* (1990), which won the 1990 Governor General's Literary Award for illustration. Priscilla Galloway has retold a number of Greek myths, including *Aleta and the Queen: A Tale of Ancient Greece* (1995), *Atalanta: The Fastest Runner in the World* (1995), and *Daedalus and the Minotaur* (1997). All are illustrated by Normand Cousin. It is interesting to note that myths and legends have spawned many phrases in the English language. Greek myths in particular have generated phrases such as "the Midas touch," "Pandora's box," "Herculean effort," and "a Trojan horse."

Legends are stories told about real people and their feats or accomplishments. Usually the narratives are mixed with superstition, and they expand and enhance the actual exploits of their heroes. Legends are closely related to myths, but they do not contain supernatural deities as myths do. The stories of Beowulf, King Arthur, Robin Hood, William Tell, Davy Crockett, and Johnny Appleseed are legends. From reading myths and legends, children are encouraged to seek explanations for the phenomena in their lives—

to ask questions about modern "legendary" figures and heroes and perhaps relate them to the possibilities inherent in their own lives.

Fables

The origin of the fable is thought to reside with a Greek slave named Aesop, who lived in the 6th century BC. Experts, however, believe there were many sources of the fable, since it is found worldwide. Fables are fictional tales that are meant to entertain though they also contain a moral. They usually have only two or three characters, frequently talking animals who possess humanlike characteristics. Fables are popular with young children today largely because of the presence of the talking animals and the humour the stories contain. Fables such as "The Town Mouse and the Country Mouse" and "The Tortoise and the Hare" remain particular favourites with children. There are also many variations of "The Lion and the Mouse" and "The Raven and the Fox."

The Oral Tradition of Storytelling

True storytelling calls upon stories that are part of the tradition of oral literature, stories that have many versions and can be modified to suit audience and purpose. These are the stories that are handed down within families or within cultural groups. The Aboriginal peoples of Canada, the United States, Australia, and New Zealand have a rich fund of stories, some of which are ritual stories that may not be shared with the general public. Families also have their stories and storytellers—stories of early settlement in homesteads on the prairie, stories of great-grandfathers who worked on the trans-Canada railway, stories of great hardship, illnesses, long journeys at sea, family treasures, and great adventures. These are the stories that cannot easily be written down and neatly illustrated. They are stories that have a special significance to the listener and frequently appeal to a small audience. This is the difference between storytelling and "performing" a text.

Children in the elementary grades generally enjoy a good storyteller. They enjoy hearing a senior citizen speak of times past in a small community, and they enjoy collecting the stories of community members. True storytelling demands discipline so that a story is captured and shaped to suit the audience and the purpose for its telling. A rambling recollection of an event that occurred a number of years ago is not the same thing as a story. Thus, teachers who wish to engage in storytelling, or to have their students tell stories in the classroom, should hone their storytelling skills. This includes perfecting the nuances of chosen vocabulary, intonation, facial expressions, and hand gestures, as well as ensuring that stories have cohesion, development, and appropriate closure, just as a good written tale does. Storytelling must also be rehearsed in the same way that any performance is rehearsed before it is shared with an audience.

Teachers can make full use of storytelling in their classrooms and help children develop as storytellers by having them read many different versions of a traditional story and then retell it in their own way. In this way children can invest the oral story with their own thoughts and feelings, story and storyteller becoming one. Two excellent resource books for teachers are *And None of It Was Nonsense: The Power of Storytelling in the Classroom* by Betty Rosen (1988) and *Stories to Tell* by Bob Barton (1992). Rosen describes her thinking, preparation, follow-up work, and lessons. The book also includes selections of her students' work. Barton has put together a set of resource materials for storytelling, and draws on his experiences as a Canadian storyteller/teacher/writer. He encourages teachers to tell their own stories, including the songs, rhymes, jingles, chants, and sayings they remember. Barton connects the worlds of storytelling, drama, games, movement, and role-play in the creation of new stories, reminding us that stories can be revisited and remade again and again. In *Stories in the Classroom*, Bob Barton and David Booth (1990) collaborated in furthering their work on storytelling, drama, and response to literature. It provides another valuable resource for teachers.

POETRY FOR CHILDREN

The nursery rhymes, songs, and jingles of their infancy constitute a core of literature for most children. Poetry has a major role to play in the language arts curriculum. This section presents selections of poems, poetic forms, and poetic devices appropriate for the elementary grades.

Many adults remember clearly the nursery rhymes, jingles, skipping songs, and playground chants they heard when they were preschoolers. Opie and Opie (1963) refer to these oral rhymes as "the true waifs of our literature in that their original wordings, as well as their authors, are usually unknown" (p. 7). Many of these rhymes, now considered suitable only for the nursery, were not originally intended for children. They stem from old ballads, political lampoons, and "worldly songs." The Opies spent more than 20 years collecting and researching nursery rhymes, and the section of incidental notes at the back of their collection, *The Puffin Book of Nursery Rhymes*, provides fascinating insights into the history of many rhymes in the book. Young children continue to enjoy nursery rhymes, with their unusual words, frequent nonsense, and compelling rhythms.

As adults we also remember the deeply meaningful and emotive poems read to us by family members and teachers, poems such as "Meg Merrilies" by John Keats and "The Highwayman" by Alfred Noyes. Refrains and particularly humorous stanzas from poems such as "The Adventures of Isabel" by Ogden Nash also remain fixed in our memories. We may remember writing poems in school or responding to poems in response journals or through drama activities. Huck, Hepler, Hickman, and Kiefer (2004, p. 350) write that

> Poetry can both broaden and intensify experience, or it might present a range of experiences beyond the realm of personal possibility for the individual listener. It can also illuminate, clarify, and deepen an everyday occurrence in a way the reader never considered, making the reader see more and feel more than ever before. For poetry does more than mirror life; it reveals life in new dimensions.

Poetry communicates experience by appealing to both the thoughts and feelings of the reader. Every word is carefully chosen by the poet for the nuances and emotive meanings it conveys. Children usually need to experience poetry as being pleasurable and often amusing before they can experience its more beautiful and philosophical aspects. Poetry should be as much a part of the literary world of children as contemporary realistic fiction or picture books are. Learning to understand and appreciate poetry is an ongoing process, as it is with other forms of literature. Children are more likely to enjoy poetry if they have experienced it from their earliest days, through nursery rhymes, jingles, and songs. Nursery rhymes and skipping rhymes cannot be considered poetry, but they do lay the foundation for later journeys into poetic language.

Defining poetry is a challenge, for many contemporary poets are breaking the traditional expectations of poetry, both in content and form. Words are placed across the page, at angles, and in bunches. Contemporary poetry is written about subjects not previously dealt with (taking the garbage out, watching father eat mashed potatoes at dinner time, listening to a fight between parents). However, poems continue to make children laugh, ponder, imagine, remember, and see the world in new ways. Indeed, poetry helps to develop insights and new understandings.

As Booth and Moore (1988) write, "Children's poetry has a special appeal: the form and language of poetry speaks directly to the child, to their senses, their imaginations, their emotions, their feelings, their experiences of childhood" (p. 22). Experience tells us that children are not interested in static poems that describe the seasons, weather, or events in nature. Rather, they are interested in poems of action, rhythm, rhyme, and energy that invite them to participate and relate to their everyday experiences. Children are naturally rhythmical. From the earliest nursery rhymes to the poems of Dennis Lee, a musical rhythm pervades the text. Children are generally intrigued by the sound of language as they play with it and learn its melody.

Sharing Poetry with Children

Children become readers and appreciators of poetry by experiencing poetry with adults who enjoy, read, and share poetry with them. Hearing the skilfully crafted arrangement of the sounds of a poem read aloud is one of the primary pleasures of poetry. Although enunciation is a fundamental component of any kind of oral sharing of poetry, it is also vital that poetry be read interpretively. This means that a reader must learn to focus on the emotive meanings conveyed by a poem, whether those meanings are playful or wistful. When children hear Sheree Fitch read her poems aloud, they are entranced by her sheer energy and engagement with the words:

> I've a yearning
> That is burning
> A desire for Higher learning
> I would like
> To go to college
> To improve upon
> My knowledge....

(From *If You Could Wear My Sneakers* by Sheree Fitch [poetry] and Darcia Labrosse [illustrations]. © 1997 Sheree Fitch and Darcia Labrosse. Reprinted with the permission of Doubleday Canada Limited.)

Readers of poetry, whether adults or children, consider the mood they wish to set when reading a poem aloud. The interpretation of a poem is greatly influenced by how a reader varies its tempo, volume, rhythm, pitch, and juncture. Briefly,

- *tempo* refers to how slowly or quickly words or lines are read,
- *volume* refers to loudness,
- *rhythm* describes emphasis or stress,
- *pitch* refers to the lowering or raising of the voice, and
- *juncture* describes the location and length of pauses.

Teachers and students may vary these elements when reading poetry and then discuss if and how the changes affected their interpretations of the poems.

Choral reading and the implementation of drama strategies enhance children's understanding and awareness of poetry. Sound effects, mime, puppets, shadow plays, and role-playing are dramatic techniques that can be used when working with poetry in the classroom.

Poetic Devices

Rhyme is a very common element of poetry. Indeed, some children believe rhyme to be the sole determining feature of poetry. The poems of Michael Rosen, Dennis Lee, Jack Prelutsky, and Shel Silverstein are contemporary works whose use of rhyme, rhythm, and playfulness forms part of their appeal. Although rhyme is a popular device of poets, children may need to expand their definition of poetry if they are to enjoy more sophisticated poems in later years.

Comparison is another device used by poets. The use of *similes*, explicitly comparing one thing with another using the words "like" or "as," and the use of *metaphors*, comparing two things by implying that one is like the other, are two common comparison techniques used by poets. A beautifully illustrated picture book of similes is *As Quick as a Cricket* (Woods, 1982). A tongue-in-cheek collection of similes for older readers is *As: A Surfeit of Similes* (Juster, 1989). A further poetic device used by writers is *alliteration*—the repeated use of the same initial consonants in consecutive words or the use of words that are close in proximity and produce a pattern of the same or similar sounds. Chris Van Allsburg used alliteration in his alphabet book *The Z Was Zapped* (1987). *Some Smug Slug* (Edwards, 1996) is another example of the use of alliteration to tell a tale.

Onomatopoeia is a device wherein writers use sound words (e.g., *splash*, *slurp*, *boing*) to make the writing more vivid and sensory. The elements of tempo, volume, stress, and pitch can be manipulated in ways to assist in conveying the meaning and imagery of sound words. *Machine Poems* (Bennett, 1993) and *Click, Rumble, Roar: Poems About Machines* (Hopkins, 1987) are collections of poems that contain many examples of onomatopoeia. The repetition of words and phrases is another device used by many poets. For example, in the book *A Dark Dark Tale* (Brown, 1981), the author repeats the words "dark, dark." As the poem continues, each location described in the text as "dark, dark" progressively decreases in size. The poem begins, "Once upon a time there was a dark, dark moor" and the next dark, dark location is a wood, and the next one a house, and then a door, and so on.

Imagery and *figurative language* are other important poetic elements that play a role in poetry for children. Langston Hughes's poem "City" (1950) creates the image of the city as a bird, and Carl Sandburg (1944) likens the fog descending on a city to a cat in his poem "Fog." The language, imagery, and rhythm of poetry interact in creating the emotional force of a poem. Langston Hughes's poem entitled "Poem" (1960) evokes a powerful emotional response in most readers, as does "Listening to Grownups Quarrelling" by Ruth Whitman (1968).

Forms of Poetry

One of the most popular forms of poetry with children is *narrative poetry*, poetry that tells a story. One narrative poem that has been reproduced in picture book format is *The Cremation of Sam McGee*, written by Robert Service and illustrated by Ted Harrison (1987). *Lyric* and *free verse* are two other forms of poetry enjoyed by children. Lyric poetry frequently describes a mood or feeling and elicits strong emotions about the subject of the poem. Although free verse poetry generally lacks rhyme, this type of poetry allows poets great freedom in creating their own rules of rhythm. Emotional language and imagery are important elements of free verse. The topics of free verse poetry are often abstract or philosophical.

Haiku and *cinquain* are forms of poetry that have prescribed structures. Haiku is a form of poetry originating in Japan; a haiku is a three-line poem with the first and last lines each having five syllables and the middle line having seven syllables. Traditionally, haiku dealt with topics associated with nature or the seasons, but modern haiku is written about a much broader range of subjects. A cinquain, a five-line stanza, is structured around 22 syllables in a 2-4-6-8-2 syllable pattern.

Rhyme, rhythm, and sound are important poetic elements that influence students' opinions of poems (Tompkins and Hoskisson, 1995). Edward Lear popularized *limericks*, now a favourite form of poetry among children and adults alike, in his book, *The Complete Book of Nonsense* (1846, 1946). Limericks are usually humorous or silly five-lined verses, with the first and second lines rhyming with the fifth line and the shorter third and fourth lines rhyming with each other. Often the fifth line is a repetition of the first line. Two books of limericks are *The Book of Pigericks* (Lobel, 1983) and *The Hopeful Trout and Other Limericks* (Ciardi, 1989).

Concrete poems are arranged in a particular manner on a page in order to create an image or visual shape of the poem's subject. For example, in the poetry collection *A Hippopotamusn't* (Lewis, 1990), Lewis has written a concrete poem about the flamingo, cleverly arranging the words in a flamingo shape. Concrete poetry is meant to be seen even more than heard. This form of poetry often lacks a rhythm or rhyming pattern. *Seeing Things: A Book of Poems* (Froman, 1974) and *Concrete Is Not Always Hard* (Pilon, 1972) are two collections of concrete poetry.

Picture Book Versions of Poems

There are many picture book versions of single poems, including Robert Frost's "Stopping by Woods on a Snowy Evening," illustrated by Susan Jeffers (1978), and Eugene Field's "Wynken, Blynken and Nod," also illustrated by Susan Jeffers (1982). Jan Brett (1991) has illustrated a picture book version of "The Owl and the Pussy Cat" by Edward Lear, and Ed Young (1988) has illustrated Robert Frost's poem "Birches." Ted Rand has illustrated two poems: "My Shadow" (1990) by Robert Louis Stevenson and "Arithmetic" (1993) by Carl Sandburg.

In the picture book *In Flanders Fields: The Story of the Poem by John McCrae* (1995), Linda Granfield not only presents "In Flanders Fields" but also shares information about the poet and his experiences working in a field hospital. She describes the living conditions and daily routines of the soldiers and provides information about World War I. She also explains the origin of the symbolic gesture of wearing a poppy. The illustrator, Janet Wilson, travelled to Flanders to do research for her paintings because she wanted them to be as accurate as possible.

Canadian poet sean o huigin has written many poems for children. Much of o huigin's work is traditional humorous light verse. Two serious works written by o huigin and published in picture book format are *Atmosfear* (1985), an antipollution poem with a cautionary message, and *The Ghost Horse of the Mounties* (1983), a poem based on an event that took place in 1874 when a violent thunderstorm stampeded the horses of the first Mounties in Manitoba. In 1983, *The Ghost Horse of the Mounties* became the first children's poetry book ever to win the Canada Council Children's Literature Prize.

Poetry Collections

Many books of poetry are collections of one individual's works. Examples include:

- *Dogs and Dragons, Trees and Dreams* (Kuskin, 1980)
- *A Light in the Attic* (Silverstein, 1981)
- *The New Kid on the Block* (Prelutsky, 1984)
- *Roomrimes* (Cassedy, 1987)
- *Day Songs, Night Songs* (Priest, 1993)
- *Demi's Secret Garden* (Demi, 1993)
- *Beast Feast* (Florian, 1994)
- *If You Could Wear My Sneakers* (Fitch, 1997)

Byrd Baylor, David McCord, John Ciardi, Dennis Lee, and Myra Cohn Livingston are also known for collections of their poetry.

Many poetry books are specialized collections of poems related to a single theme or topic—for example, snow, dinosaurs, monsters, dragons, magic, festivals, machines, Halloween, and nightmares. General anthologies of poetry are useful for teachers to have on hand. Notable anthologies include *The Oxford Book of Poetry for Children*, compiled by Edward Blishen (1963); *The Random House Book of Poetry* by Jack Prelutsky (1983);

Box 10.8 Poetry Resources

Balaam, J. and Merrick, B. (1989). *Exploring poetry: 5–8*. Sheffield, UK: National Association for the Teaching of English.

Bouchard, D. (1993). *If you're not from the prairie*. Vancouver: Raincoast Books.

Fleischman, P. (1985). *Joyful noise: poems for two voices*. New York: Harper and Row.

Foster, J. and Paul, K. (2000). *Pet poems*. Oxford: Oxford University Press.

Goldstein, B. (ed.). (1993). *Birthday rhymes, special times*. New York: Delacorte.

Harrison, M. and Stuart-Clark, C. (comp.). (1995). *The New Oxford treasury of children's poems*. Toronto: Oxford University Press.

Janeczko, P. (2001). *A poke in the I*. Cambridge, MA: Candlewick Press.

Larrick, N. (ed.). (1991). *To the moon and back*. New York: Delacorte.

Lee, D. (1974). *Alligator pie*. Toronto: Macmillan Canada.

Mayo, M. (2000). *Wiggle waggle fun: Stories and rhymes for the very very young*. Toronto: Random House.

Merrick, B. (1991). *Exploring poetry: 8–13*. Sheffield, UK: National Association for the Teaching of English.

Numeroff, L. (2002). *Sometimes I wonder if poodles like noodles*. New York: Aladdin Paperbacks.

Prelutsky, J. (1993). *The dragons are singing tonight*. New York: Greenwillow Press.

Prelutsky, J. (1996). *A pizza the size of the sun*. New York: Greenwillow Books.

Priest, R. (2002). *The secret invasion of bananas*. Victoria, BC: Cherrubim Books.

Rosen, M. (1984). *Quick, let's get out of here*. New York: Dutton.

Silverstein, S. (1974). *Where the sidewalk ends: Poems and drawings*. New York: Harper.

Steig, J. (1988). *Consider the lemming*. New York: Farrar, Straus, and Giroux.

Stepanek, M. (2002). *Celebrate through heart songs*. New York: Hyperion.

The New Wind Has Wings: Poems from Canada, compiled by Mary Alice Downie and Barbara Robertson (1984); *Til All the Stars Have Fallen* by David Booth (1989); and *Images of Nature: Canadian Poets and the Group of Seven* by David Booth (1995). A number of poetry anthologies suitable for use in elementary school classrooms are listed in Box 10.8 on page 305.

INFORMATION BOOKS

Nonfiction or information books are an important learning resource for use across the curriculum. Nonfiction books must be current, accurate, and appealing to children. This section presents various types of nonfiction books, as well as criteria for evaluating nonfiction materials.

Information books (also known as nonfiction literature) play a major role in every elementary classroom, for it is this genre that provides the resource material for most teaching across the entire curriculum. Through reading about a topic from many sources and from a number of different perspectives, students are able to construct a fuller understanding of the topic. Each piece of information and each point of view helps to create a broader picture in the mind of the student and provides the fertile ground for new meanings to develop. Meaning, after all, resides in the individual learner. Many children in the primary grades (and earlier) thoroughly enjoy reading nonfiction materials, and it is this genre that caters to the special interests of students and provides them with the resources they need for pursuing their avocation. However, it is only recently that educators have recognized children's interests and pleasure in reading nonfiction materials and have begun to teach children how to read expository texts as well as narrative texts.

Doiron (1994) comments that "the primacy of fiction in our literacy programs" is being challenged, and Pappas (1991) maintains that a lack of exposure to nonfiction text translates into a lack of opportunity to write nonstory compositions. The result, Pappas believes, is that most children are unprepared for the expository writing of secondary school. Clearly, children need both narrative and non-narrative reading and writing experiences. Now, with children in even the primary grades being encouraged to write reports and projects using nonfiction materials for information, educators are teaching youngsters how to use the index of a book, the glossary, and the table of contents, as well as how to browse through a book quickly to see from the pictures and the headings if the book is going to be helpful or interesting.

There are at least eight major types of nonfiction books for children:

1. photo-documentaries
2. "how-to" books
3. question and answer formats
4. experiment and activity books
5. sequential explanation (survey) books
6. field guides
7. biographies
8. narrative nonfiction

Some of these nonfiction books are designed to be used as reference materials and have a typical expository format. Others are intended to be read from beginning to end, more like a work of fiction, and consist of narrative text.

Nonfiction material has improved a great deal in quality and presentation over the last ten years. Many of the nonfiction materials still on library shelves from the 1970s look dull and uninviting compared with more recent publications. The explosion in technology, allowing for the superb reproduction of photographs, maps, and other graphics and a more interesting and accessible page layout, has created a splendid new age of nonfiction, especially for young readers.

Many awards have been specifically created for nonfiction books. These include the Information Book Award sponsored by the Children's Literature Round Tables of Canada, the Orbis Pictus Award for Outstanding Nonfiction for Children established by the National Council of Teachers of English (in the United States), the Boston Globe–Horn Book Award established jointly by the *Boston Globe* and *The Horn Book Magazine* (United States), and the *Times* Educational Supplement Information Book Awards (United Kingdom). The designation of these awards is a mark of the increasing recognition accorded nonfiction books, as well as a recognition of children's strong interest in informational materials. It is also an indication that the quality of nonfiction materials has improved sufficiently to merit awards specifically for the genre.

Criteria for Evaluating Nonfiction Books

The information available in any subject area grows rapidly over time. Keeping a nonfiction collection up to date is a major challenge and a major expense for any school or library. Books published on a topic ten or fifteen years ago are likely to be out of date today. It is therefore important that nonfiction books be purchased for the school or classroom library with discrimination, and with the aid of library selection tools such as *CM: Canadian Materials*, *The Horn Book Magazine*, *School Library Journal*, *Teacher Librarian*, or *Booklist*. It is also important that the books made available to children be current, and that they not be allowed to remain on the shelves for years without being reviewed. A list of evaluation criteria for nonfiction books is presented in Box 10.9.

The *accuracy* and *authenticity* of material is probably the most difficult criterion for educators to assess. The first thing to look for in any nonfiction book is an indication from the author(s) that either they have the expertise themselves (as with Beatty and Geiger, 1992, in *Buried in Ice: Unlocking the Secrets of a Doomed Arctic Voyage*), or they have consulted with experts in the creation of the book (as in the Starting with Space series from Kids Can Press). The latter series contains excellent illustrations, clear explanations, and interesting activities for readers to complete either at home or at school. The books in the series have a glossary, an index, a table of contents, *and* an acknowledgment of the assistance provided by the scientists at the Royal Ontario Museum (McLaughlin Planetarium). This last piece of information tells the reader that the information contained in the book has come from a reliable source. Whatever is provided for the reader, however, the main criterion for selecting a book must be compatibility with the reader's own background knowledge of the subject. Teachers play a crucial role in assisting their students to select books that are appropriate in content—books that are neither too simple nor conceptually overloaded.

The *format* of nonfiction books is an especially important area to evaluate. Some nonfiction books are too "busy" in their layout for young readers. The visual effect is one of overload, as the reader has to attend to too much input at one time. A pleasing book in terms of content and format is *You Are the Earth* (Suzuki and Vanderlinden, 1999), a book that explores how the four physical elements of air, water, earth and fire, contribute to life on earth. It is a book readers will likely pick up and read in occasional short bursts rather than use as a reference book or for a sustained read. Many activities are included in the book, which children can complete themselves, and the illustrations are of a high quality. This book is suitable for a classroom collection, and is one of the better books of its kind.

Unfortunately, many science books are printed without colour photographs and diagrams. They may contain lots of interesting information and ideas for children, but they

---

Box 10.9 Criteria for Evaluating Nonfiction Books

Format

- Is the book well made so that it will stand up to wear?
- Is the page design uncluttered?
- Is the book visually appealing? Does it invite the reader to browse through it?
- Does it pique the reader's interest?
- Are there enough visuals and enough colour to make the book appealing?

Organization and Style

- Is the material presented in a clear and unambiguous way?
- Does the book create a feeling of reader involvement and convey a positive tone?
- Does the author use vivid and interesting language?
- Is the content structured clearly and logically, with appropriate subheadings?
- Are there reference aids such as a table of contents, index, bibliography, glossary, and appendix?

Content

- Is the content presented in a manner that allows children to connect it with their own experiences?
- Where content has been simplified, does it retain accuracy?
- Does the book include the author's sources as well as additional information for keen readers who want to learn more?
- Is the book current and does it reflect (and mention) current research activity in the field?
- Are the qualifications and experiences of the authors presented?
- Does the book avoid stereotypes and present differing viewpoints?
- Is a distinction made among fact, theory, and opinion?
- Does the book foster a scientific method of inquiry?

Graphics and Illustration

- Are there appropriate and sufficient maps, charts, and diagrams to add to the reader's understanding of the text?
- Are the graphics and illustrations an appropriate size?
- Are the graphics and illustrations clearly understandable and well labelled?
- Do the maps, charts, and diagrams contain appropriate detail?

Source: Based on F. Smardo Dowd, "Trends and evaluative criteria of informational books for children," in E. Freeman and D. Person (eds.), *Using nonfiction trade books in the classroom: From ants to zeppelins* (Urbana, IL: National Council of Teachers of English, 1992), pp. 34–43.

are not laid out or planned in ways that make them accessible for young readers. The books usually contain black-and-white drawings that, in combination with the black-and-white text, do little to help children stay focused on the various units of meaning presented on each page. Too much information is presented in the same format for readers to be able to easily pick out which information belongs together. Children can become overwhelmed by the amount of information, even if it is in the form of a diagram or drawing, and they may close the book and move on to something else. Colour photographs and drawings help young readers move their eyes and their attention around the page from one unit of meaning to another more easily. *The Disaster of the Hindenburg* (Tanaka, 1993) is well formatted, allowing the focus of attention to move smoothly from text to diagram to photograph and back to text. The format helps the reader take in the information and make sense of it.

Narrative Nonfiction

Some of the most fascinating nonfiction materials published recently are narrative texts that incorporate details and explanations into a story. These books are not easy to come by. David Suzuki sought to use narrative in his Nature All Around series. Some of the books in the series work better than others, but all remain blatantly didactic, consisting of what is basically a lecture-tour by a mother, father, or other character in the story. The aesthetic experience afforded by these books does not meet the informative value.

Snowflake Bentley (Martin, 1998) is a book of narrative nonfiction that won the Caldecott Medal in the United States in 1999. William Bentley, a Vermont farmer/photographer, had a special interest in exploring and photographing natural phenomena. During the early part of the 20th century, Bentley created photographs that demonstrated that no two snowflakes are alike and that each one is startlingly beautiful. At the time, Bentley's work with snow was often misunderstood. His book *Snow Crystals* and his "lantern slides" were, however, well respected and were used by many colleges and universities. Author Jacqueline Briggs Martin accompanies the gentle story with sidebars containing snippets of information and explanations of Bentley's work. The woodcuts created by illustrator Mary Azarian bring the story beautifully to life.

Anastasia's Album (Brewster, 1996) is a most interesting Canadian work of narrative nonfiction consisting of photographs, watercolours, and hand-decorated pages capturing the life of Tsar Nicholas's youngest daughter. The story of the Romanov family is told from the perspective of Anastasia herself, and includes excerpts from her diaries and letters as well as the recollections of family friends. The book makes interesting and compelling reading for adults as well as children, and does not "talk down" to a child audience.

Theodoric's Rainbow, written by Stephen Kramer (1995) and illustrated by Daniel Mark Duffy, tells the story (much of it through pictures) of Theodoric of Freiberg, a German philosopher and theologian who was one of the first people to experiment in science (rather than philosophize). Theodoric discovered how drops of water reflect and refract light. He then went on to develop the first geometrically correct explanation of the rainbow. The text is straightforward and well written, and children from Grade 3 onwards (and possibly earlier) will find this beautiful book fascinating.

Thunderstorm! (Tripp, 1994) is a book that describes the large and small changes that take place in the atmosphere when weather fronts move. Such changes warn animals and humans to seek shelter from the explosive forces of a storm. The book, illustrated by Juan Wijngaard, tells in narrative style how a thunderstorm develops over one farm, building

Box 10.10   A Selection of High-Quality Nonfiction Books

Anholt, L. (1998). *Stone girl, bone girl: The story of Mary Anning*. New York: Orchard Books.

Baker, J. (1995). *The story of Rosy Dock*. New York: Greenwillow Books.

Bishop, N. (1997). *The secrets of animal flight*. New York: Houghton Mifflin.

Godkin, C. (1995). *Ladybug garden*. Markham, ON: Fitzhenry & Whiteside.

Heller, R. (1999). *Color, color, color*. New York: Puffin.

Mann, E. (1996). *The Brooklyn Bridge*. New York: Mikaya Press.

Prager, E. (2000). *Sand*. Washington, DC: National Geographic Society.

Schlein, M. (1996). *The puzzle of the dinosaur bird*. New York: Dial Books for Young Readers.

Sis, P. (1996). *Starry messenger*. New York: Farrar Straus Giroux.

in intensity and transforming quiet farmland into nature's most spectacular sound and light show.

One of the best-known books of narrative nonfiction for young children is the award-winning Australian book *Where the Forest Meets the Sea* by Jeanie Baker (1987). It is an innovative picture book that chronicles the reflections of a young boy exploring the rainforest of northern Queensland with his father. The illustrations (also done by Baker) consist of relief collage constructed from a mix of natural materials, including lamb's wool, fabric, and leaves. The result is a rich three-dimensional perspective on the rainforest that invites the reader to explore the secrets of the forest and the majesty of nature. The boy plays, imagines, wonders, and questions: "Will the rainforest still be here when we come back?" No answers are provided, no didacticism. It is left to the reader to ponder the question.

These and other well-written, well-illustrated nonfiction books for children have moved the genre into a new era. A few exemplary nonfiction books are listed in Box 10.10. They truly are books to be read purely for pleasure, and not only for the information they offer. And ultimately, though written for children, they make compelling reading for all ages.

At the beginning of this chapter, Jennifer wondered how she could include nonfiction literature in her reading program. This last section of the chapter has provided examples of books she might suggest to her students. These books provide educators with opportunities for teaching and creating new meaning for students, and provide children with opportunities to reflect on and appreciate the artistic presentation and well-crafted texts of this genre.

SUMMARY

Scholars such as Meek (1988) and Wells (1986) have demonstrated how children who are read to in their preschool years and who learn to appreciate literature are much more likely to experience success in their literacy development and in their learning in school. They are also more likely to read for pleasure when they are adults. Learning from this, educators have embraced the concept of literature-based reading instruction, and many have created language arts programs based on the many genres of trade books available. Consequently, children's literature is incorporated into most language arts programs in Canada, whether it is used to balance a basal reading series or used as the foundation for the literacy program.

A wide range of top-quality literature is available for children in the elementary grades. The picture book genre is growing most rapidly in terms of scope and quality. Many picture books are produced for students in upper elementary and junior high schools. Likewise, most novels for children are available in paperback and include fantasy, contemporary realistic fiction, historical fiction, time-slip fantasy, mystery, and horror. Modern classics—books such as *Charlotte's Web* (White, 1952) and *Angel Square* (Doyle, 1984)— are part of the cultural heritage of youngsters. Traditional stories, poetry, and storytelling all play a role in the repertoire of literary materials and activities with which children engage. Books of all genres continue to create opportunities for children to take on the four roles of the reader as described by Freebody and Luke (1990): code breaker, text participant, text user, and text analyst. Mastering these four roles not only enhances a child's reading ability, it also contributes to the lifelong pleasures he or she will have from reading.

The quality and number of nonfiction books available for the classroom have increased markedly over the last fifteen years. Current technology has helped to create colourful, interesting, and understandable diagrams, charts, and maps. Graphics are generally appealing, and photographs are reproduced with greater clarity than ever before. Authors of nonfiction material for children must write intelligently for an audience that has access to more information than was ever previously available. Such materials must therefore be current, accurate, well-designed, and interesting, for they are competing with the Internet, television, and movies as sources of information for students. However, good nonfiction literature for children must also be aesthetically appealing to a wide audience, including adults. This is especially the case in books of narrative nonfiction where information is embedded in a contextualized narrative. Frequently such stories are accompanied by illustrations rendered by well-known artists.

As language arts programs increasingly incorporate works of children's literature as instructional resources, teachers are finding they must be knowledgeable about books, authors, and illustrators, and must be able to talk with children about the books they are reading. Teachers regularly recommend books of all genres to children. This means that teachers increasingly read books written for children and are familiar with the reading interests of their students. If teachers enjoy books and welcome children into the world of literature, their students are also likely to enjoy books and become lifelong readers.

SELECTED PROFESSIONAL RESOURCES

Huck, C., Hepler, S., Hickman, J., and Kiefer, B. Z. (2004). *Children's literature in the elementary school* (8th ed.). Dubuque, IA: McGraw-Hill. This American text remains one of the most encompassing of resources on children's literature. It is an excellent source of information on the different genres of literature, the history of children's literature, author and illustrator profiles, and planning for instruction in the elementary school. The book provides a wealth of background information, and is a useful reference tool for classroom teachers and teacher-librarians. A database on CD-ROM accompanies the text. Over 4000 books can be accessed by author, title, genre, and more. Full bibliographic information, plus the approximate interest level (by grade) is provided for each book. Unfortunately, very few Canadian books are listed.

Vandergrift, K. *Kay Vandergrift's special interest page.* Available: scils.rutgers.edu/%7Ekvander. This noncommercial site was developed by Kay Vandergrift, the Associate Dean and Director of the Information, Technology and Informatics Program in the School of Communication, Information and Library Studies at Rutgers University, New Jersey. The site contains lists of picture books, juvenile novels and young adult literature, as well as lists of multicultural and multiethnic books, many of them Canadian. The comprehensive lists include Aboriginal, Islamic, traditional, and feminist literature. Videos about children's authors and illustrators are available, as well as articles on featured authors and books. Sections of the site are devoted to a history of children's literature, literature applicable to teaching topics across the curriculum and resources to support teaching.

The children's literature web guide. Available: www.acs.ucalgary.ca/~dkbrown. This site, created by David K. Brown, is an attempt to gather together and categorize the growing number of Internet resources related to books for children and young adults. Much of the information found on these Web pages is provided by schools, libraries, and commercial enterprises involved in the book world. The site is internationally known for its rich connections to various lists: best books of the year, book awards, authors and illustrators on the Web, discussion groups, children's literature organizations, conferences, and book reviews. Brown has compiled his lists from a variety of both print and Internet sources. He takes a thorough look at each site before adding it to his list. His site is valuable to teachers, librarians, parents, book professionals (writers, editors, booksellers, and storytellers), as well as children. David K. Brown is director of the Doucette Library of Teacher's Resources, University of Calgary. He has several years of experience in children's materials and educational resources, and is based in the Faculty of Education. He believes that an important part of his mandate is to promote both children's literature and electronic sources of information such as the Internet.

CHILDREN'S BOOKS NOTED IN CHAPTER TEN

Ahlberg, J. and Ahlberg, A. (1978). *Each peach pear plum.* London: Kestrel Books.

Avi. (1981). *Who stole the Wizard of Oz?* New York: Alfred A. Knopf.

Babbitt, N. (1975). *Tuck everlasting.* New York: Farrar, Straus and Giroux.

Baker, J. (1987). *Where the forest meets the sea.* New York: Greenwillow Books.

Beatty, O. and Geiger, J. (1992). *Buried in ice: Unlocking the secrets of a doomed Arctic voyage.* Mississauga, ON: Random House.

Bennett, J. (1993). *Machine poems.* Don Mills, ON: Oxford University Press.

Blishen, E. (comp.). (1963). *The Oxford book of poetry for children.* London: Oxford University Press.

Booth, D. (1989). *Til all the stars have fallen.* Toronto: Kids Can Press.

Booth, D. (1995). *Images of nature: Canadian poets and the Group of Seven.* Toronto: Kids Can Press.

Brandis, M. (1996). *Rebellion: A novel of Upper Canada.* Erin, ON: The Porcupine's Quill.

Brett, J. (illus.). (1991). *The owl and the pussy cat.* (Poem by Edward Lear). New York: Putnam.

Brewster, H. (1996). *Anastasia's album.* Toronto: Penguin Books.

Brouillet, C. (1996). *The Chinese puzzle.* Charlottetown: Ragweed Press.

Brown, R. (1981). *A dark, dark tale.* New York: Scholastic.

Browne, A. (1981). *Hansel and Gretel.* London: Julia MacRae Books.

Browne, A. (1986). *Piggybook.* New York: Alfred A. Knopf.

Browne, A. (1989). *The tunnel.* London: Julia MacRae Books.

Buchan, B. (1975). *The dragon children.* Richmond Hill, ON: Scholastic-TAB.

Buffie, M. (1987). *Who is Frances Rain?* Toronto: Kids Can Press.

Bunting, E. (1988). *Is anybody there?* New York: Harper & Row.

Burningham, J. (1977). *Come away from the water, Shirley.* London: Cape.

Byars, B. (1996). *Dead letter.* New York: Viking.

Byars, B. (1997). *Death's door.* New York: Viking.

Cassedy, S. (1987). *Roomrimes.* New York: Thomas Crowell.

Ciardi, J. (1989). *The hopeful trout and other limericks.* New York: Houghton Mifflin.

Coerr, E. (1993). *Sadako.* (E. Young, illustrator). New York: Putnam.

Cooper, S. (1969). *The dark is rising.* New York: Collier Macmillan.

Creech, S. (1994). *Walk two moons.* New York: HarperCollins.

Curtis, C. (1995). *The Watsons go to Birmingham—1963.* New York: Delacorte.

Dahl, R. (1961). *James and the giant peach.* New York: Puffin Books.

Davidge, B. and Wallace, I. (1993). *The mummer's song.* Toronto: Groundwood Books.

Demi. (1993). *Demi's secret garden.* New York: Henry Holt & Co.

Downie, D. and Robertson, B. (comp.). (1984). *The new wind has wings: Poems from Canada.* Toronto: Oxford University Press.

Doyle, B. (1984). *Angel square.* Toronto: Douglas & McIntyre.

Edwards, P. (1996). *Some smug slug.* New York: HarperCollins.

Ellis, S. (1998). *The back of beyond.* Toronto: Groundwood Books.

Fitch, S. (1997). *If you could wear my sneakers.* Toronto: Doubleday Canada.

Florian, D. (1994). *Beast feast.* New York: Harcourt Brace.

Froman, R. (1974). *Seeing things: A book of poems.* New York: Thomas Y. Crowell.

Galdone, P. (1974). *Little Red Riding Hood.* New York: McGraw-Hill.

Galloway, P. (1995). *Aleta and the Queen: A tale of ancient Greece.* (N. Cousin, illustrator). Toronto: Annick Press.

Galloway, P. (1995). *Atalanta: The fastest runner in the world.* (N. Cousin, illustrator). Toronto: Annick Press.

Galloway, P. (1997). *Daedalus and the Minotaur.* (N. Cousin, illustrator). Toronto: Annick Press.

Garner, A. (1967). *The owl service.* London: William Collins & Sons.

Graham, K. (1908). *The wind in the willows.* New York: Scribners.

Granfield, L. (1995). *In Flanders Fields: The story of the poem by John McCrae.* (J. Wilson, illustrator). Toronto: Lester.

Harrison, T. (illus.). (1987). *The cremation of Sam McGee.* (Poem by Robert W. Service). New York: Greenwillow.

Hopkins, L. B. (1987). *Click, rumble, roar: Poems about machines.* New York: Thomas Y. Crowell.

Howe, D. (1996). *Bunnicula: A rabbit tale of mystery.* New York: Simon & Schuster.

Hughes, L. (1950). "City." In *The Langston Hughes reader.* New York: Harold Ober Associates.

Hughes, L. (1960). "Poem." In *Don't you turn back: Poems by Langston Hughes.* L. B. Hopkins (ed.). New York: Knopf.

Hughes, M. (1980). *The keeper of the Isis light.* London: Mammoth.

Hutchins, P. (1969). *Rosie's walk.* London: Bodley Head Press.

Hyman, T. S. (1983). *Little Red Riding Hood.* New York: Holiday House.

Innocenti, R. (1985). *Rose Blanche.* Mankato, MN: Creative Education.

Jacques, B. (1987). *Redwall.* New York: Philomel.

Jeffers, S. (illus.). (1978). *Stopping by woods on a snowy evening.* (Poem by Robert Frost). New York: Dutton Books.

Jeffers, S. (illus.). (1992). *Wynken, Blynken and Nod.* (Poem by E. Field). New York: E. P. Dutton.

Juster, N. (1989). *As: A surfeit of similes.* New York: William Morrow.

Kodama, T. (1995). *Shin's tricycle.* New York: Walker.

Konigsburg, E. L. (2002). *Silent to the bone.* New York: Aladdin Paperbacks.

Kramer, S. (1995). *Theodoric's rainbow.* (D. M. Duffy, illustrator). New York: W. H. Freeman & Co.

Kuskin, K. (1980). *Dogs and dragons, trees and dreams.* New York: Harper & Row.

Lawson, J. (1992). *The dragon's pearl.* (Paul Morin, illustrator). Toronto: Stoddart.

Lear, E. (1946 [1846]). *The complete book of nonsense.* New York: Dodd, Mead.

Lee, D. (2001). *The cat and the wizard.* Toronto: Key Porter Books.

L'Engle, M. (1962). *A wrinkle in time.* New York: Farrar, Straus and Giroux.

Lewis, C. S. (1950). *The lion, the witch and the wardrobe.* New York: Macmillan.

Lewis, J. P. (1990). *A hippopotamusn't.* New York: Dial Books for Young Readers.

Lisle, J. T. (1989). *Afternoon of the elves.* New York: Orchard Books.

Little, J. (1985). *Lost and found.* Toronto: Penguin Books Canada.

Little, J. (1991). *Once upon a golden apple.* Markham, ON: Viking.

Lobel, A. (1983). *The book of pigericks.* New York: Harper & Row.

Lowry, L. (1993). *The giver.* Boston: Houghton Mifflin.

Lunn, J. (1979). *The twelve dancing princesses.* (L. Gal, illustrator). Toronto: Methuen.

Lunn, J. (1981). *The root cellar.* New York: Scribners.

Macaulay, D. (1990). *Black and white.* New York: Houghton Mifflin.

McNicoll, S. (1996). *The big race.* Richmond Hill, ON: Scholastic Canada.

Martin, J. B. (1998). *Snowflake Bentley.* Boston: Houghton Mifflin.

Maruki, T. (1980). *Hiroshima no pika.* New York: Lothrop, Lee & Shepard Books.

Mayer, M. (1989). *The twelve dancing princesses.* (K. Craft, illustrator). New York: Morrow.

Mollel, T. (1990). *The orphan boy.* (P. Morin, illustrator). Toronto: Oxford University Press.

Montgomery, L. M. (1908). *Anne of Green Gables.* London: L. C. Page & Company.

Morimoto, J. (1987). *My Hiroshima.* Sydney, Australia: Collins.

Norton, M. (1952). *The borrowers.* San Diego: Harcourt.

o huigin, s. (1983). *The ghost horse of the Mounties.* Windsor, ON: Black Moss Press.

o huigin, s. (1985). *Atmosfear.* Windsor, ON: Black Moss Press.

Ormerod, J. (1981). *Sunshine.* Harmondsworth, UK: Puffin Books.

Ormerod, J. (1982). *Moonlight.* Harmondsworth, UK: Puffin Books.

Ormerod, J. (1990). *The frog prince.* (D. Lloyd, illustrator). New York: Lothrop, Lee & Shepard Books.

Parks, R. (1980). *Playing Beatie Bow.* Ringwood, Australia: Penguin Books Australia.

Paterson, K. (1992). *The king's equal.* (V. Vagin, illustrator). New York: HarperCollins.

Pearce, P. (1958). *Tom's midnight garden.* London: Oxford University Press.

Pearson, K. (1986). *The daring game.* Markham, ON: Puffin Books.

Pearson, K. (1987). *A handful of time.* Markham, ON: Viking Kestrel.

Pearson, K. (1989). *The sky is falling.* Markham, ON: Viking Kestrel.

Pearson, K. (1998). *This land.* Markham, ON: Viking.

Pilon, A. (1972). *Concrete is not always hard.* New York: Xerox Education.

Priest, R. (1993). *Day songs, night songs.* Toronto: Groundwood Books.

Prelutsky, J. (1983). *The Random House book of poetry.* New York: Random House.

Prelutsky, J. (1984). *The new kid on the block.* New York: Greenwillow Books.

Pullman, P. (1996). *The golden compass.* New York: Knopf.

Rand, T. (illus.). (1990). *My shadow.* (Poem by Robert Louis Stevenson). New York: Putnam.

Rand, T. (illus.). (1993). *Arithmetic.* (Poem by Carl Sandburg). New York: Harcourt Brace.

Raskin, E. (1990). *The Westing game.* Morton Grove, IL: Albert Whitman & Co.

Richler, M. (1975). *Jacob Two-Two meets the hooded fang.* Toronto: Puffin Books.

Richler, M. (1987). *Jacob Two-Two and the dinosaur.* Toronto: Puffin Books.

Richler, M. (1995). *Jacob Two-Two's first spy case.* Toronto: McClelland & Stewart.

Roberts, K. (1988). *Hiccup champion of the world.* Vancouver: Douglas & McIntyre.

Roberts, W. D. (1988). *Megan's island.* New York: Macmillan.

Rounds, G. (1993). *The three billy goats Gruff.* New York: Holiday House.

Rowling, J. K. (1998). *Harry Potter and the sorcerer's stone.* New York: A. A. Levine Books.

Rylant, C. (1986). *Night in the country.* New York: Bradbury Press.

Sandburg, C. (1944). "Fog." In *Chicago poems.* New York: Harcourt Brace & Co.

Sanderson, R. (1990). *The twelve dancing princesses.* New York: Little, Brown & Co.

Scieszka, J. (1989). *The true story of the three little pigs.* New York: Scholastic.

Shreve, S. (1987). *Lucy Forever & Miss Rosetree, shrinks.* New York: Alfred A. Knopf.

Shura, M. F. (1989). *The mystery at Wolf River.* New York: Scholastic.

Silverstein, S. (1981). *A light in the attic.* New York: Harper & Row.

Smucker, B. (1977). *Underground to Canada.* Toronto: Clarke, Irwin.

Spalding, A. (1995). *Finders keepers.* Victoria, BC: Beach Home.

Spinelli, G. (1990). *Maniac Magee.* Boston: Little, Brown & Co..

Stine, R. L. (1992). *Welcome to the dead house* (Goosebumps Series). New York: Scholastic.

Sutcliff, R. (1958). *Warrior scarlet.* Harmondsworth, UK: Puffin Books.

Suzuki, D. and Vanderlinden, K. (1999). *You are the earth: From dinosaur breath to pizza from dirt.* Vancouver: Greystone Books.

Tanaka, S. (1993). *The disaster of the Hindenburg.* Richmond Hill, ON: Scholastic/Time Quest.

Taylor, C. (1987). *The doll.* Toronto: Douglas & McIntyre.

Thomas, G. and Crossley-Holland, K. (1985). *Tales from the Mabinogian.* New York: Overlook Press.

Tolkien, J.R.R. (1937). *The hobbit.* Boston: Houghton.

Toten, T. (1995). *The onlyhouse.* Red Deer, AB: Red Deer College Press.

Tripp, N. (1994). *Thunderstorm!* (J. Wijngaard, illustrator). New York: Dial Books.

Trivizas, E. (1993). *The three little wolves and the big bad pig.* London: William Heinemann.

Truss, J. (1977). *A very small rebellion.* Edmonton: J. M. Lebel Enterprises.

Truss, J. (1982). *Jasmin.* Vancouver: Douglas & McIntyre.

Valgardson, W. D. (1997). *Garbage creek.* Toronto: Groundwood Books.

Van Allsburg, C. (1987). *The z was zapped.* New York: Houghton Mifflin.

Van Allsburg, C. (1992). *The widow's broom.* New York: Houghton Mifflin.

Van Draanen, W. (1998). *Sammy Keyes and the hotel thief.* New York: Alfred A. Knopf.

Waddell, M. (1986). *The tough princess.* (P. Benson, illustrator). London: Walker Books.

Wallace, I. (1994). *Hansel and Gretel.* Toronto: Douglas & McIntyre.

White, E. B. (1952). *Charlotte's web.* New York: Harper and Row.

Whitman, R. (1968). "Listening to grownups quarrelling." In *The marriage wig and other poems.* New York: Harcourt Brace & Co.

Wiesner, D. (1988). *Free fall.* New York: Lothrop, Lee & Shepard Books.

Wiesner, D. (1991). *Tuesday.* New York: Clarion.

Wiesner, D. (1992). *June 29, 1999.* Boston: Houghton Mifflin.

Wild, M. (1991). *Let the celebrations begin!* (J. Vivas, illustrator). Adelaide, Australia: Omnibus Books.

Wilson, E. (1983). *The Kootenay kidnapper.* Don Mills, ON: Collins.

Wilson, B. (1995). *Harold and Harold.* Porters Lake, NS: Pottersfield Press.

Winthrop, E. (1985). *The castle in the attic.* New York: Bantam Skylark.

Woods, A. (1982). *As quick as a cricket.* New York: Child's Play International.

Wynne-Jones, T. (1992). *Zoom upstream.* (E. Beddows, illustrator). Toronto: Douglas & McIntyre.

Wynne-Jones, T. (1993). *Some of the kinder planets.* Toronto: Douglas & McIntyre.

Wynne-Jones, T. (1994). *The book of changes.* Toronto: Douglas & McIntyre.

Wynne-Jones, T. (1995). *The maestro.* Toronto: Douglas & McIntyre.

Wynne-Jones, T. (1999). *Lord of the fries and other stories.* Toronto: Douglas & McIntyre.

Young, E. (illus.). (1988). *Birches.* (Poem by Robert Frost). New York: Henry Holt & Company.

REFERENCES

Barthes, R. (1970, trans. 1974). *S/Z: An essay.* New York: Hill & Wang.

Barton, B. (1992). *Stories to tell.* Markham, ON: Pembroke.

Barton, B. and Booth, D. (1990). *Stories in the classroom.* Markham, ON: Pembroke.

Booth, D. and Moore, B. (1988). *Poems please! Sharing poetry with children.* Markham, ON: Pembroke.

Campbell, J. (1988). *The power of myth.* New York: Doubleday.

Dickson, R. (1998). Horror: To gratify, not edify. *Language Arts*, 76 (2), 115–122.

Doiron, R. (1994). Using nonfiction in a read-aloud program: Letting the facts speak for themselves. *Reading Teacher*, 47 (8), 616–623.

Eco, U. (1978). *The role of the reader.* Bloomington, IN: Indiana University Press.

Freebody, P. and Luke, A. (1990). "Literacies" programs: Debates and demands in cultural contexts. *Prospects*, 5 (3), 7–16.

Freeman, E. and Person, D. (eds.). (1992). *Using nonfiction trade books in the classroom: From ants to zeppelins.* Urbana, IL: National Council of Teachers of English.

Holdaway, D. (1979). *The foundations of literacy.* Gosford, Australia: Ashton Scholastic.

Huck, C. S., Hepler, S., Hickman, J., and Kiefer, B. Z. (2004). *Children's literature in the elementary school* (8th ed). Dubuque, IA: McGraw-Hill.

Hunt, L. C. (1970). The effect of self-selection, interest and motivation upon independent, instructional and frustration level. *Reading Teacher, 24* (2), 146–151.

Keifer, B. (1995). *The potential of picturebooks: From visual literacy to aesthetic understanding.* Englewood Cliffs, NJ: Prentice-Hall.

Meek, M. (1988). *How texts teach what readers learn.* Stroud, UK: Thimble Press.

Opie, I. and Opie, P. (1963). *The Puffin book of nursery rhymes.* Harmondsworth, UK: Penguin Books.

Pantaleo, S. (1994). Teacher influence on student response to literature. PhD dissertation, University of Alberta, Edmonton, AB.

Pappas, C. (1991). Fostering full access to literacy by including information books. *Language Arts, 68* (6), 449–461.

Perry, L. A. and Butler, R. P. (1997). Are Goosebumps books real literature? *Language Arts, 74* (6), 454–456.

Rosen, B. (1988). *And none of it was nonsense: The power of storytelling in the classroom.* Richmond Hill, ON: Scholastic-TAB.

Tompkins, G. and Hoskisson, K. (1995). *Language arts: Content and teaching strategies* (3rd ed.). Englewood, NJ: Prentice-Hall.

Vanderhaeghe, G. (1996). *The Englishman's boy.* Toronto: McClelland & Stewart.

Wells, G. (1986). *The meaning makers.* Portsmouth, NH: Heinemann.

Chapter

Responding to Literature

Reader Response

- Learning Through Response
- Response Groups
- Literature Response Journals
- Readers' Workshop
- Literature Circles
- Novel Studies
- Alternative Modes of Response
- Dependent Authorship

Responding to Literature

Book Selection

- Guidelines for Appropriate Selection of Children's Literature
- Censorship of Children's Materials
- Issues and Controversies

Canadian Literature

- Why Canadian?
- Books by Aboriginal Canadians

When Shawn began his student teaching in a Grade 5 classroom, the teacher told him he would be working with the students as they engaged in response groups. She invited him to suggest a few novels the students might enjoy. Shawn wanted to choose some Canadian books but wasn't sure which titles would be most appropriate. He also wanted to suggest books the children would enjoy, but not something controversial that might run the risk of offending the school community. Shawn began researching current titles and began to think about how the language arts teaching strategies he had learned in his course work would fit into response group activities. How, for example, could Halliday's functions of language (1969) help him? Where would dramatic response be most appropriate, and in what ways could he help the children to become involved in writing response journals?

This chapter addresses Shawn's questions about how teachers can facilitate literary response and how they can go about selecting literature for the classroom. As an introduction to these topics, cast your mind back to your own early reading instruction. What and where did you read in school? Was more than one reading series or more than one grade level of material used in your classroom? Did you visit the school library regularly and check out books to take home? Did the classroom have its own collection of books? Were you allowed to read some books and not others? Who decided what you could and could not read? Did you participate in response activities such as group discussions, puppet shows, or journal writing about the books and stories you were reading? Did your teacher read books aloud to the whole class regularly, and talk with the class about well-known authors and illustrators and their work? These same questions are important for teachers to consider when planning a balanced literacy program for their own classrooms. The decisions they make about these items will deeply affect the literacy programs they develop and implement with their students.

READER RESPONSE

The first section of this chapter explains what is meant by reader response and what response "looks like" in a classroom. As well, many activities are described for use in the elementary language arts program.

Reader response refers to the events that occur within a reader when a piece of text is read. Rosenblatt (1978) maintains that text is simply squiggles on a page until a reader reads it. When a reader reads the print, *something* happens within the reader. That "something" is often labelled "response." The response might be boredom, confusion, interest, sadness, empathy, or joy, but a reading event is never undertaken without a variety of responses. People respond to all kinds of events in their everyday lives—a menu read in a restaurant, a movie seen at the cinema, news from a friend, a television show, international news on the radio, a song, a play, an editorial in the newspaper. Response is part of the human condition, part of our interactions with the people and the world around us. It is part of the meaning-making process, and as such, response to literature is an important component of a language arts program.

Rosenblatt (1978) refers to the reading experience as a transaction between *text* and *reader*, a transaction that creates the *poem*, or what Rosenblatt terms the "lived-through experience with the text." Readers respond to the "poem" (a term used broadly by Rosenblatt to mean the transactional experience) as they read, after they read, and when they reflect on or recapture their reading experience. Rosenblatt maintains that a response is dictated to a considerable extent by the purpose for reading or, in other words, by the *stance* from which the reader approaches the text. A stance can be anywhere on a continuum from efferent at one end, where the reader seeks information of some kind, to aesthetic at the other, where the reader focuses on appreciating what is read. Response fluctuates along this continuum as we read. At one moment a reader may be reading for the pure pleasure and appreciation of a work, and the next moment might be noticing something interesting and memorable in the text, or something that relates to a piece of information received from a different source in the recent past. For example, when reading *The Doll* (Taylor, 1987), a reader may first be appreciating the artistry of the language and the tantalizing nature of time-slip fantasy. Then, suddenly, his or her attention might shift to a focus on prairie fires and the devastation they can cause to farmland and livestock—

a thought that can be connected with a newspaper article he or she read the previous day. The reading experience thus moves from an aesthetic stance to a more efferent stance.

The extremes of response on this continuum can be demonstrated by two quite different reading events. When someone is reading a first-aid manual to treat an injury, the reading has a very pragmatic purpose—to allow the reader to gain essential information that will directly affect his or her behaviour in the immediate future. The reading of a first-aid manual is *efferent reading*, at the far end of the continuum. When that same person is reading a novel, however, the purpose is likely to be to allow him or her to gain a deeper understanding of the human experience. As readers engage with a novel, they enter into the space of the novel and disconnect themselves from the time of their own existence as well as their own ongoing or chronological time. This is where Rosenblatt (1978) uses the term "lived-through experience with the text" to describe an *aesthetic reading* (Cooper, 1985, p. xiv). A good book is almost certain to evoke a deep personal engagement, whether that turns out to be one involving angst or one involving pleasure.

Teachers can provide opportunities for children to respond aesthetically to a text whether that text is in a reading series or in a trade book. Rosenblatt maintains that "once the work has been evoked, it can become the object of reflection and analysis, according to the various critical and scholarly approaches" (Farrell and Squire, 1990, p. 106). In other words, a text first evokes an aesthetic or "lived-through" response and then evokes a more efferent response as the reader consciously thinks about the text and the reading experience. For example, a short story such as "Tashkent" (in *Some of the Kinder Planets*, by Tim Wynne-Jones, 1993) may be read in such a way that the reader enters the story's time, identifying with the protagonist's illness and recuperation, and leaving behind the more immediate concerns of the world. When reflecting on the story, however, the reader constructs meaning (on the basis of the text) that may relate to other stories or poems, to geographical facts, to information the reader already possesses, or to the reader's own life or that of a friend. When readers reflect in this way, they reenter ongoing chronological time and engage in a more efferent response. A *totally* efferent response to "Tashkent" might include summarizing the story as we retell it to a friend, locating in an atlas the place names mentioned in the story, or comparing the story with a poem that has a similar theme. These transactions form the cornerstone for the creation of possible meanings, as well as for coming to understand how texts work.

What is seen of response to literature in a classroom is like the tip of an iceberg: much of it remains out of sight (Purves and Rippere, 1968). Teachers can keep the following points in mind as they engage students with literature:

- The extent to which students show their responses in a classroom context depends very much on the reading abilities of the individual children.
- The depth of response students demonstrate depends very much on the level of trust they feel in the classroom environment.
- People in general do not share feelings and thoughts if they don't feel safe.
- If children are taught that there is one "right" response to a piece of literature (usually the teacher's response or interpretation), they are less likely to express their own responses.
- Through sharing and discussing responses, students discover that meaning can be negotiated and constructed in a multitude of equally valid ways.
- When students are encouraged to respond to texts and to engage in dialogue with themselves, their peers, and teachers about books, they are more likely to see that meaning is created by the learner, and that multiple ways of knowing and responding to literature are valid and necessary.

- Students who share their responses to literature and have their responses accepted respectfully are likely to become more thoughtful and critical readers than those students who do not experience a fair exchange of responses.

Learning Through Response

Children learn a great deal through responding to literature. They discover how texts work, what constitutes a good book, how language can be used in different ways to create different meanings and effects—in short, how to become readers, not just people able to read. As a result of active responding, children are likely to take ownership of the reading process and come to understand that literature can be interpreted in many varied ways. However, as Rosenblatt (1978) says, some responses are more legitimate or appropriate than others because a response must be based in the text read. Through learning to respect and honour their own interpretations of what they have read, students gain the confidence to become more critical in their thinking about texts, more creative in their own writing, and much more capable in their ability as language users and language learners. In effect, they take on the four roles of the reader (Freebody and Luke, 1990) described in Chapter Ten: code breaker, text participant, text user, and text analyst.

Literature can be the basis for an entire language arts program in the elementary classroom, for the nature of reading and response encourages children to integrate their knowledge, make personal sense of it, and express it through movement, the visual arts, music, drama, writing, and dialogue. Thomson (1987) reminds us that "the development of a mature response to literature involves a progressive movement from close emotional involvement to more distanced reflective detachment, and from an interest in self to an interest in other people and the human condition" (p. 153). This means that the process of response almost always begins with an aesthetic, personal experience of the text—the very experience that a response activity in the classroom aims to encourage and facilitate.

Response Groups

One important vehicle for exploring a text is the response group. Adult readers have discovered the pleasures of reading clubs, where members read a book in their own time and then come together as a group to discuss the book and explore interpretations of it. A reading club is a response group. Such groups play a valuable role in the elementary language arts classroom.

Teachers and researchers have discovered that children benefit from *orally* sharing and shaping their responses to books. As they share their own responses and listen to the ways in which other readers have responded to a book, children become aware that no two readers read in the same way or create meaning in the same way. In the process of discussion, their attention is drawn to details they might have missed, and they are called to think about things that, as individual readers, they might not have thought about.

Taking part in a response group can be a fascinating experience. It can also be a frustrating experience if readers want everyone in the group to respond to a book in the way in which *they* have responded to it. Research conducted by Eeds and Wells (1989) formed the foundation for *Grand Conversations* (Peterson and Eeds, 1990), a book that underscores the importance of dialogue in constructing meaning from a text. Peterson and Eeds (1990, p. 21) write: "The lecture model places knowledge outside the students for them to passively receive; dialogue recognizes that knowledge is something students actively construct." The authors provide many suggestions and insights for teachers who work with response groups, including ideas for selecting books, facilitating literature study, and evaluating responses to literature. They also reiterate that children need time in class just for reading, and that children should not be expected to do all of their reading outside class time.

Critical to the success of response groups is that teachers respect each child's ideas and not impose their own ideas on the class. There are many occasions when teachers have to put their own feelings and opinions aside to listen to the students' voices. Classroom discussions can be extremely enlightening for a teacher and can provide a springboard for choosing and creating alternative ways of responding to books. The role of the teacher in literature response groups is that of sensitive guide, helping to create links from the text to actual life experiences and to other texts, and inserting literary insights at appropriate moments. Peterson and Eeds (1990) maintain that comments such as "Let's think more about that" can help children reflect on their reading and deepen their responses to the reading. Talking with students about a book is likely to be a more effective teaching strategy than asking direct questions such as "What was your favourite part of the story, and why?" because it immediately creates a possible connection to the child's own life and demands a personal engagement with the text.

Stanley Fish (1980) says, "Not only does one believe what one believes, but one teaches what one believes, even if it would be easier and safer and more satisfying to teach something else" (p. 364). If we believe that teaching reading means asking children questions, requiring them to provide a retelling of almost every story they read, or picking out the main ideas from a chapter in a book, then our teaching of reading will betray those beliefs. Langer (1994) writes: "The thought-provoking literature class is an environment where students [and teachers] are encouraged to negotiate their own meanings by exploring possibilities, considering understandings from multiple perspectives, sharpening their own interpretations, and learning through the insights of their own responses" (p. 207). She goes on to remind us that response is based as much on the reader's own personal and cultural experiences as it is on the particular text and its author. In closing, Langer says, "In instructional contexts of this sort, that treat all students as thinkers and provide them with the environment as well as the help to reason for themselves, even the most "at-risk" students can engage in thoughtful discussions about literature, develop rich and deep understandings, and enjoy it too" (p. 210).

Literature Response Journals

Literature response journals provide children with opportunities for reflection on what they are currently reading. They are not the same as personal journals or learning logs, but, as Parsons (2001) explains, they usually consist of a notebook, folder, section of a binder, or an electronic file "in which students record their personal reactions to, questions about, and reflections on what they read, view, write, represent, observe, listen to, discuss, do, and think and how they go about reading, viewing, writing, representing, observing, listening, discussing or doing" (p. 9). Response journals are usually intensely private and personal, for they depict exactly how a reader interprets a text and responds to it. When teachers read students' response journals, they try to be sensitive to the nature of the writing and aware of the privileged position they hold in accessing this material. They do not correct grammar or spelling errors, but try to respond to the content, reading in the role of "fellow reader," not as an "authority" on the text. The Grade 2 children who wrote the following entries in response to *Miss Rumphius* (Cooney, 1982) certainly were not focusing on correct spelling as they completed their entries. In these peer-dialogue journals, they wrote an entry, exchanged journals with a partner, and then wrote a response to their partner's entry. The teacher did not draw attention to their invented spelling, but instead complimented the pair on their interesting exchange and added a comment about her own dislike of some aspects of gardening.

Melissa: This story reminds me of me becos I alwiys wanted to plant a garden over in they emtey lot acros from us but my mom sade it wood be to mush work, but I'm saving my alowince for some plants and flowers so I can plant some ther.

Stuart: I like planting flowers and vegebals but I hate it when I have to take a slug off a flower there so slimy and ugly but I kind of have a indoor green house that I got from Scholastic books.

In response to *Two Bad Ants* by Chris Van Ahlsburg (1988), the two wrote:

Melissa: This reaminds me of wen I went to the mountins and I fownd a wered object it looked like a melted tin but it was verry hard to bend. at ferst I thot I wood end up richer than my parentes but I endied out not beaing rich atole. Do you think the ants were beaing gready or wanted to try their musteyris cristels that we know is sugar. It also reaminds me of the time my brother fownd a white rock and thot it was a cristel and he came in yelling mom—mom I fownd a white crustel.

Stuart: The rock your brother found probely had shiny minirels in it but doase your brother still have the rock.

Melissa: he still thinkes ther cristeles so he heas got tuns.

Literature response journals work most effectively when they are open-ended and unstructured. However, students need to know the expectations, requirements and routines associated with them. For example, students need to know how often they are expected to write in their journal, how their journal writing will be assessed, how often the teacher will read the journal, and how they are expected to record the titles and other pertinent information about the books they read. Parsons' book *Response Journals Revisited* (2001) suggests a number of organizational strategies teachers can use in the upper elementary/middle years grades. Parsons also emphasizes that teachers must make time in the classroom for reading as well as for responding, and that students can respond to "read-aloud" sessions as well as to their silent reading.

Directing children to focus their responses on some specific aspect of the text such as plot, setting, characters, or theme does *not* appear to be as effective as leaving the response options open to the students, providing suggestions only where necessary. However, cueing questions can be very effective in getting students started on writing a response. These are not a prescribed set of questions provided by the teacher, but may include such questions as: "After reading this far, what more do you hope to learn about what these characters plan to do, what they think, feel and believe, or what happens to them?" (Parsons, 2001, p. 37). Response writing, like any other type of writing, is learned. Children who are not used to writing in the expressive voice (see Chapter Seven) may need some time to get used to the idea that this is an acceptable form of writing. It is not a matter of learning *what* to write, but rather of learning what to focus on and *how* to write a response.

Teachers keep in mind that a student's written responses to a text are part of the student's meaning making. Written responses rely heavily on the child's ability to comprehend what has been encountered through the reading. For this reason, teachers engage their students in strategies that will help them to comprehend the text as well as shape a reflective response to it. Successful response writing is partly about making the invisible "visible." As a first strategy in helping them to write a response, teachers assist their students in identifying some of the invisible processes of reading. Teachers explain to their students that successful readers use two types of voices while they are reading. The first can be referred to as the Reciting Voice, which is the voice in the reader's head that says the words found on the page. The second voice can be referred to as the Conversation Voice, which is the voice in the reader's head that responds to what the reader is reading.

Many students are unaware that their Conversation Voice needs to be present for good reading to take place. As a result they use only the Reciting Voice and they need to be taught how to develop their Conversation Voice. One way to aid in this development is to have students pay attention to their thoughts while watching a television show or a movie. Students initially seem to find it easier to recognize their Conversation Voices in this context rather than trying to "hear" it while reading. Teachers can model this process by sharing the types of conversations they experience while watching an appropriate in-class movie. Students can join the discussion by sharing what their Conversation Voices were saying. Responses in the Conversation Voice might vary from predicting to questioning or sharing an opinion about something that happened in the movie.

Teachers also provide their students with modelling through a strategy referred to as Think Aloud. This strategy shows students how an expert reader makes sense of text. "By sharing your thinking out loud, you make the elusive process of comprehension more concrete" (Tovani, 2000, p. 26). If students are aware of the tools needed to make text meaningful they will be more able to respond with greater depth in their response journals. The Think Aloud strategy is straightforward and requires little planning. The following outlines how a teacher might model this strategy:

1. Select a short piece of text: the first page of a novel, a couple of pages of a picture book, or a small piece of nonfiction material.
2. On an overhead transparency of the text, point to the words as you read aloud.
3. Stop your reading from time to time and share what your Conversation Voice is saying by "thinking aloud."

Using the picture book *Thank You, Mr. Falker* (Polacco, 1988), for example, a teacher might make the following comments during the first two pages of the book: "I wonder why the grandpa is pouring honey on the book; I remember when I learned to read in Grade 1; I loved it when my grandma would read to me, because she always read to me in a rocking chair; why is Trisha not able to read? I think Trisha is going to have troubles learning to read."

After the teacher models the process, the students can practise their Conversation Voices while reading instructional level text. They may record their thoughts on a separate piece of paper or on a Post-It Note. With the Post-It Note they can mark the pages in the book that evoked the response. Alternatively, they might write responses in the margin of a photocopied page from the book. The teacher can then provide opportunities for the students to share their Conversation Voices with a partner, the teacher, and perhaps with the entire class. The teacher and students together can begin to identify and record on a class chart the types of Conversation Voices used during reading. Below is an example of some of the Conversation Voices successful readers use while reading.

Predicting
Visualizing
Disagreeing
Agreeing
Questioning
Clarifying
Reminding
Summarizing
Inferring
Relating

Teachers can also model journal writing for their students using the Think Aloud strategy, recording their responses on an overhead acetate or on chart paper. Once students become comfortable writing in their response journals, teachers may continue to model written responses but without Thinking Aloud. Teachers write their own responses while the students are writing theirs. Because writing in a response journal involves the complex processes of both reading and writing, some students may struggle with the task. Below are some suggestions for providing support to such students.

- Encourage the students to work at "listening" for one of the Conversation Voices identified on the class chart and write their response in that voice.
- Encourage struggling writers to record their responses in picture or point form rather than sentences.
- Encourage them to read the teacher's modelled responses as a springboard for getting started themselves. Perhaps the teacher's response reminds them of something they thought about when they read the text, or that they were confused about and might now write about.
- Before students begin writing in their response journals encourage them to share past entries or thoughts they might include in their latest entry.

Any response to literature that students might write is shaped by the text itself. Some texts, such as *Gorilla* by Anthony Browne (1983) or *Julie* by Cora Taylor (1985), invite immediate responses, though the responses will differ significantly from one reader to another. Most readers readily identify with the protagonists of these two stories and can empathize with the situation in which the characters find themselves. Other texts, such as *The Golden Compass* by Philip Pullman (1995), may at first appear strange, complex, or even baffling. The text may generate many questions before a reader can shape a response to it, and the response is likely to change as the reading progresses.

Whether the reader's response to a book is tentative and questioning, or confident and fully engaged, teachers and researchers have found that the written responses of children to books demonstrate what the children know, what and how they think, and just exactly how they have comprehended a text. Thus, there is little need for having a child retell the story to ascertain whether he or she has understood a book or not. It is clear, for example, that Ron, in Grade 5, not only enjoyed *The Dragon Children* (Buchan, 1975), but also understood the complex plot:

> I really liked this book because there were two mysteries in the whole book. One of the mysteries was if the crook would make it out of town in time, and if John, Scott, Cathy and Steven would get the crook or not. The other mystery was to find out who or what Steven really was. I figured out what Steven was by putting all the clues together. At the end of the book I found out who

Steven was. At first I thought that Steven was a ghost (even though he was) that the crook had drowned in the river. I was half right about that.

It was a surprise to me when John, Scott, and Cathy found out that the crook wasn't who they thought he was. It surprised me because when Steven told John that the crook was driving a green car with a license plate number 5K-206 it wasn't the crook driving it. Instead it was the man who had come with his family for their vacation. The man did seem like a crook though because when he was walking through the woods with his son, it looked like he had kidnapped the child.

My favorite part, though, was when Scott sneaked up behind the real crook and poked the needle in his back-end. I liked it because it really made me laugh.

Ron wrote this response about how he played detective as a reader in order to fit all the pieces of the story together, making meaning and unravelling the two mysteries. The response demonstrates how Ron engaged with the text, and how he experienced a more distanced response to the book rather than a personal identification with the characters and their actions.

Mitch, in Grade 5, wrote the following dialogue journal entry in response to Chapter 3 of *The Iron Man* (Hughes, 1968), which the teacher had read aloud to the class:

I think the Iron Man will be like the machine in the scrap metal yard that gets rid of the metal. The Iron Man will be happy, the farmers will be happy and Hogarth can visit the Iron Man all the time. Who were the people that had the picnic on the hill and will they show up again? If the Iron Man is controlled by something, who or what is it and what will it think of the Iron Man being so happy? If there is more Iron Men does the Iron Man we know about keep in touch with them? If he does, maybe our Iron Man will tell the others and they will come too. I like how the author called all the metal delicacies. I can see how the chain is spaghetti and maybe the knobs on the bed were choco-late covered candy. Brass covered iron. I don't understand how different kinds of metals have different kinds of tastes. What do you think the Iron Man's favorite kind of metal is? … What will happen when the Iron Man runs out of food at the metal scrap yard? Will they bring him food from other towns? Do you think the Iron Man will ever go back to the sea? Maybe if he leaves the scrap yard all the townsfolk will look for him at the sea. Do you know if the farmers filled up the hole? I sure hope so. It would be disastrous if some-body fell down the hole. If somebody did fall down the hole, maybe the Iron Man will help them out and then he might not be hated so much. Is the Iron Man hated? I think it starts out in the story that the Iron Man was hated but now I think maybe he is more liked.

Mitch's response is like "stream of consciousness" writing. He has put onto paper the many questions raised for him as he listened to this chapter of the story, and has high-lighted some of the images in Hughes's writing. The response demonstrates the engage-ment Mitch experienced as he listened to the story, processing the thoughts that went through his mind about this chapter. Mitch moved quickly from one idea to another, not stopping long to reflect on any one aspect of the chapter, but trying to capture the excite-ment and wonder evoked by this modern fairytale. Mitch makes predictions about the fate of the Iron Man, accurately foretelling the Iron Man's role in the community and the shift

Two children sharing a literature response journal.

in the populace's perceptions as the Iron Man becomes an ally of the people instead of an enemy to be defeated.

Literature response journals provide opportunities for teachers to deliver instruction and feedback to students that is student-oriented as well as text-oriented. Response journals do not replace discussion, they reinforce and support discussion. Response journals provide a place for children to slow down their thinking and reflect on their reading (and on their group discussions), asking questions, wondering, predicting, and synthesizing. Here children can genuinely work at seeking to understand how literature weaves its magic, how reading is accomplished, and how books work.

Readers' Workshop

Readers' workshop was a term made popular by Nancie Atwell in the 1980s. The second edition of her book *In the Middle: New Understandings About Writing, Reading and Learning* (1998) continues her exploration of children's reading and response. A complaint frequently voiced by children is that they are given very little time in school to actually *read*. Instead, they are required to devote most of their time to activities *about* reading. Like Peterson and Eeds (1990), Atwell suggests that if children are to truly enjoy the reading experience, time for reading as well as for learning about reading must be established in school. She maintains that because children read magazines, TV guides, and other such material out of school, teachers play an important role in encouraging students to broaden their reading repertoire by selecting novels, poetry, plays, biography, and works of nonfiction when they are in school. The books, however, should be of interest to the students and, where appropriate, self-selected.

Atwell proposes a readers' workshop format where most of the in-class time is spent reading, and mini-lessons are used for what Purves (1993) suggests is "schooling in the teaching of reading and literature." Atwell offers the following guidelines for conducting a readers' workshop:

- Have children come to the workshop prepared with a book in their possession that they are ready to read or are already in the process of reading. The book should be self-selected from either the classroom or the school library. Readers' workshop is not a time for making book selections.
- Regardless of grade level, ensure that students have a sustained and uninterrupted time for reading. Suitable time lines for readers' workshops vary from grade level to grade level. Grades 5 to 7 require 20–30 minutes for reading. Younger students

require much less, depending on their ability to sustain silent reading. Thus in Grades 1 and 2, the reading time might be only ten minutes.

- Encourage children not to talk or disturb others during reading time, though they may sit or recline anywhere, depending on the physical constraints of the classroom.
- Help students understand that quiet time is important when reading. Most readers cannot read fluently if there is noise around them, or if they are trying to attend to more than one activity at once.

Mini-lessons, whether planned or spontaneous, should usually be brief (say, between five and fifteen minutes), and designed in response to the students' needs. A mini-lesson may be

- a discussion of a topic (e.g., the need for quiet time during reading, the procedures and agendas for response groups, how the classroom library is organized, classroom literary resources, organizing a reading folder and keeping a record of books read, self-assessment procedures, and goal setting);
- a book-share by the teacher (reading part of a book to the class), a book talk by the teacher or a group of students, or some other presentation of activities completed by students *in response* to a book they have read;
- a presentation on a particular author, where the teacher shows the class a number of books by that author (information about authors is available in libraries in publications such as *Meet Canadian Authors and Illustrators* [Gertridge, 2002] or the book series *Something About the Author* [ed. Commaire, annual]); or
- a further exploration of a book in response groups, journal writing, or alternative response activities.

The key role of the teacher in a readers' workshop is to facilitate students' learning as they progress from personal interpretations and understandings ("My question is …," "It reminds me of … ," "I don't understand why …") to shared meanings ("This story is about …") and on to negotiated meanings ("We think the writer wanted us to understand that …"). The readers' workshop is a place where students can read, take ownership of their reading, and respond in their own language to the material they have selected to read. They discuss their ideas about a text with other readers and come to shared and negotiated understandings of the meanings of the stories, poems, and plays they are reading.

Purves (1993) has emphasized that reading in school can never be like reading out of school, because in school it is the teacher's job to facilitate children's growth in book selection, reading skill, confidence, fluency, and ability to express thoughts and opinions and to engage in critical and creative thought. As Purves writes: "I urge us to see our task in schools as helping students read literature and understand the culture, to speculate on the ideas and the imaginative vision, and to speculate on the nature and the use of the language that is the medium of the artistic expression" (p. 360). Much of this can be achieved, we believe, in well-handled readers' workshops.

Literature Circles

In his book *Literature Circles: Voice and Choice in Book Clubs and Reading Groups*, Daniels (2002) writes, "Literature circles are small, temporary discussion groups whose members have chosen to read the same story, poem, article or book. While reading each group-assigned portion of the text (either in or outside of class), members make notes to help them contribute to the upcoming discussion, and everyone comes to the group with ideas to share" (p. 2). In other words, literature circles are student-led discussion groups.

Each literature circle in a classroom is likely to be reading a different book, but the groups meet regularly according to a schedule. The teacher acts as a facilitator for the groups. Role sheets, which give a different role to each group member, are often used at first as they help to guide the students in the roles they agree to take on. Daniels emphasizes that the aim is to make the role sheets obsolete. After using role sheets once or twice, students usually opt to work without them as they learn how to tailor the group processes to meet their own needs. Roles might include:

- *Questioner.* Develops a list of questions the group might like to discuss—generally helps to the group to talk over the big ideas.
- *Connector.* Finds connections between the book and the world outside (the school, the community, events at other times and places).
- *Literary luminary.* Locates a few special sections of the text the group might like to hear read aloud—emphasis is on interesting, funny, powerful or puzzling sections.
- *Illustrator.* Draws some kind of picture or representation related to the text.
- *Summarizer.* Prepares a brief summary of the day's reading—the essence of it.
- *Researcher.* Digs up background information on any topic related to the book or the author/illustrator.
- *Word wizard.* Looks out for a few especially important words—new, interesting, strange, or puzzling.

Daniels' system is highly organized, and can be both interesting and enjoyable for students. Most teachers find that literature circles provide an excellent structure for beginning group work in response to literature. Many teachers report that students no longer need the role sheets after they have participated in the system two or three times. The students learn how to organize the groups themselves and understand the possibilities response groups can offer for discussion of innumerable topics and ideas related to their reading. Teachers need to be aware that literature circles can become mechanistic and, if due care is not taken, can function from an efferent stance. The greatest learning is likely to take place when students write in response journals in addition to discussing their reading in a response group, and engage in the unstructured "grand conversations" described by Eeds and Wells (1989).

Novel Studies

The term *novel study* is used to describe a range of group activities that encourage and facilitate students' reading and responding to novels. At the elementary school level, novel studies provide a vehicle for children to experience a novel in a small group setting, much like a book club or response group. Novel studies can be conducted with a whole class of children, though they can usually be separated into small groups for many of the discussions and activities. Novel studies can also be conducted in small groups of four to six students, as in a literature circle.

Multiple copies of novels are necessary for a novel study, so it is most economical to involve no more than five or six children with one novel at any one time. Prepared novel study sets are usually prepackaged in groups of six books. Many teachers complete one whole-class novel study at the beginning of the year to set out the expectations for novel studies and to establish guidelines and procedures for novel study activities. After the initial whole-class study, teachers usually work with small groups, as in a literature circle.

Successful novel study requires creating a classroom community where reading is important and students and teachers behave like "real readers." As highlighted by both Atwell (1998) and Daniels (2002), children benefit from opportunities to self-select reading material and from having substantial time to read independently. Students can be assigned to groups on the basis of their approximate reading speeds, or they can self-select a reading group on the basis of their interest in the novel. The group chooses a book to read, and the group members meet regularly to discuss the book and complete response activities. The activities can be designed by the students or suggested by the teacher.

In preparation for the group activity, the students agree to achieve specific goals for each meeting. The goals may include reading a certain number of pages before the meeting, or accomplishing certain tasks such as answering questions raised in the previous meeting. This is a way of "thinking back and thinking ahead." It provides students with a means of synthesizing their reading, making predictions, asking questions and negotiating meaning with the group. During the discussion time, the teacher circulates about the room, listening to the ongoing conversations and participating where appropriate. Once the discussions are complete, each group sets a new reading goal that can be recorded on a small chart posted at the front of the classroom. The teacher can monitor the reading goals to ensure they are appropriate for the various groups. The students spend the rest of the period reading their novels, writing in their response journals, or engaging in alternative response activities. The teacher can either read silently during this time or assist individual students with their responses.

Journal responses can be written at any time during the reading of a novel: the midpoint, on completion of the texts, or (as more frequently happens) during the reading. The students can decide on the content of their responses (there is no particular structure or format for the entries), but they are encouraged to select and write in depth about one or two ideas, images, feelings, memories, or thoughts they experienced during or after their reading. This helps the students to explore, extend, or develop their reading experiences. Some students relate the story to other books, movies, or experiences in their lives; some evaluate a situation or a character, or put themselves in a character's position in the book and discuss what they would feel or do and why; and others discuss the author's writing purpose, style, or techniques.

Reading instruction also occurs in a novel study when individual students or groups of students require assistance in dealing with comprehension difficulties, selecting novels, or organizing themselves to meet their goals. Because students in this activity are largely independent in their work, they need to be aware of the expectations for novel studies, such as when it is appropriate to write in their response journals and when to hand responses in to the teacher. It is also important that children know where to find the novels they are interested in reading, the procedures for signing out books, and any other classroom routines related to this study activity.

As mentioned above, a number of prepackaged novel studies are available for use in classrooms. A word of caution: many commercial novel studies are not of high quality and include exercises more like the ones found in old-fashioned reading series (formerly called "basal readers"). This approach has been referred to as the **basalization** of children's literature—turning the work of literature into skill-building exercises (or "dummy runs" as Britton, 1970, called them). Teachers use their professional judgment when assessing the value of such resources for their own classrooms. They keep in mind their own objectives in working with literature in the classroom, and the needs of the students they teach.

Alternative Modes of Response

As children begin to read, continue reading, and finish reading a novel, they can engage in many interesting activities that will help them explore, interpret, and more fully understand the text. Chapter Twelve on drama strategies includes examples of activities that might be part of a novel study. Benton and Fox (1985) also provide a rich source of activities for promoting children's explorations and meaning-making from books. Their suggestions for working with *Tuck Everlasting* (Babbitt, 1975) include

- creating a timeline,
- drawing portraits of the characters,
- "hot-seating" the characters,
- writing character sketches,
- interviewing characters for a talk show,
- making wanted posters for Mae Tuck (a character in the book),
- creating a map of the story's setting, and
- writing an imaginary diary entry as the character Winnie.

These activities encompass the full spectrum of response, from aesthetic to efferent. Halliday's (1969) functions of language (discussed in Chapter Two of this text) also provide a solid foundation for creating a diverse range of purposeful language activities for children as they respond to and explore novels. In the rest of this section, more than a dozen examples of response activities are described, using *Awake and Dreaming* by Kit Pearson (1996) as the sample novel.

Awake and Dreaming is the story of a young girl named Theo and her "flower child" mother, Rae. Theo dreams of being part of a stable, loving family with her own room and brothers and sisters to play with. She loves reading and often loses herself in a book, the school library being her only source of pleasure. Rae is an immature and irresponsible parent who lives in poverty and moves from one apartment to another regularly. She and Theo live on welfare and supplement their income by begging on the streets of Vancouver. When Rae moves in with her new boyfriend, Cal, Theo must go to live with her Aunt Sharon in Victoria. While on the ferry, Theo falls asleep and awakens to find herself in a house in Victoria—part of a family at last. But is it real?

Here are a number of drama strategies that could be used to facilitate response to the story:

Hot-Seating. Rae has arrived home from panhandling in downtown Vancouver. Theo is exhausted from dancing to recorded music. In groups of three, students take turns "hot-seating" the characters from this chapter of the book (Chapter Three). The teacher will likely need to model this strategy first if the children are not familiar with it. In the role of Cindy (or one of the other characters) the teacher can take questions from the students about Cindy's thoughts and feelings about Rae and her lifestyle. Following this, the students take turns "being" Theo, Rae, or Cal (Rae's boyfriend) and entertain questions from the other two students in the group. Students draw on their own experiences and previous knowledge to create answers to the questions that will fit the context of the story.

Tableaux. Theo is sitting in a seat on the ferry watching the other children in the lounge playing. Theo notices a woman in a baggy tweed coat watching her. A girl speaks to Theo and invites her to join their group. They go outside onto the deck together, playing and "flying" in the wind. Rae reappears, and Theo panics. The next thing Theo hears is a steady dripping of rain as she awakens in a soft warm bed. In groups of four to six, students can create tableaux—still pictures of these scenes. Each group first decides what it wants to include in its tableau, and plans who will take the role of each character. Once this is determined, the students take up their positions, perhaps by acting out a brief portion of the story and freezing the action at a given moment. The children then orchestrate the tableau so that it becomes an artistic and aesthetically pleasing portrayal of the scene.

Students can imagine this as either a photograph or as a diorama exhibit in a museum. Rereading Chapter 6 will help the students discover the details of the situation and portray their interpretations of it. Each group is given the opportunity to show its tableau to the rest of the class.

Thoughts-in-the-Head. While engaged in their tableaux, the teacher touches each character gently on the shoulder. At the touch, the students, in role, say what thoughts are going through their minds at that moment. If any students do not wish to speak, they may remain silent and the teacher moves on to the next character.

Puppets. Many different kinds of puppets can be created to put on a play of some part of the story. From paper lunch bag, sock, or paper-plate puppets to more elaborate creations, students generally enjoy this activity. Some groups of students may want to script the play first; others may simply create the dialogue as they go. Either way, all groups should have the opportunity to rehearse before sharing their work.

Readers' Theatre. Readers' theatre is a form of oral presentation in which scripts are read aloud rather than memorized. Participants read their parts expressively and use their voices, gestures, and facial expressions to communicate images, events, and actions in the minds of audience members. In readers' theatre, the characters may sit on stools or a high bench to read their parts. Often, to identify themselves, the participants wear an item of clothing typical of the character they are "reading." Thus, Theo might wear a tattered sweatshirt or jacket. For this dramatic activity, the teacher may need to rewrite or script portions of the original text or provide students with instructional assistance as they create the readers' theatre script themselves.

Character Profile. Students select a character from the book and dress as that character. Each student enters the classroom donned in appropriate attire and tells the other students about him or herself. Drawing on the novel, the student describes the character and the significant events that have happened to him or her (as the character). Classmates may ask the character questions.

These activities represent only a few of the many drama strategies that can be used in a literature or language arts program. More drama strategies for use in reader response are presented in Chapter Twelve. Drama activities frequently take longer than might be expected and they should not be rushed. Throughout their drama work, students are encouraged to talk with one another about their interpretations, opinions, likes and dislikes, and personal "pictures" of the characters and setting. This oral processing enhances the students' personal engagement with the text, and can help them have a more satisfying and memorable experience with a book. Only one or two of the above activities should be selected for use with any one text. A common option is to have groups of children in a classroom work on different activities, which makes sharing the sessions with one another all the more interesting. Readers are usually curious about other readers' interpretations of the work under consideration.

Visual art activities have the same appeal as the drama strategies suggested above, allowing children to become actively involved in creating an artifact representative of their responses. Drawing, painting, and making models, dioramas, wall charts, and portraits are just a few of the activities that give children the opportunity to display their responses to a text. For the book *Awake and Dreaming*, the following activities could be considered:

- *Photograph album.* Students create a "photograph album" of the Caffrey family during Theo's early life and later when she and Rae move to Vancouver.

"Photographs" can consist of pictures taken from magazines, or they can be created by the children themselves, either with a camera or with art supplies. A caption can be added beneath each image. The students can explain why they chose to include their images in their albums.

- *Scrapbook*. In a similar manner to the photograph album, students make a scrapbook of the mementos of Theo's families—both the Caffreys and the Kaldors. Students can make notes, menus, pet paw prints, and other such memorabilia from Theo's life and her encounter with the character Cecily Stone.

- *Mapping*. Students create large and colourful maps of the area of Victoria where Theo lived with the Kaldors and where she eventually met Cecily Stone. The map is not necessarily intended to be a realistic depiction of Victoria, but can be created from the description provided in the text. Alternatively, students could map the journey Theo took from Vancouver to Victoria. If students wish to locate a real map of the area and base their renditions on it, this will also extend their learning.

- *Silhouettes*. Individually or in small groups, students draw on transparencies a silhouette of a character from the story. The finished drawings can be displayed using the overhead projector. What features have the artists given the various characters? Why are these features important?

- *Drawings*. After reading parts of the book or the entire book, students draw scenes, characters, or various aspects of their own interpretation of the story. Drawing can elicit some insightful responses from students that might not otherwise be captured. Students may also want to write about their drawings.

- *Book covers*. Students usually have very definite ideas about the appropriateness of a book cover. Some students may want to design an alternative cover for *Awake and Dreaming*. The graphics used, the positioning of the title and author's name, and the colours are all important elements in creating a book's initial appeal. A book cover can invite a reader into the text or be a factor in dissuading him or her from reading the book. An important facet of a student's response to a book can be found in the alternative cover he or she might design. Covers created by students can be displayed along with other items profiling the novel.

- *Dioramas*. Any setting from a book can be used as the starting point in creating a diorama. A number of settings in *Awake and Dreaming* lend themselves to this kind of interpretation (e.g., the cemetery). Dioramas are frequently made from large shoeboxes, and many odds and ends of materials can be carefully put together to create an effective representation of the setting and atmosphere of the novel as a whole. Dioramas can provide an enticement for other students to read the book.

- *Advertisements*. If a reader had to create a poster advertising *Awake and Dreaming*, what would it be like? Most students are familiar with movie posters, but what would a publishing company look for in a poster designed to promote a book? What would a prospective reader want to know about the book? What ambiance could be created through a poster? What colours would be most effective in portraying this story? After students have read a novel, an advertising poster can be an exciting way to share their responses to the book with the rest of the class.

- *Wall charts*. There are many kinds of wall charts students can develop to help themselves understand a book. For *Awake and Dreaming*, students might consider creating a family tree to show the relationships noted in the story, or a timeline that tracks the story's events or records Theo's moves from one apartment to another.

Benton and Fox (1985) suggest that teachers, when considering various oral, dramatic, visual, and written response activities, ask themselves two fundamental questions: "Will this activity enable the reader to look back on the text and to develop the meanings he has already made?" and "Does what I plan to do bring reader and text closer together, or does it come between them?" (p. 108). Activities that meet the criteria set by Benton and Fox will extend students' reading transactions, enhance students' meaning making from the text, and avoid any unnecessarily lengthy examination of the text that may detract from the reading experience.

Dependent Authorship

Adams (1987) coined the phrase "dependent authorship" to describe activities that invite students to write from within the world of the literary text. The writing depends on the original text, since it is based on knowledge and understanding of that text. Meyers (1997) suggests a number of dependent authorship activities, including writing

- a dream that a character in the book may have,
- a flashback that illuminates a character and some aspect of the character's personality,
- a flashforward that extends the story,
- a continuation of the work, picking up where the author left off,
- an interior monologue that captures the unspoken thoughts of a character,
- a poem or song that could appear in the work,
- a diary entry for one of the characters,
- a new passage that incorporates a character from another story into this work, and
- letters a character might have written.

Children have also written diary entries by Theo after she met Cecily Stone; a letter from Theo to the character Anna, ten years after the story ended; a report by the social worker, Ms. Sunter, after her conversation at school with Theo; a poem by Rae after her move to Victoria; a dream of Sharon's; a biography about Cecily Stone; and a new passage incorporating Polly from Sarah Ellis's book *Pick-Up Sticks* (1991), wherein Polly helps Theo settle into her new life with her Aunt Sharon in Victoria.

Dependent authorship activities can be generated by teachers when they have a thorough knowledge and understanding of Halliday's seven functions of language (1969). Keeping in mind the primacy of the purposes of language enables teachers to develop learning activities that are authentic language acts. Dependent authoring is conducted from "inside" the literary work, and always takes the student into a deeper understanding of it. It also underscores the intertextual elements of any piece of writing, "recognising that every literary work is a wellspring for others" (Meyers, 1997).

> This section of the chapter has provided both a theoretical perspective on reader response and a demonstration of how these elements can be woven into learning activities for children. Response groups, journals, literature circles, novel studies, and dramatic and visual responses all hold possibilities for enhancing children's meaning making in relation to the literature they read and hear in the classroom.

ASSESSING RESPONSE ACTIVITIES

Response activities are usually conducted in small groups or as individual writing activities. Teachers assess student growth during these activities on an ongoing basis and the assessment practices are usually formative—they help the teacher to monitor children's development and they provide input into instructional planning. When students are engaged in group activities, assessment is usually completed through teacher observations—listening to and talking with students as they discuss books and engage in various response activities—artistic, dramatic and written. The listening and speaking assessment practices suggested in Chapter Two are particularly applicable here. Teachers also carefully read or examine the products of group work and engage in conversations with their students about such artifacts and the production of them.

Because well-planned and -implemented response activities encourage children to use high-level critical and creative thinking skills, teachers listen for such things as how children interpret their reading; how they apply their ideas to the world around them, both in and out of school; how they attend to the language of a book; what they are learning as a result of their reading; how they dialogue with other students in their group; how they listen and acknowledge the ideas of others; what questions they raise; and how they express their own ideas and responses. Teachers therefore keep anecdotal notes, checklists, conference notes, work samples, and portfolios, and occasionally they create tests and whole-class activities in order to gain information about their students' learning.

The assessment of response journals is most effective when teachers read their students' journals frequently, and take the time to respond to the entries, either in brief notes in the journal itself, or on Post-It notes stuck onto the relevant pages. Teachers usually take in four or five journals every few days so that they can respond to their students' ideas regularly, and students receive feedback on their entries in a timely fashion. The teacher engages in a brief written conversation with students, noting interesting comments,

---

Box 11.1 Assessment Guide for Response Journals

Level	Criteria
Noncompliant	Insufficient reading
	Insufficient number and/or length of responses
	Content superficial or perfunctory
	Student-teacher conference required
Functional	Sufficient reading accomplished
	Sufficient number and length of responses
	Responses characterized by: frequent retelling, likes and dislikes, occasional relating to personal experience, some prediction
Extended	All routines established plus some additional reading and responding
	Responses additionally characterized by: brief retelling when necessary, frequent relating to personal experience, prediction, offering reasons for opinions and conclusions
Independent	All routines established plus considerable additional reading and responding
	Responses additionally characterized by: recognition of characters' motivations, linking cause and effect, opinions usually supported by evidence from the text, awareness of author/illustrator's purposes

applauding thoughtful ideas and asking questions that encourage deeper thinking about an issue. Teachers write notes to themselves about a students' work immediately after reading the journals, and they also provide feedback to the student regarding how they're functioning and how they can improve their work. Teachers refrain from making summative judgments about journal work and they do not give grades. Instead they often devise a simple rubric based on performance criteria and divided into levels. These rubrics include information that will help students understand what they do well plus how they can improve their work. In his book *Response Journals Revisited*, Parsons (2001) presents a number of checklists for teachers and students and some basic rubrics for assessing response journals. These are based on teacher expectations and routines agreed upon in the classroom in regard to working with response journals. Box 11.1 presents an assessment guide based on Parson's suggestions.

BOOK SELECTION

This section of the chapter explores the definition of good literature and who has the right to make that determination. Which awards are devoted to children's literature? Which books should be selected for use in the classroom, and how are decisions made?

The confounding question facing most elementary school teachers is: Who decides what constitutes a "quality" book for children?

Over the years, it has generally been accepted that children, parents, teachers, and librarians are all involved in making the decisions. In fact, however, many of the most prestigious awards for children's literature are made by library and other associations whose awards committees consist solely of adults. (Examples include the Amelia Francis Howard-Gibbon Award and Governor General's Award in Canada, the Caldecott and Newbery Awards in the United States, and the Kate Greenaway and Carnegie Medals in the United Kingdom.) We know that children's choices of "good" literature frequently vary from adult choices. Children enjoy books that involve mystery, excitement, humour, and adventure. Teachers, on the other hand, think it is more important that the reader be interested in, and able to identify with, the characters in a story (elements, not surprisingly, ranked much lower by children). Thus teachers and librarians often recommend books to children that may be good for the adult reader even though they hold no particular appeal for children. The result is that children often learn to ignore these book suggestions.

A number of Children's Choice Awards exist at the regional level in Canada and at the state level in the United States. Voting for the awards is often conducted through the schools in collaboration with local public libraries. In order to vote, students must have read a certain number of titles from a list created by teachers and librarians. The list consists of recent books but not necessarily those published in the last year. The Silver Birch Award in Ontario, the Manitoba Young Reader's Choice Award, the Rocky Mountain Book Award in Alberta, and the Red Cedar Award in British Columbia are examples of children's choice awards in Canada. The awards are highly regarded by authors and illustrators and they provide children with a chance to show their support for the books they like. Unfortunately, these awards are not generally given high regard. This has prompted many observers to question the perceived significance of children's interests and opinions about books, and the intended purpose of the more prestigious awards.

We have to ask: If a book is good, what is it good *for*? Is it a challenging reading experience that will delight readers and help them become *better* readers by showing them something new? Is it a good book for taking on vacation and reading on the beach? Is it a good book for teaching more about language arts skills, or for helping readers learn how to do something of special interest to them, such as keeping a successful tropical aquarium? Is it a good book because it enables the reader to escape from real life and see life differently? In trying to answer questions such as these, teachers, librarians, and even scholars of children's literature are coming to realize how difficult it is to describe the specific characteristics or features of "quality" literature. A book that demonstrates how to create a healthy tropical aquarium will differ enormously from a book of short stories. A book that a person finds so notable that he or she wants to keep a copy for a long time is likely to be very different from the pocket book picked up as reading material for a long plane trip. Clearly then, describing quality in each of these cases must vary according to the format of the book, the purpose of the author, and the purpose, interests, and reading experiences of the reader.

Guidelines for Appropriate Selection of Children's Literature

When selecting materials to include in a classroom or school library, teachers and teacher–librarians make every effort to choose books that meet the needs of both children and the curriculum. Knowledge of child development and the literary quality of books, as well as knowledge of the provincial programs of study and of curriculum expectations, help teachers make appropriate selections. Critics might say that "book selection" is simply a code for a librarian's own brand of censorship, but as Roberts (1996, p. 19) asserts, there are distinct differences between selection and censorship:

> Selection is a positive process that supports intellectual freedom when the selector considers resources in a holistic manner with the intent of including as many as possible in the library collection. Resources are selected objectively, according to set criteria, without regard for a selector's personal biases. Conversely, censorship is a negative process in which the censor searches for reasons, either internal or external, to exclude a resource.

Sound selection decisions are guided by the quality of reading and learning, even when, as Booth (1992, p. 9) says, "reading reveals unpleasant truths or viewpoints opposed to those of a particular parent or child, as long as the child is deemed capable of dealing with such ideas."

The selection of print materials for use in schools is a complex issue, for it is difficult to say in a public education system who should decide what children should and should not read. There is also a difference between making book selections for a school library and selecting material that will be used for teaching purposes in a classroom. The debate involves freedom of expression and beliefs about what is appropriate for children, what is moral and what is immoral, and what is acceptable and not acceptable in society. It is highly likely that most children will confront difficult and disturbing ideas as they grow up. Reading and discussing a broad range of literature can help children become critical thinkers and thoughtful human beings capable of making sound judgments, both as individuals and as members of society.

The selection debate relates directly to the discussion of emancipatory or critical constructivism presented in Chapter One of this textbook. It is a compelling and difficult issue, and one that teachers are frequently required to address.

In 1974, the Canadian Library Association issued a statement on intellectual freedom that was subsequently adopted by the Canadian School Library Association. Two parts of that statement are of particular relevance for educators. The first asserts that it is a person's fundamental right to have access to all expressions of knowledge, creativity, and intellectual activity and to be able to express one's thoughts publicly. The second states that libraries must guarantee and provide access to all expressions of knowledge and intellectual activity, including those elements that conventional society might deem unacceptable or unpopular (Canadian Library Association, 1974). Thus, anyone who endorses this statement, and who thereby advocates selection as opposed to censorship of materials, still has the right to object to certain books if he or she so chooses, but not to insist on their removal from library shelves so that others are denied access to them. Advocates of book selection also respect the child's intellectual freedom (and innate common sense) and believe that adults have an obligation to be honest with children. This approach to selection does not argue that all books for children are of equal quality and equal value, or that they are even appropriate for children of all ages, but it does assert that children have the right of access to the best literature and learning resources available.

The most important things teachers can do when engaged in selecting of reading materials are to be aware of their own biases and values; to stay current with issues, themes, and book publications and reviews; and to maintain files of policy statements, useful resources, procedures for dealing with challenges to materials, and guidelines from recognized authorities. ("Challenges" are those occasions where books or other materials are considered by an individual or group to be inappropriate for the audience, and a request is made for the material to be removed from the classroom or library.) Many professional resources and tools are available to aid teachers and librarians in selecting books. By far the best resources are professional journals. *CM: Canadian Review of Materials*, published by the Manitoba Library Association, is available online at www.umanitoba.ca/cm. It provides book reviews and profiles of Canadian authors and illustrators. *Canadian Children's Literature*, published by the University of Guelph, Ontario, provides reviews of Canadian publications as well as articles about Canadian children's literature. *Teacher Librarian Today*, published by the Learning Resources Council of the Alberta Teachers' Association, and *School Libraries in Canada*, the journal of the Canadian School Library Association (published by the Canadian Library Association) contain book reviews, author/illustrator profiles, and well-informed articles on school librarianship in Canada. *Teacher Librarian*, published jointly in Canada and the United States (out of Vancouver and Seattle), presents articles that reflect literature-related concerns common to both countries. Other worthy professional journals include *Language Arts*, *The Reading Teacher*, and *The Horn Book*.

In addition to the journals, a variety of other resources are available to help teachers with book selection. One of these is the *Our Choice* catalogue, issued annually by the Canadian Children's Book Centre in Toronto. It lists recommended materials published each year in Canada, including fiction and nonfiction books, videos, CD-ROMs, and audiocassettes and CDs. Also helpful is the *Canadian Book Review Annual*, an evaluative guide to Canadian-authored, English-language publications. It reviews the year's scholarly publications, reference materials, and publications for children. The emphasis is on analyzing and evaluating materials, with brief descriptions of the books reviewed.

As this section has shown, many book selection tools are available in Canada for students such as Shawn (introduced at the start of this chapter), and for inservice teachers who want to engage their students with the very best of children's literature. Information about book censorship is also available. Since censorship and challenges to books and periodicals in school libraries are unpredictable and usually emotional, it is critical that teachers try to remain up to date and well informed about processes for dealing with book challenges. We discuss these issues in the next section.

Censorship of Children's Materials

As already noted, there is a clear difference between selecting materials for use in schools and censoring these materials. Where book selection uses positive criteria to determine which books to place in a collection—what Nodelman (1992) calls the "books we approve of"—censorship seeks to remove, suppress, or restrict books *already present* in a collection. Censorship is generally ineffective in ensuring that only the most "appropriate" of books are read by students, yet it can be extremely disruptive to the life of a school. Occasionally, a **challenged book**, removed from library shelves, will become a bestseller and read more widely than if it had not been challenged.

School libraries and classrooms encounter far more challenges to books than public libraries in North America (Schrader, 1996). This makes it imperative that teachers and librarians be informed on the issues and prepared to debate the relative merits of the materials selected for use in their schools. Educators have a responsibility to fulfill their professional obligations to learners by providing students with the very best in children's literature, meaning material that challenges children to think critically and explore new ideas and perspectives. Teachers have a further role, however, which is to help their students become more thoughtful and critical about their own choices of reading materials, and to help them develop their abilities to think for themselves and make sound judgments.

Teachers are often surprised to see which children's books are commonly challenged. *Bridge to Terabithia* (Paterson, 1977), *The Paper Bag Princess* (Munsch, 1980), *Thomas's Snowsuit* (Munsch, 1985), *Who Is Frances Rain?* (Buffie, 1987), and *Harry Potter and the Sorcerer's Stone* (Rowling, 1998) have all had censorship threats in recent years. Jenkinson (1994) found that challenges to books increased in Manitoba in the ten-year period between 1983 and 1993. The authors challenged most often in Jenkinson's study were Robert Munsch (*Giant: Or, Waiting for the Thursday Boat*, 1989, and *A Promise Is a Promise*, 1988), Roald Dahl (*Revolting Rhymes*, 1982, and *The Witches*, 1983), Alvin Schwartz (*Scary Stories to Tell in the Dark*, 1981), and William Steig (*The Amazing Bone*, 1976). The top ten reasons Jenkinson identified for challenges were:

1. concerned witchcraft or the supernatural (24 percent),
2. contained or concerned violence (18 percent),
3. contained material inappropriate for an immature audience (12 percent),
4. described or showed explicit sex (10 percent),
5. contained questionable morality (9 percent),
6. described or showed nudity (9 percent),
7. contained obscenities (8 percent),
8. contained profanities (7 percent),
9. contained sexism or role stereotypes (6 percent), and
10. contained beliefs contrary to those of a particular religious ideology (5 percent)

In addition to challenges are the indirect instances of censorship, in which books simply go missing, have pages removed, or are ripped up or defaced. Censorship can also be an attempt by special-interest groups to protect themselves against ideas or beliefs that may threaten their status. *Maxine's Tree* by Diane Leger-Haskell (1990), for example, was challenged in 1992 by members of the IWA-Canada on British Columbia's Sunshine Coast as being "emotional and an insult to loggers" (Nodelman, 1992, p. 132). The religious right is particularly noted for making censorship demands in schools because many members of such religious groups often have problems with public schools and with the whole notion of secular education.

Explicit procedures detailing how book complaints will be received and reviewed can be set up by school boards or by individual schools. Information about past legal rulings, groups behind challenges, and approaches to resisting challenges is available from organizations such as the Book and Periodical Council (Toronto), the Canadian Library Association (Toronto), the National Council of Teachers of English (Urbana, Illinois), and the International Reading Association (Newark, Delaware). An extremely useful publication is *The Students' Right to Read*, published by the National Council of Teachers of English (1982). The book includes sample forms for collecting a statement of concern from a complainant, a sample letter to a complainant, instructions for establishing an evaluating committee, and suggestions for evaluating the complaint.

The National Council of Teachers of English and the International Reading Association have recently developed a CD-ROM resource, *Rationales for Challenged Books* (National Council of Teachers of English, 1998), which includes more than 200 rationales for over 170 commonly challenged materials for kindergarten through Grade 12 (though the emphasis is on publications for Grades 7 to 12). Publications are listed both by title and author on this Web-type resource, and information is provided about book challenges and what can be done by schools and libraries to counter challenges.

Issues and Controversies

The most recent flurry of challenges and censorship activities has involved picture books depicting same-sex family relationships (gay and lesbian couples). The 1998 court case in Surrey, BC, regarding *Asha's Mums* by Rosamund Elwin (1990), *Belinda's Bouquet* by Leslea Newman (1998), and *One Dad, Two Dads, Brown Dad, Blue Dad* by Johnny Valentine (1994) was not about whether children should have access to these books in the school library but whether the books should be used in classrooms for teaching purposes. The debate underscores the complex nature of censorship and reminds teachers how difficult it can be to ensure that all children have access to books about a range of social and family contexts, while not insisting that all children read the same books.

No less controversial has been the issue of racial discrimination in literature. In the middle to late 20th century, it was not uncommon to find books for children that were explicitly racist in their treatment of blacks or Native North Americans. When many of these books were originally published, however, society in general was not as aware of the appalling discrimination portrayed in them. Since the 1948 Universal Declaration of Human Rights by the United Nations General Assembly, book publishers and educators have fought hard to prevent the publication of books that are clearly discriminatory.

In the first edition of *The Bobbsey Twins* (Hope, 1904), for example, the reader was told what a good mother Flossie was to her dolls, for she protected them from a black doll given to her by one of the servants. Flossie told her friends that the doll didn't really belong in the family. However, since Flossie's mother explained that there were "no asylums for black orphans," the doll was allowed to stay with the others—separated from them by a piece of cardboard. Given the nature of American society at that time, it was hardly surprising to see such blatant racial discrimination in a book for children. What is surprising is that the piece was not removed from the book until the 1950s.

One of the earliest "multicultural" books in North America was *The Story of Little Black Sambo* (Bannerman, 1899), set in India but with illustrations depicting black characters. Although Bannerman's book has received much criticism for its racial stereotyping, the story has remained hugely popular. It has been retold numerous times, and was recently published in two new editions. *The Story of Little Babaji* (Bannerman and Marcellino, 1996) contains the original text, except that the characters are given authentic Indian names. Fred Marcellino's illustrations place the story clearly in India. *Sam and the Tigers: A New Retelling of Little Black Sambo*, written by Julius Lester and illustrated by Jerry Pinkney (1996), depicts black characters but the fantasy setting (Sam-sam-sa-mara) removes it from any specific geographic location.

Stereotypical images abound in literature, from the works of Shakespeare to *Anne of Green Gables* (Montgomery, 1908) and *The Adventures of Huckleberry Finn* (Twain, 1885, 1963). The central feature of many of the American classics containing racist stereotypes was the presence of "indolent, happy-go-lucky slaves" (Miller-Lachmann, 1992). Other books, such as *The Five Chinese Brothers* (Bishop, 1938), seemed to promote the stereotype that all Chinese people look alike. Such books now provide a springboard for discussing issues such as racism, slavery, social class, and stereotyping in general.

Literature portrays all aspects of human nature, and children's literature is no exception. Through the library collections that teachers make available in schools, students can learn to appreciate the human condition, to discriminate good from bad and just from unjust, and to make sense of the world and their feelings toward it in a new and deeply personal way. As they select literature for children, teachers face the challenge of putting their own feelings and biases aside and presenting a balanced and equitable view of our diverse global community.

CANADIAN LITERATURE

In this section, we address the reasons why it is important for Canadian children to read Canadian literature as well as international literature, and suggest many book titles that are specifically Canadian in context.

Over the years, Canadians have become accustomed to receiving media largely from the United States and Britain. Children's print materials are no exception. Most professional books currently available for teachers, especially those about multicultural literature, are from the United States, and they largely (and sometimes entirely) refer to American books. However, the stories and experiences of Hispanic Americans, African Americans, Chinese Americans, and other ethnic and cultural groups are not necessarily parallel to those of Canadians.

It is well accepted that children need to see their own culture represented in the books they read. In the 1980s, Canadian publishing companies increased their publication of Canadian trade books for children and young adults. Today, many excellent children's books are written and produced in Canada. The Canadian Children's Book Centre in Toronto (CCBC) publishes lists of books, and information about authors. More information about CCBC is presented in Box 11.2.

Why Canadian?

Literature can be a powerful vehicle for the transmission of national culture anywhere in the world. Diakiw has written that in "most culturally homogeneous countries, children grow up hearing and learning the stories that define their culture … and these shared sto-

Box 11.2 The Canadian Children's Book Centre

The Canadian Children's Book Centre (commonly referred to as the CCBC), located in Toronto, was established in 1976. The organization provides information to members on current Canadian books, and their authors and illustrators. The Centre contains a collection of Canadian children's materials available for browsing by members of the society, and extensive files on Canadian authors, illustrators, and the Canadian book publishing industry. The newsletter *The Children's Book News* highlights what's new and exciting in the Canadian children's book world, including information about Canadian Children's Book Week. *Our Choice*, published annually, is a guide to the year's best books, audio recordings, videos, and CD-ROMs. Online resources include industry news, a calendar of events, a guide to Canadian Children's Book Awards, and a listing of Children's Literature Roundtables across the country. Reference services are available to members by phone, fax or email. Online resources include links to publishers' sites and a complete list of Canadian Children's Book Awards. For information contact: CCBC, 40 Orchard View Boulevard, Suite 101; Toronto, ON M4R 1B9. Online at: www.bookcentre.ca. Phone: (416) 975-0010. Fax: (416) 975-8970. For inquiries email: info@bookcentre.ca.

ries lie at the heart of a culture's identity" (1997, p. 37). He argues that there are powerful commonplaces in Canada's culture and identity—shared values that most Canadians can identify with—and that school is an important place to explore, discuss, and debate these. One way to uncover these is through Canadian stories and literature. "Literature, arts and crafts, music, dance, film, and poetry blend together over time to crystallize an image that says, 'This is who we are'" (Diakiw, 1997, p. 37).

Canada prides itself on its "cultural pluralism" and the importance of accepting different races, ethnicities, languages, and cultures. Nieto describes this as "a model based on the premise that all newcomers have a right to maintain their languages and cultures while combining with others to form a new society reflective of all our differences" (1992, p. 307). Yet Bissoondath (1998) warns that Canada's policy of multiculturalism could lead to a reinforcement of stereotypes and a "gentle marginalization" of those who accept and display their ethnic heritage. He maintains that Canadian multiculturalism has emphasized difference and has retarded the integration of immigrants into the Canadian mainstream. Bissoondath writes that "we need to focus on programs that seek out and emphasize the experiences, values and dreams we all share as Canadians, whatever our colour, language, religion, ethnicity or historical grievance. And pursue acceptance of others—not merely tolerance of them" (1998, p. 22).

If children are to know themselves and Canada they need frequent opportunities to access resources that are Canadian and which depict Canadian culture and identity (see, for example, the *Proud Canadian Kids* Web site available at proudcanadiankids.ca/index.htm). Although it is also essential that Canadian children have opportunities to read about Canadian people and Canadian places in the literature they encounter, until the last 20 years or so there was very little Canadian children's literature available and there was little Canadian readers could identify with. Most Canadian children grew up with a canon of British literature.

Today, a wide range of high-quality children's literature is published all across Canada, and some of that literature is published by school districts and by relatively small publishing houses. This has had an impact on children's reading across the country, for now students can read about Canadian people and places, from Peggy's Cove and Saskatoon to Ungava Bay and Yellowknife. When they read Canadian materials, children can imagine the prairie, mountains, or seacoast, and they learn more about Canada and who they are as Canadians. Many scholars and writers have suggested that the land, the actual environment or physical landscape of Canada, characterizes Canadian literature. *The Doll* by Cora Taylor (1987) is a time-slip novel set in Fort Carlton, Saskatchewan, *Rebellion* by Marianne Brandis (1996) is a novel set in historical Toronto, *The Fishing Summer* (Jam, 1997) is a picture storybook set on Canada's east coast. Each of these books provides different insights into Canada and what it means to be Canadian, and each is profoundly reliant upon the landscape in which it is set. Perhaps through reading Canadian literature, children can develop pride in being Canadian and an appreciation and understanding of Canada's role in the global community. Defining our identity as Canadians is a continuing process and one in which our students have a role.

From Canadian books such as those noted above, children not only learn about Canada and being Canadian, they also learn that Canadian people can be authors and illustrators, and that authors and illustrators live in places where the students might also live. Authors become real people, and writing and illustrating become possible professions. Well-known authors and illustrators now visit schools on a regular basis, and some of the hard work and the craft of writing and illustrating are demonstrated to children as they listen to artists speak about and read their published work. Several organizations across Canada, such as the Young Alberta Book Society (see Box 11.3), exist for the sole purpose of enhancing literacy development and introducing Canadian authors and illustrators to children in schools. Box 11.4 presents a list of Canadian fiction suitable for children in Grades 4 to 7.

In addition to fiction materials, good nonfiction books about Canada have been written and published by Canadians. In *To the Top of Everest* (Skreslet and MacLeod, 2001) Laurie Skreslet relates his experiences in becoming the first Canadian to reach the summit of Mount Everest, a feat he accomplished in 1982. The book is filled with stunning photographs of the mountain and the climbers, as well as a first-person account of the perils encountered during the adventure. Skreslet recalls the long years of preparation, and recounts how he had to overcome fear and learn how to survive in the thin air and harsh weather conditions. The book is visually appealing and well laid out, with sidebars explaining various aspects of the expedition. The text is immensely readable and appeals to a wide range of readers, adults as well as children. A list of recent Canadian nonfiction books is presented in Box 11.5.

Box 11.3 The Young Alberta Book Society

The Young Alberta Book Society is an advocate for the literary arts and a year-round resource for information on Alberta authors and illustrators and their works. The organization provides displays of Alberta children's books at relevant conferences throughout Alberta and organizes *Chrysalis*, an annual celebration of children's books that involves readings by authors, illustrators, and storytellers in schools and public libraries across the province. The society's mailing address is 2nd Floor, Percy Page Centre, 11759 Groat Road, Edmonton, Alberta, T5M 3K6; its email address is info@yabs.ab.ca; and its Web site is www.yabs.ab.ca.

Box 11.4   A Selection of Canadian Literature for Grades 4 to 7

Bedard, M. (1990). *Redwork*. Toronto: Lester & Orpen Denys.

Bishop, M. (2001). *Tunnels of time*. Regina: Coteau Books.

Bly, D. (1993). *The McIntyre liar*. Edmonton: Tree Frog Press.

Brouwer, S. (1993). *The accidental detectives:* Shortcuts. Wheaton, IL: Victor Books.

Buffie, M. (1987). *Who is Frances Rain?* Toronto: Kids Can Press.

Buchholz, K. (1999). *How Lone Crow became Magpie*. Winnipeg, MB: Pemmican.

Doyle, B. (1984). *Angel square*. Toronto: Groundwood Books/Douglas& McIntyre.

Ellis, D. (1999). *Looking for X*. Toronto: Groundwood Books.

Ellis, S. (1997). *Back of beyond*. Toronto: Groundwood.

Godfrey, M. (1988). *Send in Miss Teeny Wonderful*. Richmond Hill, ON: Scholastic TAB.

Horvath, P. (2001). *Everything on a waffle*. New York: Farrar Strauss Giroux.

Hughes, M. (1980. *The keeper of the Isis light*. London: Mammoth.

Lunn, J. (1997). *The hollow tree*. Toronto: Alfred A. Knopf Canada.

Oppel, K. (1997). *Silverwing*. Scarborough, ON: HarperCollins.

Scrimger, R. (1998). *The nose from Jupiter*. Toronto: Tundra Books.

Spalding, A. (1995). *Finders keepers*. Victoria, BC: Beach Holme Publishing.

Smucker, B. (1989). *Jacob's little giant*. Toronto: Puffin Books.

Taylor, C. (1985). *Julie*. Saskatoon: Western Producer Prairie Books.

Wilson, E. (2001). *The Emily Carr mystery*. Toronto: HarperCollins.

Box 11.5   A Selection of Canadian Nonfiction for Children

Beatty, O. and Gieger, J. (1992). *Buried in ice: Unlocking the secrets of a doomed Arctic voyage*. Mississauga, ON: Random House.

Bondar, B. (1993). *On the shuttle: Eight days in space*. Toronto: Greey de Pencier Books.

Brewster, H. (1996). *Anastasia's album*. Toronto: Penguin Books Canada.

Corriveau, D. (2002). *First peoples: The Inuit of Canada*. Minneapolis, MN: Lerner.

Dudley, K. (1997). *Wolves: The untamed world*. Calgary: Weigi Educational.

Granfield, L. (2001). *Where poppies grow: A World War I companion*. Toronto: Stoddart Kids.

Hill, L. (1993). *Trials and triumphs: The story of African-Canadians*. Toronto: Umbrella Press.

Kenna, K. (1995). *A people apart*. Toronto: Somerville House.

London, J. (1993). *The eyes of Grey Wolf*. San Francisco: Chronicle Books.

Raskin, L. and Pearson, D. (1998). *52 days by camel*. Toronto: Annick Press.

Reevers, N. and Froman, N. (1992). *Into the mummy's tomb: The real life discovery of Tutankhamen's treasures*. Richmond Hill, ON: Scholastic.

Shell, B. (1997). *Great Canadian scientists*. Vancouver: Polestar.

Shemie, B. (1997). *Houses of China*. Montreal: Tundra Books.

Swanson, D. (1994). *Safari beneath the sea*. Vancouver: Whitecap Books.

Tanaka, S. (1998). *The buried city of Pompeii: What it was like when Vesuvius exploded*. Richmond Hill, ON: Scholastic.

Ulmer, M. (2001). *M is for maple*. Chelsea, MI: Sleeping Bear Press.

Zhang, S.N. (1995). *The Children of China: An artist's journey*. Montreal: Tundra Books.

Books by Aboriginal Canadians

In recent years, many excellent books for children have been created by Aboriginal Canadian authors and illustrators. The works of George Littlechild, Michael Arvaarluk Kusugak, Thomas King, Richard Van Camp and Tomson Highway have become particularly popular. George Littlechild's book *This Land Is My Land* (1993) is a particularly stunning introduction to Aboriginal literature, with personal stories about Littlechild's family members and ancestors. The short narratives are unforgettable in their intensity and poignancy. Littlechild writes and paints about his experiences in boarding school and recalls memories, many of them tragic, of family members. He speaks excitedly about his first visit to New York City, and describes the development of his artwork. The book ends optimistically, with Littlechild telling about the current revival of Aboriginal culture and traditions and emphasizing the pride he feels in his ancestry.

Tomson Highway's two books for young readers, *Caribou Song* (2001) and *Dragonfly Kite* (2002), are the first two books in a trilogy, *Songs of the North Wind*. The books are superbly illustrated by well-known Canadian artist Brian Deines, and the text of the books is presented in Cree and English. Both stories tell of the magical adventures of two brothers, Joe and Cody, as they play together, encountering wildlife and entertaining themselves in the beautiful northern Manitoba summer.

Two Pairs of Shoes by Esther Sanderson (1990) is a picture storybook about Maggie, and two special gifts she receives for her eighth birthday. Maggie's mother gives her a pair of shiny, black patent-leather shoes, and her *kokom* (grandmother) gives her a pair of hand-made beaded moccasins. Grandmother tells Maggie, "From now on you must remember when and how to wear each pair." The author has dedicated the book to "all children who walk in two pairs of shoes."

Michael Kusugak has produced many well-received picture books, most of them illustrated by Vladyana Krykorka. One of the best known is *Northern Lights: The Soccer Trails* (1993). The book embodies the life and spirit of the Inuit people of the North. Each double-page spread consists of a full-page illustration on one side and the text, adorned with a beadwork flower or motif set above or below, on the other. The children's toys, the dogs, and the landscapes are depicted by Krykorka in dazzling colours that capture the tones of the Arctic and the unique flavour of the Inuit culture. *Hide and Sneak* (1992) by the same author/illustrator team also captures the traditional culture and way of life in the Arctic. The book contains illustrations surrounded by Inuit script opposite each page of English text. It is a celebration of the mythology and traditional symbolism of Inuit culture.

Box 11.6 features a selection of books by Aboriginal Canadian authors and illustrators.

The chapter began with Shawn, a preservice teacher beginning a student teaching experience in a Grade 5 classroom. This section of the chapter has attempted to answer Shawn's questions about a teacher's role in engaging children with books. By now, Shawn understands the valuable role played by children's encounters with literature in helping them understand themselves and their world. By providing multiple ways for children to respond to literature, the teacher clearly demonstrates the many options a reader has when constructing personal and shared meanings. In a democratic society such as Canada's, a reader is free to make informed choices about reading material. As a teacher guides children in their book selections, demonstrating respect for multiple viewpoints and lifestyles is a key consideration.

Box 11.6 Children's Material by Aboriginal Canadians

Ahenakew, F. (1999), *Wisahkecahk flies to the moon*. Winnipeg, MN: Pemmican.

Bouchard, D. and Vickers, R.H. (1990). *The elders are watching*. Tofino, BC: Eagle Dancer Enterprises.

Bruchac, J. (1993). *Fox song*. Toronto: Oxford University Press.

Bruchac, J. (2000). *Crazy Horse's vision*. New York: Lee & Low Books.

Condon, P. (2000). *Changes*. Saskatoon, SK: Gabrial Dumont.

Highway, T. (2002). *Dragonfly kite*. Toronto: HarperCollins.

Highway, T. (2001). *Caribou song*. Toronto: HarperCollins.

King, T. (1992). *A coyote Columbus story*. Toronto: Groundwood Books.

Kusugak, M. (1990). *Baseball bats for Christmas*. Toronto: Annick Press.

Kusugak, M. (1993). *Northern lights: The soccer trails*. Toronto: Annick Press.

Littlechild, G. (1993). *This land is my land*. Emeryville, CA: Children's Book Press.

Loewen, I. (1993). *My kookum called today*. Winnipeg: Pemmican.

McLellan, J. (1989). *The birth of Nanabosho*. Winnipeg: Pemmican.

Oliviero, J. and Morrisseau, B. (1993). *The fish skin*. Winnipeg: Hyperion Press.

Paul-Dene, S. (1992). *I am the eagle free (sky song)*. Penticton, BC: Theytus Books.

Sanderson, E. (1990). *Two pairs of shoes*. Winnipeg: Pemmican.

Van Camp, R. (1997). *A man called Raven*. San Francisco: Children's Book Press.

Van Camp, R. (1998). *What's the most beautiful thing you know about horses?* Markham, ON: Children's Book Press.

Yerxa, L. (1993). *Last leaf first snowflake to fall*. Toronto: Groundwood Books.

SUMMARY

"Reader response" refers to the events that occur within a reader when he or she reads a piece of text. That response is part of the meaning-making process, and as such it is an important component of a language arts program. Rosenblatt (1978) maintains that a response to literature is dictated to a considerable extent by the purpose for reading or the *stance* from which the reader approaches the text. A stance can be anywhere on a continuum from efferent at one end, where the reader seeks information of some kind, to aesthetic at the other, where the reader focuses on appreciating what is read. A text first evokes an aesthetic or "lived through" response, and then evokes a more efferent response as the reader consciously thinks about the text and the reading experience.

Through reading works of literature and responding to them, children come to understand how texts work, what constitutes a good book, how language can be used in different ways to create different meanings and effects—in short, how to become readers, not just people able to read. Children are more likely to take ownership of the reading process and to understand that there is no right "answer" to literature when they are invited to respond to a text (though, as Rosenblatt says, some responses are more legitimate or appropriate than others). Responses to literature can be captured and represented in written, oral, visual, or dramatic form.

An important vehicle for exploring a text is the response group, which works very much like a reading club. Teachers and researchers have discovered that children benefit from orally sharing and shaping their responses to books, and successful group work can enhance the enjoyment children experience in their reading. Literature response journals provide children with opportunities for written reflection on what they are currently reading, as do literature circles, novel studies, readers' workshops, and drama and art activities. There are also many "dependent authoring" activities that enhance children's enjoyment and understanding of literature.

When selecting materials to include in a classroom or school library, teachers and teacher–librarians must make every effort to choose books that meet the needs of children as well as the needs of the curriculum. The selection of print materials for use in schools is a complex issue, for it is difficult to say in a public education system who should decide what children should and should not read. There is, however, a clear difference between selecting materials for use in schools and censoring these materials. Where book selection uses positive criteria to determine which books to place in a collection, censorship seeks instead to remove, suppress, or restrict books already present in a collection. Guidelines for handling complaints about books can be established by school boards or by individual schools, and many agencies provide guidelines for creating such processes.

Educators understand that when children read aesthetically, they may identify with the characters, setting, or events of a story. However, until the last 20 years or so, Canadian children had little they could identify with in the literature available to them. Most Canadian children grew up with a canon of British and American literature. Today, a wide range of high-quality children's literature is published across Canada, some of that literature is published by school districts and relatively small publishing houses. Canadian literature for children is now noted and characterized by its multicultural nature, and there are many excellent Aboriginal Canadian authors and illustrators creating books for children. Perhaps through reading Canadian literature, children can develop pride in being Canadian and an appreciation and understanding of Canada's role in the global community. Defining our identity as Canadians is a continuing process and one in which our students have a role.

SELECTED PROFESSIONAL RESOURCES

Egoff, S. and Saltman, J. (1990). *The new republic of childhood: A critical guide to Canadian children's literature in English*. Toronto: Oxford University Press. Egoff and Saltman's classic text (originally published in 1967) provides a history of children's literature in Canada and an overview, genre by genre, of the rich diversity of Canadian titles available for children in the elementary and middle years. The authors provide insightful discussion of books, topics, themes, issues, illustrators, and authors. The book is an excellent resource for Canadian teachers, with a detailed index and complete bibliographies of the materials referenced in each chapter.

CM: *Canadian Review of Materials*. Available: www.umanitoba.ca/cm. CM has been published by the Manitoba Library Association since 1995. It is an electronic reviewing journal issued biweekly from September to June every year. Reviews of materials of interest to children and young adults are provided, with a maple leaf symbol denoting Canadian materials, and a globe symbol indicating non-Canadian materials (but that have a Canadian distributor). Also included are author and illustrator profiles, interviews, and publishing news. Back issues are online from 1995 onward and access is completely free of charge. The journal provides an archived collection of items from the years 1971 to 1994, when the journal was published by the Canadian Library Association (in print form) under the title *CM: A Reviewing Journal of Canadian Material for Young People.*

CHILDREN'S BOOKS NOTED IN CHAPTER ELEVEN ━━━━

Babbitt, N. (1975). *Tuck everlasting.* New York: Farrar, Straus and Giroux.

Bannerman, H. (1899). *The story of Little Black Sambo.* New York: Frederick A. Stokes and Company.

Bannerman H. and Marcellino, F. (1996). *The story of Little Babaji.* New York: Michael di Capua Books (HarperCollins).

Bishop, C. (1938). *The five Chinese brothers.* New York: Coward, McCann & Geoghegan.

Brandis, M. (1996). *Rebellion: A novel of Upper Canada.* Erin, ON: The Porcupine's Quill.

Browne, A. (1983). *Gorilla.* New York: Alfred A. Knopf.

Buchan, B. (1975). *Dragon children.* Richmond Hill, ON: Scholastic-TAB.

Buffie, M. (1987). *Who is Frances Rain?* Toronto: Kids Can Press.

Cooney, B. (1982). *Miss Rumphius.* New York: Viking Penguin.

Dahl, R. (1982). *Revolting rhymes.* London: Jonathan Cape.

Dahl, R. (1983). *The witches.* New York: Farrar, Straus and Giroux.

Ellis, S. (1991). *Pick-up sticks.* Toronto: Groundwood Books.

Elwin, R. (1990). *Asha's mums.* Toronto: Women's Press.

Hope, L. L. (1904). *The Bobbsey Twins.* New York: Grosset & Dunlap.

Hughes, T. (1968). *The Iron Man.* London: Faber and Faber.

Jam, T. (1997). *The fishing summer.* Toronto: Groundwood Books/Douglas & McIntyre.

Kusugak, M. (1992). *Hide and sneak.* (V. Krykorka, illustrator). Toronto: Annick Press.

Kusugak, M. (1993). *Northern lights: The soccer trails.* (V. Krykorka, illustrator). Toronto: Annick Press.

Leger-Haskell, D. (1990). *Maxine's tree.* Victoria, BC: Orca Books.

Lester, J. (1996). *Sam and the tigers: A new retelling of Little Black Sambo.* (J. Pinkney, illustrator). New York: Dial Books for Young Readers.

Littlechild, G. (1993). *This land is my land.* Emeryville, CA: Children's Book Press.

Montgomery, L. M. (1908). *Anne of Green Gables.* London: L. C. Page & Company.

Munsch, R. (1980). *The paper bag princess.* Toronto: Annick Press.

Munsch, R. (1985). *Thomas's snowsuit.* Toronto: Annick Press.

Munsch, R. (1989). *Giant: Or, waiting for the Thursday boat.* Toronto: Annick Press.

Newman, L. (1998). *Belinda's bouquet.* Anola, MB: Blue Heron Enterprises.

Paterson, K. (1977). *Bridge to Terabithia.* New York: HarperCollins.

Pearson, K. (1996). *Awake and dreaming.* Toronto: Puffin/Penguin.

Polacco, P. (1988). *Thank you, Mr. Falker.* New York: Philomel Books.

Pullman, P. (1995). *The golden compass.* New York: Ballantine Books.

Rowling, J. K. (1998). *Harry Potter and the sorcerer's stone.* New York: A. A. Levine Books.

Sanderson, E. (1990). *Two pairs of shoes.* Winnipeg: Pemmican.

Schwartz, A. (1981). *Scary stories to tell in the dark.* New York: HarperCollins.

Skreslet, L. and MacLeod, E. (2001). *To the top of Everest.* Toronto: Kids Can Press.

Steig, W. (1976). *The amazing bone.* New York: Farrar, Straus and Giroux.

Taylor, C. (1985). *Julie.* Saskatoon: Western Producer Prairie Books.

Taylor, C. (1987). *The doll.* Toronto: Douglas & McIntyre.

Twain, M. (1963 [1885]). *The Adventures of Huckleberry Finn.* New York: Washington Square Press.

Valentine, J. (1994). *One dad, two dads, brown dad, blue dad.* Boston: Alyson Wonderland Publications.

Van Allsburg, C. (1988). *Two bad ants.* Boston: Houghton Mifflin.

Wynne-Jones, T. (1993). *Some of the kinder planets.* Toronto: Douglas & McIntyre.

REFERENCES

Adams, P. (1987). Writing from reading: "Dependent authorship" as a response. In B. Corcoran and E. Evans (eds.), *Readers, texts, teachers*. Portsmouth, NH: Boynton/Cook.

Atwell, N. (1998). *In the middle: New understandings about writing, reading and learning* (2nd ed.). Portsmouth, NH: Boynton/Cook.

Benton, M. and Fox, G. (1985). *Teaching literature: Nine to fourteen*. London: Oxford University Press.

Bissoondath, N. (September 1998). No place like home. *New Internationalist*, 20–22.

Booth, D. (1992). *Censorship goes to school*. Markham, ON: Pembroke Publishers.

Britton, J. (1970). *Language and learning*. Harmondsworth, UK: Penguin Books.

Canadian Library Association. (1974). Statement on intellectual freedom. 29th Annual Conference, Winnipeg, MB.

Commaire, A. (ed.). (published annually since 1971). *Something about the author*. Detroit: Gale Research.

Cooper, C. (1985). *Researching response to literature and the teaching of literature*. Norwood, NJ: Ablex.

Daniels, H. (2002). *Literature circles: Voice and choice in book clubs and reading groups*. Portland, ME: Stenhouse.

Diakiw, J. (1997). Children's literature and Canadian national identity: A revisionist perspective. *Canadian Children's Literature*, 23 (3), 36–49.

Eeds, M. and Wells, M. (1989). Grand conversations: An exploration of meaning construction in literature response groups. *Research in the Teaching of English*, 23 (1), 4–29.

Egoff, S. and Saltman, J. (1990). *The new republic of childhood: A critical guide to Canadian children's literature in English*. Toronto: Oxford University Press.

Farrell, E. and Squire, J. (eds.). (1990). *Transactions with literature: A fifty year perspective*. Urbana, IL: National Council of Teachers of English.

Fish, S. (1980). *Is there a text in this class? The authority of interpretive communities*. Cambridge, MA: Harvard University Press.

Gertridge, A. (2002). *Meet Canadian authors and illustrators: 60 creators of children's books*. Toronto, ON: Scholastic Canada.

Halliday, M.A.K. (1969). Relevant models of language. *Educational Review*, 22 (1), 26–37.

Jenkinson, D. (1994). The changing faces of censorship in Manitoba's public school libraries. *Emergency Librarian*, 22 (2), 15–21.

Langer, J. (1994). Focus on research: A response-based approach to teaching literature. *Language Arts*, 71 (3), 203–211.

Meyers, D. (1997, Fall). Dependent authorship: A dependable teaching activity for reading and writing critically and creatively. *Statement*, 20–22.

Miller-Lachmann, L. (1992). *Our family, our friends, our world*. New Providence, NJ: R. R. Bowker.

National Council of Teachers of English. (1982). *The students' right to read*. Urbana, IL: National Council of Teachers of English.

National Council of Teachers of English. (1998). *Rationales for challenged books* [CD-ROM]. Urbana, IL: National Council of Teachers of English.

Nieto, S. (1992). *Affirming diversity*. New York: Longman.

Nodelman, P. (1992). We are all censors. *Canadian Children's Literature*, 68, 121–133

Parsons, L. (2001). *Response journals revisited: Maximizing learning through reading, writing, viewing, discussing, and thinking*. Markham, ON: Pembroke.

Peterson, R. and Eeds, M. (1990). *Grand conversations*. Richmond Hill, ON: Scholastic-TAB.

Purves, A. (1993). Toward a re-evaluation of reader response and school literature. *Language Arts*, 70 (5), 348–361.

Purves, A. and Rippere, V. (1968). *Elements of writing about a literary work: A study of response to literature*. NCTE Research Report No. 9. Urbana, IL: National Council of Teachers of English.

Roberts, E. A. (1996). A survey of censorship practices in public school libraries in Saskatchewan. MLIS thesis, University of Alberta, Edmonton, AB.

Rosenblatt, L. (1978). *The reader, the text, the poem: The transactional theory of the literary work*. Carbondale, IL: Southern Illinois University Press.

Schrader, A. (1996). Censorproofing school library collections: The fallacy and futility. *School Libraries Worldwide*, 2 (1), 71–94.

Thomson, J. (1987). *Understanding teenagers' reading: Reading processes and the teaching of literature*. Norwood, Australia: Australian Association for the Teaching of English.

Tovani, C. (2000). *I read it, but I don't get it: Comprehension strategies for adolescent readers*. Portland, ME: Stenhouse Publishers.

Chapter 12

Drama in the Elementary Classroom
By Patricia A. Payne

Drama and Literacy Development

- Scenario I
- Scenario II
- Scenario III

Drama in the Elementary Classroom

Teacher Concerns Related to Drama

- Learning the Language of Drama
- Using Role
- Management
- Time
- The Concert
- Assessment

Planning and Teaching Drama

- Teaching Drama: Interpretation of Literature
- Teaching Drama: Process Drama

Classification of Drama

- Drama as Playing
- Drama as a Process for Learning
- Drama as Interpretation of Literature
- Drama as Theatre

From School Time to Drama Time

- Using Pictures
- Transforming Text
- Representing New Ideas
- Scenario IV
- Scenario V
- Scenario VI

DRAMA AND LITERACY DEVELOPMENT

The chapter begins with a description of three classroom scenarios. The discussion following each example serves to highlight

- the power of drama for literacy development, and
- issues facing teachers as they begin their drama journey.

The remainder of the chapter outlines the different forms of dramatic activity that support literacy development.

Scenario I

Teacher: I would like you to get into small groups and practise your parts for the play. Today we will practise reading our lines, and tomorrow you will have time to act them out.

During the next few days the students rehearse their plays for a performance to another class. Some children forget their lines, the shy students find it difficult to project their voices, the audience becomes more restless and inattentive. Classroom management becomes more problematic, and the teacher becomes more frustrated. She reevaluates the educational merits of this type of drama activity and wonders how she can improve her strategies to facilitate the implementation of drama.

This scenario mirrors the school experience of many preservice teachers. It reflects the view of drama as performance: performing a play to peers or to a larger, unknown audience—at the school concert, for example. When I announce to my students in the introductory language arts class, "Next class will be a drama workshop," trepidation is written across their faces. This initial apprehension is reflected in their learning log comments. For example:

> In elementary school, drama was a word I hated to hear. It was only done occasionally and was worth many marks, which put a great deal of stress in the situation, especially for someone like me who was shy. (Lynne De Boyle, 1999)

> Drama meant the school concert—I did not enjoy "being on show." Drama as a tool for learning rather than performance sake—this is pretty much a new way for me to look at drama. (Danielle Couillard Fash, 1999)

> In my education I didn't do drama until junior and senior high, so when you said that we'd be doing drama today, my heart began to beat quickly. I was afraid to do anything for fear that I would make a fool of myself. (Christine Ventura, 1999)

A slightly different perception of drama is revealed by inservice teachers who choose to participate in the senior drama methods course. These teachers are exploring new ways to enhance their teaching of language arts. Like the teacher in Scenario I, they have often tried to implement some form of drama because they value active learning, but—also like that teacher—they have had less than satisfactory experiences. "To me, incorporating drama into my teaching meant painful, time-consuming preparations" (Flynn and Carr, 1994, p. 39).

Some teachers have a tendency to blame themselves for their lack of success, so they take a drama course to improve their strategies. They expect to learn ways of helping their students act out plays. These preservice and inservice teachers have developed a concept of drama that is difficult to implement in elementary school: *drama as performance*. Therefore, a different understanding of what drama is and what it involves needs to be explored.

New theories about language and language learning bring forth fresh insights and require new concepts and labels. For example, "reading readiness" has been replaced by the term "emergent literacy." The first label represents a behavouristic perspective, the second a developmental one. Such new terms represent new understandings, and these in turn shape classroom practices. The *Memory Box* drama, which is described in the next section, is an example of drama practices that have been shaped by a new understanding of drama. Here, drama is used to provide a context for learning—specifically, a context for the purposeful use of language. This form of drama is referred to as *process drama*.

Scenario II

Mr. Hughes, a teacher at Florence MacDougall Community School, High Level, Alberta, has read Mary Bahr's story *The Memory Box*, to his Grade 3 class. This story tells of a young boy's visit to his grandparents' cottage during the summer holidays. During this visit his grandfather gets lost. His grandmother explains to her grandson that his grandfather has Alzheimer's disease. Together they make plans to assemble a memory box. The teacher uses this story idea for the following dramatic activity.

Episode I

Teacher-in-role: [A friend of the grandfather; he is talking to the whole class, which is seated around his chair]: Well, friends, you all know my dear buddy has Alzheimer's and I think you all know that he has a special birthday coming soon. So, I'd just like to read this letter I received from his grandson and see what you think. [Reads the letter from the grandson requesting help from friends and family to help with a birthday celebration.] Well, what do you think? Can we do it?

Student: We could bring photos to help him remember.

Teacher-in-role: That's a great idea! [The discussion continues and the class contributes several possibilities.]

Teacher-in-role: Well, you seem keen to help, so I'll write and tell him we'll get organized for this party. [Moves from the chair and "re-enters" as teacher.]

Teacher: You certainly had lots of great ideas. We will work on these tomorrow.

Episode II

Teacher: Let's see if we can use some of your suggestions to organize this celebration. [Through the teacher's questioning, the more general ideas from Episode I are shaped into concrete, specific details. "We need to think about Grandpa's life," "What did he do?" "What events will we celebrate?" "How?" "What is our relationship to him?" and "How will we help him remember?" are a few of the key questions that focus the drama.]

Teacher: Let's chart these ideas so we don't forget them. [Chart developed, as shown on the next page.]

Teacher: We have all these ideas, so ...? What do we need to do next?

Student: We need to decide who we are going to be. I want to be his fishing buddy, I love fishing!

Student: We have to make up our memory and then make something to help Grandpa remember.

Examples from the Planning Chart			
What did Grandpa do?	How old was he?	Who was he with when it happened?	Represented by
(a) Caught the biggest fish in the tournament	• 35 years	• Friends Jim and Tom	• Picture of a fish, certificate, news article reporting the event
(b) Invented a special beaver trap	• 45 years	• Colleagues Bill and Jack from Fisheries and Wildlife Department	• Diagram of the trap; oral descriptions, a beaver story, reasons for the invention
(c) Great teller of stories	• 72 to present	• Children, grandchildren	• Book, picture of a character from the story

[Plans are negotiated, and the students complete the activities outlined in Episode III.]

Episode III

Students choose their role and create their memory, first orally, then in writing. Students are then grouped according to roles and shared events. For example, all the fishermen collaborate on the same story. Some stories are modified to avoid repetition and contradictions. Finally, memory objects are assembled.

Episode IV

Teacher-in-role:

[as Grandpa's friend] All sit quietly until I bring our dear friend to this celebration. We have the birthday cake? When he walks in the door, sing "Happy Birthday." [Teacher exits the circle and re-enters slowly as Grandpa, signalling the change with a pair of spectacles, a walking stick, and slow steps. Keeping his eyes down, he enters, muttering.]

Objects to signify role

Teacher-in-role:

[as Grandpa] What day is it today? I know it's supposed to be something important. ... Who are all these people?

Students-in-role:

Happy Birthday! [The memories are shared with Grandpa. After the last object is presented, the teacher places his stick and glasses on the chair, steps out of the circle, and becomes the narrator.]

Teacher-as-narrator:

Grandpa treasured the memory box: it gave him so much pleasure. His grandson is grown up now and he too treasures that box. It reminds him of all the happy times he spent with his grandparents at the cottage. [Pauses a moment, and then steps back into the circle as teacher.]

Teacher:	The drama went very well today. You all stayed in role and there

Teacher:

Reflection on the drama

The drama went very well today. You all stayed in role and there was no giggling. Well done! [The students reflect on this imagined experience and compare it with their personal experience of dealing with elderly and sick people.]

This new understanding of drama stems from the pioneering work of Dorothy Heathcote, a British drama educator. (See, for example, Heathcote, 1972.) Working with students in this way has been labelled "group drama," "**contextual drama**," "drama as a medium for learning," "drama for understanding," "role drama," and, as used in this chapter, "process drama." Each one of these labels signifies a critical attribute of this new understanding of drama. As Neelands (1992, p. 5) says, this way of working with students involves using drama as "an important means of constructing and experiencing the social contexts within which the different functions and uses of language can be identified and developed."

Once teachers have participated in a process drama, they quickly see that this strategy can easily become part of their regular teaching and that time-consuming preparations are not required. They recognize the potential of process drama to support learning in all areas of the curriculum, and they have no difficulty grasping the new insights about drama. The teachers try out these ideas with their classes and share their experiences enthusiastically with other teachers in drama workshops. Through sharing, they receive further support and reinforcement from their peers, which encourages them to continue implementing process drama in all areas of the curriculum. Listening to one of them speak, you would hear comments such as, "This writing is amazing for this child. She has hardly written anything all year. The drama provided an excellent prewriting activity," and "This child, in role, spoke in front of the whole class for the first time."

However, once the drama workshop ends, so does a lot of this support. What happens then? Drama is still not used extensively in elementary schools, even though research demonstrates that it supports student learning (Schaffner, 1985). It seems a good thing to do, but few teachers do it. Why? The teacher's insights following the next scenario illuminate this paradox. In my role as a language arts consultant, I was requested by Nicole McGillivray, a first-year teacher, to teach a lesson that demonstrated how **drama strategies** support literacy development. It was January of the school year, and these Grade 1 students were just beginning to write. The time available for the lesson was 40 minutes.

Scenario III

I chose to use the following poem by A. A. Milne (1928, p. 30) as a stimulus for oral and written language development.

The More It Snows

> The more it
> SNOWS-tiddely-pom,
> The more it
> GOES-tiddely-pom
> The more it
> GOES-tiddely-pom
> On
> Snowing.
>
> And nobody
> KNOWS-tiddely-pom,

How cold my
TOES-tiddely-pom
How cold my
TOES-tiddely-pom
Are
Growing.

The poem was recited in a variety of ways:

- I read the poem, modelling expressive intonation.
- I read the poem while the class tapped out the beat of "tiddely-pom" as they said the words.
- I divided the class in half and had them use an antiphonal arrangement:
  - Group I: The more it SNOWS
  - Group II: Tiddely-pom
  - Group I: The more it GOES ...
- Each group had the opportunity to recite the other group's lines.
- We said the poem together as we tapped out the rhythm.

After the choral work had been completed, most of the students had memorized the poem and shared their accomplishment. The poem was recited in unison once more and was followed by the *narration* described below.

Teacher-narration, imaging:	Close your eyes. [Waits for quiet and slowly continues.] You are tucked in your bed. In a moment you are going to get out of bed and go to the window. [Pauses.] See yourself getting out of bed, move over to the window, and open the drape. You are so happy ... It's been snowing! What can you see? [Pauses.] You get dressed quickly and go outside to play. [Pause.] Keep your eyes closed and imagine playing in the new snow near your house. [Pause.] I am going to come round and tap you on the shoulder, and I want you to speak out loud and say what you are doing. [The teacher moves to first child, taps the shoulder.]
Voice-in-the-head:	Child I: I am making a snow angel.
	Child II: I am shovelling the path.
	Child III: [No response. Teacher moves to the next child.]
	Child IV: I am making footprints. I make my name. [The process continues until the students have had an opportunity to respond.]

After this activity, the students transformed their images and oral sentences into written form. Many of the students wished to share their efforts, so their work was folded into the poem.

I then divided the class into small groups and gave each group an opportunity to present. The group lined up facing the front of the class. The students recited the poem using the antiphonal arrangement. At the end of the poem, each person stepped forward and read a sentence while displaying a picture. Each presentation of the picture was punctuated by the refrain "tiddely-pom." To complete the presentation, the class created an additional line that was recited in unison, "Oh! I do-o-o-o hope it keeps on snowing!" This informal presentation was shared with another class at the Grade 1's request.

In planning this lesson, I selected strategies that I thought Nicole might be able to incorporate into her own teaching repertoire: *imaging* and *voice-in-the-head*. I also needed to demonstrate how these strategies supported literacy development. Nicole's analysis suggests that these intents were realized.

Nicole: The way you focused the class was great. Getting them to close their eyes and then slowly and quietly providing them with cues to help them create a picture in their head really helped. They had no trouble sharing their ideas. I could use that. What's it called?

Pat: Imaging.

Nicole: Yes, I could use imaging. It is more effective than saying, "Pretend you have just woken up, it's been snowing. What do you see?" Imaging gives the students more time to think, and the activity of walking around the classroom and tapping them on the shoulder as a signal to share their ideas was also effective. It did not stop the flow of the lesson, and those students who needed more thinking time could take it. They were also encouraged by other students' ideas. That way of doing it—

Pat: Voice-in-the-head.

Nicole: Voice-in-the-head allowed them to stay with their image.

Pat: They did well reciting the poem. You have obviously done some choral work with them.

Nicole: Yes, but I usually have them chant repetitive phrases from poems and stories. "Fee, fie, fo, fum" from "Jack and the Beanstalk," "I'll huff and I'll puff and I'll blow your house down" from "The Three Little Pigs"—chants like that. I do it spontaneously and the kids enjoy it. What I liked was the way these activities supported the writing process. I had no one saying, "I don't know what to write."

Pat: Yes, imaging, voice-in-the-head, and chanting are three drama strategies that are fairly easy to implement, particularly in this lesson. Although the children were seated at their desks, they remained actively involved.

Nicole: Yes, they were involved. I would not have counted those activities as drama. I thought drama meant active … active in the sense of physical activity. I know you don't mean that here. [Points to another poem.] I could use similar strategies with this nursery rhyme.

Nicole's analysis of this lesson highlights several important points. First, the connections between the general teaching strategies familiar to most teachers and the less familiar drama strategies need to be made explicit. Second, the shift that is required of the teacher to move a class from school time to drama time, from the here and now of the classroom to the "as if" world of drama, demands closer scrutiny. (Examples illustrating this transition are described later in the chapter.) Nicole recognized the shift that was required. "Yes, I could use imaging, instead of saying, 'Pretend you have just woken up, it's been snowing. What do you see?'" She also articulated the other benefits of using such strategies—there is more time to think, the flow of the lesson is not interrupted, activities are connected to help the students compose. She was able to identify how the drama strategies were part of the writing process.

Later, chatting with the teacher of the class who had viewed the poetry presentations, Nicole had further insights.

Teacher:	My kids enjoyed the presentation. Thanks for sharing. My Grade 1's love to do *choral speech*.
Nicole:	Yes ... and my class loved the drama strategies.
Teacher:	Choral speech is drama?
Nicole:	[Provides a synopsis of the lesson.] So you see the drama strategies, imaging and voice-in-the-head, were used to help the students compose their sentences, but these strategies were not part of the presentation of the poem.
Teacher:	You could use imaging and voice-in-the-head to help with reading comprehension, too.
Nicole:	Yes?
Teacher:	For example, imaging. Let's say you were going to read the story of Goldilocks. You could take the sentence, "She went through the wood!" The students could image the scene, and then their oral responses could be translated into a collective picture. The class picture could be compared with the illustration in the story book. I could also see using these strategies with illustrations to develop predicting skills.
Nicole:	How?
Teacher:	[Points to a picture of the three bears returning to find their house in disarray. Consternation is reflected in their faces.] "You are the father bear ... say out loud what you are thinking." When the students have had an opportunity to respond as the three characters, you can continue the story to verify or modify the students' thinking in role.
Nicole:	Great idea! I think I could do that kind of drama.

Nicole McGillivray shared this lesson idea with another Grade 1 teacher, Anna McAskile, who provided a number of writing samples after she had taught the drama lesson. Exhibits 12.1 and 12.2, on page 358, were composed as a result of the imaging and voice-in-the-head strategies. Exhibits 12.3 and 12.4, on page 359, represent the elaboration of these ideas completed in another lesson.

In Scenario III, imaging, voice-in-the-head, and narration were strategies that were part of the composing process. When the product, the poem, was presented, these processes

Exhibit 12.1 Brittany's Representation of Her Imaging

I feel like the sky is full of fluffy marshm for me to eat

Brittany Straub

were not visible. Many teachers are using similar strategies in their daily teaching but don't count them as "drama," because their conception of drama is equated with performance. Like Nicole, once they are aware of this misconception of drama and are cognizant of the slight shift required to use these strategies in a more conscious manner, they feel "I can do that!" When drama is incorporated as part of the writing process, it can be efficient and effective—it does not have to be time-consuming and painful.

Similar insights were gained by preservice teachers who recently participated in a one-hour drama workshop as part of the introductory language class at the University of Alberta. The students listened to a traditional folk tale, *The Three Sillies*, in which a man, woman, and daughter behave stupidly. A young gentleman refuses to marry the daughter until he sees three sillies sillier than these three. Of course he does, and in true folk tale fashion, the young gentleman and the daughter live happily ever after. After hearing the story, the class was instructed to work in a small group to create a frozen picture, or *tableau*, of one scene from the story. First, voice-in-the-head was added to this tableau, which then led to a short *improvisation* of the scene. After the story was enacted, each group created a new silly situation and shared the improvisation with the class.

Exhibit 12.2 Kyle's Representation of His Imaging

I feel like I'm flying. in the ske.

Kyle Didzena

Exhibit 12.3 Brittany's Elaboration of Story Idea from Imaging

> One day I wokeup. I saw the snow falling. I putc on my close and whent outside And I saw the snow falling. I liked the snow it was beutful. It looked like marshmallows it was a beutifl white. The snow cuverd the groud.

Brittany Straub

The culminating activity of the workshop was for each group to share its new version of the story in written form. Boxes 12.1 and 12.2 (page 360) are two examples from the same improvisation, one written as a newspaper article, the other as a narrative piece.

The following learning log comments indicate that the preservice teachers understood how drama can support literacy development:

> I didn't realize (until today) that drama fits into the language arts curriculum. Now, though, it seems very obvious to me! (Yvonne Mik, 1999)

> As I am such a hands-on learner, I can see how this process will internalize the learning for students. When you explained the writing process—brainstorming ideas, putting ideas together, and writing the first draft—it was easy to see how this same process happened in our group when we were creating our tableau of another silly solution. (Danielle Couillard Fash, 1999)

Table 12.1 on page 361 highlights the connection between drama and literacy by analyzing the two drama lessons ("The More It Snows" and *The Three Sillies*) in relation to the writing process.

Exhibit 12.4 Kyle's Elaboration of Story Idea from Imaging Activity

> One day I wock up and I drest up and wet outside and I toucka jump Wen I touck th jump I feel like I'm flying in the ske. I was on my toboggan. I wet down the big hill

Kyle Didzena

Box 12.1   A Silly Story: Sink or Drink

If you're at the brink of sinking, why not try drinking! Drinking the water in the boat that is! It's an odd response, but that is exactly what a group of tourists did when they discovered a hole in their boat while on a zoo cruise in the swamps of Louisiana. Tourists along the shore of the alligator-infested waters could be heard shouting "Jump, jump!" The gang onboard the boat, however, countered these nasty directives with "Drink, drink." They used whatever they could find on the boat—straws, teacups, and their hands—to literally drink the water away. Luckily, a passing patrol boat saw their desperate situation and came to the rescue. Wouldn't Mark Twain have made a good story out of this!

Source: Katherine Weber, workshop participant, 1999. Reprinted with permission.

The scenarios in this introduction provide you with a glimpse of the range of activities we label "drama." The discussions have outlined some of the benefits and perceived difficulties associated with implementing drama in the elementary classroom, and three major ideas were noted:

- Our understanding of drama shapes our classroom practices.

- Our understanding of the connections between the drama process and the reading and writing processes eliminates time-consuming preparations, as drama is seen as part of, not apart from, literacy instruction. Drama is viewed not as a curricular frill—something to be done if there is time—but as a process for learning. Drama provides a context for meaningful literacy activities.

Box 12.2   A Silly Story: There's a Hole in the Boat!

It was a hot July day. Sharlene and her friends watched the sun dance off the clear blue water as they rowed the boat in unison. As the sun beat down on their golden shoulders, they felt as though the world could not be more perfect than it was at the exact moment. Suddenly, one of the girls in the back screamed, "There's a hole in the boat!"

Sure enough, water came pouring in the boat from a hole as large as a tennis ball. No one knew how the hole came to be.

"What should we do?" one girl cried. Several suggestions were made and each one was tried in its turn.

"Make juice out of it and drink it," Angie suggested.

"Use your shoe to scoop it out," exclaimed another.

"Soak it up with a rag," offered Mary.

"Stuff Lisa in it," Angie said with a nervous giggle.

"Make another hole so the water can seep back out!" Jane cried.

The girls tried in vain to stop the water, but it kept oozing in. Finally, the most sensible idea came up, "Let's all jump out of the boat!" And so they did. The girls splashed wildly in the blue water while the boat slowly sank.

Source: Yvonne Mik, workshop participant, 1999. Reprinted with permission.

- Our understanding of the similarities between familiar, generic teaching strategies and less familiar drama strategies supports a change in teacher stance. This change of stance from "expert/I am in charge" to "negotiator/storyteller" is a prerequisite if the teacher wants the class to explore the "as if" world of drama. This change in stance—reflected in the language and gestures of the teacher—enables the teacher to use appropriate drama strategies to implement the various dramatic forms.

When teachers' actions are shaped by this knowledge, their apprehension about using drama in the classroom diminishes, and they begin their drama journey. The remainder of this chapter provides further elaboration of these insights, with examples of classroom practice.

CLASSIFICATION OF DRAMA

Our understanding of drama shapes our classroom practices.

Drama is like language in that one uses it to learn about events, issues, and relationships. Drama is taught not so students become better at doing it, but as a way of helping them understand the world.

Girls going into a tableau

Table 12.1 Drama and Writing

Writing Process	Grade 1	Preservice Teachers
Idea Generation		
1. Stimulus	Poem, "The More It Snows"	Story, *The Three Sillies*
2. Method of presentation	Choral work by teacher and students	Storytelling by the teacher
3. Drama strategies	• Imaging • Voice-in-the-head	• Tableau • Voice-in-the-head • Improvisation
First draft	Picture and sentence	Dramatization of a new silly solution
Second draft	Elaboration of picture and sentence	Dramatization transformed into writing
Revision	Not completed	Peer conferencing
Edit	Not completed	Final copies produced
Publication/celebration	Presentation of the poem to another class	Display

It can be used across the curriculum. As students become engaged in drama activities and become familiar with a variety of strategies, their drama skills do improve. Like language, drama skills are taught in context as the students explore meanings of stories, poems, issues, and events. The term "drama" applies to a wide range of activities, from the informal dramatic play of a young children's tea party or the informal classroom presentation of a puppet play, to the more formal production of a school play with an audience. Table 12.2, a modification of Bolton's 1979 **classification of dramatic forms**, highlights the differences among these various concepts of drama.

Drama as Playing

Drama as playing is a very important type of activity, because it fosters the social and intellectual development of the young child. As Vygotsky (1978, p. 102) says, "Children at play are always above their average age, above their daily behaviour; in play, it is as though they were a head taller than themselves." This type of drama places the least demand on the teacher, who simply provides time and space for the play to occur. The students decide how long they will play, with whom, and what the play will be about.

This type of drama as playing should be encouraged in young children. Classrooms in kindergarten that support this activity will have a designated space and prop box for dramatic play. Sometimes teachers will structure this space to support the themes the class is studying. The space may become a house, restaurant, hospital, post office, or store. Dramatic play fosters social skills, verbal abilities, cooperation, and symbolic representation, as illustrated in the following example:

An Example of Dramatic Playing

(Two children in a kindergarten class are playing with large interlocking construction blocks.)

Richard:	Let's make this into a castle. [Points to the structure he has built.]
Marilyn:	Yes, and this [placing skipping rope around the structure] can be the water and this [placing large block over the rope] can be the bridge.
Richard:	What are you going to be?
Marilyn:	I'm going to be the bridge keeper.
Richard:	I'm going to look after the castle. [They continue planning their play.] Come and let's eat.
Marilyn:	Okay. I have to put up this bridge first ... a dragon might come. [Makes the noise of the bridge going up as she imitates a winding action.]
Richard:	Dinner is ready. [Uses the rest of the blocks to create a table.]

Table 12.2 Drama As ...

	Playing	Process for Learning	Interpretation	Theatre
Critical attributes	• Spontaneous • No specific end • No practice required • Duration of the play determined by students	• Context is created through negotiation by students and teacher, who take roles to explore an event, issue, or relationship. • Dramatic tension is necessary to move drama forward. • It appears spontaneous but the language and actions are prompted by the demands of the situation, which is carefully structured by the teacher. • Reflection is crucial.	• Author's ideas are represented. • A variety of different modes of expression are used: dramatization, story theatre, readers' theatre, choral speech, puppetry.	• Parts are assigned. • Lines are memorized and rehearsed for an audience.
Examples	Playing at castles (p. 362)	Planning a celebration (p. 352)	Dramatization of stories and poems (p. 354)	High school drama performances
Age	Young children, 3 to 6 years	All ages	All ages	Older students
Teacher's role	• Provides space and time in the classroom for playing to occur.	• Negotiator—helps students create the context. • Facilitator—helps students understand their roles. • Provides tension. • Guides students to seek a solution.	• Selects literature to be interpreted. • Teaches specific drama skills. • Coaches students to improve skills	• Director—chooses the play, auditions, organizes rehearsals to polish students' skills to performance level.
Educators	Vygotsky (1978)	Bolton (1979), Booth (1986), Heathcote (1972), Neelands (1992), O'Neill et al. (1977), Bowell and Heap (2001)	McCaslin (1996), Moffett (1983), Stewig (1983)	Sporre (1993)

Marilyn: Hey, I want those blocks for my bridge.

Richard: No, they're mine.

[The squabble terminates the cooperative dramatic play.]

For young children's dramatic play to work, they tacitly agree to abide by certain rules related to time, space, and people. These rules shape the dramatic play. The rules of this situation are "We agree to be in a castle" (space); "Our story happened a long time ago" (time); "We agree to take on the roles of drawbridge keeper and castle keeper" (people); and "We agree to do and say what we think those people did and said in that time and place" (space, time, and people). The first part of this dramatic play is concerned with negotiating the rules of the drama game so the play can begin. In order to sustain belief in their play, the children use a variety of strategies. The play terminates when a rule is broken. The drawbridge keeper comes out of role, and the young child demands ownership of the blocks.

The analysis of drama as playing in Table 12.3 illustrates some of the strategies used by young children in spontaneous play. The strategies used in the *Memory Box* drama described earlier are more structured versions of the ones that have their genesis in children's play. Table 12.4 illustrates the structured drama strategies used in this drama.

Process drama appears outwardly spontaneous, like drama as playing, but it is carefully structured by the teacher to help students achieve new insights and understanding.

Drama as a Process for Learning

In *process drama*, the teacher often works in role and facilitates the action from within the dramatic context. For example, in Scenario II, the teacher-in-role as Grandpa's friend worked with his friends and relatives (students) to plan an appropriate celebration. Rather than acting out a story with a defined beginning, middle, and end, this form of drama is more concerned with creating dramatic contexts within which teacher and pupils explore themes, issues, and relationships. As in dramatic play, the participants first construct the meaning of the dramatic situation so they can work within it.

Drama as Interpretation of Literature

The choric presentation of A. A. Milne's poem "The More It Snows" described earlier is an example of *drama as interpretation of literature*.

Transforming text into a drama presentation is a means of helping students understand, interpret, and compose stories and poems. This form of drama is used as a way of representing ideas from a story or poem. Students are encouraged to interpret literature through a variety of **dramatic forms** of expression: *dramatization, puppetry, readers' theatre, choral speech,* and *choric drama.* Most often, these forms are shared with classmates. When they are polished and rehearsed for a general audience—such as a school assembly or school concert—they move toward drama as performance.

Drama as Theatre

Drama as theatre places great demands on students as actors and the teacher as director. A great deal of time and energy is spent in rehearsing, and the educational gains may be

Table 12.3 Emerging Drama Strategies: Drama as Playing

Strategy	Examples
1. Use of objects to build belief	Use of interlocking blocks. "Let's make this into a castle."
2. Defining space	Skipping rope represents water. "This can be the water and this can be the bridge."
3. Use of role	"I'm going to be the bridge keeper."
4. Narration	They did their work and then it was time for supper.
5. Movement	Act out making the supper, winding the drawbridge.
6. Soundtracking	Imitates the noise of the bridge being lifted.
7. Dialogue	Dialogue to negotiate rules: "Let's make this into a castle." Dialogue in role: "I have to put up this bridge."

Table 12.4 Structured Drama Strategies: Drama as a Process for Learning

Strategy	Examples
1. Use of objects to build belief	Glasses and a walking stick used to support the teacher in role as Grandpa.
2. Defining space	Children seated in a circle to define the drama space.
3. Use of role	Participants decide on a specific role in relation to the main character (friends, family members).
4. Narration	Teacher: "Grandpa treasured the memory box. It gave him so much pleasure."
5. Movement	A group of friends enact the catching of the prized fish to remind Grandpa of the event.
6. Soundtracking	Not used in this drama.

7. Dialogue	• Dialogue for negotiation:
	  Teacher: "Can we do it?"
	  Student: "We could bring photos to help him remember."
	• Dialogue in role:
	  Teacher
	  as Grandpa: "What day is it today? I know it's supposed to be something important."

minimal, although such an enterprise probably strengthens home and school relations. This chapter does not address this form of drama.

It is important to understand the differences among these four classifications of drama, because our understanding shapes what we do in classrooms. As illustrated in Figure 12.1, "I did drama today" could represent a range of activities, depending on the teacher's interpretation of the term "drama."

PLANNING AND TEACHING DRAMA

Consider the statement "I did drama today using Bahr's *The Memory Box*." For a teacher who views drama as interpretation of literature, this sentence summarizes certain strategies and procedures: dividing the story into scenes, assigning characters, practising the scenes, and then sharing the presentation with peers. For a teacher who equates drama with process drama, this statement would mean selecting the type of strategies and procedures outlined in Scenario II. Drama as interpretation of literature places the teacher outside the play as director, guide, and coach. The process approach places the teacher inside the drama as he or she takes on various roles to support the work.

These two types of drama have represented two different perspectives on drama education and have been thoroughly debated. Should drama be taught as an art form or should it be used as a process for learning? This "either-or" approach is represented below.

- *Educator 1*. To use drama to interpret literature we must first fashion the tool. (Implications for instruction: discrete activities to improve voice, gesture movement, and dialogue before enacting a play.) (Supports drama as an art form.)
- *Educator 2*. Drama is about exploring what it means to be human. We are human; we do not need to practise it. (Implications for instruction: teacher in role with the students negotiates a dramatic context to explore human events and issues.) (Supports drama as a process for learning.)

These two views, drama as an art form (Way, 1967) and drama as a process for learning (Heathcote, 1972) have been the cause of much debate. A more fruitful discussion of these two views is described by Wolf, Edmiston, and Enciso (1997) as they see both approaches supporting literacy development. They differentiate these two approaches by highlighting the emphasis placed on the particular piece of literature used within the drama lesson. A literal interpretation of the text—saying a poem, enacting a scene—is described as "working at the heart of the text." When the literature is used as a starting point to explore issues and events it is described as "working at the edges of the text." For example, the poem "Tiddely-Pom," (described in a lesson at the beginning of this chapter) plays a central role in the drama lesson. Close attention is paid to each word on the page. The focus is on the interpretation of the actual words of the poem: this lesson is "working at the heart of the text." The text *The Memory Box* is used in a different way. It is not interpreted literally, but the idea suggested in the text of old age and loss of memory is explored with the students. The drama lesson incorporated the theme of the text, but the resulting drama did not represent any particular scene from the story. The drama explored the implications of memory loss in a specific, concrete way: these lessons represent "working at the edges of the text." Both approaches support literacy development.

The next section of this chapter provides specific lesson ideas for teaching these two types of drama. Important to keep in mind, however, are the following points:

Figure 12.1   Different Conceptions of Drama

Drama as Playing
The teacher sets up the play area as a restaurant. The children play at being cooks, waiters, customers.

Process Drama
Teacher selects a story, decides on a focus, and adopts a role to create a context for problem solving.

"I did drama today."

Drama as Interpretation
Teacher selects a story and guides the children through a series of procedures until the dramatic product is complete.

Drama as Theatre
Parts are assigned, and students practise a scene. The teacher directs.

- All of these lessons have been taught to elementary children by either university students as part of a drama project or by me in response to a teacher's request for strategies to support literacy development. The selection of strategies presented in these lessons is limited to ones that beginning drama teachers could appropriate more readily.

- All of these lessons were part of, not apart from, the language arts curriculum. The teachers saw drama as a context for language learning, because in "doing drama," all the six language arts were included. When children complete a play for reader's theatre, they have an opportunity to repeat and practise their part. Such opportunities for oral interpretation develop fluency in reading in a purposeful context. Listening, talking, viewing, and representing are used throughout the dramas. When children are representing their ideas through tableau, the rest of the class is viewing and interpreting the meaning. In creating a tableau, students need to talk and listen to one another to shape their representation. Not all drama activity involves writing, but the examples described earlier illustrate the drama–writing connection.

Our understanding of the connection between the drama process and the reading and writing processes eliminates time-consuming preparations, as drama is seen as part of, not apart from, literacy instruction. Drama is viewed not as a curricular frill—something to be done if there is time—but as a process for learning. Drama provides a context for meaningful literacy activities.

Teaching Drama: Interpretation of Literature

Dramatization

This dramatic form involves transforming stories and poems using improvisation. The students are guided and coached by the teacher.

Primary Level

Caps for Sale (Slobodkina, 1947)

The teacher reads the story, which involves a peddler and monkeys, to the class. While the peddler rests in the forest, monkeys, hiding in the trees, steal his caps. When the peddler finds out, he gets angry. He shakes his fist, stamps his foot, and throws his own cap on the ground. The monkeys then imitate him, so he is able to retrieve his caps. As a literature response activity, the teacher dramatizes the story with the whole class.

Teacher-as-narrator: So the peddler went to sell his caps, he packed his tray.

Movement: All the children portray the peddler and enact the story, adding limited dialogue as the teacher narrates.

Teacher-as-narrator: The peddler went back to town shouting …

Chant (children):

Student: Caps for sale!

Primary Level

The Three Billy Goats Gruff

Storytelling: The teacher has read the story to the children before the lesson. The class sits around her in a circle. She invites them to help her retell the story by joining in the refrain,

Chant: "Who's that trip-trapping over my bridge?" This invitation to join in the story is signalled by the teacher's posture, voice, tone, and pause. "Class, when I raise my hand like this, you say, 'Who's that trip-trapping over my bridge?'" When the students have listened to the retelling of the story, the teacher moves into the *dramatization*.

Teacher:

Relaxation activity
Find a space. Lie on the floor. As I count to ten, you become more and more relaxed. Eyes closed. One … two … [Teacher moves around the room to see if the children are following directions and then continues with the story.] You are beginning to wake … stretch … put on your trousers … [The teacher narrates the process of getting dressed, and children mime the actions.]

Movement (parallel action):

Teacher-as-narrator: You walk slowly and heavily out of your house. You are so, so big … [When the teacher sees the children have attained the movement quality of a giant she continues.] Stop, Mr. Troll, and listen. Trip-trap-trip-trap. Troll, you say …

Chant (class): [Teacher signals, and class responds in unison.] Who's that trip-trapping over my bridge?

[This dramatic sequence is repeated for the three goats. The combination of narration by the teacher and parallel action by the students can be used for any story. As the teacher narrates, all students assume the same role simultaneously. These strategies are most suitable for younger students, who require more active participation.]

Teacher-in-role
(as the big billy goat): Mr. Troll, I am going to butt you with these horns. [Moves out of role, which is signalled by change in posture and voice.] On the count of three you are butted in the stomach and fall into the river. Let's practise that part. [When the students have practised, the teacher moves back into role.] Move, Mr. Troll, I am warning you. I have very dangerous horns. I will count to three: one, two, … three. [The children collapse on the floor, and the teacher moves out of role and narrates the ending of the story.] The goat joined the other goats, and they lived happily ever after.

Upper Elementary Level

King of the Cats (Jacobs, 1973)

Story synopsis: The sexton's wife is sitting by the fire with her big black cat, Tom. Her frightened husband returns home from work. He tells her that while he was digging a grave he saw six black cats carrying a coffin covered with a purple pall with a crown on top. As the sexton watched the service, the leader of the cats turned to him and said, "Go, tell Tom Tildrum that Tim Tildrum is dead." When the sexton spoke these words to his wife, their cat Tom flew up the chimney, never to be seen again. The teacher selects one scene from the story to begin the drama.

Teacher:

Tableau

The sexton was digging the grave, and when he looked up, he was so scared. If he had taken a picture of that scene, what would it look like? I would like you to get into groups of seven and create that picture. [Students create two tableaux: one depicts the cats entering the churchyard, the other shows the cats kneeling around the grave.]

Teacher: Let's look at these different frozen pictures. Look at the tableaux and tell me one thing you really liked. Give one suggestion for improvement.

Sally: They are not being silly. All their faces and bodies are sad, like this [demonstrates]. They could make it better by all holding the coffin at the same height.

Teacher:

Reflection

Can you try Sally's suggestion? You did well to stay so serious for so long. Well done! We've really improved at staying in drama time. [The process continues, and the teacher reinforces the improvement in drama skills and helps the students to incorporate the suggestions. The improvement in the movement quality of the frozen pictures reinforces the commitment to the drama.]

Teacher: Voice-in-the-head	Move into your tableau. As I come around and tap you on the shoulder, tell me one thought. If you can't think of anything to say, just put your head down and I'll move on. [The teacher moves to the tableau depicting the grave scene and taps Mary on the shoulder.]
Mary: Individual memory	I'll miss you Tim. [Her response is inaudible to the rest of the class. Rather than spotlight the child by asking her to repeat the sentence in a louder voice, the teacher encourages a choral response. "Excellent Mary. Say after me, class, 'I'll miss you, Tim.'" The process continues and the students contribute their individual memories of Tim. "I'll remember the time you helped me win the alley fight." "You looked after me when I was sick." "You helped me find Dick Whittington, my master. Thank you, Tim."]
Teacher: Improvisation, action, and dialogue	Some very interesting thoughts, lots of great stories there. Let us now add *movement* and *dialogue*. You will begin in tableau, come alive for a few seconds, and then freeze again. [The Grade 4 students practise their short improvisations and share them with the class. The sharing is important, since drama skills are taught in context. The students practise the skill (such as slowly picking up the coffin) in order to clarify the meaning of the story. Shaping the movement quality deepens the aesthetic experience for the students.]

The dramatization of such folk tales can be extended in a variety of ways, as Table 12.5 illustrates.

When dramatizing stories with students, the key to success is to select a small part of the story with strong action qualities. Many folk tales have this characteristic. With primary children, *parallel action* is more appropriate than tableau. Young children like to move, and tableaux are too static. In the stories *The Three Billy Goats Gruff* and *Caps for Sale*, the same strategies were used. The teacher

- selected a story with a strong line of action,
- chose one or two short scenes to be enacted,
- analyzed the movements of the characters and included these descriptions in the narration: (e.g., "Troll, you walk very slowly to the bridge"),
- gave all children the same role and chose scenes in which the characters were clearly defined, and
- folded in simple dialogue, such as "Caps for sale!" and "Who's that trip-trapping over my bridge?"

These same principles can be applied in transforming text into a puppet play.

Puppetry

When using puppetry in the classroom, it is important to simplify puppet construction. The puppets help the students move into the imaginary world of drama. Many shy children find security in this form of drama. They can hide behind the puppet theatre as attention is focused on the puppet. Puppet plays should not be scripted, because students find it difficult to read scripts and manipulate the puppets at the same time. To organize students for puppetry, consider these guidelines:

- Provide guidance and materials for puppet construction.
- Help students select an appropriate part of the story. Select a small part with strongly defined action.

Table 12.5 Extension Activities from *King of the Cats*

Strategy	Examples
1. Music	• One class focused more on dramatic movement and music, and the story became a dance drama.
2. Writing	• Another class folded in different literacy activities, including stories, eulogies, résumés for the position of king.
3. Drama	• One class moved into contextual drama and had a meeting to decide the next heir apparent.
4. Drawing	• One class, at Halloween, made the story into a shadow play. They used cutouts placed on the overhead projector and recorded the dialogue and sound effects.

- Provide practice time. Put a time limit on the practice and then evaluate. At this point, the first attempt can be appreciated and improved. Group process skills can be reinforced. It is often these procedural concerns that deter teachers from drama work—"It takes too much time and energy" (Edwards and Payne, 1994).
- Celebrate puppet plays by inviting another class to watch the polished performance.

Readers' Theatre

Readers' theatre is a form of oral interpretation in which a group of readers performs written texts using a script. This activity provides a meaningful context for practising reading aloud. Commercially printed scripts are available, but students can prepare their own scripts. Guidance from the teacher is needed to facilitate this task, since children need assistance with:

- *Choosing a story.* The story needs to be short, with lots of dialogue and a variety of characters.
- *Organizing the cast.* The class needs to be grouped according to the number of characters involved in the story.
- *Transforming the story into a script.* Initially, the teacher may model this process with the whole class.

As the students become more proficient at transforming story into play, they can create their own scripts. This transformation of text to script involves students in a close reading of the text, which is an excellent context for developing comprehension abilities. Readers' theatre is more akin to a radio play, except that the readers are visible and can use gestures and facial expressions to portray meaning. This form is more appropriate for older students (Grades 3 to 6).

Readers' theatre gives students practice in reading aloud and making oral interpretations. Oral interpretation is also a major focus of choral speech and choric drama.

Choral Speech

Choral speech is the art of interpreting text as a group. The following nursery rhymes have been selected to demonstrate the variety of ways they can be interpreted. Older students can use these same strategies with more age-appropriate poems. Choral work can be as informal as students chanting repetitive phrases while the teacher reads a story, or as formal as students performing a poem for an audience, to be judged at a drama festival. For more formal presentations, there are four basic ways that text can be approached for choric work to achieve variety.

Line-by-Line Arrangement. Scenario III, in which the poem "The More It Snows" was used, is an example of arranging poetry line by line. Each child, or group of children, chants one line.

Antiphonal. The class is divided into two groups: one group recites the first verse, and the other group recites the second verse. This process is continued throughout the poem. For example:

Group 1:   Pussy Cat, Pussy Cat
            Where have you been?
Group 2:   I have been up to London
            To visit the Queen.
Group 1:   Pussy Cat, Pussy Cat
            What did you there?
Group 2:   I frightened a little mouse
            Under the chair.

Cumulative. One voice begins and others are added throughout the poem.

Student 1:   For want of a nail a shoe was lost.

Students 1
and 2:   For want of a shoe a horse was lost.

Students 1,
2, and 3:   For want of a horse the general was lost.

Students 1,
2, 3, 4:   For want of a general the battle was lost.
              [Pause]

Student 1:   All for the want of a nail.

Unison. All students say all parts. Unison is not very appropriate for elementary children because the meaning of the text is obscured by the singsong pace of the group. It takes practice to effectively interpret a poem in unison. Students prefer to spend time adding action, dialogue, and props to their choral interpretation. With these additions, choral speech becomes choric drama. Choric drama is a combination of dramatization and choral speech. For example, John Ciardi's "Mummy Slept Late and Daddy Fixed Breakfast" (1962) lends itself to this form of drama. A group of children can improvise Daddy preparing breakfast while the rest of the class recites the poem.

All these forms of drama can be used in the elementary classroom to help students develop an appreciation of literature. In the process of transforming text into drama, students use many skills that support the comprehension and composition of stories. As Moffett (1983, p. 114) says, "For any narrative, what improvisation does is to translate what happened into what is happening, thus making the abstraction of the story come alive in the present moment."

Transforming a text into a dramatic improvisation involves students moving between these different levels of abstraction, from what happened to what happens. This process becomes internalized by the students and shows up in their written stories as dialogue (present tense) and narration (past tense). Hence, their literacy development is supported by "working at the heart of the text" (Wolf, Edmiston, and Enciso, 1997).

Process drama also supports literacy development through the exploration of text. This approach is not concerned with transforming written text into a dramatic form, but rather with using drama to understand concepts and issues represented by the text. "Working at the edges of the text" (Wolf, Edmiston, and Enciso) provides students with a social context to use language for a variety of purposes in a variety of ways, hence providing further support for the development of literacy skills.

Teaching Drama: Process Drama

A brief overview of process drama was provided earlier in this chapter. It was noted that, while process drama outwardly appears to be spontaneous (like dramatic playing), in fact it is structured through careful planning (unlike dramatic playing). Planning for this structured spontaneity can benefit from some of the recent insights generated by a number of drama educators, notably those included in the References section of this chapter.

The 1972 film *Three Looms Waiting* illustrates very effectively some of the principles that are fundamental to process drama. Although somewhat dated, the film shows Heathcote, the pioneer of this work, demonstrating the powerful affective quality of this kind of drama. This intensity can be akin to that experienced by small children who are deeply absorbed in dramatic play. Following is an example of a process drama in which the students involved achieved this kind of intensity. Their work had the spontaneous quality of dramatic play, but this spontaneity was achieved through careful planning and the use of several drama strategies.

Process Drama: An Example

The story *Old Henry*, by Joan Blos (1987), deals with a social studies theme. This drama was used with a Grade 2/3 class and represents three hours of instruction. Old Henry is a new resident in the village. He is very untidy, and the villagers try to help him. Old Henry refuses help, and conflict ensues.

Phase 1—Establishing the Life and Activity of the Village

Read story:	The teacher reads the story up to the episode where the men try to help Henry.
Imaging:	Children are asked to close their eyes and imagine what Henry's house might look like.
Discussion:	They share their ideas, and the teacher draws Henry's house as they provide the detail.
Drawing:	[The class begins to concretize context as a way of building belief, as a way of stepping into the imaginary world of Old Henry.]
Imaging:	The teacher continues the imaging exercise. "Close your eyes. You also live in this community. Who are you? What does your house look like? Draw your house." [Students are encouraged to adopt the role.] The teacher rolls out a large piece of paper, places Mr. Henry's house at one end, and asks the students to place their house on the map and draw the other important build-

ings. As the children are working on the activity, the teacher walks around feeding information and giving suggestions "I wonder who lives here?"

Mapping: "Maybe I can find information about Mr. Henry from the shopkeeper?" As children begin to accept the lures, the teacher reinforces their roles. Child says: "Mr. Henry comes into my shop for his parrot seed."

Subtle questions and responses:

Teacher: "Oh, so you know something about him then?"

Phase 2—Establishing the Community

Gossip strategy: The teacher asks the class to sit around the map. "There seem to be a lot of stories going around our community about Mr. Henry. Maybe we could share these? It may help us to know how to deal with him. Please introduce yourself and share a story if you have had dealings with Mr. Henry. I am the mayor and I know he's honest because he pays his taxes." Students share their stories about Mr. Henry. [This activity builds the character of Mr. Henry, giving the students a chance to move into role.]

Teacher-in-role: The mayor calls a town meeting.

Defining space: Chairs are set up in a formal manner. A child is selected to role-play the clerk of the court.

Use of ritual: The mayor asks all the "citizens" to introduce themselves and say what they do. This process is done very formally. The teacher uses the role as mayor to control: "Order, please." [Ritual slows down the drama and gives students time to deepen belief.]

Teacher-in-role (formal manner represents authority figure):   The mayor says, "Clerk of the court, please read out the charges."

Use of documents: The clerk reads, "City bylaw 99: Failure to keep town tidy. City bylaw 11: Failure to shovel snow. City bylaw 63: Failure to pay fines." [These documents can be prepared by the teacher alone or with the children out of drama time; use of formal language sustains belief.] The mayor states, "I, the mayor of this town, am hereby opening the floor for discussion."

Storytelling: Children provide eyewitness accounts.

Meeting: The mayor closes the meeting with the following statements: "I am hereby appointing special community task forces to find a solution to our problem." [The class is divided into groups, and the groups discuss their ideas. Students become "experts" on solving problems as members of the task force.] The mayor continues with his speech: "Please have a full written report to present at the next council meeting."

Teacher-in-role: Town meeting—the groups present their solutions [reports written out of drama time]. [Teacher/mayor leaves the room and comes back as Mr. Henry.]

Phase 3—Injecting the Tension

Improvisation: Mr. Henry rejects all proposals. He tells the community members they are intolerant and informs them of his departure.

Phase 4—Seeking a Solution

Documents are written out of drama time but help to consolidate ideas: the community members modify proposals and generate other solutions in the form of news reports, letters to Mr. Henry, and diary entries.

During the reflection on the drama, the students discussed the impact of their solutions on themselves and Mr. Henry. The class reflected on the similarities of the dramatic situation to a local political issue. "We've done our best; we've been responsible. Mr. Henry needs to cooperate. It's just like what's happening with our hockey team. Let them go, the hockey team and Mr. Henry." This example once again illustrates the generalization of experience from one situation to another. After the reflection on the drama, the class compared their handling of the situation with that of the author, Joan Blos.

In this drama, the planning was broken down into four phases (Littledyke and Baum, 1986). These phases overlap and the boundaries are not rigid.

Phase 1. Establishing the life and activity of the village

- Creating the context and roles

Phase 2. Establishing the meaning of village life

- Villagers share stories about Mr. Henry
- Villagers cope with the problem

Phase 3. Injecting the tension

- Mr. Henry rejects the village proposals and calls the citizens intolerant

Phase 4. Seeking a solution

- Villagers modify proposals
- Villagers decide Mr. Henry has to take some responsible action

In the first phase, the emphasis is on building belief in the drama through tasks—imaging, drawing, and mapping. In the second phase, the tasks become less important and the students are asked to reflect on village life. They share their stories about Mr. Henry and review his status using a variety of strategies, teacher-in-role, gossip, defining space, ritual, documents, storytelling, meeting, eyewitness accounts, and news reports. In phase 3, the villagers' suggestions are rejected and Mr. Henry leaves. Sometimes the tension in the drama is introduced gradually. For example, one villager says, "I hope Mr. Henry accepts our proposal because his art shop brings many new people to the village. They spend a lot of money." In phase 3 of this drama, the element of surprise is used: the teacher switches roles from being the mayor to being Henry instantly. Phase 4 follows the logic suggested by the students. Students put their own solutions into operation, writing letters, news reports, and diary entries, setting them into the context of their own lives during the reflection phase. In each of these phases, the teacher plans for certain events to occur. However, the outcome of these events is not so predictable, as the students create their characters and make suggestions. It is this unpredictability that gives this work its energy. The students feel empowered when their suggestions are translated into action. It is the teacher's use of a variety of strategies to structure the students' suggestions that makes this succeed.

FROM SCHOOL TIME TO DRAMA TIME

What does the teacher need to understand, do, and say to transport students from the "here and now" of the classroom to the imagined world of drama?

In the planning phase, the teacher has to understand the differences among the four major types of drama (see Table 12.2) in order to select the type most suited for the purpose. It is at this point that confusion often arises about the connection between a dramatic form and a drama strategy. Is the strategy of tableau a part of dramatization, choric drama, or process drama? Is chanting a refrain (choral speech), a dramatic form, or a drama strategy? To clarify this confusion, I compare writing and drama to highlight the connection between form and strategy. Teachers understand that a variety of forms (poems, stories, reports) can be developed by using a common strategy—brainstorming, for example—to generate ideas for writing. They also realize that some strategies are more appropriate for specific forms. Using the pattern of a familiar story to compose a new story or using an interview to gather data for a report are examples of form-specific strategies. Likewise, some drama strategies, tableau and voice-in-the head, can be used to develop a variety of dramatic forms, whereas a strategy like teacher-in-role is more specific to process drama. Understanding the relationship between strategy and form permits teachers to maximize the use of a few strategies to access a variety of dramatic forms. Following are several descriptions of the use of tableau and voice-in-the-head. The following examples are ordered from simple to complex in terms of organization and classroom management.

Using Pictures

In the first example, the teacher provides each group in the class with a picture depicting a scene of pioneer life. The students are asked to select one character and imagine what he or she is thinking. These thoughts are shared, and the teacher identifies the drama strategy as voice-in-the-head. In the second example, the teacher provides each group in the class with a new set of pictures and the instruction to "be like waxworks in a museum to represent the people in the picture." The groups share the representations, and the teacher names this drama strategy as tableau. Tableau is an efficient strategy for representing information quickly.

Transforming Text

In the third example, the teacher reads a story and instructs students to "create a tableau with voice-in-the-head" of one scene from the story. And in the fourth example, the teacher provides a general statement—for example, "The people leave." The students create a tableau that illustrates this idea. Headlines from the newspaper can also provide many ideas for this kind of activity.

Representing New Ideas

In the fifth example, students listen to part of a story and are asked to create an ending using tableau. These endings are compared with the one in the text. The students can also use tableau and voice-in-the-head to create new stories. Sixth, students use these strategies in social studies to represent life in the past and present. Each group of students presents two tableaux, one showing an aspect of life in pioneer times (e.g., farming), and the second representing farming in the present day.

As these drama strategies are presented, they are not extended into a particular dramatic form. Rather, they are providing an alternative way of representing ideas related to different learning outcomes in different curriculum areas. Tableau and voice-in-the-head require additional strategies to create a particular dramatic form. However, students can move easily from the static tableau to improvisation. "Your tableau comes alive for 30 seconds. What will you do or say?" or "Now add movement and words to your tableau to explain what is happening." Such guidance moves students smoothly into drama time.

The decision to extend these activities depends on the comfort level of the teacher. Some teachers require more controlled and gradual ways of moving from school time to drama time. The social health of the class also influences such decisions. These activities provide possible ways of making this transition, and with additional strategies, the teacher can access a variety of dramatic forms. Table 12.6 outlines some additional drama strategies that could have been used to extend the dramas described previously in this chapter. These examples include dramas based on Bahr's *The Memory Box*, Galdone's *The Three Sillies*, and Milne's poem "The More It Snows."

In the drama described earlier in this chapter, the teacher, using Bahr's *The Memory Box*, chose to employ a class discussion to generate ideas that were chanted and then used to plan the drama. The same outcome could have been achieved through the tableau strategy. There would have been more talk in less time, and the ideas would have been shared very effectively and efficiently.

Our understanding of the similarities between familiar, generic strategies and less familiar drama strategies supports a change in teacher stance. This change of stance from "expert/I am in charge" to "negotiator/storyteller" is a prerequisite if the teacher wants the class to explore the "as if" world of drama. This change in stance—reflected in the language and gestures of the teacher—enables the teacher to use appropriate drama strategies to implement the various drama forms.

Once teachers have experienced the efficiency of using drama, they are encouraged to incorporate more drama strategies into their teaching repertoire. As already noted, drama is another way of learning, not an additional curriculum subject. The following teacher

Table 12.6 Forms and Strategies

Form	Strategy	Activity
Dramatization (*The Three Sillies*)	1. Tableau 2. Voice-in-the-head 3. Narration	Students create a scene from the story using strategies 1 and 2. The teacher uses narration to link the scenes.
Choric drama ("The More It Snows")	1. Tableau 2. Voice-in-the-head 3. Antiphonal arrangement	The class is divided into three groups. Two groups recite the poem using strategy 3; the other group creates the tableau of each verse and incorporates strategy 2.
Process drama (*The Memory Box*)	1. Tableau 2. Voice-in-the-head 3. Use of role	"Let's imagine I have a photograph album of Grandpa's life. Create a tableau of one of these photos." The ideas presented are used to move into role.

scenarios illustrate drama strategies that achieve similar learning outcomes to the more familiar language arts strategies. The crucial difference between the two types of strategies is the stance and language of the teacher. Using drama generally encourages more student participation than the non-drama approaches.

Scenario IV

Let's examine the drama strategy "gossip" to illustrate these points just discussed. Mr. Henry, a story character from *Old Henry* by Joan Blos (review the example of process drama detailed earlier) has moved into the village and is creating problems for all the residents. The teacher asks the students to form small groups and take the role of the villagers. She directs them to "share the rumours and gossip you have heard around the village." After the gossip session, one student from each group shares the rumours discussed, and these are listed on a chart by the teacher. In this way, all the possible ideas for the drama can be examined more critically out of drama time. Because students understand that gossip is not necessarily "true," they know that their responses will not be wrong.

This drama strategy encourages uninhibited participation and uncritical acceptance of responses. The goal of this activity is to generate a quantity of ideas—in effect, it is a form of brainstorming. The shift required is a change in teacher stance from "I am in charge" to "we are in this together," which is manifested in tone, gesture, and language. This shift involves a change in the language of the teacher from "Get into groups and brainstorm as many ideas as you can and then we will chart them on the board," to "You are all a little upset at Mr. Henry's behaviour. He's bothered you, and you've heard lots of rumours and gossip about other things he has done. You meet your friends in the village, and you begin to share the rumours you have heard." The first example is the typical language of instruction, the second is the language of the storyteller. The brainstorming activity engenders a more impersonal response ("He is a litterbug"), whereas the gossip strategy promotes a narrative response ("I saw him at the park and he threw his litter on the grass").

Scenario V

Mr. Hughes, at Florence MacDougall Community School in High Level, Alberta, begins by reading articles and stories to his class about the life of Houdini, the magician. After the reading is completed, he moves into role as Houdini's press secretary:

Teacher-in-role: Welcome. I am Mr. Brown, Mr. Houdini's press secretary. You must be the newspaper reporters. Now as you can imagine, Mr. Houdini has a very tight schedule and his time is limited. In order to make this conference efficient, I would like you to prepare some questions before he arrives so there is no repetition. I will have to limit the time so he can make his next appointment.

Rather than giving explicit instructions, Mr. Hughes chooses his words very carefully. The students know their role and task; the press of time adds creative tension to the drama. Out of role, the teacher monitors the group discussions, and when he thinks the students are prepared, he moves back into role as Houdini.

Teacher-in-role: Good morning. My press secretary tells me you have some questions for me?

The press conference is completed, and Houdini leaves before all questions are answered. The "reporters" are disappointed, so, out of role, Mr. Hughes gives his students time and resources to find the answer to these questions on their own. Their reports are published in the school newspaper. In his comments about the lesson, Mr. Hughes said, "I like this story because I *am* a magician and I can demonstrate a few tricks. I did this story last year, but I used the KWL strategy [see Chapter Five]. It worked well, but the class was more engaged this time; it showed in their writing." When asked what had prompted him to incorporate drama, he explained it this way: "In my first year of teaching I needed more control. When you use drama, you give the students more decision-making power—but there is always the anxiety they may not come up with anything! After teaching for a year, I realize I can take back the control by saying, "Let's stop. This drama is not working. What can we do?" After I had used role in the *Memory Box* drama, I felt more confident to try it with this story. The students had no difficulty relating to me as teacher, Houdini's press secretary, and Houdini. My change in posture and language keyed them to these role changes."

The control issue is very important, particularly in process drama. The teacher is part of the drama and has to guide the students from within the role. If students are uncooperative, it does not work and it is important to hand back the responsibility to the class—saying, for example, "We need to fix this. Any suggestions?" Because our notion of drama as performance is so embedded in our consciousness, we tend to equate stopping a lesson with interrupting and spoiling a play. But this shouldn't be so. Just as we examine and practise group process skills in other situations (such as writing conferences and literary response groups), so we should have no hesitation in applying the same procedures to drama situations.

Scenario VI

The students read the story "Red Riding Hood" and, guided by teacher questions, they create a story grammar (see Chapter Five). The purpose of this strategy is to help students understand the structure of a story. This same learning outcome can be achieved by using tableau and improvisation along with narration. The students act out the problem and the solution; the teacher connects the scenes through narration.

Not only can narration act as a link between different scenes, it can also help teachers focus the attention of students on smaller pieces of a whole text. For example, the story *King of the Cats* uses narration very effectively. Compare the following samples of teacher language: "Make a tableau of the part where the cats come to the grave and scare the sexton" and "The sexton was digging the grave and, when he looked up, he was very, very scared. Make a tableau of what he saw." The first example is the language of instruction, the second is the language of storytelling. Narration provides the same information, but it has more affective resonance: if narrated with appropriate expression, it can create a dramatic tension or provide an appropriate atmosphere that deepens the students' belief in the drama. It can also be used to summarize an end to a drama to effect closure. For example, in the *Memory Box* drama, the teacher moves out of role as Grandpa and moves into the role of narrator to bring the drama to a satisfying closure: "Grandpa treasured the memory box: it gave him so much pleasure." These uses of narration—introducing, linking, or closing dramatic action—save time because they eliminate unnecessary repetition of text. To use narration successfully, the teacher adopts the language of the storyteller to create an atmosphere appropriate to the dramatic context.

All of these scenarios describe ways in which a teacher can facilitate the students' engagement in the "as if" world of drama. These last three scenarios demonstrate the links among the more familiar language arts strategies—brainstorming, KWL, story grammar (see Chapter Five)—and the less familiar drama strategies of gossip, teacher-in-role, improvisation, and narration. Such strategies can be used in all areas of the curriculum. Table 12.7 (page 382) lists the strategies used in the dramas throughout this chapter.

TEACHER CONCERNS RELATED TO DRAMA

Edwards and Payne (1994) studied teachers in a drama support group for two years. During that time, many concerns about implementation were raised. Some of those concerns are described here.

Learning the Language of Drama

The teachers reported experiencing the most difficulty with terms used to label strategies in the process approach to drama. This issue was addressed earlier in this chapter in the section "Classification of Drama." Throughout this chapter, the labels of the forms and strategies have been referred to often so that the reader can learn the labels in the context of the dramatic situation. The strategies are noted in the margin or italicized when they are first introduced in the body of the text. Table 12.7 on p. 382 summarizes all of the strategies.

Using Role

Initially, the teachers in Edwards and Payne's 1994 study had some difficulty stepping into role. They found it helpful to pattern their role on a character from literature (Mr. Henry, Houdini) or to take on a role endowed with authority (such as a mayor or press secretary). These roles have a similar stance as the teacher role and permit the teacher to have some degree of control over the dramatic events.

Some teachers have found it helpful to step into role by using a hand puppet. They speak to the class as if they are the puppet. Other teachers step into role for only a few minutes and then step out of role to continue the drama. This way of working was exemplified by Mr. Hughes in his use of role in the *Memory Box* drama on page 352. As teachers become more at ease with this strategy, they find it more efficient to use a variety of roles to move the drama along quickly. Mr. Hughes did exactly this in a later drama when he took on the role of Houdini and the press secretary. Other teachers jump right into role and are able to fold in a variety of strategies to accomplish their learning outcomes. *Old Henry* is an example of a more complex drama. However, if you examine the planning phases in the *Memory Box* drama, you will notice that Mr. Hughes did not go through all of the planning phases detailed in the *Old Henry* drama. The context, roles, and tension (phases 1, 2, and 3) were provided by the story. His use of narration and the letter from the grandson moved the class quickly to phase 4, seeking a solution. The drama strategies associated with process drama enable teachers to integrate drama as part of the curriculum. These smaller episodes, such as the ones previously described, are easier to manage than a drama that is continued over several lessons. The decision to use role depends on the teacher's comfort level and control needs.

Management

For the teachers in Edwards and Payne's study, management issues arose when they initially introduced drama into their classrooms. The following rules alleviated these concerns:

- Have a signal for stopping. This can be a verbal command, such as "freeze," or some other signal.
- Clarify the boundaries of the drama space. Avoid the gym.
- Establish cooperation. Review the classroom rules.
- Use a drama "eye." This term represents the rule "We agree to enter this 'as if' world of drama." Following is one teacher's description of how she developed this rule:

I role-played a short sequence and then asked the students to describe my actions and to explain how they arrived at their meaning. Through discussion these young students could articulate the difference between using your real eyes and using your "drama eyes"—between school time and drama time. The students practised using their drama eyes by demonstrating various activities, for example, eating their favourite food. They also practised identifying my

Table 12.7 Summary of the Strategies

Strategy	Page Location
Chant	368, 369
Defining space	374
Documents	353, 374
Drawing	358, 373
Gossip	374, 378
Imaging	355, 373
Improvisation	358, 370, 375
Individual memory	370
Mantle of the expert	375
Mapping	374
Movement: parallel action	368
Narration	352, 353, 357, 368, 369, 374, 379
Objects to signify role	353
Reflection	354, 369, 375
Relaxation activity	368
Ritual	374
Storytelling	374
Tableau	358, 369, 376–77, 380
Teacher-in-role	352, 353, 357, 368, 369, 374, 379
Voice-in-the-head	355, 356, 357, 358, 370

It is not always necessary to use these strategies as part of a drama lesson. They can be used as an alternative response to demonstrate understanding in all areas of the curriculum (see Chapter 11, pp. 330–32).

actions as being in school time or drama time. It is important to remind students, particularly young students, of this distinction. At times, the emotions experienced in drama seem very real, and it is imperative that students can step out of drama time into school time to reflect on these feelings. Obviously, I want my students to be involved with, but not overwhelmed by, the drama experience. My students always have the choice of stepping out of drama time. I usually place a chair outside the boundary of the drama space and the students can go there if they feel uncomfortable during the drama. I have noticed when I use the term "drama eyes" rather than "pretend," off-task behaviour is minimized. (Jewel Bondar, special education teacher, 1994)

These rules can be reviewed with the class at the end of the lesson, and as Mr. Hughes pointed out, it is permissible—desirable even—to stop the drama when it does not appear to be going well. Again, language is important. "What can we do to fix it?" is better than "I don't like what's happening here."

Time

Many of the drama strategies discussed here can be used as part of the regular curriculum as illustrated throughout this chapter. Drama does not need a special time or place. Nevertheless, finding time to implement drama was perceived as a difficulty by the teachers in the study. This concern is not specific to drama, but to all meaning-centred approaches. In classrooms where pupils are actively involved in learning, there will be lots of talk and writing, which are crucial for clarifying meaning.

The Concert

During Edwards and Payne's two-year study, the teachers were perceived by their staff as the drama experts and were responsible for the annual school concert. The following guidelines facilitated this task:

- Use a presentational mode of drama. The forms presented in the section "Teaching Drama: Interpretation of Literature" would be appropriate.
- Where possible, allow the students to improvise dialogue and practise until they are fluent. This avoids scriptwriting and memorizing.
- Make the presentation as visual as possible, since most auditoriums have poor acoustics.
- Limit the amount of individual dialogue, since young students cannot project their voices sufficiently. Dialogue for a play can be recorded and the actions mimed. Choral work can be used.
- Allow students to choose how they will participate—for example, as performers, props makers, or scriptwriters.

Assessment

The teachers in the study discussed the importance of assessing their lessons by reviewing the drama rules with the class. These teachers were using process drama to achieve certain learning outcomes, so they judged the success of the drama in terms of achieving these outcomes. When drama strategies were used as part of the writing process, the teachers noted a marked improvement in the quality of student writing. To assess each one of the dramatic forms listed under drama as interpretation of literature, one could devise a checklist specific to the particular form. The professional resources outlined at the end of the chapter would aid teachers in this task.

SUMMARY

The first part of this chapter describes several classroom scenarios that illustrate the range of activities labelled "drama." The way preservice and inservice teachers define drama determines their attitudes toward teaching drama and shapes their classroom practices. The next section of the chapter outlines four major conceptions of drama: drama as playing, drama as a process for learning, drama as interpretation of literature, and drama as theatre. These different types of drama make different demands on students and teachers. This chapter focuses mainly on two of these forms: drama as interpretation of literature and process drama. These forms can be readily integrated into the language arts program. Several lessons described make explicit the connections between drama and literacy. These connections underscore the importance of drama as a meaning-making process.

Throughout this chapter, numerous dramatic strategies are illustrated across a variety of dramatic forms. The similarities and differences between these less familiar drama strategies and those that are the more familiar, general teaching strategies are highlighted to encourage teachers to include drama in their language arts program. The last part of the chapter details the ways in which teachers can move their students into the dramatic context, and addresses some of the common concerns voiced by teachers beginning this drama journey.

SELECTED PROFESSIONAL RESOURCES

Baldwin, P. (1997). *Stimulating drama: Cross curricular approaches to drama in the primary school.* London: National Drama. This text is a collection of lessons implemented in various primary classrooms. These lessons include: detailed plans, description of drama strategies and facsimiles of children's work arising from these drama lessons.

Barton, B. (1980). *Tell me another.* Markham, ON: Pembroke. This book is an excellent introduction to storytelling.

Booth, D. (1986). *Games for everyone.* Markham, ON: Pembroke. This book outlines a variety of practical drama games to develop cooperation, problem solving, and movement. Each game is clearly described, with suggestions for follow-up activities.

Bowell, P. and Heap, B. S. (2001). *Planning process drama.* London: Dalton Fulton Publishers. A very comprehensive book that deals with the planning of process dram. Each step of the planning process is illustrated with numerous examples. The authors use a question and answer technique to guide the reader through the process. The various charts and diagrams are helpful in consolidating the concepts related to process drama.

Kitson, N. and Spilby, I. (1997). *Drama 7–11. Developing primary teaching skills.* New York: Routledge. A practical guide to the teaching and planning of process drama. The authors describe the teaching approaches of an inexperienced drama teacher and a drama specialist. Their analysis of these two approaches is very helpful because it encourages the novices to begin and the seasoned drama teachers to develop their skills further.

Neelands, J. (1992). *Learning through imagined experience.* New York: Cambridge University Press. This book integrates the theory and practice of contextual drama very effectively. The relationship between drama and language is illustrated throughout, with many examples of drama strategies and units of study related to various curriculum areas.

Neelands, J. and Goode, T. (2000). *Structuring drama work.* Cambridge University Press. A revised version of Neelands' classic text which defines a wide range of drama strategies/conventions and provides excellent examples of each of these strategies.

O'Neill, C., Lambert, A., Linnell, R., and Warr-Wood, J. (1977). *Drama guidelines.* London: Heinemann. This book is a classic, not only for its content, but also for its format. The lessons presented in this chapter are modelled on this text. Difficult ideas are made accessible through the use of clear language and sample lessons.

Schwartz, L. (1988). *Drama themes: A practical guide for teaching drama.* Markham, ON: Pembroke. This is an excellent resource for teachers beginning work in drama. It contains many practical suggestions for using literature and drama in the language arts program.

Tarlington, C. and Verriour, P. (1983). *Offstage: Elementary education through drama.* Toronto: Oxford University Press. This is a comprehensive text containing games, drama exercises, examples of role dramas, and suggestions for drama as performance.

Toye, N. and Prendville, F. (2000). *Drama and traditional story for the early years.* London and New York: Routledge and Falmer. This text describes 16 full dramas and provides a further 30 starting points for other dramas. Traditional stories used include: *Little Bo Peep,*

Cinderella, Sleeping Beauty, Humpty Dumpty, The Pied Piper, Hansel and Gretel, and *The Three Billy Goats Gruff*. These dramas are carefully planned and linked specifically to literacy outcomes.

Winston, J. and Tandy, M. (2001). *Beginning drama 4–11.* (2nd ed). London: Dalton Futlon Publishers. This text provides excellent examples of the progression of skills for drama as an art form. It also clearly illustrates how drama can be used to achieve specific learning outcomes across the curriculum. Particularly helpful is Chapter 6 which clearly and sensibly outlines the procedures for producing the school concert.

CHILDREN'S BOOKS NOTED IN CHAPTER TWELVE ▬▬▬

Bahr, M. (1992). *The memory box*. Toronto: Albert Whitman.

Blos, J. (1987). *Old Henry*. New York: William Morrow.

Ciardi, J. (1983 [1962]). "Mummy slept late and Daddy fixed breakfast." Included in J. Prelutsky, *The Random House Book of Poetry* (p. 147). New York: Random House.

Galdone, P. (1981). *The three sillies*. New York: Houghton Mifflin.

Jacobs, J. (1973 [1854]). "King of the cats." In *Starting points in reading*. Toronto: Ginn and Company.

Milne, A. A. (1983 [1928]). "The more it snows." In *The house at Pooh Corner*. Illustrated by E. H. Shepard. Included in J. Prelutsky, *The Random House Book of Poetry* (p. 30). New York: Random House. © 1928 by E. P. Dutton, renewed © 1956 by A. A. Milne. Used by permission of Dutton Children's Books, a division of Penguin Putnam Inc.

Slobodkina, E. (1947). *Caps for sale*. New York: W. R. Scott.

REFERENCES ▬▬▬▬▬

Baldwin, P. (1997). *Stimulating drama: Cross curricular approaches to drama in the primary school*. London: National Drama.

Barton, B. (1980). *Tell me another*. Markham, ON: Pembroke.

Bolton, G. (1979). *Towards a theory of drama in education*. London: Longman.

Booth, D. (1986). *Games for everyone*. Markham, ON: Pembroke.

Bowell, P., and Heap, B. S. (2001). *Planning process drama*. London: Dalton Fulton Publishers.

Edwards, J. and Payne, P. (1994). A drama support group: Context for teacher change. *Youth Theatre*, 8 (3), 19–23.

Flynn, R. M. and Carr, G. A. (1994). Exploring classroom literature through drama: A specialist and a teacher collaborate. *Language Arts, 71*, 38–43.

Heathcote, D. (1972). *Three looms waiting: A BBC omnibus programme*. [Film]. Ipswich, UK: Concord Films.

Kitson, N., and Spiby, I. (1997). *Drama 7–11. Developing primary teaching skills*. New York: Routhedge.

Littledyke, M. and Baum, C. (1986). Structures for drama. 2D, 5 (2), 72–78.

McCaslin, N. (1996). *Creative drama in the classroom and beyond*. New York: Longman.

Moffett, J. (1983). *Student-centered language arts and reading*. Boston: Houghton Mifflin.

Neelands, J., and Goode, T. (2000). *Structuring drama work*. Cambridge University Press.

Neelands, J. (1992). *Learning through imagined experience*. New York: Cambridge University Press.

O'Neill, C., Lambert, A., Linnell, R., and Warr-Wood, J. (1977). *Drama guidelines*. London: Heinemann.

Schaffner, M. (1985). Drama and language. 2D, 4 (2), 35–44.

Schwartz, L. (1988). *Drama themes: A practical guide for teaching drama*. Markham, ON: Pembroke.

Sporre, D. J. (1993). *The art of theatre*. Englewood Cliffs, NJ: Prentice-Hall.

Stewig, J. W. (1983). *Informal drama in the elementary language arts program.* New York: Teachers College Press.

Tarlington, C. and Verriour, P. (1983). *Offstage: Elementary education through drama.* Toronto: Oxford University Press.

Toye, N., and Prendville, F. (2000). *Drama and traditional story for the early years.* London and New York: Routledge and Falmer.

Vygotsky, L. S. (1978). *Mind in society: The development of higher psychological processes.* M. Cole, V. John-Steiner, S. Scribner, and E. Souberman (eds.). Cambridge, MA: Harvard University Press.

Way, B. (1967). *Development through drama.* Harlow: Longman.

Winston, J., and Tandy, M. (2001). *Beginning drama 4–11.* (2nd ed.). London: Dalton Fulton Publishers.

Wolf, S., Edmiston, B., and Enciso, P. (1997). Drama worlds: Places of the heart, head, voice and hand in dramatic interpretation. In J. Flood, S. Bryce Heath, and D. Lapp (eds.), *Handbook of research on teaching literacy through the communicative and visual arts* (p. 492). New York: Simon and Schuster Macmillan.

Chapter 13

Critical, Media, and Technological Literacies

Critical Literacy

- Critical Reading
- Nature of Critical Literacy
- Planning for Instruction
- Questions
- Materials
- Examples
- Issues and Challenges

Media Literacy

- Stances to Media Literacy
- Goals and Forms of Media Literacy
- Media Education in Canada
- Media Literacy Instruction
- Issues and Challenges

Critical, Media, and Technological Literacies

Technological Literacy

- The Role of Computers in Education
- The Canadian Context
- Learning with Computers
- Evaluating Computer Software
- The Internet
- Challenges and Issues

Throughout her undergraduate program, Manprit Gill used her computer as a tool to conduct research on assigned and self-selected topics, to communicate with other students, her professors, and educators in other parts of the world, and to write and present papers related to course assignments. Through her interaction with the World Wide Web, she was aware that most of the material presented there is not refereed, that much of it represents corporate interests, and that at least some of it is racist, sexist, and pornographic in nature. She is convinced that the Internet provides a teaching and learning resource of enormous potential but has many questions.

Some of Manprit's questions relate to the use of technology with elementary children. She wonders if many of the computer and video "games" she has seen students playing are taking valuable time away from the development of computer and other literacy skills. She also recalls her own frustration when conducting research on the Web of finding that links lead her either to material of questionable quality or to material with very little relationship to the topic she was researching. Her critical analysis of material on the Web has lead to an increased awareness of bias evident in other texts as well, particularly in newspapers and magazines but also in materials designed for use by children in schools. Manprit has many questions.

- How can she help children become aware of the biases built into texts—of whose interests are being served and whose are not? How can children become critical users of the Internet and other texts?
- What about magazines, television, films, photographs, videotapes, and recordings? How do these contribute to children's language and literacy learning, and how can they become critical consumers?
- How are computers used in elementary classrooms, and does use of this technology increase children's learning?
- How can the Internet be used to effectively enhance elementary students' learning, language, and literacy development?

This chapter begins with a focus on **critical literacy** partly because we believe that this perspective provides the most appropriate framework for media and technological education, but also to provide you with a way to help children understand whose interests are represented in other texts as well. From this perspective, the goal of instruction is to help children learn to critically interrogate all texts, whether in books, the media or on the Internet, so that their understandings reflect the social, political, and power relations embedded in those texts. Only from this perspective are children able to gain control over media and other technologies, and make use of their understandings of all texts for personal and social transformation.

CRITICAL LITERACY

We begin our discussion of critical literacy with a description of critical reading, which most of you likely experienced in elementary school. We then contrast critical reading and critical literacy and provide suggestions for implementing critical literacy instruction in elementary classrooms.

Critical Reading

Traditionally, critical reading has involved children differentiating fact from opinion, good from bad, and reality from fantasy. In addition, children have evaluated ideas as valid, invalid, or questionable, and detected and critiqued propaganda techniques (Irwin and Baker, 1989). These activities are based on the assumption that there is an objective truth against which to judge ideas, and hence, reflect a transmission model of knowledge. Some critical reading activities, most obviously detecting and critiquing propaganda techniques, highlight the importance of closely examining an author's intentions to determine hidden meanings.

One only has to watch television on Saturday mornings to find out how many advertisements are directed at children. Critical reading of advertisements helps children become aware of techniques used to convince, persuade, or get an individual to believe or buy something. Most educators who recommend work in this area provide a set of concepts to guide children's thinking and talking about these techniques. Typical of such sets is the one in Table 13.1 adapted from Manzo and Manzo (1997). Teachers provide advertisements for children to discuss in class, children find examples of different types of advertisements to discuss with their classmates, and children write advertisements individually or in small groups. The major purpose of these activities is to help children become critical consumers of ideas and advertisements, not to label propaganda techniques.

Table 13.1 Propaganda Techniques

Label	Description	Example
Bandwagon	Everyone is doing it; go along with the crowd.	"More people drink ____ than any other cola."
Testimonial	A famous person uses, believes, or does something.	"I use ____ shampoo every day to keep my hair shiny and beautiful."
Plain folks	People that look like "you and me" suggest we use, believe, or do something.	"I've been washing clothes for many years and ____ really works."
Snob appeal	This is the opposite of plain folks.	"If you want to be part of the 'in' generation, buy ____."
Name calling	A person, thing, or movement is put down.	"Nerds like poetry."
Glittering generalities	Using popular terms to describe an idea, person, or activity.	"It's time for a change. Vote ____."
Scientific link	Scientific terms are used to make something seem better than it is.	"Four out of five doctors surveyed recommend ____."

In the past, the purpose of critical reading activities was to help children live in an increasingly complex world. Now the purpose of these types of activities is to prepare them to survive and compete in a rapidly expanding information world and in the global marketplace.

Nature of Critical Literacy

In contrast with critical reading, critical literacy reflects a fundamentally different view of knowledge and learning.

> In essence, students of critical literacy approach textual meaning as a process
> of construction ...; one imbues a text with meaning rather than extracting
> meaning from it. More important, textual meaning is understood in the con-
> text of social, historic, and power relations, not solely as the product or inten-
> tion of an author. Further, reading is an act of coming to know the world (as
> well as the word) and a means to social transformation. (Cervetti, Pardales,
> and Damico, 2001, p. 5)

In relation to the models we presented in Chapter One, critical literacy is clearly based on a social **constructivist** view of knowledge and learning.

The purpose of critical literacy instruction is to empower teachers and students to actively participate in a democracy and move literacy beyond text to social action (Cadiero-Kaplan, 2002). The ultimate goal of social action is the creation of a fairer and more just society for all people regardless of race, culture, class, or gender.

Critical literacy has been defined in several different ways by literacy educators and theorists. Lewison, Flint, and Sluys (2002) reviewed definitions presented over the past 30 years and synthesized them into the following four dimensions:

- disrupting the commonplace (seeing the everyday through new lenses to consider new frames from which to understand experience),
- interrogating multiple viewpoints (standing in the shoes of others to understand experience and text from our own perspectives and the viewpoints of others),
- focusing on sociopolitical issues (stepping outside the personal to interrogate how sociopolitical systems and power relationships shape perceptions, responses, and actions), and
- taking action and promoting social justice.

Although these dimensions are not sequential, Lewison, Flint, and Sluys found that teachers just beginning to implement critical practices focused more on the first two or three dimensions than on the last one.

A flurry of articles on critical literacy has appeared both on the Internet and in professional journals in the last few years. Indeed, there is a danger of critical literacy becoming yet another bandwagon in language arts education. In their four resources model, Luke and Freebody (1997) argue that analyzing and critiquing texts is only one of four necessary reading and writing practices. In addition to being a text analyzer, readers and writers also need to develop resources for code breaking (word identification and spelling), text participation (constructing meaning), and text use (using texts for pragmatic purposes).

Luke and Freebody note that these are not four discrete practices, nor are they stages to be dealt with in turn. Instead, Luke and Freebody recommend that teachers attend to code, meaning, pragmatic, and critical elements of reading and writing at all stages and levels. As Cadiero-Kaplan (2002, pp. 378–379) notes, "Even children as young as four and five years old can engage in critical dialogue on issues of race and skin colour."

Although many writers advocate the inclusion of critical literacy in classrooms, development and implementation of critical literacy instruction is not easy because of the complexity of the issues involved (Green, 2001). As a beginning point, Wilson (2002, p. 129) suggests nurturing children in "classroom societies where they each feel valued, regardless of class, culture, race, or gender, and where the curriculum they live helps them better know and understand one another." We present more specific suggestions below including objectives for instruction, frameworks for planning lessons, questions and materials to foster critical literacy, and examples of critical literacy lessons.

Planning for Instruction

Curriculum Documents

Curriculum documents from across all regions of Canada use the word *critical* when stating outcomes and objectives for language arts instruction. From Ontario west, outcomes tend to be focused more on critical reading than on critical literacy. For example, the *Western Canadian Protocol for Collaboration in Basic Education: The Common Curriculum Framework for English Language Arts: Kindergarten to Grade 12* (1998, p. 3) includes the development of "thoughtful and critical interpretations of a variety of texts" as one goal of instruction. The *Ontario Curriculum: Grades 1–8: Language* (1997, p. 28) states that an essential aspect of the reading process is to "examine the ideas critically (e.g., distinguish between fact and opinion; use other resources to verify facts)."

In contrast, curriculum documents from Quebec and the Atlantic provinces explicitly include critical literacy as a goal of language arts programs. The Quebec *English Language Arts Program of Study* (2001, p. 72) includes the following statement:

> The noted Brazilian educator, Paulo Freire, described literacy as knowing how to "Read the world and the word." This program is centred in the connection between the learner's world and words, since language is both a means of communicating feelings, ideas, value, beliefs and knowledge, as well as a medium that makes active participation in democratic life and a pluralistic culture possible.

A key feature in *Foundation for the Atlantic Canada English Language Arts Curriculum* (1996, p. 2) is an emphasis on the personal, social, and cultural contexts of language learning and the power that language has within these contexts. More specifically,

> This curriculum encourages students to recognize the power of language to define and shape knowledge, self and relational positions in society. This curriculum encourages students to explore how forms of language construct and are constructed by particular social, historical, political and economic contexts. It encourages students to understand how their own and others' uses of language have social effects.

Even at the primary level (*Atlantic Canada English Language Arts Curriculum: Grades K–3*, 1999), curriculum documents stress the need for children to recognize how texts construct our understandings of race, gender, class, age, ethnicity, and ability in order to give them the means to bring about social justice and democracy.

Although all Canadian curriculum documents value critical reading and/or critical literacy, they provide little information to help teachers plan critical literacy lessons for the classroom. That is the purpose of the remaining material on critical literacy presented in this chapter.

Lesson Framework for Informational Texts

For informational texts, Dillon (1997) suggests the following five steps:

1. *Problem posing.* The teacher begins with either children's questions or introduces mandatory topics in content subject areas by problematizing them. For example, Bigelow (1989) introduced a unit on the arrival of Columbus in the Americas by picking up one of his student's purses and claiming that he could keep it because he "discovered" it. The students protested but quickly saw the parallel, beginning their study of Columbus' discovery of the "New" World from the problems of who lands belong to and why, and what consequences exist today because of what happened.

2. *Research and reflection.* Students use information from two major sources to try to answer the questions posed—what they already know (through talking with each other or writing freely in learning journals), and information from external sources (e.g., books, Internet, encyclopedias, videos, other people, field trips).

3. *Sharing.* After children have collected information individually or in small groups, they share their insights. The purpose of this sharing is to help them probe more deeply into the nature of the problem. Dillon believes that this step is important because many children begin at the surface of a question but with time probe more deeply and redefine the problem. For example, after dealing with their initial questions, the children in Bigelow's class generated a new and more significant question. Why did school textbooks give only one whitewashed version of an event? Redefining the problem may lead to another cycle of problem posing, research and reflection, and sharing.

4. *Go public.* Presentations can take many forms—oral presentations, dramatizations, written reports, posters, media presentations, and photographs. This stage serves the following purposes:
   - Presentations often helps students discover more about what they were trying to say or write.
   - Learners join a community of other authors and knowers as well as the larger public discussion of ideas.
   - Presentations serves as prompts to other learners and other critical inquiries.

5. *Taking action.* Dillon believes that, while in many ways this is the most important step, it must be viewed as optional since only the learners can decide what action they feel ready to undertake. The students in Bigelow's class wrote to the publishers of social studies textbooks, pointing out the distortions in their material on Columbus' arrival in the Americas. Other students might feel comfortable only in changing their own behaviour in the classroom or school context. The taking-action step is important because it helps students feel that they have power to change things, to exert some control over their lives, and to make a difference. This sense of action, influence, and control is often referred to as empowerment.

Lessons with Narrative Texts

The following lesson framework for stories was adapted from guidelines presented by Dillon (1997) and from notions of perspective presented by Whitehead (2002).

1. *Analysis of text.* The children begin by talking about what they think the author meant. Instructional techniques presented in Chapter Five can be used to facilitate their construction of meaning in this step.

2. *Discussion.* The teacher guides the children in a discussion, encouraging them to interrogate the text by asking one or more of the following types of questions.
   - *Comparison.* What other stories or events are like this text?
   - *Clarification.* What would I have done in the place of a particular character in the story?
   - *Perspective.* What difference would it make if the main character were a (boy, girl, man, woman, person from a different culture, person with a disability, poor person, older person, younger person)?
   - *Issue.* What is the general issue I see in the story? (Several questions in Box 13.1 can be used to help children identify issues.) In what situations do I live this issue? What do we think regarding this issue? As children share their reflections, they attempt to reach a consensus but also acknowledge the diversity of views. The teacher might also share his or her view as one voice in the discussion.

Box 13.1   Questions to Interrogate Texts

- Who wrote this text?
- Why did the author write this text?
- What is the author's experience and expertise on this topic?
- What does the author have to gain from writing this text?
- What evidence supports what the author wrote?
- What do other authors write about this topic?
- Who benefits from this text?
- What voices are being heard?
- Whose voices are left out?
- Is there another point of view?
- How are the (girls, boys, women, men, mothers, fathers, grandmothers, grandfathers, etc.) portrayed in this text?
- What is this text saying about (boys and girls, men and women, the elderly, people from different cultures, people with a disability, people living in poverty)? Is this true for all members of this group?
- What difference would it have made if the main character were a (boy, girl, man, woman, person from a different culture, person with a disability)?
- What is the world like for people in the text?
- Which people have power in this text?
- Is this fair?
- What is the author's underlying message?
- Violence was used to deal with a problem in this text. What other ways could the problem have been solved?
- How has the author used language to position the reader?
- What are the design features of this text? Why were they included?
- What is the author's underlying message?
- Violence was used to deal with a problem in this text. What other ways could the problem have been solved?
- How has the author used language to position the reader?
- What are the design features of this text? Why were they included?

3. *Make decision/take action.* How will I behave differently? How could I try to change things?

There are two major goals of this type of teaching—first, awareness of an issue or problem, and second, new action or behaviour based on this awareness. The teacher's role is not to point out correct answers but to help children generate their own insights and decisions, and to try to decide on collective action for the common good. Dillon sees this as democracy in action.

Questions

The questions presented in Box 13.1 are designed to invite children to interrogate the assumptions embedded in texts as well as their own assumptions. These questions were gleaned from several sources (Leland, Harste, Ociepka, Lewison, and Vasquez, 1999; Luke and Freebody, 1997; Wason-Ellam, 2002; Wilson, 2002). Initially, teachers guide children in their thinking by presenting these questions during discussions. Eventually, the goal is for children to ask themselves these types of questions as they read and write.

Some of the questions in Box 13.1 are appropriate for children at all ages while others are more appropriate for children in the upper elementary grades. In addition, some questions are appropriate for both stories and informational texts while others are appropriate for only one of these types of texts.

Materials

Both informational and narrative texts can be interrogated by children. In relation to informational texts, social studies materials are particularly appropriate for this type of work. Edelsky (1994) writes about a teacher who has her fifth-grade students look at social studies materials on the Pilgrims and Indians and ask themselves the following questions:

- Who wrote this?
- Whose idea is it?
- Do you think this is the way Aboriginal people would tell it?
- Who benefits from this version of the story?
- How do they benefit from it?

In the Canadian context, books about such topics as the Riel rebellion and exploration of the West by the French and English can be critiqued in a similar way.

Although most narrative material can be used for critical literacy lessons, some educators have identified specific texts that are particularly appropriate for this use. Wason-Ellam (2002) calls these critically conscious stories; Lewison, Flint, and Sluys (2002) refer to them as social issues books; and Leland, Harste, Ociepka, Lewison, and Vasquez (1999) use the term *critical books*.

Leland, Harste, Ociepka, Lewison, and Vasquez (1999) developed the following criteria to identify critical books:

- They don't make difference invisible, but rather explore what differences *make a difference*.
- They enrich our understanding of history and life by giving voice to those who traditionally have been silenced or marginalized.
- They show how people can begin to take action on important social issues.
- They explore dominant systems of meaning that operate in our society to position people and groups of people.
- They don't provide "happily ever after" endings for complex social problems.

Leland, Harste, Ociepka, Lewison, and Vasquez (1999) assume that a diversity-and-difference model of education serves multilingual and multicultural societies (such as those in the United States and Canada) better than the conformity-and-consensus model that currently permeates education systems. In the Appendix, we list several children's books written by authors from different cultures for use with children in elementary classrooms. In Box 13.2, we present titles and brief descriptions of critical books that have been recommended by Wilson (2002), Lewison, Flint, and Sluys (2002), Wason-Ellam (2002), and Leland, Harste, Ociepka, Lewison, and Vasquez (1999) for critical literacy instruction.

Box 13.2 Books for Developing Critical Literacy

Brinkloe, J. (1988). *Playing marbles*. In this picture storybook, a young girl draws a circle to play marbles but two boys try to take over the circle.

Browne, A. (1998). *Voices in the park*. This story presents the perspectives of four different people in a park, e.g., one mother does not want her son to play with a girl who did not look like them.

Bunting, E. (1994. *A day's work*. This story stresses hard work and the desperation of and consequences for people who can't find work.

Bunting, E. (1991). *Fly away home*. This story is about a father and son living in an airport and trying to blend into the crowd because they are homeless.

Bunting, E. (1998). *Your move*. This picture storybook tells the story of two brothers aged six and ten who are tempted to join a gang.

Cowen-Fleetcher, J. (1994). *It takes a village*. This story deals with the communalism of African village life.

Fenner, F. (1991). *Randall's wall*. This is the story of a young boy who is ostracized by his classmates. He is unclean and smells because there is no running water in his home.

Fletcher, R. (1998). *Flying solo*. This chapter book tells what happens when a substitute teacher doesn't show up and the class runs the things by themselves. The story is told from the perspective of different students.

Hesse, K. (1998). *Just juice*. This chapter book tells the story from the point of view of a chronically truant nine-year-old child who stays at home with her unsuccessful father and pregnant mother.

Isadora, R. (1991). *At the crossroads*. This picture storybook provides a snapshot of day to day life in the black townships of South Africa.

Kaplan, W. (1998). *One more border: The true story of one family's escape from war-torn Europe*. This picture book (historical nonfiction) tells the story of a Jewish family that escaped from Europe to Canada during the late 1930s to avoid persecution.

Lorbiecki, M. (1998). *Sister Anne's hands*. This picture storybook relates the author's childhood experience of racial intolerance when a classmate sent a note with a racial slur to the teacher who was a black nun.

McGovern, A. (1997). *The lady in the box*. This story is about two children who develop a relationship with a homeless stranger.

McKee, D. (1987). *Tusk tusk*. In this picture storybook, all elephants were either white or black and they hated and fought each other. The peace-loving elephants hid in the jungle and when they emerged were all grey. They lived happily until they noticed they had different-sized ears and the story continues.

Munsch, R. (1980). *The paperbag princess*. This picture storybook presents the story of a princess who saves a prince from a dragon.

Myers, C. (2000). *Wings*. A new boy in school celebrates his difference despite ridicule from classmates and adults until one quiet girl befriends him.

Van Camp, R. (1998). *What's the most beautiful thing you know about horses?* The author is from the Northwest Territories and on a bitterly cold day stays inside and asks his family and friends to respond to the question in the title of this picture book. A range of answers set up possibilities to talk about stereotypes, ethnic differences, animal rights, and other issues.

Continued

Box 13.2 Books for Developing Critical Literacy *continued*

Waboose, J. B. (1997). *Morning on the lake*. This picture storybook presents a story of intergenerational love between an Ojibway boy and his grandfather.

Winthrop, E. (1985). *Tough Eddie*. This story is about a young boy who acts tough but has a secret—at home, his favourite toy is a dollhouse.

Woodson, J. (2001). *The other side*. This picture book tells a story of friendship across a racial divide and presents accurate and respectful images of individuals from two cultures.

Examples

Example 1: *Beauty and the Beast* (Mayer and Mayer, 1978)

Temple (1993, pp. 91–93) provides the following example of a critical literacy lesson with a group of second- and third-grade children. The teacher asked the following questions about *Beauty and the Beast* to help the children critically examine their assumptions about gender roles in society: Suppose Beauty had been kind and clever but not prettier than her sisters. Do you think the author is suggesting that we should be more like Beauty or more like her sisters? Suppose Beauty had been a boy in this story, and the Beast had been a girl.

As they discussed answers to these questions, the children dealt with issues such as the high value placed on outward appearance in our society, compared with inner qualities. One child said, "You don't judge people by how pretty they are. You judge them by how nice and kind and loving they are." The children also talked about how some of the time they themselves were like the "snotty" sisters and sometimes they were like Beauty, recognizing that there is good and bad in all of us. In relation to gender roles, one child summed it up with "What bugs me is that in the fairytales, the guys are always doing things outside, and the girls are just basking around in their beautiful dresses."

Example 2: *People* (Spier, 1980)

In another example, Finazzo (1997) presents a lesson using the book *People* to expose children to diversity among people around the world and to help them identify diversity in their own classroom. The lesson proceeds through the following steps:

- The teacher begins by having the children talk briefly about how they are all the same (e.g., they are all wearing clothing, they all have shoes on).
- The teacher then reads the book, and at the end asks the children to talk about what ways people in the world are alike. As the children share ideas, the teacher writes these similarities on a chart labelled *Alike*.
- Next, the children talk about differences, and the teacher writes these on another chart labelled *Different*.
- The teacher then asks the children to take off their shoes and put them in a pile. The children separate the shoes into different groups—shoes with laces, shoes with buckles, slip-on shoes, shoes with Velcro fasteners. Then they sort the shoes again by colour, and again by size.
- The same activity is repeated using other features for sorting—eye, hair, and skin colour, languages spoken at home, number of people in families. The children talk about the differences and similarities in the groups.
- The lesson ends by having the children create a collage from old magazines to illustrate diversity among people in the world.

Example 3: Mothers

Luke, Comber, and O'Brien (1996, cited in Cervetti, Pardales, and Damico, 2001) describe how one first-grade teacher utilized questions to help the children in her class learn to analyze how mothers are constructed in catalogues that sell Mother's Day gifts. The children read and interrogated catalogues with the help of the following questions (p. 7):

- How are the mothers in the catalogues like real mothers? How are they not?
- What mothers are not included in the catalogues?
- Who are the people giving presents to the mothers?
- Where do children get the money to buy presents?
- Who produces these catalogues?
- Why do catalogue producers go through all this trouble to make sure you know what is available?

After this critical examination, the children realized that the catalogues only represented a narrow aspect of mothers' lives—the part linked to consumerism. They then engaged in social action stemming from their new understandings. They realized that their mothers were not represented so they researched their mothers and other mothers in their community. They also reconceptualized what Mother's Day meant to them; the day is less about buying gifts and more about being with their mothers.

Example 4: *Rose Meets Mr. Wintergarten* (Graham, 1994)

Wilson (2002) shares several critical literacy lessons conducted with primary classes in Australia. The one selected for inclusion here involves a book entitled, *Rose Meets Mr. Wintergarten*. In this book, Rose's family moves next door to an elderly man. Rose's house is portrayed in the book as brightly coloured and a place where there is much happy activity. Mr. Wintergarten's house is grey, and the local children tell frightening stories about him. This all changes when Rose goes to retrieve her ball from Mr. Wintergarten's property.

The teacher guided the group of primary children through the following steps:

- The teacher read the story aloud to the children.
- The children responded in writing to the question, "In this story, what is life like for Mr. Wintergarten?" The children generated responses such as, "He was very sad because he had no friends" (p. 131).
- The teacher read the story a second time and asked the children to respond to the question, "Was it fair that Mr. Wintergarten lived as he did? The children provided responses such as, "It is not fair for Mr. Wintergarten because he is alone and doesn't have any friends" (p. 133).
- Finally, the children discussed the elderly people they knew by responding to the following types of questions: Did they live alone in dark houses? Is it true that all old people live alone and are grouchy?

Beyond Examples

The major goal of the examples provided in this section is to transform both the curriculum and children's thinking. According to Freire (1970), the development of critical awareness of inequities and injustice is the first step in social change. Much of this change will be situated at the classroom and school levels, with both teachers and children taking responsibility for change. For example, in relation to gender equity the following actions can be taken at the classroom level:

- Teachers ensure that learning materials are appropriate, representing the two genders fairly and equally so both boys and girls have appropriate role models.
- Learners of both genders are encouraged to be actively involved in the learning process.
- Teachers and children agree that stereotypical language referring to males and females is not acceptable in the classroom, and they are vigilant in their reading of other authors' work and in their own classroom interactions and writing to detect and exclude this type of language.

Overall, teachers and children create classroom contexts and school communities in which all children are valued regardless of gender, age, race, exceptionality, or class.

Issues and Challenges

One issue in critical literacy instruction relates to the wide range of diversity portrayed in children's literature, including differences in family structure, ethnicity, gender, age, exceptionalities, values, socioeconomic status, and ways of communicating. Although this literature provides opportunities for children to see both themselves and their families portrayed by authors, some parents feel uncomfortable when children are exposed to family structures and values different from their own. As indicated in Chapter Eleven, parents and community groups are challenging the use of some books in schools and even their availability in school libraries.

In addition to the question of censorship, a major challenge teachers face in work on critical literacy is what to do when a child's meaning is quite different from their own. Lewis (1993) describes the difficulty she had with one boy's response to "The Pelican and the Crane" (Lobel, 1980). In this fable, a pelican comes to tea at the crane's house and is very sloppy and wasteful, all the time wondering aloud why nobody ever invites him anywhere. At the end of the story, the pelican says he hopes he will be invited back. The crane says, "Perhaps, but I am so busy these days." The moral given by the author is, "When one is a social failure, the reasons are as clear as day." But Rick felt sorry for the pelican because he was a klutz and was critical of the crane for telling a lie. He generated a very different moral for the story, "Give people a chance." What would you do if you were Rick's teacher? Lewis attempted to persuade Rick of her meaning because she felt it was her responsibility to help him understand texts in ways that match the expectations of those in power. However, she had limited success and suggested that instead she should have legitimized Rick's interpretation by helping him compare his moral to that presented by Lobel, discussing how readers might interact with this text to arrive at different conclusions.

Teachers have also reported difficulty knowing how to respond when they overhear disparaging remarks made by students to peers such as, "I hate black people" (Lewison, Flint, and Sluys, 2002). Lewison, Flint, and Sluys suggest that the most appropriate response is to plan and conduct critical literacy lessons focused on racism. Teachers also have difficulty during critical literacy lessons when students respond in ways that are biased against those with less power. In one example presented by Lewison, Flint, and Sluys, a novice fifth-grade teacher read aloud the book *Randall's Wall* (Fenner, 1991) about a boy who is ostracized by his classmates because he is unclean due to no running water in his house. When asked what might happen if Randall joined their classroom, the students' responses were similar to those of the children in the story; they discussed not befriending Randall for fear of jeopardizing their status with peers. It took considerable discussion to help children begin to "understand how they are constructed by larger power structures" (Lewison, Flint, and Sluys, 2002, p. 387).

We are just beginning to figure out how to help children develop critical literacy in elementary classrooms. We know that children need to work in groups rather than individually, and that interrogating text is at the heart of this type of instruction. While critical thinking is important, however, the ultimate goal is taking action for social justice.

MEDIA LITERACY

In this section, we describe the range of media that children experience in their daily lives, and then present goals for instruction in using multimedia materials in language arts programs. We discuss some ways teachers use media as vehicles for instruction, and identify issues and challenges they face.

Children today are immersed in a multimedia world. Nearly all Canadian homes (99 percent) have at least one television set, and nearly two-thirds own more than one. Children between the ages of two and eleven years watch approximately 18 hours of television each week. U.S. data show that 68 percent of families with children between the ages of two and seventeen own video game equipment and that 57 percent of children have a TV and 39 percent have video game equipment in their bedrooms. While lower-income Americans are less likely to own a computer, their children are more likely to have a TV in their bedrooms and spend more time with media than their counterparts in higher income families (Media Awareness Network, www.media-awareness.ca/eng/issues/stats/index.htm).

Luke (1997) estimates that by the age of 18 years, the average child has watched 14 000 hours of TV as compared to spending 12 000 hours in school. Children are also surrounded with other media, including photography, recordings, radio, film, videotape, video games, computers, the performing arts, and virtual reality (Whipple, 1998). "From infancy, children are indeed immersed in the texts of popular culture, and their understanding of narrative, of good versus evil, of heroes and heroines, gender, race, and social power, is learned from those texts" (Luke, 1997). By the time they arrive at school, children have already well-established values and understandings learned from family, TV, and from the artifacts of popular culture they grew up with.

At the same time, children have more spending money today than ever before. In the 1950s, three or four children had to compete for whatever spending money one working parent chose to give them. In the 1990s, one or two children received funds from two working parents. Twenty-five percent of all prime-time and weekend daytime commercials advertise food, 50 percent of which is "junk" food (Ontario Media Literacy Homepage, www.angelfire.com/ms/MediaLiteracy/Demo.html). The average viewer sees some 20 000 advertisements on TV per year, and by age six, the average child has seen 14 000 violent on-screen images (Luke, 1997).

Stances to Media Literacy

There are at least three stances that parents and educators take toward media and popular culture—protection, pleasure, and preparation (Considine and Haley, 1999). Many parents and teachers, who grew up in a very different world, view television from the perspective of negative content and social consequences, and believe that children need protection from these effects. They view children as duped viewers who need to be emancipated from "bad habits" and "incorrect readings" (Luke, 1997). Parents who take this stance often censor their children's TV viewing, and teachers censor or denigrate TV talk in the classroom. Pedagogy becomes a tool against students' pleasure derived from TV and other popular culture.

The pleasure stance is often associated with areas such as music, drama, and art in schools. Some educators believe that the arts should be redefined to incorporate **media literacy**, including both viewing and media production. Others set pleasure as one of the goals of viewing and representing in language arts curricula.

Most educators take a preparation stance to media literacy. They believe that in addition to helping students construct or analyze information from media sources and develop appreciation of media presentations, we need to teach them the critical viewing, reading, and thinking skills that will help them to recognize textual distortion, resist manipulation, and generate alternatives to media messages. This critical analysis enables teachers and students to determine whether texts promote or subordinate people according to gender, race, class, culture, sexual preference, or some other criteria. Similar to critical interrogation of books, this kind of critique is motivated by values such as equality, democracy, and social justice (Semali, 2002).

Luke (1997, p. 25) concludes:

> Not to attend to these new cultural forms and texts, not to teach children the value and constructedness of our media and mediated understandings of how these texts structure experience, knowledge, and social relations, is pedagogically and politically irresponsible.

In concurrence with Luke, we suggest that media literacy be taught within a critical literacy framework.

Goals and Forms of Media Literacy

We believe that the goal of media literacy is to provide students with skills and strategies for dealing critically with the media and the role they play in their lives. Specifically, media literacy includes (Ontario Ministry of Education, 1989; Pailliotet, Semali, Rodenberg, Giles, and Macaul, 2000)

- the skills, knowledge, and attitudes necessary for interpreting the way media present reality,
- an appreciation and aesthetic understanding of media texts,
- the ability to identify and examine the cultural practices, values, and ideas contained in media texts,
- the ability to produce one's own multimedia texts,
- the analysis of media and popular texts from a critical perspective to engage students in personal transformation and growth as well as increased democratic and ethical actions in and out of the classroom.

There are three major types of media forms:

- *Electronic media.* Radio, television, film, CDs, DVDs, videos, telephones, computers, cameras, video games
- *Print media.* Newspapers, magazines, comics, interactive books, advertising, junk mail, travel brochures, posters, graffiti, electronic zines (a list of children's magazines is presented in Chapter 14)

- *Popular culture.* Stardom, celebrity-making, shopping malls, toys, clothing trends, fashion fads, fast food, theme parks, slang (Ontario Media Literacy Homepage, www.angelfire.com/ms/MediaLiteracy/Introduction.html)

This is not an exhaustive list, but it does provide some indication of the range of texts that can be used in media education.

Media Education in Canada

In 1987, Ontario was the first province to mandate the inclusion of media education in the curriculum. Media education became a mandatory component of English courses from Grades 7 to 12, and the *Media Literacy Resource Guide* was developed by the Ontario Ministry of Education (1989). During the 1990s, regions and provinces across Canada revised their language arts curriculum documents for elementary schools, and media education is strongly represented in these documents.

- The *Foundation for the Atlantic Canada English Language Arts Curriculum* (1996) identifies media literacy and visual literacy as essential components of English language arts programs.
- The *Western Canadian Protocol* (1997) acknowledges the importance of analysis and construction of media texts in outcomes for viewing and representing.
- The *Ontario Curriculum Grades 1–8 Language* (1997) includes media literacy in the Oral and Visual Communication strand. Outcomes include both analysis and creation of media works of many types.
- In its *English Language Arts Program of Study* (2001), the Quebec Ministry of Education includes media literacy as an integrated component, expanding the term *text* to include a wide range of media texts as well as popular texts such as comics, ads, and posters.

The Media Awareness Network, based in Ottawa, provides a more complete overview of media education in Canada with links to each province (www.media-awareness.ca/eng/med/bigpict/meinca.htm).

Media Literacy Instruction

Media literacy is not a body of knowledge or a skill but a way of thinking that is always evolving. To become media-literate is to raise questions about what we are watching, reading, listening to, writing, or developing into a media presentation. Some ways to develop media literacy follow.

Media Log

Quantitative analyses are often used in primary media education as a lead-in to other types of analysis. For example, children might be asked to note how much time they spend with varied media such as TV, music, computers, and video games. Students can also be asked to keep a record of the content viewed. Many are surprised at the content and how much time they spend in front of TV or computer screens. This type of analysis can lead to students setting time management goals based on the insights they gained from mapping their viewing habits (Pailliotet, Semali, Rodenberg, Giles, and Macaul, 2000).

Children might also be asked to count the number of times a product name appears in an advertisement to discuss the use of repetition and foregrounding to persuade a viewer/reader and to associate promises with the product name. Alternatively, children can count and list the number of superlatives in an advertisement to see how an "old" product reinvents itself by claiming to be new and improved (Luke, 1997).

Close Analysis

Media experiences go by so quickly that we rarely have time to reflect on them. The first step in this method is to isolate a particular media message and replay it several times. First, students write down everything they can about the visuals—lighting, camera angles, pacing, and uses of colour. Luke (1997) notes that the use of pinks, pastels, fade-ins, and slow pacing predominate in commercials aimed at females. In contrast, ads aimed at males use primary colours, quick jump shots, close-ups, and fast pacing. Shots of women commonly use a downward camera angle whereas those of males use upward angles to signify power and authority.

After students have analyzed the visuals, they are turned off and the sound track is played by itself. The students write down all the words that are spoken. Who says them? What kind of music is used? Are there other sounds? What purposes do they serve?

This type of analysis helps students notice what the media text is really saying underneath the surface—values expressed and unexpressed, lifestyles endorsed or rejected, how different people might react differently to it, and whether they accept the message of this media text and why (Thoman, 1999).

Deep Viewing

Watts Pailliotet (Watts Pailliotet, Semali, Rodenberg, Giles, and Macaul, 2000) has identified the following six areas for deep viewing:

- *Action/sequence*. What happens? When and for how long?
- *Forms*. What objects are seen? What are their characteristics?
- *Actors/words*. What is said and by whom? How is it said and heard?
- *Closeness/distance*. What types of movement occur?
- *Culture/context*. To whom might this text be targeted? What symbols do you notice? What do they mean to you? What might they mean to others?
- *Effects/process*. What is seen? What is missing? What is the quality?

Watts Pailliotet recommends teaching each of the areas in turn and then dividing a class into groups. The teacher distributes six different coloured cards to each student, each displaying one of the six viewing characteristics and related questions. As the students view a media text, the teacher pauses two or three times and invites students to hold up cards that reflect the elements of viewing they experience in each segment. One student serves as the recorder for each group and they write group members' observations and interpretations on a deep viewing guide. These are then shared with the whole class for discussion. The teacher focuses the discussion by asking questions such as:

- What impact does the ad/Web site have on you and why?
- Which effects influenced you the most and why?
- How do you know this ad/Web site is credible?
- Is this something we want people to value?
- What more do you want to know about this ad/Web site?

After viewing more and less effective ads and Web sites, students create their own media productions.

Action Learning

Thoman (1999) recommends the following model for developing a spiral of inquiry that leads to increased comprehension, critical thinking, informed judgment, and action and advocacy. It is a four-step process.

Awareness. The students engage in an activity designed to lead them to the insight, "Oh, I never thought of that before." For example, they might count the number of violent incidents in a children's cartoon or imitate various stances of female models in fashion ads and magazines.

Analysis. The teacher asks questions to guide a discussion of how the construction of any media text contributes to the meaning we make of it. Thoman recommends using how and what rather than why questions to encourage deep analysis. For example:

- How does the camera angle make us feel about the product being advertised?
- What difference would it make if the car in the ad were blue instead of red?
- What do we know about a character from her dress, makeup, and jewellery?
- How does the music contribute to the mood of the story being told?

Reflection. In this step, students look deeper to ask, "So what?" and "What ought we to do?" Students might want to consider ethical values or democratic principles when reflecting on the message they construct from a media text. For example, they might consider how groups based on disability, gender, nationality, or racial identity are stereotyped, marginalized, or excluded.

Action. Students decide on possible actions, which range from examining media texts differently in the future (internal change) to sending an email to a company questioning the messages implied by their ad or Web site.

Intertextual Instruction

Teachers are becoming increasingly aware of the way media can complement conventional literacy instruction (Flood, Heath, and Lapp, 1997). Hobbs (1997, p. 8) points out that "Many educators have discovered that the analysis of contemporary media can build skills that transfer to students' work with the written word." In her research, Mackey (2002) found that students who move daily between print and other media use similar strategies to read in both.

Whipple (1998) has demonstrated how rich intertextual connections can be when woven between literature and film. He argues that students are often much more familiar with the film/video **genre** because of its pervasiveness and are often more comfortable responding to it. In addition, says Whipple, by using both print and film, teachers can invite many students who are considered "at risk" in predominantly print learning environments to participate in classroom discourse, to become part of the classroom learning community, and to be validated as learners and people. Students learn to read actors' body and language expressions and the details of setting and action, and they draw on background knowledge to anticipate and judge the events as they unfold.

Luke (1997) also writes about media literacy as providing an opportunity to use the texts that children are familiar with in order to move them toward print-based literacy. She feels that students labelled reluctant readers might be transformed into active participants by giving them access to a medium in which they are experts, one for which they have a significant amount of prior knowledge.

Issues and Challenges

Whipple argues that either we can become resentful and reject the pervasive influence of children's home viewing habits and practices or "we can look upon them as an opportunity to support literacy development and to make connections with more traditional media (i.e., written text)" (1998, p. 146). That said, a major challenge for teachers rests on how learning about and with media can be fit into an already overcrowded curriculum.

Another challenge for teachers involves changing a long-held belief by many that TV and popular culture are "low" culture. Luke (1997) recommends that teachers become familiar with texts from youth culture (e.g., video games, TV programs) prior to bringing them into the classroom. Even then, students may view any attempt to bring popular culture into the school as co-opting what they value most about such culture, its marginality (Alvermann and Hagood, 2000). Asking students to critique TV shows or other popular culture in the public forum of the classroom often involves children giving the teacher what they think he or she wants (a negative response to the text) rather than what is going on in their heads. This is more true of middle-class than working-class children who often resist the teacher's critical interpretations of media texts.

One way to partially deal with this challenge is to focus critical interrogation on school texts as well as popular culture and media texts. Another is to take seriously and acknowledge the different meanings students construct and the pleasure they derive from popular culture and media texts while guarding against slipping into a "vacuous celebration of individual taste, pleasure, or personal responses" (Luke, 1997, p. 46).

A final challenge for teachers who incorporate media into their instructional program rests on how their students' learning growth can be assessed. Although many provincial and local school authorities advocate integrating media literacy into the curriculum, few acknowledge students' achievement in viewing and representing. Large-scale provincial achievement tests still focus on measuring the traditional language arts skills of reading and writing. Even when students are asked to view and respond to a video, the "required responses" are evaluated according to fairly conventional criteria (Hobbs, 1997). Similarly, very few school districts provide space to report children's learning growth in media literacy.

TECHNOLOGICAL LITERACY

In this section we focus on communication and information technology and, because of what is currently happening in schools, we deal almost exclusively with computers.

In the latter part of the 20th century, our society developed a strong belief in technology. People envisioned and anticipated the "good life" with technology at its core: a computer on every desk, a diminishing need for writing abilities, everything they needed at the touch of a button. In spite of the fact that this vision has not materialized, computers are still viewed by many people as being "synonymous with human progress" (Postman, 1992, p. 12).

In reality, computers have not revolutionized schools to the extent that many people predicted (Anderson and Speck, 2001). Nor is there solid research evidence to support the effectiveness of technology-based instruction. However, there is a small body of research to support the utility of word processing and the Internet for writing (Baker, 2000), and hypertext and the addition of speech to print on computers for reading (National Reading Panel, 2000).

In light of this growing evidence, the International Reading Association produced a position statement in 2002 supporting the integration of information and communication technology (ICT) into the curriculum. "To become fully literate in today's world, students must become proficient in the new literacies of ICT" (International Reading Association, 2002, p. 1). This position statement also supports assessment practices that include the Internet and word processing, as well as equal access to ICT.

The Role of Computers in Education

In 1980, Taylor proposed a framework for understanding the application of computers in education. He suggested that the computer can could function in one of three modes: as tutor, as tool, and as tutee. As tutor, the computer is used to monitor student learning and provide practice, taking the role of instructor. As tool, the computer functions as an assistant, helping with handling and creating information. And as tutee, the computer takes the role of learner, where children are given opportunities to program and solve problems through their own directions to the computer.

More recently, these functions were reconceptualized by Jonassen (1996), who writes about the differences among learning *from* computers, learning *about* computers, and learning *with* computers. He maintains that, during the 1970s and 1980s, educators mainly saw "learning from" (computer-assisted instruction) and "learning about" (computer literacy) as possibilities for computer use in the classroom. Courses in computer-assisted instruction and computer literacy abounded. Yet, as Jonassen points out, we do not necessarily need to know about the computer in order to use one in our daily lives. In response, educators have moved beyond courses *about* the computer to learning *with* computers.

Jonassen and other educators (such as Reinking, 1997, and Leu, Karchmer, and Leu, 1999) are at the forefront of a move toward encouraging teachers to work with computers as cognitive tools—what Jonassen (1996) calls "mindtools"—in the classroom. Jonassen defines these as "computer-based tools and learning environments that have been adapted or developed to function as intellectual partners with the learner in order to engage and facilitate critical thinking and higher order learning" (p. 9). Mindtools include spreadsheets, databases, semantic networks, expert systems, computer conferencing, computer programming, microworld learning environments, and multimedia and **hypermedia** construction. These tools can

- provide a scaffold for meaningful thinking,
- assist children in recognizing and setting purposes for learning,
- aid children in asking questions,
- assist learners in finding information,
- help learners analyze and organize what they have learned, and
- assist learners in representing and revising their new and emerging understandings.

These computer tools "actively engage learners in the creation of knowledge that reflects their comprehension and conception of the information rather than focusing on the presentation of objective knowledge" (Jonassen, 1996, p. 10).

An example of a software program that provides children with a mindtool is Kidspiration for younger children (K to Grade 5) and Inspiration for older students. Kidspiration provides children with tools to

- brainstorm ideas with pictures and words,
- organize and categorize information visually,
- create stories and descriptions using visual tools, and
- explore new ideas with though webs and visual mapping.

Both Kidspiration and Inspiration are designed to help children organize information, understand concepts, and express their thoughts in language arts, social studies, and science.

Before moving to the next section, spend a few minutes thinking about what roles computers have played in your own learning. How did your teachers use computers when you were in school, and was there any difference when you attended university courses on computers? Although we recognize that learners are at different points in their knowledge and facility with computers, we believe that the major focus in language arts classrooms should be on learning *with*, rather than *about* and *from*, computers.

The Canadian Context

Although not all provinces and territories have developed curriculum documents on information and communication technologies at the elementary level, those that have use a model of integration into other areas of the school curriculum rather than mandating stand-alone courses. In Quebec, for example, the program of studies includes ICT as a cross-curricular competency (*English Language Arts Program of Study*, 2001). Similarly, Nova Scotia (Nova Scotia Department of Education and Culture, 1999) recommends that information technology be integrated into the school curriculum. Nova Scotia's vision statement identifies learning outcomes for five components of IT:

- basic operations and concepts,
- productivity tools and software,
- communications technology,
- research, problem solving, and decision making, and
- social, ethical, and human issues.

In Alberta, the ICT curriculum is designed to be infused within core courses and programs. The goal is to prepare students to use ICT in effective, efficient, and ethical ways. Outcomes are organized around three interrelated categories (Alberta Learning, 2000–2003, pp. 1–2):

- communicating, inquiring, decision making, and problem solving (ability to use a variety of processes to critically assess information, manage inquiry, solve problems, do research, and communicate with a variety of audiences),
- foundational operations, knowledge, and concepts (understanding the nature and effect of technology, the moral and ethical use of technology, safety issues, and basic computer, telecommunication, and multimedia technology operations), and
- processes for productivity (ability to use a variety of productivity tools for text composition, data organization, graphical, audio, and multimedia composition and manipulation, and electronic communication, navigation, and collaboration)

In material presented in the remainder of this chapter, we recognize the full range of outcomes included in curriculum documents, and frame our suggestions for teaching information and communication technology within both social constructivist and critical literacy perspectives.

Learning with Computers

A major way that students learn *with* computers is by using them for productivity. From reading, writing, spelling, charting ideas, using and creating databases, and working with spreadsheets, to importing clip art and audio recordings into a presentation and using the Internet to access information, technological production tools lend themselves to enhancing students' language learning. Although databases, **hypertext**, and hypermedia are often thought of as primarily productivity tools, they also have the potential to be used for problem solving and higher-level thinking.

In order for students to learn *with* computers, however, they need to learn some basics about how to use a computer. Some of these basics include:

Teacher with children at a computer.

- using keyboarding skills
- applying basic computer operations (such as saving to a disk, clicking on an icon, using and organizing files)
- applying safety procedures
- uploading and downloading text and graphics

As students master such features as word wrapping, moving paragraphs, deleting words or sentences, and spell-checking, they save time and reduce effort, which provides extra time for them to think about content (Sharp, 1999).

An important concern for teachers is when and how keyboarding skills should be taught. Many children who have no developed typing skills waste a great deal of time using the two-finger hunt-and-peck method. Most educators agree that children do need to be taught keyboarding skills, using either computer programs designed for this purpose or more traditional teaching techniques. We recommend that keyboarding be taught as soon as children are using word processors to compose on a more or less frequent basis.

Word Processing

One of the most common ways computers serve as production tools in elementary language arts classrooms is in word processing. Children use word-processing technology to compose, revise, edit, and print a wide variety of written compositions, including:

- creative writing
- reports across the curriculum
- journal entries and letters to authors
- class or school newspapers
- invitations and programs for school events

It is difficult to recommend specific word processing programs for use in elementary classrooms, because new computing technology and programs are constantly emerging. With this in mind, we provide a sampling of currently available programs in Table 13.2. Children are most commonly introduced to word processing around Grades 2 and 3, although some word processing programs (such as KidWorks Deluxe) are available for younger children.

Table 13.2 Word Processing Programs for Elementary Students

Title/Platform	Level	Features
AppleWorks 6.2 (Windows/Mac)	Ages 9 and up	• Contains six applications—word processing, spreadsheet, page layout, database, painting, and presentations. • The word processor has file, edit, format, and spell-check features. • AppleWorks makes it possible to incorporate text, spreadsheets, digital photos, images, sounds, and movies into a single document. • The word processor allows the user to import text and graphics from other software programs into the text being created and to export texts, graphs, database, and graphics created with AppleWorks into a presentation program such as Hyperstudio.
Student Writing Center (Windows/Mac)	Grades 4 to 9	• The program emphasizes a writing process approach as well as writing across the curriculum. • Supports the stages of writing through prewriting, drafting, revising, editing, and publishing. • Templates allow students and teachers to create different types of documents including reports, newsletters, journals, letters, and signs • Special borders, clip art, and letterhead choices add detail and interest to documents. • Includes automatic bibliography creator, title page maker, footnotes, and endnotes.
Storybook Weaver Deluxe 2.0 (Windows/Mac)	Grades K to 8	• Allows children to create, write, and publish their own illustrated stories by placing, moving, and sizing pictures on the screen. • Children choose borders and text colour and select from hundreds of colourful graphics or use a scanner to copy their own photos into the story. • They may also select from a range of sound effects and music. • Once the scene is set, children write the story at the bottom of the screen in either English or Spanish. • The story can be edited and printed. • There is a modified spell-checker and a text-to-speech feature to allow children to hear their stories read aloud.
KidWorks Deluxe (Windows/Mac)	Ages 4 to 9	• Includes both a word processor and a paint program. • Optional features include sending and receiving stories on the Internet and accessing online help. • Children can change font, size, style and colour, spread the story across multiple pages, and add stickers and sound effects. • The program is able to read the story the children have written or they can record it themselves. • The paint feature includes drawing, filling in shapes, adding backgrounds, adding words, stickers, animated stickers and sound effects. • Stories and multimedia presentations can be saved, printed, or sent via email.

Continued

Table 13.2 Word Processing Programs for Elementary Students *continued*

Title/Platform	Level	Features
Kid's Media Magic 2.0 (Windows/Mac)	Grades K to 4	• Includes word processing, rebus writing, and multimedia. • Hundreds of words with visual and auditory clues are provided. • Has an integrated paint program. • Children can illustrate their presentations with thousands of photos, graphics, movies, and sounds. • Features a rebus writer and text anticipator. • Includes spell-check, thesaurus, text-to-speech, record sound, and unique shape book publishing options.

Databases and Spreadsheets

Students and teachers use databases to collect, organize, retrieve, and analyze information. These tools are especially useful when students are dealing with large amounts of information.

Databases. A database is a collection of data or information stored in a computer. It helps students sort information by fields and categories, providing a structure so that information can be manipulated and patterns or relationships noted.

To use database applications on the computer, children must be familiar with the concept of a database. This is most easily explained through examples children encounter in their own lives. The library catalogue is such an example. Computerized police records are another example that children see in movies and on television shows. Stolen vehicles, for example, are listed in a database that can be accessed immediately by the police if someone sees and reports an abandoned vehicle on the street.

Every database has a structure, a way in which it is organized to allow for the rapid retrieval of the information it contains. The structure includes file names, field headings, and data strings. Sorting information is an important function of a database. Information can be arranged alphabetically, numerically, or in chronological order. Fields can be sorted alphabetically from A to Z or from Z to A. If the fields are numeric, they can be arranged in the order of magnitude, from lowest to highest or highest to lowest. They can also be arranged according to date and time. Database programs also allow for changing and updating data as well as for adding and deleting information in the file. In some classrooms, children develop a database related to the books they read during the year. By sorting the database, students are able to find out how many students selected certain authors or topics. At the elementary level, some teachers set up the database and children use it to learn to make predictions, gather data, and input their own data.

According to Sharp (1999, p. 105), "a database is a perfect tool for teaching higher level critical thinking skills such as the ability to hypothesize, draw inferences, and use Boolean logic." Sharp goes on to explain that in addition to helping students develop higher-level thinking skills, databases support student learning of content material in any area of the curriculum. Once children have accessed information, they can reorganize it and make comparisons, developing new insights from this reorganization. The power of the database for inquiry lies in the ways it helps students to engage in creative thinking, predicting, and making generalizations and comparisons. It will only reach this potential, however, if the teacher asks the kinds of questions that develop this type of thinking.

A wide selection of database programs is available on the market, with varying prices and capabilities. Some are separate programs, while others are integrated with capabilities such as telecommunication, charting, word processing, and spreadsheet. Some examples of integrated software programs that are appropriate for elementary classroom use are AppleWorks, ClarisWorks for Kids, and Microsoft Works.

Spreadsheets. Spreadsheets are composed of numbered rows and lettered columns that intersect to form cells. They allow one to use numbers, letters, or a combination in the cells and are used to organize numeric information. The spreadsheet software calculates, sorts, and creates graphs.

Teachers and students use spreadsheets to analyze, graph, and compare and contrast data, and to predict or infer solutions to a problem (Anderson and Speck, 2001). For example, elementary children are capable of creating their own surveys, collecting data, and organizing it on spreadsheets. In relation to media literacy, they can keep track of how long they spend watching TV, playing video games, reading comic books, doing homework, or reading books. This information can be recorded on a spreadsheet and then converted to a bar graph, a particularly useful tool for making comparisons.

Most spreadsheet programs are capable of producing three types of graphs and charts—line graphs, bar graphs, and pie charts.

- Line graphs are most effective for displaying trends or continuous information over time, for example the amount of rainfall in inches that fell over a year.
- Bar graphs do not display continuous data well but instead are most useful for comparisons such as the one described above.
- Pie charts effectively display percentages (Anderson and Speck, 2001).

As with databases, most spreadsheets used in schools are part of integrated software programs such as AppleWorks and Microsoft Works. Spreadsheets are used more commonly in mathematics, social studies, and science than in language arts education.

Multimedia

In the 1970s and 1980s, the term *multimedia* was used to refer to technological combinations such as slide–tape presentations and interactive video. Today, the term refers to the integration of media such as sound, text, graphics, animation, and full-motion video into a single computer system. It is a computer-based method of presenting information in an interactive mode. The sophistication of current personal computers has made it possible for people to become publishers, artists, and video producers themselves (Jonassen, 1996). Children in school today belong to a "video generation" and are more apt to engage with multimedia presentations than with a single medium such as text.

According to Pan and Zbikowski (1997), multimedia applications and artificial speech technology make writing more appealing to students, enabling them to incorporate sound, drawing, video, and pictures in their compositions. In particular, synthetic speech can be a very stimulating way of adding dialogue between writer and audience and can serve to reduce inhibitions about beginning to write. As well, by composing with media other than text, students can learn to become more critical users of media in their everyday lives.

With multimedia resources and publication of students' work, young authors can now engage their readers through all the senses (Pan and Zbikowski, 1997). Because this allows for presenting information in a nonlinear, interactive way, students are able to develop a greater sense of the interconnectedness of different kinds of information. This helps them organize complex information in many media from different sources according to a particular theme. Galloway (1994) found that when students used the multimedia video tool QuickTime in writing compositions, their motivation and interest in the task increased.

Kevin Tok, a Grade 6 student at Sacred Heart School in Edmonton, created and presented a futuristic creation myth using PowerPoint presentation software. He downloaded background music from the Web (theme music from *Star Wars* and *2001: A Space Odyssey*), as well as animated cartoon characters, clip art, and graphics that he incorporated into his presentation. As he presented his story to the class, he "built" his story by having the text "fly in" from various sides of the screen, and the text was superimposed against a background of space scenes that he downloaded from the NASA Web site. His classmates were able to view Kevin's presentation on the large-screen monitor permanently mounted at the front of the classroom. Two pages from this presentation are presented in Exhibit 13.1.

Exhibit 13.1 A Grade 6 Child's PowerPoint Presentation

How the Universe Was Formed

By Kevin Tok

Aldaris returned to his creator giving him all the elements. "Well done Aldaris, " he said to Aldaris. Zel'naga absorbed the elements and created a black hole which brought comets, meteoroids and asteroids. He made them collide and create planets. He called the Fire God to merge his best stars to form the sun. He found a planet made from pure rock and made a comet to hit earth to create water and plants so that life could be there. All the planets were in the Sun's gravity which kept them balanced. Other planets and pieces went on beyond the stars. As the first animals and humans arrived on earth, new life began on Earth.

Hypertext and Hypermedia

Most of the electronic books and multimedia packages listed in this chapter use **hypertext**. Unlike conventional printed text, which is linear and read from beginning to end, in hypertext, text, images, sound, and actions are linked in nonsequential associations that allow the reader to go through a topic in any order (Sharp, 1999). As Jonassen (1996, p. 188) says:

Hypertext is super-text because the reader has much greater control of what is read and the sequence in which it is read. It is based on the assumption that the organization the reader imposes on a text is more personally meaningful than that imposed by the author.

The organization of hypertext is usually achieved through links, or "hot buttons," on which the reader clicks and is connected to yet another chunk of text. The use of computer word-processing systems and the Internet have made most learners familiar with the use of hypertext. Hypertext allows the reader to control the sequence in which information is accessed as well as the speed with which it is accessed.

Hypermedia is simply the combination of hypertext with multimedia systems. Hypermedia is computer software that is used to organize various types of multimedia information (such as sound, graphics, text, video, and animation) into a system so that the information can be accessed, retrieved, and modified easily (Wilhelm, Friedemann, and Erickson, 1998). Like hypertext, the different forms of information are linked together so that a user can move from one form to another in a nonlinear mode. Hypermedia components range from sound-enhanced documents that can be used on any computer to "stacks" (such as HyperStudio, described below) that carry sound, animation, and colour (Sharp, 1999).

Jonassen (1996) suggests that the most effective way to use hypertext in the classroom is to have learners create their own hypertexts that reflect their personal understandings and perspectives. There are a number of powerful commercial software packages for producing hypermedia presentations. Three of those that have been developed for use by children are described in Table 13.3.

Table 13.3	Hypermedia Presentation Software for Children	
Title/Platform	**Level**	**Features**
Hyperstudio 4.0 (Mac/Windows) www.hyperstudio.com	Ages 9 to adult	• Provides the basics of multimedia in an easy-to-learn and flexible environment. • Features drag-and-drop technology. • Provides an extensive media library of background layouts, scrolling text, clip art, animation, and/or sound created or selected by the student. • Material from other software programs installed on the computer, such as AppleWorks, can be imported. • Graphs, maps, graphics, photos, data cards, video clips, sound bites, diagrams, and text from the Internet and from many CDs can be imported. • Provides a morph tool to create special effects and images.
MicroWorlds 2.0 (Windows/Mac) www.microworlds.com	Grades 2 and up	• Has drag-and-drop technology for music, pictures, videos, Web pages, shapes, sounds, and QuickTime VR. • Includes drawing tools. • Enlarges and shrinks shapes. • Displays MicroWorlds projects on the Web. • Provides a Web Player for Internet browsers. • Macintosh projects can be transferred to Windows and vice versa.

Continued

Table 13.3 Hypermedia Presentation Software for Children. *continued*

Title/Platform	Level	Features
Leonardo's Multimedia Toolbox, V2 (Windows/Mac) www.leo.nec.com	Grades 4 to 12	• Customizable toolsets include animation, sound and video editing, spreadsheets, and charting. • Captures Internet content and embeds live Web sites within projects. • Provides hyperlink buttons for building interactive projects. • Provides over 300 interactive project templates, art and sound clips, and rubber stamp sets. • Features special music composition and mathematics tools.

Elementary school children have created HyperStudio presentations on myriad topics, from ancient Greece to space travel and ecology. A research project (Ver Velde, Knight, and Shushok, 1997) conducted in a school in Arizona examined the learning of kindergarten/Grade 1 children (through a unit on weather) and Grade 6 children (through a unit on careers). The project was designed to determine whether this tool brought about children's learning, or alternatively, whether it was simply a means for children to show what they had already learned. While all the children completed writing assignments throughout the respective unit, it was the students who also created a multimedia presentation through HyperStudio who clearly showed a better grasp of the subject. Children deemed "at risk" seemed especially successful in enriching their HyperStudio stacks with detailed content and information.

As with databases, a considerable amount of decision making is involved in developing hypermedia presentations. Student-created hypermedia, according to Wilhelm, Friedemann, and Erickson (1998, p. 15), "encourages students to name themselves as readers, writers, and learners and supports them in the achievement of better reading, idea development, sense of audience, classifying, organizing, collaborating, representing understandings, revising, and articulating and applying critical standards about the quality of work." And as with all software, it is how hypermedia is used in the classroom that will determine whether children go beyond productivity to inquiry in their learning.

Myers and Beach (2001) provide a pedagogical frame for helping children use hypermedia to engage in critical inquiry into how words, symbols, and actions construct our social worlds. This frame involves the following six recursive inquiry strategies:

1. *Immersing.* Students use hypermedia software to collect and link images and texts related to a specific aspect of their social world, for example, those of adolescent females scanned from magazines and ads.

2. *Identifying.* Students identify concerns, issues, and dilemmas, for example identifying how magazines portray females to achieve the purposes of the beauty industry.

3. *Contextualizing.* By pulling images out of their original context and recontextualizing them through hypermedia, students develop further awareness of the issue, for example, how magazine images position adolescent females in relation to commercialism and consumerism.

4. *Representing.* Students use hypermedia to present their own beliefs or to explain how texts are used to achieve certain purposes.

5. *Critiquing.* Students analyze how literacy practices promote certain meanings while marginalizing other possibilities. This is often accomplished by juxtaposing texts to create a critique of opposing values and identities.

6. *Transforming.* This involves changing one's actions and words to construct more desirable identities, relationships, and values.

Electronic Books

The major focus in our description to this point has been on having children use computer software to create and represent ideas. However, materials produced by hypertext and hypermedia also have the potential to maximize the constructive and creative dimensions of reading. This is where electronic books come in.

An *electronic book* is a piece of software that has many features similar to those of a traditional book. The major difference is that the electronic book is accessed by a computer. Anderson-Inman and Horney (1999) provide the following general guidelines as to what may be considered an electronic book:

- It has an electronic text, and the text is visually presented to the reader.
- The software adopts the metaphor of a book in a significant way. For example, there may be a table of contents, and the information screens are referred to as "pages." Bookmarks may also be inserted.
- The visual text is primary, and any other media are used mainly to support the text.

Children are able to access electronic books that incorporate a range of multimedia enhancements. Thus, in addition to reading the text, children interact with illustrations, graphics, and animations. It is also becoming common for electronic books to have embedded speech, either pronunciations of individual words or spoken versions of the whole text. Overall, these enhancements can make the text more comprehensible and enriching for readers at all levels of expertise.

Some electronic books published on CD-ROMs (such as encyclopedias) are primarily for reference, while others have a strong pedagogical or instructional nature. This latter group of books is designed to support the needs of a variety of readers. For example, books by key historical writers may contain links that describe the sociocultural context in which the texts were written, while additional links may explicate literary devices or provide interpretations of difficult passages. Some are designed to support learning and studying by providing a large-scale network of graphics, related documents, video, and sound. Finally, some electronic books are intended simply for entertainment, and the feature links are designed to enhance the reader's enjoyment. As with any classroom reading, it is contingent upon the teacher to guide students toward reading experiences that will help them achieve the teacher's and the students' reading goals. A brief overview of selected electronic books on CD-ROM is presented in Table 13.4.

One concern about computerized books is that the audiovisual effects and other options may distract children from the actual text. Another concern is that children will listen to the stories and engage in little, if any, reading themselves. A major disadvantage of electronic books on CD-ROM is that they cannot be read without a computer with a CD-ROM drive and a relatively sophisticated operating system (Anderson-Inman and Horney, 1999). Still, electronic books have three advantages over traditional formats. First, they are searchable, meaning that the user can easily track down information simply by entering key words or phrases into the computer's Find function. This is particularly helpful when students are searching for information in a large document, such as a CD-ROM encyclopedia.

Table 13.4 Selected Electronic Books on CD-ROM

Title/Platform	Level	Features
Encarta Encyclopedia 98 (CD-ROM for Windows and Mac)	Ages 9 to 12	• Interactive, full-range encyclopedia. • Allows students to access information through a book of contents, an index, information arranged by categories, and a find feature. • An outline feature is available. • There are photographs, animation, QuickTime movies, sound maps, and diagrams to elaborate the text. • Graphics and text can be imported into word processing and presentation programs. • Text and graphics can be printed.
World Book Encyclopedia (CD-ROM and Internet; Windows/Mac) www.worldbook.com	Ages 10 to adult	• A partial list of features include videos, maps, simulations, animations, photos, and sound. • The texts are enabled and "Homework Wizards" provide support and guidance. • Internet pages are devoted to both student learning and teacher resources. • Students can access the World Book archives as well as linking to thousand of related Web sites.
Discis Books (CD-ROM for Windows/Mac) www.discis.com	Ages 4 to 12	• This series contains several titles by Canadian author R. Munsch, including *The Paperbag Princess*. • The text is read aloud with phrases highlighted as they are read. • Music accompanies the reading and pages turn automatically or with the mouse. • The child can click on pictures or words which are then named.
Living Books Series (CD-ROM for Windows/Mac) www.kidsclick.com/living_books.htm	Ages 4 to 8	• Features animated stories and poetry. • Children have a choice of having the text read to them with accompanying animations and sound effects *or* playing in the story, whereby they animate illustrations with a click of the mouse.
WiggleWorks (CD-ROM for Windows/Mac) teacher.scholastic.com/readingprograms/wiggleworks	Kindergarten to Grade 3	• This is a multimedia literacy program referred to as the "Scholastic Beginning Literacy System." • There are three levels within each grade and each grade has 24 books on disk or CD-ROM. • The series also includes children's books, teacher's guides, audiotapes, an assessment package, and other support materials. • For each electronic book, children can (1) have the book read to them, (2) read and request help with words, (3) modify the pictures and text and print their modified book, (4) write their own story. • A magnetic board is available for word building and children can develop a personal word list to serve as a writing resource • There is a built-in management system for teachers.

Second, electronic books are modifiable, meaning that a reader can change and adapt their font size and format as needed. This feature is particularly useful for students who have visual problems. Readers can also often choose a preferred language, as many electronic books come in more than one language. Other electronic books allow the reader to add personal notes and images and to annotate the text.

The third main advantage of electronic books is that they are enhanceable, which means that the student or teacher may add resources to them to enhance text processing and comprehension. Thus, the reader may also access embedded definitions, explanations, and pictures designed to enhance meaning construction or extend understanding.

Evaluating Computer Software

We provide both general guidelines and a detailed checklist to help teachers evaluate computer software.

In the early stages of the development of software intended to enhance reading and writing abilities, much of the material produced had the appearance of worksheets. Hall and Martin (1999) point out that most educational software still focuses on drill and practice exercises, mainly because such software is relatively easy to implement and manage in the classroom. In addition, choices of software are often not made by teachers but by people outside the classroom, and such choices are often dictated by cost and based on a limited knowledge of which software is appropriate for classroom use.

In our view, it is teachers who need to make choices about software, yet the steady stream of new educational programs constantly challenges them to make instructional decisions about which software best supports their literacy program. When teachers are asked to make decisions about software, they often have only very sketchy criteria for making the most productive decisions.

Hall and Martin (1999) provide general guidelines that busy teachers may use for appraising educational software. They suggest that teachers examine the software to determine whether

- it has clear objectives,
- the implied objectives are appropriate,
- it is age-appropriate,
- it has supportive graphics and supportive text,
- it provides immediate feedback and encourages cooperative learning and critical thinking,
- it provides authentic scenarios and is easily integrated,
- the student maintains control, and
- it is accessible to special populations and represents the diversity of society.

Shade (1996, p. 18) provides this general guideline for teachers who are trying to make appropriate software choices: "Avoid drill-and-practice software. Look for software that allows the child to make decisions about what she wants to do and which she can operate with little help." In other words, select software that focuses on helping children learn *with* rather than *from* computers. Shade also cautions teachers to: "Avoid large, integrated learning systems. Look for software that allows the child to set the pace and stop anytime, experiment, operate from a picture menu, and control the interaction" (p. 19).

Shade suggests that a useful checklist of software can be grouped according to child, teacher, and technical features. These features have been adapted for the checklist presented in Table 13.5. Another useful reference for teachers is Reading Online (www.

readingonline.org/home.html), which has a section devoted to reviews—often done by classroom teachers—of current software. Overall, the most important consideration when selecting computer software still remains the needs of learners.

Table 13.5 Educational Software Review

Title:

Publisher:

Intended ages:

(A = Acceptable   N.A. = Not acceptable)

Features	A	N.A.	Comments
Student Learning Considerations			
Child can independently operate			
Child controls pace and interaction			
Navigating directions are precise and clear			
Menu uses pictures or icons			
Speech supports operations			
Graphics and text mutually supportive			
Supports intended curriculum outcomes			
Objectives are clearly identifiable			
Engages student interest			
Encourages active learning:			
• Problem solving/decision making			
• Critical thinking			
Provides appropriate feedback			
Encourages self-evaluation and monitoring			
Technical Considerations			
Easy to install and set up			
Minimal "wait" time for responses			
Can be customized			
Can be accessed by students with special needs			
Presents diverse population			
Value (cost/educational benefits)			
Additional Features			
•			
•			
•			
Overall Assessment			

Source: Adapted from D. D. Shade, "Software evaluation," *Young Children*, September 1996.

Computer software is only part of the technology picture. With the advent of the Internet, there has been an explosion in the amount of computer-based materials children are exposed to in both home and school contexts.

The Internet

The Internet and the Web make it possible for learners to access thousands of archives all over the world. Library catalogues, text files, games, graphics, and organizational databases are available on almost any subject. Bulletin boards, computer conferencing, online journals, news networks, and discussion groups are totally changing the face of both information retrieval and learning.

In this edition of our textbook, we assume that most preservice and inservice teachers are familiar with basic terms related to the Internet and with email and Internet addresses. For those who are not, this information is available on the Web at the following sites (Greenlaw, 2001):

- www.december.com/web/text/index.html (provides a collection of many guides and tutorials available on the Internet)
- www.internet101.org (provides the basics on using the Internet, including information on email, newsgroups, and chat rooms)
- www.imagescape.com/helpweb/welcome.html (provides information on the basics of using the Internet, email, newsgroups, listservs, and chat rooms)

Teachers engage children with the Internet for three purposes: reading and researching information, publishing their written work, and communicating and collaborating. We use these headings to organize information in the remainder of this section.

Reading and Researching Information

Social Construction of Meaning. The Internet is an ideal environment for the social construction of meaning. As children navigate through a wide variety of information sources, they discriminate between important and unimportant information, respond to email, and engage with other students in electronic chat sessions. In this process, what counts as knowledge is under constant construction, as the "knowledge base on the Internet becomes a function of social interaction among its users" (El-Hindi, 1999).

Learning on and with the Internet promotes the active construction of meaning for several reasons:

- *Currency.* Learners have immediate access to current information. Nearly all major newspapers publish online versions, and research findings in most fields are now available. Many Web sites are continuously upgraded.
- *Relevancy.* Learners can choose lines of inquiry and pursue personal interests. Topics are linked and cross-referenced to enable Web crawlers to navigate their own inquiry pathways.
- *Immediacy.* Students can learn about events almost as they happen.
- *Multiple perspectives.* Learners using Web links can view and appraise the same information from a number of viewpoints.
- *Multiple dimensions.* The same event, concept, or topic is often available in multiple formats—text, chart, video, and sound.

It is the very currency and immediacy of the Internet, however, that causes both students and teachers their greatest frustration as Web sites appear and disappear overnight. By the time this book is published, several of the Web sites we reference in this chapter will likely no longer be available or their Web addresses will have changed.

E-Books. In addition to electronic books on CD-ROM, there are also e-books available on the Internet. Most of them are presented page by page, and they nearly always provide an oral reading of the text. The major difference between these books and those on CD-ROM is that the latter have more sounds, animation, and interactivity.

Some e-books can be read on the Internet at no cost. The Internet Public Library hosted by the School of Information at the University of Michigan (www.ipl.org/div/kidspace/storyhour) is one source of free e-books for children. Several others are listed by David Brown at the University of Calgary on his site (www.ucalgary.ca/~dkbrown/stories.html).

Many sites sell e-books or subscriptions to an e-book site. E-books can be downloaded from these sites onto desktop computers or small portable reading devices such as palm pilots, laptop computers, or penpads. While e-books do not replace books, they are useful in circumstances where physical books are not available. Most reading on the Web, however, involves hypertext documents which are essentially manuscripts rather than books.

Reading Hypertext on the Web. A major question involves the extent to which reading on the Web is the same as or different from reading conventional print materials. Sutherland-Smith (2002) uses the term *Web literacy* to refer to finding, scanning, digesting, and storing Internet information. While these skills appear to be similar as those used with print, Sutherland-Smith believes that Web literacy involves "expanding critical reading skills to incorporate evaluation of visual and nontextual features and a greater use of associative logic" (p. 663). According to her, reading Web-based text:

- permits nonlinear strategies of thinking
- allows nonhierarchical strategies
- offers nonsequential strategies
- requires visual literacy skills to understand multimedia components
- is interactive, with the reader able to add, change, or move text
- enables a blurring of the relationship between reader and writer (Sutherland-Smith, pp. 664–665)

Burbules (1997) adds that the volume of information, the speed of information access, and the structure of the Web as a series of interlinked points differentiates Web reading from reading of printed texts.

Strategies for Web Reading. Sutherland-Smith (2002) recommends the following strategies for teaching Web reading.

1. *Use the "snatch-and-grab" reading technique.* Rather than having children read each text they find on the Web to the end, students skim text to identify a key word or phrase and grab the text onto disk or save the site as a bookmark. Once they have compiled these texts, students read them in a more detailed manner and cull references after a closer scanning. This technique emphasizes the broad nature of searching and helps students obtain a great deal of material in a limited time.

2. *Focus on refining keyword searches.* Teachers explicitly teach students to narrow the scope of their keyword search to find information more efficiently. For

example, narrowing a search from the phrase *printing press* (which located 595 hits) to *invention of* or *history of the printing press* refines the search, resulting in 12 sites for *history* and two for *invention*.

3. *Use the "chunking technique."* Sutherland-Smith coined this term to show students ways to break down a complex topic into manageable sections or chunks. For example, when researching the creation of a national airline such as Qantas, the teacher explains how students can think about the topic in chunks—when and why it was created, and its effect on remote communities. Students then brainstorm words to use as a search focus, beginning with one before moving to the next focus.

4. *Provide shortcut lists to sites or search engines.* Teachers can provide preset lists of shortcuts or bookmarks to reliable sites and hints for students to effectively organize their lists of Web addresses.

5. *Limit links.* One strategy to assist weaker students is to limit the number of links they follow. This helps these students refocus on key words or questions and keep on track.

6. *Evaluate nontextual features (images, graphics).* Students need to learn how to decode visual images and not regard them merely as illustrations. They also need to learn to evaluate visual images and to discern discrepancies between visual images and text information.

Internet Workshop. Leu (2002) recommends that teachers use Internet Workshop as an instructional framework to develop the "new" literacies students need in order to read material on the Internet. This framework consists of the following four steps.

1. Locate a site on the Internet with content related to a classroom unit and set a bookmark for the location. This limits random surfing and exploration of sites unrelated to the unit, a safety issue for children in the younger grades. One strategy for locating these sites is to use a search engine organized for teachers and children that also screens out inappropriate sites. Leu suggests the following search engines:
   • Yahooligans (www.yahooligans.com)
   • Ask Jeeves for Kids (www.ajkids.com)
   • KidsClick! (sunsite.berkeley.edu/KidsClick!)

2. Design an activity related to the learning goals of your unit. Purposes include:
   • to introduce students to a site you will use in your unit
   • to develop important background knowledge for the unit
   • to develop navigation skills
   • to help children think more critically about information they find on the Internet

   Leu notes that it is important to provide an open-ended activity for students so they bring back different information from the Internet. He suggests creating an activity sheet with open-ended questions to serve as a guide. Example: "Be a detective. What clues can you find at Kids Web Japan (bookmarked) to indicate that the information at this site comes from the government of Japan? Write them down and bring these clues to Internet Workshop. How did you find them? Write down the strategies you used" (Leu, 2002, p. 468).

3. Complete the research activity, either by scheduling a period in the school computer lab (if available) or by assigning children to a schedule if there are one or two computers in the classroom.

4. Have students share their work. The concluding step is a short workshop session in which students share and compare the information they discovered, talk about their

developing critical literacy skills, and raise new questions to be explored in the curriculum unit. Some of these can serve as the focus of further Internet Workshops.

Publishing Students' Writing

Children who interact with the Internet become aware that the information they see is available to anyone, anywhere, anytime. When they see their own efforts on the Internet, they become motivated to read and write more (Gerzog and Haugland, 1999).

Several Web sites are dedicated to publishing children's work. Two noncommercial sites are listed below:

- KidsSpace (www.kids-space.org) is an international site that invites children to send stories, includes a penpal box, and hosts children's individual home pages.
- KidPub (www.kidpub.org/kidpub) invites children to submit their stories.

Many schools have developed their own Web sites, and some publish children's written work on these sites.

Communicating and Collaborating

Leu, Karchmer, and Leu (1999) describe the changing face of literacy instruction as "envisionments" that "take place when teachers and children imagine new possibilities for literacy and learning, transform existing technologies to construct this vision, and then share their work with others." They give an example of an envisionment where teachers and students in Tasmania, as part of a cultural study, developed and posted on the Internet a traditional Indonesian folk tale. This activity was picked up by a class in Indonesia, and through email, the two classes learned about each other's culture. After reading about the experiences of the two classes, a school in the Netherlands integrated the original story into their own envisionment for literacy and learning. As other classrooms visit the original sites, numerous creation stories and myths from around the world are being made available on the Internet, and a rich curriculum resource developed by teachers and students is available for all to access and use.

Internet Project. Leu, Karchmer, and Leu (1999) recommend use of an instructional framework called *Internet project* to coordinate learning experiences developed and exchanged between two or more classrooms over the Internet. Internet projects may be either more permanent Web site projects or temporary (Leu, 2001).

One Internet project highlighted by Leu is the Flat Stanley project coordinated by Dale Hubert, a Grade 3 teacher in London, Ontario. This project is based on the book *Flat Stanley* by Jeff Brown (1996). Most Flat Stanley projects begin with a group making a Flat Stanley on paper and contributing several entries in a journal about his experiences. They send their Flat Stanley by mail to a collaborating class. The receiving class adds several journal entries describing Flat Stanley's experiences with them and returns Flat Stanley and the journal to the sender. Sometimes a group plans a route for Flat Stanley to several classes before returning home. Many groups send journal entries by email to all classrooms participating in the project. Information on Flat Stanley projects can be found at flatstanley.enoreo.on.ca.

Some of the other Internet Projects described by Leu (2001) are presented below:

- Journey North (www.learner.org/jnorth) is a global study of wildlife migration.
- Poetry Post (www.mecca.org/~graham/day/poetrypost) features poems written by children around the world.

- Book Raps (rite.ed.qut.edu.au/oz-teachernet/index.php) provides a forum for the discussion of books via email.
- Books on Tape (www.booksontapeforkids.org) is designed to link Internet Project with social action. The goal of this project is to provide excellent children's literature and a read-aloud tape to at least 100 children's hospitals in the United States.

Links to several other projects are provided at Mrs. Silverman's Webfolio at kids-learn.org.

Temporary Internet Projects are designed by teachers for a specific curriculum need. These teachers post their projects at locations on the Internet to attract collaborating classrooms. Project descriptions may be posted at several locations including:

- SchoolNet's Grassroots Project Gallery (www.schoolnet.ca/grassroots/e/project.centre/index.asp) in Canada
- Global SchoolNet's Internet Project Registry (www.gsn.org/pr/index.cfm) in the United States

Global Communication. In many ways, depending on how much opportunity students have to access the Internet, email and chat rooms are replacing the telephone as the preferred medium of information exchange for today's students. According to Bruce (1999), "Using new communication and information technologies, teachers and students are discovering more ways to communicate with others to make things, to learn about the world, and to express themselves."

In addition to sharing information and viewpoints via email and chat rooms, students are beginning to share themselves and their creativity through designing personal Web pages using tools now available. "Young people, and those not so young, are using the richly intertextual, multimedia canvas not just to learn, but to teach the world about themselves" (Bruce, 1999). These Web pages often incorporate background music, personal photographs, video segments, graphics, the imaginative use of fonts, colour, backgrounds, and clip art to create rich personal statements that are shared with others. All invite response, and most conclude by letting readers know "I love to get email!"

In the worldwide "chat" community, English-speaking students can post any of their new language learning for response and support from native speakers of the language. And access to these sites is not restricted to English speakers. New translation technologies such as Systran, available on the AltaVista site (babel.altavista.com/tr), allow Web users to translate their messages instantly from one language to another and post them on the Web. Such translation technology allows students to

- talk with friends who speak different languages
- "read" the news in a foreign language and then translate it to check its meaning
- write on a topic, translate it, post it, and wait for responses
- choose a topic, translate it, search with the translated terms, specify results in the target language, and then translate the pages that look interesting

Issues and Challenges

Effect of Technology on Learning

The major issue surrounding the use of computers in literacy programs is whether they produce better learning than conventional approaches. Several studies have explored the use of the computer in relation to quality and quantity of student writing, but the results have yielded somewhat contradictory findings (Sharp, 1999). These contradictory results appear to reflect the differences in implementation of not only word processing but other computer applications as well.

Students' literacy learning via computers is tied very strongly to the expertise of their teacher. Teachers who are considered "experts" in the use of computers in the classroom tend to guide their students in computer activities that support learning (Dillon and Gabbard, 1998). Wright (2001) concluded from her review of research on use of technology with young children that how computers are used appears to be more important than if computers are used at all. In his study of changes in third-grade children's computer literacy, Hackbarth (2000) similarly also noted that quality of access was an important factor.

Research into the effects of Internet use on literacy learning is very limited, both because of the network's relative infancy and because of the fact that the technology is changing faster than our ability to evaluate its utility using traditional approaches (Leu, Karchmer, and Leu, 1999). Because the technology is constantly changing, it is likely that by the time research results are published, they may reflect the effect of an obsolete technology or procedure.

Equity Issues

Carvin (2000, p. 56) calls the "digital divide" one of the most important civil rights issues facing our modern information economy. Basically, the digital divide is the increasing gap between people and groups who do and those who do not have access to information technology. In the United States, families earning over $75 000 per year are 20 times more likely to have home Internet access than those at the lowest income levels. And the discrepancy does not end at home.

Olson and Sullivan (1993) note that older schools frequently incur greater costs in acquiring computers because of the rewiring that must be completed for Internet access in the classrooms. In addition, there is a tendency for schools in richer communities to teach programming skills, whereas schools in poorer districts use computer-assisted instruction. Olson and Sullivan argue that the use of computers in the schools appears to be doing little to equalize opportunities across class, and that it indeed may lead to greater inequalities.

In an attempt to increase access to technology in Canadian schools, the federal government operates a national Computers for Schools (cfs-ope.ic.gc.ca) program in cooperation with provincial and territorial governments and the private and volunteer sectors. The program collects and refurbishes surplus computers from government and private-sector sources and distributes them free to schools and libraries across the country. Since its inception in 1993, CFS has provided more than 300 000 computers and currently distributes more than 60 000 computers per year.

Professional Development

As indicated above, the impact of instruction using technology is directly related to the expertise of teachers. With limited funding available for education, schools have often focused on acquisition of hardware and software rather than on professional development. Schools are also faced with the problems associated with provincially and locally mandated curriculum that is not supported with appropriate funding and technical support for teachers. Often curriculum initiatives are "added" to an already full professional development agenda for teachers.

In order to assist teachers and schools, the Canadian government has set up Canada's SchoolNet (www.schoolnet.ca), a site that provides multimedia resources, references, and unit and lesson plans. Information is also available for students and teachers at other sites such as the Telus Learning Connection (www.2Learn.ca), Kathy Schrock's Home Page (kathyschrock.net), and Classroom Connect (www.classroom.com). A more critical perspective on technology in the classroom is presented by Jamie McKenzie in his online journal, *From Now On: The Education Technology Journal* (www.fno.org).

Quality and Safety Issues

On the one hand, the Internet is "a priceless source of invaluable, easily accessed research material, and on the other a certifiable rubbish heap of useless facts and misinformation" (Anderson and Speck, 2001). It is a testimony to free speech with no governing body to censor or evaluate the quality of information.

It is important to establish safeguards for children when using the Internet. Teachers and parents need to prevent (1) exposure to sexually explicit, violent, racist, and sexist material, (2) communication with questionable people, and (3) children providing personal information such as address and telephone number that could jeopardize their safety. Gerzog and Haugland (1999) recommend that teachers and parents provide guidelines to children such as those at SafeKids (www.safekids.com). There are also several filtering software programs that can be used to set parameters to determine what resources children are able to access, although some schools are avoiding use of these programs because they may limit student access to relevant data. Three examples are:

- SurfControl (www.surfcontrol.com)
- Net Nanny (www.netnanny.com)
- CyberPatrol (www.cyberpatrol.com)

In addition to safety issues, teachers are faced with the critical issues of how credible online "shared" information is and how students can be prepared to evaluate the opinions and views that they access, including detecting distortion, bias, and outright prejudice. One way is to focus on assessing "the credibility of the advocates for different claims [rather] than on verifying the truth of their claims" (Leu, Karchmer, and Leu, 1999). Whatever the case, the Internet provides a compelling reason for students to develop the critical literacy skills discussed in the first part of this chapter. Ultimately, students need to learn to actively question both the content of the writing that is being presented and the sources from which it originates. In order to achieve this goal, teachers need to ask the types of questions outlined in the section of this chapter on critical literacy to guide students' interactions with information on the Internet.

> While we recognize the great potential of the Internet to facilitate children's language and literacy learning, we also urge caution. It is not the technology itself that results in learning, but how that technology is used and integrated into the language arts program.

SUMMARY

Critical reading has been included in reading programs for several decades and involves such skills as differentiating fact from fiction, good from bad, and the detection of propaganda devices. It is based on a transmission view of knowledge and learning. In contrast, critical literacy reflects a social constructivist view and involves students in learning to read the world (as well as the word) as a means to personal and social transformation.

In order to assist teachers with critical literacy instruction, this chapter presented frameworks for planning critical literacy lessons, questions to encourage children to interrogate texts, a list of books that highlight social issues, and examples of critical literacy lessons. It is challenging to teach critical literacy because of the complexity of social and political issues, the attitudes of some parents toward dealing with these issues in schools, and the difficulty of handling comments and questions related to sexism, racism, and discrimination.

Children live in a multimedia world. In addition to computer software and the Internet, they are exposed to films, television, photographs, and recordings in their daily lives. Although educators have not always viewed these media as appropriate vehicles for instruction, increasingly we are becoming aware of the potential of these media to enrich children's constructions of meaning, and all provinces and territories across Canada now include media literacy as part of the mandated language arts curriculum. Most educators view preparation of students to critically analyze and create media texts as the major purpose of media literacy education.

Instructional techniques to develop media literacy include media logs, close analysis, deep viewing, action learning, and intertextual instruction. Some of the challenges facing teachers include fitting media literacy instruction into an already overcrowded curriculum, their own negative views toward television and popular culture, and the fact that media literacy is rarely included in assessment of language arts achievement.

In light of growing evidence that computers have the potential to increase student achievement, several provinces have developed programs to integrate or infuse information and communication technologies into curriculum areas. Jonassen (1996) identifies three potential roles for computers in children's learning: learning *from* computers, learning *about* computers, and learning *with* computers. He recommends that teachers and children work *with* computers as cognitive tools or, as he calls them, mindtools. Word processing, database, spreadsheet, multimedia, and hypermedia software can be used by children for productivity and for problem solving and the development of higher levels of thinking.

There is a proliferation of software on the market, and more appears daily. It is important that teachers evaluate software to ensure that it will facilitate the learning of children in their classrooms. Shade (1996) recommends that teachers take into account child, teacher, and technical features when evaluating software.

The Internet provides learners with access to an enormous amount of information. Learning on the Internet is current, relevant, immediate, and multidimensional, and it involves multiple perspectives. Children learn to access information and conduct research on the Internet though developing specific strategies for Web reading and by involvement in Internet workshops. They are able to share their writing by publishing it on Web sites designed for a worldwide audience. They also communicate with other children around the world through Internet projects and communication tools such as email and chat rooms.

However, research on the impact of the Internet is in its infancy, and teacher expertise is critical to effective use of computers with students. In addition, unequal access to the Internet both at home and at school is creating a "digital divide," and there is a need for both teachers and children to deal with quality and safety issues related to information on the Web.

SELECTED PROFESSIONAL RESOURCES

Considine, D. M. and Haley, G. E. (1999). *Visual messages: Integrating imagery into instruction* (2nd ed.). Englewood, CO: Teacher Ideas Press. This text provides teachers with a comprehensive overview of media literacy. The authors lead clearly and concisely from background information on a particular media to teaching suggestions and extensions identified with the grade level for which they are appropriate. The authors suggest a critical "student-centred approach" to media inquiry as they deal with how topics such as eating disorders, sex, violence, and alcohol are presented in the media.

Media Awareness Network. Available: www.media-awareness.ca. This is a Canadian site that offers practical support for media education in the home, school, and community. For educators, it provides teaching units, student handouts, and background material on media education across the curriculum. It is sponsored by a wide range of corporate, government, and professional groups.

MediaChannel.org. Available: www.mediachannel.org/classroom. MediaChannel.org is a nonprofit, public interest site dedicated to global media issues. It is concerned with the political, cultural, and social impacts of the media. The site provides a Teachers' Toolkit including lesson plans, activities, and ideas.

Reading Online. Available: www.readingonline.org. This is the online journal of the International Reading Association. Reading Online contains articles that deal with all aspects of the literacy curriculum, including critical issues, electronic classrooms, international perspectives, research, and reviews. The key focus is on classroom applications of emerging technologies. Teachers can access archival material, as well as take part in online discussions with the authors of current articles and other classroom teachers.

SOFTWARE AND CHILDREN'S MATERIALS NOTED IN CHAPTER THIRTEEN

AppleWorks 6.2. (2002). Cupertino, CA: Apple Computer.
Browne, A. (1998). *Voices in the park*. New York: DK Publishing.
Bunting, E. (1994). *A day's work*. New York: Clarion Books.
Bunting, E. (1994). *Fly away home*. New York: Clarion Books.
Bunting, E. (1998). *Your move*. New York: Harcourt Brace & Co.
Brinkloe, J. (1988). *Playing marbles*. New York: Morrow Junior Books.
ClarisWorks for Kids. (1997). Santa Clara, CA: Claris.
Cowen-Fletcher, J. (1994). *It takes a village*. New York: Scholastic Press.
Discis: Helping children read and learn. (1994). Buffalo, NY: Discis Knowledge Research.
Encarta Encyclopedia 98. (1997). Redmond, WA: Microsoft.
Fenner, F. (1991). *Randall's wall*. New York: HarperCollins.
Fletcher, R. (1998). *Flying solo*. New York: Clarion Books.
Graham, B. (1994). *Rose meets Mr. Wintergarten*. Ringwood, Victoria: Puffin Books.
Hesse, K. (1998). *Just juice*. New York: Scholastic Press.
HyperStudio 4.0. (2000). El Cajon, CA: Roger Wagner.
Inspiration 7. Portland, OR: Inspiration Software.
Isadora, R. (1991). *At the crossroads*. New York: Greenwillow.
Kaplan, W. (1998). *One more border: The true story of one family's escape from war-torn Europe*. Toronto, ON: Groundwood Books.
Kid's Media Magic Version 2.0 (1999). Hood River, OR: Humanities Software, Inc.
Kidspiration: Build strong thinking skills with visual learning. (2000). Portland, OR: Inspiration Software.
KidWorks Deluxe. (1996). Torrance, CA: Davidson & Associates.
Leonardo's Multimedia Toolbox, V2. (1998). Rancho Cordova, CA: NEC Solutions (America) Inc.
Living Books. Novato, CA: Broderbund Software (several titles with different dates of publication).
Lobel, A. (1980). *Fables*. New York: Harper & Row.

Lorbiecki, M. (1998). *Sister Anne's hands*. New York: Dial Books for Young Readers.
Mayer, M. and Mayer, M. (1978). *Beauty and the beast*. New York: Aladdin.
McGovern, A. (1999). *The lady in the box*. New York: Turtle Books.
McKee, D. (1987). *Tusk tusk*. London: Beaver Books.
Microsoft Works. (1998). Redmond, WA: Microsoft.
MicroWorlds 2.0. Highgate Springs, VT: Logo Computer Systems Inc.
Munsch, R. (1980). *The Paperbag princess*. Toronto: Annick Press.
Myers, C. (2000). *Wings*. New York: Scholastic.
Spier, P. (1980). *People*. New York: Doubleday.
Storybook Weaver Deluxe 2.0. (1996). Minneapolis, MN: MECC.
Student Writing Center. (1995). Minneapolis, MN: Learning Company.
Toliver, P. R. and Johnson, Y. (1997). *Microsoft PowerPoint*. Reading, MA: Addison-Wesley.
Van Camp, R. (1998). *What's the most beautiful thing you know about horses?* San Francisco: Children's Book Press.
Waboose, J. B. (1997). *Morning on the lake*. Toronto, ON: KidsCan Press.
WiggleWorks: Scholastic beginning literacy system. (1994). New York: Scholastic.
Wilder, L. I. (1953). *Little house on the prairie*. New York: Harper.
Winthrop, E. (1985). *Tough Eddie*. New York: E. P. Dutton.
Woodson, J. (2001). *The other side*. New York: Putnam's Sons.
World Book encyclopedia. (1995). Chicago: World Book.

REFERENCES

Alberta Learning. (2000–2003). Information and communication technology. Available: www.learning.gov.ab.ca/k_12/curriculum/bySubject/ICTpofs.pdf.
Alvermann, D. E. and Hagood, M. C. (2000). Critical media literacy: Research, theory, and practice in "new times." *Journal of Educational Psychology*, 93 (3), 193–205.
Anderson, R. S. and Speck, B. W. (2001). *Using technology in K–8 literacy classrooms*. Columbus, OH: Merrill Prentice Hall.
Anderson-Inman, L. and Horney, M. (1999). Electronic books: Reading and studying with supportive resources. *Reading Online*. Available: www.readingonline.org/electronic/elec_index.asp?HREF=/electronic/ebook/index.html.
Atlantic Canada English Language Arts Curriculum: Grades K–3. (1999). Governments of New Brunswick, Newfoundland and Labrador, Nova Scotia and Prince Edward Island. Available: www.gnb.ca/0000/publications/curric/englangartsk-3.pdf.
Baker, E. A. (2000). Instructional approaches used to integrate literacy and technology. *Reading online*. Available: www.readingonline.org/articles/baker/index.html.
Bigelow, W. (1989). Discovering Columbus: Rereading the past. *Language Arts*, 66 (6), 635–643.
Bruce, B. (1991). Roles for computers in teaching the English language arts. In J. Flood, J. M. Jensen, D. Lapp, and J. R. Squire (eds.), *Handbook of research on teaching the English language arts* (pp. 536–541). New York: Macmillan.
Bruce, B. (1999). Learning through expression. *Reading online*. Available: www.readingonline.org/electronic/elec_index.asp?HREF=/electronic/jaal/Dec_Column.html.
Burbules, N. C. (1997). Rhetorics of the Web: Hyperreading and critical literacy. Available: faculty.ed.uiuc.edu/burbules/ncb/papers/rhetorics.html.
Cadiero-Kaplan, K. (2002). Literacy ideologies: Critically engaging the language arts curriculum. *Language Arts*, 79 (5), 372–381.
Carvin, A. (2000). Mind the gap: The digital divide as the civil rights issue of the new millennium. *MultiMedia Schools*, 7 (1), 56–58.
Cervetti, G., Pardales, M. J., and Damico, J. S. (2001). A tale of differences: Comparing the traditions, perspectives, and educational goals of critical reading and critical literacy. *Reading online*. Available: www.readingonline.org/articles/cervetti.

Chang, L. and Osguthorpe, R. (1990). The effects of computerized picture-word processing on kindergartners' language development. *Journal of Research in Childhood Education, 5,* 73–83.

Considine, D. M. and Haley, G. E. (1999). *Visual messages: Integrating imagery into instruction* (2nd ed.). Englewood, CO: Teacher Ideas Press.

Dillon, A. and Gabbard, R. (1998). Hypermedia as an educational technology: A review of the quantitative research literature on learner comprehension, control, and style. *Review of Educational Research, 68* (3), 322–349.

Dillon, D. (1997). The political: Changing our lives through literacy. In V. Froese (ed.), *Language across the curriculum* (pp. 227–248). Toronto: Harcourt Brace Canada.

Edelsky, C. (1994). Education for democracy. *Language Arts, 71* (4), 252–257.

El-Hindi, A. (1998). Exploring literacy on the Internet. *The Reading Teacher, 51,* 694–700.

El-Hindi, A. (1999). Beyond classroom boundaries: Constructivist teaching with the Internet. *Reading online.* Available: www.readingonline.org/electronic/elec_index.asp?HREF=/ electronic/RT/constructivist.html.

English language arts program of study. (2001). Quebec Ministry of Education. Available: www.meq.gouv.ca/degj/program/pdf/educprog2001bw/educprog2001bw-051.pdf.

Finazzo, D. A. (1997). *All for the children: Multicultural essentials of literature.* New York: Delmar.

Flood, J., Heath, S. B., and Lapp, D. (eds.). (1997). *Handbook of research on teaching literacy through the communicative and visual arts.* Old Tappan, NJ: Simon and Schuster.

Foundation for the Atlantic Canada English language arts curriculum. (1996). Governments of New Brunswick, Newfoundland and Labrador, Nova Scotia, and Prince Edward Island. Available: apef-fepa.org/pdf/english.pdf.

Freire, P. (1970). *Pedagogy of the oppressed.* New York: Herder and Herder.

Galloway, J. P. (1994). Effects of QuickTime multimedia tools on writing style and content. In J. Wills, B. Robin, and D. A. Wills (eds.), *Technology and teacher education annual* (pp. 94–97). Charlottesville, VA: Association for the Advancement of Computing in Education.

Gerzog, E. H. and Haugland, S. W. (1999). Web sites provide unique learning opportunities for young children. *Early Childhood Education Journal, 27* (2), 109–114.

Green, P. (2001). Critical literacy revisited. In H. Fehring and P. Green (eds.), *Critical literacy: A collection of articles from the Australian Literacy Educators' Association.* Newark, NJ: International Reading Association. Available: www.reading.org/store/content/286c.html.

Greenlaw, J. C. (2001). *English language arts and reading on the Internet: A resource for K–12 teachers.* Upper Saddle River, NJ: Merrill Prentice-Hall.

Hackbarth, S. (2000). Changes in students' computer literacy as a function of classroom access to computers and teacher utilization. *TechTrends, 44* (4), 30–33.

Hall, V. G. and Martin, L. E. (1999). Making decisions about software for classroom use. *Reading Research and Instruction, 38* (3), 187–196.

Hobbs, R. (1997). Literacy for the information age. In J. Flood, S. B. Heath, and D. Lapp (eds.), *Handbook of research on teaching literacy through the communicative and visual arts* (pp. 7–14). Old Tappan, NJ: Simon and Schuster.

Hodgins, K. (1999). Reading on the internet. Unpublished paper. University of Alberta, Edmonton, AB.

International Reading Association. (2002). *Integrating literacy and technology in the curriculum: A position statement of the International Reading Association.* Newark, DL: Author. Available: www.reading.org/pdf/technology-pos.pdf.

Irwin, J. H. and Baker, I. (1989). *Promoting active reading comprehension strategies: A resource book for teachers.* Englewood Cliffs, NJ: Prentice-Hall.

Jonassen, D. (1996). *Computers in the classroom: Mindtools for critical thinking.* Englewood Cliffs, NJ: Prentice-Hall.

Leland, C., Harste, J., Ociepka, A., Lewison, M., and Vasquez, V. (1999). Exploring critical literacy: You can hear a pin drop. *Language arts, 77* (1), 70–77.

Leu, D. J. (2001). Internet project: Preparing students for new literacies in a global village. *Reading Teacher*, *54* (6), 568–572.

Leu, D. J. (2002). Internet workshop: Making time for literacy. *Reading Teacher*, *55* (5), 466–472.

Leu, D. J., Jr., Karchmer, R. A., and Leu, D. D. (1999). The Miss Rumphius effect: Envisionments for literacy and learning that transform the Internet. *Reading online*. Available: www.readingonline.org/electronic/elec_index.asp?HREF=/electronic/RT/rumphius.html.

Lewis, C. (1993). "Give people a chance": Acknowledging social differences in reading. *Language Arts*, *70* (6), 454–461.

Lewison, M., Flint, A. S., and Van Sluys, K. (2002). Taking on critical literacy: The journey of newcomers and novices. *Language Arts*, *79* (5), 382–392.

Logan, R. K. (1995). *The fifth language: Learning a living in the computer age.* Toronto: Stoddart.

Luke, A. and Freebody, P. (1997). Shaping the social practices of reading. In S. Muspratt, A. Luke, and P. Freebody (eds.), *Constructing critical literacies: Teaching and learning textual practice* (pp. 185–225). Cresskill, NJ: Hampton Press.

Luke, C. 1997. Media literacy and cultural studies. In S. Muspratt, A. Luke, and P. Freebody (eds.), *Constructing critical literacies: Teaching and learning textual practice* (pp. 19–49). Cresskill, NJ: Hampton Press.

Manzo, A. V. and Manzo, U. (1997). *Content area literacy: Interactive teaching for active learning.* Columbus, OH: Prentice-Hall.

Mackey, M. (2002). *Literacies across media.* New York: Routledge/Falmer.

Media Awareness Network. Available: www.media-awareness.ca.

MediaChannel.org. Available: www.mediachannel.org/classroom.

Myers, J. and Beach, R. (2001). Hypermedia authoring as critical literacy. *Reading online.* Available: www.readingonline.org/electronic/elec_index.asp?HREF=/electronic/jaal/3-01_Column/index.html.

National Reading Panel. (2000). *Teaching children to read: An evidence-based assessment of the scientific research literature on reading and its implications for reading instruction.* Washington, DC: National Institute of Child Health and Human Development. Available: www.nationalreadingpanel.org.

Nova Scotia Department of Education and Culture. (1999). *Vision for the integration of information technologies within the Nova Scotia public school system.* Halifax, NS: Author. Available: ftp://ftp.ednet.ns.ca/pub/educ/lrt/vision_e.pdf.

Olson, C. P. and Sullivan, E. V. (1993). Beyond the mania: Critical approaches to computers in education. In L. L. Stewin and S.J.H. McCann (eds.), *Contemporary educational issues: The Canadian mosaic* (pp. 424–441). Toronto: Copp Clark Pitman.

The Ontario curriculum: Grades 1–8: Language. (1997). Ontario Ministry of Education. Available: www.edu.gov.on.ca/eng/document/curricul/curr971.html.

Ontario Ministry of Education. (1989). *Media literacy resource guide.* Toronto: Queen's Printer for Ontario.

Pan, A. C. and Zbikowski, J. M. (1997). Emerging technology for writing instruction: New directions for teachers. *Computers in the Schools*, *13* (3/4), 103–118.

Postman, N. (1992). The ideology of machines: Computer technology. In N. Postman (ed.), *Technopoly: The surrender of culture to technology* (pp. 107–122). New York: Alfred A. Knopf.

Reading Online. Available: www.readingonline.org.

Reinking, D. (1997). Me and my hypertext: A multiple digression analysis of technology and literacy. *Reading online.* Available: www.readingonline.org/articles/art_index.asp?HREF=/articles/hypertext/index.html.

Semali, L. (2002). Crossing the information highway: The web of meanings and bias in global media. *Reading online.* Available: www.readingonline.org/new_literacies/semali3.

Shade, D. D. (1996). Software evaluation. *Young Children*, *51*, 17–21.

Sharp, V. (1999). *Computer education for teachers* (3rd ed.). Boston: McGraw-Hill.

Sutherland-Smith, W. (2002). Weaving the literacy Web: Changes in reading from page to screen. *Reading Teacher, 55* (7), 662–668.

Taylor, R. (1980). *The computer in the school: Tutor, tool, tutee.* New York: Teachers College Press.

Temple, C. (1993). Suppose Beauty had been ugly? Reading against the grain of gender bias in children's books. *Language Arts, 60* (2), 89–93.

Thoman, E. (1999). Skills and strategies for media education. *Educational Leadership, 56* (5), 50–54.

Ver Velde, P., Knight, M., and Shushok, K. (1997). *An assessment of the effects of student-produced multimedia productions upon the learning of academic content in elementary classrooms.* Report on applied research project sponsored by Northern Arizona University Office of Research and Graduate Studies. Flagstaff, AZ.

Wason-Ellam, L. (2002). Interwoven responses to critically conscious stories. *Query, 31* (1), 21–26.

Watts Pailliotet, A., Semali, L., Rodenberg, R. K., Giles, J. K., and Macaul, S. L. (2000). Intermediality: Bridge to critical media literacy. *Reading Teacher, 54* (2), 208–219.

Western Canadian protocol for collaboration in basic education: *The common curriculum framework for English language arts*: *Kindergarten to Grade 12.* (1998). Available: www.wcp.ca.

Whipple, M. (1998). Let's go to the movies: Rethinking the role of film in the elementary classroom. *Language Arts, 76* (2), 144–150.

Whitehead, D. (2002). "The story means more to me now": Teaching thinking through Guided Reading. *Reading, 36,* 33–37.

Wilson, L. (2002). *Reading to live: How to teach reading for today's world.* Portsmouth, NH: Heinemann.

Wilhelm, J. D., Friedemann, P. D., and Erickson, J. (1998). *Hyperlearning: Where projects, inquiry, and technology meet.* York, ME: Stenhouse.

Wright, C. (2001). Children and technology: Issues, challenges, and opportunities. *Childhood Education, 78* (1), 37–41.

Chapter

Planning and Organizing Language Arts Programs

Program Planning

- Balance Revisited
- Components of Classroom Organization

Selecting Materials

- Language Arts Series
- Trade Books
- Nonbook Resources
- Selecting a Range of Topics and Materials
- Thematic Organization

Organizing Children, Time, and Space

- Whole-Class Instruction
- Grouping Children for Instruction
- Individual Activities
- Scheduling Time Blocks
- Time Guidelines
- Organizing Space

Meeting the Needs of All Children

- Views of Individual Differences
- Reading Intervention
- Children from Non-Mainstream Homes
- Limited English-Language Facility
- Learning Differences
- Mild Mental Disabilities

Planning and Organizing Language Arts Programs

Parents as Partners

- Home Environment and School Success
- Building Partnerships with Parents
- Reporting to Parents

very day when the children enter David Paul's Grade 2 classroom, they are greeted with a letter to them on the chalkboard. In the letter, David tells about unusual class activities they will do that day or comments on class events from the day before. Today, the children read the letter and David helps them use words on the classroom word wall as a resource when identifying unfamiliar words. On other days, David presents the letter as a minimal-cues message.

David then draws the children together on the floor in a group and reads them a poem about a dragon to set the theme for the group composition they will write later. As he reads, he stops at the end of some lines to give the children an opportunity to predict meaningful words.

Next, David tells the children that they are going to write a composition together about an imaginary pet dragon. He planned this instructional activity because he has noticed that many children in the class are having difficulty generating and organizing ideas in their compositions. As the children in the class brainstorm ideas, David writes them on the whiteboard. Then, with the assistance of his questions, the children organize the ideas into groups. As they do so, David uses coloured markers to circle ideas in each group—for example, how the pet dragon looks, what it does, and what it eats. The children discuss what they want to write and then dictate ideas while David records their ideas on chart paper. The completed composition is then read as a whole, and some suggestions are made for revisions. The revised composition, revision marks and all, is placed in the writing centre.

While the group is still intact, David and the children discuss how they will use their remaining time. He provides them with a sign-up chart to control the number of children who choose to work at each centre as well as to keep a record of what activities each child completes during the week. Some children indicate that they are going to continue writing a composition from their writing files. Others decide to read independently or write a response in their journal to a book they are reading. One group of children chooses to play a dragon game David has developed to reinforce a problematic spelling pattern (final *e*). Another group works on a puppet play based on a story they had read in class.

While the children are working independently or in small groups, David asks six children to join him at a small table in the corner of the room where he conducts a directed reading–thinking activity (see Chapter Five) with a level-one text. He has noticed that these children are making limited use of their own knowledge when they read. Their responses to what they are reading tend to focus on story details rather than on linking story events or characters to their own lives. He will provide guided reading for another small group tomorrow, but will continue to work with this group in subsequent lessons until they are able to make more effective use of both print- and knowledge-based information.

With five minutes left before recess, David asks the class to come back together to share what they learned that morning. One child talks about a book she is reading, and another shares a piece of writing. The children working on the puppet play say they have completed their puppets and are ready to share their play with the class the next day.

The children in this classroom were involved in a variety of listening, talking, reading, and writing activities during the 90-minute period described as well as during other parts of the school day. They worked with the teacher, with other children, and by themselves. They completed some assigned activities and were able to select others based on their interests and skills. The children moved from one activity to another with very little waiting or off-task behaviour. This did not happen by accident, but rather reflects careful planning and organization of the program. Careful planning leads to meaningful learning for children, which in turn motivates them and reduces behaviour problems. Planning and organization are key to effective classroom management.

- How did David Paul plan the day described above?
- How can classrooms be organized to ensure that children are involved in balanced language arts programs?
- How can children be grouped to meet individual needs?
- How do teachers decide the amount of time to schedule for different aspects of language arts?
- How can the physical space in classrooms be organized to maximize children's learning?
- How can a language arts program be organized to meet the range of individual differences found in any one classroom?

These are only a few of the questions you will ask yourself as you sit down to plan the language arts program in your classroom.

In the previous chapters in this text, we focused heavily on instructional techniques for speaking, listening, reading, writing, viewing, and representing. But that is only part of the story. In this chapter, we discuss how to put these pieces together in a classroom context to meet the needs of all learners.

PROGRAM PLANNING

We begin this chapter by revisiting the final section in Chapter One, where we discussed balance in language arts programs. We then identify the dimensions that teachers consider as they organize their classrooms to maximize learning.

Balance Revisited

When language arts educators write about balance, they generally refer to the need for work on word identification and comprehension in reading and on meaning and mechanics (e.g., spelling, punctuation, and handwriting) in writing. However, as indicated in Chapter One, teachers who hold a social constructive perspective view "balance" from a broader perspective. They are interested in balancing not only *what* they teach but also *how* they teach and interact with children.

Even the *what* of language arts programs is itself not a simple matter of deciding how much emphasis to place on words and meaning. Important choices must be made about how much time to spend on each strand of language arts—reading, writing, speaking, listening, viewing, and representing. In relation to the *how* of language arts, all teachers are faced with even more difficult decisions. These include

- how much time to allocate for teaching and to having children practise using strategies and skills,
- when to provide explicit instruction and when to foster implicit learning,
- how to differentiate expectations, materials, and activities to meet the language needs of all learners,
- how to help children learn new strategies and develop automaticity in using the strategies they have learned,
- when to provide assistance to scaffold children's learning and when to have them work independently,
- how to balance your control of children's learning with opportunities for them to control their own learning, and
- how to decide when children should work alone or with other children.

The answers to questions such as these begin with the words "It depends." Several factors affect the decisions you will make. Some of these include the needs of individuals and groups of children, the stages children have reached in their learning, the resources available in your school, the program of studies mandated by provincial and territorial governments, your theoretical orientation to language arts and learning, and the philosophy of your school and school district. As indicated at several points throughout this text, no one answer will be appropriate for all children at any one time or for any one child all the time. Organizational patterns change as children grow and change, but, increasingly, educators are recommending that balance is critical to effective language arts programs (International Reading Association, 1999).

The planning process always begins with children's learning needs. We described techniques earlier in this text for assessing children's oral language, emergent literacy, reading, and writing abilities. Another crucial piece of information that guides planning involves the provincial and territorial curriculum documents for language arts education. (A list of

Web sites for these documents was provided in Chapter One.) These documents delineate objectives or expectations to be reached in each strand of language learning. One of your tasks in planning is to determine which objectives each child has already achieved and what he or she needs to learn next. Other tasks involve selecting appropriate materials, scheduling language arts time, organizing the physical space in the classroom to facilitate children's learning, and planning whole-class, small group, and individual instruction and activities.

Components of Classroom Organization

Different classrooms reflect different views of language learning. When desks are arranged in rows and children face the front, the focus is generally on teacher talk, with the teacher making most decisions about what children do and when they do it. When teachers arrange children's desks in groups with the children facing one another, they encourage student talk and cooperative learning. Other decisions you will make about the use of space include

- where to place the teacher's desk,
- whether to set up reading and writing centres,
- whether to have a classroom library in addition to the school library, and
- where to place computer and other equipment.

Space is just one of the variables teachers consider as they plan and organize their classrooms to facilitate children's learning.

Time is also a crucial variable. Most jurisdictions recommend that a minimum amount of time be scheduled for language arts instruction at each grade level. In Alberta, for example, the provincial government recommends that 30 percent of the school day be spent on Language Arts in Grades 1 and 2 and that 25 percent be spent on Language Arts in Grades 3 through 6 (www.learning.gov.ab.ca/k_12/curriculum/instruct.pdf). However, teachers have flexibility within this time allocation to decide whether to organize language arts instruction in one or two large time blocks or to devote small time blocks to specific skills or activities. They also make decisions about how to allocate time to ensure that children receive a balanced language arts program.

A third variable teachers take into account when planning a language arts program is materials and equipment. As with time, provincial and territorial governments recommend materials for use in language arts instruction at each grade level. A list of these materials is available at www.curriculum.org/csc/resources/provincial.shtml. Teachers make decisions such as the following:

- the extent to which language arts series are used as compared with **trade books**
- the range of levels of reading materials included in classrooms
- who selects materials or topics—children, teachers, or both
- whether materials are organized thematically or some other way

Finally, the most critical variable teachers take into account when planning language arts programs is the children themselves. How can children be organized to maximize their learning? Teachers make daily decisions about when, why, and how to organize whole-class, small group, and individual activities.

In the next four sections of this text, we describe ways teachers organize materials, children, time, and space to meet the need of learners in their classrooms.

SELECTING MATERIALS

We begin this section by describing different types of materials commonly used in language arts programs as well as issues related to their use. We then discuss the need to select a range of topics and materials, and offer suggestions about how to organize thematic units.

Language Arts Series

Basal reading series have dominated the teaching of reading in North America since the early part of the 20th century. These series generally consist of teacher's guides, student anthologies, student workbooks, and other materials such as tests, worksheets, audiotapes, and computer software. Goodman, Shannon, Freeman, and Murphy (1988) indicate that basal readers were developed in the first two decades of the 20th century to reflect the learning theories and research of that time and a concern about the quality of reading instruction. The explicit instructions in teacher's guides and structured skill development for students were presented as a solution to this concern. The promoters of basal series believed that all teachers needed to do was follow the instructions in the guides and children would learn to read. Although this promise of basal readers has never been realized, Goodman, Shannon, Freeman, and Murphy (1988) reported that more than 90 percent of elementary school teachers in the United States were still using basal reading series in the 1980s.

Initially, basal reading series in Canada were essentially Canadianized versions of series from the United States (Murphy, 1991). However, over the past 25 years, Canadian series have been developed in this country, and they are quite different from those produced in the United States. One major difference is the attempt by Canadian publishers to produce integrated language arts series rather than focusing primarily on reading.

Another major difference involves the inclusion of more children's literature. In the past, basal reading series in the United States were criticized for including so much material written specifically to teach reading. Even when children's literature was included, it was often adapted to such an extent that it is almost unrecognizable (Goodman, Shannon, Freeman, and Murphy, 1988). In contrast, many Canadian series developed in the 1980s and 1990s made an effort to offer high-quality children's literature, and by the early 1990s, this was occurring in series produced in the United States as well (Hiebert, 1999).

Language arts series have continued to evolve in the late 1990s. At this time, the most widely recommended series across Canada include *Gage Cornerstones* (1999), *Collections* (1999), and *Nelson Language Arts* (2000). These series continue to integrate the six language arts and feature Canadian content, but balance is becoming more prominent. Another change involves the attempt by publishers to correlate teacher resource books with the learning outcomes identified in curriculum documents from different regions of the country, resulting in a different edition for each region. *Gage Cornerstones* provides further links to provincial curriculum on the Internet (www.cornerstones.gagepub.ca). In addition to resource books, core teacher materials include assessment handbooks, blackline masters, and, for *Collections*, learning strategy cards. At the Grades 1 and 2 levels, core children's materials include small anthologies or mini theme books, sets of levelled library or little books, and audiocassettes and/or CD-ROM audio sets. At Grades 3 to 6, all three series provide anthologies with a variety of genres as well as media resources.

Collections also includes genre books and novels. Supplementary materials vary by series and include such things as writing handbooks, chapter books, and alphabet flip charts.

Although language arts series have changed a lot since the days of Dick and Jane, they still place considerable power and control in the hands of publishers rather than teachers and children (Shannon, 1989). Language arts series determine not only what children read, but also what teachers do with these materials. When these types of materials are used in language arts programs, the major challenge is for teachers and children to remain in charge of the programs, selecting from and adapting the materials provided rather than using them in a rigid, inflexible manner. Teachers are the experts about the interests and needs of the children in their classrooms, and hence teachers are in the best position to critically examine the materials in language arts series to determine whether, when, and how they can be used to meet their students' needs.

Trade Books

In the past decade, trade books have become the primary material for beginning reading instruction in many North American classrooms (Hiebert, 1999). Those teachers who continue to use language arts series frequently supplement them with trade books. This is what David Paul does in his classroom, exposing the children to a wide range of materials, not just a Canadian language arts series.

The use of children's books either as the core of language arts programs or in addition to basal series has become so widespread that two chapters of this textbook are devoted to describing children's literature and how to use it in elementary classrooms. In addition, a list of children's literature is presented by grade level in the Appendix. However, including children's literature in classrooms may not necessarily lead to a significant change in the nature of language arts instruction.

In the early 1990s, Jobe and Hart (1991, p. 147) expressed concern about what they called "the basalization of children's literature." Jobe and Hart noted that what many teachers were doing with children's books was very similar to what they did with stories in traditional basal reading materials. In novel studies, for example, many teachers still assigned a chapter to be read and ten questions to be answered, developed fill-in-the-blank worksheet exercises about the stories, and asked children to define words on a list from the story and use them in a sentence.

By the mid-1990s, another agenda was being imposed on children's books, namely guided reading. This agenda, grounded in New Zealand reading programs, was presented for widespread consumption in North America by Fountas and Pinnell in 1996. They argue that guided reading is a critical component of instructional programs in language arts, and that to be effective, children need to be matched with "just-right" texts. To achieve this match, they used the following factors to place children's books at increasing levels of difficulty:

- length of the book,
- appearance and placement of print on the page,
- degree of support of pictures,
- complexity and familiarity of concepts,
- predictability to the text, and
- proportion of unique or repeated words to familiar words

Fountas and Pinnell (Fountas and Pinnell, 1999; Pinnell and Fountas, 2002) provide lists of books levelled from kindergarten through Grade 6, including a variety of formats (picture books, short stories, chapter books) and both fiction and nonfiction.

Although guided reading has increased the focus on developing strategic readers (Fawson and Reutzel, 2000), some educators are becoming concerned about whether this type of text progression fits the instructional needs of all children at all points in their literacy development (Brabham and Villaume, 2002). Routman (2000, p. 84) cautions that for children above a beginning level of reading "levels can actually be limiting factors, because they don't take into account students' varying interests, background knowledge, and motivation." Szymusiak and Sibberson (2001) worry that sometimes teachers concentrate on moving children to the next level of text rather than on helping them learn and use strategies they really need. We worry that the aesthetic aspect of reading will be lost in the emphasis on levels and strategies.

Few educators disagree that young children need levelled texts in order to learn to read. The question is on how beginning-reading texts should be levelled. Although predictable texts are useful in helping children develop many understandings and concepts during the emergent stage of learning to read, some children have difficulty shifting attention to print and developing strategies for using letter–sound relationships. These children might benefit from another form of text progression based on systematic phonics instruction (Brabham and Villaume, 2002). Progressions of decodable text support children as they develop and practice phonics knowledge in connected text. However, they often involve contrived language that is difficult to comprehend, and may result in too heavy a reliance on knowledge of letter sounds.

It is clear that no single type of text or levelling system will meet the needs of all children. One option is to use several different single-criterion progressions in order to provide a balanced view of reading to children. Another is to use current materials and sort them according to different criteria for different children in relation to their instructional needs. Yet a third option is to use materials that meet several criteria. Some Dr. Seuss books, such as *Green Eggs and Ham* (1960), do just this, although Hiebert (1999) indicates that these books often introduce too many different words too quickly for children experiencing difficulty learning to read. For these children, new texts need to be generated, incorporating the repetitive and rhythmic nature of **predictable books** with a low density of high frequency words and multiple exemplars of one or more **rimes**.

Nonbook Resources

Sometimes we imply to children through what we do and say that books are the only legitimate source of reading materials. Yet, when we think about all the different items we read each day, books are only one of many reading sources. Some of the other items we read in a normal day include newspapers, magazines, TV guides, brochures, advertisements, signs, labels, and a range of texts on the Internet. If we want children to become literate and read widely for both information and pleasure, we need to ensure that they read a wide variety of materials in school.

Most young children are aware of print in their environment before they go to school. They know the sign for McDonald's, and they can identify their favourite cereal by looking at the box. When they begin school, they encounter print in their classrooms, including their names; the names of their classmates; the days of the week and months of the year on the calendar; words on tape recorders, computers, and other equipment; words on charts; and labels in work centres. By making this print the focus of instruction, teachers build on children's experiences with printed language and help children make use of it. In Chapter Three, we included suggestions to help teachers use **environmental print** to foster children's literacy learning.

For children beyond the emergent level, the list of nonbook materials includes such items as

- pamphlets and brochures from a variety of sources (e.g., travel agencies, tourism bureaus, flyers, and advertisements)
- newspapers
- magazines
- material on the Internet and computer software

Because we are so inundated with advertisements trying to convince us to buy products, children benefit from learning to read these materials critically. For example, a Grade 6 class might discuss advertisements for jeans, discussing why the models are always young and attractive. A discussion of critical and media literacy was included in Chapter Thirteen, with one section devoted to the detection of common propaganda devices used in advertisements and other materials.

Newspapers are a source of print that most of us read nearly every day. We read newspapers for both entertainment and information about current news and events in our area. We read them to decide where to shop for groceries and which movies to go to. Many local newspapers employ education specialists and provide newspapers and suggestions for their use to classroom teachers upon request.

There are also newspapers and magazines designed specifically for children. Materials are available at a range of reading levels and focus on a variety of areas, including outdoor life, science, and popular culture. Some of those available are listed in Box 14.1. These materials can be used for several instructional activities, particularly in relation to content-area reading. They provide up-to-date information on a range of topics related both to curriculum and children's interests. Morrow and Lesnick (2001) provide research to support the positive contributions that magazines make to classroom and literacy experiences of children.

With the explosion of technology in classrooms, children are increasingly reading material on the Internet or in language arts software programs. All of the children's magazines

---

Box 14.1 Children's Periodicals

Let's Find Out and Storyworks

- *Let's Find Out* (kindergarten): Mini-books, news stories, classroom photo stories, activity pages
- *Storyworks* (Grades 3 to 5): Fiction, nonfiction, poetry and classroom plays, interviews with authors, hands-on activities, student-written book reviews

Scholastic Canada Limited
www.scholastic.ca/magazines/index.htm

Your Big Backyard and Ranger Rick

- *Your Big Backyard* (ages 3 to 7): Photo stories, activities
- *Ranger Rick* (ages 7 and up): Nonfiction, fiction, photo stories, activities, environmental tips about wildlife around the world

National Wildlife Federation
www.nwf.org/kids

Continued

Box 14.1 Children's Periodicals *continued*

National Geographic Explorer

- Grades 3 to 6: Nonfiction, photo stories, activities for junior members of the National Geographic Society

National Geographic Society

www.nationalgeographic.com

Ladybug, Spider and Cricket

- *Ladybug* (ages 2 to 6): Stories, poems, activities, games, songs, crafts, some nonfiction
- *Spider* (ages 6 to 9): Stories, articles, games, activities, jokes
- *Cricket* (ages 9 to 14): Stories, folk tales, biographies, science fiction, cartoons, poems, activities, crafts, crossword puzzles, nonfiction

Cricket Magazine Group

www.cricketmag.com

Weekly Reader

- Children's newspapers at a variety of age and grade levels

Weekly Reader Corporation

www.weeklyreader.com

Chirp, Chickadee, and Owl

- *Chirp* (ages 3 to 6): Read-out-loud stories, puzzles, games, crafts
- *Chickadee* (ages 6 to 9) and *Chirp* (Ages 2 to 6): Stories, nonfiction, activities, games
- *Owl* (ages 9 to 12): Nonfiction, activities, puzzles, news stories, contests

Chirp, Chickadee, and Owl Magazines

- These are Canadian.

www.owlkids.com

Sesame Street

- (Ages 2 to 6): Stories, poems, activities, posters, children's drawing and writing

Children's Television Workshop

www.ctw.org

Highlights for Children

- (Ages 2 to 12): Stories, puzzles, games, activities, jokes, riddles

www.highlights.com/magazine

listed in Box 14.1 have Web sites that provide further literacy experiences and activities. Several other programs and Web sites are described in Chapter Thirteen, along with suggestions and cautions for their use. Like all other materials, those on the computer are only appropriate if they meet the needs of specific children in your classroom and are integrated into the curriculum.

Selecting a Range of Topics and Materials

Whether or not teachers use a basal series as part of the language arts program, we recommend that a wide range of printed materials be available in classrooms. By including materials that cover a range of reading levels, all children have the opportunity to read both challenging and independent material every day. Having material on a range of topics and cultures provides at least some material related to each child's interests.

From the available materials, we recommend that children be allowed to choose at least some of the fiction and nonfiction books they read. When all materials are selected by someone else (the publisher or teacher), children do not gain a sense of ownership or control over their own reading. They often feel that they are reading for someone else rather than for themselves. David Paul gives children in his classroom control over what they read by allocating fifteen minutes every day to Drop Everything and Read (DEAR) right after lunch. This is a time when all the students read books of their own choice.

Similarly, children need opportunities to write on topics of their own choice. Not only does this take advantage of the unique knowledge and experience that each child brings to the classroom, but it also helps children feel like writers. If children learn to rely on story starters to serve as a beginning point for their writing, they may not develop a sense that their writing belongs to them. This does not mean that teachers will never assign specific books or topics, but that at least some of the time children can select what they read and write. On the day described at the beginning of this chapter, David Paul selected a writing topic to help children learn how to brainstorm and organize ideas before writing. When writing independently, the children wrote on topics of their own choice.

Thematic Organization

The most common way language arts materials are organized is according to themes. This organization is evident in most of the language arts series developed in Canada, with suggestions for teachers to provide children with opportunities to talk, read, and write about, as well as view and represent, ideas related to each theme. Some teachers go beyond the language arts and develop interdisciplinary or cross-curricular thematic units (Ritter, 1999; Vogt, 1997), integrating social studies, science, mathematics, art, music and other subjects with the language arts. Several advantages of **thematic organization** have been identified.

- Children transfer knowledge and skills from one context to another. In addition to integrating strategies across the language arts, they build upon their knowledge base and connect what they know with what they are learning.
- Children examine a topic more closely, going beyond the superficial to develop in-depth conceptual ways of thinking about information.
- By selecting books on a common topic at a variety of reading levels, the needs of learners at varying levels of reading proficiency can be met.
- Thematic organization also leads to opportunities for children to work cooperatively on a common topic or problem.
- Reading and writing tasks are relevant and contextualized, and children use a range of media to gather and represent information.

When considering whether to organize materials thematically, teachers also need to be aware of some potential disadvantages. One is that even when the teacher selects the theme in consultation with the children in the classroom, some children will be more interested in it and have a greater sense of ownership than others. Another potential problem is that the theme might take precedence over curriculum concerns, with the result that goals in a specific subject area become secondary in importance. The most sensible approach is to make links when appropriate, but not to force links that distort curriculum goals or fail to serve children's learning needs.

Thus, while there are many advantages to thematic organization, several factors must be taken into account when planning thematic units. The most important of these is children's learning needs, but other factors include mandated outcomes, available resources, and district initiatives. Vogt (1997) provides many helpful suggestions for developing thematic instruction. She recommends that themes be selected that are not only interesting to children but substantive enough to challenge them to seek information beyond what they already know, e.g., preserving and protecting Earth. To facilitate planning, she suggests using a web to develop a teaching plan for the thematic unit. This web shows cross-curricular connections and includes a variety of reading materials and contextually embedded activities. Vogt provides an example at www.eduplace.com/rdg/res/vogt.html.

ORGANIZING CHILDREN, TIME, AND SPACE

Before you read this section, try to recall how your language arts classrooms were organized when you were in elementary school. Did you have your own desk or were you seated at a small table with other children? Did your teacher provide reading instruction to the whole class or were you in a small group? Did you have a separate time each day allocated for spelling, reading, and writing instruction? The decisions teachers make about how they organize children, time, and space for language arts instruction reflect the goals and philosophy of their program.

In a review of literature on grouping practices up to the early 1990s, Barr and Dreeben (1991) noted that, in the primary grades, most reading instruction was provided in ability groups, while in the intermediate grades, whole-class instruction was dominant. In the 1990s, there was increase in whole-class instruction in many primary classrooms as well. When organizing children for instruction, Fountas and Pinnell (1996) recommend that teachers keep the following in mind:

- There is a wide range of experience, knowledge, and skills among any group of elementary children.
- Every child is different from every other child in some knowledge and skill.
- Children progress at different rates.

For these reasons, we recommend that children be organized in different ways throughout the school day, and that time and space be organized to facilitate whole-class, small group, and individual instruction and practice.

Whole-Class Instruction

There are several advantages of whole-class instruction. Talking and working together as a whole class helps to develop a community of learners—a community in which children help and respect one another. Children learn a great deal from one another. This learning is enhanced when children are provided with the opportunity to interact with others of differing abilities rather than only with those at a similar level of language achievement. Whole-class instruction is also an efficient use of teacher time. When introducing children to a new theme or strategy, it is more efficient to work with all of them at the same time than to teach the same thing to each child individually.

Wiseman (1992) recommends two types of activities for use with the whole class: instructional or focus time, and sharing time. At the beginning of each day, many teachers bring children together to explain what they will do for the day. Some give children an opportunity to be involved in planning, and help them to set goals for their own learning. Many teachers also teach a strategy or introduce a new genre to the whole class. In the example at the beginning of this chapter, David Paul used a minimal-cues message to teach strategies for identifying words to all the children in his class. He also read a poem to the class and had the children brainstorm ideas for a writing project. The amount of time spent on large group instruction varies with the day and needs of the children.

Sharing time near the end of the language arts time block gives children an opportunity to talk about what they have accomplished and to evaluate their learning. They may discuss books they have read, read aloud what they have written, or talk about what they have learned. Taberski (2000) suggests having children talk about what they learned about themselves as readers or writers and what worked so well that they might try it again. This provides the children and the teacher with an opportunity to evaluate the effectiveness of instruction and serves as the basis for planning the next day's objectives and activities.

Because of individual differences in language development and needs, however, whole-class instruction needs to be supplemented with other ways of organizing children. If all instruction is provided to the class as a whole, the more-able readers and writers will spend much of their time completing activities designed to teach them what they already know how to do. Conversely, the less-able readers and writers will often be involved in activities beyond their **zone of proximal development**.

Grouping Children for Instruction

Ability Grouping

The major purpose of ability grouping is to produce a more homogeneous group in terms of reading needs, making it easier for the teacher to plan and give appropriate instruction. Despite the long history of ability grouping, recent reviews of research about it have produced few conclusive findings to either support or refute its impact on reading achievement. As a result, many educators are now questioning the value of this grouping practice (e.g., Barr and Dreeben, 1991; Indrisano and Paratore, 1991). Ability grouping may offer some advantage to academically gifted students, but results are far from clear even for this group and questionable for average- and low-ability groups. Even when teachers are very careful in the names they select for different groups, children know which group is high and which is low. This has negative implications for the self-esteem of children in the low group.

Researchers have also investigated whether children are taught reading differently in high-ability as compared with low-ability groups. Again the findings are inconsistent, although some studies indicate a stronger focus on decoding for low-ability students, more emphasis on critical thinking for high-ability students, and a lower rate of engaged time for low-ability students (Indrisano and Paratore, 1991). In light of these findings, ability grouping has come under considerable criticism. Some teachers have abandoned the practice, moving to whole-class instruction instead.

While this solves the problems created by ability grouping, many educators believe that it does not meet the need of children to receive reading and writing instruction in their zone of proximal development. In order to meet this need, Fountas and Pinnell (1996) recommend combining grouping by similar reading abilities and text level with a wide range of other types of heterogeneous groups. They feel that grouping children on the basis of reading skill and experience is required for guided reading to be effective, but that in contrast to traditional ability grouping, these groups need to be dynamic. Any grouping is tentative and subject to change based on observations of the children's progress during instruction. These groups are more permanent than the skill needs groups described below, but far less fixed than the traditional so-called three-ring circus. And, perhaps most importantly, children are grouped in other ways for the remainder of their language arts instruction.

Other Ways to Group Children

In the classroom described at the beginning of this chapter, David Paul organized children into interest groups, research groups, special-needs groups, and pairs. All these groupings are far less permanent than ability groups. Interest groups in his classroom are sometimes set up for one day, for example, when children come together to play a game. Other groups, such as the one working on the puppet play, stay together for several days.

- *Interest groups* are generally made up of children at different ability levels. They tend to exist for a relatively short time, disbanding when their purpose has been achieved.
- *Research groups* are similar to interest groups in that they are temporary, although teachers are generally instrumental in a research group's formation. In addition, the focus of the research group is on a topic that the children research rather than on completing an activity or pursuing an interest. Often the teacher and students together set specific goals, and a written or oral presentation is produced at the end. Like interest groups, these groups are frequently composed of children of varying ability levels.
- *Special-needs groups* are set up for different reasons than interest or research groups. Through careful classroom observation, teachers identify an aspect of reading, writing, listening, or talking in which several children need help. David Paul identified several children who needed to make greater use of their own knowledge as they read. He brought these children together into a small group for a few lessons to help them understand the importance of their knowledge and develop strategies for using it as they read. Once the objectives for special-needs instruction have been met, these groups are disbanded.

Collaborative pair: two Grade 3 children reading a book together.

- In *collaborative pairs*, children work together on a common activity, helping one another at points of difficulty. David organized the children in his classroom into collaborative pairs for part of the language arts time. Each pair found a space and shared books. While one child read, the other listened. This gave each child much more reading practice than is the case when children read orally in groups or the whole class. Because the children chose the books themselves, the books interested them and were also at an appropriate level. Collaborative pairs are also appropriate for other types of activities, such as problem solving and writing (Indrisano and Paratore, 1991).

- A more common way of organizing children into pairs involves *peer tutoring*, either with same-age or cross-age dyads. Generally, a more proficient reader or writer is paired with one who is less proficient, and they complete a specific activity designed to facilitate skill development. This type of pairing can also be used when children need to access information from a common text in social studies or science. The child who has developed sufficient skills and strategies to construct meaning from the text reads it to the child who has not yet reached this level of reading proficiency. Another type of activity that is appropriate for peer tutoring is paired reading (see Chapter Six). As with most types of grouping, research has yielded conflicting results on peer tutoring, although it works best when programs are structured, short in duration, and focused on specific skills (Indrisano and Paratore, 1991). According to Topping (1989), both the child being tutored and the one doing the tutoring benefit from the experience.

Cooperative Learning

Many of the groupings described above lend themselves well to cooperative learning. Slavin (1980, p. 315) defines cooperative learning as a technique in which "students work on learning activities in small groups and receive rewards or recognition based on their group's performance." Golub (1994) provides several examples of cooperative groups in the language arts classroom.

- In one scenario, two students work together to complete a writing task, discussing what they will say and how they will say it. When they finish writing, they hand in one paper with both names on it.
- In another scenario, a group of students attempting to make sense of a poem first jots down questions about the poem and then discusses and shares different interpretations. The understanding the students come to as a group is different and often deeper than most children could have constructed individually.
- Still another example involves different students completing different parts of the same project and meeting regularly to discuss what they are doing. Again, one paper is handed in as a result of this work.

Cooperative learning changes the traditional authority structure of classrooms by placing more control in the hands of children. Another major difference is that, instead of each child being evaluated individually, children work together and are evaluated as a group. This encourages them to work cooperatively rather than competitively (which happens when teachers organize children into groups but still base rewards on individual achievement). Some of the additional benefits claimed for cooperative learning groups include (Mayfield, 1992)

- increased exchange of ideas,
- development of social skills,
- wider acceptance and respect for other children, and
- increased learning.

Individual Activities

There is little doubt that children need classroom time to read and write in order to become good readers and writers. It is not enough to allow children to select a book for reading or to write something of their own choice after they complete their other work, or to suggest that they do these types of activities at home. Independent reading and writing must be scheduled into each school day. Cunningham and Allington (2003) indicate that self-selected reading and writing are inherently multi-level, with each child working at an appropriate level of difficulty.

Scheduling Time Blocks

In allocating time, teachers are faced with deciding whether to divide language arts into a series of separate time periods devoted to different aspects of language arts, or to designate large time blocks for language arts (or a cross-curricular thematic unit) and organize a range of activities within these blocks.

Short Time Blocks

A major advantage of short time blocks is accountability: it is relatively easy to account for how much time has been spent on each aspect of the language arts curriculum. For example, if parents are concerned about spelling, you can assure them that a certain number of minutes are devoted exclusively to spelling instruction every week. This way of allocating time also provides a great deal of predictability for the children. They know what they will be doing at each point during the school day.

There are, however, also several disadvantages to organizing different aspects of language arts into separate time slots. First, it does little to foster links between talking, reading, and writing. For example, when phonics is taught in a separate ten-minute block each day, some children will not see its relevance for writing or reading. Second, separate time blocks make it difficult for the teacher to pursue children's needs and interests as they arise in the classroom. Instead of teaching children a strategy when they need it, the teaching is put on hold until the appropriate time in the school day. In addition, just when children get really interested in a topic they are discussing, it is often time to switch to another subject area. Third, short time blocks necessitate many changes in activity during the day, and a considerable amount of time is lost during transitions between activities. Children may spend up to 20 percent of the time allocated to language arts in transition between activities (Benterud, 1983).

Long Time Blocks

An alternative to short time blocks is to organize one or two larger daily time blocks for language arts and to include language learning opportunities in other subject areas as well. The major disadvantage of this type of organization is the difficulty of balancing time spent on each area of the language arts. Careful planning and record keeping are necessary to ensure that each child receives a balanced language arts program. However, the advantages far outweigh the disadvantages. There is more flexibility to pursue children's interests and learning needs. Activities are not cut off while children are still engaged in meaningful learning, nor are activities prolonged to fill a predetermined time slot when children are no longer interested or learning.

Time Guidelines

Each teacher's actual daily timetable will depend on many factors, including the requirements of the school system or provincial department of education; the philosophy of the school; times allocated for recess, lunch break, gym, and library; the grade level involved; and children's learning needs. Some general guidelines for allocating time are provided in Tables 14.1 and 14.2.

Cunningham and Allington (2003) suggest organizing instruction into four time blocks for language arts each day, in addition to including times for opening routines and summary activities. The four blocks they specify are

Table 14.1 Guidelines for Allocating Time in Primary Language Arts

Activities*	Kindergarten to Beginning Grade 1	Grades 1 to 3
Opening and closing routines	10–15 minutes	15–25 minutes
Reading to children	10–15 minutes	10–20 minutes
Shared reading and writing	20–30 minutes	10–15 minutes
Reading and writing instruction	20–30 minutes	40–60 minutes
Independent reading	10–15 minutes	15–30 minutes
Independent writing	10–15 minutes	15–30 minutes

*These are scheduled daily. Other activities such as drama are scheduled less frequently.

Table 14.2 Guidelines for Allocating Time in Upper Elementary Language Arts

Activities	Frequency	Time Allocation
Reading to children	Daily	15–20 minutes
Independent reading	Daily	20–30 minutes
Reading instruction	2 or 3 times each week	20–30 minutes
Writing instruction	2 or 3 times each week	30–40 minutes
Independent writing	2 or 3 times each week	20–30 minutes
Other activities*	Once each week	15–20 minutes

*Sharing a piece of reading or writing, reading with a buddy, and drama.

- guided reading,
- self-selected reading,
- writing, and
- working with words.

The guided reading component involves instruction to help children develop and use strategies as they read. The self-selected reading component involves the teacher reading aloud to children, shared reading, and children reading independently. The writing component involves shared writing, writer's workshop, and independent writing (Fountas and Pinnell, 1996).

Although most activities are completed every day in primary classrooms, some are completed less frequently with upper elementary students because older children often require longer time blocks for activities. The following guidelines are adapted from those presented by Cunningham and Allington (2003):

- *Every day.* Teacher reads books and other types of materials (e.g., newspapers, magazines) aloud to students, children read something they choose, and children do a word wall activity.
- *Two or three times a week.* Children participate in guided reading activity and a focused writing lesson, the teacher models writing, children write on a topic of their own choice, and children work with words.
- *Once a week.* Children share something they have written and something that they have read, read to or with a younger child, and do research related to a topic. One-third of the class revises, edits, and publishes a piece of writing.

It is important to keep in mind when using the guidelines in either Table 14.1 or 14.2 that the times recommended extend across subject boundaries, since language use is involved in all areas of the curriculum. This is particularly true at the upper elementary level, where a considerable amount of the reading and writing children do relates to social studies and science units.

As with everything else in language arts, there is no one best time schedule for all classrooms. We recommend that time schedules be used in a flexible way, extending the time for activities when children are obviously learning and discontinuing activities when they are not. The goal is to consistently provide the types of learning experiences described above without becoming a slave to your time schedule.

Organizing Space

You will not have much control over the amount of space or type of equipment or furniture in your classroom, but you do have control over how that space and furniture are arranged. The physical arrangement of the classroom reflects the goals and philosophy of your language arts program.

Whole-Class, Small-Group, and Individual Activities

The children's desks in David Paul's classroom are organized in rows. He uses this physical arrangement at the beginning of the day for large-group instruction when children discuss the minimal cues message on the chalkboard. On the day described, he then asked the children to push aside the desks in the middle of the room to create a space for them to sit on the floor while he read them the poem. He preferred this arrangement so the children would be closer to the book and to one another.

In some classrooms, a rug in one corner provides a place for children to come together for whole-class discussions, to listen to their teacher read, and to share what they have accomplished. Children can also be organized for whole-class activities by having their desks placed together in groups, as shown in Figure 14.1, so that everyone can view the board and screen. Tables can easily replace groups of desks in this arrangement.

In David Paul's classroom, children work together in groups in many different locations:

- They play learning games at a table placed at the perimeter of the room.
- They sit together in pairs on the floor or at adjacent desks to read books to one another.
- On the day recounted, a small group joined the teacher at a table for a lesson using the directed reading–thinking activity.

Figure 14.1 Physical Arrangement of the Classroom

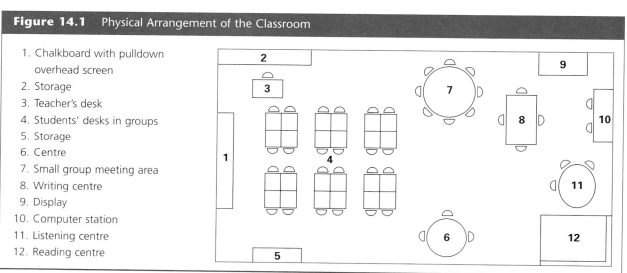

1. Chalkboard with pulldown overhead screen
2. Storage
3. Teacher's desk
4. Students' desks in groups
5. Storage
6. Centre
7. Small group meeting area
8. Writing centre
9. Display
10. Computer station
11. Listening centre
12. Reading centre

The classroom organization depicted in Figure 14.1 places a high value on children working together. In addition to organizing desks in groups, a table on one side provides a place for children to come together to work with the teacher or to work with one another on projects.

In David Paul's classroom, most independent activities are completed by children at their desks. Having desks arranged in rows facilitates independent work, although children are still able to consult with their neighbour if they need help. The children in David's classroom also often find a quiet space on the floor when they are working independently.

While the classroom depicted in Figure 14.1 is more conducive to small-group than individual work, children do have individual desks, and there are many spaces around the perimeter of the room where children can go to work alone. The reading centre, in particular, is appropriate for both group and individual reading.

Learning Centres

Many teachers set up learning centres in order to provide opportunities for children to work together in groups. Some centres, such as reading or writing centres, are permanent.

Reading centres generally include a classroom library; comfortable rugs, chairs, or cushions; and often a listening centre with taped stories. Morrow (1989) recommends that

- materials selected for reading centres appeal to a variety of interests,
- materials be at a range of reading levels,
- materials include all the types of children's literature described in Chapter Ten, as well as newspapers and magazines,
- new books and materials be introduced to the centre regularly to ensure continued interest, and
- children be involved in planning and managing the reading centre, developing rules for its use, naming it, and keeping it neat.

Writing centres often include a display area for children's writing, materials for writing, and at least one computer and printer. Morrow (1989) also recommends including materials for making books, and placing books made by children in the reading centre to share with other children.

Other centres are less permanent, often being set up on a thematic basis related to topics in social studies, science, and other subject areas. While learning centres can be very useful in facilitating children's language development and cooperative learning, one caution is in order. Sometimes centres seem to be valued for their own sake rather than for how they contribute to learning and curricular goals. As with computers and other instructional tools, learning centres need to be integrated into the curriculum to maximize their usefulness.

There is no one magic way to organize classrooms so that all children's needs are met all the time. The key to effective classroom organization is flexibility in organizing materials, time, space, and children. The challenge of organizing an effective language arts program becomes even greater when the learning needs of children considered by many to be at-risk are taken into account. The next section of this chapter focuses on the wide range of children in today's classrooms.

MEETING THE NEEDS OF ALL CHILDREN

We have indicated throughout this text that the goal of language arts teachers is to maximize the language learning of *all* children in their classrooms. We begin this section by briefly outlining how children with special needs have been viewed over the last 40 years. We then present the characteristics of effective intervention programs and describe one program that has been widely implemented across North America in recent years. Finally, we discuss instructional implications for children who come from non-mainstream cultural backgrounds, speak English as a second language, or are labelled as having learning problems.

Views of Individual Differences

Labels for special-needs children are socially constructed, reflecting societal views of individual differences rather than anything inherently "wrong" with the children being labelled. The fact that labels change across time is one indication of their social nature. In the 1960s, for example, terms such as "emotional disturbance," "mental retardation," "cultural deprivation," and "neurological dysfunction" were widely used to label children who experienced difficulties learning in schools. Programs were funded to meet the needs of children given these labels. Included were compensatory programs for children living in poverty and labelled culturally deprived.

With the advent of the learning disabilities explanation for reading problems in the 1970s, compensatory programs for children from poor homes were replaced with remedial programs. Most definitions of learning disabilities had clauses that excluded children with sensory deficits, mental handicaps, or cultural deprivation from the learning disabilities category. These clauses effectively prevented most minority children from accessing remedial reading programs provided through learning disabilities funding.

The sociopolitical nature of learning differences is also reflected in changes in the way services have been provided for at-risk children. For many years, segregated classrooms and schools were the most prevalent and preferred system for educating these students. Children were labelled according to conditions (e.g., mental, physical, emotional, cultural, and learning deficits), and placement was based on this categorization. Some children with severe disabilities were denied education in publicly funded schools. However, in the mid-1970s, legislation was passed in the United States protecting the rights of individuals with disabilities. Since then there has been a sharp movement away from segregated classes and toward educating children in the "least restrictive environment" (Wilson and Cleland, 1985, p. 331).

The impact of this legislation was felt in Canada and, in conjunction with the passing of the Canadian Charter of Rights and Freedoms in 1985, resulted in several provinces passing laws that require school boards to provide education for all students (Crealock and Bachor, 1995). In the 1980s, there was a strong trend in Canadian classrooms away from segregation to mainstreaming for special-needs children. Students were integrated for either all or part of the school day for instruction in regular classrooms.

During the 1990s, **inclusive education** was the dominant theme in special education. While the mainstreaming movement in the 1980s attempted to help special-needs children gain greater access to regular classrooms, inclusive education is aimed at having normal settings and experiences recognized as the right of all students (Saskatchewan Special Education Review Committee, 2000). Many educators view inclusive education as a crucial step in changing discriminatory attitudes and developing a more inclusive society. Crucial to the success of inclusive education, however, is the availability of a range of service options close to the classroom to meet the needs of all children. We describe the types of services that help children with special needs learn to read in the next section.

Reading Intervention

Many children—some estimates are as high as 25 percent—from mainstream homes have difficulty learning to read. Estimates are even higher for children from non-mainstream homes. In this section, we begin by outlining characteristics of successful intervention programs and then describe one program that exemplifies many of these characteristics.

Characteristics of Effective Programs

Several articles appeared in the 1990s describing characteristics of effective reading intervention programs (Wasik and Slavin, 1993; Pikulski, 1994; Spiegel, 1995). Some of these characteristics are as follows:

1. *Early intervention.* Most educators agree that intervention needs to occur early. Children who are behind their peers fall further and further behind, widening the gap between good and poor readers across the elementary grades. Prolonged failure has negative consequences for children's self-concepts which, in turn, negatively affects their learning. By intervening in Grade 1, the cycle of failure can be prevented.

2. *Increased reading time.* Another characteristic of effective intervention is increased time spent reading. In many traditional remedial programs, children spend far more time completing workbooks or worksheets than reading books or other materials. It is through extensive reading of connected texts (not isolated words or letters) that children consolidate reading strategies and develop automaticity.

3. *Increased reading instruction.* Closely related to increased reading time is the need for teachers to devote more time to reading instruction for at-risk learners. As Spiegel (1995) notes, this enhances children's opportunity to learn. Rather than providing instruction in short time blocks once or twice per week, effective intervention involves consistent, daily reading instruction.

4. *Quality instruction.* Instructional time alone is not sufficient. For intervention to be most effective, quality of instruction is also important. In high-quality programs, ongoing assessment provides a foundation for instructional decisions. Rather than providing a prescribed program for all children, programs are designed around each child's needs and strengths. Direct instruction is required, focusing on strategies and the *how to* of reading rather than specific bits of information presented in isolated ways (Pinnell, Fried, and Estice, 1990).

5. *Teacher training.* Intervention programs using certified teachers are more effective than those using paraprofessionals or volunteers. Indeed, the most effective programs, such as *Success for All* and *Reading Recovery*, include an ongoing professional development component.

6. *Individual or small-group instruction.* The most effective intervention involves instruction for individuals or small groups (no more than four or five children). This type of intervention is expensive in the short term, but if children catch up with their peers and need no or little additional intervention, the long-term savings can be considerable.

7. *Coordination with excellent classroom instruction.* Finally, intervention is more effective when children's total reading program is taken into consideration. For maximum impact, children need to receive excellent and coordinated instruction both in their classroom and intervention programs.

Reading Recovery

An intervention program that reflects most of the characteristics listed above and has been widely researched is Reading Recovery. This program was developed and trademarked by Marie Clay in the 1970s and has been implemented nationwide in New Zealand. Children making the slowest progress in reading after one year in school are identified, and in addition to classroom reading instruction, they receive one-on-one instruction for 30 minutes daily over a period of 10 to 20 weeks (Clay, 1993).

Reading Recovery consists of two components: an instructional component for children and a professional development component for teachers. The first step in Reading Recovery is a detailed assessment of the child's reading, followed by two weeks of instruction in which the child is engaged in reading and writing activities the teacher knows he or she can do. This is a time for confidence- and relationship-building. Then the teacher moves into instruction, and each 30-minute lesson includes the following activities:

- The child rereads two or more familiar books.
- The teacher takes a running record of the child reading yesterday's new book and teaches strategies.
- The teacher and child work with letter identification (if necessary) and making and breaking words.
- The child writes one or two sentences using the "hearing sounds in words" technique described in Chapter Six.
- The child rearranges the sentences that have been cut up by the teacher or child.
- The teacher introduces and previews a new book with the child.
- The child reads the new book with support as needed.

While reading and rereading books, teachers provide feedback on reading strategies being used or emerging. The goal of the program is to help children develop independent, self-generating systems for promoting their own literacy. The difficulty of new books increases gradually, ensuring that children experience success. Children are discontinued from the program when they have caught up to the average reading level of peers in their classrooms.

The professional development component of the program is an integral part of Reading Recovery. Clay has designed a three-tier system of professional development involving Reading Recovery trainers, teacher-leaders, and teachers. Teacher-leaders and teachers continue to receive professional development as long as they are involved in a Reading Recovery program.

Reading Recovery has expanded rapidly in North American since its introduction in the 1980s. Over one million students have been served in the 17 years since it was introduced in the United States (Reading Recovery® Council of North America, 2001). Reading Recovery was first provided in Ontario schools in 1988 and since that time, it has expanded to nine provinces and the Yukon Territory (Canadian Institute of Reading Recovery™, 2000). By the end of the 2001/2002 school year, Reading Recovery was being offered in 1544 schools by 2023 Reading Recovery teachers to nearly 14 000 children across Canada (Gregory, 2002).

Data collected in the United States and Canada shows that Reading Recovery works for most children. Data across the 17 years of implementation in the United States showed that 81 percent of the children who completed at least 20 weeks of lessons were performing within the average range of their classmates when discontinued from the program. In Canada, the comparable figure for 1999/2000 was 79 percent, with 73 percent of all children who participated in the program being successfully discontinued.

Independent research shows that the program helps most children, at least in the short term (Glynn, Bethune, Crooks, Ballard, and Smith, 1992; Pinnell, Lyons, DeFord, Bryk, and Seltzer, 1993; Center, Wheldall, Freeman, Outhred, and McNaught, 1995; Shanahan and Barr, 1995; Moore and Wade, 1998). It is important to note, however, that not all researchers or educators view the bulk of the research as supportive. In May 2002, for example, a group of researchers circulated an open letter on the Internet criticizing Reading Recovery and providing an alternative interpretation of the evidence (www.nrrf.org/rrletter_5-02.pdf).

Overall, most research shows that Reading Recovery works, but like all programs it does not work for all children. Some research indicates that ex–Reading Recovery children maintain their gains after they complete programs (Reading Recovery® Council of North America, 2002), but their rate of progress depends on several factors. One is clearly the nature of the program they are placed in. Another involves home and community factors. As Pinnell, Fried, and Estice (1990) point out:

Reading Recovery is promising, but it is not *the* answer. There is no one answer to problems in education. Many of the children served by *Reading Recovery* remain in the potentially-at-risk category because of economic circumstances. Children may learn to *read* through *Reading Recovery*, but they do not turn into different children even though many adopt a much more positive attitude toward school. Poor children are still poor. Highly mobile families still move. (Pp. 294–295)

The remainder of this section is devoted to a discussion of at-risk children. We focus on high-incidence groups (children from non-mainstream backgrounds, children learning English as a second language, and children with mild disabilities) rather than on low-incidence groups (children with visual impairments, hearing impairments, and severe mental disabilities). When children from low-incidence groups are placed in regular classrooms, most jurisdictions have services available to help teachers develop individual education plans.

Children from Non-mainstream Homes

As indicated in Chapter One, there is considerable evidence that literacy is related to sociocultural variables. Literacy levels are lower among the poor than the rich, among rural than urban populations, and among minorities.

Explanations for Lack of Success

Jacobs and Jordan (1993) outline several explanations that have been given to account for the relative lack of success of children from non-mainstream homes in our schools. Most explanations place the responsibility for low school achievement on the cultural groups themselves. One explanation, now widely discredited, claimed that social class and IQ were largely the result of genetic differences. A more widely held view is that the child's home and community may be at fault by failing to provide the experiences, attitudes, and values the child needs to succeed in school. As a result, proponents of this explanation believe that children arrive at school with deficient language and cognitive development.

Both of these views have been reflected in a century of Aboriginal education in the United States and Canada (Deyhle and Swisher, 1997). Although there is considerable research to show that First Nations children are not inherently inferior, attitudes and beliefs of inferiority continue to contribute to a self-fulfilling prophesy for many of these children. The notion of *cultural deprivation*, a term that came into vogue in the 1960s, persists in the minds of many educators and has fuelled assimilationist solutions such as boarding schools and immersion of First Nations children in public schools.

This is also true for children living in poverty. A coalition of 19 groups concerned about poverty in Canada states:

Our kids are not deficient. They are simply different. By blaming the parents and children, these deficit theories divert attention from the education system and how it operates to produce certain outcomes, including failure. (End Legislated Poverty, 1993, p. 137)

Rather than blaming minority groups for the apparent shortcomings that children bring to school, social constructivists shift the focus to schools and society. Schools are seen as reproducing hierarchical social relationships and streaming groups into different economic slots. Those who hold this viewpoint claim that schools contribute to inequality by valuing the cultural capital (ways of talking, acting, and socializing) of mainstream children while devaluing that of others. According to Ogbu (1993), as non-mainstream children grow older and recognize inequalities within the school and restricted job opportunities in society, many demonstrate resistance to mainstream values and drop out of school. However, Deyhle and Swisher (1997) indicate that some First Nations students report feeling "pushed out" of schools.

Multicultural Education

Multicultural education, according to Banks and Banks (1989), is the affirmation of equal opportunities for all children to learn regardless of gender, class, race, ethnicity, or culture. It also encompasses global awareness and recognition of racism, prejudice, discrimination, and equity issues. Multicultural education "begins with the child's understanding of self and the building of self-esteem, moves to an understanding and acceptance of others, and finally expands to a development of concern for larger problems and issues outside the child's immediate environment" (Finazzo, 1997). From this perspective, the focus of multicultural education goes well beyond issues of culture to include differences in family structure, ethnicity, gender, age, exceptionalities, values, socioeconomic status, and ways of communicating.

To some educators, multicultural education means integrating artifacts and literature from other cultures into the curriculum. In Chapters Ten and Eleven, we list several children's books written by authors from different cultures, including Canadian Aboriginals, for use with children in elementary classrooms. What teachers do with these books depends on the model of multiculturalism that underlies their instruction.

Sleeter and Grant (2003) describe five different approaches to multicultural education. The goals, instructional practices, and school-wide concerns associated with these approaches are summarized in Table 14.3. The first, the Difference Model, involves teaching exceptional and culturally different children, and aims to help these children become as "mainstream" as possible. A central idea behind the difference orientation is cultural continuity. We identified some cultural discontinuities for Aboriginal children entering Canadian schools in Chapter One. Teachers working from this perspective attempt to adjust instruction in the classroom to match the learning and communication styles children bring to school. This model has been the basis for many compensatory and special education programs.

The purpose of the Human Relations Model is to help students communicate with, accept, and get along with people who are different from themselves, to reduce stereotypes that students have about people, and to help students feel good about themselves. Neither this model nor the Difference Model described above directly confront the inequalities that exist among groups.

Advocates of the remaining three approaches are concerned with social and economic equality. The Single-Group Model identifies a specific group (e.g., Aboriginals, working-class Canadians) and attempts to raise the status of the group through education. Programs are designed to provide information about the group and the effect of discrimination on the group. Students are helped to think through issues from a critical perspective and to act on their insights to transform unjust social conditions.

The Multicultural Model extends the goal of social justice and equal opportunity to all individuals and groups, and promotes equity in the distribution of power. The goal is not to integrate those who have been left out into society, but rather to change the fabric of that society. The Social Reconstructivist Model has much the same long-term goals as the Multicultural Model, but focuses more specifically on the preparation of citizens to reach these goals. It uses many of the same instructional practices as several other models of multicultural education, including:

Table 14.3 Five Approaches to Multicultural Education			
Approach	**Goal**	**Practices**	**School-wide Concerns**
Difference Model	• Help lower-class, minority, and exceptional students fit into existing social structures • Build bridges between the student and the demands of the school	• Make instruction relevant to students' experiential background • Fill in gaps in knowledge and skills • Use students' first language to teach English • Use special classes as temporary aids to fill in knowledge • Decorate the classroom to show minority group members integrated into mainstream society	• Involve minority parents in supporting the work of the school
Human Relations Model	• Promote feelings of unity, tolerance, and acceptance within existing social structures	• Teach lessons about stereotyping, name calling, and individual differences • Include contributions of all groups in the class • Use cooperative learning • Decorate the classroom to reflect the uniqueness and accomplishments of all students	• Promote school-wide activities aimed at peace and unity • Make sure that school policies and practices do not put down or leave out people
Single-Group Model	• Promote structural equality for an identified group	• Teach units about the culture of the selected group, how the group has been victimized, and current issues facing the group • Build on students' learning styles, especially the learning styles of the identified group • Decorate the classroom reflecting the culture and contributions of the identified group • Have representatives of the group involved in class activities, e.g., as guest speakers	• Employ faculty members of the identified group

Continued

Table 14.3   Five Approaches to Multicultural Education   *continued*

Approach	Goal	Practices	School-wide Concerns
Multicultural Model	• Prepare citizens to work actively toward social structural equality and cultural pluralism	• Organize content around social issues involving racism, classism, sexism, and disabilities, and around experiences and perspectives of several different groups • Teach critical literacy and social action skills • Involve students in democratic decision making • Build on learning styles and use cooperative learning • Decorate the classroom to reflect social action themes and cultural diversity	• Involve the school in local community action projects • Make sure staffing includes diverse racial, gender, and disability groups • Make sure extracurricular activities include all student groups • Make sure building is accessible to all people
Social Reconstructivist Model	• Promote structural equality and cultural pluralism (mosaic)	• Organize units around contributions of several different groups • Teach critical literacy and analysis of alternative viewpoints • Make curriculum relevant to students' backgrounds and promote use of more than one language • Build on students' learning styles and promote cooperative learning • Decorate the classroom to reflect cultural pluralism and nontraditional gender roles • Library materials portray diverse groups in diverse roles	• Involve parents of minority groups actively in school • Make sure staffing includes diverse racial, gender, and disability groups • Make sure extracurricular activities include all student groups • Make sure building is accessible to all disabled people

Source: Based on ideas presented by C.E. Sleeter and C.A. Grant, *Making choices for multicultural education: Five approaches to race, class, and gender* (Danvers, MA: John Wiley & Sons, 2003).

- starting where students are and relating curriculum to their experiential background
- promoting cooperative learning
- building on students' learning styles
- avoiding biased evaluation procedures

In addition to these practices, students are actively involved in democratic decision making within the school and are taught critical thinking and social action skills. The school often becomes involved in social action projects in the local community. Critical literacy (see Chapter Thirteen) is a central component of language arts programs that adopt Multicultural and Social Reconstructivist models of education.

Information for teachers and children on social action can be found at a Web site enti-tled Kids and Teens: Action Without Borders (www.idealist.org/kt). This site provides links to a comprehensive list of organizations and projects initiated by children around the world. Another site, YouthVoice.net (www.indiana.edu/~ythvoice), contains a useful sec-tion on social action tools developed by Barbara Lewis.

Limited English-Language Facility

Canada's current immigration policy is producing a steady flow of non-English-speaking immigrants. It is likely that teachers at some point in their careers will have children with limited or no English language proficiency in their classrooms. For all children learning English as their second language (ESL), the goal of instruction is twofold: to help them learn English and to help them move ahead cognitively (Allen, 1991).

Developing Language Proficiency

As indicated in Chapter One, most non-English-speaking children are immersed in class-rooms where English is the language of instruction, often without any special assistance to support them as they learn English. Watts-Taffe and Truscott (2000, pp. 258–259) believe that the following basic principles of language development hold for both native-English speakers and students learning English as a second language:

- Reading, writing, listening, speaking, and thinking develop in an integrated manner.
- Language learning works best when children use language for meaningful purposes.
- What constitutes meaningful language learning is affected by an individual's prior experiences, culture, and goals.
- Language learning works best when children are encouraged to take risks, experi-ment, and make mistakes.
- Modeling and scaffolding are critical to successful language learning.

According to Cummins (1994), language proficiency includes both social and academic aspects. Social language is often informal and is usually accompanied by facial expres-sions, gestures, and body language. Because this context is rich, precise vocabulary and standard grammar are not necessary for successful communication. In addition, there is often time for multiple attempts at communication, and the individuals involved are usu-ally there by choice and have an authentic desire to communicate.

In contrast, academic language is tied to academic thinking and reasoning, is often con-text-reduced, and takes place in limited time frames. Not surprisingly, social language skills develop more quickly than academic language skills. Increasing the degree to which learning situations are context-rich is one way to facilitate the development of both the language and academic competence of ESL students (Watts-Taffe and Truscott, 2000).

Instructional Practices for ESL Students

Perhaps the most crucial thing that teachers of ESL children can do is immerse them in meaningful language experiences. This can be facilitated by

- selecting reading materials written with natural language patterns rather than con-trived material with limited vocabulary,
- using visual aids such as pictures and films, as well as gestures and facial expres-sions, to clarify meaning,

- building in comprehension checks and responding to requests for clarification (Pica, Young, and Doughty, 1987),
- providing language instruction in a meaningful context (e.g., a learning centre set up as a store), and
- providing opportunities for children to work together in pairs and small groups with their English-speaking peers on meaningful tasks that involve purposeful talk.

It is unclear whether speaking more slowly or pausing between sentences, clauses, and phrases assists low-proficiency English speakers (Derwing, 1990). We do know that idiomatic expressions are very confusing for second-language learners, and hence, when they are used, teachers need to explain their meanings.

Writing is one avenue for meaningful language use and, when combined with forms of visual expression, can be a safe haven for students going through a silent stage in their transition to a new language and culture. It is important that the initial focus be on content rather than conventions such as spelling and grammar. Watts-Taffe and Truscott (2000) suggest encouraging students to substitute the word in their own language for an English word they don't know to help them build confidence and focus on meaning. With their teacher's help, students then go back to the writing and replace these words with the English equivalents.

Shared reading also provides a rich context for the literacy learning of children with limited English proficiency. Big books (see Chapter Three) are ideal to use with these children because of the support given by pictures. It is important to point to pictures during discussion of the story to help children link meaning to words being used in the story. Picture storybooks (listed in Chapter Ten) also provide a rich resource for helping children develop language and literacy knowledge. By watching the teacher run his or her finger under the printed words during reading, children who have been exposed to different writing systems (e.g., Mandarin or Hebrew) develop an understanding about the directional characteristics of the English language. When reading books aloud, teachers can pause to indicate a change in events, use exaggerated intonation to emphasize key concepts, change the pitch or volume to stress certain aspects of the story, and use gestures to accompany actions in the story.

Most provinces have developed resource materials for helping teachers provide appropriate instruction for ESL students. Two of the more recently developed ones appear on the Ontario (edu.gov.on.ca/eng/document/curricul/esl18.pdf) and British Columbia (www.bced.gov.bc.ca/esl) Ministry of Education Web sites.

Learning Differences

As noted at the beginning of this section, all labels for learning differences are socially constructed, and the term *learning disabilities* is no exception. The notion of learning disabilities can be traced back to the work of James Hinshelwood who, in the late 1800s, began to study and write about what he called "congenital word-blindness." He hypothesized that the source of learning problems lay in children's brains, and this view persists to this day. In the 1920s, Samuel T. Orton, an American neurologist, replaced the term *congenital word-blindness* with *strephosymbolia* (mixed symbols), and this term was, in turn, replaced by *dyslexia*. In the 1960s, *learning disabilities* began to be used widely by educators, as it continues to be used today. "Dyslexia" is used primarily by medical practitioners.

The following definition was adopted by the Learning Disabilities Association of Canada in January 2002 (www.ldac-taac.ca/english/defined/definew.htm):

> "Learning disabilities" refers to a number of disorders which may affect the acquisition, organization, retention, understanding or use of verbal or nonverbal information. These disorders affect learning in individuals who otherwise demonstrate at least average abilities essential for thinking and/or reasoning. As such, learning disabilities are distinct from global intellectual deficiency.

The definition also indicates that learning disabilities interfere with acquisition of one or more of oral language, reading, writing, and mathematics, and may also involve difficulties with organizational skills, social perception, social interaction, and perspective taking. The definition includes the recognition that learning disabilities are due to genetic and/or neurobiological factors but not primarily due to hearing or vision problems, socioeconomic factors, cultural or linguistic differences, lack of motivation, or ineffective teaching.

Both the terms *learning disabilities* and *dyslexia* reflect a medical model: a problem needs to be labelled to indicate what's wrong with an individual before appropriate treatment can be prescribed. Indeed, in medicine, treatment follows logically from a diagnosis. If individuals have a bacterial infection, a doctor prescribes antibiotics and they get better. This is not the case for children who have difficulty learning to read. Being labelled as dyslexic does not lead directly to one's treatment, but it does have some other results.

For the child and the child's parents, the terms are both a help and a hindrance. On the one hand, they help parents feel that they did not do anything wrong in raising their children and give them a sense that they finally have an answer to the frustrating question of why their child is having difficulty learning to read. The terms also replace more derogatory labels such as "dumb," "lazy," or "bad."

On the other hand, because conditions such as dyslexia and a learning disability are viewed as relatively permanent, people view themselves as deficient learners for the rest of their lives. Hence, while the labels might bring relief in the short term, they can be devastating for some individuals in the long term. Another problem involves the locus of responsibility for the problem. What the learning disabilities movement has done is remove the spotlight from society (homes, communities, and schools) and place it squarely on the child. From this perspective, there is little need to consider the effectiveness of the school programs children are in or the social conditions they live in (Coles, 1987).

Instead of placing the responsibility for reading problems within children's heads, we recognize that reading difficulties may have multiple causes, including factors both within and outside of children. The combination of factors is different for each child who has difficulty learning to read. The effects of these factors also vary, from children who engage in word calling (pronouncing words correctly but not constructing meaning) to children who have so much difficulty processing print that the meaning they construct reflects very little of the author's message. Other children have developed strategies for dealing with print but read so little that they have to direct most of their attention to word identification and therefore have little left for making meaning. The variations go on and on. Regardless of the nature of the child's problem, however, there is often a mismatch between the child's needs and the instructional program in the classroom. Most of these children are asked to read material that is far too difficult for them, either because they have inadequate strategies for processing cues in words, or because they have insufficient background knowledge of the concepts involved.

Lipson and Wixson (1991) recommend that reading diagnosis focus on three areas:

1. analysis of the child's reading strategies and abilities,
2. analysis of teaching techniques and materials being used in the classroom, and
3. examination of the match between them and the needs of the child

This approach is relatively unique in textbooks on reading difficulties. Most others focus almost exclusively on within-child variables and do not consider reading instruction as a possible source of the problem. This is not a finger-pointing or blaming exercise, but rather a recognition that both the source of and the solution to the child's difficulties lie in the interaction between the child and the instructional context. Our goal as teachers is to maximize the match between the child's needs and the instruction we provide.

Mild Mental Disabilities

Crealock and Bachor (1995) estimate that approximately 2 to 5 percent of the population have a mild mental disability. As with learning disabilities, mental disability is generally considered to reside in the individual. However, again, it is people who decide who is and is not mentally disabled. For example, some say an IQ between 55 and 80 indicates a mental disability, while others choose between 52 and 67. Other evidence of the social nature of mental disabilities is the fact that minority groups, children with behaviour problems, and males are overrepresented in this group (Gillespie-Silver, 1979). In addition, changing social values are reflected in different labels for children in this group over time. Learners we now label as having mild cognitive disabilities (Alberta), mild intellectual disabilities (Ontario and British Columbia), or mild intellectual impairment (Quebec) were previously referred to as mentally retarded or handicapped.

The major distinguishing feature of these learners labelled as having mild mental disabilities is that they progress through the same stages of cognitive development as people of average intelligence, but at a slower rate (Bond, Tinker, Wasson, and Wasson, 1994). Similarly, language development in this group is slowed down but not qualitatively different. Hence, most of the teaching techniques suggested in this book are just as appropriate for children with mild mental handicaps as for other children. The major difference is the rate at which instruction proceeds, with numerous opportunities for repetition and practice. However, as with all children, the goal is to determine each child's individual needs and to match instruction as closely as possible to those needs.

Social constructivists view individual differences among children not as deficits, but as factors to take into account when planning instruction. We believe that appropriate instruction, not labelling, is the key to language learning.

PARENTS AS PARTNERS

The International Reading Association recommends that teachers implement effective strategies to include parents as partners in the literacy development of their children (Armbruster and Osborn, 2002). This is a recognition that school success begins at home, and that parents are the first and most important people in the education of their children. Research shows that parental involvement of almost any kind is related to school achievement in general and that there is a strong relationship between a child's home environment and success in learning to read and write at school.

Home Environment and School Success

Children who are successful in acquiring school-based literacy tend to come from homes with the following characteristics (Armbruster and Osborn, 2002):

- Literacy is valued and parents model an interest in reading and writing.
- An abundance of print materials is available.
- Academic achievement is encouraged.
- Parents frequently read to and with children.
- Parents provide a language-rich environment.
- Parents are involved with their children's academic growth in school.

This does not mean that all children who come from homes with these characteristics develop literacy easily or that all children who do not have these advantages experience school failure. It also does not mean that homes that do not have these characteristics are bad places for children to grow up.

In their study of low-income families in one American neighbourhood, Taylor and Dorsey-Gaines (1988) painted a picture of adaptation and survival rather than failure and deficiency. Despite inadequate housing, lack of essential services, limited access to higher education, and restricted job opportunities, the families they studied not only survived, but were active members in a literate society. The challenge for the teacher is to acknowledge, value, and accommodate the literacy knowledge all children bring to the school context and to build partnerships with their parents.

Building Partnerships with Parents

Including parents as partners in their children's literacy development is not a one-way relationship with information going from the teacher to the parents. Parents from different cultural backgrounds can provide valuable information on cultural forms of literacy and how they view their child's literacy development. However, some of these parents believe that when they send their child to school, they turn over responsibility of their child's education to that institution (Christie, Enz, and Vukelich, 2003). Communication with all parents is essential to the promotion of parental involvement.

One way to promote parental involvement is by encouraging them to work with their children on literacy activities at home. Teachers can (Arbruster and Osborn, 2002):

- Elicit support for reading by encouraging parents to read to and with their children and to talk about books being read, by having them encourage their children to read independently, and by encouraging them to help their children get a library card and use their local public library.
- Provide materials and methods for parents to use with their children. Christie, Enz, and Vukelich (2003) suggest sending book bags home with children. Each bag contains three or four books and informal, interactive activities for extending children's language and literacy abilities. Each bag also contains two response journals (one for the child and one for the parent). For parents who do not speak English, Christie, Enz and Vukelich suggest including tapes and tape recorders. Each bag includes an inventory so parents and children can ensure that they return everything in the bag.

- Build bridges between home and school literacy by including books in the bag from the parents culture, by having children interview older relatives in families with a strong oral tradition, and by inviting family members to the classroom to share their literacy traditions.

Parents can find a wealth of ideas on working with their children from the National Parent Information Network on the Internet (www.npin.org). Although this site was developed for parents in the United States, many ideas included in newsletters and articles will be of use to parents in Canada as well.

Another way teachers can encourage involvement of parents is by communicating with them about language arts instruction in their classroom. Parent-teacher conferences and open houses are common ways to do this, but it is better to use the following strategies to keep parents informed throughout the year (Armbruster and Osborn, 2002):

- Invite parents into the classroom as observers, guest speakers, and volunteers.
- Send home letters, newsletters, and students' work. Along with samples of a student's work, teachers send an explanation of the nature of the assignment and what it tells about the child's school progress.
- Call or visit parents. This will be most effective if at least some of the time the teacher is calling to talk about what the child does well at school.

Perhaps one of the least effective ways to communicate with parents is through report cards, but we provide some suggestions in the next section for increasing their usefulness.

Reporting to Parents

Parents have a right to know how their children are progressing in school relative to widely held expectations, and they generally *want* to know. But what is the most effective way of conveying this information to them? Report cards have changed greatly in the past 15 years, and an increased range of alternatives to the report card is now being used. These include parent–teacher–student conferences, portfolios to demonstrate student achievement, and student journals and anecdotal notes to show a record of student performance. Many of these strategies are used in conjunction with the more formal report card.

Teachers accumulate information about children's learning throughout the weeks of schooling. Many keep a file on each child with notes about her or his progress. Samples of writing, reading checklists, and other such instruments are kept in the file. At reporting time, the teacher converts this information into a grading system. Most teachers struggle with this task for a long time. How do we best represent the efforts of children in their schooling? There is no simple and straightforward answer to this question, and most teachers find their own way to amalgamate the data. Grades need to be accompanied by other, more descriptive reporting methods in order to have much value to parents, and most report cards make provision for teacher comments in addition to grades.

Report cards are usually sent home three times each year in the elementary grades. Sometimes report cards are distributed to the children (especially the first one of the year) only when parents attend a parent–teacher–student conference at the school. This ensures that parents fully understand the report card, and that they also see evidence of what their child is doing in school.

Even more helpful is ongoing communication between the school and home of the type indicated earlier in this section. Some teachers also provide regular interim progress updates through a dialogue journal of some type to keep parents and their child informed. This helps to ensure that the information in report cards is not a surprise.

A recent development in reporting to parents is the student-led conference. Here, the students are in charge, each selecting the material to show his or her parents and explaining what these materials mean in terms of his or her progress. Obviously, the teacher plays a crucial role in preparing the children and materials for the conference. The teacher ensures that the children are well prepared, have selected appropriate materials to share, and can say why these materials reflect their growth and achievement.

If portfolios are kept on an ongoing basis, student-led conferences are much easier to arrange. Portfolios were discussed in Chapters Three, Four, and Nine. Student learning logs and journals can also be used to demonstrate a child's learning. A selection of material from the portfolio can be used in the parent–child conference. Parents do not need to see everything their child has done. Students will have taken some work home on a daily or weekly basis before report time. Material in the portfolio is chosen for a particular reason, some of it by the child and some by the child and teacher together.

> We end this text on a familiar refrain: no one way of communicating with parents is best for all families. What will work best for each family is dependent upon cultural, linguistic, and economic factors.

SUMMARY

While no organizational structure is best for all classrooms, a major goal is to foster and support balanced language arts teaching and learning. Teachers take four major components into account as they plan and organize language arts programs: materials, time, space, and children.

Traditionally, basal reading series have provided the material for language arts programs throughout Canada and the United States. More recently, there has been a movement to increased use of children's literature and nonbook materials as well. Whether or not teachers choose to use a basal series, we believe that it is important that teachers make a wide range of materials available. These materials need to reflect the range of cultural backgrounds and the reading levels of the children. Many teachers select and organize materials according to themes, but the most important criterion to use when selecting any material, whether a book, magazine, videotape, or computer program, is the extent to which it is consistent with the philosophy of the language arts program and will contribute to children's language learning.

When making decisions about the organization of time, space, and children, teachers need to provide for whole-class instruction, small group work, and independent practice. Whole-class instruction is effective for helping children set learning objectives, for teaching new strategies to all children, for reading to children, and for evaluating their accomplishments.

Ability groups have traditionally dominated language arts classrooms, but more educators are now recommending a range of grouping practices to meet the diverse abilities and interests of children. These include interest, research, special needs, and paired groupings. Cooperative learning rather than individual competition is becoming increasingly common in elementary language arts classrooms. Learning centres are one way to encourage children to work in groups. It is also important that children have opportunities to read and write independently each day and that at least some of the time they choose what they read and write about. Allocating time for one or two large daily time blocks for language arts provides flexibility and facilitates integration.

One of the biggest challenges language arts teachers face is meeting the needs of all children in their classrooms. Labels for children with special needs are social constructions that have been used over the past 40 years to decide who receives special assistance. In recent years, there has been a shift away from providing special assistance outside of regular classrooms to inclusive education.

Intervention programs can break the cycle of failure when they occur early, provide increased time for reading and reading instruction, provide high-quality reading instruction, use certified teachers, involve one-on-one or small-group instruction, and are coordinated with excellent classroom instruction. Reading Recovery is an intervention program that meets most of these requirements.

Increasing numbers of children are entering schools with English as their second language. It is important that these children understand what they see and hear, and that they be immersed in meaningful learning experiences. The labels "learning disabilities" and "mild mental disabilities" are both social constructions, and as for all children, the teacher's main goal is to maximize the match between each child's needs and the classroom teaching.

Another challenge for teachers is how to include parents as partners in the language and literacy development of their children. Teachers build partnerships by encouraging parents to work with their children at home on literacy activities and by communicating with parents about the language arts instruction in their classrooms.

SELECTED PROFESSIONAL RESOURCES

Booth, D. (1994). *Classroom voices: Language-based learning in the elementary school.* Toronto: Harcourt Brace. The focus of this book is the language-based learning program in one Ontario school. The first two chapters are on planning and organizing programs. A special feature is the inclusion of numerous teachers' and children's stories throughout the book.

Fountas, I. C. and Pinnell, G. S. (1996). *Guided reading: Good first teaching for all children.* Portsmouth, NH: Heinemann. The major question Fountas and Pinnell attempt to answer in this book is how a teacher can provide young readers with materials and instruction that fit their individual levels of development. The authors present a blueprint for a balanced literacy program, including how to provide guided reading instruction, what components to include in programs, and how to organize classrooms to implement these programs.

Sleeter, C. E. and Grant, C. A. (2003). *Making choices for multicultural education: Five approaches to race, class, and gender.* Danvers, MA: John Wiley & sons. In this book, Sleeter and Grant describe five approaches to multicultural education. For each model, they discuss major goals, target students, practices related to curriculum and instruction, classroom decorations, support services, and school-wide concerns. At the end of each chapter, they present specific classroom examples.

CHILDREN'S MATERIALS NOTED IN CHAPTER FOURTEEN

Collections. (1999). Scarborough, ON: Prentice Hall Ginn Canada.

Gage cornerstones: Canadian language arts. (1999). Toronto: Gage Educational Publishing Company.

Nelson language arts. (2000). Scarborough, ON: Nelson Thomson Learning.

Seuss, Dr. (1960). *Green eggs and ham.* New York: Random House.

REFERENCES

Allen, V. G. (1991). Teaching bilingual and ESL children. In J. Flood, J. M. Jensen, D. Lapp, and J. R. Squire (eds.), *Handbook of research on teaching the English language arts* (pp. 356–364). New York: Macmillan.

Armbruster, B. B. and Osborn, J. H. (2002). *Reading instruction and assessment: Understanding the IRA standards*. Boston, MA: Allyn & Bacon.

Banks, J. A. and Banks, C. A. (eds.). (1989). *Multicultural education: Issues and perspectives*. Boston: Allyn & Bacon.

Barr, R. and Dreeben, R. (1991). Grouping students for reading instruction. In R. Barr, R. L. Kamil, P. B. Mosenthal, and P. D. Pearson (eds.), *Handbook of reading research, Volume II* (pp. 885–910). New York: Longman.

Benterud, J. G. (1983). Four first-graders' use of reading time during the language arts period in their natural classroom setting. MA thesis, University of Alberta, Edmonton, AB.

Bond, G. L., Tinker, M. A., Wasson, B. B., and Wasson, J. B. (1994). *Reading difficulties: Their diagnosis and correction*. Boston: Allyn & Bacon.

Booth, D. (1994). *Classroom voices: Language-based learning in the elementary school*. Toronto: Harcourt Brace.

British Columbia Ministry of Education. (1999). *English as a Second Language Learners: A Guide for Classroom Teachers*. Available: www.bced.gov.bc.ca/esl.

Brabham, E. G. and Villaume, S. K. (2002). Leveled text: The good news and the bad news. *Reading Teacher*, 55 (5), 438–441.

Canadian Institute of Reading Recovery™. (2000). *1990–2000 Research Report*. Available: www.cirr.ca/9900research.htm.

Center, Y., Wheldall, K., Freeman, L., Outhred, L., and McNaught, M. (1995). An evaluation of Reading Recovery. *Reading Research Quarterly*, 30 (2), 240–261.

Christie, J., Enz, B., and Vukelich, C. (2003). *Teaching language and literacy: Preschool through the elementary grades*. Boston, MA: Allyn & Bacon.

Clay, M. M. (1993). *Reading Recovery: A guidebook for teachers in training*. Portsmouth, NH: Heinemann.

Coles, G. S. (1987). *The learning mystique*. New York: Pantheon Books.

Crealock, C. and Bachor, D. (1995). *Instructional strategies for students with special needs*. Scarborough, ON: Allyn & Bacon Canada.

Cummins, J. (1994). The acquisition of English as a second language. In K. Spangenberg-Urbschat and R Prichard (eds.), *Kids come in all languages: Reading instruction for ESL students* (pp. 36–62). Newark, DE: International Reading Association.

Cunningham, P. M. and Allington, R. L. (2003). *Classrooms that work: They can all read and write* (3rd ed.). New York: Longman.

Derwing, T. M. (1990). Speech rate is no simple matter: Rate adjustment and NS-NNS interaction. *Studies in Second Language Acquisition*, 12 (3), 303–313.

Deyhle, D. and Swisher, K. (1997). Research in American Indian and Alaska Native education: From assimilation to self-determination. In M. Apple (ed.), *Review of research in education* (pp. 113–194). Washington, DC: American Educational Research Association.

End Legislated Poverty. (1993). Poverty and school performance. In S. Baxter (ed.), *A child is not a toy* (pp. 133–143). Vancouver: New Star Books.

Fawson, P. C. and Reutzel, D. R. (2000). But I only have a basal: Implementing guided reading in the early grades. *Reading Teacher*, 54 (1), 84–97.

Finazzo, D. A. (1997). *All for the children: Multicultural essentials of literature*. New York: Delmar.

Fountas, I. C. and Pinnell, G. S. (1996). *Guided reading: Good first teaching for all children*. Portsmouth, NH: Heinemann.

Fountas, I. C. and Pinnell, G. S. (1999). *Matching books to readers: Using leveled texts in guided reading, K–3*. Portsmouth, NH: Heinemann.

Gillespie-Silver, P. (1979). *Teaching reading to children with special needs*. Columbus, OH: Charles E. Merrill.

Giroux, H. A. (1987). Critical literacy and student experience: Donald Graves' approach to literacy. *Language Arts*, 64 (2), 175–181.

Glynn, T., Bethune, N., Crooks, T., Ballard, K., and Smith, J. (1992). Reading Recovery in context: Implementation and outcome. *Educational Psychology*, 12, 249–261.

Golub, J. N. (1994). Cooperative learning. In A. C. Purves (ed.), *Encyclopedia of English studies and language arts* (pp. 298–299). New York: Scholastic.

Goodman, K., Shannon, P., Freeman, Y. S., and Murphy, S. (1988). *Report card on basal readers*. Katonah, NY: Richard C. Owen.

Gregory, D. (2002). *The Canadian Institute of Reading Recovery™ National implementation data (2001–2002)*. Preliminary report prepared for the Board of Directors, Canadian Institute of Reading Recovery™.

Hiebert, E. H. (1999). Text matters in learning to read. *Reading Teacher*, 52 (6), 552–566.

Indrisano, R. and Paratore, J. R. (1991). Classroom contexts for literacy learning. In J. Flood, J. M. Jensen, D. Lapp, and J. R. Squire (eds.), *Handbook of research on teaching the English language arts* (pp. 477–487). New York: Macmillan.

International Reading Association. (1999). *Using multiple methods of beginning reading instruction: A position statement of the International Reading Association*. Newark, DL: Author. Available: www.reading.org/pdf/methods.pdf.

Jacobs, E. and Jordan, C. (1993). Understanding minority education: Framing the issues. In E. Jacob and C. Jordan (eds.), *Minority education: Anthropological perspectives* (pp. 3–13). Norwood, NJ: Ablex.

Jobe, R. and Hart, P. (1991). The basalization of children's literature. *Reflections on Canadian Literacy*, 9 (3 & 4), 147–150.

Kids and Teens: Action Without Borders. Available: www.idealist.org/kt.

Learning resources—Provinces and territories, Curriculum Services Canada. Available: www.curriculum.org/csc/resources/provincial.shtml.

Lipson, M. Y. and Wixson, K. K. (1991). *Assessment and instruction of reading disability: An interactive approach*. New York: HarperCollins.

Mayfield, M. I. (1992). Organizing for teaching and learning. In L. O. Ollila and M. I. Mayfield (eds.), *Emerging literacy: Preschool, kindergarten and primary grades* (pp. 166–195). Boston: Allyn & Bacon.

Moore, M. and B. Wade. (1998). Reading and comprehension: A longitudinal study of ex–Reading Recovery students. *Educational Studies*, 24 (2), 195–202.

Morrow, L. M. (1989). Designing the classroom to promote literacy development. In D. S. Strickland and L. M. Morrow (eds.), *Emerging literacy: Young children learn to read and write* (pp. 121–134). Newark, DE: International Reading Association.

Morrow, L. M. and Lesnick, J. (2001). Examining the educational value of children's magazines. *The California Reader*, 34 (2). Available: www.childmagmonth.org/learning/Research.pdf.

Murphy, S. (1991). Authorship and discourse types in Canadian basal reading programs. *Reflections on Canadian Literacy*, 9 (3 & 4), 133–138.

Ogbu, J. U. (1993). Frameworks—variability in minority school performance: A problem in search of an explanation. In E. Jacobs and C. Jordan (eds.), *Minority education: Anthropological perspectives* (pp. 83–111). Norwood, NJ: Ablex.

Ontario Ministry of Education. (2001). English as a second language and English literacy development: A resource guide. Available: edu.gov.on.ca/eng/document/curricul/esl18.pdf.

Pica, T., Young, R., and Doughty, C. (1987). The impact of interaction on comprehension. *TESOL Quarterly*, 21, 737–758.

Pikulski, J. J. (1994). Preventing reading failure: A review of five effective programs. *Reading Teacher*, 48 (1), 30–39.

Pinnell, G. S. and Fountas, I. D. (2002). *Leveled books for readers: Grades 3–6*. Portsmouth, NH: Heinemann.

Pinnell, G. S., Fried, M. D., and Estice, R. M. (1990). Reading Recovery: Learning how to make a difference. *Reading Teacher, 43,* 282–295.

Pinnell, G. S., Lyons, C. A., DeFord, D. E., Bryk, A. S., and Seltzer, M. (1993). Comparing instructional models for the literacy education of high-risk first graders. *Reading Research Quarterly, 29* (1), 10–38.

Reading Recovery® Council of North America. (2001). Reading Recovery facts and figures (U.S. 1984–2001). Available: www.readingrecovery.org/sections/reading/facts.asp.

Ritter, N. (1999). Teaching interdisciplinary thematic units in language arts. ERIC Digest D142 (ED436003). Available: www.ed.gov/databases/ERIC_Digests/ed436003.html.

Routman, R. (2000) *Conversations.* Portsmouth, NH: Heinemann.

Saskatchewan Special Education Review Committee. (2000). *Directions for diversity: Enhancing supports to children and youth with diverse needs.* Regina, SK: Saskatchewan Learning. Available: www.sasked.gov.sk.ca/k/pecs/se/docs/review/committee.pdf.

Shanahan, T. and Barr, R. (1995). Reading Recovery: An independent evaluation of the effects of an early instructional intervention for at-risk learners. *Reading Research Quarterly, 30* (4), 958–996.

Shannon, P. (1989). The struggle for control of literacy lessons. *Language Arts, 66* (6), 625–634.

Simner, M. L. (1993). A position paper on beginning reading instruction in Canadian schools. *Canadian Journal of School Psychology, 9* (1), 96–99.

Slavin, R. E. (1980). Cooperative learning. *Review of Educational Research, 50,* 315–342.

Sleeter, C. E. and Grant, C. A. (2003). *Making choices for multicultural education: Five approaches to race, class, and gender.* Danvers, MA: John Wiley & Sons.

Spiegel, D. L. (1995). A comparison of traditional remedial programs and Reading Recovery: Guidelines for success for all programs. *Reading Teacher, 49* (2), 86–96.

Szymusiak, K. and Sibberson, F. (2001). *Beyond leveled books: Supporting transitional readers in Grades 2–5.* Portland, MA: Stenhouse Publishers.

Taberski, S. (2000). *On solid ground: Strategies for teaching reading K–3.* Portsmouth, NH: Heinemann.

Taylor, D. and Dorsey-Gaines, L. (1988). *Growing up literate: Learning from inner-city families.* Portsmouth, NH: Heinemann.

Topping, K. (1989). Peer tutoring and paired reading: Combining two powerful techniques. *Reading Teacher, 42* (7), 488–494.

Vogt, M. E. (1997) Cross-Curricular Thematic Instruction. Available: www.eduplace.com/rdg/res/vogt.html.

Wasik, B. A. and Slavin, R. E. (1993). Preventing early reading failure with one-to-one tutoring: A review of five programs. *Reading Research Quarterly, 28* (2), 179–200.

Watts-Taffe, S. and Truscott, D. M. (2000). Using what we know about language and literacy development for ESL students in the mainstream classroom. *Language Arts, 77* (3), 258–264.

Wiener, R. B. and Cohen, J. H. (1997). *Literacy portfolios: Using assessment to guide instruction.* Columbus, OH: Merrill.

Wilson, R. M. and Cleland, C. J. (1985). *Diagnostic and remedial reading for classroom and clinic.* Columbus, OH: Charles E. Merrill.

Wiseman, D. L. (1992). *Learning to read with literature.* Boston: Allyn & Bacon.

YouthVoice.net. Available: www.indiana.edu/~ythvoice.

Appendix

Children's Literature by Grade Level: Fiction and Nonfiction for Recreational Reading

Preschool to Kindergarten

Fiction

Adoff, A. (1991). *Hard to be six.* New York: Lothrop, Lee & Shepard.

Ahlberg, J. and Ahlberg, A. (1978). Each peach pear plum. London: Kestrel Books.

Alborough, J. (1992). *Where's my teddy?* Cambridge, MA: Candlewick Press.

Brett, J. (1999). *Gingerbread baby.* New York: Putnam's Sons Publishers.

Brown, M. W. (1982). *Goodnight moon.* New York: Harper Collins Publishers.

Brown, R. (1985). *The big sneeze.* New York: Mulberry Books.

Browne, A. (1985). *Willie the champ.* New York: Knopf.

Carle, E. (1968). *The very hungry caterpillar.* New York: World Books.

Day, A. (1985). *Good dog, Carl.* New York: Simon & Schuster.

Falconer, I. (2000). *Olivia.* New York: Atheneum.

🍁 Fernandes, E. (2000). *Sleepy little mouse.* Toronto: Kids Can Press.

🍁 Gay, M. (2002). *Stella, fairy of the forest.* Toronto: Douglas & McIntyre.

🍁 Gay, M. (1999). *Stella, star of the sea.* Toronto: Groundwood Books.

Hutchins, P. (1969). *Rosie's walk.* London: Bodley Head Press.

🍁 Levert, M. (2001). *An island in the soup.* Toronto: Groundwood Books.

🍁 Morgan, A. (2001). *Matthew and the moonlight wrecker.* Toronto: Stoddart Kids.

Ormerod, J. (1981). *Sunshine.* Harmondsworth, UK: Puffin/Penguin.

Ormerod, J. (1982). *Moonlight.* Harmondsworth, UK: Puffin/Penguin.

Rathmann, P. (1994). *Goodnight, gorilla.* New York: G. P. Putnam's Sons.

Rosen, M. and Oxenbury, H. (1989). *We're going on a bear hunt.* London: Walker Books Ltd.

🍁 Schwartz, R. (2001). *The mole sisters and the moonlit night.* Toronto: Annick Press.

Sis, P. (2001). *Ballerina!* New York: Greenwillow Books.

Sis, P. (1998). *Fire truck.* New York: Greenwillow Books.

🍁 Vaage, C. (1995). *Bibi and the bull.* Edmonton, AB: Dragon Hill Press.

Waddell, M. (1992). *Can't you sleep, Little Bear?* Cambridge, MA: Candlewick Press.

Waddell, M. (1992). *Owl babies.* Cambridge, MA: Candlewick Press.

Wild, M. and Legge, D. (2001). *Tom goes to kindergarten.* Sydney, Australia: ABC Books.

Non-Fiction

Base, G. (2001). *The waterhole.* New York: Viking. (All ages.)

Bradley, K. B. (2001). *Pop! A book about bubbles.* New York: HarperCollins Children's Books.

Brown, R. (2001). *Ten seeds.* New York: Alfred A. Knopf/Random House Children's Books.

🍁 Everts, T. and Kalman, B. (1995). *Horses.* Niagara-on-the-Lake, ON: Crabtree Publishing.

Rockwell, A. (1999). *One bean.* New York: Walker Publishing Company.

Rockwell, A. (2001). *Bugs are insects.* New York: HarperCollins.

🍁 Swanson, D. (2001). *Animals can be so sleepy.* Vancouver: Greystone Books.

Tafuri, N. (1999). *Snowy flowy blowy.* New York: Scholastic Press.

Kindergarten to Grade 2

Fiction

🍁 Bailey, L. (2001). *The best figure skater in the whole wide world.* Toronto: Kids Can Press.

🍁 Bedard, M. (2000). *The wolf of Gubbio.* Toronto: Stoddart Publishing.

🍁 Bogart, J. (1997). *Jeremiah learns to read.* Richmond Hill, ON: North Winds Press.

♣ Delaronde, D. (2000). *Little Métis and the Métis Sash.* Winnipeg, MB: Pemmican Publications, Inc.

♣ Eyvindson, P. (1994). *The night Rebecca stayed too late.* Winnipeg, MB: Pemmican Publications.

♣ Gillard, D. (2001). *Music from the sky.* Toronto: Groundwood Books.

♣ Gillmor, J. (2000). *Yuck, a love story.* Toronto: Stoddart Publishing.

♣ Gilman, P. (1992). *Something from nothing.* Richmond Hill, ON: North Winds Press.

♣ Gilman, P. (1998). *Pirate Pearl.* Markham, ON: North Winds Press.

♣ Gregory, N. (2000). *Wild Girl and Gran.* Calgary, AB: Red Deer Press.

♣ Hartry, N. (2000). *Jocelyn and the ballerina.* Markham, ON: Fitzhenry & Whiteside.

Hoffman, M. (1991). *Amazing Grace.* New York: Dial.

♣ Hundal, N. (1999). *Melted star journey.* Toronto: HarperCollins Canada.

Hutchins, P. (1986). *The doorbell rang.* New York: Greenwillow Books.

♣ Hutchins, H. (1997). *Shoot for the moon, Robyn.* Halifax, NS: Formac Publishing.

♣ Kusugak, M. (1998). *Arctic stories.* Toronto: Annick Press.

♣ Leedahl, S. (1999). *The bone talker.* Red Deer, AB: Red Deer Press.

♣ London, J. (2001). *What the animals were waiting for.* Markham, ON: Scholastic Canada Ltd.

♣ Manuel, L. (1997). *Lucy Maud and the Cavendish cat.* Toronto: Tundra Books.

Moser, B. (2001). *The three little pigs.* Boston: Little, Brown & Company.

♣ Oberman, S. (1997). *By the Hanukkah light.* Toronto: McClelland & Stewart.

♣ Oppel, K. (2001). *Peg and the whale.* Toronto: HarperCollins Canada Ltd.

Polacco, P. (1990). *Just plain fancy.* New York: Bantam.

Rathmann, P. (1995). *Officer Buckle and Gloria.* New York: G. P. Putnam's Sons.

♣ Sadler, A. (2001). *Sandwiches for Duke.* Toronto: Stoddart Books.

Sanderson, R. (2001). *Cinderella.* Boston: Little, Brown & Company.

Sis, P. (2000). *Madlenka.* New York: Greenwillow Books.

♣ Thompson, R. (2000). *The follower.* Markham, ON: Fitzhenry & Whiteside.

♣ Thurman, M. (1993). *One, two, many.* Toronto: Viking Kestrel.

♣ Tibo, G. (2000). *The cowboy kid.* Toronto: Tundra Books.

Waddell, M. and Oxenbury, H. (1991). *Farmer duck.* London: Walker Books, Ltd.

♣ Wallace, I. (2000). *Duncan's way.* Toronto: Groundwood Books.

Ward, H. (2001). *The animals' Christmas carol.* Brookfield, CN: The Millbrook Press. (All ages.)

♣ Wilson, B. (2001). *A fiddle for Angus.* Toronto: Tundra Books.

Non-Fiction

Baker, J. (1987). *Where the forest meets the sea.* New York: Greenwillow Books.

Bernard, R. (2001). *Insects.* Washington, DC: National Geographic Society.

Bunting, E. (1993). *Red fox running.* New York: Houghton Mifflin Company.

Cole, H. (1998). *I took a walk.* New York: Greenwillow Books.

Cowley, J. (1999). *Red-eyed tree frog.* New York: Scholastic Press.

Davies, N. (2001). *Bat loves the night.* Cambridge, MA: Candlewick Press.

♣ Douglas, A. (2000). *Before you were born: The inside story!* Toronto: Owl Books.

George, T. C. (2000). *Jellies: The life of jellyfish.* Brookfield, CN: Millbrook Press.

Grindley, S. (1997). *Polar star.* Atlanta, GA: Peachtree Publishers.

Horenstein, H. (1999). *A is for ... ? A photographer's alphabet of animals.* San Diego: Gulliver/Harcourt Brace.

Kessler, C. (2001). *Jubela.* New York: Simon & Schuster Books.

King, D. (1997). *The flight of the snow goose.* London: HarperCollins.

♣ Kusugak, M. (1996). *My Arctic 1, 2, 3.* Toronto: Annick Press.

Lehn, B. (1998). *What is a scientist?* Brookfield, CN: The Millbrook Press.

Posada, M. (2000). *Dandelions: Stars in the grass.* Minneapolis, MN: Carolrhoda Books/Lerner.

Zuchora-Walske, C. (2000). *Leaping grasshoppers.* Minneapolis, MN: Lerner Publications.

Grade 2 to Grade 3

Fiction

Ahlberg, A. and Briggs, R. (2001). *The adventures of Bert.* Toronto: Penguin Books. Ltd.

♣ Brownridge, W. (1995). *The moccasin goalie.* Victoria, BC: Orca Books.

♣ Brownridge, W. (1997). *The final game.* Victoria, BC: Orca Books.

Bunting, E. (1994). *Smoky nights.* New York: Harcourt Brace.

♣ Eyvindson, P. (1996). *Red parka Mary.* Winnipeg, MB: Pemmican Publications Inc.

Fox, M. (1989). *Wilfred Gordon McDonald Partridge.* New York: Kane Miller.

♣ Gilmore, R. (1999). *A screaming kind of day.* Markham, ON: Fitzhenry & Henry.

♣ Graham, G. (1998). *The strongest man this side of Cremona.* Red Deer, AB: Red Deer College Press.

🍁 Hume, S. E. (2001). *Red moon follows truck*. Victoria, BC: Orca Book Publishers.

🍁 Hundal, N. (2001). *Number 21*. Markham, ON: Fitzhenry & Whiteside.

🍁 Jam, T. (1998). *The stoneboat*. Toronto: Groundwood Books.

🍁 Jam, T. (2001). *The kid linet*. Toronto: Groundwood Books.

🍁 Kulyk Keefer, J. (2000). *Anna's goat*. Victoria, BC: Orca Book Publishers.

🍁 Lawson, J. (1999). *Bear on the train*. Toronto: Kids Can Press.

🍁 Lawson, J. (1992). *The dragon's pearl*. Toronto: Stoddart.

🍁 Lawson, J. (1997). *Emma and the silk train*. Toronto: Kids Can Press.

🍁 Lebox, A. (2001). *Wild bog tea*. Toronto: Groundwood Books.

🍁 Miller, R. (2002). *The bear on the bed*. Toronto: Kids Can Press.

🍁 Mollel, T. M. (1999). *My rows and piles of coins*. Markham, ON: Clarion Books.

🍁 Morck, I. (1996). *Tiger's new cowboy boots*. Red Deer, AB: Red Deer College Press.

Paterson, K. (1992). *The king's equal*. New York: HarperCollins Publishers.

🍁 Reynolds, M. (1999). *The prairie fire*. Victoria, BC: Orca Book Publishers.

🍁 Reynolds, M. (2000). *The magnificent piano recital*. Victoria, BC: Orca Book Publishers.

🍁 Richler, M. (1987). *Jacob Two-Two and the dinosaur*. Toronto: Puffin Books.

🍁 Richler, M. (1995). *Jacob Two-Two's first spy case*. Toronto: McClelland & Stewart, Inc.

🍁 Simmie, L. (1995). *Mr. Got to Go*. Red Deer, AB: Red Deer College Press.

Trivizas, E. (1993). *The three little wolves and the big bad pig*. London: William Heinemann Ltd.

🍁 Van Camp, R. (1998). *What's the most beautiful thing you know about horses?* Markham, ON: Children's Book Press.

Waddell, M. (1986). *The tough princess*. London: Walker Books.

Non-Fiction

Adler, D. A. (1999). *How tall, how short, how faraway?* New York: Holiday House.

Arnosky, J. (1996). *All about owls*. New York: Scholastic Hardcover.

🍁 Bateman, R. and Archbold, R. (1998). *Safari*. Toronto: Penguin Books Canada/Madison Press.

🍁 Hodge, D. (2000). *The kids book of Canada's railway and how the CPR was built*. Toronto: Kids Can Press.

Kroll, V. (1994). *The seasons and someone*. New York: Harcourt Brace & Company.

Kudlinski, K. (1999). *Dandelions*. Minneapolis, MN: Lerner Publications.

London, J. (1999). *Baby whale's journey*. San Francisco: Chronicle Books.

🍁 Mackin, B. (2001). *Soccer the winning way*. Vancouver: Greystone Books.

Martin, J. B. (1998). *Snowflake Bentley*. Boston: Houghton Mifflin.

McMillan, B. (1995). *Nights of the pufflings*. Boston: Houghton Mifflin Company.

🍁 Milich, Z. (2001). *The city ABC book*. Toronto: Kids Can Press.

Montgomery, S. (1999). *The snake scientist*. Boston: Houghton Mifflin.

🍁 Morton, A. (1993). *In the company of whales: From the diary of a whale watcher*. Victoria, BC: Orca Books.

Moss, M. (2000). *This is the tree: A story of the baobab*. London: Frances Lincoln Limited.

Pratt-Serafini, K. J. (2001). *Salamander rain: A lake and pond journal*. Nevada City, CA: Dawn Publications.

🍁 Pringle, L. (1991). *Batman: Exploring the world of bats*. New York: Charles Scribner's Sons.

Pulley Sayre, A. (2001). *Dig, wait, listen: A desert toad's tale*. New York: Greenwillow Books.

Singer, M. (2001). *Tough beginnings: How baby animals survive*. New York: Henry Holt Books for Young Readers.

Walker, A. M. (2001). *Fireflies*. Minneapolis, MN: Lerner Publications.

Wallace, K. (1998). *Gentle giant octopus*. Cambridge, MA: Candlewick Press.

Yolen, J. (1998). *Welcome to the icehouse*. New York: G. P. Putnam's Sons.

Yolen, J. (2001). *Welcome to the river of grass*. New York: G. P. Putnam's Sons.

Grade 3 to Grade 4

Fiction

Ahlberg, J. and Ahlberg, A. (1993). *It was a dark and stormy night*. London: Viking.

🍁 Andrews, J. (2000). *Out of the everywhere*. Toronto: Stoddart Publishing.

🍁 Baker, J. (1995). *The story of Rosy Dock*. New York: Greenwillow Books.

Bunting, E. (1991). *Fly away home*. New York: Clarion.

Browne, A. (1983). *Gorilla*. New York: Alfred A. Knopf, Inc.

🍁 Carrier, R. (1985). *The hockey sweater*. Montreal: Tundra Books.

🍁 Fitch, S. (1997). *If you could wear my sneakers!* Toronto: Doubleday. (Poetry)

🍁 Gauthier, G. (1995). *Mooch forever*. Tr. S. Cummins. Halifax, NS: Formac Publishing.

🍁 Gilmore, R. (2000). *Mina's spring of colours*. Markham, ON: Fitzhenry & Whiteside.

🍁 Highway, T. (2001). *Caribou song*. Toronto: HarperCollins. (In Cree and English.)

- Highway, T. (2002). *Dragonfly kite.* Toronto: HarperCollins. (In Cree and English.)
- Jam, T. (1997). *The fishing summer.* Toronto: Groundwood Books/Douglas & McIntyre.
- Keens-Douglas, R. (1992). *The nutmeg princess.* Toronto: Annick Press.
- Kusugak, M. (1993). *Northern lights: The soccer trails.* Toronto: Annick Press.
- Laurence, M. (1979). *The olden days coat.* Toronto: McClelland & Stewart.
- Lottridge, C. B. (1997). *Wings to fly.* Toronto: Groundwood Books.
- McCugan, J. (1994). *Josepha: A prairie boy's story.* Red Deer, AB: Red Deer College Press.
- Provensen, A. (2001). *The master swordsman and the magic doorway: Two legends from ancient China.* Toronto: Simon & Schuster Books for Young Readers.
- Roberts, K. (2001). *The thumb in the box.* Toronto: Groundwood Books.
- Spalding, A. (1999). *Phoebe and the gypsy.* Victoria, BC: Orca Book Publishers.
- Van Camp, R. (1999). *A man called Raven.* San Francisco: Children's Book Press.
- Wallace, I. (1999). *Boy of the deeps.* Toronto: Groundwood Books.
- Watts, I. M. (2000). *Remember me.* Toronto: Tundra Books.

Non-Fiction

- Anholt, L. (1998). *Stone girl, bone girl: The story of Mary Anning.* New York: Orchard Books.
- Baker, J. (1991). *Window.* New York: Greenwillow Books.
- Collard, S. B. (2000). *The forest in the clouds.* Watertown, MA: Charlesbridge.
- Dewey, J. O. (1999). *Antarctic journal: Four months at the bottom of the world.* New York: HarperCollins Publishers.
- Funston, S. (2000). *Mummies (Strange science).* Toronto: Owl Books.
- Godkin, C. (1997). *Sea otter inlet.* Markham, ON: Fitzhenry & Whiteside.
- Godkin, C. (1989). *Wolf Island.* Markham, ON: Fitzhenry & Whiteside.
- Granfield, L. (1999). *High flight: The story of World War II.* Toronto: Kids Can Press.
- Granfield, L. (1997). *Silent night.* Toronto: Tundra Books.
- Greenwood, B. (2001). *Gold rush fever: A story of the Klondike, 1898.* Toronto: Kids Can Press.
- Hancock, P. (1998). *The kids' book of Canadian prime ministers.* Toronto: Kids Can Press.
- Harrison, T. (1992). *O Canada.* Toronto: Kids Can Press.
- Hurst, C. O. (2001). *Rocks in his head.* New York: Greenwillow Books.
- Kalman, B. (1998). *Pioneer life: From A to Z.* New York: Crabtree Publishing.

- Kramer, S. (1995). *Theodoric's rainbow.* New York: W. H. Freeman & Co.
- Levine, S. and Johnston, L. (2000). *The science of sound and music.* New York: Sterling Publishing.
- Mann, E. (1996). *The Brooklyn Bridge.* New York: Mikaya Press.
- Maydak, M. (2001). *Salmon stream.* Nevada City, CA: Dawn Publications.
- Owens, A. M. and Yealland, J. (1999). *Canada's maple leaf: The story of our flag.* Toronto: Kids Can Press.
- Redman, I. (2001). *The elephant book: For the Elefriends campaign.* London: Walker Books.
- Rhodes, R. (2001). *A first book of Canadian art.* Toronto: Owl Books/Greey de Pencier Books. (All ages.)
- Siebert, D. (1991). *Sierra.* New York: HarperCollins.
- Skreslet, L. and Macleod, E. (2001). *To the top of Everest.* Toronto: Kids Can Press Ltd. (All ages.)

Grade 4 to Grade 5

Fiction

- Browne, A. (1998). *Voices in the park.* Toronto: Doubleday Canada Ltd.
- Collington, P. (1997). *A small miracle.* New York: Alfred Knopf.
- Creech, S. (1994). *Walk two moons.* New York: HarperCollins Publishers.
- Cumyn, A. (2002). *The secret life of Owen Skye.* Toronto: Groundwood Books.
- Curtis, C. P. (1995). *The Watsons go to Birmingham—1963.* New York: Bantam Doubleday Dell/Delacorte.
- Godfrey, M. and O'Keeffe, F. (1991). *There's a cow in my swimming pool.* Richmond Hill, ON: Scholastic Canada Ltd.
- Godfrey, M. (1994). *Just call me Boom Boom.* Richmond Hill, ON: Scholastic Canada.
- Lottridge, C. B. (1992). *Ticket to Curlew.* Toronto: Groundwood Books.
- MacAulay, D. (1995). *Shortcut.* Boston: Houghton Mifflin.
- MacGregor, R. (1997). *The Screech Owls series.* Toronto: McClelland & Stewart.
- Major, K. (2000). *Eh? to Zed: A Canadian ABeCedarium.* Calgary, AB: Red Deer Press.
- Mollel, T. (1990). *The orphan boy.* Toronto: Oxford University Press.
- Morin, P. (1998). *Animal dreaming: An aboriginal dreamtime story.* Toronto: Stoddart Kids.
- Muller, R. (2001). *The happy prince.* Toronto: Stoddart Kids.
- Oberman, S. (2000). *The wisdom bird: A tale of Solomon and Sheba.* Honesdale, PA: Boyds Mills Press.
- Oberman, S. (1994). *The always prayer shawl.* Honesdale, PA: Boyds Mills Press.

Scrimger, R. (1998). *The nose from Jupiter.* Toronto: Tundra Books.

Scrimger, R. (2000). *A nose for adventure.* Toronto: Tundra Books.

Spalding, A. (1995). *Finders keepers.* Victoria, BC: Beach Holme Publishing.

Taylor, C. (1987). *The doll.* Toronto: Douglas and McIntyre.

Valgardson, W. D. (1996). *Sarah and the people of Sand River.* Toronto: Groundwood Books.

Valgardson, W. D. (1997). *Garbage Creek.* Toronto: Groundwood. (Short stories.)

Wiesner, D. (1991). *Tuesday.* New York: Clarion.

Wynne-Jones, T. (1993). *Some of the kinder planets.* Toronto: Groundwood. (Short stories.)

Non-Fiction

Atkins, J. (1999). *Mary Anning and the sea dragon.* New York: Farrar, Straus & Giroux.

Beatty, O. and Geiger, J. (1992). *Buried in ice: Unlocking the secrets of a doomed Arctic voyage.* Mississauga, ON: Random House.

Cone, M. (1992). *Come back salmon.* San Francisco: Sierra Club Books for Children.

Goodman, S. E. (2001). *Claws, coats and camouflage: The ways animals fit into their world.* Brookfield, CN: Millbrook Press.

Goodman, S. E. (2001). *Seeds, stems and stamens: The ways plants fit into their world.* Brookfield, CN: Millbrook Press.

Granfield, L. (1993). *Cowboy: A kid's album.* Toronto: Groundwood Books.

Granfield, L. (1995). *In Flanders Fields: The story of the poem by John McCrae.* Toronto: Lester Publishing.

Kerley, B. (2001). *The dinosaurs of Waterhouse Hawkins.* New York: Scholastic.

Napier, M. (2002). *Z is for Zamboni: A hockey alphabet.* Chelsea, MI: Sleeping Bear Press.

Rainey, K. (1999). *Shooting hoops and skating loops: Great inventions in sports.* Toronto: Tundra Books.

Simon, S. (1999). *Tornadoes.* New York: Morrow Junior Books.

Suzuki, D. and Vanderlinden, K. (1999). *You are the earth.* Vancouver: Greystone Books.

Swanson, D. (1994). *Safari beneath the sea.* Vancouver: Whitecap Books.

Tanaka, S. (1996). *Discovering the iceman.* Richmond Hill, ON: Madison Press/ Scholastic Canada.

Tanaka, S. (1997). *The buried city of Pompeii: What it was like when Vesuvius exploded (I was there).* Richmond Hill, ON: Scholastic Canada.

Ulmer, M. (2001). *M is for maple: A Canadian alphabet.* Chelsea, MI: Sleeping Bear Press.

Zoehfeld, K. W. (2001). *Dinosaur parents, dinosaur young: Uncovering the mystery of dinosaur families.* New York: Clarion Books.

Grade 5 to Grade 6

Fiction

Bastedo, J. (2001). *Tracking Triple Seven.* Calgary, AB: Red Deer Press.

Buffie, M. (1987). *Who is Frances Rain?* Toronto: Kids Can Press Ltd.

Clark, J. (1995). *The dream carvers.* Toronto: Viking.

Dueck, A. (1996). *Anywhere but here.* Red Deer, AB: Red Deer College Press.

Ellis, D. (1999). *Looking for X.* Toronto: Groundwood Books.

Ellis, D. (2002). *Parvana's journey.* Toronto: Groundwood Books.

Ellis, S. (1997). *Back of beyond.* Toronto: Groundwood. (Short stories.)

Farmer, N. (1994). *The ear, the eye and the arm.* New York: Puffin Books.

Freeman, B. (1998). *Prairie fire!* Toronto: James Lorimer & Company Ltd., Publishers.

French, J. (2001). *Hitler's daughter.* London: Collins.

Galloway, P. (1995). *Atalanta: The fastest runner in the world.* Toronto: Annick Press.

Horrocks, A. (1996). *Breath of a ghost.* Toronto: Stoddart Kids.

Horrocks, A. (2000). *Topher.* Toronto: Stoddart Publishing.

Horvath, P. (2001). *Everything on a waffle.* New York: Farrar Strauss Giroux.

Hughes, M. (1998). (Ed.). *What if … ? Amazing stories.* Toronto: Tundra Books.

Hutchins, H. (1997). *The Prince of Tarn.* Toronto: Annick Press.

Jocelyn, M. (2000). *Earthly astonishments.* Toronto: Tundra Books.

Little, J. (2001). *Orphan at my door: The home child diary of Victoria Cope.* Markham, ON: Scholastic Canada Ltd.

McLaughlin, F. (1990). *Yukon journey.* New York: Scholastic, Inc.

McNicoll, S. (1994). *Bringing up Beauty.* Toronto: Maxwell Macmillan.

Oppel, K. (1997). *Silverwing.* Scarborough, ON: HarperCollins.

Oppel, K. (2002). *Firewing.* Toronto: Harper Collins.

Pearson, K. (1996). *Awake and dreaming.* Toronto: Viking.

Sachar, L. (2000). *Holes.* New York: Dell Yearling.

Silverthorne, J. (1996). *The secret of Sentinel Rock.* Regina, SK: Coteau Books.

Spinelli, J. (1990). *Maniac Magee.* New York: Little, Brown.

Wilson, E. (1995). *The Inuk mountie adventure.* Toronto: HarperCollins Canada Ltd.

Withrow, S. (1998). *Bat summer.* Toronto: Groundwood Books.

Yee, P. (1996). *Ghost train.* Toronto: Groundwood Books.

Wynne-Jones, T. (1999). *Lord of the fries.* Toronto: Groundwood. (Short stories.)

Non-Fiction

- Batten, J. (2002). *The man who ran faster than everyone: The story of Tom Longboat.* Toronto: Tundra Books.
- Brewster, H. (1996). *Anastasia's album: The last tsar's youngest daughter tells her own story.* Toronto: Madison Press.
Chorlton, W. (2001). *Woolly mammoth: Life, death and rediscovery.* New York: Scholastic, Inc.
- Cummings, P. and Cummings, L. (1998). *Talking with adventurers.* Washington, DC: National Geographic Society.
- Fisher, L. E. (1999). *Alexander Graham Bell.* New York: Atheneum Books for Young Readers.
- Granfield, L. (1997). *Circus.* Toronto: Greenwood Books.
- Granfield, L. (2001). *Where poppies grow: A World War I companion.* Toronto: Stoddart Kids.
- Greenwood, B. (1998). *The last safe house: A story of the underground railway.* Toronto: Kids Can Press.
Holler Aulenbach, N. and Barton, H. A. (2001). *Exploring caves: Journeys into the earth.* Washington, DC: National Geographic Society.
Kennett, D. (2000). *Olympia: Warrior athletes of ancient Greece.* New York: Scholastic.
- Littlechild, G. (1993). *This land is my land.* Emeryville, CA: Children's Book Press.
- Raskin, L and Pearson, D. (1998). *52 days by camel: My Sahara adventure.* Toronto: Annick Press.
- Savage, C. (2001). *Born to be a cowgirl.* Vancouver: Greystone Books.
Sis, P. (1996). *Starry messenger.* New York: Farrar, Straus and Giroux.
Tripp, N. (1994). *Thunderstorm!* New York: Dial Books.
Webb, S. (2000). *My season with penguins: An Antarctic journal.* Boston: Houghton Mifflin Inc.
Wright-Frierson, V. (1999). *A North American rainforest scrapbook.* New York: Walker & Co.

Grade 6 to Grade 7

Fiction

Almond, D. (2000). *Kit's wilderness.* New York: Delacorte Press.
- Barwin, G. (2001). *Seeing stars.* Toronto: Stoddart Kids.
- Brandis, M. (1996). *Rebellion: A novel of Upper Canada.* Erin, ON: The Porcupine's Quill.
- Brooks, M. (1998). *Bone dance.* Toronto: Groundwood Books.
- Carter, A. (2000). *The girl on Evangeline Beach.* Toronto: Stoddart Kids.
Creech, S. (2000). *The wanderer.* New York: HarperCollins.
- Demers, B. (1999). *Willa's new world.* Regina, SK: Coteau Books.

- Doyle, B. (2001). *Mary Ann Alice.* Toronto: Groundwood Books.
- Fairbridge, L. (1995). *Stormbound.* Toronto: Doubleday Canada.
Freeman, S. (1997). *The cuckoo's child.* New York: Disney Press.
- Friesen, G. (1998). *Janey's girl.* Toronto: Kids Can Press.
- Friesen, G. (2000). *Men of stone.* Toronto: Kids Can Press.
Gavin, J. (2001). *Coram boy.* New York: Farrar, Straus and Giroux.
Griffin, A. (1998). *The other shepards.* New York: Hyperion Books for Children.
Hesse, K. (2001). *Witness.* New York: Scholastic Press.
- Holeman, L. (1998). *Mercy's birds.* Toronto: Tundra Books.
- Hughes, M. (2002). *The maze.* Toronto: HarperCollins Canada Ltd.
- Johnston, J. (1994). *Adam and Eve and Pinch-me.* Toronto: Lester Publishing.
O'Roark, F. (2000). *Dovey Coe.* New York: Atheneum Books for Young Readers.
Kindl, P. (1997). *The woman in the wall.* Boston: Houghton Mifflin.
Lowry, L. (2000). *Gathering blue.* Boston: Houghton Mifflin.
- Lunn, J. (1997). *The hollow tree.* Toronto: Alfred A. Knopf Canada.
- Martel, S. (1980). *The king's daughter.* Vancouver: Douglas and McIntyre.
Nicholson, W. (2000). *The windsinger.* New York: Mammoth.
Price, S. (2000). The Sterkarm handshake. New York: HarperCollins Children's Books.
Pullman, P. (1995). The golden compass. New York: Ballantine Books.
Rees, C. (2001). Witch child. Cambridge, MA: Candlewick Press.
Rubinstein, G. (1995). Galax arena. New York: Simon & Schuster Books for Young Readers.
- Slade, A. (2001). *Dust.* Toronto: HarperCollins.
- Stenhouse, T. (2001). *Across the steel river.* Toronto: Kids Can Press Ltd.
- Trembath, D. (1996). *The Tuesday Café.* Victoria, BC: Orca Book Publishers.
Wolff, V. (1993). *Make lemonade.* New York: Scholastic Inc.
Winton, T. (1999). *Lockie Leonard, scumbuster.* New York: Margaret K. McElderry Books.
Wynne-Jones, D. (1998). *The lives of Christopher Chant.* New York: Greenwillow Books.
- Wynne-Jones, T. (2000). *The boy in the burning house.* New York: A Melanie Kroupa Book/Farrar Straus Giroux.
- Wynne-Jones, T. (1995). *The maestro.* Toronto: Groundwood Books.

Glossary

aesthetic response is a term coined by American educator Rosenblatt (1989) to describe the enjoyment or appreciation a reader feels while reading a text. An aesthetic response is not concerned with comprehension, word meanings, recall, or learning, but with the deep personal engagement of reader and text. Aesthetic responses are not necessarily pleasurable; some texts can be deeply moving and cause stress or discomfort rather than pleasure, but this is still considered to be an aesthetic response.

alphabetic principle refers to the understanding that letters in written words stand for sounds in spoken words. Children demonstrate this understanding when they are able to map letters onto sounds to spell words, or sounds onto letters to identify words.

automaticity is the ability to carry out a complex act rapidly and without conscious awareness or control. An important characteristic of automaticity is that an individual can perform a complex skill or act while at the same time performing another that may not be automatic. As readers become proficient and are able to identify most of the words in texts automatically, they are able to direct their mental resources to constructing meaning. Most experts feel that children need to engage in extensive reading to achieve automaticity.

balanced language arts is a philosophical perspective or set of beliefs about what kinds of language knowledge children need and how these kinds of knowledge can be developed. First, there are multiple kinds of knowledge about language that children need to develop including (1) knowledge about words (how to identify, spell, and associate meaning with them), (2) knowledge

about understanding, responding, and creating meaning, and (3) positive attitudes to reading and writing. Second, there are multiple effective sources of knowledge including the teacher, parents, and other children. Finally, there are multiple ways of learning through which children gain varied sorts of knowledge about language (Fitzgerald, 1999).

basal reading series are sets of materials for teaching reading and language arts. These series generally consist of teacher guides, student anthologies, workbooks, and supplemental materials such as assessment materials, big books, correlated **trade books**, audiovisual aids, and computer software. Initially, basal series focused almost exclusively on reading, but in recent years they have included other areas of language arts as well. Basal series derive their name from the original intention that they form the basis of a program of instruction in reading.

basalization occurs when a **trade book** (i.e., a published work of literature) is treated in a classroom in the same way as a basal reader. Trade books have different lessons to teach children than basal readers. The objective of working with trade books is to teach children how to become readers. The ways in which texts work, and the enormous variety of text styles and formats, become apparent to readers of trade books. The essence of working with trade books is that children enjoy the reading experience and learn about the vast range of books available and the delight that reading can produce.

challenged books are those that groups or individuals have attempted to censor by having them removed from the shelves of libraries, especially in schools. Not all challenges result in the removal of a book. Specific procedures are usually

followed in dealing with a challenge to a book, and a committee of parents and teachers usually makes the final decision about whether a book should be removed from a school library.

chapter books are beginning novels for children that are designed to facilitate the reader's transition from a reliance on illustrations for creating meaning (as is done with **picture books**) to a stronger reliance on text. Many chapter books are available for young readers, and a number of publishing companies are producing specific series of chapter books (e.g., Hodge Pog Publishing). Like picture books, chapter books include all of the major **genres** of literature. An example of a chapter book is *Harold and Harold* by Budge Wilson (1995).

children's literature is a term used in this book to refer to those print materials (fiction, nonfiction, magazines, and poetry) that possess an aesthetic quality, are written primarily with an audience of young readers in mind, are acknowledged by critics to meet high standards, are well written and illustrated, and provide children with pleasurable and challenging reading experiences.

classification of dramatic forms is based on the way drama is implemented: as part of dramatic play, as a way of interpreting text, as part of a performance for an audience, or as a way of creating a context for learning. Dramatic play, drama as interpretation of literature, **contextual drama**, and drama as theatre make different demands on students and teachers.

constructivism is a theory of learning in which individuals use their knowledge to build or make meaning. Texts are viewed as providing cues to possible meanings rather than as containing meaning themselves. Readers are viewed as active meaning makers rather than passive receivers of meaning, and, because of variations in background knowledge, they construct variable meanings of the same text.

contemporary realistic fiction is imaginative writing that accurately reflects life as it is lived today. Events and situations in such stories could conceivably happen to people living in the real world. Young readers consistently select contemporary realistic fiction as their preferred **genre.** Stories are often about characters growing up in the world and their manner of coping with the problems and dilemmas of the human condition. Examples of contemporary realistic fiction are *Pick-Up Sticks* by Sarah Ellis (1991) and *The Maestro* by Tim Wynne-Jones (1995).

context cues are knowledge and linguistic cues that help a reader construct meaning when reading. Linguistic cues involve both syntactic (**grammar** or word order) and semantic (meaning) aspects of language. When children use context cues, they make predictions and monitor their reading in terms of what sounds right and makes sense.

contextual drama is concerned with creating dramatic contexts within which teacher and students explore themes, issues, and relationships. As in dramatic play, the participants in a contextual drama construct the meaning of the dramatic situation as opposed to representing the ideas of an author or poet. Contextual drama has the spontaneous appearance of drama as play, but in fact it is carefully structured by the teacher to help students achieve new insights and understanding. Thus, contextual drama often requires the teacher to work in role and to facilitate the drama from within the context.

critical literacy goes beyond providing students with conventional reading and writing skills to equipping them to critically examine how written language reflects power structures and inequali-

ties. It involves interrogating texts from different perspectives and taking action to promote social justice.

cuing systems are the three systems of **semantics**, **syntax**, and **graphophonics** that are used by readers and writers to make meaning from printed symbols. Pictures, diagrams, and charts also act as cues for readers to construct meaning, but "cuing systems" usually refers to the text-based systems discussed in this book.

cursive writing is handwriting in which the letters are connected to one another with a continuous flow from one stroke to another. The most prevalent form of handwriting today is a combination of printing and cursive writing, with printed uppercase letters and cursive lowercase letters.

dialect is a variety of a spoken language that is used in a geographic region or by members of a social class. Every dialect has distinctive patterns, rules, and features. Regional dialects are much less pronounced now than they were 50 years ago, but speech in the southeastern part of the United States, the north of England, the east coast of Australia, and maritime Canada are examples of dialects that remain distinct. The advent of radio, television, and movies has brought a more standard version of spoken language into our homes and schools.

dialogue is conversation about a topic (either written or spoken) among any number of people. Unlike in a debate, no one tries to "win" or to make his or her particular view prevail. In a dialogue, the focus is on the stream of meaning flowing among and through the participants. A partnership is created with the other people based on compassion, acceptance, and a sincere interest in the others. In dialogue, when a mistake is discovered, everybody gains.

discourse is a linguistics term used to describe a continuous stretch of spoken or written language longer than one sentence. Frequently, "discourse" is reserved

for spoken language and the term "text" for written language. Discourse is also used to refer to specific topics or types of language (e.g., the discourse of high finance). As well, discourse can be perceived as process and text as product.

drama strategies are the ways in which the drama form is created. Examples of strategies are narration, tableau, and voice-in-the-head. Such strategies can be used to create a variety of forms, though some are specific to a particular form (e.g., teacher-in-role is used mainly in **contextual drama**).

dramatic forms include storytelling, puppetry, choral speech, choric drama, readers' theatre, dramatization, and story theatre. All dramatic forms require students to create or interpret meaning within the "as if" world of drama. The forms described in this text require language to express this meaning. Scripts, props, and movement are also used. A particular combination of attributes defines a particular dramatic form.

efferent response is a term coined by American educator Rosenblatt (1989) to describe a response to literature where the intent is to focus on what can be learned, observed, and taken away from the reading. Focused on gaining information, an efferent response is at the opposite end of the continuum from an aesthetic response.

emergent literacy is a term that was developed during the early 1980s to refer to the **literacy** development of young children. Sulzby (1985) defines emergent literacy as the reading and writing concepts, attitudes, and behaviours that precede and develop into conventional literacy. Emergent literacy begins early in children's lives at home, involves interactions with print, and is part of, rather than separate from, reading and writing development.

environmental print is print in the home and community, such as on McDonald's signs and cereal boxes. The term is also used to refer to print in the classroom, such as labels, signs, calendars, charts, and lists used to organize the room.

expository writing is a form of writing that provides information, detailed explanations, judgments, and supporting examples. It may be persuasive or argumentative writing.

expressive writing is a term used by James Britton (Britton et al., 1975) to describe one of the three **voices** of writing (the others being *poetic* and *transactional*). Expressive writing is found in diaries, journals, and personal letters, where the writer's intent is to share personal points of view, ideas, thoughts, and questions. Expressive writing aims to communicate the personal identity of the writer.

fantasy is a **genre** of literature that engages and stimulates the reader's imagination and gives free rein to endless possibilities. The reader is taken to worlds where animals and toys can speak, where people can travel across time and into completely fictional worlds. Modern fantasy is rooted in folk tales, myths, and dreams. Examples of modern fantasy literature include *Charlotte's Web* by E. B. White (1952) and *The Dark Is Rising* by Susan Cooper (1969).

genre refers to the different literary and linguistic forms and functions of various texts. **Narrative**, for example, is different in form and function from expository text, which is different again from persuasive or descriptive text. Genre also refers to categories of literature such as myth, fable, poetry, **fantasy**, and **contemporary realistic fiction**. Each of these genres meets different functions and uses a variety of different forms to achieve the intentions of the text.

grammar is an ambiguous term that has been largely replaced today by the term **syntax**. However, where "grammar" is used, it refers to three distinct perspectives on language: (1) systemic-functional grammar is a description of the choices made by language users based on context and intention in order to create meaning (e.g., see Halliday, 1969); (2) generative-transformational grammar is a description of how language actually works as a process and is based on language universals (e.g., see Chomsky, 1957); and (3) prescriptive grammar focuses on the rules of language and how language *should* work. Where most grammar taught in the first part of this century was prescriptive (frequently dealing with inappropriate usage as in *seed* and *saw*, most grammar taught today is descriptive and functional, and more like (1) or (2).

graphophonics refers to the print–sound relationship of text. Graphic cues generally include letters, letter clusters, words, and parts of words. **Phonics** refers to the relationships between graphic cues and sounds. Graphophonic cues are one of the **cuing systems** that help readers to identify words as they read. The reader identifies words by relating speech sounds to letters and letter clusters.

Guided Reading is a teaching process designed to assist children in becoming independent, fluent readers by scaffolding their selection and application of a variety of effective reading strategies. Guided Reading lessons progress through three steps: (1) the teacher provides an introduction to the story to assist children in building or expanding background information; (2) the children participate in supported reading; and (3) the children may be invited to participate in an extension or follow-up activity.

heuristics—sometimes used to refer to educated guessing—is a process of discovery through exploration. Linguist Michael Halliday labelled one of the seven functions of language he identified as being heuristic. Some instructional methodology is based on heuristics in an attempt to have learners make discoveries for themselves and thus be more likely to have a meaningful learning experience than by simply being told.

high fantasy is a **genre** of literature usually involving a quest, elements of the mystical or magical, time travel, and time warps, and frequently takes place in a fictional setting and with a fictional language. Examples include *A Wizard of Earthsea* by Ursula LeGuin (1968) and *The Golden Compass* by Philip Pullman (1996). High fantasy is based on mythology (frequently Celtic). Elementary school children are aided in their reading of high fantasy when they have some familiarity with mythology.

historical fiction is a **genre** of literature set in a specific place and time in the past. It requires a great deal of research, descriptive detail, and authentic language to be credible. Good historical fiction is both an aesthetic and an efferent reading experience. The reader will learn history from it, and will also appreciate and identify with the lives and concerns of the characters.

hypermedia is computer software that is used to organize and manage various types of multimedia information (such as sound, graphics, text, video, and animation) into a system so that information can be accessed, retrieved, and modified easily. The different forms of information are linked so that a user can move from one form to another in a nonlinear manner.

hypertext is nonlinear writing. Text is linked so that the reader is able to go through a topic in any order. Readers have greater control over what they read and the sequence in which they read it than with traditional texts.

inclusive education is a framework or philosophy that schools should accommodate all children regardless of their physical, intellectual, social, emotional, linguistic, or other characteristics. Regular education experiences are recognized as the right of all students. The intent is to create educational contexts in which all students are valued and supported with a range of services accessible to meet their needs.

instructional reading level is the level of reading instruction that a child needs in order to make maximum progress learning to read. The material must be just difficult enough to help children develop reading strategies with the support of instruction. On an informal reading inventory, this is the highest level at which a child is able to accurately identify 90 percent of the words and answer 70 percent of the comprehension questions.

integration is the organization of language arts into a unified curriculum so that reading, writing, speaking, and listening are taught together rather than separately. Another level of integration involves teaching and learning language arts in other subject areas. A third level involves integrating experiences inside and outside of school.

invented spelling refers to a child's first attempts at transcribing spoken language into print symbols before learning the conventions of standard spelling. Children pay particular attention to the sounds of language, and invented spelling is a reflection of this focus.

levelled text refers to reading materials that represent a progression from more simple to more complex and challenging texts. Some text progressions are based on readability formulas, others on letter–sound relationships, and still others on multiple criteria related to language predictability, text format, and content.

literacy is a term generally associated with reading and writing, but it has been defined in many different ways. Basic literacy is the ability to read and write. Functional literacy is frequently defined as those reading and writing skills needed by people to do everyday tasks such as write cheques and read instructions on a medicine bottle. **Critical literacy** goes beyond conventional reading and writing to an interrogation of texts and taking action to promote social justice. In recent years, the term has been extended to other forms of representation such as **media literacy** and computer literacy.

manuscript printing, sometimes called *manuscript writing*, is the first form of

written language taught to children and consists of individual letters that are not connected. There are a number of styles of manuscript writing, but all of them are plain, easy to recognize, and easy for children to learn.

metacognition is awareness and control of the thinking processes involved in developing an ability. In reading, metacognition includes knowledge of factors that affect reading, of reading tasks, and of reading strategies. The regulative or control dimension of metacognition in reading involves planning and monitoring.

media literacy is concerned with the process of *understanding* and *using* mass media. It is also concerned with helping students develop an informed understanding of the nature of mass media, the techniques used by them, and the impact of these techniques. It aims to increase students' understanding and enjoyment of how media work, how they produce meaning, how they are organized, and how they construct reality. Media literacy also aims to provide students with the abilities and skills to *create* media products (Ontario Ministry of Education).

metafiction is a **narrative** mode used by authors to provide a constant and deliberate reminder that a book is something an author and reader create together, something that is not real but fictional and that is open to many interpretations. The device has been used by authors since the time of Chaucer. It is the opposite of literary realism. By drawing attention to how texts are structured, works of metafiction can show readers how texts "mean." Techniques used to this end include obtrusive narrators who directly address the reader, situations where characters and narrators change places, the insertion of parodies of other texts, typographic experimentation, and the mixing of **genres** and **discourses**. Works of metafiction usually employ any number of these techniques in combination. *Black and White* by David Macaulay (1990) and *Piggybook* by Anthony Browne (1986) are examples.

metalinguistic awareness is the growing awareness and ability we have to think and talk about language as a formal code. With children, it refers to understanding terms such as *letter*, *word*, *sentence*, and *sound*.

miscues is a term coined by Goodman (1969) for errors during oral reading. Goodman believes that analyzing oral miscues gives insights into the reading process, since miscues result from the same cues and processes as correct responses.

morphology is the study of the structure of words, specifically the ways in which morphemes (the smallest units of meaning in a language) combine to create meanings. An example of a morpheme is *s*, which denotes plural in English. Hence *dog* means one creature, and *dogs* means more than one. Suffixes and prefixes are also morphemes. Morphology is one of the essential **cuing systems** readers use to make sense of the printed word. Morphology is distinct from **syntax** in that syntax deals with the meaning of language at the level of sentences and phrases.

narrative consists of a story or a succession of related events. These events are frequently organized according to cause and effect or chronology. Narratives include descriptions of settings, events, and characters, as well as comments and observations. Narratives can have the structure of a story or a much looser structure without opening and closing sequences.

native speaker ability is the ability to use language in many situations to accomplish a wide range of purposes. Idiomatic language, **pragmatics**, and **dialect** are all important in native speaker ability.

onset is the initial consonant or consonants in a syllable. The **rime** is the vowel and remaining consonants in a syllable after the onset.

performance assessment refers to assessment in which students demonstrate what they can do by actually doing it. Rather than using paper and pencil tests, teachers use their best judgment to evaluate performance along a continuum defined by increasingly demanding performance criteria. These criteria are written descriptions that capture quality performance at various levels of achievement. This form of assessment is frequently used for children's writing.

persuasive writing is used to persuade others to do something, buy something, or believe something. Advertising, editorials, political campaign literature, religious tracts, and much of the unsolicited junk mail that arrives in mailboxes consists of persuasive writing. Children use persuasive writing when they create a poster presentation about a favourite book they have read or write a letter asking the school principal to consider changing a school rule.

phonemic awareness is the ability to segment sounds (phonemes) in spoken words. For example, the spoken word *cat* consists of three separate phonemes, one related to each letter in the written word. Research shows that performance on phonemic awareness tasks is related to the beginning of reading acquisition.

phonetics refers to the way sounds are articulated and produced. The term is often used to describe the way children spell, sounding out a word so they can articulate individual sounds (*phonemes*) within a word and transcribe them into print symbols.

phonics is the relationship between letters and their spoken sounds. Analytic or whole-word phonics is the association of sounds with larger clusters of letters such as phonograms or word families (e.g., *ight*). Synthetic phonics is the association of sounds with individual letters or letter clusters and the blending of these sounds to identify words.

phonology, sometimes called phonemics, is the study of the patterns of sound that create meaning in language. In any one language, a number of sounds

(phonemes) combine to produce words and meanings.

picture books are books in which illustrations play an integral role in creating meaning. Picture books are not the same as illustrated books, where meaning does not depend on illustrations. In a picture book, text and pictures work together. Good examples of picture books are *Each Peach Pear Plum* by Janet and Allan Ahlberg (1976) and *The Tunnel* by Anthony Browne (1989).

poetic writing is a term used by James Britton (Britton et al., 1975) to describe one of the three **voices** of writing (the others being expressive and transactional). Meant to have an aesthetic element to it, poetic writing consists of poetry and also fictional writing, including **narrative** and description. The purpose of poetic writing is purely pleasure or satisfaction on the part of the writer and audience. (Poetic writing is not necessarily pleasurable to read; it can, in fact, cause distress or discomfort for the reader.)

polysemic is a **semantics** term that describes words with more than one meaning. A polysemic text allows the reader to draw inferences, make judgments, and interpret the text in several ways. Examples of polysemic texts are *Rosie's Walk* by Pat Hutchins (1969) and *The Golden Compass* by Philip Pullman (1996). A text that is not polysemic provides a narrower reading experience for accomplished readers.

portfolio assessment uses a compilation of work done by a child over a period of time. Frequently, the portfolio items are selected by the learner or by the teacher and learner together. Items included in a portfolio are chosen with deliberation in order to demonstrate what a learner can do. Teachers find portfolios useful in demonstrating a child's learning to parents and administrators, and in explaining to children what they need to focus on and what learning must be accomplished next. Portfolios also give teachers an opportunity to reflect on

their teaching and the learning their students are engaged in. Portfolios provide children with an opportunity to see the range of work they have done over time and to assess what they are accomplishing.

pragmatics is the study of how speakers create meaning. The emphasis in pragmatics is on the context of language use and on the intentions and presuppositions of the speakers. The focus is on what an individual speaker means and on how that meaning is communicated. Pragmatics examines relatively short stretches of language compared with **discourse** analysis, which studies linguistic patterns in longer stretches of language.

predictable books, a term coined by Goodman (1969), are books that make reading easy for emergent readers. They have the following characteristics: the pictures support the text; large chunks of text are repeated; and the language has cadence, rhythm, or rhyme that supports the reading of the text. *Brown Bear, Brown Bear, What Do You See?* (Martin, 1972) and *Each Peach Pear Plum* (Ahlberg and Ahlberg, 1976) are examples of predictable books.

reading readiness is the notion that children need to reach an appropriate stage of development in order to learn to read. Maturationists believe that reading instruction should be delayed until children reach this stage of development, whereas developmentalists believe that prereading experiences can hasten children's development.

reading series (See **basal reading series.**)

realistic fiction (See **contemporary realistic fiction.**)

recounts are "tellings" of past experiences that focus on specific events. They are sequential and are usually based on the direct experience of the author. However, recounts may also be imaginative or outside the author's experience. Although the purpose is to tell what happened, a recount may also involve the author's personal interpretation of events (as in an eyewitness account of an incident).

rime. (See **onset**.)

schemata (plural; singular *schema*) are organized mental frameworks that develop through repeated exposure to ritualized experiences such as playing baseball, eating in restaurants, or singing on car trips. Schemata influence our expectations and impose structure on the information we receive.

semantic map or web is a diagram that shows relationships among ideas. It consists of nodes containing key words, with connecting lines between the nodes. Teachers and students use semantic maps or webs to organize ideas about concepts, texts, or units of study.

semantics is the meaning component of language. It does not simply refer to the denotational meanings of words but also to the ways in which words are used, in both the actual choice of one word rather than another and the connotations created by those words. A semantic system includes idioms and compound words and the unique ways that words are used in different situations.

standardized tests are norm-referenced tests comparing a student's performance with that of other students. These tests are developed by administering a test to a large number of students (the standardization group) to develop norms.

strategy is an overall plan for performing a task. One strategy can be used in several learning situations. In contrast, skills are more specific and used in the service of a strategy. Examples of strategies include predicting words and meanings, summarizing, and monitoring.

syntax (formerly **grammar**) is a linguistic term that refers to the structure of sentences. In the English language,

syntax consists largely of word order. English is a non-inflected language; it does not depend on specific inflectional word endings to denote the role of a word in a sentence.

text structure is the pattern or organization of ideas in a text. There are two major types of texts: **narrative** (story) and expository (informational). Knowledge of text structure helps us to construct meaning for texts when reading and writing.

thematic organization is a way of organizing learning matter around a central concept (such as courage), the work of a particular author, or a topic (such as farms). The theory is that learning will be facilitated and deepened by connecting ideas to one another. Thematic units may be organized within language arts or extended across other areas of the curriculum as well.

time-slip fantasy is a **genre** of literature that involves the main character or protagonist in two eras. An object often enables the character to slip from one era to the other. In *Who Is Francis Rain?* by Margaret Buffie (1987), the object is a pair of spectacles. In *Playing Beatie Bow* by Ruth Parks (1980), the object is a piece of fabric on a dress. In time-slip fantasy, the protagonist explores issues in the past that lead to an understanding of current issues.

trade books are books published by publishing companies as works of literature and not as educational texts. Books published as part of an educational program and intended for use in schools are usually referred to as *textbooks*.

transactional theory, also called *transactive theory*, is based on the work of Louise Rosenblatt (1978) and posits that meaning comes from a transaction between a reader and a text in a specific context. Readers rely on the text itself and on their background knowledge,

experiences, and world view to construct meaning while reading. The focus is on the reader's response to texts.

transactional writing is a term used by James Britton (Britton et al., 1975) to describe one of the three **voices** of writing (the others being expressive and poetic). Like **expository writing**, with which it is often used interchangeably, transactional writing is meant to accomplish a specific practical goal. Business letters, reports, term papers, report cards, recipes, and shopping lists are all examples of transactional writing.

voice is a term used in writing that refers to the combined effects of the writer's purpose, style, tone, and other intangibles, such as commitment, energy, conviction, and personality. Also used to refer to the three voices or types of writing: **expressive writing**, **poetic writing**, and **transactional writing**.

whole language is a philosophy about learning, language, and the nature of relationships between children and adults. Meaning is seen as the essence of language learning, and children are viewed as learning language through using it. Language is also seen as indivisible and as personal, social, and cultural. Practices that have been associated with whole language include involving children in real reading and writing, immersing them in a print-rich environment that includes quality **children's literature**, and basing assessments on observations of children using language in the classroom.

zone of proximal development is a term coined by Vygotsky (1978) to refer to a level of difficulty just beyond that which a child can handle independently but at which he or she can manage with help from others. Providing children with the opportunity to work with others on problems or tasks at this level maximizes learning.

Index

Martin, Bill, Jr., *Brown Bear, Brown Bear, What Do You See?*, 89–90, 92, 100
Martin, Jacqueline Briggs, *Snowflake Bentley,* 309
Martin, L.E., 416
Martin, R.J., 197
Maruki, T., *Hiroshima No Pika,* 291
Masking, in word identification, 167, 182–83
Math and Literature (Burns), 225
Mathemathics, writing in, 224–25
Math Is Language Too (Whitin & Whitin), 225
Matrices, 233
Matthew effect, 184
Maugham, Somerset, 297
Maxine's Tree (Leger-Haskell), 338
Mayer, Marianna
  Beauty and the Beast, 396
  Twelve Dancing Princesses, The, 298
Mayer, Mercer, *Beauty and the Beast,* 396
Mayfield, M.I., 444–45
McAskile, Anna, 357
McGillivray, Nicole, 354–57
McKenzie, Jamie, *From Now On: The Education Technology Journal,* 424
McKeown, M., 146, 147
McLaughlin Planetarium, 307
McNicoll, Sylvia, *The Big Race,* 292
Meaning
  construction of, 18, 112–13, 117–18, 124
  phonics and, 19–20
  reading and, 3
  words and, 19–20
  and written language, 72
Media
  action learning, 403
  bias in, 388
  education, 401
  electronic, 400
  income and ownership, 399, 423
  intertextual instruction, 403
  language development and, 388
  literacy development and, 388
  print, 400
  See also Multimedia; Nonbook resources
Media Awareness Network, 401
Media literacy, 399–404
  forms of, 400–401
  goals of, 400
  instruction, 401–3
  logs, 401–2
  pleasure stance, 400
  preparation stance, 400
  protection stance, 399–400
Media Literacy Resource Guide (Ontario Ministry of Education), 401
Meek, M., 286
Meet Canadian Authors and Illustrators (Gertridge), 327
"Meg Merrilees" (Keats), 301
Memory Box, The (Bahr), 351, 366, 377, 378, 380, 381
Mental disabilities, 460
Metacognition, 140
Metafiction, 288

Metalinguistic awareness, 43
Metalinguistic knowledge, 75
Metaphors, 303
MicroWorlds, 412
Middle-class children, 13
Milne, A.A., "The More It Snows," 354–57, 364, 377, 378
Mindtools, 405
Mini-lessons, readers' workshops and, 327
Minimal-cue messages, 105, 168, 182, 183, 442
Miscues, 84–86, 90
  in oral reading, 128–30, 183
  See also Cues
Misspellings, 210, 263, 264
Moffett, James, 48, 194–95, 213, 372
Mollel, T., *The Orphan Boy,* 299
Moonlight (Ormerod), 288
Moore, B., 302
Moorhouse, Ms., 30, 33, 47, 63
"More It Snows, The" (Milne), 354–57, 364, 377, 378
Morimoto, J., *My Hiroshima,* 291
Morin, Paul, 299
Morning messages, 105, 182
Morphemes, 34
Morphett, M.V., 68
Morrow, L.M., 438, 449
Moss, G., 16
Mothers, images of, 397
Mrs. Silverman's Webfolio, 422
Multicultural education, 454–57
Multiculturalism, 341
Multicultural literature, 153
Multicultural Model, of multicultural education, 454–55, 456
Multimedia, 410–11
Multiple-choice test items, 121
Mummer's Song, The (Davidge and Wallace), 291
Mummy Slept Late and Daddy Fixed Breakfast (Ciardi), 372
Munsch, Robert
  Giant, 338
  Paper Bag Princess, The, 338
  Promise Is a Promise, A, 338
  Thomas's Snowsuit, 338
Murphy, S., 131, 436
Murray, Donald, 221
Myers, J., 413
My Hiroshima (Morimoto), 291
My Shadow (Stevenson), 304
Mystery stories, 294
Myths, 295–97, 299–300

Narration, 46
  and drama, 380
Narrative texts
  critical literacy and, 392–93
  nonfiction, 309–10
  poetry, 303
  structure, 125, 153–54
  writing, 256–57
Nash, Ogden, "The Adventures of Isabel," 301
National Anti-Poverty Organization, 11